INTERNATIONAL ECONOMIC LAW SERIES

General Editor: John H. Jackson

EVIDENCE, PROOF, AND FACT-FINDING IN WTO DISPUTE SETTLEMENT

Evidence, Proof, and Fact-Finding in WTO Dispute Settlement

MICHELLE T. GRANDO

OXFORD
UNIVERSITY PRESS

OXFORD
UNIVERSITY PRESS

Great Clarendon Street, Oxford OX2 6DP

Oxford University Press is a department of the University of Oxford.
It furthers the University's objective of excellence in research, scholarship,
and education by publishing worldwide in

Oxford New York

Auckland Cape Town Dar es Salaam Hong Kong Karachi
Kuala Lumpur Madrid Melbourne Mexico City Nairobi
New Delhi Shanghai Taipei Toronto

With offices in

Argentina Austria Brazil Chile Czech Republic France Greece
Guatemala Hungary Italy Japan Poland Portugal Singapore
South Korea Switzerland Thailand Turkey Ukraine Vietnam

Oxford is a registered trade mark of Oxford University Press
in the UK and in certain other countries

Published in the United States
by Oxford University Press Inc., New York

First published 2009

British Library Cataloguing in Publication Data
Data available

Library of Congress Cataloging-in-Publication Data
Data available

Typeset by MPS Limited, A Macmillan Company
Printed in Great Britain
on acid-free paper by
CPI Antony Rowe, Chippenham, Wiltshire

ISBN 978–0–19–957264–9

1 3 5 7 9 10 8 6 4 2

Foreword

Michelle Grando has written an important and valuable book on *Evidence, Proof, and Fact-Finding in WTO Dispute Settlement.* While the overall assessments of the World Trade Organization's dispute settlement mechanism have been generally positive, careful analyses of specific decisions sometimes reveal serious problems in legal approach and reasoning, as well as inconsistencies with prior decisions. These problems have been particularly apparent in respect of the Appellate Body's treatment of evidence and burden of proof issues. Even if these problems have not led to 'wrong' decisions, and in my view, they have not done so to any significant extent, the problems merit careful examination. In particular, compared to cases in the GATT years, WTO cases have become much more factually complex—especially in the subsidies and SPS areas—but under other agreements as well. It would clearly be desirable for the WTO system to have a more coherent approach to such basic issues. I expect Dr Grando's masterful examination of evidence, proof and fact-finding in WTO dispute settlement will become the definitive work on these issues.

Dr Grando's book makes a particularly useful contribution by discussing in some detail the theoretical issues that are crucial to any rigorous analysis of how fact-finding should be conducted and the burden of proof allocated. In legal proceedings where factual questions arise, it is often impossible to be absolutely positive as to what the facts actually are or were—documents can be interpreted in different ways; individuals may have varying recollections of what happened. In evaluating evidence and burden of proof rules, it is useful to consider such issues as (i) which party is best able to produce relevant evidence; (ii) what level of certitude is required to make a factual finding; (iii) what are the consequences in a given type of case of a mistaken finding; as well as (iv) general due process considerations that are more familiar to lawyers. These issues are typically not considered in WTO dispute settlement cases—even where they would be particularly relevant. For example, the risks of a mistaken finding in an SPS case, which might lead to the introduction of a devastating pest, is arguably much more serious than a mistaken finding in a trade remedy case, where the economic consequences may be much less. The book performs an extremely valuable service in introducing some of the scholarly thought on these issues at the outset.

The book's background discussion of the way in which common and civil law systems deal with these issues is very helpful. As Dr Grando perceptively notes in her introduction '[I]t is not uncommon for practitioners to seek to reproduce local practices in international proceedings. ... [W]hen parties have different expectations on how the process of fact-finding should function, problems are bound to arise. . . . [T]he development of a common language that all operators can understand and speak is of utmost importance.' Indeed, I was struck while serving as Director of the WTO's Legal Affairs Division, which provides legal advice to WTO panels, that common and civil lawyers often had difficulty in effectively communicating with each other. Everyone understood that common law and civil law treat procedural issues somewhat differently—a fact usually ascribed to the difference between an adversarial and an inquisitorial approach. But there was often only the most superficial understanding of the differences and the underlying reasons for those differences. As a consequence, lawyers often talked past each other without realizing it. Dr Grando's examination of the differences should be required reading for lawyers involved in WTO cases. Her discussion of burden of proof, standards of proof, and presumptions is particularly helpful for thinking about how WTO dispute settlement might approach these issues in a more coherent way.

The core of the book is, of course, Dr Grando's critique of WTO case law on the allocation of the burden of proof. She sets out the key WTO jurisprudence, starting with the 1997 *US Wool Shirts and Blouses* case—the first Appellate Body discussion of the burden of proof issue and the case religiously cited ever since by every panel—through the 2008 *India Additional Import Duties* case. As she demonstrates, the Appellate Body's decisions on burden of proof and, in particular, how burden of proof issues should be dealt with in respect of exceptions and exclusions, are not consistent and often are not well reasoned. Dr Grando provides an analytical framework for dealing with these issues and proposes a coherent approach. As interest grows in reforming WTO dispute settlement in order to improve and perfect an already admirable system, one can legitimately hope that her ideas will be taken seriously. Indeed, since no treaty changes are needed, but rather only a more coherent approach by the Appellate Body, one can hope that this volume will have a significant impact on its future jurisprudence on burdens of proof.

All in all, this is a superb book; it is quite well written and a pleasure to read. Anyone with an interest in WTO dispute settlement would greatly profit from reading it.

William J Davey
Champaign, Illinois
July 2009

General Editor's Preface

The WTO (World Trade Organization) is now one of the world's most powerful international economic institutions, and so it is not surprising that it receives much scholarly and policy professional attention, including many published books. The Oxford University Press is at the forefront of this publishing activity, with many distinguished books on the WTO already published. This book by Michelle Grando is perfectly deserving of an honor place in the OUP IEL series, but it is also relatively unique in addressing a very procedural slice of problems which however can have a large impact on the world trading system as well as critical influence on specific cases. Her book, developed from her SJD thesis at University of Toronto in Canada under guidance from Professor Trebilcock, is a welcome addition to the WTO analytic literature.

The basic focus of this book is proof and fact-finding in the WTO dispute processes. This has often been characterised as one of the significant weaknesses of the otherwise admirable WTO dispute settlement system. This WTO DS System has only limited resources for fact-finding while such activity becomes increasingly important particularly as scientific facts become critical in the resolution of some cases. The procedures established by the treaty language (especially the Dispute Settlement Understanding (DSU)) leave open much detail. As Professor Davey's excellent overview introduction explains, Dr Grando's book fills an important gap in the analytical scholarship for the WTO. This book therefore has major usefulness to the practitioners who must struggle with the procedural dimensions of the complex WTO DS system.

Dr Grando's book is remarkable also for its structure and organization. It is very thorough, very scholarly and balanced, with much reference to the relevant literature. This work disaggregates the many concepts of fact-finding (e.g. burdens of proof, allocation of those burdens, which participants in the DS process bear various responsibilities, etc.). It notes at the outset that there are multiple policy goals for the fact-finding in the WTO DS system, and some of these goals clash, forcing some balancing process by the DS panels and Appellate Body. The table of contents itself reflects this careful analytical approach, and in addition introductory passages for each chapter and concluding remarks for those chapters reflect this.

It is a quality work which will be welcomed by scholars, practitioners, and other policy professionals.

John H. Jackson

Acknowledgements

First and foremost, I would like to thank my SJD supervisor at the University of Toronto, Professor Michael J. Trebilcock. Without his support and encouragement this fascinating journey might not have happened. I am grateful for his guidance throughout my masters and doctoral studies, and the writing of this book. Professor Trebilcock has taught me the most important lesson any professor could ever teach a student, namely, to think critically. He is not only a great scholar, but also a wonderful person.

I am also grateful to Professors Andrew Green, Petros Mavroidis, and Lorne Sossin for their participation in my SJD advisory committee. I am particularly indebted to Professor Petros Mavroidis who, despite his busy schedule due to his commitments with Columbia University and the University of Neuchatel, always found time to discuss, read and comment on drafts of this study.

Professor William Davey (University of Illinois) was the external reviewer of my thesis. His comments were extremely helpful in enhancing some of my arguments, in both the context of my SJD defence and when I was revising the manuscript for this book. I am grateful for the time he spent in reviewing previous versions of this study and the guidance he provided.

I am also deeply indebted to Professor John H. Jackson for hosting me at the Georgetown University Law Center and for the support he provided to this project—first, my SJD thesis and later, this book. I wrote most of this study while at Georgetown Law, where I had the honour of assisting Professor Jackson with the Journal of International Economic Law (JIEL). The stimulating conversations we had during our weekly JIEL meetings helped me clarify and develop some of the ideas contained in this book. Professor Jackson has inspired many students and scholars working in the field of international economic law and I feel privileged to have had the opportunity to work with him and have his support.

A special thank you goes to friends and colleagues who found time to read and provide me with comments on drafts of different parts of this study, including Jane Bradley, Lothar Ehring, Renato Gomes, Mark Herlihy, Gary Horlick, Hiromi Yano, and Alan Yanovich. Many others discussed different aspects of this study with me and I am thankful to them for their time and thought-provoking conversations: Scott D. Andersen, James Bacchus, Professor Jutta Brunnée, Professor John Crook, Barbara Eggers, Tracey Epps, Gonzalo Flores, Patricio Grané, Susan Hainsworth, Mark Kantor, Reto Malacrida, Yves Renouf, Professor Hans Smit, Eric Solovy, Debra Steger, and Eric White.

I would like to express my gratitude to the University of Toronto and Professor Michael Trebilcock for the financial support provided for my doctoral studies and the research for this book. Without their support, I would not have been able to write it.

Thanks are also due to Oxford University Press, in particular John Louth, Merel Alstein, and Lucy Page, and the copy-editor Ceri Warner, for all their help and efficiency in producing this book.

Finally, my deepest thanks are owed to my family, especially my parents, and Isamu Matsuyama for all their support and encouragement.

Contents—Summary

Table of Cases xvii
List of Abbreviations xxxiii

Introduction 1

1. Optimizing the Process of Fact-Finding 9
2. Basic Concepts 68
3. Functioning of the Burden of Proof 103
4. The Allocation of the Burden of Proof 151
5. The Main Actors in the Process of Fact-Finding and the Development of the Factual Record 231

Conclusion 354

Appendix: Understanding on Rules and Procedures Governing the Settlement of Disputes 365

Bibliography 387
Index 407

Contents

Table of Cases xvii
List of Abbreviations xxxiii

Introduction **1**
I. Background 1
II. Outline of the Book 4

1 Optimizing the Process of Fact-Finding **9**
Introduction 9
I. Legal Adjudication and the Process of Fact-Finding 10
A. The goals of legal adjudication 10
B. Optimization of goals 17
C. Managing uncertainty and the risk of error 19
II. The WTO Dispute Settlement System 21
A. A system of legal adjudication 21
B. The goals/values of the system 28
C. The institutional and procedural framework 42
Concluding Remarks 66

2 Basic Concepts **68**
Introduction 68
I. The Concept of the Burden of Proof 70
A. General scope 70
B. Differences between the common law and the civil law systems 74
C. Proceedings before international courts and tribunals 80
D. Does the burden of proof shift? 83
II. Standard of Proof 86
A. General scope 86
B. Differences between common law and civil law systems 87
C. Proceedings before international courts and tribunals 89
III. Presumptions 93
A. General scope 93
B. International law including WTO law 96
Concluding Remarks 101

3 Functioning of the Burden of Proof **103**
Introduction 103
I. The '*Prima Facie* Case' or 'Presumption' Approach 105

A. Exploring the meaning of '*prima facie* case' 105
B. The uses of a '*prima facie* case' in WTO dispute settlement 108
C. Concluding remarks on the meaning of '*prima facie* case' 132
II. The 'holistic' or 'weighing of all evidence' approach 132
A. What is the holistic approach? 132
B. The favoured approach for WTO dispute settlement 135
III. The Standard of Proof for WTO Dispute Settlement 137
A. The importance of setting a standard of proof 137
B. Considerations when setting the standard of proof 138
C. Is the *prima facie* case standard ever optimal? 142
Concluding Remarks 149

4 The Allocation of the Burden of Proof 151

Introduction 151
I. The Current Status of the WTO Rules 152
A. The problem at issue 152
B. The WTO jurisprudence 155
II. Critique of the WTO Jurisprudence 168
A. Have panels and the Appellate Body been consistent? 168
B. Are the criteria relied upon effective? 179
III. What are the Alternatives? 190
A. A look at domestic and international law 190
B. Can law and economics analysis help? 199
C. What are the options for the WTO dispute settlement system? 202
D. *India—Additional Import Duties*: a paradigm shift? 215
IV. Allocation of the Burden of Proof in Article 21.5 of the DSU Compliance Cases 217
A. 'Regular' Article 21.5 proceedings 218
B. Post-suspension of concessions Article 21.5 proceedings 219
Concluding Remarks 223
Annex: Text of Relevant Provisions from WTO Agreements 225

5 The Main Actors in the Process of Fact-Finding and the Development of the Factual Record 231

Introduction 231
I. The Panel as a Reviewer 233
A. Trade remedies agreements 233
B. SPS and TBT Agreements 239
C. Final considerations 245
II. The Panel as the Original-Trier-of-Facts 246
A. Context: institutional and procedural framework 246
B. The role of the disputing parties 250
C. The role of the panel 304
Concluding Remarks 351

Conclusion **354**

The route to optimizing the process of fact-finding 354
Conceptual clarity 355
The prima facie *case requirement* 355
The standard of proof for WTO dispute settlement 356
Determining that the standard of proof is met 357
Allocation of the burden of proof 358
Burden of pleading 358
Avoiding decisions based on the burden of proof 359
Duty of cooperation 359
The role of the panel in promoting cooperation 360
Alternatives to managing asymmetries of information 361
Confidential information 362
Panel-controlled disclosure 363
Active panel 363
Final considerations and way forward 364

Appendix: Understanding on Rules and Procedures Governing the Settlement of Disputes **365**

Bibliography 387
Index 407

Table of Cases

A. GATT CASES

Panel Report, *Canada — Administration of the Foreign Investment Review Act*, adopted 7 February 1984, BISD 30S/140 at para. 5.20 186
Panel Report, *Canada — Import Restrictions on Ice Cream and Yoghurt*, adopted 5 December 1989, BISD 36S/68 186
Panel Report, *European Economic Community — Restrictions on Imports of Dessert Apples — Complaint by Chile*, adopted 22 June 1989, BISD 36S/93 186
Panel Report, *European Economic Community — Restrictions on Imports of Apples — Complaint by the United States*, adopted 22 June 1989, BISD 36S/135 186
Panel Report, *Japan — Restrictions on Imports of Certain Agricultural Products*, adopted 2 March 1988, BISD 35S/163 186
Panel Report, *Panel on Japanese Measures on Imports of Leather* ("*Japan — Leather II (US)*"), adopted 15 May 1984, BISD 31S/94 ....99, 100
Panel Report, *Panel on Norwegian Procurement of Toll Collection Equipment for the City of Trondheim*, adopted 13 May 1992, BISD 40S/319 186
Panel Report, *Swedish Anti-Dumping Duties*, adopted 26 February 1955, BISD 3S/81 186
Report of the GATT Panel, *United States — Countervailing Duties on Fresh, Chilled and Frozen Pork from Canada*, DS7/R, adopted July 11, 1991, BISD 38S/30 186
Panel Report, *United States — Measures Affecting Alcoholic and Malt Beverages*, adopted 19 June 1992, BISD 39S/206 186
Panel Report, *United States — Restrictions on Imports of Tuna*, September 1991, unadopted, BISD 39S/155 186
Panel Report, *United States Section 337 of the Tariff Act of 1930*, adopted 7 November 1989, BISD 36S/345 186
Panel Report, *United States — Taxes on Petroleum and Certain Imported Substances* ("*US — Superfund*"), adopted 17 June 1987, BISD 34S/136 ....99, 100

B. WTO CASES

Appellate Body Report, *Argentina — Measures Affecting Imports of Footwear, Textiles, Apparel and Other Items*, WT/DS56/AB/R and Corr.1, adopted 22 April 1998, DSR 1998:III, 1003 . . . . 50, 52, 55, 274, 335

Appellate Body Report, *Australia — Measures Affecting Importation of Salmon*, WT/DS18/AB/R, adopted 6 November 1998, DSR 1998:VIII, 3327 . . . . 31, 52, 57, 61, 242, 245

Appellate Body Report, *Brazil — Export Financing Programme for Aircraft*, WT/DS46/AB/R, adopted 20 August 1999, DSR 1999:III, 1161 . . . . 47, 73, 161, 170–1, 175, 177, 296

Appellate Body Report, *Brazil — Export Financing Programme for Aircraft — Recourse by Canada to Article 21.5 of the DSU*, WT/DS46/AB/RW, adopted 4 August 2000, DSR 2000: VIII, 4067 . . . . 167, 179, 218

Appellate Body Report, *Brazil — Measures Affecting Desiccated Coconut*, WT/DS22/AB/R, adopted 20 March 1997, DSR 1997:I, 167 . . . . . . .30, 47

Appellate Body Report, *Brazil — Measures Affecting Imports of Retreaded Tyres*, WT/DS332/AB/R, adopted 17 December 2007 . . . . .63, 213

Appellate Body Report, *Canada — Certain Measures Concerning Periodicals*, WT/DS31/AB/R, adopted 30 July 1997, DSR 1997:I, 449 . . . . .60, 65

Appellate Body Report, *Canada — Continued Suspension of Obligations in the EC — Hormones Dispute*, WT/DS321/AB/R, adopted 14 November 2008 . . . . .30, 33–4, 63, 97, 135, 220–22, 242, 244, 341–2

Appellate Body Report, *Canada — Measures Affecting the Export of Civilian Aircraft*, WT/DS70/AB/R, adopted 20 August 1999, DSR 1999:III, 1377 . . . . .36, 38, 55, 61, 113, 114, 124, 130, 250, 252, 261–3, 265–7, 270, 274, 277, 281, 283–4, 317, 331, 335, 348

Appellate Body Report, *Canada — Measures Affecting the Importation of Milk and the Exportation of Dairy Products — Second Recourse to Article 21.5 of the DSU by New Zealand and the United States*, WT/DS103/AB/RW2, WT/DS113/AB/RW2, adopted 17 January 2003 . . . . 92, 152, 298

Appellate Body Report, *Canada — Measures Relating to Exports of Wheat and Treatment of Imported Grain*, WT/DS276/AB/R, adopted 27 September 2004 . . . . .116, 253

Appellate Body Report, *Chile — Price Band System and Safeguard Measures Relating to Certain Agricultural Products*, WT/DS207/AB/R, adopted 23 October 2002 . . . . .30, 31, 48, 115, 258, 343–4

Appellate Body Report, *Chile — Price Band System and Safeguard Measures Relating to Certain Agricultural Products — Recourse to Article 21.5 of the DSU by Argentina*, WT/DS207/AB/RW, adopted 22 May 2007 . . . . .60, 62, 112, 120, 121, 219

Appellate Body Report, *Dominican Republic — Measures Affecting the Importation and Internal Sale of Cigarettes*, WT/DS302/AB/R, adopted 19 May 2005, DSR 2005:XV, 7367 344

Appellate Body Report, *European Communities — Anti-Dumping Duties on Imports of Cotton-Type Bed Linen from India — Recourse to Article 21.5 of the DSU by India*, WT/DS141/AB/RW, adopted 24 April 2003 . . . . 40, 110, 122, 134, 311

Appellate Body Report, *European Communities — Conditions for the Granting of Tariff Preferences to Developing Countries*, WT/DS246/AB/R, adopted 20 April 2004, DSR 2004:III, 925 . . . . 71, 163, 170, 173, 177, 185, 211–2

Appellate Body Report, *European Communities — Customs Classification of Certain Computer Equipment*, WT/DS62/AB/R, WT/DS67/AB/R, WT/DS68/AB/R, adopted 22 June 1998, DSR 1998:V, 1851 . . . . . . .30, 48

Appellate Body Report, *European Communities — Customs Classification of Frozen Boneless Chicken Cuts*, WT/DS269/AB/R, WT/DS286/AB/R, and Corr.1, adopted 27 September 2005 48

Appellate Body Report, *European Communities — Export Subsidies on Sugar*, WT/DS265/AB/R, WT/DS266/AB/R, WT/DS283/AB/R, adopted 19 May 2005 . . . . .31, 57, 60, 61, 64, 66, 99, 344

Appellate Body Report, *European Communities — Measures Affecting Asbestos and Asbestos-Containing Products*, WT/DS135/AB/R, adopted 5 April 2001, DSR 2001:VII, 3243 . . . . .59, 244, 338

Appellate Body Report, *European Communities — Measures Affecting the Importation of Certain Poultry Products*, WT/DS69/AB/R, adopted 23 July 1998, DSR 1998:V, 2031 62

Appellate Body Report, *European Communities — Measures Concerning Meat and Meat Products (Hormones)*, WT/DS26/AB/R, WT/DS48/AB/R, adopted 13 February 1998, DSR 1998:I, 135 . . . . .38, 54, 55, 57, 61, 62, 100, 104, 105, 119, 121, 157–9, 170, 172, 174, 177, 180–1, 186, 206, 240–2, 244, 299–300, 344

Appellate Body Report, *European Communities — Regime for the Importation, Sale and Distribution of Bananas*, WT/DS27/AB/R, adopted 25 September 1997, DSR 1997:II, 591 . . . . .32, 49, 99, 100, 258, 344

Appellate Body Report, *European Communities — Regime for the Importation, Sale and Distribution of Bananas — Recourse to Article 21.5 of the DSU by the United States*, WT/DS27/AB/RW/USA and Corr.1, adopted 22 December 2008 . . . . .99, 193

Appellate Body Report, *European Communities — Selected Customs Matters*, WT/DS315/AB/R, adopted 11 December 2006 . . . . 48, 56, 57, 60, 106, 123, 343

Appellate Body Report, *European Communities — Trade Description of Sardines*, WT/DS231/AB/R, adopted 23 October 2002, DSR 2002: VIII, 3359 . . . . .57, 106, 123, 160, 170, 172, 195, 205, 221, 296–7, 311, 337

Appellate Body Report, *Guatemala — Anti-Dumping Investigation Regarding Portland Cement from Mexico*, WT/DS60/AB/R, adopted 25 November 1998, DSR 1998:IX, 3767 . . . . .47, 343

Appellate Body Report, *India — Additional and Extra-Additional Duties on Imports from the United States*, WT/DS360/AB/R, adopted 17 November 2008 . . . . .3, 135, 166, 170, 173, 180, 196, 216, 252, 254, 260

Appellate Body Report, *India — Patent Protection for Pharmaceutical and Agricultural Chemical Products*, WT/DS50/AB/R, adopted 16 January 1998, DSR 1998:I, 9 . . . . 30, 54, 71, 120, 253, 260, 289

Appellate Body Report, *India — Quantitative Restrictions on Imports of Agricultural, Textile and Industrial Products*, WT/DS90/AB/R, adopted 22 September 1999, DSR 1999:IV, 1763 . . . . 61, 113, 122, 130, 167, 295, 336

Appellate Body Report, *Japan — Measures Affecting Agricultural Products*, WT/DS76/AB/R, adopted 19 March 1999, DSR 1999:I, 277 . . . . 195, 300, 346

Appellate Body Report, *Japan — Measures Affecting the Importation of Apples*, WT/DS245/AB/R, adopted 10 December 2003 . . . . . .32, 57, 72, 113, 242

Appellate Body Report, *Korea — Definitive Safeguard Measure on Imports of Certain Dairy Products*, WT/DS98/AB/R, adopted 12 January 2000, DSR 2000:I 48, 49, 82, 111, 112, 115, 316, 344

Appellate Body Report, *Korea — Taxes on Alcoholic Beverages*, WT/DS75/AB/R, WT/DS84/AB/R, adopted 17 February 1999, DSR 1999:I, 3 . . . . .61, 291

Appellate Body Report, *Mexico — Anti-Dumping Investigation of High Fructose Corn Syrup (HFCS) from the United States — Recourse to Article 21.5 of the DSU by the United States*, WT/DS132/AB/RW, adopted 21 November 2001, DSR 2001:XIII, 6675 . . . . 27, 30, 36, 55

Appellate Body Report, *Mexico — Definitive Anti-Dumping Measures on Beef and Rice, Complaint with Respect to Rice*, WT/DS295/AB/R, adopted 20 December 2005, DSR 2005:XXII, 10853 . . . . .47, 290

Appellate Body Report, *Thailand — Anti-Dumping Duties on Angles, Shapes and Sections of Iron or Non-Alloy Steel and H-Beams from Poland*, WT/DS122/AB/R, adopted 5 April 2001, DSR 2001:VII, 2701 . . . . .30, 47, 48, 112, 117, 236–7, 281, 315, 351

Appellate Body Report, *Turkey — Restrictions on Imports of Textile and Clothing Products*, WT/DS34/AB/R, adopted 19 November 1999 . . . . 170–1, 182

Appellate Body Report, *United States — Anti-Dumping Act of 1916*, WT/DS136/AB/R, WT/DS162/AB/R, adopted 26 September 2000, DSR 2000:X, 4793 . . . . .54, 55

Appellate Body Report, *United States — Anti-Dumping Measures on Certain Hot-Rolled Steel Products from Japan*, WT/DS184/AB/R, adopted 23 August 2001, DSR 2001:X, 4697 237

Appellate Body Report, *United States — Anti-Dumping Measures on Oil Country Tubular Goods (OCTG) from Mexico*, WT/DS282/AB/R, adopted 28 November 2005 . . . . 61, 63, 64, 116

Appellate Body Report, *United States — Continued Existence and Application of Zeroing Methodology*, WT/DS350/AB/R, adopted 19 February 2009 . . . . 47, 63, 312–4

Appellate Body Report, *United States — Continued Dumping and Subsidy Offset Act of 2000*, WT/DS217/AB/R, WT/DS234/AB/R, adopted 27 January 2003, DSR 2003:I, 375 . . . . .60, 61, 65

Appellate Body Report, *United States — Continued Suspension of Obligations in the EC — Hormones Dispute*, WT/DS320/AB/R, adopted 14 November 2008 . . . . .97, 219

Appellate Body Report, *United States — Countervailing Duties on Certain Corrosion-Resistant Carbon Steel Flat Products from Germany*, WT/DS213/AB/R and Corr.1, adopted 19 December 2002, DSR 2002:IX, 3779 . . . . .47, 312

Appellate Body Report, *United States — Countervailing Duty Investigation on Dynamic Random Access Memory Semiconductors (DRAMS) from Korea*, WT/DS296/AB/R, adopted 20 July 2005 . . . . 231–2, 235–8

Appellate Body Report, *United States — Countervailing Measures Concerning Certain Products from the European Communities*, WT/DS212/AB/R, adopted 8 January 2003 . . . . .32, 112

Appellate Body Report, *United States — Definitive Safeguard Measures on Imports of Certain Steel Products*, WT/DS248/AB/R, WT/DS249/AB/R, WT/DS251/AB/R, WT/DS252/AB/R, WT/DS253/AB/R, WT/DS254/AB/R, WT/DS258/AB/R, WT/DS259/AB/R, adopted 10 December 2003, DSR 2003:VII, 3117 . . . . .62, 237–8

Appellate Body Report, *United States — Definitive Safeguard Measures on Imports of Circular Welded Carbon Quality Line Pipe from Korea*, WT/DS202/AB/R, adopted 8 March 2002 121

Appellate Body Report, *United States — Definitive Safeguard Measures on Imports of Wheat Gluten from the European Communities*, WT/DS166/AB/R, adopted 19 January 2001, DSR 2001:II, 717 . . . . 232, 236, 265, 269, 278, 286, 317

Appellate Body Report, *United States — Final Dumping Determination on Softwood Lumber from Canada*, WT/DS264/AB/R, adopted 31 August 2004, DSR 2004:V, 1875 . . . . .60, 65

Appellate Body Report, *United States — Import Measures on Certain Products from the European Communities*, WT/DS165/AB/R, adopted 10 January 2001, DSR 2001:I, 373 54
Appellate Body Report, *United States — Import Prohibition of Certain Shrimp and Shrimp Products*, WT/DS58/AB/R, adopted 6 November 1998, DSR 1998:VII, 2755 . . . . 55, 311, 314, 337
Appellate Body Report, *United States — Import Prohibition of Certain Shrimp and Shrimp Products — Recourse to Article 21.5 of the DSU by Malaysia*, WT/DS58/AB/RW, adopted 21 November 2001, DSR 2001:XIII, 6481 40
Appellate Body Report, *United States — Investigation of the International Trade Commission in Softwood Lumber from Canada — Recourse to Article 21.5 of the DSU by Canada*, WT/DS277/AB/RW, adopted 9 May 2006 237–8
Appellate Body Report, *United States — Laws, Regulations and Methodology for Calculating Dumping Margins ("Zeroing")*, WT/DS294/AB/R, adopted 9 May 2006 315
Appellate Body Report, *United States — Measures Affecting the Cross-Border Supply of Gambling and Betting Services*, WT/DS285/AB/R, adopted 20 April 2005 . . . . 3, 52, 110, 116, 118, 169, 212–4, 253, 258, 349–50
Appellate Body Report, *United States — Measure Affecting Imports of Woven Wool Shirts and Blouses from India*, WT/DS33/AB/R and Corr.1, adopted 23 May 1997, DSR 1997:I, 323 . . . . . . 15–7, 39, 55, 104, 106, 119, 123, 153–4, 169–70, 174–5
Appellate Body Report, *United States — Safeguard Measures on Imports of Fresh, Chilled or Frozen Lamb Meat from New Zealand and Australia*, WT/DS177/AB/R, WT/DS178/AB/R, adopted 16 May 2001, DSR 2001:IX, 4051 236–8
Appellate Body Report, *United States — Standards for Reformulated and Conventional Gasoline*, WT/DS2/AB/R, adopted 20 May 1996 . . . . 153, 158, 169
Appellate Body Report, *United States — Subsidies on Upland Cotton*, WT/DS267/AB/R, adopted 21 March 2005 . . . . 32, 47, 48, 62, 63, 64, 72, 73, 153, 290
Appellate Body Report, *United States — Subsidies on Upland Cotton — Recourse to Article 21.5 of the DSU by Brazil*, WT/DS267/AB/RW, adopted 20 June 2008 . . . . 40, 62, 63, 64, 93, 134, 342
Appellate Body Report, *United States — Sunset Reviews of Anti-Dumping Measures on Oil Country Tubular Goods from Argentina*, WT/DS268/AB/R, adopted 17 December 2004 . . . . 30, 48, 60, 117
Appellate Body Report, *United States — Sunset Reviews of Anti-Dumping Measures on Oil Country Tubular Goods from Argentina — Recourse to*

Article 21.5 of the DSU by Argentina, WT/DS268/AB/RW, adopted 11 May 2007 40

Appellate Body Report, *United States — Tax Treatment for "Foreign Sales Corporations"*, WT/DS108/AB/R, adopted 20 March 2000, DSR 2000:III, 1619 . . . . 36, 252

Appellate Body Report, *United States — Tax Treatment for "Foreign Sales Corporations" — Recourse to Article 21.5 of the DSU by the European Communities*, WT/DS108/AB/RW, adopted 29 January 2002, DSR 2002:I, 55 . . . . 162, 170, 175

Appellate Body Report, *United States — Tax Treatment for "Foreign Sales Corporations" — Second Recourse to Article 21.5 of the DSU by the European Communities*, WT/DS108/AB/RW2, adopted 14 March 2006 48

Appellate Body Report, *United States — Transitional Safeguard Measure on Combed Cotton Yarn from Pakistan*, WT/DS192/AB/R, adopted 5 November 2001, DSR 2001:XII, 6027 . . . . 235, 238

Award of the Arbitrators, *United States — Section 110(5) of the US Copyright Act — Recourse to Arbitration under Article 25 of the DSU*, WT/DS160/ARB25/1, 9 November 2001, DSR 2001:II, 667 275

Decision by the Arbitrators, *European Communities — Regime for the Importation, Sale and Distribution of Bananas — Recourse to Arbitration by the European Communities under Article 22.6 of the DSU*, WT/DS27/ARB, 9 April 1999, DSR 1999:II, 725 284

Panel Report, *Argentina — Definitive Anti-Dumping Measures on Imports of Ceramic Floor Tiles from Italy*, WT/DS189/R, adopted 5 November 2001, DSR 2001:XII, 6241 99

Panel Report, *Argentina — Measures Affecting the Export of Bovine Hides and Import of Finished Leather*, WT/DS155/R and Corr.1, adopted 16 February 2001, DSR 2001:V, 1779 . . . . 109, 129, 134, 313

Panel Report, *Argentina — Measures Affecting Imports of Footwear, Textiles, Apparel and Other Items*, WT/DS56/R, adopted 22 April 1998 . . . . 52, 56, 253, 261, 271, 288, 335

Panel Report, *Australia — Measures Affecting Importation of Salmon*, WT/DS18/R and Corr.1, adopted 6 November 1998 . . . . 52, 73, 283, 339–41

Panel Report, *Australia — Measures Affecting Importation of Salmon — Recourse to Article 21.5 of the DSU by Canada*, WT/DS18/RW, adopted 20 March 2000, DSR 2000:IV, 2031 339

Panel Report, *Australia — Subsidies Provided to Producers and Exporters of Automotive Leather*, WT/DS126/R, adopted 16 June 1999, DSR 1999:III, 951 316

Panel Report, *Brazil — Export Financing Programme for Aircraft*, WT/DS46/R, adopted 20 August 1999 . . . . 160–1, 171, 175, 285, 296

Panel Report, *Brazil — Export Financing Programme for Aircraft — Recourse by Canada to Article 21.5 of the DSU*, WT/DS46/RW, adopted 4 August 2000 . . . . 133, 218
Panel Report, *Brazil — Export Financing Programme for Aircraft — Second Recourse by Canada to Article 21.5 of the DSU*, WT/DS46/RW/2, adopted 23 August 2001, DSR 2001:X, 5481 . . . . 217, 223, 281
Panel Report, *Brazil — Measures Affecting Imports of Retreaded Tyres*, WT/DS332/R, adopted 17 December 2007 213–4
Panel Report, *Canada — Continued Suspension of Obligations in the EC — Hormones Dispute*, WT/DS321/R, adopted 14 November 2008 . . . . 97, 195, 336, 339, 341
Panel Report, *Canada — Export Credits and Loan Guarantees for Regional Aircraft*, WT/DS222/R and Corr.1, adopted 19 February 2002, DSR 2002:III, 849 . . . . 272, 316, 329–30
Panel Report, *Canada — Measures Affecting the Export of Civilian Aircraft*, WT/DS70/R, adopted 20 August 1999 . . . . 73, 82, 112, 113, 117, 118, 129, 130, 262, 277, 282–5, 288, 297, 301, 316–7, 329–31
Panel Report, *Canada — Measures Affecting the Importation of Milk and the Exportation of Dairy Products*, WT/DS103/R, WT/DS113/R, adopted 27 October 1999 . . . . 134, 152
Panel Report, *Canada — Measures Affecting the Importation of Milk and the Exportation of Dairy Products — Recourse to Article 21.5 of the DSU by New Zealand and the United States*, WT/DS103/RW, WT/DS113/RW, adopted 18 December 2001 . . . . 152, 219, 279, 283, 316
Panel Report, *Canada — Measures Affecting the Importation of Milk and the Exportation of Dairy Products — Second Recourse to Article 21.5 of the DSU by New Zealand and the United States*, WT/DS103/RW2, WT/DS113/RW2, adopted 17 January 2003 . . . . 92, 122, 152
Panel Report, *Canada — Measures Relating to Exports of Wheat and Treatment of Imported Grain*, WT/DS276/R, adopted 27 September 2004 . . . . 133, 273, 279, 287, 347
Panel Report, *Canada — Patent Protection of Pharmaceutical Products*, WT/DS114/R, adopted 7 April 2000 . . . . 155, 170, 173, 195
Panel Report, *Chile — Taxes on Alcoholic Beverages*, WT/DS87/R, WT/DS110/R, adopted 12 January 2000 . . . . 254, 270, 332
Panel Report, *Dominican Republic — Measures Affecting the Importation and Internal Sale of Cigarettes*, WT/DS302/R, adopted 19 May 2005 . . . . 133, 155, 170, 179, 336
Panel Report, *European Communities — Anti-Dumping Measure on Farmed Salmon from Norway*, WT/DS337/R, adopted 15 January 2008 329

Panel Report, *European Communities — Anti-Dumping Duties on Imports of Cotton-Type Bed Linen from India*, WT/DS141/R, adopted 12 March 2001 235
Panel Report, *European Communities — Anti-Dumping Duties on Imports of Cotton-Type Bed Linen from India — Recourse to Article 21.5 of the DSU by India*, WT/DS141/RW, adopted 24 April 2003 110
Panel Report, *European Communities — Anti-Dumping Duties on Malleable Cast Iron Tube or Pipe Fittings from Brazil*, WT/DS219/R, adopted 18 August 2003 . . . . .112, 255
Panel Report, *European Communities — Conditions for the Granting of Tariff Preferences to Developing Countries*, WT/DS246/R, adopted 20 April 2004 . . . . 162, 173, 176–7, 183
Panel Report, *European Communities — Export Subsidies on Sugar, Complaint by Brazil*, WT/DS266/R, adopted 19 May 2005 . . . . . . .55, 131, 153, 281, 283, 296
Panel Report, *European Communities — Measures Affecting Asbestos and Asbestos-Containing Products*, WT/DS135/R and Add.1, adopted 5 April 2001 . . . . .142, 339
Panel Report, *European Communities — Measures Affecting the Approval and Marketing of Biotech Products*, WT/DS291/R, WT/DS292/R, WT/DS293/R, Corr.1 and Add.1, 2, 3, 4, 5, 6, 7, 8 and 9, adopted 21 November 2006 . . . . .160, 163, 170, 172, 280–1, 321, 339–40
Panel Report, *European Communities — Measures Affecting the Importation of Certain Poultry Products*, WT/DS69/R, adopted 23 July 1998 281
Panel Report, *European Communities — Measures Concerning Meat and Meat Products (Hormones), Complaint by Canada*, WT/DS48/R/CAN, adopted 13 February 1998 . . . . 119, 121, 129, 157, 172, 180, 339–40
Panel Report, *European Communities — Measures Concerning Meat and Meat Products (Hormones), Complaint by the United States*, WT/DS26/R/USA, adopted 13 February 1998 119
Panel Report, *European Communities — Protection of Trademarks and Geographical Indications for Agricultural Products and Foodstuffs, Complaint by the United States*, WT/DS174/R, adopted 20 April 2005 336
Panel Report, *European Communities — Regime for the Importation, Sale and Distribution of Bananas, Complaint by Ecuador*, WT/DS27/R/ECU, adopted 25 September 1997 100
Panel Report, *European Communities — Regime for the Importation, Sale and Distribution of Bananas, Complaint by Guatemala and Honduras*, WT/DS27/R/GTM, WT/DS27/R/HND, adopted 25 September 1997 258
Panel Report, *European Communities — Regime for the Importation, Sale and Distribution of Bananas, Complaint by the United States*, WT/DS27/R/USA, adopted 25 September 1997 290

Panel Report, *European Communities — Regime for the Importation, Sale and Distribution of Bananas — Recourse to Article 21.5 of the DSU by the European Communities*, WT/DS27/RW/EEC and Corr.1, 12 April 1999, DSR 1999:II, 783 27
Panel Report, *European Communities — Selected Customs Matters*, WT/DS315/R, adopted 11 December 2006 . . . 52, 73, 127, 256, 273–4, 328
Panel Report, *European Communities — Trade Description of Sardines*, WT/DS231/R and Corr.1, adopted 23 October 2002 . . . . 73, 159, 195, 273, 336
Panel Report, *Guatemala — Definitive Anti-Dumping Measures on Grey Portland Cement from Mexico*, WT/DS156/R, adopted 17 November 2000, DSR 2000:XI, 5295 99
Panel Report, *Japan — Measures Affecting Agricultural Products*, WT/DS76/R, adopted 19 March 1999 . . . . .130, 131, 339, 346, 348
Panel Report, *Japan — Measures Affecting Consumer Photographic Film and Paper*, WT/DS44/R, adopted 22 April 1998, DSR 1998:IV, 1179 . . . . . 142, 339, 342
Panel Report, *Japan — Measures Affecting the Importation of Apples*, WT/DS245/R, adopted 10 December 2003 . . . . 206, 252, 339–41
Panel Report, *Japan — Measures Affecting the Importation of Apples, Recourse to Article 21.5 of the DSU by the United States*, WT/DS245/RW, 23 June 2005 71
Panel Report, *Japan — Taxes on Alcoholic Beverages*, WT/DS8/R, WT/DS10/R, WT/DS11/R, adopted 1 November 1996 86–7
Panel Report, *India — Additional and Extra-Additional Duties on Imports from the United States*, WT/DS360/R, adopted 17 November 2008 . . . . . . 3, 165, 173, 180, 197, 216, 331
Panel Report, *India — Measures Affecting the Automotive Sector*, WT/DS146/R, WT/DS175/R and Corr.1, adopted 5 April 2002 . . . . 93, 109, 168, 177–8, 324
Panel Report, *India — Patent Protection for Pharmaceutical and Agricultural Chemical Products, Complaint by the United States*, WT/DS50/R, adopted 16 January 1998 . . . . 73, 119, 120
Panel Report, *India — Patent Protection for Pharmaceutical and Agricultural Chemical Products, Complaint by the European Communities*, WT/DS79/R, adopted 22 September 1998, DSR 1998:VI, 2661 . . . . .103, 119
Panel Report, *India — Quantitative Restrictions on Imports of Agricultural, Textile and Industrial Products*, WT/DS90/R, adopted 22 September 1999 . . . . .130, 166–7, 178, 273, 336
Panel Report, *Indonesia — Certain Measures Affecting the Automobile Industry*, WT/DS54/R, WT/DS55/R, WT/DS59/R, WT/DS64/R and Corr.1, 2, 3, and 4, adopted 23 July 1998, DSR 1998:VI, 2201 . . . . 38, 270, 277

Panel Report, *Korea — Anti-Dumping Duties on Imports of Certain Paper from Indonesia*, WT/DS312/R, adopted 28 November 2005 286
Panel Report, *Korea — Definitive Safeguard Measure on Imports of Certain Dairy Products*, WT/DS98/R and Corr.1, adopted 12 January 2000 . . . . 104, 128, 133, 235
Panel Report, *Korea — Measures Affecting Imports of Fresh, Chilled and Frozen Beef*, WT/DS161/R, WT/DS169/R, adopted 10 January 2001.
Panel Report, *Korea — Measures Affecting Trade in Commercial Vessels*, WT/DS273/R, adopted 11 April 2005 . . . . 218, 265, 268, 270, 284, 323–4
Panel Report, *Korea — Taxes on Alcoholic Beverages*, WT/DS75/R, WT/DS84/R, adopted 17 February 1999 . . . . 109, 134, 281, 290
Panel Report, *Mexico — Anti-Dumping Investigation of High Fructose Corn Syrup (HFCS) from the United States*, WT/DS132/R and Corr.1, adopted 24 February 2000, DSR 2000:III, 1345 291
Panel Report, *Thailand — Anti-Dumping Duties on Angles, Shapes and Sections of Iron or Non-Alloy Steel and H-Beams from Poland*, WT/DS122/R, adopted 5 April 2001 . . . . .133, 316
Panel Report, *Turkey — Measures Affecting the Importation of Rice*, WT/DS334/R, adopted 22 October 2007 . . . . . . 38, 120, 121–2, 252, 261, 265, 267, 269–70, 277, 282, 286, 316–7, 335
Panel Report, *Turkey — Restrictions on Imports of Textile and Clothing Products*, WT/DS34/R, adopted 19 November 1999, DSR 1999:VI, 2363 . . . . .100, 182
Panel Report, *United States — Anti-Dumping Act of 1916, Complaint by the European Communities*, WT/DS136/R and Corr.1, adopted 26 September 2000 118
Panel Report, *United States — Anti-Dumping Measures on Certain Hot-Rolled Steel Products from Japan*, WT/DS184/R, adopted 23 August 2001 71
Panel Report, *United States — Anti-Dumping Measures on Oil Country Tubular Goods (OCTG) from Mexico*, WT/DS282/R, 20 June 2005 116
Panel Report, *United States — Anti-Dumping and Countervailing Measures on Steel Plate from India*, WT/DS206/R and Corr.1, adopted 29 July 2002 . . . . 71, 118, 235, 256
Panel Report, *United States — Continued Existence and Application of Zeroing Methodology*, WT/DS350/R, adopted 19 February 2009 312
Panel Report, *United States — Continued Suspension of Obligations in the EC — Hormones Dispute*, WT/DS320/R, adopted 14 November 2008 . . . . .97, 219, 339
Panel Reports, *United States — Definitive Safeguard Measures on Imports of Certain Steel Products*, WT/DS248/R, WT/DS249/R, WT/DS251/R, WT/DS252/R, WT/DS253/R, WT/DS254/R, WT/DS258/R, WT/DS259/R, and Corr.1, adopted 10 December 2003 280

Panel Report, *United States — Definitive Safeguard Measures on Imports of Wheat Gluten from the European Communities*, WT/DS166/R, adopted 19 January 2001 . . . . 235, 266, 278, 284, 286, 316
Panel Report, *United States — Definitive Safeguard Measures on Imports of Circular Welded Carbon Quality Line Pipe from Korea*, WT/DS202/R, adopted 8 March 2002 . . . . 288, 316, 326–30
Panel Report, *United States — Final Dumping Determination on Softwood Lumber from Canada*, WT/DS264/R, adopted 31 August 2004 235
Panel Report, *United States — Import Prohibition of Certain Shrimp and Shrimp Products*, WT/DS58/R and Corr.1, adopted 6 November 1998 . . . . 73, 339
Panel Report, *United States — Imposition of Countervailing Duties on Certain Hot-Rolled Lead and Bismuth Carbon Steel Products Originating in the United Kingdom*, WT/DS138/R and Corr.2, adopted 7 June 2000 . . . . 278, 288, 328
Panel Report, *United States — Measures Affecting the Cross-Border Supply of Gambling and Betting Services*, WT/DS285/R, adopted 20 April 2005 . . . . 3, 106, 109, 113, 114, 117, 123, 214, 280, 349–51
Panel Report, *United States — Measures Affecting the Cross-Border Supply of Gambling and Betting Services — Recourse to Article 21.5 of the DSU by Antigua and Barbuda*, WT/DS285/RW, adopted 22 May 2007 280
Panel Report, *United States — Measure Affecting Imports of Woven Wool Shirts and Blouses from India*, WT/DS33/R, adopted 23 May 1997 . . . . 118, 156, 171, 180, 235
Panel Report, *United States — Restrictions on Imports of Cotton and Man-made Fibre Underwear*, WT/DS24/R, adopted 25 February 1997 . . . . 68, 111, 155, 280, 292
Panel Report, *United States — Section 110(5) of the US Copyright Act*, WT/DS160/R, adopted 27 July 2000, DSR 2000:VIII, 3769 . . 72, 153, 254
Panel Report, *United States — Section 211 Omnibus Appropriations Act of 1998*, WT/DS176/R, adopted 1 February 2002 . . . . 109, 336
Panel Report, *United States — Sections 301-310 of the Trade Act of 1974*, WT/DS152/R, adopted 27 January 2000, DSR 2000:II, 815 . . . . 71, 104, 109, 134
Panel Report, *United States — Safeguard Measures on Imports of Fresh, Chilled or Frozen Lamb Meat from New Zealand and Australia*, WT/DS177/R, WT/DS178/R, adopted 16 May 2001 288
Panel Report, *United States — Standards for Reformulated and Conventional Gasoline*, WT/DS2/R, adopted 20 May 1996 . . . . 68, 153, 155, 169
Panel Report, *United States — Subsidies on Upland Cotton*, WT/DS267/R, and Corr.1, adopted 21 March 2005 . . . . 56, 68, 109, 112, 153, 163–4, 170–3, 176, 257, 264, 266, 270–1, 275, 282, 288, 303, 313, 316, 328–9, 331, 348

Panel Report, *United States — Subsidies on Upland Cotton – Recourse to Article 21.5 of the DSU by Brazil*, WT/DS267/RW and Corr.1, adopted 20 June 2008 153
Panel Report, *United States — Tax Treatment for "Foreign Sales Corporations"*, WT/DS108/R, adopted 20 March 2000 153
Panel Report, *United States — Tax Treatment for "Foreign Sales Corporations" — Second Recourse to Article 21.5 of the DSU by the European Communities*, WT/DS108/RW2, adopted 14 March 2006 217

C. OTHER INTERNATIONAL CASES

ADF Group Inc. v The United States of America, ICSID Case No. ARB(AF)/00/1, Award of 9 January 2003 322
Asian Agricultural Products Ltd v Republic of Sri Lanka, ICSID Case No. ARB/87/3, Award of 27 June 1990 198
Asylum (Colombia v Peru), Judgment of 20 November 1950, International Court of Justice, Reports of Judgments, Advisory Opinions and Orders (1950) 72
Biwater Gauff (Tanzania) Ltd. v United Republic of Tanzania, ICSID Case No. ARB/05/22, Procedural Order No. 2, 24 May 2006 . . . . .282, 312
Case Concerning the Application of the Convention on the Prevention and Punishment of the Crime of Genocide (Bosnia and Herzegovina v Serbia and Montenegro), Judgment of 26 February 2007, available at http://www.icj-cij.org/docket/index.php?p1=3&p2=3&k=f4&case=91&code=bhy&p3=4 (visited on 11 April 2008) 91
Case Concerning Avena and other Mexican Nationals (Mexico v United States of America), Judgment of 31 March 2004, International Court of Justice, Reports of Judgments, Advisory Opinions and Orders (2004) 198
Case Concerning the Barcelona Traction, Light and Power Company, Limited (New Application: 1962) (Preliminary Objections) (Belgium v Spain), Judgment of 24 July 1964, Separate Opinion of Judge Bustamante, International Court of Justice, Reports of Judgments, Advisory Opinions and Orders (1964) 314
Case Concerning the Barcelona Traction, Light and Power Company, Limited (New Application: 1962) (Belgium v Spain), Judgment of 5 February 1970, Separate Opinion of Judge Jessup, International Court of Justice, Reports of Judgments, Advisory Opinions and Orders (1970) 264
Case Concerning the Factory at Chorzow (Claim for Indemnity) (Merits), Judgment of 13 September 1928, Permanent Court of International Justice, Series A., No. 17, (1928) 291
Case Concerning the Land and Maritime Boundary between Cameroon and Nigeria (Preliminary Objections) (Cameroon v Nigeria), Judgment of

11 June 1998, International Court of Justice, Reports of Judgments, Advisory Opinions and Orders (1998) 198
Case Concerning Military and Paramilitary Activities in and against Nicaragua (Jurisdiction and Admissibility) (Nicaragua v United States), Judgment of 26 November 1984, International Court of Justice, Reports of Judgments, Advisory Opinions and Orders (1984) 198
Case Concerning Military and Paramilitary Activities in and against Nicaragua (Merits), Judgment of 27 June 1986, International Court of Justice, Reports of Judgments, Advisory Opinions and Orders (1986) 71
Case Concerning United States Diplomatic and Consular Staff in Tehran (United States of America v Iran), Judgment of 24 May 1980, International Court of Justice, Reports of Judgments, Advisory Opinions and Orders (1980) 73
Combustion Engineering, Inc., et al. v The Islamic Republic of Iran, et al., Partial Award No. 506-308-2, 18 February 1991, 26 Iran-U.S. Claims Tribunal Reports 60 (Cambridge: Grotious Publications, 1992) 90
Daniel Dillon (USA) v United Mexican States, 3 October 1928, Concurring Opinion of Commissioner Nielsen, 4 Reports of International Arbitral Awards 368 (Millwood, Kraus Reprint Co., 1974) 144
Fairen Garbi and Solis Corrales Case, Judgment of 15 March 1989, Inter-American Court of Human Rights, Series C, No. 6 (1989) 91
Fisheries Jurisdiction (Merits) (United Kingdom v Iceland), Judgment of 25 July 1974, International Court of Justice, Reports of Judgments, Advisory Opinions and Orders (1974) 71
Fisheries Jurisdiction (Merits) (United Kingdom v Iceland), Judgment of 25 July 1974, Separate Opinion of Judge de Castro, International Court of Justice, Reports of Judgments, Advisory Opinions and Orders (1974) 72
Flexi-Van Leasing, Inc. v. Iran, Case no. 36, 15 December 1982, 1 Iran-U.S. Claims Tribunal Reports 455 (Cambridge, Grotius Publications, 1983) 92
Glamis Gold Ltd. v the United States of America, Procedural Order No. 1, 3 March 2005 322
Godinez-Cruz Case, Judgment of 20 January 1989, Inter-American Court of Human Rights, Series C, No. 5 (1989) 140
Heirs of Jules Brun v Venezuela, 31 July 1905, Report of French-Venezuelan Mixed Claims Commission of 1902 (Washington: Government Printing Office, 1906) 144
International Ore & Fertilizer Corporation, et al. v Razi Chemical Company Ltd., et al., Award No. 351-486-3, 29 February 1988, 18 Iran-U.S. Claims Tribunal Reports 98 (Cambridge: Grotious Publications, 1989) 81
Ireland against United Kingdom, Report of the Commission, 19 Yearbook of the European Convention on Human Rights (1976) 90

Ireland v. United Kingdom, Judgment of 18 January 1978, 25 European Court of Human Rights (Series A) 90
Lillie S. Kling (U.S.A.) v United Mexican States, 8 October 1930, 4 Reports of International Arbitral Awards 575 (Millwood, Kraus Reprint, 1974) 143, 252
Lockheed Corporation v The Government of Iran, The Ministry of War, and The Iranian Air Force, Award 367-829-2, 9 June 1988, 18 Iran-U.S. Claims Tribunal Reports 292 (Cambridge, Grotius Publications, 1989) 145, 146
Melczer Mining Company (USA) v United Mexican States, 30 April 1929, 4 Reports of International Arbitral Awards 481 (Millwood: Kraus Reprint Co., 1974) 81, 144–5
Middle East Cement Shipping and Handling Co. S.A. v Arab Republic of Egypt, ICSID Case No. ARB/99/6, Award of 12 April 2002 198
Oil Platforms (Iran v United States of America), Judgment of 6 November 2003, International Court of Justice, Reports of Judgments, Advisory Opinions and Orders (2003) 92
Oil Platforms (Iran v United States of America), Judgment of 6 November 2003, Separate Opinion of Judge Buergenthal, International Court of Justice, Reports of Judgments, Advisory Opinions and Orders (2003) 91–2
Oil Platforms (Iran v United States of America), Judgment of 6 November 2003, Separate Opinion of Judge Higgins, International Court of Justice, Reports of Judgments, Advisory Opinions and Orders (2003) 91–2, 140
Oil Platforms (Iran v United States of America), Judgment of 6 November 2003, Separate Opinion of Judge Owada, International Court of Justice, Reports of Judgments, Advisory Opinions and Orders (2003) 309
Pope & Talbot, Inc. v Government of Canada, Procedural Order No. 4, 29 October 1999 322
Pope and Talbot v Government of Canada, Decision by the Tribunal, 6 September 2000 282
Pope & Talbot Inc. v The Government of Canada, Award on the Merits of Phase 2, 10 April 2001 . . . . 282, 312
Salini Costruttori S.P.A and Italstrade S.P.A v The Hashemite Kingdom of Jordan, ICSID Case No. ARB/02/13, Award of 31 January 2006 198
S. D. Myers v Government of Canada, Procedural Order No. 1, 28 May 1999 322
S.D. Myers v Government of Canada, Procedural Order No. 11 (concerning confidentiality of materials produced in the arbitration), 11 November 1999 286

The Case Concerning Certain German Interests in Polish Upper Silesia (Germany v Poland), Judgment of 25 May 1926, Permanent Court of International Justice, Series A, No. 7 (1926) 71
The Case of the S.S. "Lotus" (France v Turkey), Judgment of 7 September 1927, Permanent Court of International Justice, Series A, No. 10 (1927) 98
The Corfu Channel (Merits) (United Kingdom v Albania), Judgment of 9 April 1949, International Court of Justice, Reports of Judgments, Advisory Opinions and Orders (1949) 41, 81, 91, 96, 140, 144, 197, 268
The Greek Case, Report of the Commission, 12 Yearbook of the European Convention on Human Rights (1969) 90
The Minquiers and Ecrechos Case (France v United Kingdom), Judgment of 17 November 1953, International Court of Justice, Reports of Judgments, Advisory Opinions and Orders (1953) 198
United Parcel Service of America v Government of Canada, Decision of the Tribunal Relating to Canada's Claim of Cabinet Privilege, 8 October 2004 282
United Parcel Service of America v Government of Canada, Procedural Directions and Order of the Tribunal, 4 April 2003 . . . . 285–6, 322
Velasquez Rodriguez Case, Judgment of 29 July 1988, Inter-American Court of Human Rights, Series C, No. 4 (1988) 90
William L. Pereira Associates, Iran v The Islamic Republic of Iran, Award No. 116-1-3, 19 March 1984, Concurring Opinion of Richard M. Mosk, reprinted in 5 Iran-U.S. Claims Tribunal Reports 230 (Cambridge: Grotius Publications, 1985) 90
William A. Parker (U.S.A.) v United Mexican States, 31 March 1926, 4 Reports of International Arbitration Awards 35 (Millwood, Kraus Reprint, 1974) 56, 143, 252

D. DOMESTIC CASES

In re Oxus Gold plc, MISC No. 06-82-GEB, 2007 WL 1037387 (D.H.J. April 2, 2007) 333
In re Roz Trading Ltd., 469 F.Supp.2d 1221 (N.D.Ga. Dec 19, 2006) . . 333
Rhesa Shipping Co. S.A. v Edmunds [1985] 1 WLR 948 70–1
Snell v. *Farrell*, [1990] 2 S.C.R. 311, 107 N.B.R. (2d) 94, 72 D.L.R. (4th) 289, 110 N.R. 200, 4 C.C.L.T. (2d) 229 85
Texas Dept. of Commun. Affairs v. Burdine, 450 U.S. 248 (1981) 107

List of Abbreviations

Aarhus Convention	Convention on Access to Information, Public Participation in Decision-Making and Access to Justice in Environmental Matters
ACWL	Advisory Centre on WTO Law
ALI	American Law Institute
Anti-Dumping Agreement	Agreement on Implementation of Article VI of the General Agreement on Tariffs and Trade 1994
ATC	Agreement on Textiles and Clothing
CODEX	Codex Alimentarius Commission
DSB	Dispute Settlement Body
DSU	Understanding on Rules and Procedures Governing the Settlement of Disputes
ECJ	European Court of Justice
EC	European Community
Enabling Clause	Decision of 28 November 1979 (L/4903) on Differential and More Favourable Treatment, Reciprocity, and Fuller Participation of Developing Countries
GATS	General Agreement on Trade in Services
GATT	General Agreement on Tariffs and Trade 1994
GATT 1947	General Agreement on Tariffs and Trade 1947
GATT Understanding	Understanding Regarding Notification, Consultation, Dispute Settlement and Surveillance
IARC	International Agency for Research on Cancer
IBA	International Bar Association
IBA Rules	IBA Rules on the Taking of Evidence in International Commercial Arbitration
ICC	International Chamber of Commerce
ICJ	International Court of Justice
ICSID	International Centre for the Settlement of Investment Disputes
ICSID Convention	Convention on the Settlement of Investment Disputes between States and Nationals of Other States
ICSID Arbitration Rules	Rules of Procedure for Arbitration Proceedings
ILC	International Law Commission
IMF	International Monetary Fund
JECFA	Joint FAO/WHO Expert Committee on Food Additives
MFN	Most-Favored-Nation
NAFTA	North American Free Trade Agreement
NGO	Non-Governmental Organization
ODCs	ordinary customs duties or other duties or charges of any kind imposed on or in connection with the importation

OECD	Organisation for Economic Co-operation and Development
PCIJ	Permanent Court of International Justice
Rules of Conduct	Rules of Conduct for the Understanding on Rules and Procedures Governing the Settlement of Disputes, adopted by the DSB on 3 December 1996, WT/DSB/RC/1
SCM Agreement	Agreement on Subsidies and Countervailing Measures
SPS	Sanitary and Phytosanitary
SPS Agreement	Agreement on the Application of Sanitary and Phytosanitary Measures
TBT Agreement	Agreement on Technical Barriers to Trade
TPRM	Trade Policy Review Mechanism
TRIMS Agreement	Agreement on Trade-Related Investment Measures
TRIPS Agreement	Agreement on Trade-Related Aspects of Intellectual Property Rights
UN	United Nations
UNCITRAL	United Nations Commission on International Trade Law
UNIDROIT	International Institute for the Unification of Private Law
Vienna Convention	Vienna Convention on the Law of Treaties
WIPO	World Intellectual Property Organization
WTO	World Trade Organization
WTO Agreement	Marrakesh Agreement Establishing the World Trade Organization

Introduction

I. Background

It has been noted that since the inception of the World Trade Organization (the 'WTO') the disputes, particularly their factual component, brought before the WTO dispute settlement system have become ever more complex.[1] It is arguable that this complexity is partly a function of more complex obligations, and partly a function of the increased complexity of the measures challenged under the Understanding on Rules and Procedures Governing the Settlement of Disputes (the 'DSU'). In connection with the former, the establishment of the WTO on 1 January 1995 was accompanied by an increase in the regulation of international trade. Prior to the creation of the WTO, international trade was regulated by the General Agreement on Tariffs and Trade of 1947 (the 'GATT 1947') and a handful of agreements which were not widely accepted by all GATT 1947 contracting parties. The WTO brought with it new agreements—which bind all 153 WTO Members—in the areas of trade in services, intellectual property, agriculture, and sanitary and phytosanitary (SPS) regulation, among others. In addition, disciplines contained in pre-existing agreements were further elaborated. Without attempting to conduct a comprehensive analysis of all disputes brought to the WTO, it is worth noting that as a matter of fact some of the most factually complex disputes adjudicated under the DSU have indeed involved the new disciplines. Challenges to SPS measures are particularly illustrative. There have been seven[2] cases involving the Agreement on the Application of Sanitary and Phytosanitary Measures (the 'SPS Agreement'), which all resulted in the production of substantial amounts of scientific evidence, and consultations with experts and international institutions such as the Codex Alimentarius Commission.

As for the increased complexity of the measures challenged in dispute settlement, it is fair to say that the universe of measures which constitute blatant violations of the WTO rules has diminished on account of increased awareness of the WTO agreements. Accordingly, it is less common to find cases where all

[1] See, for example, Jeff Waincymer, *WTO Litigation: Procedural Aspects of Formal Dispute Settlement* (London: Cameron May, 2002) at 530; Mireille Cossy, 'Panel's Consultations with Scientific Experts: the Right to Seek Information under Article 13 of the DSU' in R Yerxa and B Wilson (eds), *Key Issues in WTO Dispute Settlement: the First Ten Years* (Cambridge: Cambridge University Press, 2005) 204 at 204; David Palmeter & Petros Mavroidis, *Dispute Settlement in the World Trade Organization: Practice and Procedure* (2nd edn, Cambridge: Cambridge University Press, 2004) at 116; Matthias Oesch, *Standards of Review in WTO Dispute Resolution* (Oxford: Oxford University Press, 2003) at 56.

[2] Excluding compliance proceedings under Article 21.5 of the DSU.

the evidence necessary to prove a violation of a WTO agreement is the text of the allegedly inconsistent domestic regulation or legislation. As Pauwelyn noted as early as 1998, WTO panels have been flooded with evidence and this has occurred not only in disputes under the more technical agreements such as the SPS Agreement, but also in disputes under the General Agreement on Tariffs and Trade of 1994 (the 'GATT').[3]

Another possible explanation for the increased factual complexity of the disputes—and related upsurge in the amount of evidence placed on the record of the panels—is that with the judicialization of the WTO dispute settlement system WTO Members are less likely to concede the facts of the case. While dispute settlement under the GATT 1947, particularly in the earlier years, was the domain of diplomats, in WTO dispute settlement diplomats have given way to lawyers. Law firms in Brussels, Geneva, and Washington represent WTO Members in proceedings before panels and the Appellate Body. An international organization, the Advisory Centre on WTO Law, was even created to provide support for developing countries in WTO dispute settlement proceedings. The judicialization hypothesis is in line with the fact that the reported GATT panel practice of establishing a 'cluster of undisputed facts' on which a decision was based has not been effective in the context of WTO disputes.[4]

In sum, the discussion above suggests that the evolution and increased sophistication of the WTO legal system has resulted in more complex disputes requiring the resolution of complex factual questions.

Against this background, it is important to note that the DSU contains few rules—and those mostly of a general character—to guide panels in the process of fact-finding. The most directly relevant provisions are Articles 11 and 13 of the DSU, and paragraph 4 of Appendix 3 to the DSU. The latter provides that 'the parties to the dispute shall transmit to the panel written submissions in which they present the facts of the case and their arguments'. Article 13 on its turn grants panels the 'the right to seek information and technical advice from any individual or body which it deems appropriate' including the power to establish expert review groups or to consult individual experts 'to obtain their opinion on certain aspects of the matter'. At a more general level, Article 11 of the DSU provides that 'a panel should make an objective assessment of the matter before it, including an objective assessment of the facts of the case and the applicability of and conformity with the relevant covered agreements'. Clearly these provisions provide general guidance but few direct answers to specific questions regarding the process of fact-finding. Therefore, in order to render the dispute

[3] Joost Pauwelyn, 'Evidence, Proof and Persuasion in WTO Dispute Settlement: Who Bears the Burden?' (1998) 1 Journal of International Economic Law 227 at 227.

[4] Referring to the GATT panel practice of establishing a 'cluster of undisputed facts' and its fall into disuse see Christopher Thomas, 'Litigation Process Under the GATT Dispute Settlement System: Lessons for the World Trade Organization?' (1996) 30:2 Journal of World Trade 53 at 71; Pauwelyn, above n 3 at 227.

settlement system effective, panels and the Appellate Body have had to provide answers to those questions in each case.

In fact, after 158 panel reports and 94 Appellate Body reports,[5] panels and the Appellate Body have gone a long way in filling the gaps left by the WTO negotiators. In those reports, they have addressed a wide array of questions related to the process of fact-finding, including questions related to burden of proof, fact-finding powers of the panel, protection of confidential information, production of documents, and adverse inferences, among others. As panel and Appellate Body reports are publicly available, those decisions have helped the operators of the system (panelists, disputing parties, and lawyers in the WTO Secretariat) to gain a better understanding of the functioning of the process of fact-finding in WTO dispute settlement.

This book argues, however, that that patchwork approach has not been completely successful in shaping a clear and coherent process of fact-finding. It demonstrates that panels and the Appellate Body have on occasion issued inconsistent rulings, and rulings which were not in harmony with the overall structure of the WTO dispute settlement system. In other words, panels and the Appellate Body have failed to provide clear guidance on how the process of fact-finding in WTO dispute settlement functions, including with respect to issues such as the allocation of the burden of proof—which can be determinative of the outcome of a case.

The problems that may arise from lack of clear guidance are made clear in cases such as *US—Gambling* and *India—Additional Import Duties*.[6] Those cases will be examined in detail in different parts of this book, but for the moment it suffices to say that they ended with very little information being presented on core issues. If the parties and the panel had had a clear understanding of their obligations and their role in the process of fact-finding, the panels in those cases would have been able to address the core issues of the cases effectively, and the outcome of the cases (or at least some of the claims) might have been different.

Consistency and predictability are particularly important when the operators of the system come from different legal cultures. The problem becomes more acute as a greater number of WTO Members become involved in dispute settlement under the DSU. Although the majority of cases still revolve around a handful of WTO Members, among which are the European Communities and the United States, the number of non-traditional players has risen. As has been noted with respect to international commercial arbitration, 'even though logic

[5] These numbers are as of 20 May 2009, and include standard and compliance proceedings.

[6] See Panel Report, *India—Additional and Extra-Additional Duties on Imports from the United States*, WT/DS360/R, adopted 17 November 2008; Appellate Body Report, *India—Additional and Extra-Additional Duties on Imports from the United States*, WT/DS360/AB/R, adopted 17 November 2008; Panel Report, *United States—Measures Affecting the Cross-Border Supply of Gambling and Betting Services*, WT/DS285/R, adopted 20 April 2005; Appellate Body Report, *United States—Measures Affecting the Cross-Border Supply of Gambling and Betting Services*, WT/DS285/AB/R, adopted 20 April 2005.

would command that "local specificities" stay confined to national State courts', it is not uncommon for practitioners to seek to reproduce local practices in international proceedings.[7] The adoption of local procedures might work well when the parties involved come from similar legal systems. However, when parties have different expectations on how the process of fact-finding should function, problems are bound to arise. Accordingly, in an international legal system with a diverse membership, as is the case of the WTO legal system, the development of a common language that all operators can understand and speak is of utmost importance.

For those who prize flexibility, this is not to say that rigid rules covering all aspects of the process of fact-finding must be adopted. Parties should be given room to agree on their own common language. Experience, however, shows that the parties rarely agree on anything after they engage in dispute settlement proceedings. For those cases, clear guidelines would be beneficial. This could be achieved through a variety of means, ranging from amendments to the DSU at one end of the spectrum, to a line of consistent and clear panel and Appellate Body decisions at the other end, and including options such as guidelines drawn by the Dispute Settlement Body (the 'DSB') inbetween.

II. Outline of the Book

In keeping with the overarching objective of providing clear guidance to the operators of the WTO dispute settlement system, the motivation for this book is not only to provide guidance, but to provide *good* guidance. In other words, the goal is to set out an optimal process of fact-finding for the WTO dispute settlement system. With this in mind, this study seeks to determine the extent to which panels and the Appellate Body have set out optimal rules to govern the process of fact-finding through the existing jurisprudence. To the extent that that is not the case, suggestions for improvement are made.

Chapter 1 lays out the framework according to which that assessment will be conducted and suggestions developed. Pursuant to that framework, this book will seek to determine (i) whether the solutions developed by panels and the Appellate Body maximize the goals of the WTO dispute settlement system, among which are accuracy, participation, impartiality, equality, good faith cooperation, the efficient use of resources (time and money), and the protection of confidential information; (ii) whether panels and the Appellate Body have efficiently managed uncertainty and the related risk of error, which are constant features of the process of fact-finding in legal adjudication; and (iii) whether the rules developed are in harmony with the basic structure of the WTO dispute

[7] Pierre-Yves Gunter, 'Transnational Rules on the Taking of Evidence' in E Gaillard et al (eds), *Towards a Uniform International Arbitration Law?* (Huntington: Juris Publishing, 2005) 129 at 133.

settlement system laid out in the DSU. In making these assessments, particularly in relation to the last factor, this study draws on the approaches followed in the two major legal traditions of the world—the common law and the civil law—and, to the extent possible, the approaches adopted by other international courts and tribunals.

The questions examined in Chapters 2 through 5 are closely interrelated and are part of what is referred to in this book as the 'process of fact-finding' or the 'process of proof'.

The process of fact-finding is the process through which a panel formulates its conclusions with respect to the facts of a case, that is, it is the process through which the facts of a case are established. In this regard, it is important to note that panels consider and establish facts against the background of a legal provision—ie a provision in the WTO agreements. In other words, the legal provision defines at a general level the facts which must be proved; these are the elemental facts or elemental propositions. Elemental propositions are then usually broken down into more simple propositions (auxiliary propositions or auxiliary facts) each of which needs to be proved in order to prove the elemental proposition. For instance, Article III:4 of the GATT provides that '[t]he products of the territory of any contracting party imported into the territory of any other contracting party shall be accorded treatment no less favourable than that accorded to like products of national origin [. . .].' In the context of this provision, the question of whether the products at issue are 'like products' relates to an elemental fact. Proof of the 'likeness' of the products at issue may require on its turn for it to be shown that the products have the same (i) physical characteristics, (ii) end uses, and (iii) tariff classification, and that (iv) there are no differences in the consumers' perception and behaviour towards the products at issue.[8] Factors (i) to (iv) are auxiliary facts. These auxiliary facts can be further broken down into other auxiliary facts. For example, proof that the products at issue have the same physical characteristics may require the products to be shown to have the same chemical composition, size, and colour, among other factors. The word 'fact', therefore, encompasses different levels of propositions (elemental and auxiliary), all of which must be proved in order for a violation of the WTO agreements to be established. However, while elemental propositions are set by the law, auxiliary propositions will vary from case to case, especially when they are not part of a general test as is the case of factors (i) to (iv) in the likeness test—when part of a general test, auxiliary propositions can be referred to as sub-elemental propositions. In brief, the process of fact-finding is the process at the end of which conclusions are drawn with respect to auxiliary and elemental propositions, with the ultimate aim of determining whether a claim under a specific provision of the WTO agreements has been proved.

[8] In this regard, see for instance Panel Report, *Brazil—Measures Affecting Imports of Retreaded Tyres*, WT/DS332/R, adopted 17 December 2007 at para 7.415.

At this point, it is worth devoting a few words to explaining the meaning assigned to other common words used in this book. The word 'fact' was defined above. What the previous paragraph did not mention is that facts must be proved by 'evidence'. Evidence is defined as '[s]omething (including testimony, documents, and tangible objects) that tends to prove or disprove the existence of an alleged fact'.[9] When evidence is capable of demonstrating a fact, it can be said that it constitutes 'proof' of that fact. Moreover, facts are proved with the ultimate aim of proving a 'claim'. The word 'claim' is used in this book to refer to an allegation relating a specific measure to a provision of the WTO agreements—for instance, the allegation that measure *X* violates Article III:4 of the GATT because it fails to accord 'treatment no less favourable than that accorded to like products of national origin'. The party which bears the burden of proving a claim is referred to as the 'claimant' or 'proponent'; the party which does not bear the burden of proof is referred to as the 'respondent' or 'opponent'. The terms 'complainant' (or 'plaintiff') and 'defendant' are used to refer respectively to the party which sets the process of adjudication in motion and the party against which the action is brought; these terms do not convey a specific allocation of the burden of proof.

Chapters 2 through 5 cover the main aspects of the process of fact-finding including the questions of (i) which party bears the responsibility of ultimately convincing the panel of the truth of a claim; (ii) what quantum of proof is necessary to convince the panel of the truth of a claim; and (iii) what is the role of the panel and the disputing parties (complainant and defendant) in the development of the factual record on which the panel bases its decision on a claim.

Chapter 2 discusses the meaning of basic concepts such as the burden of proof, standard of proof, and presumptions. It explains how those concepts are defined in the common law system, the civil law system, and in international law. It argues that because those concepts do not have exactly the same meaning in all legal systems, WTO panels and the Appellate Body should clearly define those concepts in the context of WTO law, taking into consideration the basic structure of the WTO dispute settlement system.

The definitions laid out in Chapter 2 will be relied upon in the rest of this study. In this regard, it is worth emphasizing that there is much indeterminacy surrounding the concepts of the burden of proof, standard of proof, and presumption. This indeterminacy occurs across and even within legal systems. At least part of the blame for this lies on the fact that the expressions 'burden of proof', 'standard of proof', and 'presumption' are frequently used in a variety of different situations including everyday non-legal speech. In light of this, the reader should be willing to accept that familiar concepts may receive a different label in this book.

[9] *Black's Law Dictionary* (8th edn, St Paul: Thomson West, 2004) at 595.

Chapter 3 focuses on the question of how the concept of the burden of proof has operated in WTO dispute settlement and the related question of the degree of persuasion that panels must reach in order to determine that the burden of proof has been discharged—ie the applicable standard of proof. Some of the more specific issues discussed include: whether the claimant must meet a threshold requirement—ie it must present a minimum amount of evidence in support of its claim—in order for the proceedings to continue; whether the burden of proof shifts between the parties during the proceedings; what is the meaning of a *prima facie* case; what evidence should the panel take into account in determining that the burden of proof has been discharged; and what standard of proof should be adopted to make such determinations. Chapter 3 not only discusses the state of WTO law on these issues, but, drawing on the framework set out in Chapter 1, also makes suggestions for improving the treatment of these questions in future cases.

Chapter 4 examines the question of the allocation of the burden of proof, that is, the question of which party—complainant or defendant—must prove a certain issue or suffer the consequences of a finding against it. In light of the fact that the DSU does not address this question, Chapter 4 conducts a critical analysis of the rules that panels and the Appellate Body have developed to allocate the burden of proof between the parties. This chapter briefly reviews some of the decisions where the question of the allocation of the burden of proof was discussed. It then sets out to demonstrate that panels and the Appellate Body have not adopted a coherent approach to the allocation of the burden of proof. Most of the chapter is then devoted to developing a framework for the allocation of the burden of proof in WTO disputes. The last part of Chapter 4 briefly addresses the question of whether the burden of proof should be allocated differently in compliance proceedings under Article 21.5 of the DSU.

Chapter 5 examines the role of the panel and the disputing parties in the development of the factual record on which the panel must base its decision. The first part of the chapter explains that in certain circumstances, particularly in challenges to domestic trade remedy investigations, the role of the panel is more limited in that the factual record of the panel will essentially be restricted to the record which was developed during the domestic investigation. Chapter 5 focuses primarily on those cases where the panel develops its own factual record free from the constraints of a previous domestic investigation. In this connection, Chapter 5 argues that the disputing parties have a duty to be forthcoming in providing relevant and necessary information, and that panels not only can, but should, be actively engaged in the process of fact-finding.

In discussing the role of the disputing parties in the process of fact-finding Chapter 5 examines different aspects of the duty of the parties to cooperate in presenting information to the panel such as (i) its scope—including whether it extends to the production of confidential information; (ii) when that duty commences; and (iii) how its observance can be ensured—including the question of whether, when, and how adverse inferences can be drawn. It also examines certain obligations which WTO Members have to provide information on their measures outside the context of the panel process and the impact which these obligations have on the development of the factual record of the panel.

As for the role of the panel in the development of the factual record, Chapter 5 first explores the question of why panels should play an active role in the process of fact-finding. It then discusses the fact-finding powers of the panel which include the authority to seek and rely upon information from the disputing parties as well as any other relevant source such as WTO Members not involved in the dispute, experts, international organizations, and private parties. In connection with the discussion of the panel's authority to seek information from the disputing parties, Chapter 5 examines the question of whether the WTO dispute settlement system should follow the adjudicator-controlled disclosure model or the party-led pre-trial discovery model. The question of the limits of the authority of the panel is then taken up in the last part of Chapter 5.

This study concludes that many of the rules governing the process of fact-finding in WTO dispute settlement are not optimally designed. The concluding chapter of this book reviews the main findings in this regard and puts forward suggestions for improving different aspects of the process of fact-finding, including a brief note on how such suggestions could be implemented.

1

Optimizing the Process of Fact-Finding

Introduction

The objective of this chapter is to present some basic ideas to be used in the enterprise of understanding, assessing, and designing suggestions for improving the process of fact-finding (or process of proof) in WTO dispute settlement. In short, the goal is to establish a framework for the analysis which is undertaken in the following chapters.

With this objective in mind, this chapter is divided in two main sections. Section I provides an overview of how the process of fact-finding fits into the overall context of legal adjudication. One of the main points discussed is that the process of adjudication seeks the realization of multiple goals among which the pursuit of the truth or accuracy occupies a prominent position. Because a rational system of adjudication must seek to optimize the realization of its goals, procedures can be assessed on the basis of whether they maximize the realization of the goals of the particular system in question. Another main point is that although the pursuit of truth is a major objective, this objective is not always attainable because of the existence of other competing goals as well as the limits of human knowledge. This indicates that uncertainty and the risk of error are normal features of legal adjudication, which must be managed in order to optimize the process of proof.

Section II focuses on the WTO dispute settlement system. It explains that the WTO dispute settlement system embraced the legal adjudication model, establishing a link with the first section and thus justifying the reference throughout this book to the ideas presented in that section. It then lays out the goals of the WTO dispute settlement system which are relevant to the project of assessing that system's process of fact-finding. Section II argues that an optimal process of fact-finding cannot be designed without due regard to the basic structure of the WTO dispute settlement system. It suggests that the rules and procedures regarding the process of proof must be custom-designed for the WTO and not simply borrowed from other systems without due attention being paid to the reasons motivating the rules and procedures in those other systems—although of course this does not mean that the optimal rules and procedures for the WTO dispute settlement system cannot resemble the rules and procedures of other systems. With this in mind, the last part of the section reviews the main features of the WTO dispute settlement system, which then form the background for the following chapters.

Accordingly, this chapter concludes that an optimal process of fact-finding must (i) maximize the goals of the system of adjudication of which it is part, (ii) manage uncertainty and the risk of error efficiently, and (iii) be in harmony with the basic structure of the system of adjudication of which it is part.

I. Legal Adjudication and the Process of Fact-Finding

Adjudication is a process through which a dispute between two or more parties is referred to an impartial third party (the adjudicator) who resolves the dispute by applying authoritative legal standards (the law) to the facts presented. One of the principal characteristics of adjudication is that specific disputes are resolved on the basis of previously set authoritative standards. This contributes 'to certainty and stability, to enabling people to plan their affairs within a settled normative framework'.[1]

A. The goals of legal adjudication

1. Accuracy

Accuracy[2] or the search for the truth is considered a—if not the—major objective of adjudication.[3] In the absence of an accurate determination of the facts, the law will not be applied properly; such improper application of the law will in turn deny the attainment of the goals pursued by the substantive law. In other words, the policies underlying the law will not be realized, undermining the effectiveness of legal regulation and its benefits to society. Inaccurate decisions are also likely to reduce confidence in the process of adjudication. This may lead to more litigation 'for fewer parties would fear that truth adverse to

[1] DJ Galligan, *Due Process and Fair Procedures: a Study of Administrative Procedures* (Oxford: Clarendon Press, 1996) at 42.

[2] In this book, references to accuracy are primarily references to the accurate establishment of the facts rather than the accurate determination of the legal standards through the process of interpretation of the text of the WTO agreements or other legal instruments.

[3] See, for example, Galligan, above n 1 at 10–11; EW Thomas, *The Judicial Process: Realism, Pragmatism, Practical Reasoning and Principles* (Cambridge: Cambridge University Press, 2005) at 327; Joachim Zekoll, 'Comparative Civil Procedure' in M Reimann & R Zimmermann (eds), *The Oxford Handbook of Comparative Law* (Oxford: Oxford University Press, 2006) 1327 at 1355; William Twining, *Rethinking Evidence: Exploratory Essays* (2nd edn, Cambridge: Cambridge University Press, 2006) at 76, 83 (explaining the Rationalist theories of evidence and proof); Robert S Summers, 'Formal Legal Truth and Substantive Truth in Judicial Fact-Finding: Their Justified Divergence in Some Particular Cases' (1999) 18 Law and Philosophy 497 at 497–8; Matti S Kurkela, *Due Process in International Commercial Arbitration* (Dobbs Ferry: Oceana Publications, 2005) at 37, 126; Lawrence B Solum, 'Procedural Justice' (2004) 78 Southern California Law Review 181 at 184–5, 192, 252, 306.

their positions would come out in [adjudicative] proceedings, and so would be less disposed to settle out of court'.[4] Moreover, as law and economics scholars have explained, the accurate determination of the facts is important to the efficacy of the law in imparting efficient incentives for its observance, that is, accuracy is important for the legal system's optimization of deterrence.[5] This is explained by the fact that, on the one hand, false negatives—incorrect exoneration from liability—make committing the harmful act more attractive. On the other hand, false positives—incorrect imposition of liability—reduce the incentives to comply with the law by subjecting wrongdoers and those who comply with the law to the same penalties. False positives may also have a chilling effect on desirable conduct. For example, if adjudicators too often mistakenly find truck-drivers to be negligent, some of the drivers who are careful and rational might decide to stop driving their trucks.[6]

In addition to its role in securing the social benefits discussed above, accuracy is also crucial to the fairness of a decision. Leaving the fairness of the substantive law aside, the fairness of a decision is to a great extent dependent on its accuracy; accurate decisions are usually fair because they fulfill the promise made to the members of society that they will be treated according to the law.[7] The law is a public declaration of the rules governing a society; such declaration creates normative expectations, and the upholding of those expectations through the proper application of the law is a necessary element of fair treatment. This also applies in the context of international adjudication involving sovereign states. In the international community states are equal and sovereign and, but for certain ground rules which states are assumed to have accepted when they join the community of nations, consent is necessary for the creation of rules restricting their sovereignty.[8] Once consent has been given, it binds the state to act in accordance with what was agreed. Such binding agreements create normative expectations, and, accordingly, the upholding of such expectations is an important element of fair treatment.

[4] Summers, above n 3 at 498.

[5] See, for example, Louis Kaplow, 'The Value of Accuracy in Adjudication: an Economic Analysis' (1994) 23:1 The Journal of Legal Studies 307 at 348; Richard A Posner, 'An Economic Approach to the Law of Evidence' (1999) 51 Stanford Law Review 1477 at 1483–4; Alex Stein, *Foundations of Evidence Law* (Oxford: Oxford University Press, 2005) at 144, 148.

[6] This example is used in Stein, above n 5 at 148.

[7] For a defence of the importance of accuracy for fair treatment, see Galligan, above n 1 at 75–8. See also Kaplow, above n 5. Many scholars have also referred to the importance of accuracy for 'justice'. See, for example, Thomas, above n 3 at 327; Twining, above n 3 at 76.

[8] Thomas M Franck, *Fairness in International Law and Institutions* (Oxford: Oxford University Press, 1995) at 29. See also John H Jackson, *Sovereignty, the WTO, and Changing Fundamentals of International Law* (Cambridge: Cambridge University Press, 2006) at 36, 52, 205–6 (raising questions regarding the scope of consent, eg the extent to which consent to the rules of a treaty creating an institution also results in consent 'to the procedures in that institution which may be used to interpret the relevant treaties and to fill gaps or resolve ambiguities').

Another aspect of the link between accuracy and fairness relates to consistency of treatment. Franck notes that coherence or consistency is a key factor for a legitimate—the procedural dimension of fairness according to Franck—decision.[9] Consistency requires that a rule be applied uniformly to similar cases. This goal cannot be achieved without an accurate determination of the similarity (the factual component) of the cases.[10]

Finally, it is important to note that the fairness of a decision encourages compliance by the losing party. Thus, accurate decisions are more likely to be complied with. This feature is particularly important in international adjudication involving states since international law relies heavily on voluntary compliance.[11]

For the above reasons, the pursuit of truth—namely, maximization of accuracy in fact-determination or simply 'accuracy'—is one of the main objectives of the process of adjudication. This is even more so in international adjudication involving states. In addition to the reasons discussed above, accuracy is important in international adjudication because '[t]he vital interests of states, directly concerning the welfare of thousands of people, may be adversely affected by a decision based upon a misconception of the facts.'[12] In recognition of the importance of accurate decisions, international tribunals are generally given wide scope for the ascertainment of the truth, among other things unhampered by rules regulating the admissibility and weight of evidence, and enjoying powers to manage and participate in the gathering of information (fact-finding powers).[13] Accordingly, accuracy is a crucial basis for evaluating fact-finding institutions, rules, and procedures.

2. Goals which compete against accuracy

Although accuracy has a prominent role in adjudication, there are other values—for example, privacy, protection of confidential information, finality—which

[9] Franck, above n 8 at 30, 38. Franck explains that there are two aspects to the fairness of international law: the substantive and the procedural. The substantive aspect refers to distributive justice, that is, 'the degree to which the rules satisfy the participant's expectations of justifiable distribution of costs and benefits'. The procedural aspect refers to legitimacy, that is, 'the extent to which the rules are made and applied in accordance with what participants perceive as right process'. Ibid at 7–8.

[10] Jeremy Bentham also believed that accurate decisions are important because they uphold 'the value in stability through regular and consistent application of the law'. Galligan, above n 1 at 10.

[11] Franck argues that judicial usefulness has to do with achieving closure and that the fairness of a decision is important to achieve that goal. Analysing the fairness of the adjudicative model adopted by the International Court of Justice (ICJ), he notes that nothing a court does affects more the public perception of its fairness than the determination of the facts of the case. Franck, above n 8 at 318–19, 335, respectively.

[12] Durward V Sandifer, *Evidence Before International Tribunals* (revised edn, Charlottesville: University Press of Virginia, 1975) at 5.

[13] See, for example, Sandifer, above n 12 at 3–4; Chester Brown, *A Common Law of International Adjudication* (Oxford: Oxford University Press, 2007) at 104–17; Mojtaba Kazazi, *Burden of Proof and Related Issues: a Study on Evidence Before International Tribunals* (The Hague: Kluwer Law International, 1996) at 34–5.

also play an important role in the process of adjudication. Exactly what those other values are is a matter that varies across legal systems. Some of those values are considered important in and of themselves, and in many instances they compete against accuracy. This is so in the case of privacy, which in some legal systems requires the adjudicator to decline to receive relevant evidence gathered in violation of laws set up to protect the privacy of individuals. Similarly, the value of finality of decisions will in certain jurisdictions impede revision of a decision whose accuracy is later called into question by the uncovering of additional evidence.[14] Moreover, the goal of efficient use of resources (time and money) or efficiency, which is a function of the scarcity of resources in the real world, places limitations on the search for information with obvious consequences for the accuracy of decisions. As regards time constraints, while on the one hand the process of uncovering information may be time consuming, particularly when the dispute concerns complex factual situations, on the other hand, as the nineteenth century British politician, William Gladstone, once said 'justice delayed, is justice denied'. Financial constraints impose limits on the depth of the search for information as well as the means of proof. For example, while DNA testing may be the most precise means of proving the paternity of an individual, a blood test may be used instead because of its lower cost. Furthermore, if an amount of only $300 is in dispute, it makes little sense to expend $400 in gathering evidence, unless, of course, the non-monetary value of the dispute is higher.

In contrast, other values such as those that are usually associated with the concept of due process (or natural justice or procedural fairness)[15] are not completely independent from accuracy. In fact, while they are intrinsically important, they are also important instruments for achieving accuracy. The fact that their importance cannot be reduced to accuracy, however, means that there might be circumstances under which they might compete against accuracy.

3. Due process

As just noted, due process is largely instrumental to accuracy. This and the next few paragraphs explore this idea further. Due process is a broad concept, the boundaries of which are not clearly defined, but which is generally linked to the idea of fair treatment. The requirements which are usually associated with due process are largely instrumental to accuracy, that is to say, the due process

[14] Another example is found in the law of privileges which authorizes the withholding of relevant information provided by clients to lawyers on the grounds that this is necessary to the effective administration of justice. See Jeremy Gans & Andrew Palmer, *Australian Principles of Evidence* (London: Cavendish, 2004) at 11. Generally, see Stein, above n 5 at 3; Summers, above n 3 at 499–505, 510–11; Twining, above n 3 at 76, 199; Mirjan R Damaska, *Evidence Law Adrift* (New Haven: Yale University Press, 1997) at 121.

[15] This study views these concepts as rough synonyms. Accordingly, hereinafter it will refer only to the expression 'due process'.

requirements have been put in place largely in order to ensure accurate decisions.[16] For the purposes of this study those requirements are broadly classified under the rubrics of impartiality, participation—namely, 'knowing what is at issue' and 'having an opportunity to present arguments and supporting evidence'—and, closely related to those two values, equality of treatment. This is so because while different legal systems have developed specific doctrines of due process, those doctrines can be mostly subsumed under the broad values of participation, impartiality, and equality of treatment. For instance, the requirements extant in certain jurisdictions of meaningful and adequate notice and opportunity to call and cross-examine witnesses are related to participation, and the requirement of reasoned decisions is linked to the idea of impartiality.[17] Focusing on the values of participation, impartiality, and equality of treatment rather than specific doctrines is also appropriate in light of the fact that some of those specific doctrines of due process may have strong ties to the substantive law being applied as well as the peculiar design and preferences of the legal system in question. For example, cross-examination is considered a due process requirement in judicial trials in the United States,[18] but is not so understood in other jurisdictions—such as those of most countries in Continental Western Europe—where the parties cannot cross-examine witnesses.

3.1. Participation

Participation includes notice and an opportunity to be heard. It encompasses the ideas expressed in the maxim *audi alteram partem* (hear the other side) and the civil law *principe du contradictoire* (according to which the court must hear both parties before deciding any question raised by a party or *sua sponte*).[19]

Participation derives most of its importance from the fact that it facilitates the development of information crucial to a correct decision.[20] If parties are provided an opportunity to participate at a meaningful time and in a meaningful manner, they are likely to present information which will help adjudicators to

[16] As noted above, it is accepted, however, that the values associated with due process also have an 'intrinsic value', that is, they are important in and of themselves independently of their contribution to accurate results.

[17] External motivations for reasoned decisions include their role in promoting public understanding of the decisions and predictability.

[18] Galligan, above n 1 at 190.

[19] Jolowicz explains that there is no obvious English translation for the *principe du contradictoire* because the common law does not have a principle which is immediately equivalent. According to him, the principle 'is comparable, but not identical, to the rule *audi alteram partem*'. JA Jolowicz, 'Fact-Finding: a Comparative Perspective' in DLC Miller & PR Beaumont (eds), *The Option of Litigating in Europe* (London: United Kingdom National Committee of Comparative Law, 1993) vol 14, 133 at 141. On the *principe du contradictoire*, see Antonio Carlos de Araújo Cintra, Ada Pellegrini Grinover & Cândido R Dinamarco, *Teoria Geral do Processo* (12th edn, São Paulo: Malheiros, 1996) at 55–7; José Vizcarra Dávalos, *Teoría General del Proceso* (9th edn, Mexico City: Editorial Porrúa, 2007) at 180–1.

[20] Galligan is an avid advocate of the view that participation is important because of the 'role it plays in the proper application of authoritative standards'. According to him, '[t]he instrumental role of participation towards proper and accurate decisions provides the key to its normative justification'. Galligan, above n 1 at 131–2, see also at 92 and Chapter 4 in general.

form a better understanding of the facts to which the law must be applied. In this context, notice is valuable because it allows the parties to provide their input. Participation is an effective instrument helping to achieve accurate outcomes because, first, the parties to a dispute are often the best source of information since they are involved in the situation which gave rise to the dispute and, second, the exchange of information which is encouraged by participatory procedures is often an effective means of generating knowledge.

Although the value of participation in the process of adjudication resides in large part in its contribution towards achieving accurate decisions, there are also other justifications for participation. In the context of state-to-state adjudication, participation may also have value as a measure of respect to the sovereignty of the parties.[21] Moreover, as Solum explains, independently from its impact on accuracy, participation is essential for the legitimacy of adjudication.[22] He argues that because as a matter of fact judgments will not always be accurate, accuracy cannot be the only reason why binding judgments are legitimate. Participation provides legitimacy to a judgment which the parties believe (or even know) to be in error.[23] Accordingly, a right of participation—as opposed to actual participation, because participation may be voluntarily relinquished—is essential for the legitimacy of adjudication.

While participation is important for the accuracy and legitimacy of a decision, accuracy and legitimacy do not require unbounded participation.[24] In this regard, it is worth noting that there is a perception that in certain jurisdictions, particularly in the common law tradition, participation is given such a prominent role that the proper application of the law often gives way to the 'contest' between the parties.[25] The origin of this problem can be traced to the

[21] This is not to say that states can invoke their sovereignty to interfere with the process of adjudication; by submitting the dispute to adjudication states agree to everything that this method of dispute resolution entails, particularly to accepting the authority of the adjudicator to decide the dispute according to the law. Along these lines, Article 53 of the Statute of the International Court of Justice (ICJ) provides that the non-appearance—failure to appear before the Court or defend its case—of a party that has accepted its jurisdiction should not affect the Court's authority to rule on the matter presented to it.

[22] Solum, above n 3 at 275ff.

[23] Solum, above n 3 at 274.

[24] Galligan directly refutes the account that the most important feature of adjudication is the participation of the parties and the control they exert over the proceedings. Galligan, above n 1 at 245–6.

[25] Damaska argues that the proper application of the law plays a secondary role in the paradigmatic common law proceedings because of the primacy of the 'conflict-resolving vision.' He seems to equate the contest between the parties with conflict-resolution. However, in my view, models of adjudication which place little emphasis on the contest between the parties are equally aimed at, and capable of, resolving conflicts. In short, in my view disputes can be resolved by models that emphasize the proper application of the law or models that emphasize the contest between the parties; the difference lies in the emphasis given to the contest between the parties. See Damaska, above n 14 at 124. On the relationship between adjudication and the contest between the parties, particularly the negative impact of the latter on the accuracy of outcomes, see also Thomas E Carbonneau, 'Darkness and Light in the Shadows of International Arbitral Adjudication' in RB Lillich (ed), *Fact-Finding before International Tribunals* (Ardsley-on-Hudson: Transnational Publishers, 1992) 153 at 163–4; JA Jolowicz, 'Adversarial and Inquisitorial Models of Civil Procedure' (2003) 52 International and Comparative Law Quarterly 281 at 284–6.

adversarial proceedings. In pure adversarial systems the court is not involved in the preparation of the case; the parties have full control over their cases and present them as they think best. In short, proceedings are structured so as to allow for a contest between opposing views. Due to the partisanship of the participants, if appropriate controls are not in place, this contest might result in a distorted understanding of the facts and a consequent failure properly to apply the law. From this it is possible to conclude that unchecked participation is not necessary to achieve accurate outcomes; to the contrary, it might make the proceedings more prone to errors. As for legitimacy, the fact that many systems of adjudication do not provide for unchecked participation indicates that legitimacy can be guaranteed through a limited right of participation. Civil law proceedings may constitute a good example in this regard. Civilian proceedings are characterized by the involvement of the courts in the preparation of the case. It is for the *principe du contradictoire* to guarantee that the court will hear both sides before deciding any questions.[26] Because of the role of the court in the proceedings, the *principe du contradictoire* does not guarantee unchecked participation, but a more limited right of notice and opportunity to be heard; these ensure the legitimacy of the proceedings.

3.2. Impartiality

Impartiality is another important component of due process. One of the preconditions for impartiality is the independence of the adjudicators, namely their freedom from external interference such as through ties linking the adjudicator to one of the disputing parties. Impartiality is guaranteed through, among others, rules disqualifying from the function of adjudicator persons who may have an interest in the outcome of a dispute and requiring adjudicators to provide reasons for their decisions. These rules are justified on the grounds that they promote accurate outcomes. Bias is a subjective element interfering with the search for the truth, hence constituting a threat to accurate outcomes. Impartiality is therefore instrumental to accurate outcomes.

Other justifications for impartiality include the confidence that it inspires on the fairness of decisions. If the process of adjudication—its structure or the person of the adjudicator—is biased or appears to be biased, even though it is possible that the final conclusion is accurate,[27] perception that the process was biased raises public doubts as to the accuracy and, consequently, the fairness of that conclusion. This in turn has a negative impact on the acceptance of and compliance with such decisions. Accordingly, impartiality has an important role in delivering accurate decisions and in inspiring confidence in the fairness of those decisions.

[26] See Jolowicz, *Adversarial and Inquisitorial Models*, above n 25 at 282–3; JA Jolowicz, 'Fact-Finding: a Comparative Perspective' in DLC Miller & PR Beaumont (eds), *The Option of Litigating in Europe* (London: United Kingdom National Committee of Comparative Law, 1993) vol 14, 133 at 141.

[27] It is possible that the bias may actually skew the decision to the right direction.

3.3. Equality

Equality is another value related to due process which is generally pursued in most, if not all, models of adjudication. Its connection with accuracy is indirect, particularly through its link with the values of impartiality and participation. Equality manifests itself in many forms in the process of adjudication but in general terms it means that the disputing parties must be considered equal and, thus, be treated in the same manner.

Equality of treatment is, accordingly, related to impartiality; if both parties are treated similarly, at least to the extent that they are similarly situated, an important source of bias is eliminated. Equality of treatment also includes equal opportunities to participate in the process of fact-finding. This means that both parties must have an equal chance to present their points of view, leading to a balanced exchange of information which is often one of the most effective means of generating knowledge. Because parties are unlikely voluntarily to produce information which is detrimental to their case, if both sides do not have similar opportunities to present their views, there is a risk that relevant information will not be made available to the adjudicator.

In state-to-state adjudication, which is the case in the WTO dispute settlement system, equality finds an additional normative justification in the equality of states which is one of the basic pillars of the law of nations.[28] In this regard, Article 2.1 of the Charter of the United Nations expressly provides that the 'Organization is based on the principle of the sovereign equality of all its Members'.

B. Optimization of goals

In sum, the process of adjudication is informed by many values, that is to say, it seeks the realization of multiple goals among which the pursuit of truth or accuracy occupies a prominent position.[29] While the pursuit of accuracy may be tempered by the pursuance of other goals/values, the proper application of the substantive law is undoubtedly one, if not the, main goal of *any* system of adjudication. Other goals to be pursued, as well as their status, are defined by

[28] On the equality of states as a basic pillar of international law, see Ian Brownlie, *Principles of Public International Law* (6th edn, Oxford: Oxford University Press, 2003) at 287; Malcolm N Shaw, *International Law* (5th edn, Cambridge: Cambridge University Press, 2003) at 192–3; Franck, above n 8 at 45; Jackson, *Sovereignty and the WTO*, above n 8 at 58. See also Shabtai Rosenne, *The Law and Practice of the International Court 1920–2005* (Leiden: Martinus Nijhoff, 2006) at 1048–9 (noting that the equality of the parties is the major principle governing the procedure of the ICJ).

[29] This is in line with the rationalist tradition of evidence scholarship. Twining explains that one of the basic assumptions of the rationalist tradition is that 'the central purpose of adjudication is "rectitude of decision", that is the correct application of substantive law to facts proved to be true on the basis of relevant evidence presented to the tribunal'. The rationalist tradition, however, accepts that 'the pursuit of truth in adjudication has to be constrained by other, "extrinsic" values'. Twining, above n 3 at 199.

each system. Within this context, the main objective of any rational system of adjudication is (or at least ought to be) to optimize the realization of its goals.

Procedures, therefore, can be assessed on the grounds of whether they maximize the realization of the goals of the system of adjudication in question. When a value is neglected without proportional increases in other values, the procedure in question cannot be considered optimal.

Moreover, as noted above, some values may compete against each other, leading to situations where conflict between them may be unavoidable. When values clash, a way must be found to reconcile them. In this regard, a rational system which is guided by the objective of optimizing the realization of its goals will to the extent possible seek to estimate the comparative value of viable alternatives in terms of expected costs and benefits. Benefits and costs do not have to be monetized or expressed in a precise number, but a meaningful comparison of alternatives requires some form of commensuration. When precise commensuration of the competing considerations involved is difficult or not possible this process of comparing alternatives and assessing their 'costs' and 'benefits' is referred to as 'balancing'.[30] According to Trachtman, balancing is 'a kind of amorphous or imprecise cost-benefit analysis', in other words, 'a kind of cost-benefit analysis that recognizes the difficulty of formalizing the analysis, and seeks to achieve similar results informally'.[31] Inevitably—particularly when either-or situations arise—balancing requires at least some assignment of priorities. Directly or indirectly, each legal system makes this assignment of priorities and there are divergences across legal systems.[32] Importantly, however, as noted previously, it is of the essence of adjudication that accuracy be assigned a high, though not necessarily an overriding, priority.[33]

Balancing can be done at the legislative as well as the judicial level. At times the solution will be to expressly delegate the task of balancing to the adjudicator, who will do so on an *ad hoc* basis. This is particularly useful when the variables can be better assessed in the specific case. This occurs, for example, when adjudicators are given the discretion to decide whether to order the production of certain evidence. In this situation adjudicators must balance the goals of accuracy and efficient use of resources and decide whether the potential gains in accuracy justify the use of the resources necessary to produce the evidence in question. Section II.B of this chapter focuses on establishing the goals of the WTO dispute settlement system and ascertaining whether any priorities have been set.

[30] See Stephen E Gottlieb, 'The Paradox of Balancing Significant Interests' (1994) 45 Hastings Law Journal 825 at 839; Joel P Trachtman, 'Trade and ... Problems, Cost-Benefit Analysis and Subsidiarity' (1998) 9 European Journal of International Law 32 at 36.

[31] Trachtman, above n 30 at 36.

[32] See Damaska, above n 14 at 121 (Damaska notes that '[a] delicate balancing process is involved in determining the desired output of any legal process; we cannot determine the absolute but can only imperfectly sense the relative weight of values that come into consideration'.)

[33] This is one of the precepts of the rationalist tradition. See Twining, above n 3 at 76.

C. Managing uncertainty and the risk of error

The previous section explained that the proper application of the substantive law is one of the major goals of the process of adjudication. It also noted that accuracy is not the only value pursued and that some of the other values compete against accuracy. One of those other values is the efficient use of resources. This is dictated by the existence of resource (time and money) constraints—one of the most common obstacles on the path to accuracy. Resource constraints are a practical limitation which systems of adjudication even in affluent societies cannot avoid, since resources must also be allocated to other pressing social purposes.[34] Accordingly, the fact that the process of adjudication pursues goals which in many instances compete against accuracy indicates that accurate outcomes are not always achievable.

In any case, even if the pursuit of the truth were always the overriding goal of adjudication, accurate outcomes would still not be obtainable in all cases owing to the limits of human knowledge. In short, even if resources were unlimited and the pursuit of the truth were to override any other competing goals, adjudicators would still not be able to conclude with absolute certainty that a certain proposition was true.

The discussion above suggests that uncertainty—either because the pursuit of accuracy is not always overriding[35] or due to the limits of human knowledge—is constant in the process of adjudication.[36] Yet, adjudication is marked by the fact that a decision in one way or the other must be delivered; skepticism is not an option. Thus, strategies must be developed to deal with uncertainty and the fact that some errors will inevitably occur.

The ideas of direct and error costs may serve as valuable tools in devising rational strategies to manage uncertainty and the risk of error. One of the main objectives of a rational system is to minimize the social loss function composed of the sum of those costs. Direct (or process) costs are costs that are incurred in the process of adjudication such as the resources spent by the parties in gathering supporting evidence, expenses related to adjudicators and supporting structures, lawyers, etc. In other words, direct costs relate to the resources available for adjudication. Error costs are those costs associated with erroneous legal judgments. Error costs include costs that are carried by the community such as those

[34] See Galligan, above n 1 at 114.

[35] Summers, for instance, notes that '[f]ormal legal truth and substantive truth may diverge in a particular case, with the court finding facts that do not represent the actual truth'. He explains that this may occur by design and that '[i]f the system is well designed, and if, in a particular case of divergence, relevant rationales for such divergence are in play, the divergence is merely the price we pay for having a complex multi-purpose system in which actual truth, and what legally follows from it, comprise but one value among a variety of important values competing for legal realization'. Summers, above n 3 at 511.

[36] The rationalist tradition of evidence scholarship acknowledges this problem. In this regard, see Twining, above n 3 at 76.

related to the frustration of the objectives of the substantive law and deterrence, as well as those costs that are born by the individual states directly affected by the erroneous decision. Taking as a given a certain level of accuracy in relation to competing values and the fact that as a general rule a rational system of adjudication aims at determining the facts as accurately and as resource-efficiently as possible, thinking in terms of minimizing the sum of direct and error costs helps to create customized strategies for specific classes of disputes. For instance, where error costs are high and additional investment in fact-finding has the potential to reduce those errors, additional expenditures are justified at least to the extent that they yield corresponding reductions in error costs.

As noted above, although accurate decisions are undeniably desirable they are not always achievable. Stein explains this problem in terms of inadequacy of evidence. He argues that while ideally evidence must cover every segment of the relevant factual allegations and eliminate any dependence upon extrinsic information that determines its credibility, evidence is constantly missing in real life, so these criteria cannot be met and fact-finders have to settle for less.[37] In light of this, Stein argues, fact-finding involves risk of error in all its stages. Consequently, adjudicators must allocate such risk 'not only in their ultimate findings [...] but also in relying upon particular evidence as a basis for their findings'.[38] In other words, Stein concludes that allocation of the risk of error is a pervasive phenomenon.[39] It is, thus, important that this omnipresence of the risk of error be openly recognized and the risk of error allocated in a rational way.

But how should the risk of error be allocated? Here, again, it is helpful to resort to the social loss function composed of direct and error costs. In adjudication, errors are classified in two broad categories: false positives and false negatives. False positives are erroneous decisions in favour of the claimant—the respondent is erroneously found liable—while false negatives are erroneous decisions in favour of the respondent—the claimant does not recover when it should. When the costs of false positives and false negatives differ, error costs can be minimized by skewing the risk of error in the direction of the less costly of the errors.[40] The main advantage of this approach is that it appropriately takes account of the interests at stake since these are included in the calculation of the error costs of the decision.[41]

Another strategy for dealing with uncertainty and the risk of error is to assess the probabilities of the situation 'based on the available stock of knowledge about the common course of events'.[42] In explaining the rationalist theories of evidence Twining notes that 'this is largely a matter of common sense supplemented by specialized scientific or expert knowledge when it is available'.[43] In other words, given the resource and knowledge constraints, and in the absence of

[37] Stein, above n 5 at 64. [38] Stein, above n 5 at 64. [39] Stein, above n 5 at 64.
[40] These ideas are further explored in Chapters 3 and 4.
[41] In favour of a similar approach, see Stein, above n 5 at x, 10; Galligan, above n 1 at 43.
[42] Twining, above n 3 at 76. [43] Twining, above n 3 at 76.

case-specific evidence suggesting otherwise, focusing on what usually happens in a similar situation allows adjudicators to maximize their chances of reaching an accurate decision.[44] An example of the application of this strategy is that in determining the facts of the case adjudicators are not expected to (and, in fact, do not) investigate an unlimited number of possibilities regarding what might have happened. Instead, the focus is on the most probable options.

It has been explained up to this point that (i) the pursuit of accuracy—the proper application of the substantive law—is a defining characteristic of the process of adjudication, but that in actuality, adjudication being (ii) a multi-goal/value process bound by practical limitations such as (iii) scarcity of resources and (iv) the limits of human knowledge, (v) uncertainty and the risk of error are ubiquitous. A rational system of adjudication must strive to (vi) optimize the realization of its multiple goals, and in that process (vii) cost-benefit analysis or the more amorphous balancing analysis will be useful tools. Rational systems of adjudication must also (viii) manage uncertainty and the risk of error. Aiming at (ix) minimizing the social loss function composed of direct and error costs is a valuable tool in designing rational procedures to manage uncertainty and the risk of error, including those whose function is to (x) allocate the risk of error to one of the disputing parties. Another strategy for dealing with uncertainty and the risk of error involves the use of (xi) an estimate of the probabilities of the situation. These ideas form part of the analytical framework of this study and will be referred to throughout this study as a means to assess—as well as to suggest improvements to—the process of fact-finding in the WTO dispute settlement system.

The next section introduces the WTO dispute settlement system and discusses the values embraced by that system of dispute settlement as well as its main structural features. These will also provide a basis for the analysis of the fact-finding procedures of the WTO dispute settlement system which will take place in the following chapters.

II. The WTO Dispute Settlement System

A. A system of legal adjudication

The World Trade Organization (WTO) was created at the end of the Uruguay Round of negotiations. The Agreement Establishing the World Trade Organization (the 'WTO Agreement') came into force on 1 January 1995. The WTO Agreement functions as the 'constitution' of the WTO and has many agreements annexed to it, covering subjects such as trade in services and intellectual property. Annex 2, the Understanding on Rules and Procedures Governing the Settlement of Disputes (DSU), establishes the rules and procedures that govern

[44] This is not to suggest that adjudicators can make findings based only on probabilities, that is, without the support of case-specific evidence.

the settlement of disputes under the WTO Agreement and its Annexes—the covered agreements.[45] Although the DSU gives the parties the option of resorting to good offices, conciliation and mediation (Articles 5 and 24.2), as well as arbitration (Article 25)[46] to settle their differences, these alternatives have rarely been used.[47] Instead, most disputes are resolved under the dispute settlement procedures which begin with a short period of consultations—usually 60 days, but sometimes longer—between the parties and lead to the establishment of a panel of three individuals if the dispute is not settled during the consultation period.[48] This study focuses on these latter procedures; the expression 'dispute settlement', when employed in the context of the WTO, is used to refer to such procedures. Accordingly, it is apposite at this point to clarify the character of WTO dispute settlement.

The means of dispute settlement in international law have been broadly classified in two categories: diplomatic and legal.[49] Diplomatic methods are based on the interests of the parties and are not binding on them; they include negotiation, good offices, mediation, inquiry, and conciliation.[50] Legal methods are characterized by decisions based on the application of the law, which are binding upon the parties. Arbitration and litigation before courts such as the International Court of Justice are the classic examples of legal methods of international dispute settlement. In other words, these legal methods of dispute settlement fall under the category of 'adjudication'.

[45] Appendix 1 to the DSU contains a list of all the agreements covered by the provisions of the DSU; it excludes Annex 3, the Trade Policy Review Mechanism from its coverage. Moreover, Article 1.2 establishes that the DSU applies 'subject to such special or additional rules and procedures on dispute settlement contained in the covered agreements as are identified in Appendix 2'.

[46] Articles 21.3(c) and 22.6 of the DSU also provide for arbitration, but these are specific procedures to resolve problems relating to the implementation of decisions delivered according to the regular dispute settlement procedures whose description follows.

[47] The arbitration procedures envisaged in Article 25 of the DSU have been invoked only once in 14 years. This was in a dispute between the United States and the European Communities. Award of the Arbitrators, *United States—Section 110(5) of the US Copyright Act—Recourse to Arbitration under Article 25 of the DSU*, WT/DS160/ARB25/1, 9 November 2001, DSR 2001:II, 667. Moreover, Nottage and Bohanes note that Article 5 of the DSU has never been utilized. Hunter Nottage & Jan Bohanes, 'Arbitration as an Alternative to Litigation in the WTO: Observations in the Light of the 2005 Banana Tariff Arbitrations' in Y Taniguchi, A Yanovich & J Bohanes (eds), *The WTO in the Twenty-first Century: Dispute Settlement, Negotiations, and Regionalism in Asia* (Cambridge: Cambridge University Press, 2007) 212 at footnote 16. A mediation outside the DSU, but following procedures similar to those foreseen in Article 5, was conducted 'to examine the extent to which the legitimate interests of the Philippines and Thailand [were] being unduly impaired as a result of the implementation by the European Communities of the preferential tariff treatment for canned tuna originating in ACP states'. See Request for Mediation by the Philippines, Thailand and the European Communities, WTO Doc. WT/GC/66/Add.1, 23 December 2002.

[48] Although Article 8.5 of the DSU allows the parties to agree on a panel of five individuals, a five-person panel has never been used since the inception of the DSU.

[49] See John Merrills, 'The Means of Dispute Settlement' in MD Evans (ed), *International Law* (Oxford: Oxford University Press, 2006) 533 at 535–49.

[50] For more details on these methods, see JG Merrills, *International Dispute Settlement* (4th edn, Cambridge: Cambridge University Press, 2005); Merrills, *The Means of Dispute Settlement*, above n 49 at 535–42.

At the beginning of the pre-WTO GATT years, disputes were settled by a mechanism that was essentially diplomatic; it involved the direct participation of the Contracting Parties to the GATT—namely, the states that were signatories of the GATT.[51] Around 1952, it was decided that disputes would be referred to independent panels of experts.[52] However, this move was not followed by the establishment of rules to guide the work of the panels of experts, and panels had thus to develop their own approaches. Some panels, particularly at the beginning, saw their function as facilitating settlement; some acted as mediators.[53] Moreover, many of the earlier cases focused on the vague concept of 'nullification or impairment'—actions that harm trade and which could not have been reasonably anticipated by the complaining party at the time a concession was negotiated—rather than on establishing whether a Contracting Party had acted inconsistently with the obligations laid down in the GATT.[54] Notably, violation of an obligation was neither sufficient nor necessary to establish nullification or impairment. It was not until 1979 that dispute settlement procedures were consolidated in a document titled the Understanding Regarding Notification, Consultation, Dispute Settlement and Surveillance (the 'GATT Understanding')[55] which was adopted by the Contracting Parties. The GATT Understanding described the procedures which had been developed through practice throughout the years. Although over time dispute settlement procedures moved closer to the legal end of the diplomatic-legal spectrum,[56] the pre-WTO system was generally characterized as a diplomatic means of dispute settlement. This was due to a great extent to the fact that the reports of the panels were submitted to the Contracting Parties for approval in a process which allowed the losing party to block the adoption of the report. Another problem was that some panels did not see their function strictly as applying the law, but rather as

[51] See Michael J Trebilcock & Robert Howse, *The Regulation of International Trade* (3rd edn, New York: Routledge, 2005) at 113; John H Jackson, *The World Trade Organization: Constitution and Jurisprudence* (London: Royal Institute of International Affairs, 1998) at 66; Robert E Hudec, *The GATT Legal System and World Trade Diplomacy* (2nd edn, Salem: Butterworth, 1990) at 75–80. Abi-Saab argues that the GATT dispute settlement system was a system of conciliation. Georges Abi-Saab, 'The WTO Dispute Settlement and General International Law' in R Yerxa & B Wilson (eds), *Key Issues in WTO Dispute Settlement: the First Ten Years* (Cambridge: Cambridge University Press, 2005) 7 at 8.

[52] See Understanding Regarding Notification, Consultation, Dispute Settlement and Surveillance, L/4907, adopted on 28 November 1979, GATT, BISD 26 Supp. 210 (1980) at Annex, para 6(ii); Hudec, above n 51 at 85–7.

[53] See Jackson, *The World Trade Organization*, above n 51 at 67.

[54] Jackson notes that the ambiguous concept of nullification or impairment 'might connote a "power"—or "negotiation"—oriented approach'. Jackson, *The World Trade Organization*, above n 51 at 66, 70.

[55] Understanding Regarding Notification, Consultation, Dispute Settlement and Surveillance, L/4907, adopted on 28 November 1979, GATT, BISD 26 Supp. 210 (1980).

[56] Jackson has described this process as a move towards rule-orientation. See, for example, Jackson, *The World Trade Organization*, above n 51 at 70; Jackson, *Sovereignty and the WTO*, above n 8 at 146.

facilitating settlement, which sometimes resulted in panels crafting reports with a view to pleasing both parties.[57]

The DSU has introduced many changes which have clearly moved the WTO dispute settlement system away from the diplomatic model. It is true that the DSU requires the complaining party to engage in consultations with the opposing party before the dispute can be referred to a panel,[58] and that it encourages panels to 'give [the parties] adequate opportunity to develop a mutually satisfactory solution'.[59] These features, however, do not mean that the dispute settlement procedures have a diplomatic character. Many national legal systems encourage litigants to negotiate solutions to their grievances. Moreover, while the DSU encourages the parties to reach a mutually acceptable solution, it also requires that such solution be consistent with the covered agreements rather than be purely based on the interests of the parties.[60] It is also worth noting that as a matter of fact panels have not sought to facilitate amicable solutions between the parties.

Among the changes which have moved the system closer to the legal adjudication model is the establishment of a right to a panel. The DSU has made clear that members have a right to a panel—'a panel shall be established at the latest at the DSB meeting following that at which the request first appears as an item on the DSB's agenda.'[61] Moreover, the adoption of panel reports—and Appellate Body reports for that matter—cannot be vetoed by the losing party; reports are automatically adopted, becoming legally binding upon the parties, unless the Dispute Settlement Body (DSB) decides by consensus *not* to adopt the report.[62] These features make adjudication compulsory; the opposing party cannot block the establishment of a panel or the adoption of the panel report.

The DSU has also created a standing appeals organ, the Appellate Body, which hears appeals from rulings delivered by panels. Appeals focus on 'issues of law covered in the panel report and legal interpretations developed by the panel'.[63] This indicates that the WTO dispute settlement system places a premium on the resolution of disputes by the proper application of the law. Along these lines, although the DSU refers to the goal of 'achieving a satisfactory settlement of the matter', it qualifies this reference with a declaration that such settlement must be '*in accordance with the rights and obligations* under this Understanding and under the covered agreements'.[64] Similarly, as noted above, while the DSU encourages

[57] See JHH Weiler, 'The Rule of Lawyers and the Ethos of Diplomats: Reflections on the Internal and External Legitimacy of WTO Dispute Settlement' (2001) 35:2 Journal of World Trade 191 at 199; Donald McRae, 'What is the Future of WTO Dispute Settlement?' (2004) 7:1 Journal of International Economic Law 3 at 7 (noting that the 'function of a GATT panel fell somewhere between applying the provisions of the GATT in order to resolve the issue between the parties and seeking to reach a friendly accommodation').

[58] Article 4 of the DSU.

[59] Article 11 of the DSU.

[60] Article 3.7 of the DSU.

[61] Article 6.1 of the DSU.

[62] Articles 16.4 and 17.14 of the DSU.

[63] Article 17.6 of the DSU.

[64] Article 3.4 of the DSU [emphasis added]. In addition, Article 3.5 of the DSU provides that '[a]ll solutions to matters formally raised under the consultation and dispute settlement provisions of the covered agreements, including arbitration awards, *shall be consistent with those agreements* and shall not nullify or impair benefits accruing to any Member under those agreements, nor impede the attainment of any objective of those agreements' [emphasis added].

the parties to a dispute to reach a mutually acceptable solution, it also requires that such solution be '*consistent with the covered agreements*'.[65] Accordingly, the DSU does not endorse settlement in and of itself, independently of how and under which terms it is reached. The view subscribed by the DSU is that settlement outside the adjudication process should be in accordance with the covered agreements; when such settlement is not possible, WTO Members have agreed that disputes will be settled by independent adjudicators—panels and the Appellate Body—on the basis of the proper application of the covered agreements.

Many Articles of the DSU support the claim that WTO dispute settlement is based on the application of the law. For instance, Article 7.1 establishes that the panel's terms of reference are 'to examine, *in the light of the relevant provisions* [...] the matter referred to the DSB'; Article 11 mandates the panel to 'make an objective assessment of the matter before it, including an objective assessment of the facts of the case and the *applicability of and conformity with the relevant covered agreements*'; Article 12.7 provides that 'the report of a panel shall set out the findings of fact, the *applicability of relevant provisions* and the basic rationale behind any findings and recommendations that it makes' [emphasis added]. In short, it has been agreed that the rulings of panels and the Appellate Body applying the covered agreements must resolve the dispute. In this regard, if the challenged measures are found to be inconsistent with the relevant provisions of the covered agreements, the defendant has a legal obligation to withdraw or bring the measure into conformity with the covered agreements.[66]

This emphasis of the DSU on dispute resolution through the application of the law is appropriate since the impact of WTO disputes is not limited to the governments directly involved but extends to producers, consumers, and the public at large whether located inside or outside the jurisdiction of the governments involved.[67] In this regard, it is worth noting that the DSU requires that mutually agreed solutions be 'notified to the DSB and the relevant Councils and Committees, where any Member may raise any point relating thereto'.[68] Moreover, dispute resolution through the application of the law places less

[65] Article 3.7 of the DSU [emphasis added].

[66] See Articles 3.7, 21.1, 22.1, 22.8 of the DSU. See also, Jackson, *The World Trade Organization*, above n 51 at 85–6; John H Jackson, 'The WTO Dispute Settlement Understanding: Misunderstandings on the Nature of Legal Obligation' (1997) 91:1 The American Journal of International Law 60 at 62–3; Andreas F Lowenfeld, *International Economic Law* (Oxford: Oxford University Press, 2002) at 156. But see Judith Hippler Bello, 'The WTO Dispute Settlement Understanding: Less is More' (1996) 90:3 The American Journal of International Law 416 at 417–18 (arguing that Members do not have an obligation to bring their measures into compliance, but instead have the option of (a) providing compensation or (b) suffering retaliation).

[67] In support of this view, see, for example, Weiler, above n 57 at 196, 202. See also Trebilcock & Howse, above n 51 at 116 (recognizing the broad impact of WTO law and arguing that the dispute settlement system should be open to all groups with a stake in the outcome of the decisions, that is, that the system should be transparent, produce decisions with clear reasons for factual and legal findings, and allow the possibility of intervention through submissions).

[68] Article 3.6 of the DSU.

powerful members on an equal footing with powerful ones;[69] an important feature in an organization of 153 members, of which the vast majority are developing countries whose main trading partners are developed countries. In the same vein, dispute settlement through the proper application of the law fulfils the purpose stated in Article 3.2 of the DSU of 'providing security and predictability to the multilateral trading system'. Reliance on the understanding that similar situations will be treated similarly—a feature of a system of dispute resolution based on the law—allows Members and private parties to predict the consequences of their actions and to adjust them accordingly, as well as to understand what to expect from other actors. As Jackson notes, predictability is highly prized in the conduct of international economic relations where entrepreneurs need predictability and guidance to make 'efficient investment and market development decisions'.[70] In addition, predictability may promote amicable settlement, reducing the need to have recourse to adjudication.[71]

While other arguments can be made in support of the legal character of the dispute settlement system,[72] the arguments against such view are few and weak. The main argument in favour of the diplomatic character of WTO dispute settlement is that it is the DSB, a political organ composed of representatives of all WTO members, that establishes panels and adopts panel and Appellate Body reports, which have no legal effect if not adopted. The argument goes on to note that it is the DSB that administers the dispute settlement mechanism while panels and the Appellate Body merely 'assist the DSB in making the recommendations or in giving the rulings provided for in [...] agreement(s)'.[73] What this argument misses is that even though DSB action is necessary to establish panels and to adopt panel and Appellate Body reports, as noted above, these acts occur almost automatically because of the negative consensus rule; for a panel not to be established and a report not to be adopted, the complaining party and the winning party, respectively, would, together with the other WTO members, have to oppose those actions in the DSB meeting where they are considered—a

[69] See Weiler, above n 57 at 198 (arguing that 'the DSU makes legal resolution more attractive to Members because, for example, it can equalize egregious disparities of power which exist at the negotiation table'); Jackson, *Sovereignty and the WTO*, above n 8 at 148 (arguing that a 'dispute settlement system helps to redress asymmetries of power'). Inadequate resources to cover the costs of legal representation may still prevent some Members from bringing cases, but this, at least, is a problem which can be more easily addressed. In fact, an international organization has been created, the Advisory Centre on WTO Law, to provide support in WTO dispute settlement proceedings to developing countries. For some of the challenges to effective participation experienced by African countries, see Victor Mosoti, 'Africa in the First Decade of WTO Dispute Settlement' (2006) 9:2 Journal of International Economic Law 427.

[70] Jackson, *The World Trade Organization*, above n 51 at 60–1.

[71] See John H Jackson, 'Dispute Settlement and the WTO Emerging Problems' (1998) 1 Journal of International Economic Law 329 at 329. Jackson speculates that after 10 years the jurisprudence is already 'providing some predictability that promotes settlements or withdrawals of cases'. Jackson, *Sovereignty and the WTO*, above n 8 at 160.

[72] Some of these arguments are covered in Section II.B where the goals of the dispute settlement system are discussed.

[73] Article 7.1 of the DSU. See also Article 11 of the DSU.

rather unlikely event.[74] Moreover, it is important to note that the DSB does not use panel and Appellate Body reports as resource material to make its *own* rulings and recommendations. Instead, it adopts those reports in their entirety, making the panel and Appellate Body rulings and recommendations its own.[75] Accordingly, for all practical purposes WTO disputes are settled according to the adjudicative model.[76]

As noted above, there are distinct models of adjudication, the main ones being arbitration and judicial settlement. There has been some contention over the question of whether the WTO dispute settlement system is a system of arbitration or a judicial system. The main arguments in support of the view that the model followed is arbitration are that (i) panels are constituted *ad hoc*, (ii) the parties to a dispute can influence the composition of panels,[77] and (iii) panels have 'terms of reference'.[78] Arguments in favour of the judicial character of the system include: (i) although panels are *ad hoc*, they rely on the services of the WTO Secretariat which is in charge of maintaining institutional memory; in addition (ii) panel decisions are reviewed by the *standing* Appellate Body— the relevance of the Appellate Body is not limited to the fact that it resembles a judicial institution in its structure, mandate and conduct, but extends to the fact that by being judicial itself, the Appellate Body influences panels also to act as judicial organs at the risk of being reproached on appeal;[79] (iii) the complainant

[74] There has been only one occasion where a panel report—which did not merely record the fact that the parties reached a mutually agreed solution—was not adopted by the DSB. This occurred because the parties—complainant and defendant—did not place the adoption of the panel report on the agenda of the DSB meeting. In *EC—Bananas III*, the EC requested that a panel under Article 21.5 of the DSU be established to find that the measures it had taken to implement the rulings and recommendations of the DSB must have been presumed to conform to WTO rules unless challenged in accordance with DSU procedures. Following this request, Ecuador requested the establishment of a panel under Article 21.5 to determine whether the EC measures were consistent with the WTO agreements. The panel requested by Ecuador found that the measures that the EC had taken were not consistent with the WTO agreements. In light of this, the panel requested by the EC found that the EC could not be presumed to be in compliance with the recommendations of the DSB. The latter panel report was never adopted. Panel Report, *European Communities—Regime for the Importation, Sale and Distribution of Bananas—Recourse to Article 21.5 of the DSU by the European Communities*, WT/DS27/RW/EEC and Corr.1, 12 April 1999, DSR 1999:II, 783.

[75] Chile and the United States have submitted proposals to amend the DSU with a view to increasing the Members' control over the rulings and recommendations of panels and the Appellate Body. These proposals have not received widespread support. See Communication from Chile and the United States, WTO Doc TN/DS/W/89, 31 May 2007; Communication from the United States, WTO Doc TN/DS/W/82, 24 October 2005; Communication from Chile and the United States, WTO Doc TN/DS/W/52, 14 March 2003.

[76] Similarly, see Yuji Iwasawa, 'WTO Dispute Settlement as Judicial Supervision' (2002) 5:2 Journal of International Economic Law 287 at 290; José E Alvarez, *International Organizations as Law-makers* (Oxford: Oxford University Press, 2006) at footnote 4 to chapter 9.

[77] Article 8.5, 8.7 of the DSU.

[78] Article 7 of the DSU.

[79] In support of the judicial character of the system see Appellate Body Report, *Mexico—Anti-Dumping Investigation of High Fructose Corn Syrup (HFCS) from the United States—Recourse to Article 21.5 of the DSU by the United States*, WT/DS132/AB/RW, adopted 21 November 2001, DSR 2001:XIII, 6675 at para 36 (where the Appellate Body notes that 'as a matter of due process, and the *proper exercise of the judicial function*, panels are required to address issues that are put before them by the parties to a dispute' [emphasis added]).

does not have to obtain the agreement of the defendant to institute the proceedings; (iv) the scope of the jurisdiction and applicable law are predetermined;[80] (v) third parties with an interest in the dispute can intervene in the proceedings and have a right to have their views fully taken into account.[81] Some have preferred to solve the conundrum by referring to the system as quasi-judicial.[82] Taking into account the fact that the conduct and rulings of panels and particularly the Appellate Body have been judicial-like and the fact that the reasons in support of the judicial character of the system are stronger and more numerous than those against it, it is fair to classify the WTO dispute settlement system as judicial.[83]

For the purpose of the questions examined in this book, however, classification of the WTO dispute settlement system into one of these two categories has little practical relevance. As Brownlie notes '[i]n recent times the distinction between arbitration and judicial settlement has become formal'; the category of judicial settlement 'can properly be applied to the work of any international tribunal settling disputes between states in accordance with rules of international law'.[84] What is important to recognize is that the system has embraced the adjudicative model.

B. The goals/values of the system

Having established that the DSU provides for disputes to be settled by adjudication, it is now apposite to determine the goals/values pursued by the system which are relevant to the project of assessing the process of fact-finding in WTO dispute settlement.

[80] Features (iii) and (iv) are commonly found in treaties choosing arbitration as the means to resolve disputes between the signatories.

[81] Article 10 of the DSU.

[82] See, for example, Ernst-Ulrich Petersmann, 'WTO Dispute Settlement Practice 1995–2005: Lessons from the Past and Future Challenges' in Y Taniguchi, A Yanovich & J Bohanes (eds), *The WTO in the Twenty-first Century: Dispute Settlement, Negotiations, and Regionalism in Asia* (Cambridge: Cambridge University Press, 2007) 38 at 87; Alvarez, above n 76 at 459.

[83] In support of this view, Iwasawa, above n 76 at 291; Weiler, above n 57 at 201, 203 (Weiler notes that 'the Appellate Body is a court in all but name and it even has a constitutional dimension'); Claus-Dieter Ehlermann, 'Reflections on the Appellate Body of the WTO' (2003) 6:3 Journal of International Economic Law 695 at 697–8 (though Ehlernmann also uses 'quasi' between parentheses); Abi-Saab, above n 51 at 10; McRae, above n 57 at 8; Andrew D Mitchell, 'The Legal Basis for Using Principles in WTO Disputes' (2007) 10:4 Journal of International Economic Law 795 at 829; The Project on International Courts and Tribunals: *The International Judiciary in Context, Synoptic Chart*, November 2004, available at <http://www.pict-pcti.org/publications/synoptic_chart.html> (accessed 21 June 2007); Joost Pauwelyn, *Conflict of Norms in Public International Law: How WTO Law Relates to other Rules of International Law* (Cambridge: Cambridge University Press, 2003) at 442; Andrew Mitchell, 'Due Process in WTO Disputes' in R Yerxa & B Wilson (eds), *Key Issues in WTO Dispute Settlement: the First Ten Years* (Cambridge: Cambridge University Press, 2005) 144 at 158.

[84] Brownlie, above n 28 at 672, 675.

1. Accuracy

As in any system of legal adjudication, the pursuit of accuracy, ie the proper application of the law, is one of the main goals of the WTO dispute settlement system. The significance of accuracy is evidenced in many Articles of the DSU. Article 11 requires panels to make an 'objective assessment of the facts of the case' and Article 12.2 reveals the desire to ensure 'high-quality panel reports'. Commitment to accurate fact-finding is also expressed in Article 13 which grants panels 'the right to seek information and technical advice from any individual or body which it deems appropriate' and imposes on members an obligation to 'respond promptly and fully' to requests for information. The fact that Members other than the disputing parties are given a right to participate in the proceedings also indicates an aspiration for the law to be properly applied. Furthermore, provisions such as Article 3.2 and Article 3.5 of the DSU affirm the importance that members have placed on the attainment of the objectives pursued by the WTO agreements—notably the improper application of the law denies the attainment of the goals pursued by the substantive law. In Article 3.2, members proclaimed that the dispute settlement system 'serves to preserve the rights and obligations of Members under the covered agreements'.[85] Article 3.5 highlights that '[a]ll solutions . . . shall be consistent with [the covered] agreements and shall not nullify or impair benefits accruing to any Member under those agreements, nor impede the attainment of any objective of those agreements'. The fact that the DSU imposes an obligation on members to comply with the rulings and recommendations of the DSB also supports the view that the DSU is designed to promote the observance of the obligations contained in the WTO agreements and the consequent achievement of the policies expressed in those agreements. In this setting, the relative weight of accuracy is high because only the truth will lead to the realization of the policies embedded in the law as well as result in optimal deterrence in the long-term.

Finally, accurate outcomes are essential to inspire confidence on the part of the members and the public at large in the dispute settlement system and the WTO in general. The WTO is constantly in the spotlight; application of the law to inaccurately determined facts disserves the system by affecting the public's perception of the fairness of its decisions.[86]

2. Due process values

Although the DSU contains no direct reference to 'due process', it does contain many provisions guaranteeing participation, impartiality, and, relatedly, equality of treatment. Moreover, the general notion of due process has been frequently invoked by panels and the Appellate Body in their rulings—most references to due

[85] Under Article 23.1 and 23.2(a) Members also undertook to have recourse to the WTO dispute settlement system—rather than other means—to redress a violation of an obligation or an impediment to the attainment of any objective of the covered agreements.

[86] Importantly, as Franck notes the fairness of a decision cannot always be judged by the reaction of a losing government. Franck, above n 8 at 319 (referring to the fairness of the decisions of the ICJ).

process in the WTO jurisprudence relate to the requirement of participation.[87] In *India—Patents* and *Mexico—Corn Syrup (Article 21.5—US)*, the Appellate Body stated, respectively, that the demands of due process 'are implicit in the DSU'[88] and 'underlie and inform the provisions of the DSU'.[89] In *India—Patents*, it noted that such demands require that the parties be 'fully forthcoming from the very beginning' in stating their claims clearly and freely disclosing the facts related to those claims.[90] In *Mexico—Corn Syrup* (*Article 21.5—US)*, the Appellate Body found that due process requires litigants to raise objections explicitly.[91] According to the Appellate Body, '[o]nly in this way will the panel, the other party to the dispute, and the third parties, understand that a specific objection has been raised, and have an adequate opportunity to address and respond to it'.[92] In *Brazil—Desiccated Coconut*, the Appellate Body noted the importance of the terms of reference for due process as they provide the parties and third parties information concerning the claims at issue allowing them an opportunity to respond to those claims.[93] Along these lines, owing to the fact that the request for establishment of a panel is under normal circumstances the basis of the terms of reference of panels, panels and the Appellate Body have also indicated that those requests must be sufficiently precise—they must 'identify the specific measures at issue and provide a brief summary of the legal basis of the complaint'[94]—so as not to violate the 'fundamental rule of due process' which entitles the parties to a dispute to know the case they have to answer.[95] In *Chile—Price Band System*, the Appellate Body

[87] See Valerie Hughes, 'Accomplishments of the WTO Dispute Settlement Mechanism' in Y Taniguchi, A Yanovich & J Bohanes (eds), *The WTO in the Twenty-first Century: Dispute Settlement, Negotiations, and Regionalism in Asia* (Cambridge: Cambridge University Press, 2007) 185 at 195 (noting that '[a]lthough there is no provision in the DSU referring to due process, this requirement has become embedded in the system by virtue of the jurisprudence, and there is no question now that it forms part of the WTO dispute settlement procedure').

[88] Appellate Body Report, *India—Patent Protection for Pharmaceutical and Agricultural Chemical Products*, WT/DS50/AB/R, adopted 16 January 1998, DSR 1998:I, 9 at para 94. See also Appellate Body Report, *Chile—Price Band System and Safeguard Measures Relating to Certain Agricultural Products*, WT/DS207/AB/R, adopted 23 October 2002 at para 176 (where the Appellate Body stated that '[d]ue process is an obligation inherent in the WTO dispute settlement system'); Appellate Body Report, *Canada—Continued Suspension of Obligations in the EC—Hormones Dispute*, WT/DS321/AB/R, adopted 14 November 2008 at para 433.

[89] Appellate Body Report, *Mexico—Anti-Dumping Investigation of High Fructose Corn Syrup (HFCS) from the United States—Recourse to Article 21.5 of the DSU by the United States*, WT/DS132/AB/RW, adopted 21 November 2001, DSR 2001:XIII, 6675 at para 107.

[90] Appellate Body Report, *India—Patents (US)*, above n 88 at para 94.

[91] Appellate Body Report, *Mexico—Corn Syrup (Article 21.5—US)*, above n 89 at para 47.

[92] Appellate Body Report, *Mexico—Corn Syrup (Article 21.5—US)*, above n 89 at para 47.

[93] Appellate Body Report, *Brazil—Measures Affecting Desiccated Coconut*, WT/DS22/AB/R, adopted 20 March 1997, DSR 1997:I, 167 at 20–1.

[94] Article 6.2 of the DSU.

[95] Appellate Body Report, *European Communities—Customs Classification of Certain Computer Equipment*, WT/DS62/AB/R, WT/DS67/AB/R, WT/DS68/AB/R, adopted 22 June 1998, DSR 1998:V, 1851 at para 70; Appellate Body Report, *United States—Sunset Reviews of Anti-Dumping Measures on Oil Country Tubular Goods from Argentina*, WT/DS268/AB/R, adopted 17 December 2004 at para 161; Appellate Body Report, *Thailand—Anti-Dumping Duties on Angles, Shapes and Sections of Iron or Non-Alloy Steel and H-Beams from Poland*, WT/DS122/AB/R, adopted 5 April 2001, DSR 2001:VII, 2701 at para 88.

also invoked due process as an additional reason for panels not to be allowed to make findings with respect to claims that are not made by the litigants.[96] Finally, when declining a request to complete the analysis with respect to claims that the panel had not specifically addressed in its report,[97] the Appellate Body noted that in the absence of a full exploration by the panel of issues which would have to be engaged in, its efforts to complete the analysis 'might affect the due process rights of the participants'.[98]

2.1. Participation

The value of participation is guaranteed through many Articles of the DSU. Provisions such as paragraphs 4, 5, and 7 of Appendix 3 to the DSU secure an opportunity for the parties to be heard in writing and orally at the hearing. This is also the case with Article 15 of the DSU which gives the parties an opportunity to comment on the interim version of the panel report, allowing the panel to correct mistakes based on those comments.[99] The Appellate Body has also recognized the importance of giving the parties an adequate opportunity to participate. In the context of a request by one of the litigants to be allowed a chance to reply to arguments made by its opponent at the second oral hearing with the panel, the Appellate Body in *Australia—Salmon* stated that '[a] fundamental tenet of due process is that a party be provided with an opportunity to respond to claims made against it'.[100] Moreover, the DSU contains several Articles guaranteeing that both sides have full knowledge of all claims, arguments, and evidence so that they are able to present their views on them. It is in this spirit that Article 18.1 of the DSU prohibits *ex parte* communications with the adjudicators, Article 12.6 determines that written submissions must upon deposit be immediately distributed to the other party or parties to the dispute,[101] and paragraph 10 of Appendix 3 to the DSU establishes that oral presentations must be made in the presence of both sides and all written documents must be made available to both sides. Notice is also ensured through the requirements of Articles 4.4 and 6.2 of the DSU, and Rule 20 of the Working Procedures for Appellate Review.[102] Article 4.4

96 Appellate Body Report, *Chile—Price Band System*, above n 88 at paras 174, 176.

97 When it finds that the panel has made sufficient findings of fact or that there are sufficient undisputed facts on the record, the Appellate Body may 'complete the analysis', that is, it may (i) decide claims not addressed by the panel, or (ii) apply to the facts of the case an interpretation of a provision that is different from the interpretation applied by the panel.

98 Appellate Body Report, *European Communities—Export Subsidies on Sugar*, WT/DS265/AB/R, WT/DS266/AB/R, WT/DS283/AB/R, adopted 19 May 2005 at para 339.

99 Similarly, paragraph 6 of Appendix 4 to DSU and paragraph 6 of Annex 2 to the TBT Agreement allow the parties to comment on the report of the expert review group and the technical expert group respectively.

100 Appellate Body Report, *Australia—Measures Affecting Importation of Salmon*, WT/DS18/AB/R, adopted 6 November 1998, DSR 1998:VIII, 3327 at para 278.

101 With respect to submissions in an appeal, see Rules 21 and 22 of the Working Procedures for Appellate Review.

102 *Working Procedures for Appellate Review*, WTO Doc WT/AB/WP/5, 4 January 2005.

dictates that a request for consultations, the first step in a dispute settlement case, 'shall give the reasons for the request, including identification of the measures at issue and an indication of the legal basis for the complaint'. Similarly, Article 6.2 establishes that a request for establishment of a panel must 'identify the specific measures at issue and provide a brief summary of the legal basis of the complaint sufficient to present the problem clearly'. As discussed above, the Appellate Body understands that Article 6.2 has a due process function and has, accordingly, allowed challenges to the effect that the request for establishment of a panel was not sufficiently precise so as to provide the defendant with adequate notice of the case it had to answer. Inadequate notice, namely, failure to comply with the requirements of Rule 20.2 of the Working Procedures for Appellate Review, is also a ground for excluding a claim from the consideration of the Appellate Body.[103]

2.2. Impartiality

Demands for impartiality are present everywhere in the DSU, and are also found in the Working Procedures for Appellate Review and the Rules of Conduct for the Understanding on Rules and Procedures Governing the Settlement of Disputes (the 'Rules of Conduct').[104]

Articles of the DSU addressing the question of impartiality may be classified in two broad categories: (i) those laying down criteria with a view to guaranteeing that adjudicators and their assistants—eg the Secretariat, experts—are independent, and (ii) those establishing requirements with a view to controlling the emergence of bias or the perception thereof. Falling under the first category, Article 8.2 of the DSU contains a general requirement that panel members 'be selected with a view to ensuring the independence of the members'. Rule II of the Rules of Conduct also directs those subject to the Rules to be independent and impartial. More specific requirements are ascribed in Articles 8.3 (regarding the citizenship of panelists), 8.9 (noting that panelists 'shall serve in their individual capacities'), 17.3 (regarding the composition of the Appellate Body), Appendix 4, paragraph 3 (dealing with the composition of expert review groups) of the DSU; and in Rule 2.3 (prohibition from receiving instructions) of the Working Procedures for Appellate Review. Within the second category, Article 12.7 of the DSU compels panels to act impartially by requiring them to set out their 'findings of fact, the applicability of relevant provisions and the basic

[103] See Appellate Body Report, *United States—Subsidies on Upland Cotton*, WT/DS267/AB/R, adopted 21 March 2005 at para 495; Appellate Body Report, *United States—Countervailing Measures Concerning Certain Products from the European Communities*, WT/DS212/AB/R, adopted 8 January 2003 at paras 62, 75; Appellate Body Report, *Japan – Measures Affecting the Importation of Apples*, WT/DS245/AB/R, adopted 10 December 2003 at paras 120–8; Appellate Body Report, *European Communities—Regime for the Importation, Sale and Distribution of Bananas*, WT/DS27/AB/R, adopted 25 September 1997, DSR 1997:II, 591 at paras 148–152.

[104] WT/DSB/RC/1, 11 December 1996.

rationale behind any findings and recommendations' that they make. Moreover, checks on bias are maintained through the prohibition of *ex parte* communications with the adjudicators[105] and the specification that oral submissions be made in the presence of the parties, and all written submissions be made available to all parties.[106]

Other requirements are contained in Rules III (imposing a general disclosure obligation), VI (requiring disclosure of certain information) of the Rules of Conduct; and in Rules 2.2 (duty not the engage in conflicting activities) and 11 (regulating conflicts of interest) of the Working Procedures for Appellate Review. All these provisions indicate a strong commitment to the value of impartiality.[107] Such commitment has been reinforced in other instruments such as the Singapore Ministerial Declaration where members declared that they 'consider the impartial and transparent operation [of the DSU] to be of fundamental importance in assuring the resolution of trade disputes, and in fostering the implementation and application of the WTO agreements'.[108]

The commitment to impartiality has also been upheld by the Appellate Body. In *Canada—Continued Suspension*, the Appellate Body ruled that the panel acted inconsistently with Article 11 of the DSU and 'infringed the European Communities' due process rights' by appointing two experts to assist the panel, whose previous involvement with issues which were at the centre of the dispute gave rise to justifiable doubts as to their independence and impartiality.[109] In this connection, the Appellate Body noted that 'the protection of due process is an essential feature of a rules-based system of adjudication, such as that established under the DSU', and that such protection 'guarantees that the proceedings are conducted with fairness and impartiality'.[110]

The fact that panels are appointed *ad hoc* and that the Appellate Body members can be re-appointed for a second term are the most obvious features of the DSU which go against the idea of impartiality because of the effect that those features might have on the independence of the WTO adjudicators. Notwithstanding this caveat, it is possible to conclude that there is a serious commitment to impartiality in the DSU and that impartiality is undoubtedly a value of the WTO dispute settlement system.

105 Article 18.1 of the DSU. 106 Appendix 3, para 10 of the DSU.

107 Observers have also noted that many efforts have been made to ensure the impartiality of those involved in the process of adjudication and that those efforts have been generally successful. See, for example, Rufus Yerxa, 'The Power of the WTO Dispute Settlement System' in R Yerxa & B Wilson (eds), *Key Issues in WTO Dispute Settlement: The First Ten Years* (Cambridge: Cambridge University Press, 2005) 3 at 5; Jackson, *WTO Emerging Problems*, above n 71 at 341.

108 Paragraph 9 of the Singapore Ministerial Declaration, WTO Doc WT/MIN(96)/DEC, 18 December 1996, available at <http://www.wto.org/english/thewto_e/minist_e/min96_e/wtodec_e.htm> (accessed 1 July 2007).

109 Appellate Body Report, *Canada—Continued Suspension*, above n 88 at para 481.

110 Appellate Body Report, *Canada—Continued Suspension*, above n 88 at para 433.

2.3. Equality

As most systems of adjudication, WTO dispute settlement also pursues the value of equal treatment of the parties. On account of this, Article 18.1 of the DSU prohibits *ex parte* communications with the panel or Appellate Body, and the standard Working Procedures—Appendix 3 to the DSU—provides the parties with an equal right to make written and oral submissions. The Appellate Body has also referred to the right to equal treatment in connection with general statements on the nature and importance of due process in a system of adjudication such as that established under the DSU. In this context, in *Canada—Continued Suspension*, it noted that due process guarantees that 'one party is not unfairly disadvantaged with respect to other parties in a dispute'.[111]

WTO dispute settlement is exclusively state-to-state. The litigants are sovereign and, thus, legally equal, which provides an additional rationale for equal treatment. Importantly, however, the fact that legal or formal equality does not always translate into substantive equality is recognized in Articles of the DSU granting developing countries special and differential treatment. For instance, Article 12.10 of the DSU establishes that 'in examining a complaint against a developing country Member, the panel shall accord sufficient time for the developing country Member to prepare and present its argumentation' and Article 24.1 requires that particular consideration 'be given to the special situation of least-developed country Members' at 'all stages of the determination of the causes of a dispute and of dispute settlement procedures involving a least-developed country Member'.

It is worth noting that while the sovereign character of the litigants provides an additional justification for equality of treatment, protection of sovereignty understood as complete freedom of action is not a value embraced by the DSU[112]—the focus here is on a member's freedom to act as it pleases in the process of settling a dispute. This is so because WTO members agreed to have recourse to, and abide by, the rules and procedures of the DSU instead of having recourse to any other means to settle their grievances.[113] This view is also consonant with Jackson's view that the contemporary concept of sovereignty essentially refers to 'allocation of power'.[114] Having allocated the power to settle disputes between them to the WTO dispute settlement system, the parties must be ready to embrace what is implied in that allocation. In this regard, it is worth

[111] Appellate Body Report, *Canada—Continued Suspension*, above n 88 at para 433.

[112] Raustiala notes that sovereignty is often conflated with freedom of action. In his view, such conception does not stand up to scrutiny. He rightly observes that '[if] sovereignty is defined such that its erosion is an intrinsic part of international cooperation—a corollary of the operation of every international institution—the concept loses its meaning'. Kal Raustiala, 'Rethinking the Sovereignty Debate in International Economic Law' (2003) 6:4 Journal of International Economic Law 841 at 844, 851–2.

[113] See Articles 3.1 and 23 of the DSU.

[114] Jackson, *Sovereignty and the WTO*, above n 8 at 72 and chapter 3 in general; John H Jackson, 'Sovereignty-Modern: a New Approach to an Outdated Concept' (2003) 97:4 The American Journal of International Law 782 at 790.

noting that Judge Higgins has argued that as regards its procedures it is time for the ICJ to 'move away [...] from undue deference to the litigants by virtue of their rank as sovereign States'.[115] She notes that beyond inherent realities such as the fact that the structure of states means that pleadings will take a certain time to prepare, there is no '"value added" to reflect State sovereignty, whether in the number of rounds of written pleadings to be allowed, the length of oral pleadings to be set, whether late documents will or will not be tolerated'.[116]

3. Good faith cooperation

As in international dispute settlement in general, the value of good faith cooperation in the settlement of disputes is highly prized in WTO dispute settlement.[117] Because there is no power above sovereign states, the peaceful settlement of disputes between members of the international community depends on good faith cooperation among them. This is recognized in the Manila Declaration on the Peaceful Settlement of International Disputes, adopted by the United Nations General Assembly in 1982, which in Section I, paragraph 5 declares that 'States shall seek in good faith and in a spirit of co-operation an early and equitable settlement of their international disputes [...]'.[118] In particular, because when states agree to submit a dispute to adjudication they do so as sovereigns—that is, they make such commitment in their free will—they also implicitly assent to cooperate for the efficient development of the process.[119]

The DSU makes two direct references to 'good faith'. Pursuant to Article 4.3, following a request for consultations members undertake to 'enter into consultations in good faith'.[120] More importantly, Article 3.10 sets forth that requests

[115] Rosalyn Higgins, 'Respecting Sovereign States and Running a Tight Courtroom' (2001) 50 International and Comparative Law Quarterly 121 at 124. [116] Higgins, above n 115 at 132.

[117] Good faith cooperation is also a value embraced by many national systems of adjudication. For example, the French Civil Code in its Article 10 provides that 'Everyone is bound to cooperate with the administration of justice with a view to the revelation of the truth'. The parties are also required by the Code of Civil Procedure to 'cooperate in the conduct of fact finding measures ordered by the judge'. See Jolowicz, above n 25 at 291.

Good faith is also a general principle of international law. This principle has broad application as a source of substantive law as well as in the interpretation of treaties. For more information on those applications of the principle of good faith in WTO dispute settlement, see Helge Elisabeth Zeitler, '"Good Faith" in the WTO Jurisprudence—Necessary Balancing Element or an Open Door to Judicial Activism?' (2005) 8:3 Journal of International Economic Law 721; Marion Panizzon, *Good Faith in the Jurisprudence of the WTO* (Oxford: Hart Publishing, 2006).

[118] UN General Assembly Resolution 37/10, UN Doc A/RES/37/10, 15 November 1982, available at <http://www.un.org/documents/ga/res/37/a37r010.htm> (accessed 11 July 2009). Section II, paragraph 5 of the Declaration also urges states not to consider recourse to judicial settlement of legal disputes 'an unfriendly act between States'.

[119] Elisabeth Zoller (ed), *La Bonne Foi en Droit International Public* (Paris: Editions A Pedone, 1977) at 141.

[120] According to Article 4.2, Members also agree to '*accord sympathetic consideration* to and afford adequate opportunity for consultation regarding any representations made by another Member concerning measures affecting the operation of any covered agreement taken within the territory of the former'. [emphasis added]

to use the dispute settlement system are *not* 'intended or considered as contentious acts and that, if a dispute arises, all Members will engage in these procedures in good faith in an effort to resolve the dispute'. The value of good faith is also implicit in provisions such as Article 3.7 of the DSU. The Appellate Body in *Mexico—Corn Syrup (Article 21.5—US)* noted that the requirement in Article 3.7 that a member 'exercise its judgement as to whether action under [DSU] procedures would be fruitful' before bringing a case 'reflects a basic principle that Members should have recourse to WTO dispute settlement in good faith, and not frivolously set in motion the procedures contemplated in the DSU'.[121]

Panels and the Appellate Body have frequently resorted to the value of good faith cooperation to provide answers to questions brought before them regarding details of the organization of the process of adjudication. The Appellate Body has, for instance, linked the duty of the parties to a dispute to comply with a request from the panel to provide information under Article 13.1 of the DSU with their obligation under Article 3.10 of the DSU to engage in dispute settlement proceedings 'in good faith in an effort to resolve the dispute.'[122] The commitment to engage in dispute settlement 'in good faith in an effort to resolve the dispute' was also referred to by the Appellate Body in *US—FSC* in support of its finding that members need to raise procedural objections seasonably and promptly.[123] The Appellate Body noted in that case that '[t]he procedural rules of WTO dispute settlement are designed to promote, not the development of litigation techniques, but simply the fair, prompt and effective resolution of trade disputes'.[124]

4. Protection of confidential information

The WTO dispute settlement system has also clearly embraced the value of protection of sensitive non-public information, that is, confidential information. The DSU, as well as other agreements such as the Anti-Dumping Agreement, recognizes the importance of protecting such information. Article 17.7 of the Anti-Dumping Agreement provides that '[c]onfidential information provided to the panel shall not be disclosed without formal authorization from the person, body or authority providing such information'. Moreover, according to Article 18.2 of the DSU, 'Members shall treat as confidential information submitted by another Member to the panel or the Appellate Body which that Member has designated as confidential'.

However, while the importance of protecting confidential information is recognized, the WTO does not have an effective mechanism in place to prevent breaches of confidentiality. The Rules of Conduct enjoin panellists, members of

[121] Appellate Body Report, *Mexico—Corn Syrup (Article 21.5—US)*, above n 89 at para 73.
[122] Appellate Body Report, *Canada—Measures Affecting the Export of Civilian Aircraft*, WT/DS70/AB/R, adopted 20 August 1999, DSR 1999:III, 1377 at para 190.
[123] Appellate Body Report, *United States—Tax Treatment for 'Foreign Sales Corporations'*, WT/DS108/AB/R, adopted 20 March 2000, DSR 2000:III, 1619 at paras 165–6.
[124] Appellate Body Report, *US—FSC*, above n 123 at para 166.

the Appellate Body, arbitrators, experts, and members of the staff of the WTO and Appellate Body Secretariats to respect the confidentiality of the proceedings.[125] If found in breach of the duty of confidentiality, panellists, arbitrators, experts,[126] and members of the Appellate Body and their staff[127] may be removed from the case in question, while staff of the WTO Secretariat are sanctioned according to the Staff Regulations.[128] Importantly, however, such rules do not apply to the parties and their representatives. In sum, while the DSU orders all those involved in the proceedings to treat as confidential information that is so designated by a Member,[129] in practice the WTO has no effective mechanism in place to protect confidential information. Special procedures to protect confidential business information have been adopted by panels—but not the Appellate Body which has refused to adopt specific rules on the subject—on an *ad hoc* basis, but their establishment has not been free of complications.

It is arguable that Members did not recognize the need to establish a special mechanism to protect confidential information because, in general, the entire dispute settlement proceedings from consultations up until the publication of panel and Appellate Body reports are designed to be confidential. Confidentiality covers consultations,[130] written submissions to panels and the Appellate Body,[131] oral hearings,[132] and the record of the panel.[133] In fact, so many aspects of the proceedings are meant to be kept confidential that questions have been raised about the appropriateness of this confidentiality and demands have been made for more transparency. Some Members have, at least implicitly, recognized (i) that making the entire proceedings confidential is not necessary to protect sensitive non-public information (namely, confidential information), and (ii) that this practice may negatively affect the public's perception of the fairness of the proceedings. Accordingly, some Members have publicly disclosed their own written submissions[134] and agreed to open the meetings with the panel and the Appellate Body to the public—if not entirely, they have agreed to make available non-confidential versions of their submissions and portions of the meetings with the panel.[135]

[125] Rules II, III.2, VII of the Rules of Conduct. [126] Rule VIII.8 of the Rules of Conduct.
[127] Rule 10.5 of the Working Procedures for Appellate Review.
[128] Rule VIII.12 of the Rules of Conduct.
[129] Article 18.2 of the DSU, Appendix 3, paragraph 3 of the DSU.
[130] Article 4.6 of the DSU. [131] Article 18.2 and Appendix 3, paragraph 3 of the DSU.
[132] Appendix 3, paragraph 2 of the DSU.
[133] Article 14.1 of the DSU and Appendix 3, paragraph 3 of the DSU.
[134] Article 18.2 of the DSU expressly allows Members to do so. According to Article 18.2, '[n]othing in this Understanding shall preclude a party to a dispute from disclosing statements of its own positions to the public'.
[135] Panel hearings were open to the public for the first time in 2005 in *Canada—Continued Suspension of Obligations in the EC—Hormones Dispute* (DS321) and *United States—Continued Suspension of Obligations in the EC—Hormones Dispute* (DS320). Appellate Body hearings were also opened for the first time in the abovementioned disputes. For a detailed account of the cases in which hearings were opened to the public and the reasoning supporting the decisions to open the hearings, see Lothar Ehring, 'Public Access to Dispute Settlement Hearings in the World Trade Organization' (2008) 11:4 Journal of International Economic Law 1021.

In light of the above, it is possible to conclude that the protection of confidential information is undoubtedly a value pursued by the WTO system,[136] even though effective regulation may be wanting. Moreover, the fact that the parties have not been allowed to invoke the confidential character of information as a justification for not providing information to the panel suggests that the value of protection of confidential information cannot override the search for the truth.[137] These, however, are questions to be addressed in a later chapter of this book.[138]

5. Efficient use of resources

The limited budget of the WTO makes the efficient use of resources not only a goal but also a practical constraint.[139] Cost efficiency is also important due to the fact that the majority of the WTO members are developing countries which have limited resources to expend in dispute settlement.[140]

Panels and the Appellate Body have demonstrated that they are aware of efficiency concerns. For example, in *EC—Hormones* the Appellate Body agreed with the panel's decision to hold a joint meeting with the scientific experts in cases brought by Canada and the United States against the European Communities with respect to the same measure. According to the Appellate Body, it would be 'an uneconomical use of time and resources to force the Panel to hold two successive but separate meetings gathering the same group of experts twice, expressing their views twice regarding the same scientific and technical matters related to the same contested EC measures'.[141] The exercise of judicial economy with respect to non-essential claims is another example of the panels' awareness

[136] Ehlermann, for instance, posits that '[t]he protection of confidential information is one of the tenets of the covered agreements'. Claus-Dieter Ehlermann, 'Six Years on the Bench of the "World Trade Court": Some Personal Experiences as Member of the Appellate Body of the World Trade Organization' (2002) 36:4 Journal of World Trade 605 at 625.

[137] Panels and the Appellate Body have found that confidentiality does not provide an excuse for parties not to submit information which is otherwise necessary to determine the truth of allegations made in dispute settlement. See Panel Report, *Indonesia—Certain Measures Affecting the Automobile Industry*, WT/DS54/R, WT/DS55/R, WT/DS59/R, WT/DS64/R and Corr.1, 2, 3, and 4, adopted 23 July 1998, DSR 1998:VI, 2201 at para 14.235; Appellate Body Report, *Canada—Aircraft*, above n 122 at paras 195–6, 199; Panel Report, *Turkey—Measures Affecting the Importation of Rice*, WT/DS334/R, adopted 22 October 2007 at paras 7.99–7.107.

[138] See Chapter 5.

[139] The total budget of the WTO for 2008 was 184,891,500 Swiss francs of which 4,408,200 were allocated to the Appellate Body. The budget for dispute settlement panels, which does not include the salaries of the Secretariat, was 1,247,000, and the budget for experts was 50,000. <http://www.wto.org/english/thewto_e/secre_e/budget08_e.htm> (accessed 2 May 2009).

[140] See n 69 above regarding the Advisory Centre on WTO Law. The lack of resources to cover the costs of international adjudication is not a problem unique to the WTO. Facing similar challenges, courts and tribunals such as the Permanent Court of Arbitration and the International Tribunal for the Law of the Sea have arrangements in place to provide financial assistant to prospective litigants. See Merrills, *International Dispute Settlement*, above n 50 at 328–9.

[141] Appellate Body Report, *European Communities—Measures Concerning Meat and Meat Products (Hormones)*, WT/DS26/AB/R, WT/DS48/AB/R, adopted 13 February 1998, DSR 1998:I, 135 at para 152.

of efficiency concerns—though efficiency could be improved if panels were to adopt a procedure to inform the parties beforehand of their decision to rule on select claims only.[142]

References to resource efficiency, particularly concerning time, are everywhere in the DSU and the special rules contained in the covered agreements. According to Article 3.3 of the DSU, the 'prompt settlement' of disputes is 'essential to the effective functioning of the WTO'. Article 12.2 of the DSU determines that panel procedures should be flexible, but this flexibility should not unduly delay the panel process. Panels are enjoined to set precise deadlines for written submissions by the parties and the parties are exhorted to respect those deadlines.[143] In addition, many deadlines are set in the agreements which in certain cases are quite strict—for example the time allocated for appellate review, which must not exceed 90 days.[144] In certain cases, for instance where the dispute concerns perishable goods, shorter deadlines are called for.[145] The WTO dispute settlement system's preoccupation with time efficient proceedings is undoubtedly a reflection of the fact that impediments to the flow of trade result in daily costs to the operators affected which, if maintained for long enough, may drive some of them permanently out of business. Having a resource (time and cost) efficient process of adjudication is, therefore, an important objective which is likely to remain important in the future.[146]

6. Other values

The DSU and other dispute settlement-related provisions of the covered agreements do not directly endorse other values embraced by certain systems of

[142] The Appellate Body has upheld the idea that panels are not obliged to examine each and every claim made by the complaining party as long as they address those claims that must be addressed in order to resolve the dispute before them. See, for example, Appellate Body Report, *United States—Measure Affecting Imports of Woven Wool Shirts and Blouses from India*, WT/DS33/AB/R and Corr.1, adopted 23 May 1997, DSR 1997:I, 323 at 19.

[143] Article 12.5 of the DSU.

[144] Article 17.5 of the DSU. Only rarely the Appellate Body does not meet the Article 17.5 deadline. Moreover, in the instances where it exceeded the 90 days, the Appellate Body sought and received the assent of the parties beforehand. For two examples that occurred in 2008, see Appellate Body Annual Report for 2008, WTO Doc. WT/AB/11, 9 February 2009 at 42. For other deadlines see Articles 12.8, 12.9, 20, 21.5, 21.4 of the DSU and Articles 4.6, 4.9, 4.12, 7.5, and 7.7 of the SCM Agreement; Rules 21.1, 22.1, 23.1 23.3, 24 of the Working Procedures for Appellate Review. The shorter procedures for perishable goods have never been used.

[145] See Articles 4.8, 4.9,12.8 of the DSU, Articles 4.6, 4.9, 4.12 of the SCM Agreement.

[146] Davey is an avid advocate for reforms to further streamline the dispute settlement procedures. See William J Davey, 'Expediting the Panel Process in WTO Dispute Settlement' in ME Janow, V Donaldson & A Yanovich (eds), *The WTO: Governance, Dispute Settlement, and Developing Countries* (New York: Juris Publishing, 2008) 409 at 415–29; William J Davey, 'Evaluating WTO Dispute Settlement: What Results Have Been Achieved through Consultations and Implementation of Panel Reports?' in Y Taniguchi, A Yanovich & J Bohanes (eds), *The WTO in the Twenty-first Century: Dispute Settlement, Negotiations, and Regionalism in Asia* (Cambridge: Cambridge University Press, 2007) 98 at 120–5; William J Davey, 'The WTO: Looking Forwards' (2006) 9:1 Journal of International Economic Law 3 at 21–2.

adjudication, such as privacy and finality.[147] As regards finality, panels and the Appellate Body have, in compliance proceedings under Article 21.5 of the DSU,[148] construed several provisions of the DSU to have that effect. In *US—Shrimp (Article 21.5—Malaysia)*, when declining to entertain a claim against an aspect of the implementation measure that was the same as in the original measure and that had been found to be consistent with the WTO agreements in the original dispute, the Appellate Body found that Appellate Body reports that are adopted by the DSB 'must be treated by the parties to a particular dispute as a final resolution to that dispute'.[149] In *EC—Bed Linen (Article 21.5—India)*, the Appellate Body added that in the same manner 'an *unappealed* finding included in a panel report that is *adopted* by the DSB must be treated as a *final resolution* to a dispute between the parties in respect of the *particular* claim and the *specific* component of a measure that is the subject of that claim'.[150] In the latter case, the Appellate Body in *dicta* also established that when a panel does not rule on a claim, exercising judicial economy, 'the complainant [is] not [...] prevented from raising that same claim in a subsequent proceeding'.[151] Along these lines, in *US—Upland Cotton (Article 21.5—Brazil)*, the Appellate Body found that a party is allowed to raise the same claim in a subsequent proceeding if the claim was not resolved on the merits in the original proceedings because after reversing the panel the Appellate Body was not able to complete the analysis.[152] Because these findings have been made in Article 21.5 proceedings, there may still be scope to argue that the same claim can be brought in a totally new dispute settlement case—as opposed to a compliance procedure—based on evidence that was not known at the time when the first case was decided. In fact, this last point regarding new evidence has not been addressed even in Article 21.5 compliance proceedings.

[147] Waincymer, for example, notes that '[t]here is no express notion of *res judicata* applicable in the WTO'. Jeff Waincymer, *WTO Litigation: Procedural Aspects of Formal Dispute Settlement* (London: Cameron May, 2002) at 511.

[148] According to Article 21.5, '[w]here there is disagreement as to the existence or consistency with a covered agreement of measures taken to comply with the recommendations and rulings such dispute shall be decided through recourse to these dispute settlement procedures, including wherever possible resort to the original panel'.

[149] Appellate Body Report, *United States—Import Prohibition of Certain Shrimp and Shrimp Products—Recourse to Article 21.5 of the DSU by Malaysia*, WT/DS58/AB/RW, adopted 21 November 2001, DSR 2001:XIII, 6481 at para 97 (the Appellate Body based its conclusion on Articles 17.4 and 3.3 of the DSU).

[150] Appellate Body Report, *European Communities—Anti-Dumping Duties on Imports of Cotton-Type Bed Linen from India—Recourse to Article 21.5 of the DSU by India*, WT/DS141/AB/RW, adopted 24 April 2003 at para 93 [original emphasis] (the Appellate Body reached this conclusion by reading together Articles 16.4, 19.1, 21.1, 21.3, and 22.1. of the DSU).

[151] Appellate Body Report, *EC—Bed Linen (Article 21.5—India)*, above n 150 at footnote 115. See also Appellate Body Report, *United States—Sunset Reviews of Anti-Dumping Measures on Oil Country Tubular Goods from Argentina—Recourse to Article 21.5 of the DSU by Argentina*, WT/DS268/AB/RW, adopted 11 May 2007 at para 148.

[152] Appellate Body Report, *United States—Subsidies on Upland Cotton—Recourse to Article 21.5 of the DSU by Brazil*, WT/DS267/AB/RW, adopted 20 June 2008 at para 210.

Importantly, the mere fact, without more, that a value is pursued by a (or a group of) legal system(s) should not automatically be interpreted as an indication that that same value has been adopted by the WTO dispute settlement system. The potential impropriety of such automatic adoption of values from other systems is evidenced in the carefulness with which the ICJ dealt with the question of evidence obtained by unlawful means in *Corfu Channel*. The ICJ could have adopted the view prevalent in some jurisdictions that illegally obtained evidence is not admissible or rather opted for the position followed in other jurisdictions which allow consideration of that kind of evidence in certain circumstances.[153] Instead of doing so, the ICJ in *Corfu Channel* chose a path that avoided the question of whether it could base a finding of violation of international law on illegally obtained evidence; the Court found that other evidence on the record allowed it to come to the same conclusion.[154]

Without precluding the possibility that the WTO dispute settlement system may embrace values other than those delineated here, the analysis in this book will focus on the values of accuracy, participation, impartiality, equality of treatment, good faith cooperation, protection of confidential information, and efficient use of resources, as described above. As noted in the previous section, some of these values compete against each other and there is potential for some of them to clash. Ehlermann, for instance, refers to the tension in WTO dispute settlement between the protection of confidential information, equal treatment, and the search for the truth.[155] Different situations of tension between values will be examined throughout this study. In dealing with these tensions, the strategy will be first to avoid clashes which would require choosing a value over other(s)—that is to say, seek to maximize the realization of the multiple goals of the system. When trade-offs become necessary, high priority will be assigned to accuracy, which will generally also mean giving high priority to participation, impartiality, equality, and good faith cooperation due to their instrumental role in achieving accurate outcomes.

[153] For a brief account of the different approaches to illegally obtained evidence, see Hugh Thirlway, 'Dilemma or Chimera? Admissibility of Illegally Obtained Evidence in International Adjudication' (1984) 78:3 American Journal of International Law 622 at 627–8 (in this article, Thirlway also raises many questions regarding the applicability of domestic procedural rules to international proceedings); Damaska, above n 14 at 23–4.

[154] *The Corfu Channel* (Merits) (United Kingdom v Albania), Judgment of 9 April 1949, International Court of Justice, Reports of Judgments, Advisory Opinions and Orders (1949) at 30–42.

[155] Ehlermann, *Six Years on the Bench*, above n 136 at 625–7. Jackson also refers to the potential tensions between the various goals of the WTO dispute settlement. Jackson, *Sovereignty and the WTO*, above n 8 at 145–6.

C. The institutional and procedural framework

1. Methodological considerations

The process of fact-finding is not carried out in a vacuum; it takes place within a broader institutional and procedural framework.[156] In this regard, for example, commentators note that the origin and development of the common law rules of evidence have been largely influenced by the institution of the jury and the adversarial system of procedure.[157] It is, accordingly, necessary to understand the basic structure of the WTO dispute settlement system, in which context the process of proof unfolds. An optimal process of fact-finding for the WTO dispute settlement system cannot be devised without an understanding of this structure; different institutional and procedural arrangements have correspondingly distinct ways to optimize their processes of proof. This study, however, does not to any significant extent intend to challenge the basic structure of the WTO dispute settlement system set out by the DSU; it recognizes the value of working with existing structures and pursuing incremental change. Accordingly, while, for example, the creation of a body akin to a public prosecutor might improve the quality of decisions, it would also require fundamental changes to the system.[158] This is not therefore an issue taken up in this study.

In reviewing the framework created by the DSU, recourse will be made to comparisons of the WTO dispute settlement model with the common law and civil law models of adjudication. This is not to say that the WTO dispute settlement system must follow one or the other model; references to those two models of adjudication is intended to facilitate understanding of the main features of the WTO dispute settlement system since most international lawyers still undergo intense training in their domestic legal systems before becoming involved in international adjudication. In this regard, this study recognizes that the common law and the civil law systems are not homogenous, that is, there are many differences between common law jurisdictions just as there are many differences between civilian jurisdictions. Although these differences make it more difficult to refer to the characteristics of the two systems as a whole, this is not an impossible task. In fact, many scholars have compared different aspects of the two systems. Unless otherwise indicated, references to the common law and the civil law focus on the archetypal features of those two systems.

It must be noted, however, that those features may have been attenuated or abandoned by certain jurisdictions over time. For instance, English procedural

[156] See Damaska, above n 14 at 76; Twining, above n 3 at 216, 223. (Twining has argued for more integration between the law of evidence and the law of procedure in the common law system. It is worth noting that in the civilian tradition 'evidence law' has never been a separate subject of study.)

[157] Twining, above n 3 at 196, 201.

[158] Suggesting the institution of a public prosecutor for the WTO, see Gregory Shaffer, 'The Challenges of WTO Law: Strategies for Developing Country Adaptation' (2006) 5:2 World Trade Review 177 at 186.

law has recently been subject to reforms which have moved that system closer to the civil law tradition of continental Europe particularly as regards the powers of the judge to manage the proceedings including the process of fact-finding.[159] However, the fact that the common and civil law systems might no longer be found in their pure forms does not impair the value of comparisons with those systems as an analytical tool. This is particularly so because the design of many fact-finding procedures are still based on the archetypal features of those systems. Twining, for instance, notes that the jury system is so ingrained in the mind of common law jurists that even where jury trials are no longer in place, their influence in the rules of evidence is still to be felt.[160] Similarly, Damaska notes that the 'marginalization of jury trials has so far failed to bite deeply into common law orthodoxy and produce shifts in mainstream thinking about evidence: jury trials continue to be employed both as the institutional background for reflection on evidence and as a benchmark for shaping evidentiary rules'.[161]

Importantly, this study advocates that the WTO dispute settlement system must produce rules appropriate to its own needs and circumstances; sometimes these rules will resemble common law rules while at other times they will resemble civil law rules, and in still others they will be truly unique.[162] With an adequate understanding of the particularities of the WTO system, however, the rules of other systems can work as sources of law[163] or at least of ideas. In this connection, transnational rules of procedure may be particularly relevant since they might indicate the existence of general (or common) principles of law. Accordingly, whenever appropriate reference will be made to transnational rules such as the ALI/UNIDROIT Principles of Transnational Civil Procedure,[164]

[159] For a brief explanation of some of the English reforms, see Jolowicz, *Adversarial and Inquisitorial Models*, above n 25 at 287.

[160] Twining, above n 3 at 196, 201 (Twining considers this to be problematic).

[161] Damaska, above n 14 at 128. See also Gillian Hadfield, 'The Levers of Legal Design: Institutional Determinants of the Quality of Law' (May 2007) USC Legal Studies Research Paper No. 07-6 at 21 (noting that 'if juries today play only a small role in fact in Anglo-American courts, however, the jury tradition may nonetheless play an important role in setting the parameters for other institutional attributes of these legal regimes').

[162] Thirlway notes that there is a 'common temptation to model international procedural norms or rules on what are perceived to be analogous dispositions of municipal procedural law, without taking sufficient account either of the degree of generality, actual or potential, of the municipal law rule, or of the accuracy of the analogy involved in its transfer to the international plane'. He is critical of this approach. Thirlway, *Dilemma or Chimera*, above n 153 at 622. See also H Lauterpacht, 'The So-Called Anglo-American and Continental Schools of Thought in International Law' (1931) 12 The British Yearbook of International Law (1931) 31 at 41 (arguing that international courts and tribunals must be able to develop their own rules of procedure which should not have to coincide with the rules of the common law).

[163] This will be so when the rule can be classified as a general principle of law pursuant to Article 38.1(c) of the Statute of the International Court of Justice (ICJ).

[164] American Law Institute & UNIDROIT, *Principles of Transnational Civil Procedure* (Cambridge: Cambridge University Press, 2006).

and the IBA Rules on the Taking of Evidence in International Commercial Arbitration.[165] International rules of procedure, to the extent they exist, have special relevance since they might have been designed to respond to similar needs and circumstances.[166] Evidence of such rules can be found in the statutes or rules of procedure of international courts and tribunals as well as their decisions; these will be referred to when possible.

2. The basic models: common and civil law

There are three main structural differences between the common law and the civil law models of adjudication which have had a significant impact on the design of the process of proof in those two systems.[167]

The first difference concerns the figure of the adjudicator. The common law has traditionally employed a professional judge to resolve questions of law whereas questions of fact are allocated to the jury, namely, a group of lay people. In contrast, in the civil law model professional judges are responsible for adjudicating both questions of law and of fact.

Second, while the common law has favoured the temporal concentration of the presentation of evidence in a single event called the 'trial', the civil law opted for the episodic taking and presentation of evidence, including a (or several) hearing(s)—unlike the common law, however, the proceedings are *not* almost entirely concentrated or focused on that hearing. The trial is a continuous event where the parties present their entire case to the jury and judge; the complainant first presents arguments and evidence in support of its claims, and is then followed by the defendant. As opposed to the common law model, in the civilian model the adjudicator is furnished with information (arguments and evidence) throughout the proceedings, and thus on the occasion of the final hearing the adjudicator's knowledge of the case is already substantial. The hearing is mainly an occasion to hear witnesses and discuss arguments and evidence already set forth in the written submissions of the parties.

[165] Available at <http://www.ibanet.org/Search/Taxonomy.aspx?TaxonomyUid=283a3ddd-d500-4ebc-86c7-fb7bc364a36e> (accessed 2 May 2009).

[166] Thirlway notes that '[t]he question of the formal sources of international procedural law has not received much doctrinal attention. It is doubtful whether anything in the nature of a binding custom, as distinct from the borrowing of tried and efficient practices, can be said to exist.' HWA Thirlway, 'Procedure of International Courts and Tribunals' in R Bernhardt (ed), *Encyclopedia of Public International Law* (Amsterdam: Elsevier, 1997) vol 3, 1128 at 1128. See also Thirlway, *Dilemma or Chimera*, above n 153 at 623–6; Rosenne, above n 28 at 1021 (noting that 'there is no general theory of international legal procedural law on which detailed rules of procedure are superimposed'); Chester Brown, *A Common Law of International Adjudication* (Oxford: Oxford University Press, 2007) (arguing that a homogeneous body of rules relating to issues of procedure and remedies before international courts and tribunals is emerging; he refers to this body of rules as the 'common law of international adjudication').

[167] See Damaska, above n 14 at 4; Jolowicz, *Fact-Finding: a Comparative Perspective*, above n 19 at 134, 141–3.

The third difference between the two systems relates to the role of the parties and the adjudicator. Common law proceedings are dominated by the parties while the adjudicator is almost entirely passive, that is to say, the proceedings are adversarial. In purely adversarial proceedings the parties not only define the scope of the case, but also control the information that the adjudicator is exposed to, each party being responsible for conducting its own factual inquiries. Civil law proceedings on the other hand provide a more prominent role for the adjudicator who is in charge of managing the proceedings, including conducting factual inquiries which s/he understands necessary. For this reason, civilian procedure is often said to be inquisitorial, though in most jurisdictions, particularly as regards civil litigation, the adjudicator is not in charge of building a case for the parties while they remain passive. Thus, it may be more appropriate to say that civilian procedures have a hybrid character. In this type of proceedings, the parties determine the scope of the case, and while they are still responsible for presenting arguments and evidence in support of their contentions they do not have complete control over the formation of the record of the proceedings.

The impact of these differences between the common law and the civil law on the process of fact-finding will be noted throughout this study and include, for instance, the following: (i) concerns about the capacity of lay persons to discern 'good' from 'bad' evidence have resulted in the creation by the common law of complex rules regarding the admissibility of evidence;[168] (ii) the strictly adversarial character of common law proceedings leads to the fission of the fact-finding enterprise into two opposite cases and the association of evidence with one or the other party, while in the civil law the involvement of the adjudicator in the process of fact-finding 'reduces the bipolar tensions of factual inquiries' making evidence more easily 'conceived as [a repository] of neutral information'[169] (iii) the rigorously adversarial character of common law adjudication has also inspired the creation of rules designed to induce the parties to search and present the best evidence available—otherwise, in the absence of an independent party with fact-finding powers, the parties would likely succumb to self-interest and where possible present evidence of lower quality which would tend to support their view or at least cause them less damage; and (iv) the single event concept—the fact that the parties present their entire case including evidence at the occasion of the trial, has created the need for pre-trial discovery in common law proceedings.[170]

3. *The phases of WTO proceedings*

The following paragraphs explain the institutional and procedural framework of the WTO dispute settlement system in which context the process of fact-finding

[168] Evidence that is inadmissible cannot be received and considered by the trier of facts.
[169] Damaska, above n 14 at 76–8.
[170] Zekoll, *Comparative Civil Procedure*, above n 3 at 1335.

takes place. The question of how the basic structure of the WTO dispute settlement system relates to the structure of common law and civil law proceedings is also discussed. The goal of the following paragraphs is to provide an overview of the setting within which the questions discussed in the following chapters are situated.

WTO dispute settlement proceedings can be roughly divided in four phases: (1) establishment of the proceedings; (2) preparation for decision; (3) decision-making; and (4) appeal.

3.1. Establishment of the proceedings

Dispute settlement begins with the filing by the complaining party of a request for consultations. Such request must designate the reasons for the request, including identification of the measures at issue and an indication of the legal basis for the complaint.[171] There are three general types of complaints: (1) violation complaints; (2) non-violation complaints; and (3) situation complaints. The first type is based on the alleged violation of a provision of the covered agreements, whereas the second and third types are respectively based on the *application by a member of any measure* or the *existence of any other situation* that nullify or impair any benefits or impede the attainment of any objective under a WTO agreement which allows these types of complaints. The latter two types of complaints have been rare to non-existent in the WTO dispute settlement system.[172]

The request for consultations is brief, usually not exceeding two to three pages. Unless the opposing party does not respond or otherwise refuses to engage in consultations—in which case the complaining party can proceed to request the establishment of a panel—following the request for consultations the parties engage in confidential consultations with a view to achieving a mutually satisfactory solution consistent with the WTO agreements.[173]

If the dispute is not settled during consultations the complaining party may request the establishment of a panel. This request is made in writing and although it is normally more detailed than the request for consultations, particularly owing to the better understanding of the terms of the dispute developed during the process of consultations, it is still a brief document. The request for establishment of a panel must concern the same dispute that was the subject of consultations. This is so because when read together Articles 4.7 and 6.2 of the

[171] Article 4.4 of the DSU.

[172] It is worth noting that Article 26.2 of the DSU provides that in the case of 'situation complaints' the procedures contained in the DSU 'apply only up to and including the point in the proceedings where the panel report has been circulated to the Members. The dispute settlement rules and procedures contained in the Decision of 12 April 1989 (BISD 36S/61-67) shall apply to consideration for adoption, and surveillance and implementation of recommendations and rulings.' In the case of non-violation complaints, Article 26.1(b) of the DSU clarifies that the Member in question is not obliged 'to withdraw the measure', but can instead 'make a mutually satisfactory adjustment'.

[173] Article 4.3 of the DSU.

DSU—the former allowing a party to request a panel if consultations 'failed to settle the dispute', and the latter requiring the request for establishment of a panel to 'indicate whether consultations were held'—suggest that a request for establishment of a panel cannot refer to a dispute that was not the subject of consultations.

Pursuant to Article 6.2 of the DSU, in addition to indicating whether consultations were held, the complaining party must in its request for establishment of a panel 'identify the specific measures at issue' and 'provide a brief summary of the legal basis of the complaint'. Together, these two requirements contained in Article 6.2 comprise the 'matter referred to the DSB', which determines a panel's terms of reference according to Article 7.1 of the DSU.[174] It is precisely because the terms of reference of a panel are determined by the request for establishment of a panel that panels and the Appellate Body have taken a cautious approach to requests for excluding a matter from the terms of reference of a panel on the grounds that the matter was not consulted upon. According to the Appellate Body, there is no requirement for '"precise and exact identity" between the scope of consultations and the request for the establishment of a panel' as long as the complaining party does not expand the scope of the dispute.[175] This also means that the legal claims identified in the request for establishment of a panel do not have to be identical to those listed in the request for consultations 'provided that the "legal basis" in the panel request may reasonably be said to have evolved from the "legal basis" that formed the subject of consultations'.[176]

Panels and the Appellate Body have, however, been more rigorous when determining whether a measure and/or legal claim has been sufficiently identified so as to fall within the terms of reference of the panel. This is so because the terms of reference establish the jurisdiction of the panel and fulfill the due process objective of giving the parties and third parties information concerning the dispute allowing them an opportunity to respond to the complaining party's case.[177] In light of this, the Appellate Body has ruled that identification of the

[174] See Appellate Body Report, *United States—Countervailing Duties on Certain Corrosion-Resistant Carbon Steel Flat Products from Germany*, WT/DS213/AB/R and Corr.1, adopted 19 December 2002 at para 125; Appellate Body Report, *Guatemala—Anti-Dumping Investigation Regarding Portland Cement from Mexico*, WT/DS60/AB/R, adopted 25 November 1998, DSR 1998:IX, 3767 at para 76.

[175] Appellate Body Report, *US—Upland Cotton*, above n 103 at para 293; Appellate Body Report, *Brazil—Export Financing Programme for Aircraft*, WT/DS46/AB/R, adopted 20 August 1999, DSR 1999:III, 1161 at paras 130–2; Appellate Body Report, *United States—Continued Existence and Application of Zeroing Methodology*, WT/DS350/AB/R, adopted 19 February 2009 at para 222.

[176] Appellate Body Report, *Mexico—Definitive Anti-Dumping Measures on Beef and Rice, Complaint with Respect to Rice*, WT/DS295/AB/R, adopted 20 December 2005, DSR 2005:XXII, 10853 at para 138.

[177] Appellate Body Report, *Brazil—Desiccated Coconut*, above n 93 at 22; Appellate Body Report, *Thailand—H-Beams*, above n 95 at paras 84–5.

treaty provisions claimed to have been violated is always necessary but not always sufficient; according to the Appellate Body, there are situations in which the circumstances are such that the mere listing of treaty articles does not satisfy the standards of Article 6.2.[178] The Appellate Body has also ruled that (i) complaining parties must set out 'as such'[179] challenges as clearly as possible, stating unambiguously the specific measures of municipal law challenged and the legal basis for the allegation that those measures are not consistent with the WTO agreements;[180] (ii) although Article 6.2 does not explicitly require identification of the products to which the specific measures at issue apply, in certain circumstances it may be necessary to identify the products subject to the measures in dispute in order to appropriately identify the specific measure at issue;[181] (iii) measures enacted subsequently to the establishment of the panel may fall within the terms of reference of the panel only in very limited circumstances such as when they amend the original measure and the amendment does 'not, in any way, change the *essence of the original measure*' or when they are mere 'modifications of the legal form of the original definitive measure';[182] (iv) measures whose legislative basis have expired, 'but whose effects are alleged to be impairing the benefits accruing to the requesting Member under a covered agreement' at the time of establishment of the panel can be part of the terms of reference of the panel.[183] In short, as a general rule, the panel request must 'plainly connect the challenged measure(s) with the provision(s) of the covered agreements claimed to have been infringed'.[184]

[178] Appellate Body Report, *Korea—Definitive Safeguard Measure on Imports of Certain Dairy Products*, WT/DS98/AB/R, adopted 12 January 2000, DSR 2000:I, 3 at para 124; Appellate Body Report, *Thailand—H-Beams*, above n 95 at paras 87–8.

[179] 'As such' claims are challenges to the general operation of a measure 'without regard to [its] application in a specific instance, or at times even without regard to whether the measure [is] yet in effect'. Appellate Body Report, *US—Oil Country Tubular Goods Sunset Reviews*,above n 95 at para 165.

[180] Appellate Body Report, *US—Oil Country Tubular Goods Sunset Reviews*, above n 95 at para 173.

[181] Appellate Body Report, *EC—Computer Equipment*, above n 95 at para 67. See also Appellate Body Report, *European Communities—Customs Classification of Frozen Boneless Chicken Cuts*, WT/DS269/AB/R, WT/DS286/AB/R, and Corr.1, adopted 27 September 2005 at paras 165–8.

[182] Appellate Body Report, *EC—Chicken Cuts*, above n 181 at paras 156–9 and footnote 320 [emphasis in the original]; Appellate Body Report, *Chile—Price Band System*, above n 88 at para 139.

[183] Appellate Body Report, *European Communities—Selected Customs Matters*, WT/DS315/AB/R, adopted 11 December 2006 at 184 (referring to Appellate Body Report, *US—Upland Cotton*, above n 103 at para 263. It must be noted, however, that the reference to paragraph 263 of *US—Upland Cotton* does not necessarily support the Appellate Body's finding since that paragraph is not addressing the terms of reference of the panel, but rather the scope of consultations under Article 4.2 of the DSU).

[184] Appellate Body Report, *US—Oil Country Tubular Goods Sunset Reviews*, above n 95 at para 162. See also Appellate Body Report, *United States—Tax Treatment for 'Foreign Sales Corporations'—Second Recourse to Article 21.5 of the DSU by the European Communities*, WT/DS108/AB/RW2, adopted 14 March 2006 at para 62 (where the Appellate Body provided guidance on the elements that must be identified in a panel request under Article 21.5 of the DSU).

Importantly, faulty requests for establishment of a panel 'cannot be subsequently "cured" by a complaining party's argumentation in its first written submission to the panel or in any other submission or statement made later in the panel proceeding'.[185] If the complaining party wishes to amend the terms of the case, it must start from scratch again, ie file a new request for consultations, followed by a panel request. It is worth noting that panels and the Appellate Body have differentiated between the 'legal basis of the complaint' (the legal claims) and the arguments put forth in support of those claims.[186] While the complaining party cannot amend its claims, it can introduce new arguments at any point during the proceedings.[187]

It must be noted that as a general rule the terms of reference are determined by the complaining party through its request for establishment of a panel. Typically, the first written submission to the panel, following the complaining party's first submission, is the first occasion where the opposing party will express its views on the scope of the dispute and raise any provisions which it considers must be part of the analysis of the panel.[188] Defendants are not permitted to raise counter-complaints in the same proceedings—eventual counter-complaints must be analysed in a separate case.[189] Accordingly, just as in the common law and the civil law models of adjudication, the parties in WTO dispute settlement, particularly the complainant, have control over the scope of the dispute within the confines of the time limits set out in the DSU.[190]

Finally, regardless of the terms of the request for establishment of a panel, the jurisdiction of panels is limited to claims under the WTO covered agreements, that is to say, panels can only rule on claims brought under the covered agreements. Arguably if the parties agree otherwise in other than standard terms of reference pursuant to Article 7.3 of the DSU, a panel may have jurisdiction to rule on claims not based on the covered agreements if those claims are sufficiently related to the covered agreements.[191] There is much disagreement as to whether, when examining claims falling under their jurisdiction, panels are permitted to apply directly rules other than those contained in or incorporated by reference by the WTO covered agreements—less contentious is the view that panels and the Appellate Body can take non-WTO rules into account when *interpreting* WTO rules. The disagreement

[185] Appellate Body Report, *EC—Bananas III*,above n 103 at para 143.

[186] Appellate Body Report, *Korea—Dairy*, above n 178 at para 139.

[187] See Appellate Body Report, *Korea—Dairy*, above n 178 at paras 139–40. In this case, the Appellate Body was also careful to distinguish arguments from evidence.

[188] Defendants have, however, particularly in the last few years, challenged the specificity of the panel request in early requests for preliminary rulings.

[189] Article 3.10 of the DSU.

[190] See, for example, Jolowicz, *Adversarial and Inquisitorial Models*, above n 25 (regarding the right of the parties to determine the substance of their dispute in French (civilian) and English (common law) civil proceedings). However, some jurisdictions empower adjudicators to bring up and examine questions of public policy on their own motion.

[191] Pauwelyn, *Conflict of Norms*, above n 83 at 444.

refers in essence to the question of whether non-WTO rules can be invoked as a defense to a claim under the covered agreements, that is, as a justification for what would otherwise constitute a violation of the WTO agreements.[192] Panels and the Appellate Body have not provided a direct answer to this question,[193] and the view that non-WTO rules can be invoked as a defense is far from being widely accepted.

3.2. Preparatory stage

Following the establishment of the panel, the Secretariat together with the parties, including the Director-General of the WTO if called on to do so, compose the panel which will analyse the matter at issue and make both findings of fact and of law.[194] A panel consists of three—or, if the parties agree, five—individuals who are chosen for their qualifications and expertise on the subject-matter of the dispute among individuals with a governmental and/or non-governmental background. Panels are, therefore, experts as opposed to the laypersons that constitute the jury.

It is worth noting at this point that proposals have been put forward to create a Permanent Panel Body composed of individuals with expertise in international trade law from which the three panelists would be drawn.[195] Aimed at mitigating the costs of the creation of a full Permanent Panel Body, and maintaining the diversity of expertise of the panelists, an alternative proposal has suggested the establishment of a Permanent Body of Chairpersons from which the chair of each panel would be chosen.[196] The objective of these proposals is to (i) ensure that panels are composed of individuals who have adjudicatory experience and are well-prepared to deal with the greater complexity of legal and factual

[192] See Pauwelyn, *Conflict of Norms*, above n 83 at 459–74 (advocating the view that non-WTO rules may be invoked as a defense to a claim under a WTO rule); Joel P Trachtman, 'The Domain of WTO Dispute Resolution' (1999) 40 Harvard International Law Journal 333 at 341–2 (in support of the view that only WTO law may be directly applied by panels); Ernst-Ulrich Petersmann, *WTO Dispute Settlement Practice 1995–2005*, above n 82 at 67–9 (explaining the different points of view with respect to the applicability of non-WTO law).

[193] *Argentina—Textiles and Apparel* suggests that defenses must be based on WTO agreements. Appellate Body Report, *Argentina—Measures Affecting Imports of Footwear, Textiles, Apparel and Other Items*, WT/DS56/AB/R and Corr.1, adopted 22 April 1998, DSR 1998:III, 1003 at para 74.

[194] Article 8 of the DSU. As noted by Davey, while in the early years of WTO dispute settlement 'the Director-General was not often called upon to compose panels[,] in recent years, his involvement has become the norm'. Davey, *Expediting the Panel Process*, above n 146 at 434.

[195] See *Contribution of the European Communities and its Member States to the Improvement of the WTO Dispute Settlement Understanding*, WTO Doc TN/DS/W/1, 13 March 2002.

[196] See *Contribution from Thailand to Clarify and Improve the Dispute Settlement Understanding: Panel System*, WTO Doc TN/DS/W/31, 22 January 2003; *Contribution of the European Communities and its Member States to the Improvement and Clarification of the WTO Dispute Settlement Understanding*, WTO Doc TN/DS/W/38, 23 January 2003 at para 14; Peter Sutherland et al, *The Future of the WTO: Addressing Institutional Challenges in the New Millenium* (Geneva: World Trade Organization, 2004) at para 257.

questions which are being presented to panels;[197] (ii) 'facilitate procedural innovations and the standardization of panel working procedures';[198] (iii) 'eliminate perceived conflicts of interest that arise when trade diplomats, who have and are negotiating agreements, are asked to interpret them';[199] and (iv) improve the efficiency of the panel process, particularly in terms of the time savings which could be effectuated through scheduling and organizational efficiencies, and the elimination of the time currently devoted to the composition of the panel—the latter would not apply to the proposal for the creation of a Permanent Body of Chairpersons since the other two panelists would still have to be appointed through the regular process.[200] The creation of a Permanent Panel Body or Body of Chairpersons would certainly facilitate the implementation of some of the suggestions propounded in this book; it could not be said, however, that such body would be necessary for their implementation. The WTO Secretariat, performing the functions foreseen in Article 27.1 of the DSU,[201] could provide the necessary guidance to panels. While much criticism has been directed at the influence which the Secretariat exerts over the content of the panel reports, guidance on questions of procedure would fall squarely within the mandate of the Secretariat laid out in Article 27.1. Moreover, to the extent that more elaborate standard working procedures would help make the process more efficient, the DSB (perhaps with the help of a group of experts) could take on the task of developing such procedures. Such procedures would not have to be binding, but could instead function as guidelines.

Returning to the structure of the panel proceedings, an important feature of such proceedings is that the taking and presentation of evidence are, similarly to civil law proceedings, episodic. As a general rule, the proceedings effectively commence with the first set of written submissions, which are followed by a first meeting (hearing) with the panel, another set of written submissions and a second meeting with the panel. In normal circumstances, first written submissions are tabled sequentially, the complaining party submitting its submission first,

[197] TN/DS/W/1, above n 195 at 2; Davey, *Expediting the Panel Process*, above n 146 at 435. Examining the composition of past panels Davey notes that not many panelists have had significant litigation experience, but that 27.5% of the panelists have at least had the opportunity to build dispute settlement skills by serving on more than two panels. Most individuals (72.5%) that serve as panelists, however, only serve on one or two panels. Finally, he notes that '[t]he existence of a group of repeat panelists and repeat chairs means that most panels (62%) are composed of at least two individuals with prior panel experience'. Ibid. at 433.

[198] Davey, *Expediting the Panel Process*, above n 146 at 434.

[199] Davey, *Expediting the Panel Process*, above n 146 at 435; TN/DS/W/1, above n 196 at 2–3; Thomas Cottier, 'The WTO Permanent Panel Body: a Bridge Too Far?' (2003) 6:1 Journal of International Economic Law 187 at 195. But see TN/DS/W/38, above n 196 at para 14 (suggesting that diplomats on leave from the government could be appointed to the panel body).

[200] Davey, *Expediting the Panel Process*, above n 146 at 434; TN/DS/W/38, above n 196 at para 14; TN/DS/W/1, above n 195 at 2.

[201] Pursuant to Article 27.1 of the DSU: 'The Secretariat shall have the responsibility of assisting panels, especially on the legal, historical and procedural aspects of the matters dealt with, and of providing secretarial and technical support.'

whereas second written submissions are presented simultaneously. The first and second written submissions are expected to brief the parties' case fully; they should be accompanied by evidence to support the parties' contentions. In the first written submission, the parties must present the facts of the case and arguments relating those facts to the law. According to the Appellate Body, 'under the standard working procedures of panels, complaining parties should put forward their cases—with "a full presentation of the facts on the basis of submission of supporting evidence"—during the *first* stage of panel proceedings', which cover the proceedings up until the first meeting with the panel; similar expectations apply to the defending parties.[202] The second set of written submissions is devoted to rebuttal of the evidence and arguments advanced in the first stage of the proceedings. Ideally any evidence submitted at this stage should be restricted to rebutting evidence and arguments presented in the first stage of the proceedings. However, owing to the fact that neither the DSU nor the Standard Working Procedures of Appendix 3 establish time limits for the submission of evidence to a panel, panels and the Appellate Body have been reluctant to decline to admit evidence during the second stage of the proceedings which could have been submitted earlier.[203] In this regard, some panels have used their prerogative to adopt Special Working Procedures to impose a time limit on the submission of factual evidence not necessary for purposes of rebuttals, answers to questions, or comments made for purposes of rebutting answers provided by others.[204] On at least one occasion, however, a panel which had imposed such time limits admitted, after the expiration of the deadline, evidence which was allegedly not necessary for purposes of rebuttal on the grounds that the panel would not 'be abiding by [its] duty in Article 11 of the DSU if [it] were to rule as inadmissible evidence that may have a bearing on the Panel's findings'.[205] It is also worth noting that in terms of the admission of evidence panels are not restricted by rules of evidence, that is to say, panels can freely admit evidence, similarly to adjudicators in civil law jurisdictions.[206]

The meetings (hearings) with the panel take place after the written submissions are filed and some time is allowed for the parties and the panel to review

[202] Appellate Body Report, *United States—Measures Affecting the Cross-Border Supply of Gambling and Betting Services*, WT/DS285/AB/R, adopted 20 April 2005 at para 271.

[203] See Appellate Body Report, *Argentina—Textiles and Apparel*, above n 193 at para 80; Panel Report, *Argentina—Measures Affecting Imports of Footwear, Textiles, Apparel and Other Items*, WT/DS56/R, adopted 22 April 1998 at para 6.55.

[204] See, for example, paragraph 12 of the Working Procedures in Panel Report, *European Communities—Selected Customs Matters*, WT/DS315/R, adopted 11 December 2006, at Annex E.

[205] Panel Report, *EC—Selected Customs Matters*, above n 204 at paras 7.66, 7.70, 7.76. A similar situation arose in Panel Report, *Australia—Measures Affecting Importation of Salmon*, WT/DS18/R and Corr.1, adopted 6 November 1998 at paras 8.5–8.6; Appellate Body Report, *Australia—Salmon*, above n 100 at paras 268, 272.

[206] This is the case with international tribunals in general. See Sandifer, above n 12 at 176, 468–9 (where he notes that 'the practice of international tribunals in the admission of evidence has developed a pattern comparable to that of the liberal system of procedure of the civil law countries'). See also references in n 227 below.

those submissions. Hearings are fairly short events normally not exceeding three days, particularly when experts are not involved. At these meetings both parties are provided an opportunity to present their views orally, written versions of which must be made available.[207] Panels may put questions to the parties during the hearings and at any other time in writing. Parties are not obliged to answer all questions at the hearing; they can provide answers in writing after the meeting.[208] This flexibility is necessary given the fact that for cost reasons the parties are often not able to bring all persons involved in the case to the hearing in Geneva. This is particularly the case of the defendant, which will rarely be able to include in its delegation all persons involved in the adoption, implementation, and operation of the challenged measure(s).

Third parties (WTO Members) with an interest in the dispute have also been given an opportunity to participate in the proceedings. In practice, any Member that declares to have an interest in the dispute is admitted as a third party. Third parties can make written submissions to the panel concerning any aspect of the dispute and have the right to be heard by the panel at the first substantive meeting and to receive the first submissions of the parties.[209] While third parties have no right to participate in the second meeting with the panel, they may nonetheless be granted such an opportunity. Panels also usually put questions to third parties. Moreover, third parties are ensured a chance to make written and oral submissions to the Appellate Body.[210]

Panels examine and decide both questions of fact and of law. According to Article 11 of the DSU, panels must 'make an objective assessment of the matter before [them], including an objective assessment of the facts of the case and the applicability of and conformity with the relevant covered agreements'. As previously noted, panels may put questions to the parties and third parties. Article 13 of the DSU goes further and grants the panel the 'right to seek information and technical advice from any individual or body which it deems appropriate', and to 'consult experts to obtain their opinion on certain aspects of the matter'. Accordingly, WTO dispute settlement is not strictly adversarial; the panel has powers to intervene in the process of proof and to manage the proceedings in general. The latter power is expressly guaranteed by several provisions[211] among which Article 12.1 of the DSU grants the panel a broad power to adopt Special Working Procedures after consulting the parties to the dispute.[212]

[207] Paragraphs 5, 7, and 9 of Appendix 3 to the DSU.

[208] Paragraph 8 of Appendix 3 to the DSU.

[209] Articles 10.2 and 10.3 of the DSU, and paragraph 6 of Appendix 3 to the DSU.

[210] Article 17.4 of the DSU.

[211] For example, Articles 12.4 and 12.5 of the DSU grant the panel the authority to determine the timetable of the proceedings and impose deadlines.

[212] As regards the Appellate Body, Article 17.9 of the DSU establishes that '[w]orking procedures shall be drawn up by the Appellate Body in consultation with the Chairman of the DSB and the Director-General'. Rule 16(1) of the Working Procedures for Appellate Review provide that: 'where a procedural question arises that is not covered by these Rules, a division may adopt an appropriate procedure for the purposes of that appeal only, provided that it is not inconsistent with the DSU, the other covered agreements and these Rules'.

The power to manage the proceedings to the extent necessary to fulfil their adjudicative function has, in fact, been recognized as inherent in international courts and tribunals.[213] This is particularly so because international courts and tribunals do not benefit from comprehensive codes of procedure or guidelines. This power is of course not unlimited. In the case of the WTO, it does not extend to disregarding and amending the DSU or other dispute settlement provisions in the covered agreements.[214] This means that panels cannot adopt Working Procedures which conflict with the rules established in the DSU. Moreover, the margin of discretion of a panel is limited by the requirements of due process.[215] Practical limitations also exist. For instance, panels and international courts and tribunals cannot issue subpoenas—unless a special arrangement with the states involved is made—because they lack police powers to enforce them.

The exact extent of the inherent powers of panels is a question to be answered on a case-by-case basis. As regards questions of fact-finding, it is safe to conclude that those powers are broad since the facts must be determined as accurately as possible, within the constraints imposed by competing goals, for the law to be correctly applied[216]—this question will be examined in more detail in Chapter 5.

[213] See Mitchell, *The Legal Basis for Using Principles*, above n 83 at 828–32 (discussing the inherent powers of international courts and tribunals and those of WTO panels); Mitchell, *Due Process in WTO Disputes*, above n 83 at 158 (arguing that WTO panels have inherent powers); Pauwelyn, *Conflict of Norms*, above n 83 at 447–8 (regarding the inherent powers of WTO panels); Jackson, *Sovereignty and the WTO*, above n 8 at 206 (Jackson seems to embrace the idea that WTO panels have inherent powers when he argues that '[t]he mere fact that the original consent of nation-states included consent to a dispute settlement system, suggests a measure of deference to the results of that system, at least to the extent that such deference is necessary for the institution to be able to keep pace with rapidly changing global characteristics and therefore to be reasonably able to carry out its responsibilities in the light of its mission'); Sandifer, above n 12 at 40 (arguing that international tribunals have inherent powers); Brown, above n 166 at 55–80 (arguing that international courts and tribunals have inherent powers); Rosenne, above n 28 at 584 (on the inherent powers of the ICJ); Higgins, above n 115 (generally on the powers of the ICJ to manage its proceedings); M Aghahosseini, 'Evidence before the Iran-United States Claims Tribunal' (1999) 1:4 International Law FORUM du Droit International 208 at 208 (on the inherent powers of the Iran–United States Claims Tribunal). For a restrictive view of inherent powers, see Friedl Weiss, 'Inherent Powers of National and International Courts' in F Ortino & E -U Petersmann (eds), *The WTO Dispute Settlement System 1995–2003* (The Hague: Kluwer Law International, 2004) 177.

[214] Amendments to the DSU must follow the procedures of Article X:8 of the WTO Agreement. See also Appellate Body Report, *United States—Import Measures on Certain Products from the European Communities*, WT/DS165/AB/R, adopted 10 January 2001, DSR 2001:I, 373 at para 165 (regarding the power to amend the DSU); Appellate Body Report, *India—Patents (US)*, above n 88 at para 92 (noting that the panel's discretion under Article 12.1 'does not extend to modifying the substantive provisions of the DSU' and stating that '[n]othing in the DSU gives a panel the authority either to disregard or to modify other explicit provisions of the DSU').

[215] See Appellate Body Report, *EC—Hormones*, above n 141 at footnote 138 to para 152; Appellate Body Report, *United States—Anti-Dumping Act of 1916*, WT/DS136/AB/R, WT/DS162/AB/R, adopted 26 September 2000, DSR 2000:X, 4793 at para 150.

[216] It is worth noting again that Article 11 of the DSU requires panels to make 'an objective assessment of the facts of the case and the applicability of and conformity with the relevant covered agreements'. See also Kazazi, above n 13 at 166 (on the inherent character of the fact-finding powers of international tribunals).

This seems also to be the view of the Appellate Body, which in *US—Shrimp* stated that 'the DSU accords to a panel [...] ample and extensive authority to undertake and to control the process by which it informs itself both of the relevant facts of the dispute and of the legal norms and principles applicable to such facts'.[217] In WTO dispute settlement, in addition to the powers mentioned above, the following have been expressly recognized as inherent in the adjudicative function of panels: (i) panels can determine on their motion the existence and scope of their jurisdiction;[218] (ii) panels have the discretion not to examine each and every claim made by the complaining party as long as they address those claims that must be addressed in order to resolve the particular matter before them—namely, panels may exercise judicial economy;[219] (iii) panels have the discretion to grant 'enhanced' participatory rights to third parties;[220] (iv) panels can draw adverse inferences from a member's refusal to provide information;[221] and (v) panels have the authority to accept submissions from *amicus curiae*.[222]

As noted above, Article 13 of the DSU expressly grants panels the authority to appoint individual experts or set up expert review groups.[223] Except for cases under the SPS Agreement involving scientific or technical issues, in which case Article 11.2 of the SPS Agreement provides that 'a panel should seek advice from experts', panels have the authority to decide whether to appoint experts, that is, a panel may decide on its own motion to seek expert advice and has the discretion not to accede to a request from the parties to appoint experts.[224] In general, panels also have the discretion to decide how to seek technical advice, and how and who to appoint.[225] Article 11.2 of the SPS Agreement requires panels to consult with the parties when choosing experts. If a panel opts for establishing an expert review group, Annex 2 to the TBT Agreement and Appendix 4 to the DSU impose requirements with respect to citizenship and

[217] Appellate Body Report, *United States—Import Prohibition of Certain Shrimp and Shrimp Products*, WT/DS58/AB/R, adopted 6 November 1998, DSR 1998:VII, 2755 at para 106.

[218] Appellate Body Report, *Mexico—Corn Syrup (Article 21.5—US)*, above n 89 at para 36; Appellate Body Report, *US –1916 Act*, above n 215 at footnote 30 to para 54.

[219] Appellate Body Report, *US—Wool Shirts and Blouses*, above n 142 at 19.

[220] Appellate Body Report, *US –1916 Act*, above n 215 at para 150; Appellate Body Report, *EC—Hormones*, above n 141 at para 154; Panel Report, *European Communities—Export Subsidies on Sugar, Complaint by Brazil*, WT/DS266/R, adopted 19 May 2005 at paras 2.5–2.9.

[221] Appellate Body Report, *Canada—Aircraft*, above n 122 at paras 202–3.

[222] Appellate Body Report, *US—Shrimp*, above n 217 at paras 106–8.

[223] Article 14.2 of the TBT Agreement also foresees the possibility of a panel establishing an expert review group. Similarly, Article 19.4 of the Customs Valuation Agreement gives panels the prerogative to request the Technical Committee to carry out an examination of any questions requiring technical consideration.

[224] Appellate Body Report, *Argentina—Textiles and Apparel*, above n 193 at para 84; Appellate Body Report, *US—Shrimp*, above n 217 at para 104.

[225] See Appellate Body Report, *EC—Hormones*, above n 141 at paras 146–8 (the DSU and the SPS Agreement enable panels to 'seek information and advice as they deem appropriate in a particular case').

qualification of the individuals appointed. Those requirements are also voluntarily observed in cases where panels are not bound by them. Panels have so far opted for appointing individual experts rather than establishing expert review groups. The agreements do not regulate the procedures for individual expert consultations. Panels have put questions in writing—normally providing the parties an opportunity to comment on them—and orally during the meeting with the experts and the parties. In the case of expert review groups, Appendix 4 to the DSU and Annex 2 to the TBT Agreement provide that the experts 'may consult and seek information and technical advice from any source they deem appropriate' and that they must produce a written report which is submitted to the panel and the parties. The opinions contained in this report as well as those of individual experts are of an advisory nature, that is, panels are not obliged to follow them. In sum, experts function under the panel's authority and assist it in establishing the facts.

3.3. Decision-making stage

With the conclusion of the second meeting of the parties with the panel and the submission of the parties' answers to the questions from the panel, the panel will focus on the drafting of its report. Consonant with the fact that the panel is composed of experts in the field and that procedures have a hybrid (adversarial-inquisitorial) character, the panel can base its decision on any piece of evidence on the record which it finds relevant. While as a general rule panels are barred from making findings with respect to measures enacted subsequently to the establishment of the panel, panels are not similarly restricted from making findings *on the basis of evidence* that post-dates the establishment of the panel.[226] Furthermore, the panel has discretion to appreciate the weight and persuasiveness of the evidence before it—that is, it can freely assess the evidence before it.[227]

[226] See Appellate Body Report, *EC—Selected Customs Matters*, above n 183 at paras 188 and 254; Panel Report, *United States—Subsidies on Upland Cotton*, WT/DS267/R, and Corr.1, adopted 21 March 2005 at para 7.192; Panel Report, *Argentina—Textiles and Apparel*, above n 203 at para 6.63. Certain restrictions regarding the evidence which may be considered by a panel exist in cases where panels act as reviewers. See Part I of Chapter 5.

[227] As a general rule, international courts and tribunals can admit and evaluate evidence freely. See H Lauterpacht, 'The So-Called Anglo-American and Continental Schools of Thought in International Law' (1931) 12 The British Yearbook of International Law 31 at 42; Eduardo Valencia-Ospina, 'Evidence before the International Court of Justice' (1999) 1:4 International Law FORUM du Droit International 202 at 202, 205; M Aghahosseini, 'Evidence before the Iran—United States Claims Tribunal' (1999) 1:4 International Law FORUM du Droit International 208 at 211; Jamison M Selby, 'Fact-Finding before the Iran–United States Claims Tribunal: a View from the Trenches' in RB Lillich (ed), Fact-Finding before International Tribunals (Ardsley-on-Hudson: Transnational Publishers, 1992) 135 at 141–2; Mojtaba Kazazi, *Burden of Proof and Related Issues: a Study on Evidence Before International Tribunals* (The Hague: Kluwer Law International, 1996) at 212; VS Mani, *International Adjudication: Procedural Aspects* (The Hague: Martinus Nijhoff, 1980) at 198; Durward V Sandifer, *Evidence Before International Tribunals* (revised ed, Charlottesville: University Press of Virginia, 1975) at 15–17.

See also *William A Parker (USA) v United Mexican States*, March 31m 1926, 4 Reports of International Arbitration Awards 35 (Millwood, Kraus Reprint, 1974) at 39, para 5 of the Award.

The Appellate Body has noted in several occasions that the panel is 'not required to accord to factual evidence of the parties the same meaning and weight as do the parties'.[228] The panel also has freedom, within the boundaries of the claims made by the parties, to choose among the arguments put forward and/or to develop its own analysis.[229] The only restrictions are that the decision of the panel must be reasoned[230] and based on the information provided during the proceedings.[231]

As regards the subject of interpretation of the agreements, Article 3.2 of the DSU instructs the adjudicators to follow the 'customary rules of interpretation of public international law'. This has been understood as a reference to the rules contained in Articles 31 to Article 33 of the Vienna Convention on the Law of Treaties (the 'Vienna Convention') which are an expression of customary rules of interpretation of public international law.[232]

Pursuant to Article 12.7 of the DSU, the report of the panel must set out the 'findings of fact, the applicability of relevant provisions and the basic rationale behind [the] findings and recommendations'. If the panel concludes that the challenged measure is inconsistent with the covered agreements it must recommend that the measure be brought into conformity with the agreements.[233] Where the panel finds, pursuant to Article 26 of the DSU, that a measure 'nullif[ies] or impair[s] benefits under, or impede[s] the attainment of objectives, of the relevant covered agreement without violation thereof' the panel must recommend that the 'Member concerned make a mutually satisfactory adjustment'.[234]

An interim version of the panel report must be made available to the parties, who must be given an opportunity to comment on it. At this stage, a party has the right to request the panel to review certain aspects of the report and to hold a meeting to discuss the issues identified.[235] According to the Appellate Body, the terms of Article 15 of the DSU which provide for review of 'precise aspects of the interim report' do not allow for introduction of new evidence at this stage of the proceedings.[236] The panel is entirely free to decide whether to revise its

[228] Appellate Body Report, *EC—Selected Customs Matters*, above n 183 at para 258; Appellate Body Report, *Japan—Measures Affecting the Importation of Apples*, WT/DS245/AB/R, adopted 10 December 2003, DSR 2003:IX, 4391 at para 221; Appellate Body Report, *Australia—Salmon*, above n 100 at para 267.

[229] See Appellate Body Report, *EC—Hormones*, above n 141 at para 156; Appellate Body Report, *EC—Export Subsidies on Sugar*, above n 98 at para 286.

[230] The requirement of reasoned decisions is prevalent in civil law proceedings. It is intended, at least in part, to keep a check on adjudicators on account of their freedom to admit and evaluate evidence. See Mirjan R Damaska, *Evidence Law Adrift* (New Haven: Yale University Press, 1997) at 22.

[231] Articles 12.7 and 14.2 of the DSU.

[232] On the subject of interpretation of the WTO Agreements, see Isabelle Van Damme, *Treaty Interpretation by the WTO Appellate Body* (Oxford: Oxford University Press, 2009).

[233] Article 19 of the DSU. The same applies to the Appellate Body.

[234] Article 26.1(b) of the DSU. The same applies to the Appellate Body.

[235] Article 15 of the DSU.

[236] See Appellate Body Report, *European Communities—Trade Description of Sardines*, WT/DS231/AB/R, adopted 23 October 2002, DSR 2002:VIII, 3359 at para 301; Appellate Body Report, *EC—Selected Customs Matters*, above n 183 at para 259.

report, but it must outline in its final report the arguments made during the review stage and its views on them.

3.4. Appeal

i. General Overview

Once the panel report has been circulated to all WTO members, the parties to the dispute—excluding third parties—may within 60 days notify the DSB of their intention to appeal the findings of the panel and file a notice of appeal with the Appellate Body.[237] The notice of appeal must indicate 'the alleged errors in the issues of law covered in the panel report and legal interpretations developed by the panel', list the provisions 'that the panel is alleged to have erred in interpreting or applying', and contain an 'indicative list of the paragraphs of the panel report containing the alleged errors'.[238] Following the notice of appeal, the parties and third parties make written submissions to the Appellate Body laying out their arguments against or in support of the claims made in the notice(s) of appeal.[239] An oral hearing is then held between 35 and 45 days after the date of the filing of the notice of appeal.[240] Pursuant to Rule 28 of the Working Procedures for Appellate Review, the Appellate Body can at any time put questions to the parties or request additional memoranda.

The Appellate Body is a standing organ composed of persons 'with demonstrated expertise in law, international trade and the subject matter of the covered agreements generally'.[241] It is, therefore, a professional body.

ii. Facts on appeal: general considerations

Article 17.6 of the DSU limits appeals 'to issues of law covered in the panel report and legal interpretations developed by the panel.' Article 17.6 has been understood by some to exclude factual questions from the appellate process. However, while the Appellate Body has no fact-finding powers similar to the panel, it would be a misconstruction to interpret Article 17.6 so as to completely exclude fact-related issues from appeal. The role of the Appellate Body is not limited to reviewing abstract interpretations of the text of the WTO agreements. In addition, panels do not make separate findings of fact before proceeding to interpret and apply the law. In general, information is presented to a panel with a view to demonstrating that the specific situation in question conforms (or does not conform) to the situation envisaged in the provision at issue; when a panel makes a finding regarding the conformity of the situation with that provision, it is making a finding which is factual and legal at the same time. This is particularly so because most obligations contained in the WTO agreements have the

237 Article 16.4 of the DSU.

238 Rule 20(2)(d) of the Working Procedures for Appellate Review.

239 Rules 21, 22, and 24 of the Working Procedures for Appellate Review.

240 Rule 27 of the Working Procedures for Appellate Review.

241 Article 17.3 of the DSU.

characteristics of standards as opposed to rules. As Trachtman explains, rules are 'clear, self-executing, fully specified in advance and not in need of interpretation or construction'; standards, in contrast, provide general guidance, are not fully specified in advance, and need to be interpreted or construed.[242] The process of defining the standard will often focus on the specific circumstances of each case, making the separation between facts and law virtually impossible. A related problem is that most terms used in the WTO agreements are legal creations, that is, they do not lend themselves to empirical observation. For instance, if instead of referring to 'like products', Article III:4 of the GATT referred to 'products of the same colour', it would be fairly straightforward to conclude that the question of whether product A and product B are, say, white is a factual question. Instead, as *EC—Asbestos* demonstrates, the question of whether two products are like cannot be said to be a purely factual question. In *EC—Asbestos*, the Appellate Body reversed the panel's finding that the products at issue were 'like' even though the panel had correctly defined the concept of 'like products' and identified the criteria for determining likeness. The Appellate Body did not agree with the panel's assessment of any of the likeness criteria—not even the 'physical properties' criterion.[243]

Accordingly, distinguishing between factual and legal issues is not always easy and in most cases the mixed character of the issues will not allow such differentiation. It seems that the only questions which can easily be classified as factual are those regarding the content and credibility of the information itself—if the information is not accurate, it cannot evidence the fact that it is intended to prove. It is arguable that the distinction is not absolutely essential in a system where a professional adjudicator decides both questions of law and of fact—as opposed to systems which have lay persons deciding questions of fact and a professional adjudicator deciding questions of law.

As regards the WTO dispute settlement system, the following factors suggest that the panel is in a better position to assess the evidence and determine whether it supports a finding of inconsistency with the agreements: (i) the panel process comprises several steps and extends over several months—usually not less than nine months but in some cases more than that—while the appeals process must be completed in three months, which will include at least a couple of weeks for translation of the Appellate Body report into Spanish and French, and (ii) the Appellate Body has not been expressly granted fact-finding powers similar to those provided under Article 13 of the DSU for panels. With an understanding of these circumstances, the Appellate Body is not likely to be inclined to second-guess the panel with respect to questions which go beyond

[242] Joel P Trachtman, 'The Domain of WTO Dispute Resolution' (1999) 40 Harvard International Law Journal 333 at 337–8. Trachtman recognizes that rules are not completely specified. Rules are nonetheless closer to the 'completeness' end of the spectrum. Ibid at 350–1.

[243] Appellate Body Report, *European Communities—Measures Affecting Asbestos and Asbestos-Containing Products*, WT/DS135/AB/R, adopted 5 April 2001, DSR 2001:VII, 3243 at paras 109–26.

the abstract interpretation of the agreements;[244] but this does not mean that it *cannot* do so, namely, that it is not allowed to entertain claims that the evidence on the record does not support the findings of the panel.[245] The Appellate Body is provided with basic tools allowing it to make this kind of assessment: first, it is in possession of the complete record of the panel proceedings[246] and, second, in accordance with Article 12.7 of the DSU, the panel report indicates the reasons behind the panel's findings. As a matter of fact, there have been many cases where the Appellate Body found that the panel erred in assessing the evidence. One example is the *EC—Asbestos* decision mentioned above. Another example is *EC—Selected Customs Matters*, where the Appellate Body examined the evidence on which the panel based its finding and concluded that it could not agree with the panel that 'the United States ha[d] established a *prima facie* case with respect to its claim alleging lack of uniform administration of the successive sales provision'.[247] In this case, the Appellate Body even examined a question which was arguably purely factual, that is, the Appellate Body made a finding regarding the content of a piece of evidence upon which the panel relied.[248]

Moreover, the references in Article 17.6 of the DSU to the panel process seem to preclude the Appellate Body from expanding the factual record of the panel proceedings and basing its conclusion on evidence that was not before the panel. If the Appellate Body were to accept new information it would have to establish on its own the content and credibility of this information and provide an opportunity to the opposing party to submit evidence in rebuttal. Given the limitations of the appeal process described above, these considerations would speak against allowing new information to be submitted at the appellate stage. In fact, the Appellate Body has declined to receive new evidence.[249] In this regard, although the Appellate Body has found that 'new arguments are not *per se*

[244] For an example of this, see Appellate Body Report, *EC—Export Subsidies on Sugar*, above n 98 at para 243.

[245] This seems also to be the view of Tania Voon & Alan Yanovich, 'The Facts Aside: The Limitations of WTO Appeals to Issues of Law' (2006) 40:2 Journal of World Trade 239 at 242, 245, 258.

[246] Rule 25 of the Working Procedures for Appellate Review.

[247] Appellate Body Report, *EC—Selected Customs Matters*, above n 183 at para 270. See also Appellate Body Report, *US—Oil Country Tubular Goods Sunset Reviews*, above n 95 at paras 209–15; Appellate Body Report, *Canada—Certain Measures Concerning Periodicals*, WT/DS31/AB/R, adopted 30 July 1997, DSR 1997:I, 449 at 20–3.

[248] Appellate Body Report, *EC—Selected Customs Matters*, above n 183 at para 268.

[249] Appellate Body Report, *United States—Final Dumping Determination on Softwood Lumber from Canada*, WT/DS264/AB/R, adopted 31 August 2004, DSR 2004:V, 1875 at para 9; Appellate Body Report, *United States—Continued Dumping and Subsidy Offset Act of 2000*, WT/DS217/AB/R, WT/DS234/AB/R, adopted 27 January 2003, DSR 2003:I, 375 at paras 221–2. In *Chile—Price Band System* (Article 21.5—Argentina), the Appellate Body listed some criteria for determining whether information submitted at the appeal stage is 'new' evidence. Appellate Body Report, *Chile—Price Band System and Safeguard Measures Relating to Certain Agricultural Products—Recourse to Article 21.5 of the DSU by Argentina*, WT/DS207/AB/RW, adopted 22 May 2007 at para 13.

excluded from the scope of appellate review', it has noted that such arguments will be excluded whenever they require the Appellate Body 'to solicit, receive and review new facts that were not before the Panel, and were not considered by it'.[250]

iii. The Appellate Body's interpretation of its role in reviewing fact-related issues

The Appellate Body's interpretation of its role in reviewing fact-related issues has been contradictory, or at best not clear. In several disputes the Appellate Body found that the process of relating facts to the requirements of legal rules—ie the legal characterization of facts, or the application of the law to the facts—is an issue which may be considered on appeal.[251] However, in several other instances, it dismissed similar appeals outright on the grounds that the panel's 'weighing and assessing of the evidence' in support of the claims advanced before the panel is 'outside the scope of appellate review'.[252] The difference between these two situations is not clear; when panels weigh and assess evidence with a view to determining whether the evidence supports the claims before them, panels are relating the evidence to the requirements laid down in the provisions of the WTO agreements. At least in some cases the Appellate Body seems to have recognized the absence of a difference between these situations. For instance, in *EC—Export Subsidies on Sugar* it carefully reviewed the findings of the panel in the light of the arguments of the European Communities and concluded that it could 'find no fault with the Panel's weighing and appreciation of the evidence'[253]—if the weighing and appreciation of the evidence were outside the scope of appellate review, the Appellate Body would have no reason to review the findings of the panel.

Further confusion has been created by challenges to the panel's appreciation of the evidence in separate claims under Article 11 of the DSU. Pursuant to Article 11, 'a panel should make an objective assessment of the matter before it, including an objective assessment of the facts of the case and the applicability of and conformity with the relevant covered agreements'. The Appellate Body's treatment of some of these challenges suggests that only serious errors will lead to a violation of Article 11.[254] Particularly, in *EC—Poultry,* the Appellate Body noted that:

> [a]n allegation that a panel has failed to conduct the 'objective assessment of the matter before it' required by Article 11 of the DSU is a very serious allegation. Such an

[250] Appellate Body Report, *Canada—Aircraft*, above n 122 at para 211.

[251] See Appellate Body Report, *US—Offset Act (Byrd Amendment)*, above n 249 at para 220; Appellate Body Report, *United States—Anti-Dumping Measures on Oil Country Tubular Goods (OCTG) from Mexico*, WT/DS282/AB/R, adopted 28 November 2005 at para 195.

[252] See Appellate Body Report, *India—Quantitative Restrictions on Imports of Agricultural, Textile and Industrial Products*, WT/DS90/AB/R, adopted 22 September 1999, DSR 1999:IV, 1763 at paras 143–4; Appellate Body Report, *Australia—Salmon*, above n 100 at paras 258–61.

[253] Appellate Body Report, *EC—Export Subsidies on Sugar*, above n 98 at para 249.

[254] Appellate Body Report, *EC—Hormones*, above n 141 at 132; Appellate Body Report, *Korea—Taxes on Alcoholic Beverages*, WT/DS75/AB/R, WT/DS84/AB/R, adopted 17 February 1999, DSR 1999:I, 3 at paras 163–4.

allegation goes to the very core of the integrity of the WTO dispute settlement process itself.[255]

Moreover, in *EC—Hormones* and *Chile—Price Band System* (*Article 21.5—Argentina)*, the Appellate Body indicated that a panel violates Article 11 of the DSU if it deliberately disregards, distorts, or misrepresents the evidence, or if it makes findings that 'lack a basis in the evidence contained in the panel record'.[256] Those cases have created the impression that appeals raising questions related to facts, including those involving the application of the law to the facts, must be brought under Article 11 of the DSU and that, therefore, only serious errors will lead the Appellate Body to reverse the panel.[257] In some of the latest cases dealing with the issue, including *US—Upland Cotton* and *US—Upland Cotton (Article 21.5—Brazil)*, the Appellate Body has sought to dispel that impression.[258]

In those disputes, the Appellate Body noted that there are two different types of challenges involving questions related to facts which can be brought before the Appellate Body: first, challenges under substantive provisions involving the application of those provisions to the facts of the case; and second, challenges under Article 11 of the DSU related to questions such as the panel's appreciation and weighing of the evidence.[259] Both challenges fall under the scope of appellate review because the former involves a legal question *per se*, and the latter

[255] Appellate Body Report, *European Communities—Measures Affecting the Importation of Certain Poultry Products*, WT/DS69/AB/R, adopted 23 July 1998, DSR 1998:V, 2031 at para 133.

[256] Appellate Body Report, *EC—Hormones*, above n 141 at para 133; Appellate Body Report, *Chile—Price Band System (Article 21.5—Argentina)*,above n 249 at para 229.

[257] For examples of where this perception is manifested, see Marco Bronckers & Natalie McNelis, 'Fact and Law in Pleadings before the WTO Appellate Body' in F Weiss (ed), *Improving WTO Dispute Settlement Procedures: Issues and Lessons from the Practice of Other International Courts and Tribunals* (London: Cameron May, 2000) 321 at 321–6; Nicolas Lockhart, 'A WTO Case Study: the Cotton Dispute' in F Ortino & S Ripinsky (eds), *WTO Law and Process: The Proceedings of the 2005 and 2006 Annual WTO Conference* (London: British Institute of International and Comparative Law, 2007) 122 at 123–7. See also Ehlermann, *Six Years on the Bench*, above n 136 at 621–2 (referring to the impression and seeking to dispel it); Jan Bohanes & Nicolas Lockhart, 'Standard of Review in WTO Law' in D Bethlehem et al (eds), *The Oxford Handbook of International Trade Law* (Oxford: Oxford University Press, 2009) 378 at footnote 163 (referring to the impression and seeking to dispel it).

[258] In support of this view, see Tania Voon & Alan Yanovich, 'The Facts Aside: The Limitations of WTO Appeals to Issues of Law' (2006) 40:2 Journal of World Trade 239 at 247.

[259] Appellate Body Report, *US—Upland Cotton*, above n 103 at para 399; Appellate Body Report, *United States—Subsidies on Upland Cotton—Recourse to Article 21.5 of the DSU by Brazil*, WT/DS267/AB/RW, adopted 20 June 2008 at para 385. See also Appellate Body Report, *Chile—Price Band System (Article 21.5—Argentina)*, above n 249 at para 238 (where the Appellate Body noted that 'a claim that a panel failed to comply with its duties under Article 11 of the DSU must stand by itself and should not be made merely as a subsidiary argument or claim in support of a claim that a panel failed to apply correctly a provision of the covered agreements'. Similarly, see Appellate Body Report, *United States—Definitive Safeguard Measures on Imports of Certain Steel Products*, WT/DS248/AB/R, WT/DS249/AB/R, WT/DS251/AB/R, WT/DS252/AB/R, WT/DS253/AB/R, WT/DS254/AB/R, WT/DS258/AB/R, WT/DS259/AB/R, adopted 10 December 2003, DSR 2003:VII, 3117 at paras 498–9.

involves a factual question transformed into a legal question by virtue of its connection with Article 11 of the DSU. With respect to challenges under Article 11, the Appellate Body stated that it 'will not interfere lightly with the Panel's discretion "as the trier of facts" '.[260] The Appellate Body did not make a general statement explaining when the panel would be found to violate Article 11 of the DSU; however, in examining the specific claims before it, the Appellate Body focused on issues such as whether the panel: (i) treated the evidence even-handedly;[261] (ii) disregarded evidence;[262] or (iii) dealt with the evidence in a coherent manner.[263]

While the Appellate Body sought to draw a clear distinction between the two types of challenges, the reality is that there is no bright line between them. In fact, it is arguable that there is no real distinction between them. For instance, in *US—Upland Cotton* the Appellate Body ruled that whether the panel has properly interpreted a provision and properly applied that interpretation to the facts of the case is a legal question which 'is different from whether the Panel made "an objective assessment of the matter before it, including an objective assessment of the facts of the case", in accordance with Article 11 of the DSU.'[264] One can interpret this finding as meaning that the two questions are completely unrelated, but this would be absurd because if the panel does not properly apply the law to the facts, its assessment cannot be considered objective—unless the Appellate Body is restricting the meaning of 'objective' to 'unbiased'. Conversely, if a panel fails to make an objective assessment of the matter before it, including an objective assessment of the facts of the case, it cannot be said to have properly applied the law to the facts. The Appellate Body seems to have recognized this in *US—Anti-Dumping Measures on Oil Country Tubular Goods,* where at the outset it found that the question at issue related to a 'legal characterization of [...] facts',[265] but then concluded that in examining that question the 'Panel failed to make an objective assessment of the matter,

[260] Appellate Body Report, *US—Upland Cotton*, above n 103 at para 399; Appellate Body Report, *US—Upland Cotton (Article 21.5—Brazil)*, above n 259 at para 384; Appellate Body Report, *Brazil—Measures Affecting Imports of Retreaded Tyres*, WT/DS332/AB/R, adopted 17 December 2007 at para 186.

[261] Appellate Body Report, *US—Upland Cotton (Article 21.5—Brazil)*, above n 259 at para 292.

[262] Appellate Body Report, *US—Upland Cotton (Article 21.5—Brazil)*, above n 259 at paras 293–4. See also Appellate Body Report, *Brazil—Retreaded Tyres*, above n 260 at para 190; Appellate Body Report, *Canada—Continued Suspension*, above n 88 at para 615; Appellate Body Report, *United States—Continued Existence and Application of Zeroing Methodology*, WT/DS350/AB/R, adopted 19 February 2009 at paras 336–7, 348 (where the Appellate Body found that 'the Panel disregarded the significance of the submitted evidence when it failed to give consideration to that evidence in its totality', requiring instead that each piece of evidence by itself demonstrate the fact at issue. In light of this, the Appellate Body concluded that the panel acted inconsistently with Article 11 of the DSU).

[263] Appellate Body Report, *US—Upland Cotton (Article 21.5—Brazil)*, above n 259 at paras 292, 294–5.

[264] Appellate Body Report, *US—Upland Cotton*, above n 103 at para 399.

[265] Appellate Body Report, *US—Anti-Dumping Measures on Oil Country Tubular Goods* above n 251 at para 195.

including an objective assessment of the facts of the case, as required by Article 11 of the DSU'.[266]

The view that that there is no difference between the two questions is further supported by the fact that in several instances the reasoning employed by the Appellate Body in examining the two questions was the same.[267] For instance, in *US—Upland Cotton* (Article 21.5—*Brazil)* the United States challenged certain findings of the panel both on the grounds that the panel had incorrectly applied the law to the facts, and on the grounds that the panel failed to make an objective assessment of the facts pursuant to Article 11 of the DSU. In examining those challenges, the Appellate Body first focused on the panel's application of the law to the facts. After finding no problem with the panel's analysis in that regard, the Appellate Body turned to examine the claim under Article 11 of the DSU. Importantly, in dismissing the Article 11 challenge, the Appellate Body referred to its previous findings on the panel's application of the law to the facts. According to the Appellate Body:[268]

> As we explained above [ie when examining the claim that the panel incorrectly applied the law to the facts], the Panel did not disregard or distort the meaning and significance of such evidence, nor did it fail to provide a reasoned and adequate explanation for its conclusions in the light of plausible alternative explanations. We, therefore, find that the Panel did not fail to carry out an objective assessment of the facts, as required by Article 11 of the DSU.

In short, the Appellate Body rejected the Article 11 claim on the same grounds as it had rejected the claim that the panel had incorrectly applied the law to the facts. Conversely, in *US—Upland Cotton*, the Appellate Body dismissed a claim that the panel had incorrectly applied the law to the facts using the same reasoning it frequently applies in examining claims under Article 11 of the DSU.[269] In fact, it even quoted a passage from a decision regarding a claim under Article 11. According to the Appellate Body:

> the Panel adopted a plausible view of the facts in connection with expected prices and planting decisions, even though it attributed to these factors a different weight or meaning than did the United States. As the Appellate Body has said [Appellate Body Report, *Australia—Salmon*, paragraph 267], it is not necessary for panels to 'accord to factual evidence of the parties the same meaning and weight as do the parties'.[270]

[266] Appellate Body Report, *US—Anti-Dumping Measures on Oil Country Tubular Goods* above n 251 at para 210.

[267] For a similar opinion on this point, see Bohanes & Lockhart, above n 257 at 431–2.

[268] Appellate Body Report, *US—Upland Cotton (Article 21.5—Brazil)*, above n 259 at para 415. Similarly, see paras 398–9.

[269] This example in also used in Bohanes & Lockhart, above n 257 at 431–2. For a similar example, see Appellate Body Report, *EC—Export Subsidies on Sugar*, above n 98 at para 249 (where in the context of an 'application of the law to the facts' challenge, the Appellate Body concluded that it could 'find no fault with the panel's weighing and appreciation of the evidence').

[270] Appellate Body Report, *US—Upland Cotton*, above n 103 at para 445.

Ultimately, the difficulty of distinguishing challenges under Article 11 from challenges related to the application of the law to the facts is likely a reflection of the difficulty of distinguishing questions of law from questions of fact—the Appellate Body seems to require factual findings to be challenged under Article 11 as a way of bringing them into the scope of appellate review. As noted above, however, there is no clear difference between factual and legal issues in legal adjudication, particularly in a system such as the WTO legal system in which most obligations have the characteristics of standards.[271] Accordingly, most 'factual' issues that come before the Appellate Body are likely to have a legal component. Moreover, a strict distinction between factual and legal questions is not essential in the context of WTO dispute settlement, since the Appellate Body would not, as would a court hearing appeals from jury cases, infringe upon the democratic right of the parties to have questions of fact decided by the jury. Nor would the Appellate Body have problems in assessing the credibility of eyewitnesses, since only expert witnesses have appeared before panels.

In light of this, a better approach might be for the Appellate Body not to exclude any questions outright from appellate review, but for it to defer to the analysis of the panel when that analysis is plausible. In other words, given the practical limitations of the appellate process discussed at the outset, the Appellate Body should avoid second-guessing the panel when there are no obvious reasons to believe that the panel committed an error in deciding a fact-related question—namely, a question which involves more than the abstract interpretation of the text of the WTO agreements.

iv. The question of remand

No remand procedures are provided for in the DSU. Accordingly, whenever the Appellate Body modifies or reverses a finding of the panel regarding the meaning of the text of the agreements, the Appellate Body may have to complete the analysis in order to determine whether the measure at issue is consistent with the agreements and, therefore, 'secure a positive solution to the dispute' according to Article 3.7 of the DSU.[272] The Appellate Body has found that it will undertake such analysis only when it concludes that it can rely upon facts discussed in the

[271] Compare, for instance, the following decisions where the Appellate Body came to different conclusions regarding the 'factual' character of the questions before it. Appellate Body Report, *US—Softwood Lumber V*, above n 249 at paras 173–4 (where the Appellate Body characterized the question of whether two companies were similarly situated as a factual question); Appellate Body Report, *Canada—Certain Measures Concerning Periodicals*, WT/DS31/AB/R, adopted 30 July 1997, DSR 1997:I, 449 at 21–3 (where the Appellate Body noted that the question of whether two products are like is a legal question); Appellate Body Report, *US—Offset Act (Byrd Amendment)*, above n 249 at 217–20 (where the Appellate Body found that a challenge to the panel's reliance on certain letters was a question of law).

[272] For a more thorough understanding of the conditions under which the Appellate Body has completed the analysis as well as other issues regarding the subject of completing the analysis, see Alan Yanovich & Tania Voon, 'Completing the Analysis in WTO Appeals: the Practice and its Limitations' (2006) 9:4 Journal of International Economic Law 933.

panel report and/or information on the panel record which has not been contested by the parties.[273] In other words, the Appellate Body does not solicit or receive evidence nor does it provide an opportunity for the parties to make submissions as would happen before panels. More recent appeals indicate that the Appellate Body is aware of the possible due process implications of completing the analysis,[274] though the Appellate Body has not completely discarded this solution to the problem of what would otherwise be unresolved disputes.[275]

v. Final considerations

Although as discussed above the Appellate Body analyses facts on appeal, this analysis is dependent on the fact-finding activities undertaken during the panel process. The panel is the primary organ as far as fact-finding is concerned. Accordingly, this study will focus chiefly on the panel process. This is not to say that many of the issues discussed throughout this book are not relevant for an appeal; an example of this is the allocation of the burden of proof, discussed in Chapter 4.

4. Final considerations on the procedural framework

This brief description of the main procedural features of the WTO dispute settlement system demonstrates that the system has indeed embraced the legal adjudication model. Although the system is unique, its basic structure resembles more that of the civil law model of adjudication than that of the common law. This is so because disputes are decided by experts in the field, the taking and presentation of evidence is episodic, and both parties and adjudicators have been given an active role in the proceedings, particularly as regards the process of fact-finding. The following chapters will examine in more detail the interaction between, on the one hand, these basic features of the WTO dispute settlement system and the more detailed procedural rules described above and, on the other hand, the process of fact-finding.

Concluding Remarks

This chapter has laid out the framework within which this study will develop. It highlighted the different considerations that must be taken into account in order for the WTO dispute settlement system to have an optimal process of fact-finding. The more general ideas presented in Section I, which are summarized at the end of that section, will be referred to throughout this book with the objective of assessing and suggesting improvements to the process of fact-finding

[273] See, eg, Appellate Body Report, *EC—Export Subsidies on Sugar*, above n 98 at para 278.
[274] See Appellate Body Report, *EC—Export Subsidies on Sugar*, above n 98 at para 339.
[275] Yanovich & Voon, *Completing the Analysis*, above n 272 at 944.

in WTO dispute settlement. The ideas in Section II serve, at least in part, to establish the boundaries of the inquiry and limit the scope of possible suggestions. They are also used, however, to inform the critique of the current fact-finding rules and procedures; in other words, they are the basis for a judgment about the synergy between the rules and procedures related to the process of fact-finding and the overall scheme of the DSU.

In short, this chapter concludes that in order for the WTO dispute settlement system to have an optimal process of fact-finding it must (i) maximize the goals of the system, namely, accuracy, participation, impartiality, equality, good faith cooperation, the efficient use of resources, and the protection of confidential information; (ii) manage uncertainty and the risk of error efficiently; and (iii) be in harmony with the basic structure of the system described in the last part of this chapter.

2

Basic Concepts

Introduction

Generally speaking, because parties usually submit evidence in support of their positions and the fraction of cases where adjudicators remain in doubt after all the evidence is presented is small, issues regarding the burden of proof do not appear in most cases.[1] While this statement may provide a fair account of the issue with respect to most courts and tribunals, the same cannot be said of the WTO dispute settlement system. In the WTO, questions regarding the burden of proof were raised as early as 1996[2]—about a year after the WTO agreements came into force—and have since then been frequently debated in the jurisprudence. In fact, it would be little exaggeration to state that questions regarding the burden of proof have been raised in almost every case since then. The fact that the concept of the burden of proof is so often invoked and debated in WTO dispute settlement begs the question 'Why is this so?'

The first possible reason for the 'ubiquity' of the concept in WTO dispute settlement relates to the fact that the disputing parties have discussed a variety of issues under the heading of the burden of proof including (i) issues regarding the quantum or degree of proof necessary to prove a proposition, (ii) questions regarding evaluation of evidence—for example, a party that disagrees with the panel's assessment of the evidence sometimes argues on appeal that the panel erred in the application of the burden of proof; (iii) questions related to the allocation of the onus of presenting evidence in support of a factual allegation or a claim which is part of a panel's terms of reference, and (iv) questions regarding the allocation of the risk of non-persuasion. The indiscriminate use of the term 'burden of proof' is bound to create confusion. In light of this, one of the

[1] For example, see Claus-Dieter Ehlermann, 'Six Years on the Bench of the 'World Trade Court': Some Personal Experiences as Member of the Appellate Body of the World Trade Organization' in F Ortino & E -U Petersmann (eds), *The WTO Dispute Settlement System 1995–2003* (The Hague: Kluwer Law International, 2004) 499 at 511 (Ehlermann explains that questions related to the burden of proof have been almost absent in proceedings before the European Court of Justice).

[2] See Panel Report, *United States—Standards for Reformulated and Conventional Gasoline*, WT/DS2/R, adopted 20 May 1996; Panel Report, *United States—Restrictions on Imports of Cotton and Man-made Fibre Underwear*, WT/DS24/R, adopted 25 February 1997.

objectives of this chapter is to define the burden of proof and related concepts such as the standard of proof and presumption.

A second explanation for the frequent debate among parties regarding the burden of proof, even in cases where there is little disagreement on the raw facts of the case, relates to the fact that the content of many WTO obligations is not clear. This means that the parties may not know what must be proved. It is not rare for panels and the Appellate Body to interpret a provision differently from the parties—in the case of the Appellate Body even differently from the panels.[3] Thus, the evidence required to prove the legal standard, as interpreted by the panels and the Appellate Body, may not be automatically produced by the parties. In this context, because the panel must find against the party bearing the burden of proof when the evidence before it is insufficient, it is only natural that the question of the allocation of the burden of proof is controversial. This occurred, for instance, in *US—Upland Cotton* where the panel defined 'world market share' in Article 6.3(d) of the SCM Agreement differently from the claimant, Brazil. In that case the panel found that Brazil failed to establish a violation of Article 6.3(d) because the evidence and argumentation put forward by Brazil 'focused exclusively upon a different, and in [the panel's] view erroneous, legal interpretation of the phrase "world market share." '[4] Panels can avoid this negative effect by communicating with the parties during the proceedings and giving them an opportunity to present evidence that would address their interpretation of the legal standard—this position is advanced in Chapter 5. Moreover, the problem may become less significant as the case law evolves and the meaning of the WTO obligations becomes clearer.

Yet another reason that may explain the controversial character of the burden of proof in WTO proceedings is that it is not clear to the members what are the duties of the party that bears the burden of proof. For instance, panels and the Appellate Body have often stated that the party that bears the burden of proof must establish a *prima facie* case of violation of a WTO obligation whereupon it is for the opposing party to rebut that case or convince the panel that it has acted consistently with the obligation at issue. As will be discussed in Chapter 3, this statement can be interpreted in a variety of different ways and WTO members seem to have different views about its meaning.

The present chapter seeks to provide a general picture of the duties of the parties in the proceedings. This chapter is divided in three main sections where the concepts of the burden of proof, the standard of proof, and presumption are discussed. Each section reviews the meaning of these concepts in the common law, the civil law, and international law, including WTO law. These concepts will be referred to and further analysed in the following chapters of this book.

[3] The fact that the Appellate Body has no remand authority aggravates the situation.

[4] Panel Report, *United States—Subsidies on Upland Cotton*, WT/DS267/R, Corr.1, and Add.1 to Add.3, adopted 21 March 2005 at paras 7.1464–7.1465.

I. The Concept of the Burden of Proof

A. General scope

The burden of proof is a concept related to the law of evidence which tells us which party in a case—plaintiff or defendant—must provide proof of a determinate issue at the risk of having the adjudicator rule against it with respect to that issue.[5] This concept has two main functions. First, it distributes between the parties the task of initiating the presentation of evidence which is necessary for the adjudicator to arrive at a conclusion with respect to the issues in question. This is the organizational aspect of the burden of proof. Second, and more importantly, the burden of proof works as a rule of adjudication telling the court what to do (i) when there is not enough evidence on the record to allow the court to arrive at a conclusion, or (ii) when it is in doubt with respect to the meaning of the evidence presented, that is, when the evidence is in equipoise or equivocal.[6]

The English case *Rhesa Shipping Co SA v Edmunds*[7] provides a good example of the functioning of the burden of proof. *Rhesa Shipping* was a case regarding a ship insured against the perils of the sea which sank along the shores of Algeria. The owners of the ship claimed against the underwriters, arguing that the ship had been lost by perils of the sea. The ship had sunk and it was not possible to examine it. There were no rocks in the neighbourhood and no sign of any floating objects. The defendants argued that prolonged wear and tear opened up the plating of the ship causing it to sink. The question before the judge was 'why had the plating opened up?' The judge was persuaded by the expert evidence that it was virtually impossible for the plating to have opened up by wear and tear. He also found that it was extremely improbable that a submarine had collided with the ship causing the plate to open. The judge concluded, however, that on the balance of probabilities a submarine must have been the cause. The case went to the House of Lords. The House of Lords noted that the burden of proof was on the plaintiff and that the fact that the defendant had put forward an explanation that was not acceptable should not alter the plaintiff's obligation to prove its case. According to the House of Lords, if the judge was in doubt as

[5] Often studied (at least in the common law tradition) as part of the law of evidence, the burden of proof has been considered a matter of substantive as well as procedural law. It is possible to find rules on the burden of proof in codes and statutes setting rules of procedure as well as in codes and statutes establishing rules of substantive law. I will use the terms 'proponent' or 'claimant' to refer to the party that bears the burden of proof, and the terms 'opponent' or 'respondent' to refer to the party that does not bear the burden of proof. The terms 'complainant' (or 'plaintiff') and 'defendant' are used to refer respectively to the party which sets the process of adjudication in motion and the party against which the action is brought. These terms do not convey a specific allocation of the burden of proof.

[6] Clermont & Sherwin note that it is a 'psychological truth that equipoise is a range of probabilities rather than a point'. Kevin M Clermont & Emily Sherwin, 'A Comparative View of Standards of Proof' (2002) 50 American Journal of Comparative Law 243 at 253.

[7] *Rhesa Shipping Co SA v Edmunds* [1985] 1 WLR 948.

to the cause of the loss, the burden of proof had not been discharged. Therefore, the judge should have found against the plaintiff.

At the outset, it is important to emphasize that the burden of proof is a concept that applies to issues of fact only. That is to say, the litigants do not have to prove the law, and ambiguities in the law must be resolved by the adjudicator through interpretation. This means that the party bearing the burden of proof does not have to prove the existence or the meaning of the law; what that party must demonstrate is that the facts presented to the court fit the prescription of the law. In practice, however, the litigants also provide their opinion on legal questions with a view to influencing the court to interpret the law in a manner that favours them. The parties do not have to prove the law because the courts are assumed to know the law—*jura novit curia*.[8] This principle is generally accepted in domestic[9] and international law,[10] including WTO law.[11] However, a few exceptions apply in most jurisdictions. For example, a party invoking foreign law before a domestic court is usually required to provide proof of that law. In proceedings before international courts, as a general rule, domestic law is treated as a fact, thus the litigants must prove it as they would prove any other fact.[12] In

[8] This principle is sometimes given a broader scope, namely, that courts may freely decide which legal rules should apply to a certain set of facts. In other words, the parties would present the facts and the court would be in charge of choosing from the universe of available legal rules the specific rule that would apply to the facts presented. This understanding of *jura novit curia*, however, is not as widely accepted and is not the meaning given here to this expression.

[9] See Nicole Verheyden-Jeanmart, *Droit de la Preuve* (Brussels: Maison Larcier, 1991) at 8.

[10] See *Case Concerning Military and Paramilitary Activities in and against Nicaragua* (Merits), Judgment of 27 June 1986, International Court of Justice, Reports of Judgments, Advisory Opinions and Orders (1986) at para 29; *Fisheries Jurisdiction* (Merits) (United Kingdom v Iceland), Judgment of 25 July 1974, International Court of Justice, Reports of Judgments, Advisory Opinions and Orders (1974) at para 17. See also Mojtaba Kazazi, *Burden of Proof and Related Issues: a Study on Evidence Before International Tribunals* (The Hague: Kluwer Law International, 1996) at 43–4; Daniel Bethlehem, 'Submissions on Points of Fact and Law: Written and Oral Pleadings Before the International Court of Justice' in F Weiss (ed), *Improving WTO Dispute Settlement Procedures: Issues and Lessons from the Practice of Other International Courts and Tribunals* (London: Cameron May, 2000) 175 at 187; JC Witenberg, 'La Theorie des Preuves Devant les Juridictions Internationales' (1936) 56 Recueil des Cours 5 at 35.

[11] See Appellate Body Report, *European Communities—Conditions for the Granting of Tariff Preferences to Developing Countries*, WT/DS246/AB/R, adopted 20 April 2004, DSR 2004:III, 925 at para 105. See also Petros C Mavroidis, 'Development of WTO Dispute Settlement Procedures Through Case-Law (We Will Fix It)' in F Ortino & E -U Petersmann (eds), *The WTO Dispute Settlement System 1995–2003* (The Hague: Kluwer Law International, 2004) 153 at 167.

[12] See *The Case Concerning Certain German Interests in Polish Upper Silesia* (Germany v Poland), Judgment of 25 May 1926, Permanent Court of International Justice, Series A, No 7 (1926) at 19; Appellate Body Report, *India—Patent Protection for Pharmaceutical and Agricultural Chemical Products*, WT/DS50/AB/R, adopted 16 January 1998, DSR 1998:I, 9 at paras 65–6; Panel Report, *United States—Sections 301–310 of the Trade Act of 1974*, WT/DS152/R, adopted 27 January 2000, DSR 2000:II, 815 at para 7.18; Panel Report, *United States—Anti-Dumping and Countervailing Measures on Steel Plate from India*, WT/DS206/R and Corr.1, adopted 29 July 2002 at para 7.90; Panel Report, *United States—Anti-Dumping Measures on Certain Hot-Rolled Steel Products from Japan*, WT/DS184/R, adopted 23 August 2001 at para 7.143; Panel Report, *Japan—Measures Affecting the Importation of Apples, Recourse to Article 21.5 of the DSU by the United States*, WT/DS245/RW, 23 June 2005 at para 8.19. See also Ian Brownlie, *Principles of Public International Law* (6th edn, Oxford: Oxford University Press, 2003) at 38–40; Kazazi, above n 10 at 44–5; Witenberg, *La Theorie des Preuves*, above n 10 at 35.

addition, while general customary international law does not have to be proven by the litigants,[13] the International Court of Justice has required proof of regional customs.[14] Despite the fact that general customs do not have to be proved, as a matter of practice, on account of the fact that customary international law is based on precedents, which are factual in nature, parties usually provide evidence in support of their views.

Furthermore, the concept of the burden of proof relates to proof of the *factual basis* of a claim as a whole. In the context of the WTO this means a claim under a provision of the WTO agreements, such as Article II:1(a) of the GATT. In this context, it is important to draw a distinction between elemental propositions and auxiliary propositions.[15] Elemental propositions refer to the constitutive elements of a claim as determined by a provision of the WTO agreements. Auxiliary propositions are those that help to establish an elemental proposition; many auxiliary propositions may be necessary to establish an elemental proposition. The proponent of a claim must establish all the elements of the claim (elemental propositions) according to a certain standard of proof[16] in order to satisfy the burden of proof. For example, if a claim is brought under Article II:1(a) of the GATT,[17] the claimant must establish the elements that (i) a WTO Member has made a commitment in its Schedule to provide a certain treatment, and that (ii) the claimant has been accorded treatment that is less favourable than that specified in the Schedule of that WTO Member.

The term 'burden of proof' is sometimes used to refer to proof of individual facts—ie auxiliary propositions—alleged by the parties in the course of the proceedings. This is the sense in which the term is used when it is said that 'the party that asserts a fact is responsible for providing proof thereof'.[18] When used in this sense, the term is merely an expression of the principle that judicial decisions

[13] See *Fisheries Jurisdiction (Merits) (United Kingdom v Iceland)*, Judgment of 25 July 1974, Separate Opinion of Judge de Castro, International Court of Justice, Reports of Judgments, Advisory Opinions and Orders (1974) at 79. See also Witenberg, *La Theorie des Preuves*, above n 10 at 35; Kazazi, above n 10 at 47.

[14] See *Asylum (Colombia v Peru)*, Judgment of 20 November 1950, International Court of Justice, Reports of Judgments, Advisory Opinions and Orders (1950) at 276. See also *Fisheries Jurisdiction (Merits) (United Kingdom v Iceland)*, Judgment of 25 July 1974, Separate Opinion of Judge de Castro, International Court of Justice, Reports of Judgments, Advisory Opinions and Orders (1974) at 79.

[15] For more on this distinction see Terence Anderson, David Schum & William Twining, *Analysis of Evidence* (2nd edn, Cambridge: Cambridge University Press, 2005) at 60–1, 90–1 (see distinction between penultimate probanda and interim probanda); Alex Stein, *Foundations of Evidence Law* (Oxford: Oxford University Press, 2005) at 49.

[16] The concept of standard of proof will be discussed in the next section.

[17] Article II:1(a) of the GATT provides that: 'Each contracting party shall accord to the commerce of the other contracting parties treatment no less favourable than that provided for in the appropriate Part of the appropriate Schedule annexed to this Agreement'.

[18] The Appellate Body has recognized this difference of meaning. See Appellate Body Report, *Japan—Measures Affecting the Importation of Apples*, WT/DS245/AB/R, adopted 10 December 2003 at para 157; Appellate Body Report, *United States—Subsidies on Upland Cotton*, WT/DS267/AB/R, adopted 21 March 2005 at para 656. See also Panel Report, *United States—Section 110(5) of the US Copyright Act*, WT/DS160/R, adopted 27 July 2000, DSR 2000:VIII, 3769 at para 6.14.

must be based on verified facts rather than on unsupported allegations. When determining whether an elemental proposition has been established, a court cannot consider those auxiliary propositions which have not been supported by evidence.[19] The same applies as regards the party that does not bear the burden of proof, that is, the adjudicator cannot take into account in his decision facts which that party alleges with a view to impeding an establishment of the elemental proposition if those factual allegations are not supported by evidence.[20] The expression 'burden of proof' is consciously not used in this sense in this book.

A generally accepted exception to the rule that the parties must provide evidence in support of their allegations is the category of notorious facts of which adjudicators may take judicial notice.[21] Notorious facts are those that are generally known within the jurisdiction or field of expertise of a tribunal, or that constitute matters of public knowledge. For example, the fact that 'currencies tend to depreciate over time because of inflationary pressures, and these pressures are greatest in developing countries' is a notorious fact of which WTO panels may take judicial notice.[22]

Most legal systems will also not require proof of factual allegations that are admitted by the opposing party. This has been the practice in WTO dispute settlement as well. For example, in *Australia—Salmon*, Australia conceded that it had not conducted a risk assessment with respect to four categories of salmon products at issue, and thus, the panel concluded that Canada had successfully discharged its burden of proving that Australia acted inconsistently with Article 5.1 regarding those four products.[23] Moreover, some systems will deem a factual

[19] For examples in the WTO jurisprudence, see Panel Report, *European Communities—Selected Customs Matters*, WT/DS315/R, adopted 11 December 2006 at paras 7.216, 7.225, 7.320–7.327, 7.415–7.416.

[20] For examples in the WTO jurisprudence, see Panel Report, *Canada—Measures Affecting the Export of Civilian Aircraft*, WT/DS70/R, adopted 20 August 1999 at para 9.344; Appellate Body Report, *US—Upland Cotton*, above n 18 at para 656.

[21] With respect to domestic jurisdictions, see, for example, United States Federal Rules of Evidence, Rule 201; German Code of Civil Procedure, section 291 (for an English version, see Charles E Stewart, *German Commercial Code & Code of Civil Procedure*, (Dobbs Ferry: Oceana Publications, 2001); Brazilian Code of Civil Procedure, Article 334.I. As regards international law, see *Case Concerning United Sates Diplomatic and Consular Staff at Teheran* (United States of America v Iran), Judgment of 24 May 1980, International Court of Justice, Reports of Judgments, Advisory Opinions and Orders (1980) at 9, para 13; Bin Cheng, *General Principles of Law as Applied by International Courts and Tribunals* (London: Stevens & Sons, 1953) at 303; Keith Highet, 'Evidence, the Court, and the Nicaragua Case' (1987) 81 The American Journal of International Law 1 at footnote 160 to page 33; Witenberg, *La Theorie des Preuves*, above n 10 at 30; Bethlehem, above n 10 at 188–9.

[22] Appellate Body Report, *Brazil—Export Financing Programme for Aircraft*, WT/DS46/AB/R, adopted 20 August 1999, DSR 1999:III, 1161 at para 70.

[23] Panel Report, *Australia—Measures Affecting Importation of Salmon*, WT/DS18/R and Corr.1, adopted 6 November 1998 at paras 8.53, 8.59. For other examples, see Panel Report, *EC—Selected Customs Matters*, above n 19 at para 7.215 and footnote 427; Panel Report, *United States—Import Prohibition of Certain Shrimp and Shrimp Products*, WT/DS58/R and Corr.1, adopted 6 November 1998 at para 7.15; Panel Report, *India—Patent Protection for Pharmaceutical and Agricultural Chemical Products, Complaint by the United States*, WT/DS50/R, adopted 16 January 1998 at paras 7.51–7.52; Panel Report, *European Communities—Trade Description of Sardines*, WT/DS231/R and Corr.1, adopted 23 October 2002 at para 7.122.

allegation *implicitly* admitted unless the opposing party *explicitly* denies the allegation.[24] In systems that allow implicit admissions, parties must deny all facts asserted by their opponents or face the consequences of having the adjudicator consider the alleged facts even though no proof of them has been made. The effects attached to implicit admissions usually result (i) from a specific provision establishing that factual assertions which are not contested do not require proof, or (ii) indirectly, as a consequence of a rule of pleading requiring defendants to specifically indicate the alleged facts that they contest. The DSU contains none of these types of provisions. The parties and the panel could, however, agree to include such provisions in the Working Procedures of the panel. In the absence of such provisions in their Working Procedures, panels should not base their decisions on factual assertions made by one party that are not supported by any evidence on the record, nor have been explicitly admitted by the opposing party, nor refer to notorious facts.[25]

B. Differences between the common law and the civil law systems

Owing to variations in the structure of the proceedings the concept of the burden of proof has evolved differently in the civil law and the common law legal systems. In contrast to the common law, in the civil law system the phrase 'burden of proof' has only one meaning. It refers to the duty of each party to prove their claims, that is, to convince the judge of what is claimed. In the common law system the concept has been divided in two ideas; this division is mainly a function of how the trial is organized. The 'burden of going forward'—or duty of passing the judge, evidential burden, the burden of adducing

[24] See, for example, German Code of Civil Procedure, section 138 (for an English version, see Charles E Stewart, *German Commercial Code & Code of Civil Procedure* (Dobbs Ferry: Oceana Publications, 2001); Brazilian Code of Civil Procedure, Articles 302 and 334.III; Jan M Hebly, *The Netherlands Civil Evidence Act 1988* (Deventer: Kluwer Law and Taxation Publishers, 1992) at 11; R Verkerk, 'The Netherlands: Powers of the Judge' in CH van Rhee (ed), *European Traditions in Civil Procedure* (Antwerpen: Intersentia, 2005) 281 at 283; Harald Koch & Frank Diedrich, *Civil Procedure in Germany* (The Hague: Kluwer Law International, 1998) at 96; Verheyden-Jeanmart, above n 9 at 37.

[25] Witenberg argues that international law knows of implicit admissions. He notes that implicit admissions are a consequence of procedural rules that require a defending state to admit or expressly contest the facts alleged by the complaining state. In support of his view, he refers to the rules of the Tripartite (United States, Austria, and Hungary) Claims Commission, Article VI; the British-American Commission 1910–1925, Article XV; the French–Mexican Commission of 1924, Article XIV. Witenberg, *La Theorie des Preuves*, above n 10 at 31. The rules of the Tripartite Claims Commission can be found at Supplement to the (1927) 21 American Journal of International Law 119. Because the rules of these commissions explicitly required respondents to deny factual allegations with which they disagreed, and the scope of these commissions was narrow—they focused on settling disputes regarding damages caused by states to private parties—there seems to be little evidence to support a conclusion that the rule on implicit admissions is a general rule of international law. In fact, Article 53 of the Statute of the International Court of Justice suggests the opposite. Article 53 provides that whenever one of the parties fails to defend its case, the *Court must satisfy itself* that the claims are well founded in *fact* and law before deciding the case.

evidence, the burden of evidence—refers to the burden of showing, if called upon to do so, that 'there is sufficient evidence to raise an issue as to the existence or non-existence of a fact in issue [...]'.[26] The 'burden of persuasion'—or legal burden—refers to persuading the court to find in favour of the proponent of a certain claim at the end of the proceedings.

1. Common law

The burden of going forward is also referred to as the 'duty of passing the judge' because in a jury trial, if the party bearing the burden fails to meet it, the issue in question will not be sent to the jury for a decision. The party that bears the burden of going forward is required to adduce evidence to satisfy the court that a reasonable person could possibly rule in its favour on the basis of that evidence. Even if the party bearing the burden of going forward adduces enough evidence to successfully discharge the burden and the opponent does not provide any contrary evidence, the proponent is generally[27] not entitled to a final decision on its favour.[28]

The burden of going forward is a product of the availability of procedural motions to test the sufficiency or weight of the evidence during the trial. Without the motions the concept cannot be grasped.[29] The motions require the court to rule on the sufficiency of the evidence, and, thus, attach a legal consequence to the burden of going forward. The motions and the concept of the burden of going forward owe their origin largely to the trial by jury and the possibility of withdrawing an issue from that body[30]—though they are also available in cases tried to a judge. The specific features of those procedural motions may vary across jurisdictions, but for purposes of illustration two examples can be given.[31]

First, after the proponent of a certain issue has finished presenting evidence, ie rested his case, the opponent may interpose a motion asking the court to rule

[26] Colin Tapper, *Cross & Tapper on Evidence* (8th edn, London: Butterworths, 1995) at 122. See also John W Strong (ed), *McCormick on Evidence* (5th edn, St Paul: West Group, 1999) vol 2 at 419.

[27] It seems that the only exception to this would be those situations where the evidence presented by the proponent is overwhelmingly strong and a motion for a directed verdict in favour of the proponent is available.

[28] Fleming James Jr, 'Burdens of Proof' (1961) 47 Virginia Law Review 51 at 57; Stephen N Subrin et al, *Civil Procedure: Doctrine, Practice, and Context* (2nd edn, New York: Aspen, 2004) at 164.

[29] See Tapper (1995), above n 26 at 122, 125; Strong, above n 26 at 419–420; John Sopinka, Sidney N Lederman & Alan W Bryant, *The Law of Evidence in Canada* (2nd edn, Toronto: Butterworths, 1999) at 75.

[30] Tapper (1995), above n 26 at 125.

[31] These and other examples can be found in Subrin et al, above n 28 at 164, 449, 467–9; Richard H Field, Benjamin Kaplan & Kevin M Clermont, *Civil Procedure* (8th edn, New York: Foundation Press, 2003) at 150, 1277–98; David Crump et al, *Cases and Materials on Civil Procedure* (5th edn, Newark: LexisNexis, 2008) at 737–48; John J Barcelo, 'Burden of Proof, Prima Facie Case, and Presumption in WTO Dispute Settlement' (2009) 42:1 Cornell International Law Journal (forthcoming).

that the evidence presented is insufficient to allow a reasonable person to find in favour of the proponent. In other words, the opponent asks the court to rule against the proponent because the evidence presented is so slight that a rational trier of fact would not, based on that evidence, be able to find in favour of the proponent. If the case is tried to a jury, a decision in favour of the opponent will take the issue from the jury, ie the judge will dismiss the issue. If the motion is denied, the issue will proceed and the opponent will have an opportunity to present evidence with a view to rebutting the evidence presented by the proponent. Notably, if the opponent does not present any evidence in rebuttal, the proponent will not necessarily win. This is so because the judge in denying the motion merely decides that a rational jury could rule in favour of the proponent on the basis of the evidence presented.

Second, after the opponent has rested his or her case, the proponent may ask the judge to find that the evidence is so overwhelming that a reasonable person could not disbelieve it, that is, that no reasonable person could find against the proponent. If the judge grants the motion and the opponent does not present additional evidence so as to cause reasonable people to disagree on the conclusions to be drawn from the evidence, the issue is removed from the jury and judgment is entered in favour of the proponent—in this situation the opponent is said to have the burden of production because if the opponent does not present additional evidence the proponent will be entitled to a judgment in his or her favour.

The specific consequences of a failure to discharge the burden of going forward will depend upon which party bears the burden, the nature of the burden, and the stage of the proceedings at which the burden arises.[32] Sopinka, Lederman, and Bryant provide an example of this in the context of Canadian criminal law. If the Crown, the state prosecutor, fails to discharge the burden of going forward 'for a definitional element of an offence, the trial judge must withdraw the case from the jury and enter a verdict of acquittal'.[33] If the Crown successfully discharges the burden of going forward with respect to those elements, the burden of going forward with respect to 'a common law defence, such as drunkenness, rests on the accused. If the accused fails to adduce evidence of intoxication to satisfy the threshold test for this defence, the trial judge will not leave this issue for the jury's consideration.'[34] In other words, the judge will find against the accused on this point, and the jury will not be allowed to consider the issue of drunkenness. However, the trial judge's decision on this issue is not fatal to the accused. The Crown will still have to convince the jury according to the criminal standard—beyond a reasonable doubt—that the elements of the offence are present.

The burden of persuasion comes into play after the presentation of evidence is completed and the case is ready for judgment by the trier of fact. In a trial by

[32] Sopinka, Lederman & Bryant (1999), above n 29 at 67.
[33] Sopinka, Lederman & Bryant (1999), above n 29 at 67.
[34] Sopinka, Lederman & Bryant (1999), above n 29 at 67.

jury, it will be for the jury to decide whether an issue has been proved. The party bearing the burden of persuasion must persuade the trier of fact—according to the appropriate criminal or civil standard of proof[35]—of the truth of the facts it alleges. If after considering all the evidence on the record the trier of fact is not persuaded, the party bearing the burden of proof loses on that issue. Importantly, if the evidence allows the trier of fact to come to a determinate conclusion on the question at issue, the burden of persuasion does not play any role in the decision-making process.

2. *Civil law*

In the civil law system the burden of proof refers to the duty of each party to prove their claims, that is, to convince the judge of what is claimed. The organization of civil law proceedings differs from common law proceedings, which explains the differences in the conception of the burden of proof. Two important differences are: (i) the presentation of evidence is spread over several events—as opposed to a single event, ie the trial—and there is no rigid sequence of presentation; (ii) the procedural motions discussed above are not available in the civilian system. In light of this, there is no place for the common law distinction between the two burdens.[36] Other features of civilian proceedings which affect the understanding of the concept of the burden of proof include the fact that proceedings are to a large extent written, and that courts can play an active role in gathering information. The process (including evidence production) will begin with written submissions from both sides and extend into one or several hearings, where arguments and evidence presented with the written submissions are discussed and witnesses heard.

In civilian proceedings more emphasis is placed on written submissions than in common law proceedings, and documentary evidence is the most frequently used type of evidence. The written submission of the complainant provides a detailed account of the facts on which the claims are based, and must usually be accompanied by supporting documents and/or indicate other types of evidence, such as the name of the witnesses and the facts to which they will testify, the complainant intends to present at the hearing.[37] Where certain means of proof are required,

[35] The standard of proof in criminal cases is usually 'beyond a reasonable doubt', and in civil cases 'preponderance of the evidence'.

[36] Herzog notes, for example, that in France '[s]ince the court has to determine both the law and the facts and no procedural motion is available to test whether sufficient evidence has been introduced to permit the court to find a certain way before the court decided which way it will actually find, the distinction between the two burdens is of no practical significance'. Peter Herzog, *Civil Procedure in France* (The Hague: Martinus Nijhoff, 1967) at 310.

[37] See, for example, Brazilian Code of Civil Procedure, Articles 282, 283, 396; German Code of Civil Procedure, sections 130, 131; French Code of Civil Procedure, Articles 15, 132; AW Jongbloed, 'The Netherlands (1838–2005)' in CH van-Rhee (ed), *European Traditions in Civil Procedure* (Antwerpen: Intersentia, 2005) 69 at 86–7 (discussing provisions of the Dutch Code of Civil Procedure); Koch & Diedrich, above n 24 at 25, 78, 81–2.

normally documentary evidence, these must be attached to the written submission. Failure to do so may result in dismissal of the claim.[38] Failure to attach non-required documents or indicate other types of evidence to be produced may result in a court order requiring the claimant to amend its written submission and may eventually lead to the dismissal of the claim.[39] Accordingly, documents are introduced into evidence with the written submissions, as opposed to the common law practice of presenting documentary evidence during the hearing when it is usually authenticated by testimony.[40] As a matter of fact, at the hearing civil law judges may not accept the production of evidence that was not previously referred to in written submissions. In its written submission, the defendant must answer to the allegations and evidence presented in the complainant's submission.

The defendant's written submission must also provide a detailed account of the defendant's version of the facts. It must be accompanied by documentary evidence and/or indicate other types of evidence that will be produced at the hearing in support of all the facts alleged by the defendant, including those that merely seek to deny the facts alleged by the complainant as well as those supporting any claims adduced by the defendant.[41] As regards the defendant's own claims—ie those for which it bears the burden of proof—failure to produce required or non-required documents and to indicate other types of evidence that will be produced at the hearing will generally engender the same consequences described above with respect to the complainant. As regards denials of the complainant's allegations, failure to produce documents or indicate other types of evidence to be produced at the hearing may preclude the defendant from presenting evidence at a later time. Accordingly, in general, each party makes all efforts to develop its own evidence.

It is important to note that there are no pre-trial discovery procedures similar to those available in common law jurisdictions, but the parties are under a duty to cooperate in the production of evidence.[42] Sometimes the court will become

[38] See, for example, Brazilian Code of Civil Procedure, Article 283, 284, 366, 295.VI.

[39] See, for example, Brazilian Code of Civil Procedure, Articles 284 and 295.VI. See also P Oberhammer & T Domej, 'Germany, Switzerland, Austria (CA. 1800–2005)' in CH van Rhee (ed), *European Traditions in Civil Procedure* (Antwerpen: Intersentia, 2005) 103 at 115 (discussing provisions of the German Code of Civil Procedure).

[40] W Lawrence Craig, William W Park & Jan Paulsson, *International Chamber of Commerce Arbitration* (3rd edn, Dobbs Ferry: Oceana Publications, 2000) at 419.

[41] See, for example, German Code of Civil Procedure, sections 130, 131; Brazilian Code of Civil Procedure, Articles 300, 396; French Code of Civil Procedure, Articles 15, 67, 132; Jongbloed, above n 37 at 86–7 (discussing provisions of the Dutch Code of Civil Procedure); Koch & Diedrich, above n 24 at 25, 81–2.

[42] See Bernard Hanotiau, 'Satisfying the Burden of Proof: the Point of View of a "Civil Law" Lawyer' (1994) 10 Arbitration International 341 at 344; Verheyden-Jeanmart, above n 9 at 30–1, 42, 46; CH van Rhee, 'Introduction' in CH van Rhee (ed), *European Traditions in Civil Procedure* (Antwerpen: Intersentia, 2005) 3 at 21–2 (referring to the emphasis on cooperation in the proceedings in general); L Cadiet, 'The New French Code of Civil Procedure (1975)' in CH van Rhee (ed), *European Traditions in Civil Procedure* (Antwerpen: Intersentia, 2005) 49 at 58; Jongbloed, above n 37 at 86. See also, for example, Brazilian Code of Civil Procedure, Articles 339, 340.

involved in this process, helping the parties to gather the evidence.[43] Although civil procedure in the civil law system is to a large extent adversarial,[44] judges have the power to order production of evidence on their own motion if they believe that the evidence will help to clarify a contested issue—thus as mentioned in Chapter 1, the proceedings are hybrid adversarial-inquisitorial.[45] Usually they will do so at the request of a party.

Finally, after all the evidence is presented, the judge decides the case based on the elements which the judge finds more convincing.[46] The burden of proof becomes a question only when the evidence before the court is insufficient or in equipoise. In those situations, the court must find against the party bearing the burden of proof. According to Hanotiau, the French Supreme Court has said that 'the uncertainty or doubt subsisting after the production of evidence should necessarily be retained to the detriment of the one who had the burden of this proof'.[47]

The discussion above demonstrates that although in the civilian tradition only the party bearing the burden of proof is subject to an adverse ruling in case the evidence presented is deficient or in equipoise, the proceedings are structured in such a manner that both parties submit evidence with respect to not only their own claims but also their opponents' claims. The parties have a duty to cooperate in the production of evidence. There is no direct sanction[48] for failure to voluntarily produce evidence with respect to a claim for which the opponent bears the burden of proof. However, (i) that the respondent has no means of knowing the strength of the claimant's evidence until the judge finally decides the matter, (ii) that if evidence is submitted after a certain stage of the proceedings, normally the initial phase, it may not be accepted, and (iii) that the

[43] On the powers of judges regarding production of evidence, see Hanotiau, above n 42 at 344; Verheyden-Jeanmart, above n 9 at 21–2; Jongbloed, above n 37 at 86; A Wijffels, 'France: Powers of the Judge' in CH van Rhee (ed), *European Traditions in Civil Procedure* (Antwerpen: Intersentia, 2005) 269 at 279; Verkerk, above n 24 at 284–7; P Oberhammer & T Domej, 'Germany, Switzerland, and Austria' in CH van Rhee (ed), *European Traditions in Civil Procedure* (Antwerpen: Intersentia, 2005) 295 at 300, 304–5. See also, for example, Brazilian Code of Civil Procedure, Articles 130,355; Belgian Judicial Code, Article 871; French Code of Civil Procedure, Articles 8, 10, 144; Dutch Code of Civil Procedure, Article 22; German Code of Civil Procedure, sections 139–144.

[44] Civil procedure in civil law jurisdictions is guided by the principle of neutrality of the judge and the principle of party control (*principe dispositive*). However, civil proceedings are considered to perform a public function, which explains to a great extent some of the powers given to judges. In this regard, see Antonio Carlos de Araújo Cintra, Ada Pellegrini Grinover & Cândido R Dinamarco, *Teoria Geral do Processo* (12th edn, São Paulo: Malheiros, 1996) at 64–5 (referring to the cases of Brazil, Austria, Germany, and Italy).

[45] Judges usually have the power to call and interrogate witnesses, request the appearance and question the parties, appoint experts, order production of documents, and make inspection visits.

[46] Except in those cases where the substantive law requires a certain type of proof.

[47] Hanotiau, above n 42 at 343.

[48] The meaning of a 'direct sanction' in this context must be understood in contrast with the type of sanction that is imposed on the complainant if the complainant fails to present evidence. If the complainant does not present any evidence to support his or her allegations, the judge will inescapably find against the complainant. However, if the respondent does not present evidence, the respondent merely runs the risk of an adverse decision, that is, the judge may still find that the complainant's case is not persuasive.

judge may also on her own motion order the production of evidence,[49] serve as an incentive for the respondent to produce evidence. The proponent of a claim presents evidence because he will ultimately lose the case if not enough evidence is before the judge. Moreover, if his written submission fails to present or indicate evidence to be produced at the hearing, the judge may *sua sponte* dismiss the case before the hearing.

Finally, it is important to note that many of the disparities discussed above could be linked to a fundamental difference in the way civil litigation is viewed by the common law and the civil law. Civilian jurisdictions understand civil litigation as having a public or social dimension[50] whereas common law jurisdictions tend to view civil litigation exclusively as a private affair between the parties.[51] This difference in the fundamental conception of civil litigation has practical implications, such as the fact that judges in the civil law are given more powers to direct the proceedings including with respect to fact-finding—though the parties have control over several aspects of the proceedings and judges do not actively investigate all the contentious issues of the case.

C. Proceedings before international courts and tribunals

Proceedings before international courts and tribunals are more similar to civil law proceedings than common law proceedings. As in the civil law system, the concept of the burden of proof is not divided into the burden of going forward and the burden of persuasion.[52] There are no procedural motions to test the sufficiency of evidence and, thus, there are no intermediate rulings regarding the burden of proof.[53] The court or tribunal in charge of the case decides both issues of law and fact. The parties are also under a duty to cooperate in the production

[49] If the judge orders the respondent to produce evidence which is in the respondent's possession, failure to do so may lead the court to draw inferences against the respondent. This situation will be further explored in Chapter 5.

[50] See, for example, van Rhee, above n 42 at 11–16 (explaining how civil procedure in the civilian tradition evolved and incorporated public interest concerns); Cintra, Grinover & Dinamarco, above n 44 at 64–5.

[51] See, for example, R Verkerk, 'England and Wales: Powers of the Judge' in CH van Rhee (ed), *European Traditions in Civil Procedure* (Antwerpen: Intersentia, 2005) 307 at 307 (referring to the English legal system).

[52] Kazazi, above n 10 at 31; Chittharanjan F Amerasinghe, *Evidence in International Litigation* (Leiden: Martinus Nijhoff, 2005) at 38, 40; Durward V Sandifer, *Evidence Before International Tribunals* (revised edn, Charlottesville: University Press of Virginia, 1975) at 127; Joost Pauwelyn, 'Evidence, Proof and Persuasion in WTO Dispute Settlement: Who Bears the Burden?' (1998) 1 Journal of International Economic Law 227 at 232; Anna Riddell & Brendan Plant, *Evidence before the International Court of Justice* (London: British Institute of International and Comparative Law, 2009) at 84–5 (referring to the ICJ).

[53] As Amerasinghe notes, 'international proceedings, whether "civil" or "criminal", never consist of two distinct parts as such whereby the court needs to take a decision to proceed to the second phase only on the basis that sufficient evidence has been produced in the first phase (ie a prima facie case had been made), or to dismiss the case, if the evidence is insufficient in this respect'. Amerasinghe, above n 52 at 38.

of evidence,[54] and the adjudicators are given powers to request information.[55] Accordingly, as in the civil law system, the burden of proof becomes a question only when at the end of the proceedings the state of the evidence is such that it does not allow the adjudicator to come to a conclusion on the matter. In those situations the adjudicator must resolve the dispute by finding against the party bearing the burden of proof. Importantly, as in civilian systems, although the respondent must cooperate in the production of evidence, there is no direct sanction for the respondent's failure to voluntarily produce evidence in support of his contentions—such a failure, however, may produce many consequences as pointed out above.[56] In contrast, if the claimant fails to produce evidence and the record of the proceedings is as a result unpersuasive, the court must find against the claimant, ie the party bearing the burden of proof.[57]

[54] This duty will be discussed in detail in Chapter 5. See Kazazi, above n 10 at 119–21; JC Witenberg, 'Onus Probandi Devant les Juridictions Arbitrales' (1951) 55 Revue Generale de Droit International Public 321 at 333; Witenberg, *La Theorie des Preuves*, above n 10 at 47; Pauwelyn, *Evidence, Proof and Persuasion*, above n 52 at 232; Jacquelyn MacLennan, 'Evidence, Standard and Burden of Proof and the Use of Experts in Procedure Before the Luxembourg Courts' in F Weiss (ed), *Improving WTO Dispute Settlement Procedures: Issues and Lessons from the Practice of Other International Courts and Tribunals* (London: Cameron May, 2000) 265 at 268 (discussing the rules of the European Court of Justice); KPE Lasok, *The European Court of Justice: Practice and Procedure* (2nd edn, London: Butterworths, 1994) at 422 (discussing the rules of the European Court of Justice).

[55] The powers and role of tribunals, particularly WTO panels, will be further discussed in Chapter 5. See, for example, Statute of the International Court of Justice, Articles 48, 49, 50; International Court of Justice Rules of Court, Articles 62, 66, 67; Convention on the Settlement of Investment Disputes between States and Nationals of Other Parties, Article 43; ICSID Rules of Procedure for Arbitration Proceedings, Articles 34, 37; Rules of the Iran–United States Claims Tribunal, Article 24.3. See also Witenberg, *La Theorie des Preuves*, above n 10 at 47; International Court of Justice, *The International Court of Justice* (5th edn, The Hague: ICJ, 2004) at 53, 59; MacLennan, above n 54 at 268 (discussing the rules of the European Court of Justice); M Aghahosseini, 'Evidence before the Iran–United States Claims Tribunal' (1999) 1:4 International Law FORUM du Droit International 208 at 209 (discussing the rules of the Iran–United States Claims Tribunal). As regards WTO dispute settlement see, for example, David Palmeter & Petros Mavroidis, *Dispute Settlement in the World Trade Organization: Practice and Procedure* (2nd edn, Cambridge: Cambridge University Press, 2004) at 144 (discussing Article 13 of the DSU and noting that the WTO follows the practice of courts in the civil law system as regards the powers of the adjudicator with respect to fact-finding).

[56] These will be discussed in more detail in Chapter 5. Chapter 5 will also discuss the consequences of a failure to produce evidence directly requested by the panel.

[57] For example, in *International Ore*, the Iran–United States Claims Tribunal held that the fact that the respondents had not offered any evidence in support of their denial of the claimants' allegations did not suffice to relieve the claimants from their duty to prove their own contentions. *International Ore & Fertilizer Corporation et al v Razi Chemical Company Ltd et al*, Award No 351-486-3, 29 February 1988, reprinted in 18 Iran–U.S. Claims Tribunal Reports 98 (Cambridge: Grotius Publications, 1989) at 101, para 10 of the award. Similarly, the Mexico–United States General Claims Commission of 1923 in *Melczer Mining Co.* noted that '[c]laimant Government must produce concrete and convincing evidence and is not relieved of such requirement by fact that evidence submitted by the respondent Government is meagre'. *Melczer Mining Company (USA) v United Mexican States*, 30 April 1929, 4 Reports of International Arbitral Awards (Millwood: Kraus Reprint Co, 1974) at 482. In *Corfu Channel*, the ICJ noted that although the United Kingdom, the claimant, had contended that Albania herself had laid the mines that caused the damage to the British Navy ships, and that it had repeated this contention during the oral hearing, the United Kingdom had not furnished any evidence in support of its contention. Therefore, the Court found that it would 'pay no further attention to this matter'. *The Corfu Channel* (Merits) (United Kingdom v Albania), Judgment of 9 April 1949, International Court of Justice, Reports of Judgments, Advisory Opinions and Orders (1949) at 25.

Finally, it is widely understood that international courts and tribunals have the discretion to base their decisions on any piece of evidence on the record on which the parties had an opportunity to comment, no matter whether that evidence was submitted by the claimant or the respondent, or whether it was voluntarily submitted or submitted on the request of the adjudicator.[58] This understanding has also been applied in WTO dispute settlement. In *Korea—Dairy*, for instance, the Appellate Body rejected Korea's claim that the panel had erred in basing its conclusion that Korea acted inconsistently with the Agreement on Safeguards on evidence which had been presented by Korea rather than the European Communities (the complainant in the case).[59] Korea argued that it had not submitted the evidence at issue as evidence of compliance or non-compliance with the Agreement on Safeguards, but rather as information that might be useful in explaining the context of and background to the dispute.[60] According to the Appellate Body, in carrying out its mandate under Article 11 of the DSU, 'a panel has the duty to examine and *consider all the evidence before it*, not just the evidence submitted by one or the other party, and to evaluate the relevance and probative force of each piece thereof'.[61]

The written rules governing the proceedings of international courts and tribunals are, however, not as detailed as domestic rules of procedure. On account of this, there has been some confusion regarding the functioning of the burden of proof. Sometimes parties and tribunals use the common law terminology on the burden of proof and seek to distinguish between the burden of going forward and the burden of persuasion—this is probably due at least in part to the fact that such parties, their lawyers, or members of the tribunal have been trained in a common law jurisdiction. However, as noted above, in the absence of procedural motions to test the sufficiency of the evidence, the use of this terminology is not appropriate and only serves to create confusion. In the WTO context, for example, defendants have in several occasions asked panels to issue an intermediate ruling regarding the sufficiency of the evidence presented by the complainant. Following the tradition in international proceedings, such requests have been denied.[62] Chapter 3 will further discuss this question with respect to WTO proceedings.

[58] In this regard, see, for instance, Sandifer, above n 52 at 107 (noting that '[i]n determining whether there is sufficient evidence upon which to base an award, account may be taken of the evidence submitted by all parties to the proceedings').

[59] Appellate Body Report, *Korea—Definitive Safeguard Measure on Imports of Certain Dairy Products*, WT/DS98/AB/R, adopted 12 January 2000, DSR 2000:I, 3 at para 137.

[60] In *Canada—Aircraft*, Canada made a similar attempt to restrict some of the evidence that it presented to the examination of particular questions. Panel Report, *Canada—Aircraft*, above n 20 at paras 6.202, 6.275, 6.303.

[61] Appellate Body Report, *Korea—Dairy*, above n 59 at para 137 [emphasis added].

[62] See, for instance, Appellate Body Report, *Korea—Dairy*, above n 59 at para 145; Panel Report, *Canada—Aircraft*, above n 20 at para 9.87.

Another source of confusion relates to the use of the expression 'evidential burden'. In the common law context, the evidential burden is the burden of going forward.[63] However, this expression has been used in other contexts to refer to (i) the onus on a party asserting a particular auxiliary proposition to adduce evidence in support of it,[64] (ii) the fact that the party that bears the burden of proof must produce evidence in support of its claims, and (iii) the onus on a party to present or indicate evidence at the time it presents its written submission as a consequence of a rule requiring that party to do so.[65] The latter refers to the fact that—as noted above in the description of the general features of civilian systems—when a party is required to submit evidence with its written submission, a complete failure to enclose or indicate evidence to be produced with a view to demonstrating that its assertions have any substance may result in an early dismissal of the case. Because the expression 'evidentiary burden' is loosely used in different contexts, often to describe processes to which no separate legal consequence is attached, the use of this and other similar expressions will be avoided in this book.

D. Does the burden of proof shift?

One of the most contested issues regarding the burden of proof refers to the shifting of the burden of proof. Although there is a considerable level of agreement among commentators that the burden of proof does not shift, it is not difficult to find decisions or academic commentary mentioning the shifting of the burden of proof.[66] The issue becomes more confusing because they do not refer to exactly the same phenomenon. In the common law system there is broad consensus around the proposition that the burden of persuasion does not shift.[67] This burden is set at the beginning of a case and remains with the same party throughout the case. Therefore, if at the end of the proceedings the trier or facts

[63] Sopinka, Lederman & Bryant, for example, refer to the burden of going forward as the 'evidential burden'. Sopinka, Lederman & Bryant (1999), above n 29 at 53. Similarly, see Chester Brown, *A Common Law of International Adjudication* (Oxford: Oxford University Press, 2007) at 93.

[64] See, for example, MacLennan, above n 54 at 266; Lasok, above n 54 at 422.

[65] See, for example, Mark Brealey, 'The Burden of Proof before the European Court' (1985) 10 European Law Review 250 at 251 (discussing the rules of the European Court of Justice); Lasok, above n 54 at footnote 18 to page 423.

[66] This is particularly the case in WTO dispute settlement reports. This issue will be discussed more carefully in Chapter 3.

[67] See Tapper (1995), above n 26 at 125; Sopinka, Lederman & Bryant (1999), above n 29 at 71; James B Thayer, 'The Burden of Proof' (1890) 4:2 Harvard Law Review 45 at 60; AT Denning, 'Presumptions and Burdens' (1945) 61 The Law Quarterly Review 379 at 379; Charles V Laughlin, 'The Location of the Burden of Persuasion' (1956) 18 University of Pittsburgh Law Review 3 at 24–5.

remain uncertain, the party which is assigned the burden of persuasion bears the consequences of non-persuasion, namely, it loses with respect to that issue. This is also the understanding as regards the concept of the burden of proof in the civil law system,[68] and international law.[69]

As regards the burden of going forward in the common law, some commentators suggest in their writings that this burden shifts from one party to the other during the proceedings.[70] The burden of going forward may shift when, as discussed above, the evidence presented by the party originally bearing the burden is so overwhelming that upon her motion the judge may remove the issue from the jury and enter judgment in her favour unless the opposing party presents additional evidence. It is unlikely, however, that the burden of going forward on a certain issue will shift several times. This is so because 'conflicting evidence on a single issue would in most realistic settings leave the matter in the realm where decision is properly for the jury', namely, 'a reasonable jury could find *A* or decline to find *A*'.[71] Accordingly, when courts or commentators refer to the burden of going forward shifting back and forth, it is likely that they are using an overly broad definition of the burden of going forward which includes what has been referred to as the tactical or provisional burden.[72] The concept of tactical burden refers to the situation where a party adduces evidence as a matter of tactics and prudence.[73] For example, when the opponent denies the occurrence of an event which is central to the establishment of one of the elements of the proponent's case, it may be prudent for the opponent to provide evidence that demonstrates that the event did not occur. In other words, because the stronger the evidence presented by the proponent, the higher is the likelihood that the trier of facts will find in her favour, when the opponent sees the proponent's evidence becoming stronger he may as a matter of common sense and prudence feel compelled to present evidence to the contrary. However, if such evidence is not provided, the trier of facts may still find that the proponent's evidence is

[68] See Pauwelyn, *Evidence, Proof and Persuasion*, above n 52 at 230.

[69] See Amerasinghe, above n 52 at 43; Kazazi, above n 10 at 36; Pauwelyn, *Evidence, Proof and Persuasion*, above n 52 at 232; Robert B von Mehren, 'Burden of Proof in International Arbitration' in AJ van den Berg (ed), *Planning Efficient Arbitration Proceedings: The Law Applicable in International Arbitration* (The Hague: Kluwer Law International, 1996) 123 at 125; Aghahosseini, above n 55 at 212; David Unterhalter, 'The Burden of Proof in WTO Dispute Settlement' in ME Janow, V Donaldson & A Yanovich (eds), *The WTO: Governance, Dispute Settlement, and Developing Countries* (Huntington: Juris Publishing, 2008) 543 at 544, 550.

[70] See, for example, von Mehren, above n 69 at 124; Thayer, above n 67 at 60.

[71] Field, Kaplan & Clermont, above n 31 at 1243. See also Strong, above n 26 at 420; Clifford S Fishman, *Jones on Evidence: Civil and Criminal* (7th edn, Rochester: Lawyers Cooperative Publishing, 1992) at 281.

[72] See Sopinka, Lederman & Bryant (1999), above n 29 at 75; Tapper (1995), above n 26 at 126–7.

[73] Sopinka, Lederman & Bryant (1999), above n 29 at 74; Tapper (1995), above n 26 at 126.

not persuasive.[74] On account of this and the fact that the opponent has no means of telling when the tactical burden has been brought into existence or when it has been discharged, commentators have noted that the concept of the tactical burden has no legal significance.[75] In support of this view, the Supreme Court of Canada in *Snell v Farrel* noted that:

> It is not strictly accurate to speak of the burden shifting to the defendant when what is meant is that evidence adduced by the plaintiff may result in an inference being drawn adverse to the defendant. Whether an inference is or is not drawn is a matter of weighing evidence. The defendant runs the risk of an adverse inference in the absence of evidence to the contrary. This is sometimes referred to as imposing on the defendant a provisional or tactical burden. [. . .] this is not a true burden of proof, and use of an additional label to describe what is an ordinary step in the fact-finding process is unwarranted.[76]

The concept of the tactical burden is, therefore, not legally significant and references to it in legal decisions may confuse rather than assist the parties in understanding a decision. For these reasons, courts would be wise to refrain from stating that the burden of proof, even in the sense of the tactical burden, shifts.

Courts and commentators may also refer to the shifting of the burden of proof when the allocation of one of the burdens—the burden of going forward or the burden of persuasion—is made conditional upon the proof of some other fact.[77] Rebuttable presumptions have this effect. However, the burden of proof in this kind of situation does not actually shift; what happens is that different parties are allocated the burden with respect to different issues.[78] A similar

[74] The situation can be further illustrated by reference to the issue of alibi in a murder case. After the prosecution presents evidence of the murder and its linkage to the defendant, the defendant may choose to argue that he could not possibly have committed the crime alleged by the prosecution because at the time of the crime he was out of the country. The issue of an alibi raises a question with respect to the existence of the crime as regards the person of the defendant. In other words, the alibi is a way for the defendant to say that he did not do it. Therefore, when the defendant argues that he was out of the country when the crime occurred he is denying that he committed the crime. Although the defendant may have to provide evidence that he was out of the country if he wants the court to take this specific argument into account, this does not change the fact that the prosecution must produce enough evidence demonstrating that the defendant actually committed the crime—which includes evidence that the defendant was at the scene of the crime at the time Mr X was murdered. The prosecution, however, may not have to present evidence on the specific point that the defendant was *not* outside the country, if it can otherwise provide enough evidence to demonstrate that it was the defendant who murdered Mr X. This is because the specific point of whether the defendant was outside the country at the time the murder took place is an auxiliary proposition rather than an elemental one. The elemental proposition in this case is the authorship of the murder and this may be established through other auxiliary propositions—for example, the prosecution may present testimony from two eyewitnesses, and DNA tests showing that blood found at the scene of the crime matches the defendant's blood.

[75] See Tapper (1995), above n 26 at 127; Sopinka, Lederman & Bryant (1999), above n 29 at 75; Julius Stone, 'Burden of Proof and the Judicial Process: A Commentary on *Joseph Constantine Steamship, LTD.* v. *Imperial Smelting Corporation, LTD.*' (1944) 60 The Law Quarterly Review 262 at 267.

[76] *Snell v Farrell* [1990] 2 SCR 311, 107 NBR (2d) 94, 72 DLR (4th) 289, 110 NR 200, 4 CCLT (2d) 229.

[77] Tapper (1995), above n 26 at 126.

[78] See Laughlin, above n 67 at 25; Stone, above n 75 at 263.

situation regards multiple-issue cases where the complainant is allocated the burden of proof with respect to some issues and the defendant is assigned the burden of proof with respect to others.[79] Again, in this type of case, parties are assigned the burden of proof with respect to different issues; thus the burden of proof with respect to a specific issue remains with the same party throughout the proceedings.

II. Standard of Proof

A. General scope

The standard of proof refers to the degree of proof required to discharge the burden of proof. In other words, it refers to the degree of persuasion that the adjudicator must reach in order for the adjudicator to decide an issue in favour of the party bearing the burden of proof. Standards of proof serve as 'guides to aid the fact-finder in exercising discretion' in the fact-finding process.[80] Conversely, they help the parties to assess the strength of their cases, that is, to determine whether the evidence may justify a finding in their favour.

The standard of proof, however, does not tell the parties or adjudicators exactly what kind of evidence must be provided in order to discharge the burden of proof; it solely establishes a degree of proof that must be reached in order to discharge that burden. In this respect, where the system of legal proofs—namely, when the law determines the type of evidence that must be presented in order to prove a certain proposition—is in place, there is no role for the idea of the standard of proof. Although the principle of free evaluation of evidence is the norm nowadays, many civil codes in civilian jurisdictions still contain provisions requiring certain propositions to be proven by predetermined types of evidence.

The standard of proof should not be confused with the content of the propositions to be proved, that is, the legal standards. The legal standards are established by interpreting the language of the agreements and they determine *what* must be proved. The standard of proof defines the degree of persuasion required to establish the propositions that must be proved. For example, the panel in *Japan—Alcoholic Beverages II* mistakenly employed the term 'standard of proof' to refer to the legal standard. In that case the panel noted that if a Member could invoke protection of health in the context of an aims-and-effects test under Article III of the GATT, 'the standard of proof established in Article XX would effectively be circumvented'.[81] According to the panel, if this were the

[79] See Sopinka, Lederman & Bryant (1999), above n 29 at 71; Tapper (1995), above n 26 at 126.
[80] Anderson, Schum & Twining, above n 15 at 244.
[81] Panel Report, *Japan—Taxes on Alcoholic Beverages*, WT/DS8/R, WT/DS10/R, WT/DS11/R, adopted 1 November 1996 at para 6.17.

case 'WTO Members would not have to prove [under Article XX] that a health measure is "necessary" to achieve its health objective'.[82]

B. Differences between common law and civil law systems

1. Common law

In the common law system, the concept refers to the degree of proof necessary to satisfy the burden of going forward or the burden of persuasion. As regards the burden of persuasion, the standard of proof in civil cases is the 'preponderance of the evidence' or 'balance of probabilities'. In the United States, certain issues in civil cases require the party bearing the burden of proof to satisfy the higher standard of 'clear and convincing evidence'. In other common law jurisdictions, such as England, the predominant view is that the preponderance of the evidence standard accommodates different degrees of probability depending on the nature of the case.[83] In criminal cases, the prosecution must satisfy the standard of 'beyond reasonable doubt' in order to succeed.

Defining the preponderance of the evidence standard as requiring the proponent to present evidence which is more convincing than the opponent's evidence is misleading. Such definition disregards those situations where although the proponent has presented evidence and the opponent has presented little or no evidence to the contrary, the fact-finder is still not able to conclude that the factual proposition advanced by the proponent would likely have occurred.[84] The preponderance of the evidence standard is more appropriately defined as requiring that a proposition be shown to be more probably true than not. Such judgment that a proposition is more likely than not true must be based on the evidence that is on the record but taking into account what other evidence could have been produced, that is, the universe of available evidence related to the proposition in question. Although the judgment is probabilistic, the standard does not have to be expressed in numeric terms, ie that the adjudicator must determine that the probability that a proposition is true is 0.5 or higher in order to find for the proponent.[85] In fact, there are good reasons for not expressing the standard in those terms. First, it is difficult to justify such

[82] Panel Report, *Japan—Alcoholic Beverages II*, above n 81 at para 6.17.

[83] Anderson, Schum & Twining, above n 15 at 243–4 (discussing the differences between England and the United States); Kevin Costello, 'Administrative Law—The Burden of Proof on Judicial Review' (1993) 15 Dublin University Law Journal 134 at 140 (discussing the standard of proof applicable in cases involving administrative law in Ireland); William Wade & Christopher Forsyth, *Administrative Law* (9th edn, Oxford: Oxford University Press, 2004) at 291.

[84] See Strong, above n 26 at 422. (Strong explains that adjudicators can make this kind of judgment because they do not view the evidence in a vacuum, that is, they rely upon their own experience in order to reach a decision.)

[85] For more information on the use of probabilities in legal fact-finding see Anderson, Schum & Twining, above n 15 at 246ff.

numerical judgments 'because the events of concern either happened or did not happen *on exactly one occasion*'.[86] Second, expressing the standard in numeric terms opens the door to problems regarding the treatment of statistical evidence. If we interpret the preponderance standard as requiring a party to present evidence that the probability that a proposition is true is 0.5 or higher, 'when there is clear statistical evidence showing that the facts would be favourable to that party only in 49% of the cases', the fact-finder may feel compelled to find against that party.[87] This is so, even though a statistic does not say anything about the occurrence of the particular event at issue. In order to avoid this type of problem, Walker explains the fact-finder's task under the preponderance standard as deciding 'what is "probably true" in the sense of "being warranted by the evidence" '.[88]

As regards the burden of going forward, when the opponent requests the court to rule on the sufficiency of the evidence presented by the proponent, the court must determine whether the evidence on the record could possibly allow a reasonable person to find in favour of the proponent. The court does not decide at this point whether it is persuaded, for example, to a balance of probabilities; it merely determines whether the evidence before it could lead a reasonable person to that conclusion.[89] This standard has been referred to by some as the *prima facie* evidence standard.[90]

2. Civil law

The question of the standard of proof is less discussed in civil law jurisdictions. Codes of civil procedure and judicial decisions are silent on the question.[91] There are at least two possible reasons for this lack of interest in the question. First, trials by jury are rare—restricted to a small number of criminal cases—in the civilian system and, therefore, there is little need to give the jury clear instructions on the standards for decision. Second, many civilian jurisdictions still apply the system of legal proofs with respect to certain questions; requiring

[86] Anderson, Schum & Twining, above n 15 at 246 [emphasis added]. See also Stein, above n 15 at 80ff.

[87] Vern R Walker, 'Preponderance, Probability and Warranted Factfinding' (1996) 62 Brooklyn Law Review 1075 at 1080.

[88] Walker, *Preponderance, Probability and Warranted Factfinding*, above n 87 at 1136. Similarly, see Stein, above n 15 at 69–70, 90–2. (Stein refers to the parameters of 'probability' and 'weight'. He explains that the 'weight' parameter 'measures the extent to which the existing evidence covers the specific factual allegations in the case' and that it 'blocks any probabilistic deduction unaccompanied by case-specific evidence'.)

[89] See, for example, John Sopinka, Sidney N Lederman & Alan W Bryant, *The Law of Evidence in Canada* (Toronto: Butterworths, 1992) at 130–1; Strong, above n 26 at 417.

[90] Sopinka, Lederman & Bryant (1999), above n 29 at 67, 70; Fishman, above n 71 at 235.

[91] See Clermont & Sherwin, above n 6 at 253–4; Kazazi, above n 10 at 324; Juliane Kokott, *The Burden of Proof in Comparative and International Human Rights Law: Civil and Common Law Approaches with Special Reference to the American and German Legal Systems* (The Hague: Kluwer Law International, 1998) at xvii–xviii.

certain propositions to be proven by predetermined types of evidence obviates the need for a standard of proof.

The standard of proof in civilian jurisdictions is often described as the judge's personal conviction, but it is not clear what degree of proof is required to satisfy the personal conviction of the judge. As regards civil cases, there is support in the literature for both the view that the party bearing the burden of proof must convince the court that a proposition is more probable than not,[92] as well as for the view that the party bearing the burden of proof must convince the court beyond a reasonable doubt or that a proposition is highly probable or almost certain.[93] The fact that the standard of the personal conviction of the judge is applied in civil and criminal cases, may suggest that that standard is a high one—likely closer to beyond a reasonable doubt than to the preponderance of the evidence standard—since no court in a western legal system would convict a person of a crime on the basis of evidence that is not very close to the certainty end of the spectrum. It is also possible that in practice the courts ascribe a different meaning to the standard of the personal conviction depending on whether they are adjudicating a civil or a criminal case. However, because these standards are not articulated, this hypothesis is mere speculation.[94]

C. Proceedings before international courts and tribunals

The question of the standard of proof has been similarly neglected in proceedings before international courts and tribunals. The statutes and rules of

[92] Herzog, above n 36 at 310 (discussing the standard applicable in civil cases in France); Claude Giverdon, 'The Problem of Proof in French Civil Law' (1956) 31 Tulane Law Review 29 at 38 (discussing the standard applicable in civil cases in France); Yasuhei Taniguchi, Pauline C Reich & Hiroto Miyake (eds), *Civil Procedure in Japan* (2nd edn, Yonkers: Juris Publishing, 2002) at para 7.05[13][b] (discussing the standard of proof in civil cases in Japan); Koch & Diedrich, above n 24 at 109 (discussing the standard of proof in civil cases in Germany). Principle 21.2 of the ALI/UNIDROIT Principles of Transnational Civil Procedure states that '[f]acts are considered proven when the court is reasonably convinced of their truth'. The ALI/UNIDROIT commentary to the principles notes that this standard is essentially the same as the preponderance of the evidence standard. American Law Institute & UNIDROIT, *Principles of Transnational Civil Procedure* (Cambridge: Cambridge University Press, 2006) at 42.

[93] Kuo-Chang Huang, *Introducing Discovery into Civil Law* (Durham: Carolina Academic Press, 2003) at 53 (discussing the standard of proof applicable in civil cases in the civil law system in general, and specifically in Germany, France, and Japan); Clermont & Sherwin, above n 6 at 245–7; Hanotiau, above n 42 at 345 (discussing the standard of proof applied by the Belgian Supreme Court); Taniguchi, Reich & Miyake, above n 92 at para 7.05[13][b] (discussing the standard of proof in civil cases in Japan); Kokott, above n 91 at 18 (discussing the standard of proof in German civil cases).

[94] Clermont and Sherwin are critical of the civilian standard of the personal conviction of the judge. They argue that civilians favour the unitary standard of the personal conviction of the judge because 'suppression of the probabilistic nature of factfinding gives judgments an appearance of legitimacy'. They believe that these legitimating benefits come at cost. See Clermont & Sherwin, above n 6 at 273–4.

international courts and tribunals such as the ICJ[95] and the Iran–United States Claims Tribunal are silent on the issue. Nor has the jurisprudence of those bodies elaborated on the standard of proof that must be satisfied to prove a proposition.[96] Reflecting the influence of civilian procedure, the standard seems to be that of the conviction of the judge.[97] Again, it is not clear exactly what this standard entails. It seems that proof beyond a reasonable doubt is too high a standard for most questions in international proceedings where special consideration should be given to the fact that evidence is more difficult to gather. Accordingly, this standard has been applied only in few cases, where the nature of questions at issue warrants a higher standard, such as criminal cases, quasi-criminal, or tort claims.[98]

The European Court of Human Rights and the now extinct European Commission of Human Rights have applied the standard of beyond a reasonable doubt in certain cases.[99] In the *Irish* case, the Court stated that it adopted the beyond a reasonable doubt standard, but noted that 'such proof may follow from the coexistence of sufficiently strong, clear and concordant inferences or of

[95] Valencia-Ospina notes that Article 53 of the Statute of the ICJ could be interpreted as establishing a standard of proof for cases where a party fails to appear before the Court. Article 53 provides that the Court may rule in favour of the other party only after it has satisfied itself that it has jurisdiction, and that 'the claim is well founded in fact and law'. The Court, however, has not elaborated on this standard or found that it also applies in cases falling outside the scope of Article 53. Eduardo Valencia-Ospina, 'Evidence before the International Court of Justice' (1999) 1:4 International Law FORUM du Droit International 202 at 204.

[96] Some scattered decisions, particularly separate and dissenting opinions, of the Iran–United States Claims Tribunal refer to the preponderance of the evidence standard, but the Tribunal has not openly discussed and set a standard of proof applicable to cases brought before it. Examples of such decisions include *William L Pereira Associates, Iran v The Islamic Republic of Iran*, Award No. 116-1-3, 19 March 1984, Concurring Opinion of Richard M. Mosk, reprinted in 5 Iran–U.S. Claims Tribunal Reports 230 (Cambridge: Grotius Publications, 1985) at 231; *Combustion Engineering, Inc et al v The Islamic Republic of Iran et al*, Partial Award No. 506-308-2, 18 February 1991, reprinted in 26 Iran–U.S. Claims Tribunal Reports 60 (Cambridge: Grotius Publications, 1992) at 80, para 70 of the award. See also Kazazi, above n 10 at 348–50; Aghahosseini, above n 55 at 213. In support of the view that international courts and tribunals have not clearly articulated the standards of proof applicable in cases brought before them, see Sir Arthur Watts, 'Burden of Proof, and Evidence Before the ICJ' in F Weiss (ed), *Improving WTO Dispute Settlement Procedures: Issues and Lessons from the Practice of Other International Courts and Tribunals* (London: Cameron May, 2000) 289 at 294 (discussing the case of the ICJ); Riddell & Plant, above n 52 at 136; Thomas Buergenthal, 'Judicial Fact-Finding: Inter-American Human Rights Court' in RB Lillich (ed), *Fact-Finding before International Tribunals* (Ardsley-on-Hudson: Transnational Publishers, 1990) 261 at 271; Kazazi, above n 10 at 325; Amerasinghe, above n 52 at 232; Lasok, above n 54 at 431 (discussing the case of the European Court of Justice); MacLennan, above n 54 at 268 (discussing the case of the European Court of Justice).

[97] See, for example, Valencia-Ospina, above n 95 at 203; Cheng, above n 21 at 302; Lasok, above n 54 at 429 (discussing the standard in proceedings before the European Court of Justice).

[98] See Amerasinghe, above n 52 at 235–6; Kazazi, above n 10 at 345, 347–8.

[99] *Ireland against United Kingdom*, Report of the Commission, 19 Yearbook of the European Convention on Human Rights (1976) at 796; *The Greek Case*, Report of the Commission, 12 Yearbook of the European Convention on Human Rights (1969) at 196. For more information on the practices of the European Court of Human Rights, see Kokott, above n 91 at 197–202.

similar unrebutted presumptions of fact'.[100] A somewhat lower standard than beyond a reasonable doubt has been applied in certain cases by the Inter-American Court of Human Rights.[101] In the *Velasquez Rodriguez* and the *Fairen Garbi and Solis Corrales* cases, the Court noted that a 'finding that a State Party to the Convention has carried out or has tolerated a practice of disappearances in its territory' is particularly serious and that, therefore, the Court should apply a standard of proof 'which considers the seriousness of the charge and which [...] is capable of establishing the truth of the allegations in a convincing manner'.[102]

Similarly to other international courts and tribunals, it is possible to find only scant references to standards of proof in the jurisprudence of the ICJ. In the *Corfu Channel* case, one of the few cases where some sort of standard was articulated, the Court noted that 'proof may be drawn from inferences of fact, provided that they leave *no room* for reasonable doubt'.[103] The Court also rejected evidence 'falling short of conclusive evidence' and in making this finding it noted the exceptional gravity of the allegation.[104] The Court referred to this ruling in the *Genocide Convention (Bosnia and Herzegovina v Serbia and Montenegro)* case, where it stated that it would require 'proof at a high level of certainty'[105] and that it should be 'fully convinced that allegations made in the proceedings [...] have been clearly established'.[106] In the *Iranian Oil Platforms* case, judges Buergenthal and Higgins submitted separate opinions in which they criticized the Court for not defining the standard of proof applied.[107] Both judges questioned how the Court reached the conclusion that the evidence was 'insufficient'.[108] In another part of its judgment the Court, instead of saying that

[100] *Ireland v United Kingdom*, Judgment of 18 January 1978, 25 European Court of Human Rights (Series A) at para 161.

[101] Although the Court did not explicitly state that it was not adopting the beyond a reasonable doubt standard, it did note that the international protection of human rights should not be confused with criminal justice. *Velasquez Rodriguez Case*, Judgment of 29 July 1988, Inter-American Court of Human Rights, Series C, No 4 (1988) at 136, para 134; *Fairen Garbi and Solis Corrales Case*, Judgment of 15 March 1989, Inter-American Court of Human Rights, Series C, No 6 (1989) at 124, para 136.

[102] *Velasquez Rodriguez Case*, above n 101 at 135, para 129; *Fairen Garbi and Solis Corrales Case*, above n 101 at 123, para 132.

[103] *The Corfu Channel* (Merits), above n 57 at 18 [original emphasis].

[104] *The Corfu Channel* (Merits), above n 57 at 17.

[105] *Case Concerning the Application of the Convention on the Prevention and Punishment of the Crime of Genocide* (*Bosnia and Herzegovina v Serbia and Montenegro*), Judgment of 26 February 2007, available at <http://www.icj-cij.org/docket/index.php?p1=3&p2=3&k=f4&case=91&code=bhy&p3=4> (accessed 11 April 2008) at para 210.

[106] *Case Concerning the Application of the Convention on the Prevention and Punishment of the Crime of Genocide*, above n 105 at para 209.

[107] *Oil Platforms* (*Iran v United States of America*), Judgment of 6 November 2003, Separate Opinion of Judge Higgins, International Court of Justice, Reports of Judgments, Advisory Opinions and Orders (2003) at 233, para 30; *Oil Platforms (Iran v United States of America)*, Judgment of 6 November 2003, Separate Opinion of Judge Buergenthal, International Court of Justice, Reports of Judgments, Advisory Opinions and Orders (2003) at 286, para 41.

[108] *Oil Platforms*, Separate Opinion of Judge Higgins, above n 107 at 234, para 34; *Oil Platforms*, Separate Opinion of Judge Buergenthal, above n 107 at 286, para 41.

the evidence was 'insufficient', stated that the evidence was 'highly suggestive, but not conclusive'.[109] In her separate opinion, Judge Higgins notes that the evidence in question was detailed, significant, and pointed in but one direction; yet, the Court rejected such evidence without articulating the standard of proof applied, making it 'impossible to know how the Court reached [that] conclusion'.[110] Finally, Judge Higgins noted that as the principal judicial organ of the United Nations, the Court should 'make clear what standards of proof it requires to establish what sorts of facts'.[111]

The DSU and the dispute settlement organs have not defined the standard of proof applicable to WTO disputes either. Some have argued that in practice panels apply the preponderance of the evidence standard,[112] while others have argued that panels have applied the *prima facie* case standard.[113] In a rare pronouncement, the panel in *Canada—Dairy (Article 21.5—New Zealand and US II)* rejected the application of the standard of beyond a reasonable doubt.[114] This question will be further discussed in Chapter 3. At this point, it suffices to note that panels and the Appellate Body have not explicitly referred to the

[109] *Oil Platforms (Iran v United States of America)*, Judgment of 6 November 2003, International Court of Justice, Reports of Judgments, Advisory Opinions and Orders (2003) at 195, para 71.

[110] *Oil Platforms*, Separate Opinion of Judge Higgins, above n 107 at 234–5, paras 36–7. Judge Buergenthal also criticized the Court for changing the standard without providing any explanation. *Oil Platforms*, Separate Opinion of Judge Buergenthal, above n 107 at 288, para 44.

[111] *Oil Platforms*, Separate Opinion of Judge Higgins, above n 107 at 234, para 33.

[112] Edmond McGovern, *International Trade Regulation* (3rd edn, Exeter: Globefield Press, 1995) at 2.23-63, issue 18; Jeff Waincymer, *WTO Litigation: Procedural Aspects of Formal Dispute Settlement* (London: Cameron May, 2002) at 568. See also Tim Josling et al, 'Implications of WTO Litigation for the WTO Agricultural Negotiations' (2006) 19 IPC Issue Brief at 11 (noting that the panel in *US—Upland Cotton* 'made [its] ruling on the basis of a preponderance of the evidence from economic studies that production of cotton in the US has a significant impact on the world market price').

[113] Petros C Mavroidis, 'Development of WTO Dispute Settlement Procedures Through Case-Law (We Will Fix It)' in F Ortino & E -U Petersmann (eds), *The WTO Dispute Settlement System 1995–2003* (The Hague: Kluwer Law International, 2004) 153 at 172; European Communities' arguments in Appellate Body Report, *Canada—Measures Affecting the Importation of Milk and the Exportation of Dairy Products—Second Recourse to Article 21.5 of the DSU by New Zealand and the United States*, WT/DS103/AB/RW2, WT/DS113/AB/RW2, adopted 17 January 2003 at para 48.

[114] Canada had argued that the calculation of the average total cost of production required to show that no payments were made within the meaning of Article 9.1(c) of the Agreement on Agriculture should be based on data regarding the *cost of production of individual producers*. In the panel's view, the amount of information that would have to be gathered under this approach made it too costly and unworkable. Requiring this type of evidence would amount to imposing a standard akin to proof beyond a reasonable doubt. Panel Report, *Canada—Measures Affecting the Importation of Milk and the Exportation of Dairy Products—Second Recourse to Article 21.5 of the DSU by New Zealand and the United States*, WT/DS103/RW2, WT/DS113/RW2, adopted 17 January 2003 at para 5.67. The costs and unworkability of an approach which would require production of immense amounts of information also influenced the decision of the Iran–United States Claims Tribunal in *Flexi-Van*. See *Flexi-Van Leasing Inc v Iran*, Case no 36, 15 December 1982, 1 Iran–U.S. Claims Tribunal Reports 455 (Cambridge, Grotius Publications, 1983) at 457–461.

preponderance of the evidence standard;[115] references to a *prima facie* case, however, are found in almost every report.

III. Presumptions

A. General scope

The word 'presumption' is used in many different contexts in legal discourse. Hence, it is important to define the concept as it will be referred to in this study. In most legal systems, a presumption is a conclusion as to the existence of a fact which is unknown (the presumed fact) that is drawn from a known fact (the basic fact). Presumptions are traditionally classified into 'presumptions of fact' and 'legal presumptions' (or 'presumptions of law').

Legal presumptions are rules of law providing that proof of the basic fact requires the adjudicator to find the presumed fact. Legal presumptions are either rebuttable (presumptions *juris tantum*) or irrebuttable (presumptions *juris et de jure*). If a presumption of law is rebuttable, proof of the basic fact must lead the adjudicator to find the presumed fact, unless the opposing party persuades the adjudicator to the appropriate standard of the contrary. In other words, upon proof of the basic fact by the proponent, the opponent must prove that the presumed fact did not occur in order to avoid the consequences of the presumption.[116] If a presumption of law is irrebuttable, the proponent will succeed if it proves the basic fact, that is, '[o]n proof of the basic fact, the presumed fact is conclusively deemed to exist'.[117] Irrebuttable presumptions are rules of substantive law masquerading as presumptions.[118] For example, some jurisdictions which do not allow children to be prosecuted for crimes may state this rule in the form of a presumption, namely, that a child under a specified age is presumed incapable of committing a crime.

Presumptions of fact are those where proof of the basic fact *may* lead the adjudicator to find the presumed fact. Presumptions of fact, as the name

[115] Indirect references have been made in certain cases such as *India—Autos* where the panel noted in one occasion that the European Communities had 'not proven on balance' that a certain proposition was true. More recently, in *US—Upland Cotton* (*Article 21.5—Brazil*), the Appellate Body noted that '[t]he Panel's finding [. . .] provides a sufficient evidentiary basis for the conclusion that it is *more likely than not* that the revised GSM 102 programme operates at a loss'. Respectively, Panel Report, *India—Measures Affecting the Automotive Sector*, WT/DS146/R, WT/DS175/R and Corr.1, adopted 5 April 2002 at para 7.233 [emphasis added]; Appellate Body Report, *United States—Subsidies on Upland Cotton—Recourse to* Article 21.5 *of the DSU by Brazil*, WT/DS267/AB/RW, adopted 20 June 2008 at para 321 [emphasis added].

[116] See, for example, Tapper (1995), above n 26 at 136–7; Sopinka, Lederman & Bryant (1992), above n 89 at 107–8; Herzog, above n 36 at 314.

[117] Sopinka, Lederman & Bryant (1992), above n 89 at 104. See also Herzog, above n 36 at 314; Amerasinghe, above n 52 at 223.

[118] See Sopinka, Lederman & Bryant (1992), above n 89 at 105; Fishman, above n 71 at 305; Herzog, above n 36 at 316.

suggests, are not rules of law; rather, they are a creation of adjudicators. When certain combinations of facts recur frequently, adjudicators may refer to those facts as establishing a presumption. The presumption in this case is nothing but a logical conclusion regarding unknown facts which is derived from known facts. An example of this type of presumption is that according to which a letter posted is presumed to have reached its destination. Accordingly, presumptions of fact are more properly classified in the category of inferences[119]—they are inferences that recur in many cases.[120]

While certain rebuttable legal presumptions are nothing but a natural inference which was given special weight by the law, this is not the basis, or the *only* basis, of all legal presumptions. Legal presumptions may be designed to resolve impasses, save time and expense, correct imbalances in access to evidence, reflect probabilities, and/or pursue certain policy goals.[121] Examples are the presumption in force in some jurisdictions that provides that where two or more persons died in circumstances rendering it uncertain which one of them survived the other, the eldest is presumed to have died first, followed by the eldest of the survivors and so on, and the presumption that a child born in wedlock is legitimate.

Up until now the concept of presumption has been restricted to those situations where conclusions as to the existence of a fact (the presumed fact) are drawn from another fact (the basic fact); these may be called *presumptions with basic facts*. There are other presumptions, however, that are not structured in the same manner; they do not require proof of a basic fact. Presumptions without a basic fact are rules of substantive law whose only function is to allocate the burden of proof.[122] In other words, these are rules on the allocation of the burden of proof clothed in the language of presumptions.[123] These presumptions require that a conclusion be drawn until the contrary is proved; the party in whose favour the presumption is created does not have to prove anything. The most commonly cited example of a presumption without a basic fact is the

[119] Tapper (1995), above n 26 at 136–7; Sopinka, Lederman & Bryant (1992), above n 89 at 100; Strong, above n 26 at 434; Herzog, above n 36 at 313, 317; Amerasinghe, above n 52 at 223–4.

[120] An inference is a 'conclusion reached by considering other facts and deducing a logical consequence from them'. *Black's Law Dictionary* (8th edn, St Paul: Thomson West, 2004) at 793. Inferences are limitless and in the majority of situations they are case-specific, that is, they are conclusions which are drawn from the particular circumstances and evidence before the adjudicator which may vary from case to case.

[121] See Strong, above n 26 at 438; Sir Richard Eggleston, *Evidence, Proof and Probability* (2nd edn, London: Weidenfeld and Nicolson, 1983) at 108–9; Colin Tapper, *Cross and Tapper on Evidence* (9th edn, London: Butterworths, 1999) at 123; Régine Genin-Meric, 'Droit de la Preuve: l'Exemple Français' in JML de Freitas (ed), *The Law of Evidence in the European Union* (The Hague: Kluwer Law International, 2004) 137 at 147; Fishman, above n 71 at 308. On account of the fact that rebuttable presumptions of law affect the allocation of the burden of proof, these presumptions are usually created for the same reasons that determine the allocation of the burden of proof. The allocation of the burden of proof will be further discussed in Chapter 4.

[122] See Sopinka, Lederman & Bryant (1992), above n 89 at 98; Tapper (1999), above n 121 at 120.

[123] The question of the allocation of the burden of proof will be further discussed in Chapter 4.

rule that provides that every person is presumed to be innocent until proven guilty.

The discussion above demonstrates that the word 'presumption' can be used in many different contexts and have several different meanings and effects. Accordingly, the indiscriminate use of this word is bound to generate confusion. On account of this, if the word 'presumption' is used without any of the modifiers described, the best understanding is that which restricts the use of the word 'presumption' to a rebuttable presumption of law. The reasons for this understanding have been noted above, but can be briefly summarized as follows. First, presumptions of fact are inferences which the adjudicator may or may not draw depending on the circumstances, and as such they need no other description. Presumptions of fact do not affect the allocation of the burden of proof—this means that in the common law, neither the allocation of the burden of going forward nor of the burden of persuasion is affected.[124] Second, irrebuttable presumptions of law and presumptions without a basic fact are rules of substantive law. The former defines the scope of a legal rule and in many occasions is nothing more than a definition that is termed as a presumption. The latter is a rule whose only function is to allocate the burden of proof.

Rebuttable presumptions of law also affect the burden of proof, but in a more indirect way; they attach certain consequences to proof of particular facts (the basic fact). After the proponent proves the basic fact, the presumed fact must be taken to be established unless the adjudicator is persuaded to the appropriate standard of the contrary, that is, the opponent has the burden of proving that the presumed fact does not exist.[125] Rebuttable presumptions of law can also be understood as means of proof in that if the opponent does not prove the non-existence of the presumed fact, the proponent is considered to have proved the existence of the presumed fact upon proof of the basic fact only.

In some common law jurisdictions, particularly the United States, a presumption may have the effect of assigning (i) the burden of going forward only or (ii) the burden of going forward and the burden of persuasion. In the United States, presumptions that fix both burdens have been called 'Morgan presumptions', and those that assign the burden of going forward only have been referred to as 'Thayer presumptions'.[126] Thayer presumptions require the opponent to present some evidence contrary to the presumed fact. Once the opponent adduces some contrary evidence the presumption loses its effect and the evidence concerning the basic fact has no more than its own weight, that is, the adjudicator may still infer the presumed fact from the basic fact if in the circumstances of the case the inference is a strong one. If the proponent proves the basic fact, Morgan presumptions assign both burdens with respect to the presumed fact to

[124] See Sopinka, Lederman & Bryant (1992), above n 89 at 100; Tapper (1999), above n 121 at 122.
[125] See, for example, Tapper (1999), above n 121 at 120; Strong, above n 26 at 452.
[126] Fishman, above n 71 at 312–16.

the opponent. Commentators note that it is not clear when a presumption affects only the burden of going forward and when it affects both burdens.[127] Because the distinction between the two burdens is non-existent in civilian and international procedure, this subject is of limited relevance to this study. Accordingly, a detailed analysis of when and what specific type of presumptions have been classified as Morgan or Thayer presumptions falls outside the scope of this study.

On account of the fact that most legal systems, particularly civil law systems which share more commonalities with international procedure, adopt the view that the opponent must persuade the adjudicator of the non-existence of the presumed fact—ie if the basic fact is proved, the opponent bears the burden of proving the non-existence of the presumed fact—this is the effect ascribed to rebuttable presumptions of law (or, simply, 'presumptions') in this study.

B. International law including WTO law

It is important to note that there is disagreement as to the existence of presumptions in general international law owing to the lack of a superior authority to define the presumptions and prescribe the consequences for the burden of proof.[128] This debate, however, is irrelevant when the presumptions are clearly provided for in the text of conventions and treaties such as the WTO agreements.

Interestingly, many of the examples given by those commentators who undertake the task of identifying presumptions in general international law are in fact examples of what international courts and tribunals have found *not* to constitute presumptions. Examples include (i) an abuse of right should not be presumed; (ii) the international responsibility of the state is not to be presumed; (iii) restrictions upon the independence of states to act cannot be presumed; (iv) a sovereign state cannot be presumed to have made the substance of its debt and the validity of the obligations accepted by it in respect thereof subject to any law other than its own; (v) there is no presumption that a state necessarily had knowledge of unlawful acts committed within its territory, as found by the ICJ in *Corfu Channel*;[129] (vi) renunciation cannot be presumed; and (vii) bad faith

[127] See, for example, Strong, above n 26 at 455–6; Fishman, above n 71 at 302, 316.

[128] Sandifer, above n 52 at 141–2. See also Witenberg, *Onus Probandi*, above n 54 at 329–30 (arguing that the creation of legal presumptions falls in the realm of legislative action and that international tribunals misuse the word 'presumption'. Witenberg also argues that the presumption in favour of the regularity and necessity of governmental acts and the presumption of regularity and validity of all acts of public officials are not real presumptions in that they do not dispense with proof of the facts which result in international responsibility, nor do they alter the allocation of the burden of proof. In other words, to say that the international tribunal must presume the regularity of the activity of the state is to say that it is incumbent upon the state claiming reparation to prove the illegal act from which responsibility would result); Witenberg, *La Theorie des Preuves*, above n 10 at 46–7.

[129] *The Corfu Channel* (Merits), above n 57 at 18.

cannot be presumed.[130] Other examples cited refer to rules of substantive law, such as that good faith is a general principle which must be presumed.[131]

It is worth noting at this point that the existence and impact of the alleged presumption of good faith was considered by the panel and the Appellate Body in *Canada—Continued Suspension*.[132] In that case, the panel derived from the general principle of good faith a presumption according to which 'every party to an international agreement must be presumed to be performing its obligations under the agreement in good faith'.[133] The panel also found that such presumption can be equated with a presumption of good faith compliance with treaty obligations.[134] The panel then applied that presumption in the context of Article 22.8 of the DSU[135] to allocate to the defendant the burden of proof on the issue of whether the complainant, the European Communities, had removed the measure which had been found to be inconsistent with the WTO agreements in *EC—Hormones*.[136] In short, the panel did give the presumption of 'good faith compliance' the effect of a rebuttable presumption. The panel's interpretation was, however, reversed on appeal. According to the Appellate Body, the 'presumption of good faith attaches to the actor, but not to the action itself'.[137] Therefore, the Appellate Body concluded that while the European Communities should be presumed to have acted in good faith when adopting the implementing measure, it does not follow that the measure it adopted should be presumed to have achieved compliance. In light of this, the Appellate Body's interpretation of the presumption of good faith means that the presumption has no evidentiary value in WTO law since the question of whether a complainant has acted in good faith is unlikely to arise in WTO dispute settlement.

There are yet other rules of international law which are expressed in the language of presumptions, but which do not relate to the process of fact-finding. This is, for instance, the case of the presumption referred to in Article 33.3 of the Vienna Convention on the Law of Treaties which relates to interpretation of treaties and provides that '[t]he terms of the treaty are presumed to have the

[130] These examples are mentioned in Amerasinghe, above n 52 at 214–16; Kazazi, above n 10 at 246–8; Cheng, above n 21 at 305–6.

[131] See Amerasinghe, above n 52 at 214; Kazazi, above n 10 at 248–9; Cheng, above n 21 at 305.

[132] The issue was also considered in the parallel case *US—Continued Suspension*. See Appellate Body Report, *United States—Continued Suspension of Obligations in the EC—Hormones Dispute*, WT/DS320/AB/R, adopted 14 November 2008; Panel Report, *United States—Continued Suspension of Obligations in the EC—Hormones Dispute*, WT/DS320/R, adopted 14 November 2008.

[133] Panel Report, *Canada—Continued Suspension of Obligations in the EC—Hormones Dispute*, WT/DS321/R, adopted 14 November 2008 at para 7.317.

[134] Panel Report, *Canada—Continued Suspension*, above n 133 at paras 7.320–7.321.

[135] Pursuant to Article 22.8 of the DSU: 'The suspension of concessions or other obligations shall be temporary and shall only be applied until such time as the measure found to be inconsistent with a covered agreement has been removed [...]'.

[136] Panel Report, *Canada—Continued Suspension*, above n 133 at para 7.369.

[137] Appellate Body Report, *Canada—Continued Suspension of Obligations in the EC—Hormones Dispute*, WT/DS321/AB/R, adopted 14 November 2008 at para 315.

same meaning in each authentic text'. Another example is the presumption in favour of sovereignty. Such presumption, if it in fact exists, plays a role in defining the scope of the substantive rules of international law.[138]

Finally, it should be noted that commentators are often not able to ascertain whether international courts and tribunals use the word 'presumption' to refer to a presumption of law or a presumption of fact.[139]

A more interesting question in the context of treaty law, including the WTO agreements, is whether, in the absence of an express reference to that effect, a presumption of law is rebuttable or irrebuttable. When the provisions in question are drafted in the language of presumptions, but they function as a definition, it is clear that they are irrebuttable. This is the case, for instance, of Articles 1.1 and 2.3 of the SCM Agreement which, respectively, define a subsidy and the concept of specificity.[140] Not all cases, however, are as clear-cut. In light of the fact that irrebuttable presumptions are rules of substantive law[141] which function in a similar fashion as strict liability rules, adjudicators should be careful not to declare easily that a presumption is irrebuttable. They must determine whether there are policy considerations warranting the creation of such rules of substantive law.

Interestingly, there has been debate over the question of whether the presumption of nullification and impairment contained in Article 3.8 of the DSU is irrebuttable even though Article 3.8 expressly provides that the presumption *is rebuttable*.[142] Roessler argues that the presumption should be irrebuttable because allowing the opponent to rebut the presumption 'would lead to a denial

[138] See Brownlie, above n 12 at 288–9. Brownlie explains that the question to which this presumption refers is that of 'whether, in case of doubt as to the mode of application of rules or in case of an absence of rules, the presumption is that states have legal competence or is one of incompetence'. This was the question before the Permanent Court of International Justice in the *Lotus* case where the court stated that 'restrictions upon the independence of States cannot be presumed'. As mentioned above, several authors refer to this as a presumption related to fact-finding. This, however, was not the context in which the PCIJ stated the presumption. *The Case of the S.S. 'Lotus' (France v Turkey)*, Judgment of 7 September 1927, Permanent Court of International Justice, Series A, No 10 (1927) at 18.

[139] Kazazi and Amerasinghe recognize this problem in their studies. Amerasinghe, above n 52 at 214; Kazazi, above n 10 at 260.

[140] Article 1.1 provides that '[f]or the purposes of this Agreement, a subsidy *shall be deemed* to exist if: . . .'. Article 2.3 provides that '[a]ny subsidy falling under the provisions of Article 3 *shall be deemed* to be specific'; [emphasis added]. Other provisions that function as definitions include footnote 1 to the DSU; footnote 11 to the Anti-Dumping Agreement; footnote 1 to the TRIPS Agreement; footnote 1 to the TBT Agreement; footnote 6 to the SPS Agreement; Articles 15.4 and 15.5 of the Customs Valuation Agreement.

[141] They do not work as means of proof; rather they establish the scope of a rule.

[142] Article 3.8 provides: 'In cases where there is an infringement of the obligations assumed under a covered agreement, the action is considered *prima facie* to constitute a case of nullification or impairment. This means that there is normally a presumption that a breach of the rules has an adverse impact on other Members parties to that covered agreement, and in such cases, it shall be up to the Member against whom the complaint has been brought to rebut the charge.'

of rights'.[143] Furthermore, according to him, '[i]n a multilateral trade order that prescribes conditions of competition and therefore does not guarantee trade results but trade opportunities, the application of the concept of nullification and impairment to violation cases cannot fulfil a useful function'.[144]

Panels and the Appellate Body have noted that the presumption is rebuttable, yet they have never found that the presumption was successfully rebutted nor have they provided much guidance as to the kind of evidence that a party could adduce in order to rebut the presumption.[145] They have, however, stated what would not be suitable. For instance, in *Guatemala—Cement II*, the panel rejected Guatemala's contention that violation of the requirement contained in Article 5.5 of the Anti-Dumping Agreement—that an investigating authority notify the exporting country before an anti-dumping investigation is initiated—had not impaired Mexico's defence because Guatemala had granted the Mexican exporter an extension to respond to the questionnaire and it had not effectively initiated the investigation until Mexico had been notified. In examining the question, the panel simply restated its finding that Guatemala had not notified Mexico according to the requirements of Article 5.5, and noted that the extension of time to respond to the questionnaire had no bearing on the fact that Mexico had not been timely notified. Finally, in the panel's view, while there was a possibility that the investigation would have proceeded in the same manner had Mexico been timely notified, it was not for the panel to speculate on what would have happened had Mexico received a timely notification.[146] In *EC—Bananas III*, the panel and Appellate Body ruled that demonstration that a measure has no, or insignificant, effects on the volume of exports is not sufficient

[143] Frieder Roessler, 'The Concept of Nullification and Impairment in the Legal System of the World Trade Organization' in E -U Petersmann (ed), *International Trade Law and the GATT/WTO Dispute Settlement System* (London: Kluwer Law International, 1997) 123 at 142.

[144] Roessler, above n 143 at 141. In support of this view, he also notes that the GATS and the SCM Agreement have abandoned the notion of a rebuttable presumption of nullification or impairment. Ibid at 130.

[145] See Appellate Body Report, *European Communities—Regime for the Importation, Sale and Distribution of Bananas— Recourse to Article 21.5 of the DSU by the United States*, WT/DS27/AB/RW/USA and Corr.1, adopted 22 December 2008 at paras 469-476; *Appellate Body Report, European Communities—Export Subsidies on Sugar*, WT/DS265/AB/R, WT/DS266/AB/R, WT/DS283/AB/R, adopted 19 May 2005 at paras 293–9; Panel Report, *Argentina—Definitive Anti-Dumping Measures on Imports of Ceramic Floor Tiles from Italy*, WT/DS189/R, adopted 5 November 2001, DSR 2001:XII, 6241 at paras 6.105, 6.130; Panel Report, *Guatemala—Definitive Anti-Dumping Measures on Grey Portland Cement from Mexico*, WT/DS156/R, adopted 17 November 2000, DSR 2000:XI, 5295 at paras 6.105–6.111; Appellate Body Report, *European Communities—Regime for the Importation, Sale and Distribution of Bananas*, WT/DS27/AB/R, adopted 25 September 1997, DSR 1997:II, 591 at paras 249–53. See also Panel Report, *United States—Taxes on Petroleum and Certain Imported Substances ('US—Superfund')*, adopted 17 June 1987, BISD 34S/136 at paras 5.1.6–5.1.10; Panel Report, *Panel on Japanese Measures on Imports of Leather ('Japan—Leather II (US)')*, adopted 15 May 1984, BISD 31S/94 at 48–56.

[146] Panel Report, *Guatemala—Cement II*, above n 145 at paras 6.109, 6.111.

to rebut the presumption of nullification or impairment.[147] The panel in *Turkey—Textiles* found that it was not sufficient for the defendant to demonstrate that exports had increased; rather, the question was 'whether exports ha[d] been what they would otherwise have been, were there no WTO incompatible quantitative restrictions against imports from India'.[148] The panel also noted that the fact that India had not fully utilized its quotas did not rebut the presumption because quantitative restrictions 'lead to increased transaction costs and [. . .] create uncertainties which could affect [trade]'.[149]

Along the lines of the position advocated by Roessler, these decisions suggest that panels have focused on whether complaining parties have been guaranteed 'opportunities', namely, competitive opportunities and in the case of *Guatemala—Cement II* an opportunity to intervene in an anti-dumping investigation in a timely manner. In determining whether opportunities are provided, the focus has not been on what happened or is happening, but on what would happen if there were no violations of the agreements. This type of analysis naturally involves speculation about alternative scenarios, which analysis panels do not seem ready to undertake. Therefore, even though the presumption of nullification and impairment contained in Article 3.8 of the DSU is not *legally* irrebuttable, it is possible to conclude that it is *in fact* irrebuttable.[150] This result is not surprising or absurd since a violation of the agreements is in itself a strong basis to give rise to responsibility.

The WTO Agreements contain other rebuttable presumptions such as Article 2.5 of the TBT Agreement, Article 3.2 of the SPS Agreement,[151] and the now

[147] Appellate Body Report, *EC—Bananas III*, above n 145 at paras 252–3; Panel Report, *European Communities—Regime for the Importation, Sale and Distribution of Bananas, Complaint by Ecuador*, WT/DS27/R/ECU, adopted 25 September 1997 at para 7.398. Similarly, see Panel Report, *United States—Taxes on Petroleum and Certain Imported Substances* ('*US—Superfund*'), adopted 17 June 1987, BISD 34S/136 at para 5.1.9.

[148] Panel Report, *Turkey—Textile and Clothing Products*, WT/DS34/R, adopted 19 November 1999, DSR 1999:VI, 2363 at para 9.204.

[149] Panel Report, *Turkey—Textiles*, above n 148 at para 9.205. Similarly, see Panel Report, *Panel on Japanese Measures on Imports of Leather* ('*Japan—Leather II (US)*'), adopted 15 May 1984, BISD 31S/94 at 55.

[150] Gazzini adopts the view that the presumption in Article 3.8 of the DSU is rebuttable. He argues that the fact that the presumption 'has never been rebutted demonstrates that Members have judiciously resorted to the DSU, as required by Article 3(7) [of the DSU]'. Tarcisio Gazzini, 'The Legal Nature of WTO Obligations and the Consequences of their Violation' (2006) 17:4 The European Journal of International Law 723 at 733.

[151] In *EC—Hormones*, the Appellate Body noted that the presumption in Article 3.2 of the SPS Agreement is rebuttable. According to the Appellate Body, if a Member promulgates an SPS measure that conforms to an international standard such measure 'enjoys the benefit of a presumption (albeit a rebuttable one) that it is consistent with the relevant provisions of the SPS Agreement and of the GATT 1994';. Appellate Body Report, *European Communities—Measures Concerning Meat and Meat Products (Hormones)*, WT/DS26/AB/R, WT/DS48/AB/R, adopted 13 February 1998, DSR 1998:I, 135 at para 170.

expired Article 6.1 of the SCM Agreement.[152] Article 6.1 of the SCM Agreement established four situations under which serious prejudice to the interests of another member was presumed to exist. If a member succeeded in proving, for instance, that the total ad valorem subsidization of a product exceeded 5 per cent, serious prejudice would be found, unless, as provided in Article 6.2, the defendant succeeded in demonstrating that the subsidy in question had not resulted in any of the effects listed in Article 6.3, for example, that the subsidy did not displace or impede imports into its market. This provision was created during the Uruguay Round at a time when there was a sentiment that the serious prejudice provisions were hard to enforce in practice and did not result in credible disciplining.[153] In other words, there was a perceived difficulty in demonstrating serious prejudice, which in turn resulted in little incentive to comply with the disciplines. Accordingly, the presumption in Article 6.1 embodies more than a natural inference; it reflects a desire to respond to difficulties in demonstrating serious prejudice and to increase the efficacy of the disciplines—in other words, increase deterrence.

As will be discussed in the next chapter, panels and the Appellate Body have frequently used the term 'presumption' in a sense which does not correspond to any of the meanings ascribed to this word above. They have stated that the party bearing the burden of proof must present arguments and evidence sufficient to establish a presumption that the challenged measure is inconsistent with a provision of the WTO agreements. If a presumption of inconsistency is established it is then up to the responding party to bring arguments and evidence to rebut the presumption. Panels and the Appellate Body have used the language of presumptions to describe the process of evaluation of evidence. As argued in the next chapter, reference to presumptions in this context has confused and obscured the process of fact-finding and, therefore, should be avoided.

Concluding Remarks

This chapter reviewed the concepts of burden of proof, standard of proof, and presumption, and demonstrated that the concepts may have different meanings

[152] According to Article 31 of the SCM Agreement, Article 6.1 'shall apply for a period of five years, beginning with the date of entry into force of the WTO Agreement. Not later than 180 days before the end of this period, the Committee shall review the operation of those provisions, with a view to determining whether to extend their application, either as presently drafted or in a modified form, for a further period.' The Committee on Subsidies and Countervailing Measures held a special meeting on 20 December 1999 to conclude the review under Article 31. At that meeting, no consensus was reached by the Committee to extend Article 6.1. Accordingly, the provisions of that Article expired at the end of 1999. See Minutes of the Special Meeting Held on 20 December 1999, WTO Doc G/SCM/M/22, 17 December 2000.

[153] See Terence P Stewart (ed), *The GATT Uruguay Round: a Negotiating History (1986–1992)* (Deventer: Kluwer Law and Taxation Publishers, 1993) vol I at 893–4.

throughout different legal systems—and in some cases even within the same legal system. It was also pointed out that those concepts have the ability to influence the outcome of a dispute. For instance, a case may be decided differently depending on whether the adjudicator can find '*A*' based on evidence which suggests that '*A*' might be true, or whether the adjudicator can find '*A*' only if the evidence leaves no doubt that '*A*' is true. Hence, because those concepts are at the basis of the process of proof, it is important that they be clearly defined so that the operators of the WTO dispute settlement system understand what is expected of them at the different stages of the proceedings. Having a clear understanding of those concepts is also important at the pre-dispute settlement stage when the parties are assessing the strength of their cases. In other words, the parties' understanding of what their obligations in terms of proof will be during the proceedings is likely to influence their decision on whether to pursue dispute settlement under the DSU.

This chapter explained the meaning of the concepts of burden of proof, standard of proof, and presumption in the common law, civil law, and international law, and noted how the concepts are used in this study. The next two chapters conduct an in-depth analysis of how the concepts are employed in the WTO dispute settlement system as well as how they ought to be used in order to optimize the process of proof.

3

Functioning of the Burden of Proof

Introduction

The previous chapter introduced some basic concepts related to the process of fact-finding and briefly outlined how those concepts are applied in international dispute settlement proceedings including WTO dispute settlement. This chapter examines in more detail how panels and the Appellate Body manage the concept of the burden of proof and determine when the burden of proof has been discharged. In other words, the main issue discussed in this chapter regards the functioning of the burden of proof in WTO dispute settlement. This chapter also discusses the related question of the degree of persuasion that panels must reach in order to determine that the burden of proof has been discharged, that is, it addresses the question of the standard of proof. The chapter not only discusses the state of WTO law on these issues, but also makes suggestions for improving the treatment of these questions in future cases.

This chapter revolves around the problem posed by a series of statements made by panels and the Appellate Body regarding the functioning of the burden of proof. It is contended that although these statements are similar, a careful reading reveals substantial differences which may lead to dramatically different factual determinations. Whether the differences are intended or accidental is a question impossible to answer. This chapter is developed on the basis of the reasonable assumption that variations in the wording of those statements will lead at least some to believe that those variations reflect *differences in the meaning* of those statements.

The following exemplify the variations mentioned. In *India—Patents,* the panel found that the European Communities, the complainant, had 'established a *prima facie* case of violation with respect to Article 70.8(a) [of the TRIPS Agreement]' and that, therefore, 'the *onus* [*had shifted*] to India to bring forward evidence and arguments to *disprove* the claim by the EC'.[1] In *US—Wool Shirts and Blouses,* the Appellate Body stated that if the party bearing the burden of

[1] Panel Report, *India—Patent Protection for Pharmaceutical and Agricultural Chemical Products, Complaint by the European Communities*, WT/DS79/R, adopted 22 September 1998, DSR 1998: VI, 2661 at para 7.42 [emphasis added].

proof 'adduces evidence sufficient to raise a presumption that what is claimed is true, the *burden then shifts* to the other party, who will fail unless it adduces sufficient evidence to *rebut the presumption*'.[2] The panel in *US—Section 301 Trade Act* noted that it is for the complaining party 'to present arguments and evidence sufficient to establish a *prima facie* case in respect of the various elements of its claims' and that '[o]nce the [complainant] has done so, it is for the [defendant] to rebut that *prima facie* case'.[3] However, in the panel's view, when both parties submit evidence with respect to a certain claim, the panel's task is 'to balance all evidence on the record and decide whether [the party bearing the burden of proof] has convinced [the panel] of the validity of its claims. In case of uncertainty, i.e., in case all the evidence and arguments remain in equipoise, [the panel must] give the benefit of the doubt to the [...] defending party'.[4] Finally, in *Korea—Dairy*, the panel stated that '[a]s a matter of law the burden of proof rests with the [complainant], and does not shift during the panel process. As a matter of process before the Panel, the [complainant] will submit its arguments and evidence and [the defendant] will respond to rebut the [complainant's] claims. At the end of this process, it is for the Panel to weigh and assess the evidence and arguments submitted by both parties in order to reach conclusions as to whether the [complainant's] claims are well-founded.'[5]

India—Patents and *US—Wool Shirts and Blouses* use the words *prima facie* and presumption in a similar fashion, referring to the shifting of the burden of proof to the defendant after the complainant establishes a presumption or *prima facie* case.[6] The language of *India—Patents* suggests that the panel was referring to a 'real' shift of the burden of proof. If this is the case, the *prima facie* case is in fact the standard of proof that the complainant must meet in order to discharge the burden of proof. After the complainant has successfully discharged the burden of proof according to that standard of proof, the burden is placed on the defendant, who now seems to have the much more difficult task of disproving the proposition advanced by the complainant—while the complainant seems to be able to rely upon evidence that is further down the inferential chain connecting the evidence to the proposition advanced, the defendant must present evidence that directly shows that the complainant's theory cannot be true.

US—Section 301 Trade Act, in contrast, suggests that the *prima facie* case requirement is a threshold question much like the requirement in force in some

[2] Appellate Body Report, *United States—Measure Affecting Imports of Woven Wool Shirts and Blouses from India*, WT/DS33/AB/R and Corr.1, adopted 23 May 1997, DSR 1997:I, 323 at 14 [emphasis added].

[3] Panel Report, *United States—Sections 301–310 of the Trade Act of 1974*, WT/DS152/R, adopted 27 January 2000, DSR 2000:II, 815 at para 7.14.

[4] Panel Report, *US—Section 301 Trade Act*, above n 3 at para 7.14.

[5] Panel Report, *Korea—Definitive Safeguard Measure on Imports of Certain Dairy Products*, WT/DS98/R and Corr.1, adopted 12 January 2000, at para 7.24.

[6] The expressions '*prima facie* case' and 'presumption' as used by panels and the Appellate Body in the present context are interchangeable. The expressions '*prima facie* case' and '*prima facie* evidence' have also been used interchangeably.

civil law jurisdictions that the complainant attach or indicate in its first submission the evidence that it will produce during the oral hearing at the risk of having the case dismissed at the outset by the adjudicator—or much like a court in a common law jurisdiction would determine that the complainant has satisfied its burden of going forward, if we were to assume that motions to test the sufficiency of the evidence are available in WTO dispute settlement. After the panel establishes that the complainant has produced some evidence in support of its allegations, the *prima facie* case standard becomes irrelevant; the panel must then weigh all the evidence and decide whether there is enough evidence in support of the claim in order to meet the specified standard of proof.

Finally, *Korea—Dairy* seems to stand for the proposition that panels should weigh all the evidence before them and decide whether that evidence reaches the degree of certainty required by a specified standard of proof; statements that a complainant must present a *prima facie* case which must then be rebutted by the defendant merely describe the dynamics of the process of fact-finding before the panel, that is, they have no meaning as a matter of law.

Sections I and II of this chapter analyse in further detail these different possibilities and discuss the advantages and disadvantages of each of them. Section III examines the question of the appropriate standard of proof for WTO dispute settlement. It is important to keep in mind, as discussed in the previous chapters, that the overall structure of international proceedings including WTO proceedings is more similar to the structure of civil proceedings in civil law jurisdictions than common law jurisdictions. Important features of those proceedings are that although they have an adversarial component, the adjudicator has certain fact-finding powers and the parties have a duty to cooperate throughout the proceedings to establish the facts.

I. The '*Prima Facie* Case' or 'Presumption' Approach

A. Exploring the meaning of '*prima facie* case'

Panels and the Appellate Body have frequently referred to the concept of a *prima facie* case. They have not, however, provided a clear definition of this concept. In *EC—Hormones,* the Appellate Body defined a *prima facie* case as 'one which, in the absence of effective refutation by the defending party, requires a panel, as a matter of law, to rule in favour of the complaining party presenting the *prima facie* case'.[7] This attempt at defining a *prima facie* case is at best incomplete, in that the Appellate Body did not establish what the degree of persuasion is that would require the panel to rule in favour of the complaining party. Panels and

[7] Appellate Body Report, *European Communities—Measures Concerning Meat and Meat Products (Hormones),* WT/DS26/AB/R, WT/DS48/AB/R, adopted 13 February 1998, DSR 1998:I, 135 at para 104.

the Appellate Body have also stated in several cases that 'precisely how much and precisely what kind of evidence will be required to establish [...] a presumption [or *prima facie* case] will vary from measure to measure, provision to provision, and case to case'.[8] Again, this statement does not provide any guidance as to what constitutes a *prima facie* case. Merely stating that what constitutes a *prima facie* case varies in each specific case according to the provisions and, more importantly, the measure at issue, says nothing about what a *prima facie* case is. In other words, the only guidance this statement provides is that panels and the Appellate Body will recognize a *prima facie* case when they see one.

While it is true that it is not possible for panels to make a general statement on the type of evidence that would in every circumstance meet the requirements of a *prima facie* case, it is nonetheless possible to define in terms of degree of proof the standard of persuasion required to establish a *prima facie* case. In this regard, the literal meaning of the expression '*prima facie*' is 'at first sight; from a first impression'.[9] This would suggest that the *prima facie* case standard would be a low standard of proof, namely, a low degree of certainty involving a mere *possibility* that a proposition is true would satisfy this standard.[10] This hypothesis would be in line with the use of the expression '*prima facie* case' in international law in the context of requests for provisional measures and preliminary challenges to the jurisdiction of an international court or tribunal.[11] In both situations, all the moving party is required to show is that there is a possibility that its case is meritorious. This is so because the court or tribunal must decide whether to grant provisional measures or whether it has jurisdiction before it has heard all the evidence.

The idea of a *prima facie* case was introduced for the first time in the WTO jurisprudence in *US—Wool Shirts and Blouses* and the United States, a common

[8] Appellate Body Report, *US—Wool Shirts and Blouses,* above n 2 at 14. See also Appellate Body Report, *European Communities—Selected Customs Matters*, WT/DS315/AB/R, adopted 11 December 2006 at para 266; Appellate Body Report, *European Communities—Trade Description of Sardines*, WT/DS231/AB/R, adopted 23 October 2002 at para 270; Panel Report, *United States—Measures Affecting the Cross-Border Supply of Gambling and Betting Services*, WT/DS285/R, adopted 20 April 2005 at para 6.12.

[9] *The New Shorter Oxford English Dictionary* (Oxford: Clarendon Press, 1993) vol 2 at 2352.

[10] See, for example, James Cameron & Stephen J Orava, 'GATT/WTO Panels between Recording and Finding Facts: Issues of Due Process, Evidence, Burden of Proof, and Standard of Review in GATT/WTO Dispute Settlement' in F Weiss (ed), *Improving WTO Dispute Settlement Procedures: Issues and Lessons from the Practice of Other International Courts and Tribunals* (London: Cameron May, 2000) 195 at 236 (arguing that the 'standard for presenting a *prima facie* case is, under virtually any definition, relatively low'); Theofanis Christoforou, 'WTO Panels in the Face of Scientific Uncertainty' in F Weiss (ed), *Improving WTO Dispute Settlement Procedures: Issues and Lessons from the Practice of Other International Courts and Tribunals* (London: Cameron May, 2000) 243 at footnote 29 (noting that in any dispute settlement system the complainant is required to 'provide complete proof—not only *prima facie* evidence'); Chester Brown, *A Common Law of International Adjudication* (Oxford: Oxford University Press, 2007) at 98 (noting that *prima facie* evidence 'is the lowest degree of proof').

[11] Audley Sheppard, 'The Jurisdictional Threshold of a Prima Facie Case' in P Muchlinski, F Ortino & C Schreuer (eds), *The Oxford Handbook of International Investment Law* (Oxford: Oxford University Press, 2008) 932; Christoforou, above n 10 at footnote 29; Brown, above n 10 at 99.

law jurisdiction, was the first member to refer to the *prima facie* case in its submissions.[12] The expression '*prima facie* case' is frequently employed in common law jurisdictions, where it has been equally problematic because common law courts have not been consistent regarding the meaning of the expression.[13] It has been given at least two meanings.[14] The first is related to the concept of the burden of going forward; a *prima facie* case is the degree of proof required to satisfy the burden of going forward, that is, to withstand a motion to exclude a claim from the proceedings for failure to present sufficient evidence in support. This definition of a *prima facie* case is in line with the idea that *prima facie* is evidence which at first sight seems plausible. The other meaning equates *prima facie* with a presumption which entitles the plaintiff to prevail on its cause of action if its opponent does not contradict the evidence presented by the plaintiff.[15] The latter effect of a *prima facie* case may be prescribed by a statutory provision establishing a presumption[16]—similarly in the WTO context to Article 3.8 of the DSU discussed in the previous chapter—but this has not always been the case. The first definition rejects the notion of a *prima facie* case as a mandatory presumption in that the trier of fact is not bound to rule in favour of the party who satisfies the burden of going forward even if its opponent does not produce any evidence. In contrast, the second definition equates the notion of a *prima facie* case with a presumption in that the trier of fact must rule in favour of the party that makes a *prima facie* case in the event that the opposing party does not produce any evidence.[17] The first is the older and more frequently used of the two meanings. The fact that the *prima facie* case has been ascribed such contradictory meanings has generated confusion and prompted scholars to recommend that the expression be clarified.[18]

[12] Joost Pauwelyn, 'Evidence, Proof and Persuasion in WTO Dispute Settlement: Who Bears the Burden?' (1998) 1 Journal of International Economic Law 227 at 242–4, 246.

[13] Georg Nils Herlitz, 'The Meaning of the Term "Prima Facie"' (1991) 55 Louisiana Law Review 391 at 394. See also John Sopinka, Sidney N Lederman & Alan W Bryant, *The Law of Evidence in Canada* (2nd edn, Toronto: Butterworths, 1999) at 67–70.

[14] The United States Supreme Court made reference to the two meanings of a *prima facie* case in *Texas Department of Community Affairs v Burdine*, 450 US 248 (1981) at footnote 7.

The expression *prima facie* case may also be informally used to refer to the elements of a claim. In this regard, a judge may ask the plaintiff what the plaintiff's *prima facie case* is, by which the 'judge is asking either for an enumeration of the elements of the plaintiff's claim (or cause of action) or for a short description of the evidence as to each of those elements'. Stephen N Subrin et al, *Civil Procedure: Doctrine, Practice, and Context* (2nd edn, New York: Aspen, 2004) at 168.

[15] Herlitz above n 13 at 394. Herlitz notes that the second definition of a *prima facie* case has been credited to a mistake in the reporting of an English case of 1841. Ibid at 398.

[16] Sopinka, Lederman & Bryant (1999), above n 13 at 70. See also Clifford S Fishman, *Jones on Evidence: Civil and Criminal* (7th edn, Rochester: Lawyers Cooperative Publishing, 1992) at 307.

[17] Herlitz, above n 13 at 397.

[18] Herlitz, above n 13 at 408. Herlitz recommends that the state of Louisiana adopt the view that a *prima facie* case creates a permissive inference only. See also Sopinka, Lederman & Bryant (1999), above n 13 at 70 (they argue that the 'better view is that a *prima facie* case does not compel a specific determination unless there is a specific rule of law establishing a presumption which demands such a conclusion').

The problematic nature of the concept of a *prima facie* case in the common law as well as the fact that proceedings before international tribunals differ in many ways from proceedings before ordinary common law courts—eg the notion of the burden of going forward is foreign to international procedure—suggest that a comprehensive study of the common law case law on the notion of a *prima facie* case would be of little value in assessing the appropriateness of references to that notion in WTO dispute settlement. Hence, the following sections of this chapter will focus exclusively on the WTO jurisprudence. However, the discussion that ensues does provide further reasons for why transplanting the common law meanings of a *prima facie* case to the WTO dispute settlement system would be undesirable.

B. The uses of a '*prima facie* case' in WTO dispute settlement

This section is structured around the idea that panels and the Appellate Body have used the expression *prima facie* case in two different ways.

Sometimes a *prima facie* case seems to function as a standard of proof. As noted above, this seems to be the case if we assume that panels shift the burden of proof in the 'real' sense. In this type of situation, a *prima facie* case is the standard of proof which the complainant must meet before the burden of proof is transferred to the defendant, who then needs to demonstrate that the proposition advanced by the complainant is not true. A *prima facie* case can also function as a *final* standard of proof, that is, assuming that there is no 'real' shift of the burden of proof and that the panel focuses on balancing the evidence presented by both sides, the panel would find in favour of the complainant if it were to determine that the evidence before it reaches the degree of certainty required by the *prima facie* case standard—which degree of certainty is lower than that required by the preponderance of the evidence standard. The preponderance of the evidence standard requires the evidence to lead to the conclusion that the proposition advanced by the claimant is more likely than not to be true. Although there is no clear definition of the *prima facie* standard, it would seem that a mere possibility that the claimant's claim may be true is enough to satisfy that standard.

In other situations, the expression *prima facie* case seems to be used to refer to a threshold requirement which must be met in order for the proceedings to continue or for the panel to begin an examination of all the evidence before it. These two options are discussed in more detail below.

1. Threshold question

1.1. Is the '*prima facie* case' a threshold question?

As previously noted, some panels have suggested that the requirement for the complainant to present a *prima facie* case is a threshold question. In other words, the panel must first determine whether the complainant has presented a *prima facie* case; if the panel finds that that is the case, it can then proceed to determine on the basis of all the evidence before it whether the challenged measure is inconsistent with the WTO agreements. For example, in *US—Section 211 Appropriations Act*, the panel stated that it is for the complainant 'to submit arguments and evidence sufficient to raise a presumption' that the measures challenged are inconsistent with the WTO obligations; once the complainant does so, 'the Panel's task becomes a matter of weighing the arguments and evidence available to it to determine whether, on balance, the Panel is convinced that' the challenged measures are inconsistent with the provisions invoked.[19]

Korea—Alcoholic Beverages provides another good example. One of the issues before the panel in *Korea—Alcoholic Beverages* was whether in Korea domestic and imported alcoholic beverages were directly competitive or substitutable. The panel dismissed outright those claims regarding products for which the complainants had presented no evidence in support of their assertions. The panel noted that it could 'only make determinations with respect to the products specifically discussed by the complainants'—which included vodka, whiskies, rum, gin, brandies, cognac, liqueurs, tequila and admixtures; as regards the remainder of the products under HS 2208, the panel ruled that the complainants had 'not carried their burden of establishing a *prima facie* case'.[20] The panel then proceeded to determine whether the products for which the complainants had submitted evidence were in a directly competitive relationship with Korean soju.

A similar situation arose in *US—Upland Cotton* where the panel noted that the complainant, Brazil, had not submitted any direct evidence—not even a direct quotation from the challenged Act—with respect to its claim that the FSC Repeal and Extraterritorial Income Act of 2000 (the 'ETI Act of 2000') was inconsistent with Articles 8 and 10.1 of the Agreement on Agriculture and Articles 3.1(a) and 3.2 of the SCM Agreement. Because the facts and arguments necessary to make out the claim before the panel were entirely missing, the panel found that Brazil failed to make a *prima facie* case of inconsistency with the Agreements.[21] Therefore, the panel declined to examine the ETI Act of 2000 with a view to determining whether it was inconsistent with the agreements.

[19] Panel Report, *United States—Section 211 Omnibus Appropriations Act of 1998*, WT/DS176/R, adopted 1 February 2002 at para 8.19. Similarly, see Panel Report, *US—Section 301 Trade Act*, above n 3 at para 7.14 (described in the introduction of this chapter); Panel Report, *Argentina—Measures Affecting the Export of Bovine Hides and Import of Finished Leather*, WT/DS155/R and Corr.1, adopted 16 February 2001, DSR 2001:V, 1779 at paras 11.12–11.13.

[20] Panel Report, *Korea—Taxes on Alcoholic Beverages*, WT/DS75/R, WT/DS84/R, adopted 17 February 1999 at para 10.57.

[21] Panel Report, *United States—Subsidies on Upland Cotton*, WT/DS267/R, and Corr.1, adopted 21 March 2005 at paras 7.959, 7.974, 7.986. In a similar vein, see Panel Report, *India—Measures Affecting the Automotive Sector*, WT/DS146/R, WT/DS175/R and Corr.1, adopted 5 April 2002 at para 7.294; Panel Report, *US—Gambling*, above n 8 at para 6.217 (but compare with paragraphs 6.383, 6.398, 6.402, 6.406 where the panel seems to use *prima facie* as the final standard of proof).

Along these lines, in *US—Gambling*, the Appellate Body found that the panel had 'erred in examining whether [. . .] eight state laws were consistent with the United States' obligations under Article XVI of the GATS', [22] because the complainant, Antigua, had not provided evidence and argument demonstrating how those eight state laws operated and violated Article XVI of the GATS.[23] In other words, the Appellate Body found that Antigua had not established a *prima facie* case with respect to the eight state laws and, therefore, the panel should not have proceeded to examine whether those laws were inconsistent with Article XVI of the GATS.[24] In contrast, the Appellate Body found that Antigua had established a *prima facie* case of inconsistency of three federal laws with Article XVI, and that, therefore, the panel had not erred in examining whether those federal laws were consistent with the United States' obligations under Article XVI of the GATS.[25] In a later section of its report, the Appellate Body then examined whether the three federal laws were indeed inconsistent with Article XVI of the GATS.[26]

Finally, in *EC—Bed Linen (Article 21.5—India)*, the Appellate Body distinguished between a finding that (i) a *prima facie* case that a measure is inconsistent with the WTO agreements has not been established, and (ii) a finding that a measure is not inconsistent with WTO obligations. When examining the question of whether a claim which was rejected in a previous proceeding could be re-litigated in a compliance proceeding under Article 21.5 of the DSU, the Appellate Body stated that defendants should not 'be subject to a second challenge of the measure found not to be inconsistent with WTO obligations, merely because the *complainant failed to establish a prima facie case, as opposed to failing ultimately to persuade the original panel.*'[27] Accordingly, the Appellate Body suggested that the issue of whether a *prima facie* case has been

[22] Appellate Body Report, *United States—Measures Affecting the Cross-Border Supply of Gambling and Betting Services*, WT/DS285/AB/R, adopted 20 April 2005 at para 154.

[23] Antigua had not directly argued that the eight state laws were inconsistent with Article XVI. The panel found references to those laws in exhibits—including government reports, law review articles, and websites—submitted by Antigua. On the basis of these indirect references the panel found that Antigua had presented a *prima facie* case with respect to those laws. See Panel Report, *US—Gambling*, above n 8 at paras 6.224–6.248.

[24] Appellate Body Report, *US—Gambling*, above n 22 at para 151.

[25] Appellate Body Report, *US—Gambling*, above n 22 at paras 153–4.

[26] Interestingly, the evidence and arguments regarding the inconsistency of the three federal laws with Article XVI of the GATS were not well developed either because Antigua's arguments focused on the theory—which was rejected by the panel and the Appellate Body—that the United States had in place a 'total prohibition' on the cross-border supply of gambling and betting services which was in and of itself inconsistent with Article XVI of the GATS.

[27] Appellate Body Report, *European Communities—Anti-Dumping Duties on Imports of Cotton-Type Bed Linen from India—Recourse to Article 21.5 of the DSU by India*, WT/DS141/AB/RW, adopted 24 April 2003, DSR 2003:III, 965 at para 96. [emphasis added] In the original proceedings, India had not presented arguments in support of its claim; this led the panel to rule that India had failed to present a *prima facie* case. Panel Report, *European Communities—Anti-Dumping Duties on Imports of Cotton-Type Bed Linen from India—Recourse to Article 21.5 of the DSU by India*, WT/DS141/RW, adopted 24 April 2003 at para 6.52.

made is a question which precedes the final question of whether the panel has been persuaded of the truth of the complainant's claim.

Some commentators[28] and WTO Members also share the view that the *prima facie* case is a threshold requirement. For instance, the United States in *US—Underwear* argued that the first step in the panel's analysis should be to determine whether Costa Rica, the complainant, had brought forward factual information and legal arguments substantiating its case.[29] In *US—Gambling*, the United States requested the panel to invite Antigua to make a further submission identifying the specific measures at issue; if Antigua declined to provide further information, the United States requested the panel to make a preliminary ruling finding that all measures which Antigua had listed in the annex to its panel request—which measures were not directly discussed in Antigua's first submission—were excluded from the proceedings.[30] In *Korea—Dairy*, Korea argued that, as a threshold matter, the panel had to make a finding regarding whether the complainant had established a *prima facie* case of violation. Korea argued that the panel had ignored this step and proceeded to weigh all the evidence at the end of the proceedings.[31] In *Canada—Aircraft*, Canada protested the fact that the panel had not ruled on the preliminary issue of whether Brazil, the complainant, had made a *prima facie* case. Canada argued that this made it difficult for Canada to defend itself.[32]

1.2. Problems with the threshold theory

The cases and arguments reviewed above support the view that a *prima facie* case may be interpreted as a threshold requirement which the complainant must satisfy before the panel can examine in detail the claims of inconsistency with the WTO agreements. One of the main problems with this theory is that as a general rule panels have not issued intermediate rulings declaring that a party has not made a *prima facie* case—similarly to what would occur in common law jurisdictions if the complainant failed to meet the burden of going forward[33]—nor have they requested parties who presumably have not made a *prima facie*

[28] See, for example, Cameron & Orava, above n 10 at 235.

[29] Panel Report, *United States—Restrictions on Imports of Cotton and Man-made Fibre Underwear*, WT/DS24/R, adopted 25 February 1997 at para 5.67.

[30] Request for Preliminary Rulings by United States, 17 October 2003, at paras 22–24, found at <http://www.ustr.gov/trade-topics/enforcement/dispute-settlement-proceedings/wto-dispute-settlement> (accessed 3 August 2009).

[31] Appellate Body Report, *Korea—Definitive Safeguard Measure on Imports of Certain Dairy Products*, WT/DS98/AB/R, adopted 12 January 2000, DSR 2000:I, 3 at para 15.

[32] Panel Report, *Canada—Measures Affecting the Export of Civilian Aircraft*, WT/DS70/R, adopted 20 August 1999 at para 9.84.

[33] Taniguchi has also concluded that 'a prima facie case in the WTO is not the same as a *prima facie* case resulting from satisfaction of the burden of production in the common law'. Yasuhei Taniguchi, 'Understanding the Concept of Prima Facie Proof in WTO Dispute Settlement' in ME Janow, V Donaldson & A Yanovich (eds), *The WTO: Governance, Dispute Settlement, and Developing Countries* (Huntington: Juris Publishing, 2008) 553 at 571.

case to amend their submissions—similarly to the practice in many civilian jurisdictions in cases where the complainant fails to attach documents to its submission or to indicate other types of evidence to be produced. In fact, in *Korea—Dairy*, the Appellate Body ruled that panels are not required to rule on the question of whether the complainant has made a *prima facie* case before they proceed to examine all the evidence on the record.[34]

One of the few, if not the only, exceptions to this general pattern is *US—Upland Cotton* where the panel issued a communication during the proceedings indicating that 'on the basis of the evidence and arguments presented [up until that moment the panel was] unable to form any view on whether the ETI Act of 2000 satisfie[d] the relevant provisions of the Agreement on Agriculture'. That communication provided Brazil an opportunity to redress deficiencies in its case.[35] The panel, however, chose not to indicate any specific deficiencies in the case brought by Brazil and although Brazil acknowledged the panel's communication, it did not submit additional evidence.[36] It is also important to note that panels usually ask questions to the parties and by doing so they may indirectly indicate to the parties points where their arguments are not clear or well supported by evidence. Questions, however, may serve a variety of purposes, of which indication of a fundamental deficiency in the arguments and evidence presented by the complainant is only an instance. Among other reasons, panels may ask questions (i) to encourage dialogue between the parties; (ii) to verify whether their understanding of the complainant's claim is correct; and (iii) regarding points which are not directly relevant to the resolution of the dispute, but which would allow panels to have a better understanding of the case before them. Because the parties may not always be able to discern the purpose of a question, this is not the best manner for a panel to indicate to the complainant the existence of a deficiency which if unremedied would result in an

[34] Appellate Body Report, *Korea—Dairy,* above n 31 at paras 144–5. This ruling was referred to in Appellate Body Report, *Thailand—Anti-Dumping Duties on Angles, Shapes and Sections of Iron or Non-Alloy Steel and H-Beams from Poland*, WT/DS122/AB/R, adopted 5 April 2001, DSR 2001: VII, 2701 at para 132; Appellate Body Report, *Chile—Price Band System and Safeguard Measures Relating to Certain Agricultural Products—Recourse to Article 21.5 of the DSU by Argentina,* WT/DS207/AB/RW, adopted 22 May 2007 at para 135. See also Panel Report, *Canada—Aircraft*, above n 32 at para 9.87 ('We note that there is nothing in the DSU that requires a panel to rule on the establishment of a *prima facie* case as a preliminary matter'); Panel Report, *US—Gambling,* above n 8 at Annex B, paras 38–40; Panel Report, *European Communities—Anti-Dumping Duties on Malleable Cast Iron Tube or Pipe Fittings from Brazil,* WT/DS219/R, adopted 18 August 2003 at para 7.10 (where the panel issued a preliminary ruling denying the request of the European Communities that the panel refuse to consider certain 'claims on the basis of their alleged vagueness').

[35] Panel Report, *US—Upland Cotton*, above n 21 at paras 7.980–7.981. Although in a different context, the Appellate Body has also adopted a pro-active attitude. In *US—Countervailing Measures on Certain EC Products*, it invited the United States to further specify the terms of its Notice of Appeal. Appellate Body Report, *United States—Countervailing Measures Concerning Certain Products from the European Communities*, WT/DS212/AB/R, adopted 8 January 2003, DSR 2003:I, 5 at para 55.

[36] Panel Report, *US—Upland Cotton*, above n 21 at para 7.982.

outright rejection of the claim at issue.[37] Moreover, different panels handle questions differently; while some panels are more proactive, others are more passive.

If the *prima facie* case does not function as a prerequisite for the continuation of the proceedings, what is its function? If the panel waits until the final report to issue a decision on whether a *prima facie* case has been made the parties do not have an opportunity to respond to that ruling. In other words, complainants cannot amend their submissions to correct any deficiencies; and defendants will at that point have either incurred additional costs to respond to a poorly presented case or not have presented arguments and evidence in rebuttal—which strategy may have devastating consequences if the panel finally finds that the complainant successfully presented a *prima facie* case. As for the panel, at the stage when it is writing its final report it would be more reasonable for it to weigh all the evidence before it. Otherwise, what should the panel do with evidence on the record that was not voluntarily submitted by the complainant but which clearly suggests that the challenged measure violates the agreements? Should the panel ignore that evidence? What objectives would such a solution advance? This is clearly problematic and perhaps partly explains why panels and the Appellate Body have not completely embraced the conception of a *prima facie* case as a threshold requirement which the complainant must satisfy before the panel can fully examine the related claims of inconsistency with the WTO agreements.

Contradicting the idea of a *prima facie* case as a threshold requirement, the Appellate Body has found in several cases that when determining whether a *prima facie* case has been made, panels may consider not only the evidence submitted by the complainants but also evidence submitted by defendants and other sources including experts.[38] According to the Appellate Body, panels may

[37] For example, in *US—Gambling*, the panel addressed the following question to Antigua: 'Is Antigua and Barbuda challenging: (i) specific *legislative and regulatory provisions* that are claimed to amount to a prohibition on the cross-border supply of gambling and betting services *as such*; and/or (ii) the specific *application* of such provisions; and/or (iii) the US *practice vis-a-vis* the foreign cross-border supply of gambling and betting services? *Please identify all relevant legislative and regulatory provisions*.' Antigua could have interpreted this question as a sign that the panel believed that there was a fundamental deficiency in the presentation of Antigua's case; it could also have understood the question as an attempt by the panel to clarify its understanding of Antigua's challenge. It seems that the latter was the case, since Antigua answered that it was challenging the 'total prohibition' of gambling and betting services offered from outside the United States—which theory the panel rejected in its final report. Antigua did not point to any specific legislative and regulatory provisions nor did it provide further detail on how specific laws and regulations of the United States prohibited the cross-border supply of gambling and betting services. Panel Report, *US—Gambling*, above n 8 at Annex C, Question 10. [emphasis added]

[38] Appellate Body Report, *Canada—Measures Affecting the Export of Civilian Aircraft*, WT/DS70/AB/R, adopted 20 August 1999, DSR 1999:III, 1377 at para 192; Appellate Body Report, *Japan – Measures Affecting the Importation of Apples*, WT/DS245/AB/R, adopted 10 December 2003, DSR 2003:IX, 4391 at para 166; Appellate Body Report, *India—Quantitative Restrictions on Imports of Agricultural, Textile and Industrial Products*, WT/DS90/AB/R, adopted 22 September 1999, DSR 1999:IV, 1763 at para 142. See also Panel Report, *Canada—Aircraft*, above n 32 at

even seek information with a view to determining whether a *prima facie* case has been made.[39] These considerations support the view, which will be explored in the next section, that the *prima facie* case is a final standard of proof. Therefore, unless panels issue an intermediate ruling or clearly communicate to complainants the existence of major deficiencies in the presentation of their claims requiring them to supplement their submissions, the idea of a *prima facie* case as a threshold requirement is not useful.

1.3. Opportunity to remedy major deficiencies

Although the Appellate Body has ruled that panels are not required to issue a preliminary ruling regarding whether the complainant has made a *prima facie* case, it may be in the interests of accuracy, meaningful participation, equality of treatment, and the efficient resolution of disputes to institute a requirement broadly along those lines. In keeping with the international law tradition of encouraging cooperation between the parties and giving adjudicators broad powers to manage the proceedings, ideally such requirement should aim at providing the complainant an opportunity to remedy *major* deficiencies in the presentation of its claims. In this vein, panels should be required to communicate to complainants the existence of major deficiencies in their presentation of arguments and evidence and provide them with an opportunity to remedy those deficiencies. Although panels should do so on their own motion, nothing should impede defendants from bringing perceived deficiencies to the panel's attention. Such solution should be preferred over the creation of an obligation similar to the burden of going forward which would require the panel on the motion of the opponent to make a ruling excluding from the dispute a claim for which the complainant failed to present a *prima facie* case. The possibility of obtaining such a ruling at an early stage of the proceedings would not encourage cooperation; on the contrary, it would encourage opponents to withhold information in the hopes that the panel would exclude the complainant's claim. In this connection, it is worth emphasizing that in a system lacking pre-trial discovery in the common law sense and where the evidence is developed during the proceedings through the interaction of the adjudicator and the parties, cooperation is fundamental to the effective resolution of disputes.[40] The unitary structure of

paras 9.87–9.89; Panel Report, *US—Gambling,* above n 8 at Annex B, paras 38–40 (where the panel denied a US request for a preliminary ruling on the question of whether Antigua had made a *prima facie* case on the grounds that Antigua had 'two sets of written submissions and two panel hearings to convince the Panel that it has established a *prima facie* case').

[39] Appellate Body Report, Canada—Aircraft, above n 38 at para 192.

[40] Cameron and Orava seem to discount the importance of cooperation in the resolution of international disputes. They suggest that the defendant be given an opportunity to request a preliminary ruling on the sufficiency of the complainant's case. Their suggestion mirrors the burden of going forward and is heavily influenced by a strictly adversarial and private conception of dispute settlement. Although they note that their suggestion 'is intended to reach those egregious cases where a party has completely failed to plead its case in a manner that would entitle it to relief,' their

international proceedings, including WTO proceedings, not only contributes to, but is also necessary to foster that cooperation. Moreover, the fact that the same adjudicator decides questions of fact and of law eliminates one—and perhaps the prevailing—reason for the creation of the burden of going forward.

Even in international proceedings, however, equality between the parties and participation must be respected. What is suggested, therefore, is the introduction of a procedure that would ensure that the requirements of equality of treatment and participation are observed and which would ultimately contribute to the effective resolution of the disputes brought before WTO panels. Equality, participation, as well as efficiency, concerns suggest that major deficiencies should be cured as early as possible so that both parties have a meaningful opportunity to respond without delaying the proceedings. Accordingly, panels should examine the complainants' first submission in light of the panel request with a view to determining whether the complainants have presented arguments and evidence that at first sight would support the claims set out in the request. The evidence would not necessarily have to be all attached to the first submission, particularly when it is not in the form of documents or when the evidence is not in the possession of the complainant and the complainant provides an explanation why it has not been produced. Complainants should, however, at that stage at least indicate the evidence which they would like to produce during the proceedings. If the complainants' first submission does not contain arguments and evidence with respect to all the elements of the claims set out in the request for establishment of a panel, the panel should issue a communication to the complainant requesting it either to amend its submission or declare that it renounces the claim. This procedure would also ensure similar treatment of similar problems, namely, (i) the problem of claims that are stated in the panel request but which are not pursued in later submissions,[41] and (ii) the problem of claims that are poorly pursued through conclusory arguments. In other words, it would be clear from the initial stage of the panel proceedings which claims are being pursued by the parties.

invocation of *Korea—Dairy* as an example of such case implies that that is not so. It was clear in *Korea—Dairy* that the European Communities, the complainant, was challenging a specific safeguard measure adopted by Korea. While the first submission of the European Communities focused on evidence presented by Korea to the Committee on Safeguards as opposed to a report produced by the Korean investigating authorities, it can hardly be said that the European Communities had not presented evidence in support of its contentions or that Korea did not know the nature of the case against it. Furthermore, in its later submissions the European Communities did engage in discussions regarding the investigation report. See Cameron & Orava above n 10 at 235–6.

[41] This was the problem before the Appellate Body in *Chile—Price Band System*. In that case, the Appellate Body found that the panel had acted inconsistently with Article 11 of the DSU because the panel ruled on a claim under the second sentence of Article II:1(b) of the GATT which could have been interpreted to be part of the panel request, but which the complainant never made—ie pursued—during the proceedings. Appellate Body Report, *Chile—Price Band System and Safeguard Measures Relating to Certain Agricultural Products*, WT/DS207/AB/R, adopted 23 October 2002 at paras 153–77 [original emphasis].

The Appellate Body has laid down criteria which could serve as a guide for panels in this process. In *US—Gambling*, the Appellate Body stated that in order to satisfy the *prima facie* case requirement, the complainant must present arguments and evidence 'in relation to *each* of the elements of the claim'.[42] According to the Appellate Body, '[t]he evidence and arguments underlying a *prima facie* case [...] must be sufficient to identify the *challenged measure* and its basic import, identify the relevant *WTO provision and obligation contained therein*, and explain the *basis for the claimed inconsistency* of the measure with that provision'.[43] If the complainant presents argument and evidence that allow the panel and the defendant to identify the challenged measure and discern how that measure may possibly be inconsistent with a WTO agreement, due process is satisfied. Naturally, because similar requirements apply to the request for the establishment of a panel,[44] the first submission must present a detailed account of the claims stated in the panel request. In particular, the first submission must include supporting evidence.

Finally, it is important to note that the procedure suggested in this paragraph would not necessarily require an amendment to the DSU; it could be implemented through the working procedures of the panel, which can be adapted by panels after consultations with the parties.[45]

The same procedure should be followed with respect to claims (or defences *stricto sensu*)[46] raised by the defendant—an alternative to this procedure is discussed in Section III.C.3 of Chapter 4. This would allow the complainant to address in its second written submission the provisions raised by the defendant in its first written submission. There are no rules in the DSU disciplining claims

[42] Appellate Body Report, *US—Gambling*, above n 22 at para 140. [original emphasis].

[43] Appellate Body Report, *US—Gambling*, above n 22 at para 141 [emphasis added]. A similar logic was applied by the Appellate Body in *Canada—Wheat Exports and Grain Imports* where the Appellate Body found that 'it is incumbent upon a party to identify in its submissions the relevance of the provisions of legislation—the evidence—on which it relies to support its arguments'. Appellate Body Report, *Canada—Measures Relating to Exports of Wheat and Treatment of Imported Grain*, WT/DS276/AB/R, adopted 27 September 2004 at para 191. On the basis of the Appellate Body's ruling in *US—Gambling*, the panel in *US—Anti-Dumping Measures on Oil Country Tubular Goods* found that Mexico had established a *prima facie* case that the Sunset Policy Bulletin was inconsistent with Article 11.3 of the Anti-Dumping Agreement. In that case, the panel also interpreted the *prima facie* case as a threshold requirement in that after it found that Mexico had established a *prima facie case*, it proceeded to analyse the claims on the basis of all of the evidence on the record. Panel Report, *United States—Anti-Dumping Measures on Oil Country Tubular Goods (OCTG) from Mexico*, WT/DS282/R, 20 June 2005 at para 6.28. On appeal, after reversing the panel's findings with respect to the Sunset Policy Bulletin on other grounds, the Appellate Body declared that the panel's statement regarding Mexico's *prima facie* case was moot and of no legal effect. Appellate Body Report, *United States—Anti-Dumping Measures on Oil Country Tubular Goods (OCTG) from Mexico*, WT/DS282/AB/R, adopted 28 November 2005 at para 211.

[44] See, for example, Appellate Body Report, *US—Gambling*, above n 22 at para 141.

[45] See Article 12.1 of the DSU.

[46] The term 'defence *stricto sensu*' is used to indicate a defence which constitutes more than a mere negation of the propositions advanced by the opposing party; a defence *stricto sensu* is in this respect a distinct claim.

raised by defendants which are not referred to in the request for establishment of a panel filed by the complainant. However, just as due process requires the complainant to set out its claims in the panel request with sufficient clarity to allow the defendant 'to know what case it has to answer'[47] and ought to later require the complainant to present in its first submission arguments and evidence sufficient to identify each of its claims, due process (ie equality of treatment and participation) should also demand that the defendant raise any claims as early as possible and not later than in its first submission. This view is also bolstered by the fact that according to Article 12.6 of the DSU, 'subsequent written submissions shall be submitted simultaneously'; thus if the defendant does not raise its defences *stricto sensu* with its first written submission the complainant may be left without a meaningful opportunity to rebut the arguments and evidence submitted by the defendant. The defendant should explain its claims with sufficient clarity to allow the panel and the complainant to identify the nature of the claims. Whether the defendant has a legal obligation to present supporting evidence is a question whose answer depends on whether the defendant bears the burden of proof with respect to those defences *stricto sensu* (this is discussed further in Chapter 4). Because the parties have a duty to cooperate in the process of fact-finding, defendants must nonetheless strive to provide evidence in support of any claims that they raise.

Panels, however, have given defendants the opportunity to raise defences *stricto sensu* until as late as the second meeting with the panel.[48] Although panels and the Appellate Body have stated that defendants can raise claims after the first meeting of the panel with the parties on the condition that due process is observed,[49] allowing defendants to raise claims as late as the second meeting with the panel does not seem to promote nor ensure due process. First, complainants are not allowed to raise new claims during the proceedings, namely,

[47] Appellate Body Report, *Thailand—H-Beams*, above n 34 at para 88; Appellate Body Report, *United States—Sunset Reviews of Anti-Dumping Measures on Oil Country Tubular Goods from Argentina*, WT/DS268/AB/R, adopted 17 December 2004 at para 161.

[48] Panel Report, *Canada—Aircraft*, above n 32 at paras 9.77–9.78; Panel Report, *US—Gambling*, above n 8 at para 6.583.

[49] Panel Report, *Canada—Aircraft*, above n 32 at para 9.77; Appellate Body Report, *US—Gambling*, above n 22 at para 272. In *US—Gambling*, the United States raised for the first time in its second written submission a defence *stricto sensu* under Article XIV of the GATS. Even though Antigua did not refer to Article XIV of the GATS in its second submission, the Appellate Body found that Antigua had not been denied its due process rights. This would seem to be a clear example of denial of due process, since Antigua's opportunities to address the United States' defence *stricto sensu* were limited to the second meeting with the panel. See also Panel Report, *US—Gambling*, above n 8 at para 6.584 (where the panel noted that 'Antigua did not advance much argumentation in response to the submissions made and evidence adduced by the United States in support of its defence under Article XIV'). Fairness considerations, including equality of treatment, however, may have motivated the Appellate Body's decision, since the fact that Antigua focused its presentation of arguments and evidence on the 'total prohibition' of gambling and betting services offered from outside the United States—which theory the panel and the Appellate Body rejected—may also have denied the United States a full opportunity to defend itself with respect to the three federal laws which were ultimately found to be inconsistent with Article XVI of the GATS.

they are limited to those claims stated in their request for establishment of a panel;[50] defendants should, therefore, be held to similar standards. Second, if a claim is raised after the first set of submissions, the opportunities to present arguments and evidence regarding the new claim will not be similar to those regarding claims that have been part of the proceedings since the request for establishment of the panel. In this respect, the *Canada—Aircraft* panel's analogy to the situation where new evidence is presented after the first meeting with the panel is inappropriate.[51] New evidence relates to a claim which has been subject to debate since the beginning of the proceedings. A new claim would require the whole process of fact-finding to be set in motion. The Appellate Body in *US—Gambling* also did not seem to fully appreciate the fact that raising a new claim at a late stage of the proceedings constitutes a graver problem than presenting new evidence at a late stage.[52] In order to remedy the problem of unequal treatment of a claim raised at a late stage, panels could allow the parties to submit an additional submission entirely devoted to the new claim. However, this would inevitably delay the proceedings.

Accordingly, unless the defendant provides a reasonable justification for not raising the claim before, panels should not allow the defendant to raise claims after its first submission. Such solution would also be in accordance with the value of good faith cooperation. Along these lines, in *US—1916 Act (EC)* the panel noted that good faith implies that the parties should not withhold until the interim review stage arguments that they could be legitimately expected to have raised at a much earlier stage of the proceedings.[53]

2. Standard of proof

2.1. Prima facie as the initial standard of proof

In *US—Wool Shirts and Blouses*, the panel explained that it was for India, the complainant, to submit a *prima facie* case of violation of the ATC. After India had discharged this burden, '[i]t was then for the United States to *convince* the Panel that, at the time of its determination, *it had respected the requirements of Article 6* of the ATC'.[54] On appeal, the Appellate Body agreed with the panel

[50] In fact, this is not the only restriction imposed on the complainants. In *US—Steel Plate*, the panel declined to rule on a claim that had been stated in the panel request, explicitly abandoned by the complainant in its first submission and then restored by the complainant in its second submission. Panel Report, *United States—Anti-Dumping and Countervailing Measures on Steel Plate from India*, WT/DS206/R and Corr.1, adopted 29 July 2002 at paras 7.25–7.29.

[51] According to the Panel, 'there is nothing in the DSU, or in the Appendix 3 Working Procedures, to prevent a party submitting new evidence or allegations after the first substantive meeting. We can see no basis in the DSU to treat the submission of affirmative defences after the first substantive meeting any differently.' Panel Report, *Canada—Aircraft*, above n 32 at para 9.77.

[52] Appellate Body Report, *US—Gambling*, above n 22 at para 271.

[53] Panel Report, *United States—Anti-Dumping Act of 1916, Complaint by the European Communities*, WT/DS136/R and Corr.1, adopted 26 September 2000 at para 5.18.

[54] Panel Report, *United States—Measure Affecting Imports of Woven Wool Shirts and Blouses from India*, WT/DS33/R, adopted 23 May 1997 at para 6.7 [emphasis added].

and stated that if the party bearing the burden of proof 'adduces evidence sufficient to raise a presumption that what is claimed is true, the *burden then shifts* to the other party, who will fail unless it adduces sufficient evidence to *rebut the presumption*',[55] that is to say, to '*disprove* the claim'.[56]

In *EC—Hormones*, when analysing the complainants' claim that the measure regarding the hormone MGA was inconsistent with Article 5.1 of the SPS Agreement because it had not been based on a risk assessment, the panel ruled that it is for the complainants 'to present a *prima facie* case that the EC measures in dispute relating to MGA are *inconsistent* with the requirements of Article 5, after which the burden shifts to the European Communities to prove that it *has* complied with these requirements'.[57] On appeal, although the Appellate Body reversed some of the other findings of the panel regarding the burden of proof, the findings with respect to the hormone MGA were not affected. The Appellate Body made a general ruling that the panel should first determine whether the complainant has made a *prima facie* case of inconsistency with the SPS Agreement; if that is the case, the panel may then shift the onus to the defendant 'to bring forward evidence and arguments to *disprove* the complaining party's claim'.[58] According to the Appellate Body, the general rule requires 'a complaining party to establish a *prima facie* case of inconsistency with a provision of the *SPS Agreement* before the *burden of showing consistency with that provision* is taken on by the defending party'.[59]

In *India—Patents (US)*, the panel found that the United States, the complainant, had established a *prima facie* case of violation with respect to Article 70.8(a) of the TRIPS Agreement and that, therefore, 'the *onus [shifted*] to India to bring forward evidence and arguments to *disprove* the claim'.[60]

Finally, in one of its latest reports in *Chile—Price Bands (Article 21.5—Argentina)*, the Appellate Body stated that '[a] complaining party *will satisfy its burden* when it establishes a *prima facie* case by putting forward adequate legal

[55] Appellate Body Report, *US—Wool Shirts and Blouses*, above n 2 at 14 [emphasis added]. On page 13, the Appellate Body stated that it agreed 'with the Panel that it was up to India to present evidence and argument sufficient to establish a presumption that the transitional safeguard determination made by the United States was inconsistent with its obligations under Article 6 of the *ATC*. With this presumption thus established, it was then up to the United States to bring evidence and argument to rebut the presumption.'

[56] Appellate Body Report, *US—Wool Shirts and Blouses*, above n 2 at 16–17 [emphasis added].

[57] Panel Report, *European Communities—Measures Concerning Meat and Meat Products (Hormones), Complaint by Canada*, WT/DS48/R/CAN, adopted 13 February 1998 at para 8.255 [original emphasis]; Panel Report, *European Communities—Measures Concerning Meat and Meat Products (Hormones), Complaint by the United States*, WT/DS26/R/USA, adopted 13 February 1998 at para 8.252 [original emphasis].

[58] Appellate Body Report, *EC—Hormones*, above n 7 at para 109 [emphasis added].

[59] Appellate Body Report, *EC—Hormones*, above n 7 at para 104 [emphasis added].

[60] Panel Report, *India—Patent Protection for Pharmaceutical and Agricultural Chemical Products, Complaint by the United States*, WT/DS50/R, adopted 16 January 1998 at para 7.40 [emphasis added]. Similarly, see Panel Report, *India—Patents (EC)*, above n 1 at para 7.42.

arguments and evidence. [...] Once the complaining party has established a *prima facie* case, it is then for the responding party to *rebut it*.'[61]

i. A 'real' shift of the burden of proof?

The language of *US—Wool Shirts and Blouses, EC—Hormones,* and *India—Patents (US),* requiring the respondent to demonstrate the consistency of its measure or 'disprove the claim' with respect to which the complainant presented a *prima facie* case, suggests that panels and the Appellate Body were referring to a real shift of the burden of proof.[62] *Chile—Price Bands (Article 21.5—Argentina)* explicitly says that the claimant satisfies its burden when it establishes a *prima facie* case; from there on it is for the respondent to rebut that case.

In *India—Patents (US)*, the Appellate Body's reading of the panel ruling reinforces the view that the burden may have been shifted. According to the Appellate Body, 'after properly requiring the United States to establish a *prima facie* case and after hearing India's rebuttal evidence and arguments, the Panel concluded that *it* had "reasonable doubts" that the "administrative instructions" would prevail over the mandatory provisions of the Patents Act if a challenge were brought in an Indian court.'[63] If the burden of proof had remained with the United States throughout and the panel indeed was uncertain about whether the administrative instructions would prevail over the Patent Act, the panel should have ruled against the United States rather than India. In this situation, the Appellate Body should have found that the panel erred in finding against India—unless in the Appellate Body's view the burden had in fact shifted to India after the United States made a *prima facie* case. Moreover, the reasoning of the Appellate Body when reviewing India's measure was such that it suggests that the burden of proof was ultimately on India. For instance, the Appellate Body stated that it was not 'persuaded that India's "administrative instructions" would survive a legal challenge under the Patents Act'.[64] If the burden of proof were on the United States rather than India, a more appropriate formulation would be that the Appellate Body *was persuaded* that, given the circumstances,

[61] Appellate Body Report, *Chile—Price Band System (Article 21.5—Argentina)*, above n 34 at para 134 [emphasis added]. Similarly, see Panel Report, *Turkey—Measures Affecting the Importation of Rice*, WT/DS334/R, adopted 22 October 2007 at paras 7.9, 7.59–7.60, 7.87–7.88.

[62] Similarly, see Edmond McGovern, *International Trade Regulation* (3rd edn, Exeter: Globefield Press, 1995) at 2.23–60, issue 18; Petros C Mavroidis, 'Development of WTO Dispute Settlement Procedures Through Case-Law (We Will Fix It)' in F Ortino & E -U Petersmann (eds), *The WTO Dispute Settlement System 1995–2003* (The Hague: Kluwer Law International, 2004) 153 at 168; John J Barcelo III, 'Burden of Proof, Prima Facie Case, and Presumption in WTO Dispute Settlement' (2009) 42:1 Cornell International Law Journal (forthcoming). See also Brown, above n 10 at 96–7 (noting that in some cases the burden of proof has been shifted, but that in others the 'shift' of the burden once a *prima facie* case is established has been avoided. He notes that this practice of shifting the burden 'appears to be at variance with the manner in which most other international courts deal with the allocation of the burden of proof').

[63] Appellate Body Report, *India—Patent Protection for Pharmaceutical and Agricultural Chemical Products*, WT/DS50/AB/R, adopted 16 January 1998, DSR 1998:I, 9 at para 74 [original emphasis].

[64] Appellate Body Report, *India—Patents (US)*, above n 63 at para 70.

India's administrative instructions *would not* survive a legal challenge under the Patents Act. The formulation adopted by the Appellate Body indicates that it was for India to convince the panel and Appellate Body that its administrative instructions would survive legal challenge.[65] A similar situation occurred in *EC—Hormones*, where in an analysis limited to a single paragraph the panel determined that the complainants had made a *prima facie* case[66] after which the panel constantly referred to the European Communities as the party bearing the burden of proof. In the end the panel ruled that 'the European Communities ha[d] not met its burden of providing evidence to the Panel that its measures in dispute, in so far as they relate to the hormone MGA, are, either from a procedural or a substantial point of view, *based on* a risk assessment and that, therefore, these measures are inconsistent with the requirements of Article 5.1'.[67] The Appellate Body upheld the panel's finding with respect to the hormone MGA on the grounds that 'there was an almost complete absence of evidence on MGA in the panel proceedings'.[68] Such finding again would suggest that the burden of proof was indeed shifted to the respondent, ie the European Communities.

More recently, in *Turkey—Rice*, the panel ruled that 'the *initial burden* of proof rests upon the United States, as a complainant, to establish its *prima facie* case'; if it 'meets this test, the burden would then be on Turkey *to rebut* the said claim'.[69] In applying this ruling, the panel divided its analysis in two steps, which clearly indicate that the burden of proof was shifted. First, the panel examined all the evidence on the record with a view to determining whether the United States had established its *prima facie* case.[70] Having concluded that a *prima facie* case was established, in a separate section the panel turned to

[65] Similarly, see Appellate Body Report, *United States—Definitive Safeguard Measures on Imports of Circular Welded Carbon Quality Line Pipe from Korea*, WT/DS202/AB/R, adopted 8 March 2002 at para 188. Although in a context not related to the shifting of the burden of proof, the Appellate Body in *Chile—Price Bands (Article 21.5—Argentina)* seems to have recognized that language similar to that used in *India—Patents (US)* may be problematic in that it implies an allocation of the burden of proof. In *Chile—Price Bands (Article 21.5—Argentina)*, the panel made a series of statements which suggested that it was for Chile, the defendant, to prove that its measure was in compliance with its WTO obligations. Appellate Body Report, *Chile—Price Band System (Article 21.5—Argentina)*, above n 34 at paras 137–43.

[66] According to the panel, 'Canada argues that the European Communities has not submitted any scientific evidence which could constitute a risk assessment for the hormone MGA and that the European Communities has, therefore, *a priori*, not based its measures with respect to MGA on any risk assessment as required by Article 5.1. We find that Canada thus meets its burden of presenting a *prima facie* case of inconsistency with Article 5.1.' Panel Report, *EC—Hormones (Canada)*, above n 57 at para 9.256.

[67] Panel Report, *EC—Hormones (Canada)*, above n 57 at para 9.264. [original emphasis]

[68] Appellate Body Report, *EC—Hormones*, above n 7 at para 201.

[69] Panel Report, *Turkey—Rice*, above n 61 at para 7.59. [emphasis added]

[70] Panel Report, *Turkey—Rice*, above n 61 at para 7.61ff. Interestingly, in considering whether the United States had made a *prima facie* case, the panel did not focus only on evidence and arguments put forward by the United States.

examine whether Turkey had rebutted the *prima facie* case.[71] In this specific case, however, this shift was not problematic because the circumstances were such as to allow the panel to draw an adverse inference against Turkey. In other words, the reasons why Turkey failed to rebut the *prima facie* case were the same kind of reasons that warrant the drawing of an adverse inference against a party. Without going too deeply into the subject at this point—the requirements for the drawing of adverse inferences are discussed in detail in Chapter 5—those reasons included the fact that (i) the panel requested Turkey to produce information which was relevant and necessary to clarify the facts at issue, (ii) the information was in Turkey's possession, and (iii) the United States had no means of accessing it. In fact, the panel made a specific finding in that regard, ie it found that it was appropriate for it to draw inferences from Turkey's failure to produce the requested information.[72]

The fact that in *Canada—Dairy (Article 21.5 II)* Canada, the defendant, appealed a finding of the panel that placed on the complainants the burden under Article 10.3 of the Agreement on Agriculture of 'making a *prima facie* showing that the elements of the claimed export subsidies [were] present'[73] indicates that WTO members also have the impression that the burden is in fact shifted to the opposing party after a *prima facie* case is made by the claimant.[74] Otherwise, why would Canada appeal a finding that was beneficial to it? Canada argued that Article 10.3 sets out a reverse burden of proof[75] that requires the defendant to establish a rebuttable presumption that its measures are not inconsistent with its obligations; it would then fall upon the complainants to present evidence and argument to rebut that presumption. Canada submitted that it had presented sufficient evidence to raise a rebuttable presumption that there was no export subsidy, and that the United States and New Zealand had not successfully rebutted that presumption.[76]

The analysis in the previous paragraphs may be considered formalistic in that it is arguable that the evidence on the record would have allowed panels and the Appellate Body to arrive at the same conclusions no matter who the party bearing the burden of proof was at any given time. Even if that is the case, the fact that the language employed by panels and the Appellate Body in those cases

[71] Panel Report, *Turkey—Rice*, above n 61 at para 7.88ff.

[72] Panel Report, *Turkey—Rice*, above n 61 at para 7.106.

[73] Panel Report, *Canada—Measures Affecting the Importation of Milk and the Exportation of Dairy Products—Second Recourse to Article 21.5 of the DSU by New Zealand and the United States*, WT/DS103/RW2, WT/DS113/RW2, adopted 17 January 2003 at para 5.18.

[74] A similar view regarding the shifting of the burden of proof has been expressed by India in Appellate Body Report, *India—Quantitative Restrictions*, above n 38 at para 46; Appellate Body Report, *EC—Bed Linen (Article 21.5—India)*, above n 27 at paras 155, 174.

[75] Article 10.3 of the Agreement on Agriculture does allocate the burden of proof to the defendant. See discussion in Chapter 4.

[76] Panel Report, *Canada—Dairy (Article 21.5—New Zealand and US II)*, above n 73 at paras 15–16.

implies that the burden of proof shifts in the real sense may lead to the application of this understanding to a situation where it will indeed affect the outcome of the case—the potential consequences of a real shift of the burden of proof are discussed below. In other words, the incorrect or imprecise enunciation of rules eventually leads to errors not only of form but also of substance.[77]

ii. Critique of prima facie *case as the standard of proof*

If the burden of proof is shifted in the real sense, a *prima facie* case is in fact the standard of proof that the claimant must meet in order to discharge the burden of proof. After the claimant has successfully discharged the burden of proof according to that standard, the burden is placed on the respondent. The responding party must then disprove the proposition advanced by the claimant, that is, the respondent must prove that the proposition is not true at the risk of having the adjudicator rule against it with respect to that issue.

Therefore, shifting the burden of proof after the claimant has presented a *prima facie* case produces effects similar to those of a rebuttable presumption of law. Yet though the effects are similar, the circumstances that give rise to a *prima facie* case are not similar to the circumstances that give rise to a rebuttable presumption of law. As discussed in Chapter 2 a rebuttable presumption of law *is a rule of law* providing that proof of a basic fact requires the adjudicator to find the presumed fact; both the basic fact and the presumed fact are stipulated in the rule. It is also important to note that, as mentioned before, panels have used the expressions 'make a *prima facie* case' and 'raise a presumption' interchangeably. As just pointed out, however, the use of the word presumption in these circumstances cannot be understood to refer to a rebuttable presumption of law. In fact, it cannot even be understood to refer to a presumption of fact since the 'recurrence' element is absent—namely, the basic fact and the presumed fact are not *frequently* found together—as the Appellate Body itself made clear when it stated that 'precisely how much and precisely what kind of evidence will be required to establish [...] a presumption will vary from measure to measure, provision to provision, and case to case'.[78] Reference to a presumption in this context merely refers to the fact that the adjudicator will engage in the drawing of inferences, a process which in any event permeates the process of fact-finding[79]—though some pieces of evidence speak more directly to the fact at

[77] Aghahosseini argues that the Iran–United States Claims Tribunal has delivered many legally flawed decisions on account of the shifting of the burden of proof. M Aghahosseini, 'Evidence before the Iran–United States Claims Tribunal' (1999) 1:4 International Law FORUM du Droit International 208 at 212.

[78] Appellate Body Report, *US—Wool Shirts and Blouses*, above n 2 at 14. See also Appellate Body Report, *EC—Selected Customs Matters*, above n 8 at para 266; Appellate Body Report, *EC—Sardines*, above n 8 at para 270; Panel Report, *US—Gambling*, above n 8 at para 6.12.

[79] See, for example, John Sopinka, Sidney N Lederman & Alan W Bryant, *The Law of Evidence in Canada* (Toronto: Butterworths, 1992) at 101 (noting that 'it is the usual function of the trier of fact to draw inferences from other facts'). The Appellate Body has itself recognized that

issue (conclusive or direct evidence) while others require additional steps in the reasoning (non-conclusive or indirect evidence). Inferences permeate the process of fact-finding because there is a necessary distinction between evidence of some event and the event itself; from any piece of evidence the adjudicator 'can only infer to some degree that the event [in question] did occur'.[80]

In light of the above, it is possible to conclude that the use of an expression (ie 'presumption'), which already has a specific meaning in the context of fact-finding, to describe a process that is carried out by adjudicators on a regular basis does not add anything to our understanding of the process of proof. Therefore, panels and the Appellate Body should refrain from stating that the claimant must raise a presumption that what is claimed is true, after which the burden shifts to the respondent who will fail unless it adduces sufficient evidence to rebut the presumption.

Pauwelyn argues that instead of stating that the burden of proof shifts after the complainant makes out a *prima facie* case, panels and the Appellate Body should use the language of presumptions.[81] For the reasons just presented, this study comes to a different conclusion.[82] Moreover, Pauwelyn seems to believe that the word 'presumption' has an unequivocal and clear meaning which, as discussed above and in Chapter 2, is not the case. First, the word 'presumption' in and of itself does not say anything about the degree of persuasion that the adjudicator must reach in order to find that a presumption has been established.[83] The ordinary meaning of the word simply suggests that inferences about the fact at issue may be drawn from evidence of other facts. Second, in the area of fact-finding the word 'presumption' conveys different meanings. Rebuttable presumptions of law—or for that matter any rule which produces a similar effect such as the requirement that the burden of proof be shifted after the claimant has presented a *prima facie* case—have different implications than presumptions of fact. While a rebuttable presumption of law *requires* the adjudicator to find the presumed fact once the basic fact is proved, when faced with a presumption of fact, the adjudicator has the *discretion* to decide in the light of the circumstances of the case whether proof of the basic fact should be taken as proof of the fact at issue—ie the presumed fact. This difference also affects the

adjudicators draw inferences routinely. The Appellate Body has also noted that '[t]he DSU does not purport to state in what detailed circumstances inferences, adverse or otherwise, may be drawn by panels from infinitely varying combinations of facts'. Appellate Body Report, *Canada—Aircraft*, above n 38 at para 198.

[80] Terence Anderson, David Schum & William Twining, *Analysis of Evidence* (2nd edn, Cambridge: Cambridge University Press, 2005) at 60 (see also the following pages for more details on how adjudicators link evidence to propositions that must be proved).

[81] Pauwelyn, *Evidence, Proof and Persuasion*, above n 12 at 254.

[82] Vermulst, Mavroidis, and Waer also believe that the term 'presumption' has been misused by the Appellate Body. Edwin Vermulst, Petros C Mavroidis & Paul Waer, 'The Functioning of the Appellate Body After Four Years: Towards Rule Integrity' (1999) 33:2 Journal of World Trade 1 at 12.

[83] Similarly, see Vermulst, Mavroidis & Waer, above n 82 at 12.

options available to the respondent. The following scenarios explain the differences in options when considering facts '*A*' and '*B*'.

First scenario

Basic fact		Presumed fact
A	→ Must	B

In this scenario, the respondent must either rebut the evidence of *A* or disprove *B*, otherwise the adjudicator *must* find against the respondent.

Second scenario

Basic fact		Presumed fact
A	→ May	B

In this second scenario, the respondent may choose to rebut the evidence of *A* or present other evidence regarding the link between *A* and *B*, that is, evidence which would affect the drawing of the inference leading to the presumed fact. The respondent may also choose to disprove *B*. Importantly, in this scenario, if the respondent does not succeed in producing any evidence, the adjudicator still has to assess the evidence presented by the claimant and determine whether in the circumstances of the case evidence of *A* is sufficient—ie reaches the degree of persuasion set by the standard of proof—to support a conclusion of *B*.

One of the problems with shifting the burden of proof is that an opportunity is created for the adjudicator to decide that proof of *A* also proves *B* without a careful analysis of the link between *A* and *B*, and of whether in the circumstances of the case there would be more direct ways of proving *B*.[84] This problem will occur whenever the evidence presented by the claimant is not conclusive—namely, evidence regarding collateral circumstances from which the fact in controversy may be inferred. Therefore, a shift in the burden of proof may elevate non-conclusive evidence to the category of conclusive evidence without the support of a rule of law as is the case with rebuttable legal presumptions.[85]

[84] An opportunity for error may present itself even when there is no reference to a shift of the burden of proof. This may occur when the adjudicator divides the analysis in two steps focusing on the first step exclusively on evidence that supports a certain proposition and analysing evidence against that proposition in a second step.

[85] As noted in the introduction to Section I, in response to confusion regarding the use of the expression '*prima facie* case' in court decisions in common law jurisdictions, some scholars have argued that a *prima facie* case should not be interpreted so as to 'compel a specific determination

Moreover, because *B* is taken as a given after the shift, the respondent is then placed in a position that requires him to provide conclusive evidence of non-*B*. If the respondent fails to do so, the adjudicator will find against him even though the circumstances may be such that if a holistic examination of all the evidence on the record were to be conducted, the adjudicator would reach the conclusion that there was not enough evidence to support a finding that it was more likely than not that fact *B* had occurred. In other words, this means that the standard of proof which will allow the claimant to satisfy the burden of proof and possibly receive a ruling in his favour[86] is set at a very low level. Importantly, a system which would generally allow respondents to be found liable even though the evidence in support of the proposition advanced by the claimant is insufficient to reach a more likely than not standard—the preponderance of the evidence standard—would be clearly biased towards claimants. If the burden of proof is shifted to the respondent after the claimant makes a *prima facie* case, the respondent is assigned a more difficult task than the claimant; while the claimant is able to rely upon little evidence or evidence that is further down the inferential chain connecting the evidence to the proposition being advanced, the respondent must present compelling evidence which is capable of directly showing that the claimant's theory cannot be true.

Shifting the burden of proof to the respondent after the claimant makes out a *prima facie* case is also problematic because any doubts—ie those situations where the evidence is in equipoise—will be resolved against the respondent, whereas if the burden were not shifted, uncertainties would be resolved against the claimant. Accordingly, in the situation where, after the respondent submits some evidence in response to a *prima facie* case made by the claimant, the panel is uncertain about the facts of the case, the panel will decide against the respondent. In this context, the fact that in the absence of an intermediate ruling the respondent has no means of knowing whether the claimant has made a *prima facie* case is particularly problematic. Moreover, if the burden of proof is allocated to the respondent after the claimant presents a *prima facie* case, the reasons for allocating the burden of proof to the claimant (discussed in Chapter 4) are frustrated because the burden of proof is in effect placed on the respondent.

Finally, as noted by Pauwelyn, this technique of shifting the burden of proof after the claimant establishes a *prima facie* case can easily be employed by panels and the Appellate Body to justify result-oriented findings.[87] Panels can, on the basis of little evidence, find that the claimant has made a *prima facie* case and then rule that the respondent was not able to rebut that case. This is arguably

unless there is a specific rule of law establishing a presumption which demands such a conclusion'. Sopinka, Lederman & Bryant (1999), above n 13 at 70. See also Herlitz, above n 13 at 408.

[86] This will happen if the respondent does not succeed in proving non-*B*.

[87] Pauwelyn, *Evidence, Proof and Persuasion*, above n 12 at 258.

what happened in *EC—Selected Customs Matters* where the panel relied upon an unsubstantiated statement contained in an EC Court of Auditors report which had been issued more than five years earlier in order to find that the European Communities had acted inconsistently with Article X:3(a) of the GATT for not uniformly administering Article 147 of Commission Regulation No. 2454/93, ie the successive sales provision (allegedly some of the EC Member States required prior approval for the use of the successive sales provision, while others did not). According to the panel, although the European Communities had contested the accuracy of that statement, it had not provided any evidence in support of its assertions.[88] The panel, therefore, found in favour of the complainant because the European Communities had not presented evidence to rebut the assertion contained in the EC Court of Auditors report. On appeal, the Appellate Body reversed the panel in response to a claim by the European Communities that the panel had unduly shifted the burden of proof. The Appellate Body disagreed with the panel that the United States had established a *prima facie* case with respect to its claim that the successive sales provision had not been uniformly administered. In doing so, it explained what kind of evidence would have been necessary to establish a *prima facie* case in the specific circumstances of that case. It did not, however, provide general guidance on the quantum of proof that is necessary to make out a *prima facie.* If a standard such as the preponderance of the evidence were applicable, it seems clear that the evidence which was before the panel would not have been sufficient. However, under a *prima facie* case standard understood in its literal sense, the EC Court of Auditors report would have been enough since it indicated at least a possibility of non-uniform administration.

iii. What is behind the burden-shifting language?

It is probable that when panels and the Appellate Body state that the burden of proof shifts after the claimant makes a *prima facie* case they are not referring to an actual shift in the burden. However, if they do not mean to shift the burden in the real sense, what is behind such statements? One hypothesis is that panels and the Appellate Body are merely describing the steps they will follow in analysing the evidence placed before them, that is, they will first analyse all the evidence in favour of the proposition advanced by the claimant and afterwards they will consider all the evidence against that proposition. This is still problematic because this compartmentalization of the analysis may result in bias towards the claimant. After analysing the evidence in favour of the proposition advanced by the claimant, panels may assume that that evidence, even though indirect, proves the truthfulness of the proposition. In the next step, the panel takes the truth of the proposition as a given and requires the respondent to prove

[88] Panel Report, *European Communities—Selected Customs Matters*, WT/DS315/R, adopted 11 December 2006 at para 7.382.

its untruthfulness. As a matter of fact, this results in a real shift of the burden of proof.

A second hypothesis is that when panels and the Appellate Body refer to the shifting of the burden of proof they are actually referring to the tactical burden. Parties rarely remain quiescent in proceedings even when they do not bear the burden of proof; they submit evidence to contradict evidence produced by their opponent, behaving much like players in a ping-pong game. However, only one of the parties will suffer an adverse ruling against it if it fails to produce evidence and the record of the proceedings is, as a result, unpersuasive; the other party submits evidence based on its common sense judgement that if it does not do so the adjudicator may believe that the proposition advanced by the party bearing the burden of proof is true. In short, the tactical burden may shift during the proceedings, but the tactical burden is not *stricto sensu* the burden of proof. As discussed in Chapter 2, the concept of the tactical burden is not legally significant and references to it in legal decisions confuse rather than assist the parties in understanding the decisions.

iv. Final considerations

As noted in Chapter 2 there is strong consensus among common law, civil law, and international law scholars that the burden of proof does not shift. On account of that and the reasons discussed above, this study concludes that the burden of proof should not be shifted in WTO proceedings. In this regard, the *Korea—Dairy* panel report has, to this author's knowledge, been the only WTO dispute settlement report to explicitly recognize that the burden of proof does not shift. According to the panel:

> [a]s a matter of law the burden of proof rests with the European Communities, as complainant, and *does not shift during the panel process.* As a matter of process before the Panel, the European Communities will submit its arguments and evidence and Korea will respond to rebut the EC claims. At the end of this process, it is for the Panel to weigh and assess the evidence and arguments submitted by both parties in order to reach conclusions as to whether the EC claims are well-founded.[89]

Recapping briefly, if the burden of proof shifts to the respondent after the claimant presents a *prima facie* case, the standard of proof that the complainant must meet in order to discharge the burden of proof originally allocated to him is set at a very low level.[90] A standard of proof which is lower than the

[89] Panel Report, *Korea—Dairy*, above n 5 at para 7.24. [emphasis added] Although the Appellate Body addressed the question of the burden of proof in this case, it did not make any specific findings with respect to the panel's ruling that the burden of proof does not shift.

[90] This was arguably the case in the following cases. In *EC—Hormones* the panel found that Canada made a *prima facie* case of inconsistency with Article 5.1 of the SPS Agreement exclusively on the basis of Canada's *argument* 'that the European Communities has not submitted any scientific evidence which could constitute a risk assessment for the hormone MGA and that the European Communities has, therefore, *a priori*, not based its measures with respect to MGA on any

preponderance of the evidence standard would create a bias towards claimants which would negatively affect the impartiality of the dispute settlement system. Moreover, references in dispute settlement reports to the shifting of the burden of proof—or the requirement that the respondent rebut the presumption raised by the claimant—should be avoided even though they may not be intended to refer to a real shift of the burden. Such references do not add anything to our understanding of the process of proof, they are prone to cause confusion—since they may always be understood to refer to a real shift of the burden of proof[91]—and they may eventually lead to mistakes in the assessment of the evidence.

2.2. Prima facie as the final standard of proof

There is yet another category of cases where panels and the Appellate Body have analysed *all* evidence on the record with a view to determining whether a *prima facie* case had been made.

In *India—Quantitative Restrictions*, when analysing the claim that India did not meet the conditions of the Ad Article XVIII:11 of the GATT the panel

risk assessment as required by Article 5.1'.Panel Report, *EC—Hormones (Canada)*, above n 57 at para 9.256. In *Canada—Aircraft*, the panel concluded that the Canada Account debt financing at issue conferred a benefit under Article 1 of the SCM Agreement on the basis of: (i) a newspaper article where a senior Bombardier official was said to have acknowledged that 'Bombardier had used the Canada Account for 'a very small number of transactions' under terms of financing described as 'close to commercial'; (ii) Canada's statement that during the relevant period 'Canada Account debt financing had been provided for two "export transactions" in the civil aircraft sector', which led the panel to conclude that these two transactions were the same Bombardier transactions referred to in the newspaper article; (iii) Canada's contention that the senior Bombardier official's comment was made in reference to the Commercial Interest Reference Rates (CIRRs) established by the OECD Consensus, and (iv) Canada's statement that CIRRs 'may be above or below the market for a particular credit', which led the panel to conclude that Canada had implicitly accepted that the 'close to commercial rates' referred to by the senior Bombardier official could themselves have been below the market, and, therefore, have conferred a benefit. This evidence is very scant. The panel would have had stronger grounds to find in favour of the claimant, Brazil, if it had referred as a basis for its decision to the fact that Canada refused to provide details of the terms of the two instances of Canada Account debt financing acknowledged by Canada. See Panel Report, *Canada—Aircraft*, above n 32 at 9.216–9.224. Contrast with Panel Report, *Argentina—Hides and Leather*, above n 19 at para 11.52 (where the panel refused to make a finding of inconsistency with Article XI of the GATT on the basis of evidence that it considered 'thin' and included a newspaper article and opinion piece, a press release from the domestic industry, and a statement by a Member of the Argentine congress).

[91] For examples of this kind of understanding see John S Applegate, 'The Prometheus Principle: Using the Precautionary Principle to Harmonize the Regulation of Genetically Modified Organisms' (2001) 9 Indiana Journal of Global Legal Studies 207 at 238. (Applegate notes that '[t]he procedural approach of the WTO allocates to the challenger of a regulation the initial burden of going forward with evidence of a violation, but the ultimate burden lies with the regulator. Moreover, WTO panels give little or no deference to regulatory judgment, which intensifies the impact of the burden of proof'). Pei-San Tan, *United States – Measures Affecting Imports of Woven Wool Shirts and Blouses* (1998), online: <http://207.57.19.226/journal/vol9/No1/sr1c.html> (Date accessed: 11 May 2009). (Tan argued that the burden imposed on the complainant by the Appellate Body in *US—Wool Shirts and Blouses* was 'an attenuated burden'. He also raised the question of whether '[i]f all that is required of the Claimant State is to raise a *prima facie* case of violation, might this burden be so light as to not make the respective burdens no different than under the rule-exception approach?')

considered at the same time evidence presented by the United States, India, and the IMF (the IMF presented evidence following a request from the panel).[92] On appeal, the Appellate Body found that the panel had not erred in proceeding in this manner. According to the Appellate Body, a panel is not required to conclude that a *prima facie* case is made before it considers evidence presented at the request of the panel by experts and other organizations such as the IMF. In fact, in the Appellate Body's view, '[s]uch consideration may be useful in order to determine whether a *prima facie* case has been made'.[93] Moreover, the Appellate Body stated that there was nothing wrong with the fact that the panel 'took into account, in assessing whether the United States had made a *prima facie* case, the responses of India to the arguments of the United States'.[94]

Similarly, in *Canada—Aircraft* the panel and the Appellate Body noted that panels may need to 'seek information or advice' in order to determine whether a *prima facie* case has been made.[95] In addition, when analysing the proposition that EDC debt financing conferred a 'benefit' under Article 1 of the SCM Agreement, for example, the panel analysed all the evidence on the record including the evidence submitted by the defendant with a view to determining whether a *prima facie* case had been made.[96] On the basis of all the evidence on the record, the panel then concluded that 'there [was] no *prima facie* case that EDC debt financing confers a "benefit", and therefore constitutes a "subsidy", within the meaning of Article 1 of the SCM Agreement'.[97]

During the interim review process in *Japan—Agricultural Products II,* the panel explained that in deciding whether a *prima facie* case has been made the panel must 'examine and weigh all the evidence validly submitted' to the panel, including the expert opinions.[98] When analysing the claims at issue the panel found, for example, that after weighing the evidence and expert opinions it

[92] See Panel Report, *India—Quantitative Restrictions on Imports of Agricultural, Textile and Industrial Products*, WT/DS90/R, adopted 22 September 1999 at paras 5.201–5.213.

[93] Appellate Body Report, *India—Quantitative Restrictions*, above n 38 at para 142.

[94] Appellate Body Report, *India—Quantitative Restrictions*, above n 38 at para 142. Interestingly, in *India—Quantitative Restrictions*, the Appellate Body did not say that the burden of proof shifts; along those lines, it referred to the defendant's task after the complainant establishes a *prima facie* case as one that requires the defendant to 'rebut *the evidence adduced* in support of the inconsistency' rather than the presumption or the proposition proved by the complainant. Ibid at para 136. It is worth noting that the language of the panel report in *India—Quantitative Restrictions* suggests that the panel, differently from the Appellate Body, understood the *prima facie* case as a threshold requirement which must be met by the party bearing the burden of proof; if that requirement is met, the panel then weighs all the evidence on the record. See Panel Report, *India—Quantitative Restrictions*, above n 92 at paras 5.119–5.120, 5.176.

[95] Panel Report, *Canada—Aircraft*, above n 32 at para 9.89; Appellate Body Report, *Canada—Aircraft*, above n 38 at para 192.

[96] See Panel Report, *Canada—Aircraft*, above n 32 at paras 9.162–9.182, particularly, paras 9.166–9.174.

[97] Panel Report, *Canada—Aircraft*, above n 32 at para 9.182.

[98] Panel Report, *Japan—Measures Affecting Agricultural Products*, WT/DS76/R, adopted 19 March 1999 at para 7.10. In a later paragraph generally addressing the question of the burden of proof, however, the panel referred to the Appellate Body report in *EC—Hormones* and made a statement regarding the shifting of the burden of proof. Ibid at para 8.13.

concluded that the United States 'raised a presumption that Japan's varietal testing requirement [was] maintained without sufficient scientific evidence and that this presumption [was not] sufficiently rebutted by Japan'.[99]

Finally, in *EC—Export Subsidies on Sugar*, the panel weighed all the evidence on the record in making its findings and concluded in the end that there was *prima facie* evidence that: (i) the European Communities' total exports of sugar exceeded its quantity commitment level; (ii) the European Communities provided export subsidies within the meaning of Article 9.1(a) of the Agreement on Agriculture to what it considered to be exports of ACP/India equivalent sugar; and (iii) the European Communities provided export subsidies within the meaning of Article 9.1(c) of the Agreement on Agriculture to its exports of C sugar.[100]

In the cases reviewed in the previous paragraphs, panels and the Appellate Body did not compartmentalize their analysis of the evidence. They seem to have treated the *prima facie* case standard as the final standard of proof. Using the *prima facie* case as the final standard of proof means that the adjudicator weighs all the evidence in favour and against the proposition advanced by the claimants and decides in favour of claimants if there is a *possibility* that the proposition is true. Importantly, a finding that a proposition is *possibly* true does not necessarily translate into a finding that the proposition is more likely to be true than not—the preponderance of the evidence standard. Therefore, the main problem with using the *prima facie* case as a final standard of proof is that it may result in decisions that are biased towards the claimant.[101] This situation will occur whenever the evidence, though sufficient to demonstrate that a proposition is possibly true, is not sufficient to establish that the proposition is more likely true than not.

Although it is possible that panels and the Appellate Body do not intend to apply a low standard of proof,[102] as noted at the beginning of this section the

[99] Panel Report, *Japan—Agricultural Products II*, above n 98 at para 8.42.

[100] Panel Report, *European Communities—Export Subsidies on Sugar, Complaint by Brazil*, WT/DS266/R, adopted 19 May 2005 at paras 7.336–7.338, 8.1. It is interesting that as regards findings (ii) and (iii), the burden of proof was on the European Communities to demonstrate that it had *not* subsidized its exports which were above its reduction commitment levels. Still in paragraphs 7.337 and 7.338, findings (ii) and (iii) respectively, the panel concluded that the *complainants*—ie Australia, Brazil, and Thailand—had provided *prima facie* evidence.

[101] The fact that complainants have won the vast majority of cases brought before panels and the Appellate Body does not necessarily mean that the system is currently biased against defendants. Iida reports that the rate of violation findings from 1995 to June 2002 was 88%. Using a different methodology, Maton and Maton submit that complainants have won in over 80% of all disputes. High win rates for complainants may be explained by complainants selecting for litigation cases that they are likely to win. For the data mentioned, see, respectively, Keisuke Iida, 'Why Does the World Trade Organization Appear Neoliberal? The Puzzle of the High Incidence of Guilty Verdicts in WTO Adjudication' (2003) 23:1 Journal of Public Policy 1 at 4; John Maton and Carolyn Maton, 'Independence Under Fire: Extra-legal Pressures and Coalition Building in WTO Dispute Settlement' (2007) 2 Journal of International Economic Law at 328–9.

[102] A similar problem seems to have arisen in international arbitration. Reiner notes that in certain cases arbitrators seem to have used a very low standard of proof. According to him, in 'many cases the arbitrators may simply have insufficiently explained in the text of the award the (full) reasons for their decision.' In his view, 'even simple short-cuts in the text of the reasons should be

expression '*prima facie*' whose literal meaning is 'at first sight' connotes a low standard. Panels and the Appellate Body have not otherwise defined a *prima facie* case. The definition provided by the Appellate Body in *EC—Hormones* does not set a degree of persuasion for the *prima facie* case. Therefore, in order to prevent parties and panels from interpreting the *prima facie* case as a low standard of proof,[103] the expression *prima facie* case should not be used to refer to the final standard of proof for a decision; a more appropriate standard of proof should be adopted. This question will be addressed later in this chapter.

C. Concluding remarks on the meaning of '*prima facie* case'

The discussion in the preceding sub-sections demonstrates that panels and the Appellate Body have used the expression *prima facie* case in different contexts, which implies that the expression may have several disparate meanings. Scholars have struggled to decipher what panels and the Appellate Body mean when they refer to a *prima facie* case.[104] Moreover, as noted in the previous sub-sections, there are many problems with the uses of a *prima facie* case. On account of these considerations, this section concludes that panels and the Appellate Body should refrain from using the expression *prima facie* case in connection with the burden of proof.

Section II below will argue that panels and the Appellate Body should focus on weighing all the evidence on the record—in a similar manner to that described in section I.B.2.2 above—and determining whether the weight of the evidence allows them to reach a degree of persuasion not lower than that required by the preponderance of the evidence standard.

II. The 'holistic' or 'weighing of all evidence' approach

A. What is the holistic approach?

As previously noted, in *Korea—Dairy* the panel expressly stated that it would 'weigh and assess the evidence and arguments submitted by both parties in order

avoided. The parties feel frustrated, and not only the moral authority but also the legal validity of the decision may be affected [. . .]'. Andreas Reiner, 'Burden and General Standards of Proof' (1994) 10 Arbitration International 328 at 337.

[103] Several commentators have expressed the view that the *prima facie* case is a low standard of proof: Cameron & Orava, above n 10 at 236; Tan, above n 91; Christoforou, above n 10 at footnote 29; Douglas A Irwin & Joseph Weiler, 'Measures Affecting the Cross-Border Suply of Gambling and Betting Services (DS 285)' in H Horn & PC Mavroidis (eds), *The WTO Case Law of 2004–2005: Legal and Economic Analysis* (Cambridge: Cambridge University Press, 2008) 71 at 84.

[104] See, for example, Pauwelyn, *Evidence, Proof and Persuasion*, above n 12 at 244–6; Cameron & Orava, above n 10 at 233–4; McGovern, above n 62 at 2.23–60, 61, issue 18; Barcelo, above n 62; James Headen Pfitzer & Sheila Sabune, 'Burden-Shifting in WTO Dispute Settlement: The Prima Facie Doctrine' (2008) March:2 Bridges 18 at 18.

to reach conclusions as to whether' the claims advanced by the complainant were well-founded.[105] When analysing each of the claims raised by the complainant, the panel indeed examined all the evidence on the record and made findings that Korea acted consistently or inconsistently with the requirements of the Agreement on Safeguards with reference to that evidence and without invoking the notion of a *prima facie* case.

The panel in *Canada—Wheat Exports and Grain Imports* also made no reference to the notion of a *prima facie* case when examining the evidence before it with a view to determining whether Canada had violated its obligations under the GATT and the TRIMS Agreement. For example, in its analysis of the United States' claim that the provisions of Section 87 of the Canada Grain Act were, as such, inconsistent with Article III:4 of the GATT the panel examined all the evidence on the record. The panel then stated that after '[h]aving weighed and considered the evidence' on the record it concluded that the United States failed to establish that Section 87 was, as such, inconsistent with Article III:4 of the GATT.[106]

When considering Honduras' claim that the requirement that cigarette importers post a bond to ensure payment of taxes constituted a restriction on the importation of cigarettes that was inconsistent with Article XI:1 of the GATT, the panel in *Dominican Republic—Import and Sale of Cigarettes* analysed all arguments and evidence on the record. After examining the evidence presented by both parties, the panel concluded that in the light of all the evidence available, it was 'not persuaded' or 'convinced' that the propositions advanced by Honduras were true.[107] The panel thus found that Honduras had 'failed to establish' that the bond requirement was inconsistent with Article XI:1 of the GATT.[108]

The *Korea—Alcoholic Beverages* panel also adopted the approach of examining and weighing all the evidence on the record.[109] In that case the panel had to

[105] Panel Report, *Korea—Dairy*, above n 5 at paras 7.24–7.25. The panel in *Thailand—H-Beams* stated that it would follow a similar approach to that followed by the *Korea—Dairy* panel, that is, that it would 'weigh and assess the evidence and arguments submitted by both parties in order to determine whether Poland ha[d] established that Thailand acted inconsistently with its obligations under the AD Agreement'. Panel Report, *Thailand—Anti-Dumping Duties on Angles, Shapes and Sections of Iron or Non-Alloy Steel and H-Beams from Poland*, WT/DS122/R, adopted 5 April 2001 at para 7.49.

[106] Panel Report, *Canada—Measures Relating to Exports of Wheat and Treatment of Imported Grain*, WT/DS276/R, adopted 27 September 2004 at para 6.375. See also Panel Report, *Brazil—Export Financing Programme for Aircraft—Recourse by Canada to Article 21.5 of the DSU*, WT/DS46/RW, adopted 4 August 2000, for example, at paras 6.92–6.106.

[107] Panel Report, *Dominican Republic—Measures Affecting the Importation and Internal Sale of Cigarettes*, WT/DS302/R, adopted 19 May 2005 at para 7.265.

[108] Panel Report, *Dominican Republic—Import and Sale of Cigarettes*, above n 107 at para 7.266. Similarly, see paras 7.150–7.154. The panel generally avoided references to the *prima facie* case. Only one reference can be found at para 7.186.

[109] As noted in the previous section, the panel seems to have treated the requirement to establish a *prima facie* case as a threshold requirement. For other cases where the panel treated the

determine whether the products at issue—imported vodka, whiskies, rum, gin, brandies, cognac, liqueurs, tequila and admixtures on the one hand, and Korean soju on the other—were directly competitive or substitutable. In making this determination the panel examined the evidence presented by the complainants and the defendant concerning the physical characteristics, the end-uses, the channels of distribution and points of sale, and the prices of the products in question. The panel weighed and balanced all the evidence regarding each of those factors; with respect to each of them the panel concluded that 'overall' or 'on balance' the evidence supported a finding that the domestic and imported products were directly competitive or substitutable.[110] Accordingly, the panel concluded that 'the weight of the evidence overall supports a finding that the imported and domestic products at issue are directly competitive or substitutable'.[111]

It is also worth noting that the Appellate Body in *EC—Bed Linen (Article 21.5—India)* approved of the panel's decision to assess and weigh all the evidence before it with a view to determining whether that evidence was persuasive enough to allow the panel to come to a conclusion with respect to the question of whether the European Communities had violated Article 3.4 of the Anti-Dumping Agreement.[112]

More recently, in *US—Upland Cotton (Article 21.5—Brazil)*, the Appellate Body in reviewing a factual finding of the panel examined the evidence before the panel with a view to determining whether the programs at issue were making losses or profits. After reviewing the evidence, the Appellate Body concluded that there was 'a sufficient evidentiary basis for the conclusion that it is more likely than not that the revised GSM 102 programme operates at a loss'.[113] It is also worth noting that the Appellate Body avoided references to the *prima facie* case standard in making its findings in this case.

In the cases just described, the panels examined all the evidence on the record in order to determine whether a certain proposition was established. In other words, the panels did not divide the analytical process in steps; instead they conducted a holistic analysis of the evidence on the record. When there are multiple sources of evidence (claimant, respondent, experts among others) regarding a certain proposition, this approach requires panels to weigh all the

requirement to establish a *prima facie* case as a threshold requirement, and afterwards weighed all the evidence on the record, see Panel Report, *US—Section 301 Trade Act*, above n 3 at para 7.14; Panel Report, *Canada—Measures Affecting the Importation of Milk and the Exportation of Dairy Products*, WT/DS103/R, WT/DS113/R, adopted 27 October 1999 at para 7.34; Panel Report, *Argentina—Hides and Leather*, above n 19 at para 11.13.

[110] Panel Report, *Korea—Alcoholic Beverages*, above n 20 at paras 10.67, 10.82, 10.86, 10.94, 10.98.

[111] Panel Report, *Korea—Alcoholic Beverages*, above n 20 at para 10.95.

[112] Appellate Body Report, *EC—Bed Linen (Article 21.5—India)*, above n 27 at paras 174, 177.

[113] Appellate Body Report, *United States—Subsidies on Upland Cotton—Recourse to Article 21.5 of the DSU by Brazil*, WT/DS267/AB/RW, adopted 20 June 2008 at para 321.

evidence, and only then determine (in the light of the chosen standard of proof) whether the evidence supports a finding that the proposition is true. In those cases where there is only one source of evidence, the panel must scrutinize the evidence presented with a view to determining whether it reaches the degree of persuasion required for a finding that the proposition in question is true[114]—unless otherwise specified, references to the weighing of all the evidence on the record encompass this situation as well.

Moreover, in the cases reviewed the panels did not refer to the *prima facie* case standard when making a determination about whether the challenged measure was consistent with the WTO Agreements; rather they either stated that they were persuaded or convinced, or simply found that it had been established that the measure at issue was consistent or inconsistent with the obligation in question. Although the panels did not spell out the standard of proof adopted, the language employed conveys a degree of persuasion which is at least as high as that required to satisfy the preponderance of the evidence standard. In this regard, the Appellate Body in *US—Upland Cotton (Article 21.5—Brazil)* seems to have explicitly embraced the preponderance of evidence standard when it examined the evidence before the panel with a view to determining whether that evidence supported a conclusion that the program at issue was 'more likely than not' operating at a loss. It must be noted, however, that while the Appellate Body did not refer to the *prima facie* case standard in that case, it reverted to those references in subsequent cases.[115]

B. The favoured approach for WTO dispute settlement

In order to avoid the problems discussed in the previous section regarding the use of the expressions '*prima facie* case' and 'presumption' and references to the shift of the burden of proof, panels and the Appellate Body should follow the approach discussed in this section—ie the 'holistic' or 'weighing of

[114] Kazazi argues that if the opponent does not present evidence to challenge the evidence presented by the claimant, 'the application of the preponderance of evidence, as a standard of proof, is not possible and the proper term for the standard of proof applied is *prima facie* evidence'. This view is based on an incorrect reading of the preponderance of evidence standard as requiring the claimant to present evidence which is more convincing than the opponent's evidence. The preponderance of evidence standard is more appropriately defined as requiring that a proposition be shown to be more probably true than not. Accordingly, when only the claimant presents evidence, the adjudicator must determine whether that evidence demonstrates that the proposition in question is more probably true than not. See Mojtaba Kazazi, *Burden of Proof and Related Issues: a Study on Evidence Before International Tribunals* (The Hague: Kluwer Law International, 1996) at 348–9.

[115] See, for example, Appellate Body Report, *India—Additional and Extra-Additional Duties on Imports from the United States*, WT/DS360/AB/R, adopted 17 November 2008 at paras 185–93; Appellate Body Report, *Canada—Continued Suspension of Obligations in the EC—Hormones Dispute*, WT/DS321/AB/R, adopted 14 November 2008 at paras 358, 581.

all evidence' approach.[116] They must make clear that the burden of proof rests from beginning to end on the same party, and that that party must do more than simply provide evidence which at first sight may support the proposition that it advances. This of course does not mean that in determining whether a certain proposition has been proved the panel must examine only evidence presented by the party bearing the burden of proof. Since (i) the process of fact-finding is unitary (in the sense that there are no intermediate rulings on the sufficiency of the evidence) and dynamic, (ii) panels are not passive spectators, but instead have the right or power to 'seek information and technical advice from any individual or body which [they deem] appropriate',[117] and (iii) the parties to a dispute have a duty to cooperate in the fact-finding process, the panel should examine and weigh all the evidence on the record before attempting to arrive at a conclusion. After considering all the evidence, panels should ask themselves whether that evidence supports a conclusion that the proposition advanced is, at the very least, more likely than not to be true. The answer to this question should be spelled out in the panel report, so that the parties (and for that matter any reader) are able to understand how the panel arrived at its conclusion. If after considering and weighing all the evidence before them panels are left uncertain, ie the evidence is in equipoise, they must state this and find against the party bearing the burden of proof—which, again, is the same party from the beginning to the end of the proceedings.

Such an approach promotes transparency, impartiality, and accountability in adjudicatory decision-making and is more likely to lead to accurate outcomes. Following this approach, if a panel finds in favour of the party bearing the burden of proof on the basis of flimsy evidence this will be clear from the report—as noted before, this is not necessarily the case when panels apply the '*prima facie* or presumption' approach. A decision which is clearly not supported by the evidence will undoubtedly have its legitimacy questioned, and will also be an easier target in an eventual appeal. On appeal, the panel could be found to have violated its obligation under Article 11 of the DSU to 'make an objective assessment of the facts of the case'. Alternatively, the Appellate Body may find that the facts on which the panel relied did not justify its legal conclusion, in other words, the Appellate Body may review the panel's application of the law to the facts.[118] This will in turn create an incentive for panels to carefully consider all the evidence before them and refrain from pursuing specific results; in sum, it would work as a check on bias and increase the likelihood of achieving accurate outcomes.

[116] Along these lines, see Barcelo, above n 62. At least in part, Pauwelyn also shares a similar view; see Pauwelyn *Evidence, Proof and Persuasion*,above n 12 at 254–5.
[117] Article 13 of the DSU.
[118] For more details on appeals regarding factual issues, see Chapter 1.

III. The Standard of Proof for WTO Dispute Settlement

A. The importance of setting a standard of proof

As described in Section II above, the panels that have followed the 'weighing of all evidence' approach have not spelled out the standard of proof required to 'persuade' or 'convince' the panel of the veracity of the proposition in question. Therefore, those panels seem to apply the vague standard of 'the personal conviction of the judge' which is applied by international tribunals in general, and courts in civilian jurisdictions. As discussed in Chapter 2, there are divergent views as to what degree of proof this standard requires; some argue that it requires proof beyond a reasonable doubt while others submit that it demands that a proposition be shown to be more probable than not. A compelling reason for further specification of the standard of proof applicable in WTO disputes is the fact that the WTO Membership is diverse[119] and each Member may, based on its own legal system, have different views on what 'convincing the adjudicator' entails. Moreover, a detailed description of the standard of proof to be applied would also enhance the transparency of the process of fact-finding. Accordingly, this section is devoted to the discussion of the appropriate standard(s) of proof for WTO dispute settlement.

Before entering into a more detailed discussion of the rationales behind certain standards of proof, two issues must be addressed. First, some commentators are sceptical about the fact that differences in articulated standards of proof have any practical effect.[120] This view is valid in limited circumstances only. Although the standard of proof actually applied has no impact on the resolution of the issue in question in cases where the evidence is overwhelmingly strong/weak that it would meet/fail any standard (*prima facie* case, preponderance of the evidence, beyond a reasonable doubt), the same cannot be said where the evidence is more balanced, as illustrated in the following example.[121] *A* sues *B* on a note whose execution *B* denies. Both *A* and *B* bring witnesses; two apparently credible witnesses testify affirmatively to the execution of the note, and one more credible witness testifies negatively. The testimonies of *A*'s witnesses and *B*'s witness would have been believed if they had not been contradicted. Assuming that there is no further evidence, the fact-finder following the preponderance of the evidence standard *could* find for *A*, given a certain reaction to the three witnesses' credibility. However, the fact-finder following the beyond a

[119] As of May 2009 the WTO has 153 Members.

[120] See Kevin M Clermont & Emily Sherwin, 'A Comparative View of Standards of Proof' (2002) 50 American Journal of Comparative Law 243 at 261 (the authors note the scepticals' view, but disagree that 'the difference in articulated standards of proof has no practical effect').

[121] This example is used in a slightly different context in Clermont & Sherwin, above n 120 at 247.

reasonable doubt or highly probable standard could not come to the same conclusion.[122]

Second, it has been argued that a vague standard of proof such as the 'adjudicator's conviction' may, in contrast to more precise standards such as the preponderance of the evidence, have the advantage of providing adjudicators more discretion to take into account the various trade-offs in particular situations.[123] It must be noted, however, that although the preponderance of the evidence standard provides less room to exercise discretion, it still allows adjudicators to exercise a certain margin of discretion. When applying this standard the adjudicator determines whether a certain proposition is more probable than not on the basis of her assessment of the evidence, that is to say, the adjudicator does not apply a mathematical formula which yields an exact probability of the occurrence of the fact at issue. Moreover, providing panels less discretion in exchange for enhanced transparency and predictability may also have the desirable effects of encouraging amicable settlement and boosting the legitimacy of the dispute settlement system, which is frequently under attack from certain civil society groups and WTO members concerned about the erosion of their sovereign powers.

B. Considerations when setting the standard of proof

When thinking about standards of proof it is important to understand that in many cases it is difficult if not impossible to prove with absolute certainty that a certain fact occurred or that a proposition is true. Furthermore, the cost of producing evidence which would demonstrate conclusively that the fact occurred or that a proposition is true is sometimes prohibitive. In the light of this, many deserving parties will not be able to recover if adjudicators are required to be certain of the truth of a proposition in order to find in favour of the party bearing the burden of proof with respect to that proposition. Therefore, an absolute certainty requirement would result in many erroneous decisions and these decisions would always be against the party bearing the burden of proof and in favour of its opponent. In sum, a high standard of proof does not necessarily serve the truth.[124] Importantly for the WTO, given that the costs and the difficulty of gathering evidence tend to be significant in disputes of an

[122] The conclusion that standards of proof have practical consequences is also supported by at least some empirical data. Clermont and Sherwin admit that this data focuses on Anglo-American fact-finding and is imperfect, but in their view it nonetheless supports the conclusion that standards of proof can make a practical difference. Clermont & Sherwin, above n 120 at 262–3.

[123] Dominique Demougin & Claude Fluet, 'Deterrence Versus Judicial Error: a Comparative View of Standards of Proof' (2005) 161 Journal of Institutional and Theoretical Economics 193 at 204.

[124] Similarly, see Kuo-Chang Huang, *Introducing Discovery into Civil Law* (Durham: Carolina Academic Press, 2003) at 62.

international character,[125] an excessively high standard of proof may in fact disserve the truth.

In situations where the interests of the parties to a dispute are valued similarly—namely, when an error in favour of the claimant (false positive) costs[126] the same as an error in favour of the respondent (false negative)—bias against claimants cannot be justified. In these cases, adoption of a mid-range standard of proof that allows the claimant to recover when the evidence indicates that its claim is more probable than not corrects that bias, providing the parties similar treatment. This is the basic rationale behind the preponderance of the evidence or balance of probabilities standard.[127]

Some commentators have also argued that the preponderance of the evidence standard minimizes errors.[128] Walker disagrees with this proposition. He argues that '[w]e cannot deduce error rates for particular propositions from general principles, and therefore should not infer that a decision rule of 0.5 will in fact minimize total errors in the long run'.[129] In other words, '[w]hether the 0.5 decision rule is more effective than other rules at producing accurate findings is an entirely empirical matter that is not deducible a priori'.[130] Walker's concern seems well-founded. Accordingly, it seems that the preponderance of the evidence could be said to minimize errors only in the sense that by adopting this standard the adjudicator pursues his best chance of arriving at a decision that corresponds to the true state of affairs—this occurs whenever the adjudicator's assessment of the evidence leads him to believe that a proposition is more probable than not.

Another important rationale for the preponderance of the evidence standard is the creation of an incentive for evidence production.[131] On the one hand, if the standard of proof is set too low, the party bearing the burden of proof has no incentive to produce more than the minimal evidence required to satisfy that

[125] In support of this view, see Chittharanjan F Amerasinghe, *Evidence in International Litigation* (Leiden: Martinus Nijhoff, 2005) at 241.

[126] The word 'cost' is used in the broader sense of disutility or negative consequences associated with a certain decision, rather than in a narrower monetary sense.

[127] See Sopinka, Lederman & Bryant (1992), above n 79 at 146; Vern R Walker, 'Preponderance, Probability and Warranted Factfinding' (1996) 62 Brooklyn Law Review 1075 at 1116 (Walker argues that the preponderance of evidence standard is motivated by the goal of 'treating parties in an unbiased fashion' or of 'fairness to parties beyond minimal fairness'); John Kaplan, 'Decision Theory and the Factfinding Process' (1968) 20 Stanford Law Review 1065 at 1072; Richard A Posner, *Economic Analysis of Law* (New York: Aspen Publishers, 2003) at 617.

[128] See Alex Stein, *Foundations of Evidence Law* (Oxford: Oxford University Press, 2005) at 143–4; David Kaye, 'Naked Statistical Evidence' (1980) 89:3 The Yale Law Journal 601 at 603–5; David Kaye, 'The Limits of the Preponderance of the Evidence Standard: Justifiably Naked Stastical Evidence and Multiple Causation' (1982) 7:2 American Bar Foundation Research Journal 487 at 496–500; Clermont & Sherwin, above n 120 at 252–3; Thomas R Lee, 'Pleading and Proof: the Economics of Legal Burdens' (1997) 1997 Brigham Young University Law Review 1 at 25–6.

[129] Walker, *Preponderance, Probability and Warranted Factfinding*, above n 127 at 1104.

[130] Walker, *Preponderance, Probability and Warranted Factfinding*, above n 127 at 1101–2.

[131] Walker, *Preponderance, Probability and Warranted Factfinding*, above n 127 at 1113.

standard. On the other hand, if the standard is set too high, the party that does not bear the burden of proof will have little incentive to produce any evidence. A mid-range standard such as the preponderance of the evidence encourages both parties to provide their account of the facts and submit supporting evidence.[132]

In contrast, a higher standard of proof—that is, a higher degree of proof than usually required under the preponderance of the evidence standard—may be justified when there is a general interest in disfavouring certain claims, namely, when the costs of a false positive are higher than the costs of a false negative.[133] A higher standard of proof aims to reduce errors against respondents, which in certain circumstances are more costly. For instance, a higher degree of probability within the more probable than not range is usually required in order to prove claims of great gravity. In this vein, in her separate opinion in the *Iranian Oil Platforms* case, Judge Higgins noted the existence of a general agreement that 'the graver the charge the more confidence must there be in the evidence relied on'.[134] The gravity of the allegation was also mentioned by the ICJ in the *Corfu Channel* case as a factor determining the quantum of proof required to discharge the burden of proof.[135] The gravity of the accusation is a factor influencing the standard of proof because grave accusations carry a stigma with them which result in high reputational costs for respondents; because claimants do not incur reputational costs, at least not of the same magnitude as the respondents, there is an imbalance in this situation justifying a higher standard of proof. Along these lines, common law jurisdictions usually require a higher degree of probability—which in the United States is expressed in the standard of 'clear and convincing evidence'[136]—in civil cases where the livelihood of the respondent or individual rights are at stake.[137]

As a general rule, in WTO dispute settlement, false positives and false negatives are valued similarly. For example, in a dispute under the Anti-Dumping

[132] Walker, *Preponderance, Probability and Warranted Factfinding*, above n 127 at 1115.

[133] See Kaplan, above n 127 at 1072; Huang, above n 124 at 61; Walker, *Preponderance, Probability and Warranted Factfinding*, above n 127 at 1119.

[134] *Oil Platforms (Iran v United States of America)*, Judgment of 6 November 2003, Separate Opinion of Judge Higgins, International Court of Justice, Reports of Judgments, Advisory Opinions and Orders (2003) at 234, para 33 (Judge Higgins was criticizing the ICJ for not providing more detailed guidance on the standard of proof adopted by the Court).

[135] *The Corfu Channel (Merits) (United Kingdom v Albania)*, Judgment of 9 April 1949, International Court of Justice, Reports of Judgments, Advisory Opinions and Orders (1949) at 26. See also, *Godinez-Cruz Case*, Judgment of 20 January 1989, Inter-American Court of Human Rights, Series C, No 5 (1989) at 136, paras 135 and 140 (while the Inter-American Court of Human Rights noted that it had to apply a standard of proof which *considered the seriousness of a finding* that a government has tolerated a practice of disappearances in its territory, it also noted that the international protection of human rights cannot be confused with criminal justice.)

[136] As noted in Chapter 2, other common law jurisdictions interpret the preponderance of evidence standard flexibly so that it accommodates different degrees of probability depending on the nature of the case.

[137] See, for example,Sir William Wade & Christopher Forsyth, *Administrative Law* (9th edn, Oxford: Oxford University Press, 2004) at 291; Walker, *Preponderance, Probability and Warranted Factfinding*, above n 127 at 1119.

Agreement, in general terms the stakes are similar for the claimant and the respondent, in that the trade and related employment losses of one of the parties are the gains of its opponent, that is, the interests of both parties are similar. Moreover, in the absence of pre-trial discovery procedures similar to those available in common law jurisdictions, the WTO dispute settlement system is more heavily dependent on the cooperation of the parties. Creation of incentives for evidence production is therefore crucial for the healthy operation of the system. For these reasons, the standard of proof applicable in most WTO disputes should be the preponderance of the evidence or balance of probabilities.[138]

A slightly higher standard of proof—namely, a standard requiring a higher degree of probability—could be adopted for categories of cases where generally speaking the respondent has more at stake. As in England, the standard could still be referred to as the preponderance of the evidence or balance of probabilities, with the understanding that a slightly higher degree of probability, which could still be accommodated in the more probable than not formula, would be required. Cases under the SPS Agreement would in general be good candidates for this higher standard since not only trade, but also human, animal or plant life or health in the territory of the respondent would be affected. More obvious candidates for a higher standard of proof would be non-violation complaints under Article 26.1 of the DSU in conjunction with Article XXIII:1 (b) of the GATT, and situation complaints under Article 26.2 of the DSU in conjunction with Article XXIII:1(c) of the GATT. Non-violation nullification or impairment and situation complaints are not based on an alleged violation of a provision of the WTO agreements; rather they are based on the application of any measure or the existence of any other situation that nullify or impair any benefits or impede the attainment of any objective under a WTO agreement which allows these types of complaints. The following factors provide good reasons to require claimants to meet a higher standard of proof in order to succeed in non-violation nullification or impairment and situation complaints: first, the vagueness of the commitment under Article XXIII:1, paragraphs (b) and (c); second, the fact that in contrast to the original GATT the obligations contained in the WTO agreements cover many aspects of the regulation of international trade which would have previously fallen under the scope of Article XXIII:1(b) and (c); and third, the fact that Articles 26.1(a) and 26.2(a) of the DSU expressly require the claimant to present 'a detailed justification in support of' its claim. Along these lines, the panel in *Japan—Film* ruled that 'Article 26.1

[138] In favour of the application of the preponderance of evidence standard in WTO disputes, see Vern R Walker, 'Keeping the WTO from Becoming the "World Trans-science Organization": Scientific Uncertainty, Science Policy, and Factfinding in the Growth Hormones Dispute' (1998) 31 Cornell International Law Journal 251 at 290–1; David Unterhalter, 'The Burden of Proof in WTO Dispute Settlement' in ME Janow, V Donaldson & A Yanovich (eds), *The WTO: Governance, Dispute Settlement, and Developing Countries* (Huntington: Juris Publishing, 2008) 543 at 552.

(a) of the DSU and GATT jurisprudence confirm that this is an exceptional remedy for which the complaining party bears the burden of providing a detailed justification to back up its allegations'.[139]

C. Is the *prima facie* case standard ever optimal?

Finally, this section addresses the question of whether there are any circumstances that would justify employing a standard of proof lower than the preponderance of the evidence. As noted before, a low standard of proof such as the *prima facie* case would bias the system in favour of complainants and, more notably, allow decisions to be made on the basis of little evidence.[140] Decisions based on little supporting evidence would be questionable, affecting not only their legitimacy but also that of the dispute settlement system as a whole. If, as discussed in Chapter 4, there are reasons to provide the benefit of the doubt to the complainant, the burden of proof should be allocated to the defendant instead; this would allow the formation of an adequate factual record and, thus, address the potential accuracy and legitimacy problems just noted.

Some international tribunals seem to have used a *prima facie* case—ie a standard lower than the preponderance of the evidence—as a final standard of proof.[141] However, in most cases, though the expression *prima facie* case is used, the tribunals do not simply base their decisions on *prima facie* or suggestive evidence—the expressions '*prima facie* evidence' and 'suggestive evidence' are used in this limited context to refer to evidence which indicates that a certain proposition may possibly be true but does not allow the adjudicator to conclude that the proposition is at least more likely than not true. Instead, suggestive evidence is considered in conjunction with other surrounding facts and circumstances which indicate that the claimant's case represents the truth. In other words, although the evidence presented in support of a certain proposition is not sufficient to allow the tribunals to conclude that the proposition at issue is at least more probable than not, there are other facts and circumstances surrounding the dispute which when analysed together with the suggestive evidence allow the tribunals to arrive at such conclusion.

For example, in the frequently cited *Parker* case, the United States–Mexico General Claims Commission made a statement which suggested that whenever the claimant presented suggestive evidence and the respondent did not rebut or

[139] Panel Report, *Japan—Measures Affecting Consumer Photographic Film and Paper*, WT/DS44/R, adopted 22 April 1998, DSR 1998:IV, 1179 at para 10.30. See also Panel Report, *European Communities—Measures Affecting Asbestos and Asbestos-Containing Products*, WT/DS135/R and Add.1, adopted 5 April 2001 at para 8.271.

[140] In addition, if the standard of proof is set too low the party bearing the burden of proof has no incentive to produce more than the minimal evidence required to satisfy that standard. See Walker, *Preponderance, Probability and Warranted Factfinding*, above n 127 at 1114–15.

[141] In support of the view that international tribunals have relied on a *prima facie* case when the respondent does not submit evidence in rebuttal, see Kazazi, above n 114 at 333, 336–337, 339.

provide some reason for doubting, the Commission was prepared to rule in favour of the claimant based on the suggestive evidence.[142] The Commission, however, provided further clarification. Such clarification indicates that the Commission did *not* find that whenever respondents remain quiescent the Commission would rule in favour of the claimant on the basis of *prima facie* evidence. According to the Commission, '[i]n any case where evidence which would probably influence its decision is *peculiarly within the knowledge* of the claimant or of the respondent Government, the *failure to produce it, unexplained, may be taken into account* by the Commission in reaching a decision'.[143] The Commission took up this issue once again in the *Kling* case. The Commission noted that '[t]he mere fact that evidence produced by the respondent Government is meagre cannot itself justify an award in the absence of satisfactory evidence from the claimant'.[144] However, according to the Commission, certain inferences can be drawn from the non-production, or an unsatisfactory explanation for such non-production, of available evidence in the possession of the respondent.[145] Such inferences coupled with *prima facie* evidence could be sufficient to allow the Commission to conclude that a certain proposition was at least more probable than not.

In the *Kling* case, in the light of evidence that Mr Kling was shot in Mexican territory and of some evidence which although scarce indicated that Mexican soldiers were responsible for the shooting, the Commission gave special consideration to the fact that Mexico did not submit any information concerning the investigation of the shooting even after the Commission made a specific request for production of evidence.[146] The Commission emphasized that while Mexico denied having knowledge of the shooting, evidence on the record demonstrated that Mexican authorities had investigated the event at issue.[147]

[142] In the words of the Commission, 'when the claimant has established a *prima facie* case and the respondent has offered no evidence in rebuttal the latter may not insist that the former pile up evidence to establish its allegations beyond a reasonable doubt without pointing out some reason for doubting'. *William A Parker (USA) v United Mexican States*, 31 March 1926, 4 Reports of International Arbitration Awards 35 (Millwood, Kraus Reprint, 1974) at 39 or para 6 of the Award.

[143] *William A Parker*, above n 142 at 39 or para 7 of the Award [emphasis added].

[144] *Lillie S Kling (USA) v United Mexican States*, 8 October 1930, 4 Reports of International Arbitral Awards 575 (Millwood, Kraus Reprint, 1974) at 581.

[145] *Lillie S Kling*, above n 144 at 582.

[146] Following the Commission's request for the records of any proceedings instituted by Mexican civil or military authorities regarding the incidents out of which the claim arose, Mexico provided two letters indicating that no information had been found with respect to the killing of Kling. One of the letters noted that an ex-General, who was in command of the sector where the shooting occurred, might have been able to provide some information. Mexico, however, did not present an affidavit or report from the said General.

[147] *Lillie S Kling*, above n 144 at 577, 584. The Commission also suggested that the fact that Mexico did not investigate and prosecute the person who shot Kling would in itself render Mexico responsible.

Accordingly, on the basis of the *prima facie* evidence and the circumstances regarding Mexico's non-production of evidence, the Commission ruled in favour of the claimant.[148]

In a similar fashion, international tribunals may also take into account the difficulties faced by the claimant in securing evidence from areas outside its control. For instance, in *Corfu Channel*, the International Court of Justice noted that the exclusive territorial control exercised by a state within its frontiers may affect the capacity of the claimant state to gather and present evidence to the Court. When these circumstances are present, the Court noted that the claimant state 'should be allowed a more liberal recourse to inferences of fact and circumstantial evidence'.[149] Although in *Corfu Channel* the evidence regarding the facts at issue—ie whether Albania had knowledge of mine-laying in its territorial waters—was never classified as of a *prima facie* character, this case nonetheless indicates that the claimant's difficulties in securing evidence may be one of the circumstances, together with others such as the respondent's unwillingness to cooperate, that an international court or tribunal may weigh together with suggestive evidence.

Importantly, the claimant must also be prepared to present evidence in support of the existence of such difficulties in gathering proof, particularly when those facts are not notorious. In *Melczer Mining Company*, for example, the Mexico–United States General Claims Commission rejected the claimant's assessment of the value of the property said to have been stolen because, among other reasons, affidavits presented by the claimant referred to books which were not produced to the Commission and no convincing explanation had been

[148] See also *Melczer Mining Company (USA) v United Mexican States*, 30 April 1929, 4 Reports of International Arbitral Awards 481 (Millwood: Kraus Reprint Co, 1974) at 485–6; *Daniel Dillon (USA) v United Mexican States*, 3 October 1928, Concurring Opinion of Commissioner Nielsen, 4 Reports of International Arbitral Awards 368 (Millwood, Kraus Reprint Co., 1974) at 371. The *Brun* case adjudicated by the French–Venezuelan Mixed Claims Commission of 1902 has also been cited as an example of a case where the tribunal relied on *prima facie* evidence coupled with an inference against the respondent for not providing information in its sole possession and for not permitting the initiation of proceedings before its own courts to ascertain the facts connected with the injury and death of Mr Brun. For an example of where this case was cited, see Amerasinghe, above n 125 at 247–8. It is important to note, however, that while the tribunal noted that it might have come to a different conclusion had the respondent been more forthcoming, the evidence of the facts related to the death of Mr Brun which was placed before the tribunal was plenty to allow it to come to the conclusion that it came to, that is, that the Venezuelan government was responsible for the death of Mr Brun. In addition, the tribunal never described the evidence as being of a *prima facie* character; to the contrary, it noted that the evidence was enough to satisfy the tribunal to a 'moral certainty'. *Heirs of Jules Brun v Venezuela*, 31 July 1905, Report of French-Venezuelan Mixed Claims Commission of 1902 (Washington: Government Printing Office, 1906) at 25.

[149] *The Corfu Channel* (Merits), above n 135 at 30. See also Daniel Bethlehem, 'Submissions on Points of Fact and Law: Written and Oral Pleadings Before the International Court of Justice' in F Weiss (ed), *Improving WTO Dispute Settlement Procedures: Issues and Lessons from the Practice of Other International Courts and Tribunals* (London: Cameron May, 2000) 175 at 187, 190 (referring to the practice of the International Court of Justice).

provided for such non-production. The claimant asserted that some of the books could not be removed from Mexico because of prohibitions of Mexican law, and that other books were destroyed during the progress of the looting. The Commission set aside the affidavits noting that there was 'no specific information as to what books were destroyed or which books [were] unavailable or what particular books were relied upon in formulating the statements purported to be based upon things revealed by books which [were] available'.[150]

Some commentators have also supported the approach described in the previous paragraphs. They have carefully noted that *prima facie* evidence alone is not enough to allow a tribunal to rule in favour of the party bearing the burden of proof. However, *prima facie* evidence combined with other inferences arising from the circumstances of the dispute—such as the unexplained non-production of evidence in the exclusive possession of the respondent—may be enough to allow the adjudicator to conclude that a certain proposition is more likely than not true—the specific conditions under which inferences can be drawn from non-production of evidence are discussed in Chapter 5.[151]

Kazazi is one of the few commentators that have unqualifiedly concluded that international tribunals have ruled in favour of claims on the basis of *prima facie* evidence whenever that evidence is not rebutted.[152] In support of his view, he cites cases from the Iran–United States Claims Tribunal of which at least *Lockheed Corporation* seems to support the unqualified conclusion that a tribunal may rule in favour of the complainant on the basis of *prima facie* evidence whenever the respondent remains quiescent.[153] Importantly, assuming that Kazazi's assessment of the jurisprudence of the Iran–United States Claims Tribunal is accurate, the specific circumstances under which that tribunal has operated would not warrant extrapolating that conclusion to *all* international tribunals, particularly the WTO dispute settlement mechanism. The Iran–United States Claims Tribunal was one of the measures taken to resolve the crisis in relations between Iran and the United States which arose out of events linked to the Iranian revolution. Its mandate is largely limited to awarding damages for

[150] *Melczer Mining Company*, above n 148 at 485.

[151] Durward V Sandifer, *Evidence Before International Tribunals* (revised edn, Charlottesville: University Press of Virginia, 1975) at 170–4; Bin Cheng, *General Principles of Law as Applied by International Courts and Tribunals* (London: Stevens & Sons, 1953) at 323–6 (Cheng notes that a tribunal may be satisfied with less conclusive proof, ie *prima facie* evidence, when 'proof of a fact presents extreme difficulty' and when the opponent can easily produce countervailing evidence but chooses not to do so). In support of the application of a similar approach in domestic proceedings, see Colin Tapper, *Cross and Tapper on Evidence* (9th edn, London: Butterworths, 1999) at 129 (Tapper notes that 'a party's knowledge of essential facts may lessen the amount of evidence required to discharge an evidential burden borne by his adversary').

[152] Kazazi, above n 114 at 333, 336–7, 339.

[153] *Lockheed Corporation v The Government of Iran, The Ministry of War, and The Iranian Air Force*, Award 367-829-2, 9 June 1988, 18 Iran–U.S. Claims Tribunal Reports 292 (Cambridge, Grotius Publications, 1989) at 318–19, paras 94–7 of the award. The dissenter, however, disapproved the use of *prima facie* evidence. Ibid at 340–2.

violations of property rights and breaches of contract[154] and most of the claims before the tribunal were brought by United States nationals against the government of Iran. As the tribunal itself recognized in its awards,[155] the Iranian revolution forced many of the claimants to leave Iran in such circumstances that they did not have an opportunity to gather documents and other evidence which could be used before the tribunal to prove the facts at issue.[156]

Many international tribunals, however, do not have such limited mandates and/or operate under similar circumstances. This is particularly the case of the WTO dispute settlement system. WTO disputes are government-to-government; WTO Members challenge measures (eg laws and regulations) adopted by other Members. If a measure is found to violate a provision of the WTO agreements, the DSB requests the Member concerned to bring its measure into conformity with the agreements.[157] According to Article 22.1 of the DSU, compensation and retaliation are only 'temporary measures available in the event that the recommendations [to bring a measure into conformity] are not implemented within a reasonable period of time'.[158] Accordingly, in the WTO an erroneous decision against the defendant—ie the defendant is required to change or withdraw a measure that is actually consistent with the WTO agreements—has more serious implications than a similarly mistaken decision by a tribunal such as the Iran–United States Claims Tribunal, which merely requires the losing defendant to pay damages to the claimant. This would advise panels

[154] See Article II of the Declaration of the Government of the Democratic and Popular Republic of Algeria Concerning the Settlement of Claims by the Government of the United States of America and the Government of the Islamic Republic of Iran (Claims Settlement Declaration) 19 January 1981.

[155] For example, see *Lockheed Corporation*, above n 153 at 319, para 97 of the award.

[156] See Sayyed Khalil Khalilian, *The Law of International Arbitration* (North Vancouver: Pacific Arbitration Network, 2003) at 287.

[157] Non-violation nullification or impairment, and situation complaints are an exception to this rule. Article 26.1(b) of the DSU provides that 'where a measure has been found to nullify or impair benefits under, or impede the attainment of objectives, of the relevant covered agreement without violation thereof, *there is no obligation to withdraw the measure*. However, in such cases, the panel or the Appellate Body shall recommend that the Member concerned make a *mutually satisfactory adjustment*'. [emphasis added] The reasons discussed above for adopting a higher standard of proof for non-violation nullification or impairment complaints also explain the choice of a less demanding remedy. For the case of situation complaints, see Article 26.2 of the DSU.

[158] There is some disagreement among commentators as to whether a WTO Member has an obligation to bring its measure into compliance. Some have argued that Members may freely choose between (i) bringing their measures into conformity with the WTO agreements, (ii) providing compensation, and (iii) suffering retaliation (ie suspension of concessions or other obligations). It is this author's view that while as a matter of fact no one can coerce a Member to comply, there is nonetheless a legal obligation requiring a Member to comply. Among others, Article 22.1 of the DSU supports such conclusion. In support of the view that WTO Members may choose between one of the three options mentioned, see Judith Hippler Bello, 'The WTO Dispute Settlement Understanding: Less is More' (1996) 90:3 The American Journal of International Law 416 at 417–18. In support of the existence of an obligation to comply, see John H Jackson, 'The WTO Dispute Settlement Understanding: Misunderstandings on the Nature of Legal Obligation' (1997) 91:1 The American Journal of International Law 60 at 63.

against adopting a low standard of proof which would clearly favour the claimant. Moreover, as a general rule, conditions in the WTO system are not such as to completely deny claimants access to means of proof. In fact, as will be discussed in Chapter 5, the WTO agreements contain transparency obligations which require Members to publicize their measures affecting trade,[159] and upon request to provide information regarding those measures.[160]

In the light of the above, this section concludes that there are no circumstances justifying the application of a standard of proof lower than the preponderance of the evidence in WTO dispute settlement. Panels, however, may conclude that a certain proposition is more probable than not by considering evidence presented by the parties which *per se* would not be sufficient to justify that conclusion—ie suggestive evidence—together with certain inferences arising from the circumstances of the dispute. The fact that the respondent has not presented evidence in rebuttal is not of itself a circumstance justifying such an inference. Only under specific conditions may non-production of evidence by the respondent justify the drawing of an inference which, combined with suggestive evidence, allows a panel to conclude that a certain proposition is at least more probable than not. The discussion above indicates that at least the following conditions should be present cumulatively—Section II.B.4.1 of Chapter 5 discusses in more detail the conditions which must be observed in drawing inferences from non-production of evidence. First, the claimant must demonstrate that it has made all efforts to secure evidence which if presented would allow the panel to conclude that the proposition at issue is more probable than not. Second, it must be established that the respondent has access to evidence which if presented would allow the panel to conclude that the proposition at issue is more probable than not. Third, a convincing explanation for the non-production of such evidence is not provided by the respondent.[161] Put differently, the mere fact that the respondent does not produce evidence which is in its possession should not result in panels drawing inferences from such circumstances if the claimant could through reasonable means have secured that evidence by itself. Alternatively to the second and third conditions, the claimant could demonstrate that evidence that would support a conclusion that the proposition at issue is more probable than not is unavailable because of an act of the respondent.

[159] For example, Article X of the GATT and Article 7 and Annex B of the SPS Agreement.

[160] For instance, Article 5.8 and Annex B of the SPS Agreement.

[161] In support of these criteria, see Walker, *Preponderance, Probability and Warranted Factfinding*, above n 127 at 1125–6 (Walker argues that '[f]actfinders should be allowed, or even encouraged, to take into account in a particular case a failure to produce evidence to which a party probably has access, at least if the nonproduction is unexplained. [. . .] [T]his is a case in which the finding is warranted, despite the subjective uncertainty concerning the truth of the finding. The factfinder is not thereby changing the civil standard of proof but rather applying the traditional preponderance standard in light of the evidence in the case').

Contrary to what has been recommended here, the panel in *Canada—Aircraft* based its finding that the Canada Account debt financing at issue conferred a benefit under Article 1 of the SCM Agreement on evidence which could be, and indeed was, classified as of a *prima facie* character.[162] The panel had requested Canada to provide details of the terms of the two instances of Canada Account debt financing acknowledged by Canada. Canada refused to provide the information requested. The panel, however, did not consider Canada's refusal when making its decision. Instead the panel referred to the fact that after the claimant makes a *prima facie* case the burden of proof shifts to the respondent. Because Canada had not submitted additional evidence, the panel found that Canada had 'not rebutted the *prima facie* case against the Canada Account (a debt financing instrument)'.[163] Accordingly, in this case, the panel based its decision exclusively on *prima facie* evidence. The panel would have had stronger grounds to find in favour of the claimant, Brazil, if it had referred as a basis for its decision to the fact that Canada refused to provide relevant evidence which was in the exclusive possession of Canada.

Finally, it is important to distinguish the approach suggested above from proposals for panels, similarly to investigating authorities in anti-dumping investigations, to rely upon facts available.[164] Article 6.8 of the Anti-Dumping Agreement authorizes investigating authorities to make determinations on the basis of facts available '[i]n cases in which any interested party refuses access to, or otherwise does not provide, necessary information within a reasonable period or significantly impedes the investigation'. An investigating authority, as the title suggests, is an investigator rather than an adjudicator; unlike an adjudicator, an investigating authority does not make either-or binary findings only. Article 6.8 aims at providing investigating authorities the means to complete an investigation, make a determination, and calculate dumping margins for each investigated exporter 'even in the event that [those exporters are] unable or unwilling to provide necessary information within a reasonable period'.[165] Facts available are usually the information that petitioners provide in the application for the initiation of an anti-dumping investigation or other information to which the investigating authority has access—this usually does not include information submitted by other investigated foreign producers and exporters.[166] The investigating authority is not obliged to satisfy itself of the accuracy of that

[162] Panel Report, *Canada—Aircraft*, above n 32 at paras 9.216–9.224. See description in n 90 above.

[163] Panel Report, *Canada—Aircraft*, above n 32 at para 9.225.

[164] See Cameron & Orava, above n 10 at 229.

[165] Panel Report, *United States—Anti-Dumping Measures on Certain Hot-Rolled Steel Products from Japan*, WT/DS184/R, adopted 23 August 2001 at para 7.51 [original emphasis]. See also Judith Czako, Johann Human & Jorge Miranda, *A Handbook on Anti-Dumping Investigations* (Cambridge: Cambridge University Press, 2003) at 17; Edwin Vermulst, *The WTO Anti-Dumping Agreement: a Commentary* (Oxford: Oxford University Press, 2005) at 146.

[166] Annex II, paragraph 1 of the Anti-Dumping Agreement; Czako, Human & Miranda, above n 165 at 17.

information.[167] In a way, the use of facts available is a penalty for lack of cooperation which allows the investigating authority to make a determination independently of any belief in its accuracy. In contrast, according to the proposal advanced in the previous paragraphs: (i) suggestive evidence is considered in conjunction with other surrounding facts and circumstances, including the non-production of evidence in the possession of the respondent, which indicate that the claimant's case has merit; (ii) not every non-production of evidence by the respondent justifies the adjudicator in coming to such a conclusion; (iii) at the end the adjudicator must be able to conclude that the proposition at issue is at least more probable than not; and (iv) the adjudicator must be satisfied of the accuracy of the suggestive evidence.

In the light of the reasons provided above, the preponderance of the evidence is the appropriate standard of proof for WTO disputes. A panel should not make a finding of a violation of the WTO agreements on the basis of evidence which is not sufficient to allow the panel to conclude that the propositions being advanced by the claimant are more probable than not. Disregard of this recommendation introduces a bias in favour of claimants in the system, which in turn may affect its legitimacy.

Concluding Remarks

This chapter has discussed the question of how the concept of the burden of proof functions in WTO dispute settlement as well as the closely related question of the degree of persuasion that panels must reach in order to find that the burden of proof has been discharged—ie the applicable standard of proof. It concludes that panels and the Appellate Body have made the functioning of the burden of proof unclear by referring to the requirement that the claimant must make a *prima facie* case without explaining in any detail what this requirement entails. The jurisprudence allows that requirement to be interpreted in several different ways, none of which are in consonance with the goals and/or current structure of WTO dispute settlement system. In light of this, panels and the Appellate Body would be well advised to stop referring to that requirement. In connection with that question, they should also refrain from referring to the

[167] This conclusion follows from the text of Article 6.6 of the Anti-Dumping Agreement, which provides that '[e]*xcept in circumstances provided for in paragraph 8*, the authorities shall during the course of the investigation satisfy themselves as to the accuracy of the information supplied by interested parties upon which their findings are based'. [emphasis added] In addition, paragraph 7 of Annex II establishes that investigating authorities '*should, where practicable*, check the information from other independent sources at their disposal'. This soft command is followed by a note that '[i]t is clear, however, that if an interested party does not cooperate and thus relevant information is being withheld from the authorities, this situation could lead to a result which is less favourable to the party than if the party did cooperate'.

shifting of the burden of proof, which in its real sense should not shift from one party to another during the proceedings.

It is suggested that in deciding whether the burden of proof has been discharged, panels should weigh all the evidence before them, instead of focusing on the evidence presented by one or the other party. Moreover, in determining whether the burden of proof has been discharged, panels should in most cases be guided by the preponderance of the evidence standard. This standard ensures equal treatment, fosters cooperation, and is more likely to lead to accurate decisions than would a lower or higher standard of proof. A slightly higher standard of proof could, however, be adopted in connection with categories of claims as to which the respondent has more at stake, that is, when the costs of a false positive are higher than the costs of a false negative.

4

The Allocation of the Burden of Proof

Introduction

The importance of the burden of proof lies in the fact that it determines the outcome of a case when the evidence on the record is equivocal or scant.[1] Accordingly, it is crucial that the parties know in advance who bears the burden of proof with respect to the issues in the case. Such knowledge avoids later surprises and gives the party bearing the burden of proof an opportunity to make all efforts necessary to prove its case. Moreover, knowledge of which party bears the burden of proof may also play a role in the decision of the parties to resort to adjudication. This chapter analyses how adjudicators, particularly WTO panels and the Appellate Body, determine which party—complainant or defendant—must prove a certain issue or suffer the consequences of a finding against it. In other words, it examines the question of the allocation of the burden of proof.

As noted in Chapter 2, the kind of considerations that determine the allocation of the burden of proof may also explain the creation of some rebuttable presumptions of law. Therefore, the discussion in this chapter is also useful to understanding at least some of those presumptions. This is particularly the case of the factors analysed in Section III—'What are the alternatives?'—especially the theories of *a priori* judgments, relative-cost-of-proof, and error-cost. In other words, most rebuttable presumptions can be explained with reference to policy considerations, estimates of the probabilities of a situation, and the costs to the parties of presenting evidence, or a combination of these three factors.

Taking into account the fact that the question of the allocation of the burden of proof has not been addressed in the DSU, one of the main objectives of this chapter is to conduct a critical analysis of the rules that panels and the Appellate Body have developed to allocate the burden of proof between the parties. Section I reviews the case law and sets out the questions which will be further discussed in the following sections. Section II argues that panels and the Appellate Body have not adopted a coherent approach and that this has resulted in arbitrary allocations of the burden of

[1] The concept of the burden of proof is defined in more detail in Chapter 2. An earlier version of the present chapter was published in 2006: Michelle T Grando, 'Allocating the Burden of Proof in WTO Disputes: a Critical Analysis' (2006) 9:3 Journal of International Economic Law 615. The current chapter represents the views of the author more accurately.

proof. Section III then searches for solutions outside the realm of WTO jurisprudence. It explains that domestic law and general principles of law can provide only limited guidance. An alternative analytical framework is then developed on the basis of the law and economics literature on the burden of proof. The last part of the chapter addresses the question of whether the burden of proof should be allocated differently in compliance proceedings under Article 21.5 of the DSU.

I. The Current Status of the WTO Rules

A. The problem at issue

Article 10.3 of the Agreement on Agriculture is one of the few provisions in the agreements which directly address the question of the burden of proof—as noted in Chapter 2, presumptions such as those in Article 6.1 of the SCM Agreement, Article 2.5 of the TBT Agreement, and Article 3.2 of the SPS Agreement also affect the allocation of the burden of proof with respect to the presumed fact. According to Article 10.3, '[a]ny Member which claims that any quantity exported in excess of a reduction commitment level is not subsidized must establish that no export subsidy, whether listed in Article 9 or not, has been granted in respect of the quantity of exports in question'. The panel and Appellate Body in the *Canada—Dairy* cases noted that Article 10.3 'provides a special rule for proof of export subsidies that applies in certain disputes under Articles 3, 8, 9 and 10 of the *Agreement on Agriculture*'[2] and that this rule has the effect of moving 'the burden of proof from the complainant to the defendant'.[3] While normally it would be for the complainant to prove that the defendant provides export subsidies, under Article 10.3 the defendant must

[2] Appellate Body Report, *Canada—Measures Affecting the Importation of Milk and the Exportation of Dairy Products—Second Recourse to Article 21.5 of the DSU by New Zealand and the United States*, WT/DS103/AB/RW2, WT/DS113/AB/RW2, adopted 17 January 2003, DSR 2003:I, 213 at para 69.

[3] Panel Report, *Canada—Measures Affecting the Importation of Milk and the Exportation of Dairy Products*, WT/DS103/R, WT/DS113/R, adopted 27 October 1999 at para 7.33; Panel Report, *Canada—Measures Affecting the Importation of Milk and the Exportation of Dairy Products—Recourse to Article 21.5 of the DSU by New Zealand and the United States*, WT/DS103/RW, WT/DS113/RW, adopted 18 December 2001 at para 6.3; Panel Report, *Canada—Measures Affecting the Importation of Milk and the Exportation of Dairy Products—Second Recourse to Article 21.5 of the DSU by New Zealand and the United States*, WT/DS103/RW2, WT/DS113/RW2, adopted 17 January 2003 at paras 5.15–5.18.

In *Canada—Dairy (Article 21.5—New Zealand and US II)*, while the panel recognized that Article 10.3 requires the defendant to prove that no export subsidy has been granted in excess of its reduction commitments, it noted on paragraph 5.18 that an 'an operational interpretation of Article 10.3 requires that the Complainants make a *prima facie* showing that the elements of the claimed export subsidies are present'. On appeal, the Appellate Body disagreed with this finding of the panel. Appellate Body Report, *Canada—Dairy (Article 21.5—New Zealand and US II)*, above n 2 at para 69.

prove that no export subsidy has been granted to exports in excess of its reduction commitments.[4] Article 10.3 of the Agreement on Agriculture was interpreted in a similar manner in *US—FSC*, *US—Upland Cotton*, *US—Upland Cotton (Article 21.5—Brazil)*, and *EC—Export Subsidies on Sugar*.[5]

Apart from specific provisions such as Article 10.3 of the Agreement on Agriculture, the WTO agreements, similarly to most international treaties,[6] do not contain *general* rules regarding the allocation of the burden of proof. Panels and the Appellate Body, however, have had to deal with this question since the first disputes brought under the WTO dispute settlement system.

In one of its first decisions the Appellate Body established that 'the burden of proof rests upon the party, whether complaining or defending, who asserts the affirmative of a particular claim or defence'.[7] In order for this rule to operate, it was then necessary to define what constitutes an affirmative defence which must be proved by the defendant. Pre-WTO panels ('GATT 1947 panels') had established that exceptions such as those contained in Articles XX and XI:2(c)(i) of the GATT are defences that must be proved by the defendant.[8] This view was embraced by panels and Appellate Body as early as 1996 in *US—Gasoline*.[9] Accordingly, it would seem that the question of the allocation of the burden of proof would have been settled: the complainant would have to prove the violations of the agreements that it alleged, and the defendant would have the

[4] In *US—Upland Cotton* the Appellate Body found that Article 10.3 does not apply to unscheduled products, that is, when the export subsidy at issue regards an unscheduled product the burden of proof is on the complainant to demonstrate that export subsidies have been granted with respect to that product. Appellate Body Report, *United States—Subsidies on Upland Cotton*, WT/DS267/AB/R, adopted 21 March 2005, DSR 2005:I, 3 at para 652.

[5] Panel Report, *United States—Tax Treatment for 'Foreign Sales Corporations'*, WT/DS108/R, adopted 20 March 2000 at para 7.136; Panel Report, *United States—Subsidies on Upland Cotton*, WT/DS267/R, and Corr.1, adopted 21 March 2005 at paras 7.793ff; Appellate Body Report, *US—Upland Cotton*, above n 4 at para 644ff; Panel Report, *European Communities—Export Subsidies on Sugar, Complaint by Brazil*, WT/DS266/R, adopted 19 May 2005 at paras 7.223ff; Panel Report, *United States—Subsidies on Upland Cotton—Recourse to Article 21.5 of the DSU by Brazil*, WT/DS267/RW and Corr.1, adopted 20 June 2008 at para 14.47.

[6] The UNCITRAL Arbitration Rules is one of the few international instruments which refer to the burden of proof. It states that '[e]ach party shall have the burden of proving the facts relied on to support his claim or defence' (Article 24). The Iran–United States Claims Tribunal adopted Article 24 of the UNCITRAL Arbitration Rules as part of its Tribunal Rules of Procedure of 3 May 1983.

[7] Appellate Body Report, *United States—Measure Affecting Imports of Woven Wool Shirts and Blouses from India*, WT/DS33/AB/R and Corr.1, adopted 23 May 1997, DSR 1997:I, 323 at 14. As will be discussed in the next section of this chapter, this is one of the formulations of the rule *actori incumbit probatio*.

[8] See Joost Pauwelyn, 'Evidence, Proof and Persuasion in WTO Dispute Settlement: Who Bears the Burden?' (1998) 1 Journal of International Economic Law 227 at 235.

[9] Panel Report, *United States—Standards for Reformulated and Conventional Gasoline*, WT/DS2/R, adopted 20 May 1996 at para 6.20; Appellate Body Report, *United States—Standards for Reformulated and Conventional Gasoline*, WT/DS2/AB/R, adopted 20 May 1996. See also Panel Report, *United States—Section 110(5) of the US Copyright Act*, WT/DS160/R, adopted 27 July 2000, DSR 2000:VIII, 3769 at paras 6.13, 6.16 (referring to *US—Gasoline* in support of the proposition that the defendant bears the burden of proving exceptions).

burden of proving any exceptions contained in those agreements. This, however, is not the case.

Panels and the Appellate Body have struggled with the definition of an exception. Provisions that are very similar—all of them containing specific rules exempting members from compliance with more general rules—have been placed into two different categories: (i) provisions that establish an exception to a rule,[10] and (ii) provisions that exclude the application of other provisions.[11]

In the first case, the complainant has the burden of proving that the defendant has violated a *general* rule. This having been determined, the defendant has the burden of proving that it has complied with the requirements of the provision establishing an *exception* to that rule.

In the second case, the complainant has the burden of proving that the defendant does not fall under the situation or has not complied with the requirements of a provision which *excludes* the application of the *general* rule. If the complainant successfully discharges its burden of proof with respect to the *excluding* provision, it may then seek to establish a violation of the *general* rule. In other words, in the presence of a provision which may potentially *exclude* a Member from the application of a *general* rule, the party seeking a finding of violation of the latter—the *general* rule—must first establish that its opponent does not fall under the situation foreseen by the *excluding* provision. Therefore, while the burden of proof with respect to an exception is on the defendant, in the case of a provision that excludes the application of another the burden is on the complainant. As will be discussed in the next section, it is not easy to make this distinction. In fact, the confusing ways in which panels and the Appellate Body have described this distinction suggests that the distinction is artificial.[12] Moreover, in a few cases panels and the Appellate Body did not rely upon this distinction to allocate the burden of proof; instead they allocated the burden of proof based on other criteria.

[10] I will refer to this type of provision as 'exception provision' or 'excepting provision'.

[11] I will refer to this type of provision as 'a provision that excludes the application of another' or 'excluding provision'. A provision that excludes the application of another has also been called 'conditional right'. See, for example, Steve Charnovitz et al, 'The Appellate Body's GSP Decision' (2004) 3:2 World Trade Review 239 at 257.

[12] See Pei-San Tan, *United States – Measures Affecting Imports of Woven Wool Shirts and Blouses* (1998), online: <http://207.57.19.226/journal/Vol9/No1/sr1c.html> (accessed: on 11 May 2009) (arguing, for example, that it is difficult to distinguish *US—Wool Shirts and Blouses*—the case in which the Appellate Body first referred to excluding provisions—from other cases where the rule-exception was applied); Peter Lichtenbaum, 'Procedural Issues in WTO Dispute Resolution' (1998) 19 Michigan Journal of International Law 1195 at 1250 (arguing that the decision of the Appellate Body in *US—Wool Shirts and Blouses* left murky the manner in which Members and future panels should determine whether a particular provision or agreement is an exception or whether there are other situations where the complaining country does not have the burden of proof); Lorand Bartels, 'The WTO Enabling Clause and Positive Conditionality in the European Community's GSP Program' (2003) 6 Journal of International Economic Law 507 at 517 (arguing that the Appellate Body has characterized provisions that exclude the application of others in a confusing number of different ways).

B. The WTO jurisprudence

This section reviews the most relevant WTO cases regarding the question of the allocation of the burden of proof. The review highlights the most important aspects of the cases which will form the basis of the analysis in the next section of the chapter. Those readers who are familiar with the jurisprudence on the subject may choose to move to the next part. For ease of reference, excerpts from relevant Articles of the WTO Agreements are reproduced in the Annex to this Chapter.

US—Gasoline was the first case to go through the WTO panel and Appellate Body process. In this case the panel and Appellate Body confirmed the GATT rule that the party invoking an exception bears the burden of proving the elements of that exception. The United States had argued that its measure was justified by an exception provided in Article XX of the GATT. The panel and the Appellate Body noted that the burden of proof under Article XX of the GATT rests on the party invoking that exception, ie the United States.[13] Neither the panel nor the Appellate Body provided further reasons for their findings regarding the allocation of the burden of proof. Similar rulings were issued in *US—Underwear*, *Canada—Pharmaceutical Patents*, and *Dominican Republic—Cigarettes,* where the panels found that Article 6 of the Agreement on Textiles and Clothing (the 'ATC'), Article 30 of the TRIPS Agreement, and Article XV of the GATT, respectively, are exceptions and that, therefore, the burden of proof with respect to those provisions is on the defendants.[14]

The issue of whether a certain provision is an exception which must be proved by the defendant was more controversial in cases such as *US—Wool Shirts and Blouses*, *EC—Hormones*, *Brazil—Aircraft*, *EC—Sardines*, *EC—Tariff Preferences*, *US—FSC (Article 21.5)*, *US—Upland Cotton*, and *India—Additional Import Duties*. In these cases panels and the Appellate Body devoted considerable attention to the issue of what is an exception which places the burden of proof on the defendant. As will be discussed, in order to define what an exception is, panels and the Appellate Body sought to distinguish provisions which had previously been found to be exceptions from those that are not; they did not provide a general definition of what an exception is. In this process, they often compared the provisions at issue with Article XX of the GATT.

[13] Panel Report, *US—Gasoline*, above n 9 at para 6.20; Appellate Body Report, *US—Gasoline*, above n 9.

[14] Panel Report, *United States—Restrictions on Imports of Cotton and Man-made Fibre Underwear*, WT/DS24/R, adopted 25 February 1997 at paras 7.15–7.16; Panel Report, *Dominican Republic—Measures Affecting the Importation and Internal Sale of Cigarettes*, WT/DS302/R, adopted 19 May 2005 at paras 7.107, 7.131; Panel Report, *Canada—Patent Protection of Pharmaceutical Products*, WT/DS114/R, adopted 7 April 2000, DSR 2000:V, 2289 at para 7.16.

1. US—Wool Shirts and Blouses

Similarly to Costa Rica in *US—Underwear*, India argued in *US –Wool Shirts and Blouses* that Article 6 of the ATC is an exception, and that, therefore, the United States bore the burden of proving that it had met the requirements contained in that Article. India further argued that the language of Article 6 supported such allocation. According to Article 6, safeguard action may be taken by a Member when '[. . .] *it is demonstrated* that a particular product is being imported into its territory in such increased quantities as to cause serious damage, or actual threat thereof [. . .]' and that '[s]erious damage or threat thereof must *demonstrably* be caused by such increased quantities [. . .]'. India contended that it is for the Member taking safeguard action to *demonstrate* an increase in imports, the existence of serious damage, and a causal link between the two.[15]

The panel did not accept any of India's arguments. Instead, the panel allocated to India the burden of establishing that the safeguard measure was inconsistent with Articles 2 and 6 of the ATC.[16] In contrast with *US—Underwear*, the panel did not undertake an analysis with a view to determining whether Article 6 was an exception. The panel instead relied on the position of the litigants to allocate the burden of proof, that is, it allocated the burden of proof to India because it was the complainant in this case.

On appeal, India challenged the panel's findings regarding the burden of proof. The Appellate Body noted that it was the practice of GATT panels to place the burden of establishing a violation of the GATT on the complaining party. The Appellate Body recognized that although this was the general rule, GATT panels also applied another rule according to which the party invoking a defence, such as those found in Article XX and Article XI:2(c)(i) of the GATT, had the burden of proving it.[17] In the Appellate Body's view, the justification for the latter rule is that 'Articles XX and XI:(2)(c)(i) are limited exceptions from obligations under certain other provisions of the GATT 1994, not positive rules establishing obligations in themselves. They are in the nature of affirmative defences. It is only reasonable that the burden of establishing such a defence should rest on the party asserting it.'[18] The Appellate Body, however, found that Article 6 of the ATC is not an affirmative defence. According to the Appellate Body, 'Article 6 of the ATC is an integral part of the transitional arrangement manifested in the ATC and should be interpreted accordingly'.[19] Furthermore, the Appellate Body noted that Article 6 of the ATC contains carefully negotiated language, reflecting an equally carefully drawn balance of rights and obligations

[15] Panel Report, *United States—Measure Affecting Imports of Woven Wool Shirts and Blouses from India*, WT/DS33/R, adopted 23 May 1997 at para 5.2.

[16] Panel Report, *US—Wool Shirts and Blouses,* above n 15 at para 7.12.

[17] Appellate Body Report, *US—Wool Shirts and Blouses*, above n 7 at 16.

[18] Appellate Body Report, *US—Wool Shirts and Blouses*, above n 7 at 16.

[19] Appellate Body Report, *US—Wool Shirts and Blouses*, above n 7 at 16.

of Members.[20] In light of this, the Appellate Body found that it was upon India, the complainant, 'to put forward evidence and legal argument sufficient to demonstrate that the transitional safeguard action by the United States was inconsistent with the obligations assumed by the United States under Articles 2 and 6 of the ATC'.[21]

2. *EC—Hormones*

In *EC—Hormones*, the panel began its analysis with a general interpretative note regarding the allocation of the burden of proof in disputes under the SPS Agreement. According to the panel, 'the allocation of evidentiary burden under the SPS Agreement to the Member imposing a sanitary or phytosanitary measure flows directly from the wording of many of the provisions contained in that Agreement and in particular the first three words thereof: "*Members shall ensure that* . . ." (e.g. Articles 2.2, 2.3, 5.1 and 5.6 of the SPS Agreement).'[22]

Moreover, the panel also ruled that Article 3.3 of the SPS Agreement provides an exception to the general obligation contained in Article 3.1 of that Agreement. Therefore, according to the panel, if the complaining party demonstrates pursuant to Article 3.1 that the challenged SPS measure is not based on an existing international standard, the defending party must then prove that it has acted consistently with Article 3.3 of the SPS Agreement.[23] The panel noted that this approach was in accordance with established GATT practice, according to which, for example, the burden of proof regarding a justification under Article XX rests on the defending party.[24]

On appeal, the Appellate Body found that 'the general interpretative ruling of the Panel [was] bereft of basis in the SPS Agreement'.[25] It disagreed with the panel that

[20] The United States had argued that Article 6 constituted a critical *quid pro quo* for the acceptance of the ATC's phase-out of pre-existing quotas and integration of textiles and clothing trade into the multilateral trading system.

[21] Appellate Body Report, *US—Wool Shirts and Blouses*, above n 7 at 16.

[22] Panel Report, *European Communities—Measures Concerning Meat and Meat Products (Hormones)*, Complaint by Canada, WT/DS48/R/CAN, adopted 13 February 1998 at para 8.55 [original emphasis]. The panel's finding regarding the allocation of the burden of proof in the SPS Agreement is confusing. Similarly to other panels, the panel in this case also found that Canada and the United States, the complaining parties, had the burden of establishing a *prima facie* case of inconsistency with the SPS Agreement. However, at the same time the panel made the finding described above allocating the burden of proof to the Member imposing the SPS measure, the defending party in a case under the SPS Agreement. As noted in the previous chapter, it is possible that the panel had something else other than the burden of proof in mind when it referred to the 'evidentiary burden'. However, in the absence of further elaboration of this concept on the part of the panel, one can only wonder what exactly the panel meant. The Appellate Body interpreted the panel's statement as referring to the burden of proof. Another plausible explanation was that the panel expected the European Communities, the defending party, to place on the record all the evidence regarding the adoption of the measure at issue.

[23] Panel Report, *EC—Hormones (Canada)*, above n 22 at para 8.90.

[24] Panel Report, *EC—Hormones (Canada)*, above n 22 at footnote 393 to para 8.90.

[25] Appellate Body Report, *European Communities—Measures Concerning Meat and Meat Products (Hormones)*, WT/DS26/AB/R, WT/DS48/AB/R, adopted 13 February 1998, DSR 1998:I, 135 at para 102.

the prescriptive language of some of the provisions of the SPS Agreement—'Members shall ensure that ...'—has any bearing on the allocation of the burden of proof under that Agreement. According to the Appellate Body, there is no 'connection between the undertaking of Members to ensure, for example, that SPS measures are "applied only to the extent necessary to protect human, animal or plant life or health...", and the allocation of burden of proof in a dispute settlement proceeding'.[26] The Appellate Body, therefore, sided with the panel in *US—Wool Shirts and Blouses* in its view that the fact that a provision contains prescriptive language does not suggest any specific allocation of the burden of proof.

The Appellate Body also disagreed with the Panel's allocation of the burden of proof under Article 3 of the SPS Agreement. The Appellate Body ruled that Article 3.3 is not an exception which must be proved by the defendant. According to the Appellate Body, the general rule requiring the complaining party to establish a *prima facie* case of inconsistency with the SPS Agreement 'is not avoided by simply describing that same provision as an "exception" ...'.[27] Moreover, the Appellate Body found that the panel had misconceived the relationship between Articles 3.1, 3.2 and 3.3. According to the Appellate Body, this relationship is qualitatively different from the relationship between, for example, Article I and Article XX of the GATT. In the Appellate Body's view:

> Article 3.1 of the SPS Agreement simply *excludes from its scope of application* the kinds of situations covered by Article 3.3 of that Agreement, that is, where a Member has projected for itself a higher level of sanitary protection than would be achieved by a measure based on an international standard. *Article 3.3 recognizes the autonomous right* of a Member to establish such higher level of protection, provided that that Member complies with certain requirements in promulgating SPS measures to achieve that level.[28] [emphasis added]

Furthermore, when explaining the relationship between Articles 3.1, 3.2 and 3.3, the Appellate Body emphasized that the right of a Member under Article 3.3 'to determine its own appropriate level of sanitary protection is an important right' and that this 'is made clear in the sixth preambular paragraph of the

[26] Appellate Body Report, *EC—Hormones*, above n 25 at para 102.

[27] Appellate Body Report, *EC—Hormones*, above n 25 at para 104.

This statement seems to have been intended to address the fact that Article 3.1 uses the word 'except' in reference to Article 3.3. Another possibility is that the Appellate Body was rejecting the rule applied by GATT panels that the burden of proving exceptions such as Article XX and XI:2(c) of the GATT is upon the party invoking that exception, that is, the defendant. Such an understanding, however, would contradict the Appellate Body's own practice—eg *US—Gasoline*. Yet another possibility would be that the Appellate Body was simply stating that the fact that the complaining party asserts that a certain provision is an exception does not in and of itself turn that provision into a real exception. In order for a provision to be considered an exception it would have to comply with certain pre-requisites. The Appellate Body, however, never discussed what these pre-requisites would be.

[28] Appellate Body Report, *EC—Hormones*, above n 25 at para 104.

SPS Agreement'.[29] The Appellate Body, however, did not further explain why it considered that the relationship between Articles I and Article XX on the one hand, and the relationship between Articles 3.1 and 3.3 of the SPS Agreement on the other hand are qualitatively different.

3. *EC—Sardines*

Similar questions were raised in *EC—Sardines* in the context of the TBT Agreement. In *EC—Sardines*, the panel noted that the European Communities, the defendant, had asserted under the second part of Article 2.4 of the TBT Agreement that the international standard specified by Peru, the complainant, was ineffective or inappropriate to fulfil the legitimate objectives pursued by the challenged EC regulation. The panel found, therefore, that in line with the principle that the burden of proof rests on the party which asserts the affirmative of a particular claim or defence, the European Communities bore the burden of proving the second part of Article 2.4 of the TBT Agreement.[30] In the view of the panel, this allocation of the burden of proof is also supported by the fact that complainants are not in a position to establish what the legitimate objectives pursued by the defendant are and what factors may render the international standard inappropriate.[31] Interestingly, the panel later concluded that even though the burden of proof with respect to the second part of Article 2.4 was on the European Communities, Peru had 'provided sufficient evidence and legal arguments [...] to demonstrate that Codex Stan 94 is not an ineffective or inappropriate means to fulfil the legitimate objections pursued by the EC Regulation'.[32] This conclusion undermines the panel's earlier point that the burden of proof under the second part of Article 2.4 should be allocated to defendants because complainants are not in a position to establish the conditions laid out in that provision.

On appeal, the Appellate Body disagreed with the panel. It found that the panel's concerns about the ability of complainants to show that an international standard is ineffective or inappropriate pursuant to the second part of Article 2.4 were not justified. According to the Appellate Body, complainants have means to obtain information on the objectives of technical regulations or the specific considerations that may be relevant to the assessment of their appropriateness. Some of the options include the mechanism of Article 2.5 of the TBT Agreement,[33] the

[29] Appellate Body Report, *EC—Hormones*, above n 25 at paras 170–2.

[30] Panel Report, *European Communities—Trade Description of Sardines*, WT/DS231/R and Corr.1, adopted 23 October 2002 at para 7.50.

[31] Panel Report, *EC—Sardines*, above n 30 at para 7.52.

[32] Panel Report, *EC—Sardines*, above n 30 at para 7.114.

[33] Pursuant to Article 2.5 of the TBT Agreement, '[a] Member preparing, adopting or applying a technical regulation which may have a significant effect on trade of other Members shall, upon the request of another Member, explain the justification for that technical regulation in terms of the provisions of paragraphs 2 to 4'.

TBT enquiry points provided for in Article 10.1 of the TBT Agreement, and the process of consultations which precedes the establishment of a panel.[34]

The principal reason for overruling the panel was, however, the fact that the panel disregarded the rulings of the Appellate Body in *EC—Hormones*. The Appellate Body noted that given the similarities between Article 2.4 of the TBT Agreement, and Articles 3.1 and 3.3 of the SCM Agreement, the panel should not have disregarded the Appellate Body ruling in *EC—Hormones.*[35] According to the Appellate Body, similarly to Articles 3.1 and 3.3 of the SPS Agreement there is no 'general rule-exception' relationship between the first and the second part of Article 2.4 of the TBT Agreement; 'the circumstances envisaged in the second part of Article 2.4 are *excluded from the scope of application* of the first part of Article 2.4'.[36] Accordingly, in the view of the Appellate Body, it is for the complainant to prove not only the first but also the second part of Article 2.4.

4. *Brazil—Aircraft*

In *Brazil—Aircraft*, Canada argued that Article 27.4 of the SCM Agreement is an exception to Article 3 of that Agreement and, therefore, Brazil (the defendant) had to prove that it had complied with the conditions set out in Article 27.4. Addressing the question of which party should bear the burden of proof regarding the elements of Article 27.4 of the SCM Agreement, the panel stated that:

> Part and parcel of asserting the affirmative of a particular claim is to demonstrate that the legal provision forming the basis for that claim applies to the Member against whom that legal provision is being invoked. Naturally, there will be no inconsistency with a given provision if a Member is explicitly excluded from its scope of application or a situation is explicitly identified in the text of the Agreement as falling outside the scope of application of a particular provision. [...] Clearly, on the basis of the plain meaning of the text of the provision, developing country Members falling within Article 27.2(b) [...] do not fall within the scope of application of the prohibition contained in Article 3.1(a) until 1 January 2003.[37]

In the view of the panel, the relationship between Articles 3.1(a), 27.2(b), and 27.4 of the SCM Agreement on the one hand, and the relationship between the substantive obligations contained in Articles I or III of the GATT 1994 and the

[34] Appellate Body Report, *European Communities—Trade Description of Sardines*, WT/DS231/AB/R, adopted 23 October 2002, DSR 2002:VIII, 3359 at paras 277–80.

[35] Appellate Body Report, *EC—Sardines*, above n 34 at para 274. Perhaps for this reason the panel in *EC—Approval and Marketing of Biotech Products* invoked the similarities between Articles 3.1 and 3.3 of the SPS Agreement on the one hand, and Articles 2.2 and 5.7 of the SPS Agreement on the other hand to support its finding that Article 5.7 of the SPS Agreement is not an exception. Panel Report, *European Communities—Measures Affecting the Approval and Marketing of Biotech Products*, WT/DS291/R, WT/DS292/R, WT/DS293/R, Add.1 to Add.9, and Corr.1, adopted 21 November 2006, DSR 2006:III–VIII at para 7.2982.

[36] Appellate Body Report, *EC—Sardines*, above n 34 at para 275 [emphasis added].

[37] Panel Report, *Brazil—Export Financing Programme for Aircraft*, WT/DS46/R, adopted 20 August 1999 at para 7.50.

affirmative defences set out in the 'general exceptions' of Article XX of the GATT 1994 on the other hand, is qualitatively different.Article 27.2(b) excludes a developing country which complies with certain conditions from the scope of application of Article 3.1(a). Furthermore, in the view of the panel, although Article 27.4 would not necessarily be the legal basis for a separate claim of violation of the SCM Agreement, Article 27.4 does impose certain obligations.[38] In the light of the above, the panel concluded that Canada bore the burden of proving that Article 3.1(a) applied to Brazil—a developing country within the meaning of paragraph 27.2. Consequently, it was for Canada to establish that Brazil had not complied with the conditions stipulated in Article 27.4 of the SCM Agreement.[39]

The Appellate Body agreed with the panel's allocation of the burden of proof. Similarly to the panel, the Appellate Body noted that the 'ordinary meaning of the text of Article 27.2(b) is clear', that is, 'the prohibition of export subsidies in paragraph 1(a) of Article 3 of the SCM Agreement *does not apply* to developing country Members'.[40] The Appellate Body also emphasized that Article 27 contains 'a carefully negotiated balance of rights and obligations for developing country Members'.[41] The balance embodied in Article 27 *entitles* developing countries 'to the *non-application* of Article 3.1(a)' during a transitional period of eight years '*provided* that they comply with the specific obligations set forth in Article 27.4'.[42] Furthermore, in the view of the Appellate Body, a careful reading of paragraphs 2 and 4 of Article 27 clearly reveals that 'the conditions set forth in paragraph 4 are *positive obligations* for developing country Members, *not* affirmative defences'.[43] Accordingly, the Appellate Body embraced the distinction created by the panel between a provision establishing an affirmative defence and a provision which excludes a party or a certain situation from the application of another provision. In addition, the Appellate Body reinforced the view that Article 27.4 contains an obligation.

5. US—FSC (Article 21.5—EC)

The question of whether a provision is an exception which places the burden of proof on the defendant was raised once again in *US—FSC* (Article 21.5—EC). In that case, the United States argued that if its measure were found to be inconsistent with Article 3.1(a) of the SCM Agreement, it was nevertheless justified under the fifth sentence of footnote 59 to item (e) of the Illustrative List of Export Subsidies read in conjunction with footnote 5 of the SCM Agreement.

[38] Panel Report, *Brazil—Aircraft*, above n 37 at para 7.55.

[39] Panel Report, *Brazil—Aircraft*, above n 37 at para 7.56.

[40] Appellate Body Report, *Brazil—Export Financing Programme for Aircraft*, WT/DS46/AB/R, adopted 20 August 1999, DSR 1999:III, 1161 at para 139.

[41] Appellate Body Report, *Brazil—Aircraft*, above n 40 at para 139.

[42] Appellate Body Report, *Brazil—Aircraft*, above n 40 at para 139.

[43] Appellate Body Report, *Brazil—Aircraft*, above n 40 at para 140.

The Appellate Body concluded that footnote 59 does not alter 'the scope of the definition of a 'subsidy' in Article 1.1', nor does it alter the 'scope of item (e) of the Illustrative List or the meaning of export contingent subsidies under Article 3.1(a)'.[44] According to the Appellate Body, the fifth sentence of footnote 59, similarly to Article XX of the GATT, merely entitles Members 'to "take" or "adopt" measures to avoid double taxation of foreign-source income, notwithstanding that they may be, in principle, export subsidies within the meaning of Article 3.1(a).'[45] Therefore, the Appellate Body concluded that the fifth sentence of footnote 59 is an affirmative defence which must be proved by the defendant.

6. *EC—Tariff Preferences*

In *EC—Tariff Preferences* the panel had to determine the allocation of the burden of proof under the GATT 1979 Decision on Differential and More Favourable Treatment, Reciprocity, and Fuller Participation of Developing Countries (hereinafter the 'Enabling Clause'). The panel noted that the Enabling Clause—similarly to Articles XX, XXI, and XXIV of the GATT—does not impose an obligation on Members to provide preferences to developing countries.[46] The fact that these provisions, including the Enabling Clause, contain requirements did not, in the panel's view, alter the 'basic "non-obligatory" nature of these provisions', because the conditions contained in these provisions 'are only subsidiary obligations, dependent on the decision of the Member to take such measures'.[47] Moreover, the panel noted that the Enabling Clause not only functions similarly to other GATT 1994 provisions that the Appellate Body has characterized as exceptions (eg Articles XX, XXI, and XXIV:5 of the GATT) but it is also worded in a similar fashion, that is to say, the language of these provisions provides authorization for deviation from certain rules establishing obligations.[48] Finally, the panel noted that the policy objectives pursued by a given provision are 'not decisive in determining whether a provision is an exception or a positive rule'.[49] Accordingly, the panel concluded that the Enabling Clause is an affirmative defence which must be proved by the defendant.[50]

[44] Appellate Body Report, *United States—Tax Treatment for 'Foreign Sales Corporations'—Recourse to Article 21.5 of the DSU by the European Communities*, WT/DS108/AB/RW, adopted 29 January 2002, DSR 2002:I, 55 at para 131.

[45] Appellate Body Report, *US—FSC (Article 21.5—EC),* above n 44 at para 132.

[46] Panel Report, *European Communities—Conditions for the Granting of Tariff Preferences to Developing Countries*, WT/DS246/R, adopted 20 April 2004 at para 7.38.

[47] Panel Report, *EC—Tariff Preferences*, above n 46 at para 7.37.

[48] Panel Report, *EC—Tariff Preferences*, above n 46 at para 7.36.

In a dissenting opinion, one of the members of the panel concluded, essentially based on the wording of the Enabling Clause, that there is no a general rule-exception relationship between the Enabling Clause and Article I. Panel Report, *EC—Tariff Preferences*, above n 46 at para 9.13.

[49] Panel Report, *EC—Tariff Preferences*, above n 46 at para 7.52.

[50] Panel Report, *EC—Tariff Preferences*, above n 46 at para 7.39.

On appeal, the Appellate Body explained that:

> In cases where one provision permits, in certain circumstances, behaviour that would otherwise be inconsistent with an obligation in another provision, and one of the two provisions refers to the other provision, the Appellate Body has found that the complaining party bears the burden of establishing that a challenged measure is inconsistent with the provision permitting particular behaviour *only* where one of the provisions suggests that the obligation is not applicable to the said measure. Otherwise, the permissive provision has been characterized as an exception, or defence, and the onus of invoking it and proving the consistency of the measure with its requirements has been placed on the responding party.[51]

As the Appellate Body itself recognized, this distinction is not evident. In an analysis similar to that of the panel, the Appellate Body concluded that the Enabling Clause is an exception. The reasons for such conclusion were, first, that the ordinary meaning of the term 'notwithstanding' suggests that the 'Enabling Clause permits Members to provide "differential and more favourable treatment" to developing countries "in spite of" the MFN obligation of Article I:1'.[52] This, according to the Appellate Body, means that the Enabling Clause excepts Members from complying with Article I. Second, according to the Appellate Body, the object and purpose of the WTO Agreement and the Enabling Clause did not suggest that the Enabling Clause should not operate as an exception. The Appellate Body noted that although the Enabling Clause contributes to the furtherance of one of the objectives highlighted in the Preamble to the WTO Agreement, this does not mean that the Clause is not an exception.[53]

7. US—Upland Cotton

In *US—Upland Cotton* the United States asserted that Brazil's claims of adverse effects and serious prejudice under the SCM Agreement and Article XVI of the GATT could not be maintained unless the panel 'found that United States support measures for upland cotton do not conform to Article 13 of the Agreement on Agriculture'.[54] Brazil submitted that Article 13 of the Agreement on Agriculture is in the nature of an affirmative defence, and, therefore, the United States bore the burden of proving that its measures are in conformity with Article 13.[55]

[51] Appellate Body Report, *European Communities—Conditions for the Granting of Tariff Preferences to Developing Countries*, WT/DS246/AB/R, adopted 20 April 2004, DSR 2004:III, 925 at para 88. This test was applied in Panel Report, *EC—Approval and Marketing of Biotech Products,* above n 35 at paras 7.2968–7.2969 (where the panel found that Article 5.7 of the SPS Agreement is not an exception). For a critique of this decision, see Tomer Broude, 'Genetically Modified Rules: the Awkward Rule-Exception-Right Distinction in *EC – Biotech*' (2007) 6:2 World Trade Review 215.

[52] Appellate Body Report, *EC—Tariff Preferences,* above n 51 at para 90.

[53] Appellate Body Report, *EC—Tariff Preferences,* above n 51 at paras 94–8.

[54] Panel Report, *US—Upland Cotton,* above n 5 at para 7.287.

[55] Panel Report, *US—Upland Cotton,* above n 5 at para 7.265.

Similarly to the Appellate Body in *US—Wool Shirts and Blouses*, the panel sought to determine whether Article 13 of the Agreement on Agriculture contains positive obligations. It concluded that Article 13 does not contain positive obligations.[56] Instead, 'it sets out conditions according to which certain domestic support measures and export subsidies for agricultural products benefit from certain protection'.[57] The panel, however, did not conclude from this that Article 13 was an exception. The panel proceeded to analyse Articles 5 and 6 of the SCM Agreement and noted that both Articles expressly stated that they do not apply to subsidies for agricultural products that satisfy the conditions of Article 13 of the Agreement on Agriculture. The panel concluded on the basis of this language that '[s]atisfaction of the conditions in Article 13 is therefore a question of the scope of the obligation and the initial burden is on the complainant to adduce evidence sufficient to raise a presumption that domestic support measures do not satisfy those conditions'.[58] In the panel's view, the fact that Article 3.1 of the SCM Agreement provides that certain subsidies are prohibited '[*e*]*xcept* as provided in the Agreement on Agriculture' does not indicate that the subsidies covered by this phrase 'necessarily fall within the scope of the basic obligation in Article 3.1';[59] in other words, the panel seemed to have said that the word 'except' does not indicate that Article 13 is an exception. The panel found that this was so, because the drafters would have intended Articles 5, 6, and 3.1 to have the same effect. The panel also rejected the idea that use of the words 'notwithstanding' and 'exempt' in Article 13 necessarily indicate that Article 13 is an exception.[60] The panel concluded that Articles 3.1, 5 and 6.9 of the SCM Agreement 'alter the scope of the prohibited and actionable subsidies obligations by reference to the conditions in Article 13'.[61] Similarly, in the panel's view, the conditions contained in Article 13 define the scope of the obligations contained in those Articles of the SCM Agreement. On this basis, the panel concluded that Article 13 is not an affirmative defence.[62]

8. *India—Additional Import Duties*

In *India—Additional Import Duties*, the United States, the complainant, claimed that the Additional Duty and the Extra Additional Duty imposed by India on imports were either 'ordinary customs duties' or 'other duties or charges of any kind imposed on or in connection with the importation' (hereinafter 'ODCs') within the meaning of Article II:1(b) of the GATT. In light of this, the United

[56] According to the panel, the only positive obligation in Article 13 is the obligation to show due restraint in initiating countervailing duty investigations, but this, the panel noted, is not relevant to this dispute. Panel Report, *US—Upland Cotton*, above n 5 at paras 7.274, 7.278.

[57] Panel Report, *US—Upland Cotton*, above n 5 at para 7.274.

[58] Panel Report, *US—Upland Cotton*, above n 5 at para 7.276.

[59] Panel Report, *US—Upland Cotton*, above n 5 at para 7.277.

[60] Panel Report, *US—Upland Cotton*, above n 5 at para 7.279.

[61] Panel Report, *US—Upland Cotton*, above n 5 at para 7.282.

[62] Panel Report, *US—Upland Cotton*, above n 5 at para 7.283.

States argued, in applying the additional duty and the extra-additional duty India imposed duties in excess of those provided for in its WTO Schedule of Concessions. In response, India argued that the measures at issue were charges of the kind described in Article II:2(a) of the GATT, and hence they were not subject to the restrictions contained in Article II:1(b).

Notwithstanding the clear wording of Article II:2 of the GATT—ie 'Nothing in this Article shall prevent [. . .]'—the panel went to great length to find that the charges referred to in Article II:2 are excluded from the scope of application of Article II:1(b).[63] The panel characterized the import charges described in Article II:2(a) as being of a different nature from ordinary customs duties and ODCs.[64] According to the panel, one of the main differences between ordinary customs duties and ODCs on the one hand, and the Article II:2(a) charges on the other hand is that the former inherently discriminate against, or disadvantage, imports.[65] On account of their different nature, the panel concluded, there is no rationale for subjecting the Article II:2 charges to the disciplines of Article II:1(b).[66] The panel then noted that its view that 'Article II:2 charges are not subject to the obligations set out in Article II:1(b) has significant implications. In particular, it means that Article II:2 does not set out exceptions to the positive obligations contained in Article II:1(b)'.[67] Accordingly, the panel explained that the 'sub-paragraphs of Article II:2 do not provide affirmative defences to a claim of violation of Article II:1(b)'.[68] The panel then noted that in coming to this conclusion it was:

> [. . .] mindful of the fact that the chapeau of Article II:2 opens with the phrase '[n]othing in this Article [Article II] shall prevent . . .'. That phrase is similar to the phrase 'nothing in this Agreement shall be construed to prevent . . .' in the chapeau of Article XX of the GATT 1994 which is entitled 'General Exceptions' and which jurisprudence confirms sets out exceptions to positive obligations. However, we do not consider that a phrase like 'nothing in this Article shall prevent . . .' always and necessarily introduces an exception of the kind described above.

The panel finally concluded that in the circumstances of the case at hand, and because Article II:2 is not an affirmative defence, the United States had the burden of demonstrating that the measures at issue fall outside the scope of Article II:2(a).[69] In short, the panel's interpretation of the relationship between Articles II:1(b) and II:2 of the GATT was at least in part motivated by the

[63] The panel devoted 23 paragraphs of its report to explaining that the charges referred to in Article II:2 of the GATT are not subject to the obligations contained in Article II:1(b) of the GATT.

[64] Panel Report, *India—Additional and Extra-Additional Duties on Imports from the United States*, WT/DS360/R, adopted 17 November 2008 at para 7.141.

[65] Panel Report, *India—Additional Import Duties*, above n 64 at paras 7.130, 7.133, 7.137.

[66] Panel Report, *India—Additional Import Duties*, above n 64 at para 7.137.

[67] Panel Report, *India—Additional Import Duties*, above n 64 at para 7.148.

[68] Panel Report, *India—Additional Import Duties*, above n 64 at footnote 193 to para 7.148.

[69] Panel Report, *India—Additional Import Duties*, above n 64 at para 7.160.

objective of avoiding the characterization of Article II:2 as an exception which must be proved by the defendant.

On appeal, the Appellate Body reversed the panel's convoluted interpretation of the relationship between Articles II:1(b) and II:2 of the GATT. At the outset, the Appellate Body noted that the chapeau of Article II:2 makes clear that Article II:1(b) shall not prevent a Member from imposing on the importation of a product the kind of charges described in paragraphs (a) through (c) of Article II:2. In other words, the Appellate Body found that 'Article II:2(a), subject to the conditions stated therein, exempts a charge from the coverage of Article II:1 (b)'.[70] In allocating the burden of proof, the Appellate Body did not refer to its rulings in previous cases concerning the distinction between provisions that establish an exception to a rule, and provisions that exclude the application of other provisions. That is to say, the Appellate Body did not allocate the burden of proof on the basis of whether Article II:2(a) of the GATT was an exception or a provision that excluded the application of another provision. Instead, the Appellate Body noted that because Articles II:1(b) and II:2 are closely interrelated and the 'potential for application of Article II:2(a) is clear from the face of the challenged measures', the United States was required to demonstrate that the measures were not justified under Article II:2(a).[71]

9. *India—Quantitative Restrictions*

The panel in *India—Quantitative Restrictions* did not follow the approach adopted by other panels and the Appellate Body of allocating the burden of proof on the basis of whether a certain provision is, in the abstract, considered a claim or an affirmative defence (or exception).[72] The panel found that the rules on the burden of proof dictate that 'each party has to provide evidence in support of each of its particular assertions'.[73] This rule, according to the panel, implied that the United States had to prove 'its claims in relation to the alleged violation of Article XI:1 and XVIII:11', and India had to 'support its assertion that its measures are justified under Article XVIII:B'.[74] The panel also found that India's reference to the proviso contained in the last sentence of paragraph 11 of Article XVIII was 'in the nature of an affirmative defence'. Therefore, the panel's approach to the allocation of the burden of proof seems to have been that

[70] Appellate Body Report, *India—Additional and Extra-Additional Duties on Imports from the United States*, WT/DS360/AB/R, adopted 17 November 2008 at para 153.

[71] Appellate Body Report, *India—Additional Import Duties*, above n 70 paras 189, 192, 195.

[72] This is not to say that the panel made no reference in its Report to claims and defences. The main point here is that the panel seems to have decided whether a certain issue was a claim or a defence on the basis of the party that raised the issue, namely, issues raised by the United States were characterized as claims, whereas those raised by India where characterized as defences.

[73] Panel Report, *India—Quantitative Restrictions on Imports of Agricultural, Textile and Industrial Products*, WT/DS90/R, adopted 22 September 1999 at para 5.119.

[74] Panel Report, *India—Quantitative Restrictions*, above n 73 at para 5.119.

whoever raised a certain issue had the burden of providing proof thereof.[75] Importantly, since Article XVIII:11 is part of Article XVIII:B, it would seem that both parties had the burden of proof with respect to the points they raised under that provision.[76]

On appeal, the Appellate Body agreed with the panel that India bore the burden of proof with respect to the last sentence of Article XVIII:11.[77] The Appellate Body also found that the burden of proof with respect to the Ad Note to Article XVIII:11 rests on the complainant.[78] Similarly to the panel, the Appellate Body did not approach the question of the burden of proof on the basis of its previous rulings which sought to determine whether a certain provision was an exception which places the burden of proof on the defendant.

10. India—Autos

India—Autos arose out of further developments related to the problem presented in *India—Quantitative Restrictions*. India contended that the measures challenged by the European Communities and the United States were justified under Article XVIII:B of the GATT, and that the burden of proof with respect to that Article was on the complainants. In support of its view, India referred to the Appellate Body's finding in *EC—Hormones* that the general rule requiring a complaining party to establish a *prima facie* case of inconsistency with a provision is not avoided by simply describing that provision as an exception. Moreover India noted that in *India—Quantitative Restrictions* the panel had required the United States to prove its claim under Article XVIII:11 of the GATT. India also invoked *US—Wool Shirts and Blouses* in support of its argument that similarly to Article 6 of the ATC, Article XVIII:B of the GATT does not establish a limited exception but positive rules. Furthermore, just as Article 6 of the ATC is a fundamental part of the rights and obligations of WTO Members

[75] Panel Report, *India—Quantitative Restrictions*, above n 73 at para 5.219. A similar approach was followed by the Appellate Body in *Brazil—Aircraft (Article 21.5)*. In that case the Appellate Body noted that Brazil was seeking to use item (k) as a justification for the PROEX's inconsistency with Article 3.1(a) of the SCM Agreement. Thus, according to the Appellate Body, Brazil was, 'clearly, using item (k) to make an affirmative claim in its defence'. Therefore, the Appellate Body agreed with the panel that Brazil bore the burden of proof with respect to its alleged defence under item (k). Appellate Body Report, *Brazil—Export Financing Programme for Aircraft—Recourse by Canada to Article 21.5 of the DSU*, WT/DS46/AB/RW, adopted 4 August 2000, DSR 2000:VIII, 4067 at para 66.

[76] In paragraph 5.121 the panel noted that '[i]n the case of Article XVIII, the United States has claimed that India has violated Article XVIII:11 by maintaining balance-of-payments measures that are no longer justified. If the evidence before us supports the US position, the United States will at the same time have negated India's Article XVIII defence'.

[77] Panel Report, *India—Quantitative Restrictions*, above n 73 at para 136.

[78] Appellate Body Report, *India—Quantitative Restrictions on Imports of Agricultural, Textile and Industrial Products*, WT/DS90/AB/R, adopted 22 September 1999, DSR 1999:IV, 1763 at para 138. There was no discussion regarding the allocation of the burden of proof under the other paragraphs of Article XVIII:B.

under the ATC, Article XVIII:B is a fundamental part of the rights and obligations of developing countries under the GATT.[79]

The panel found that India misinterpreted the cases cited. According to the panel, the rule applied in those cases was the general rule on the burden of proof that a 'party claiming a violation must assert and prove its claim, and that a party asserting a defence is required to prove that the conditions for invoking that defence are met'.[80] Accordingly, in the present case, the panel concluded that because the United States and the European Communities did not assert any claims under Article XVIII:B, it was exclusively for India to prove its contentions under that Article.[81] While the panel's account of *India—Quantitative Restrictions* may be correct, it is highly questionable whether the reasoning of the Appellate Body in *US—Wool Shirts and Blouses* was as simplistic as the panel suggested.

II. Critique of the WTO Jurisprudence

The analysis in this section demonstrates that panels and the Appellate Body have failed to develop a consistent and effective approach to the allocation of the burden of proof. The analysis is divided in two parts. The first part identifies criteria that have been considered by panels and the Appellate Body when establishing whether a provision is a defence which must be proved by the defendant. These criteria are then invoked to analyse the findings of panels and the Appellate Body. The goal of this analysis is to demonstrate that those criteria have not been consistently applied which, therefore, diminishes their value in predicting the outcome of future decisions. In the second part, the analysis will focus on determining whether the criteria themselves are meaningful, that is, whether the criteria are effective in distinguishing provisions that must be proved by the defendant from those that must be proved by the complainant.

A. Have panels and the Appellate Body been consistent?

1. Distinguishing between exception *provisions and* excluding *provisions*

1.1. Identification of the criteria

A review of the WTO jurisprudence suggests that the following criteria have played a central role in determining whether a certain provision is an exception or a provision that excludes the application of another.

[79] Panel Report, *India—Measures Affecting the Automotive Sector*, WT/DS146/R, WT/DS175/R and Corr.1, adopted 5 April 2002, DSR 2002:V, 1827 at para 4.154–4.155.

[80] Panel Report, *India—Autos,* above n 79 at para 7.285.

[81] Panel Report, *India—Autos,* above n 79 at para 7.286.

(a) The *language* criterion. The 'ordinary meaning' of the words has been the starting point of panels and the Appellate Body in the interpretation of the WTO Agreements. The focus on 'text' has been so prominent that on occasion it has prompted criticism of panels and the Appellate Body.[82] Because of the prominence of the ordinary meaning of the text of the agreements in the WTO jurisprudence, it is assumed that this should be an important criterion.

(b) The *US—Wool Shirts and Blouses* criteria. The ruling of the Appellate Body in *US—Wool Shirts and Blouses* has been cited in most subsequent cases that deal with the question of the burden of proof as the authority in the matter. First, in that case, the Appellate Body said that in order for a provision to be considered an exception, it must authorize derogation, ie provide an exception, from obligations and it must *not* be a *positive rule* establishing legal obligations in itself.[83] This criterion will be referred to as the *positive rule* criterion. Second, when developing its reasoning in support of the view that Article 6 of the ATC was not an exception, the Appellate Body said that Article 6 reflects a 'carefully drawn balance of rights and obligations of Members' and that 'Article 6 of the ATC is a fundamental part of the rights and obligations of WTO Members'.[84] This suggests that the importance that the drafters placed on a certain provision is a factor that must be taken into account when determining whether a certain provision is an exception; it implies the existence of a hierarchy between provisions where exceptions are placed at a lower level of the hierarchical pyramid. This criterion will be referred to as the *hierarchical* criterion.

1.2. Analysis of the criteria

i. The language criterion. A quick look at the text of some of the provisions which were the subject of a ruling on the question of the allocation of the burden of proof reveals that most of those provisions contain some language which suggests that the drafters created a special rule deviating from other more general rules. Article XX of the GATT, and Article XIV of the GATS state '... nothing in this Agreement shall be construed to prevent ...';[85] Article XI:2(c)(i)

[82] For example, see Henrik Horn & Joseph HH Weiler, 'European Communities – Trade Description of Sardines: Textualism and its Discontents' in H Horn & PC Mavroidis (eds), *The WTO Case Law of 2002* (Cambridge: Cambridge University Press, 2005) 248 at 252; William Davey, 'The WTO Dispute Settlement System: the First Ten Years' (2005) 8 Journal of International Economic Law 17 at 22.

[83] Appellate Body Report, *US—Wool Shirts and Blouses*, above n 7 at 16.

[84] Ibid.

[85] With respect to Article XX of the GATT, see, for example, Panel Report, *US—Gasoline*, above n 9; Appellate Body Report, *US—Gasoline*, above n 9. With respect to Article XIV of the GATS, see Appellate Body Report, *United States—Measures Affecting the Cross-Border Supply of Gambling and Betting Services*, WT/DS285/AB/R, adopted 20 April 2005.

of the GATT contains the phrase '... shall not extend to the following ...';[86] Article XXIV:5 of the GATT says that '... the provisions of this Agreement shall not prevent ...';[87] Article XV:9 of the GATT states that 'Nothing in this Agreement shall preclude ...';[88] the Enabling Clause states that 'Notwithstanding the provisions of Article I...';[89] Article II:2(a) of the GATT states 'Nothing in this Article shall prevent ...';[90] Article 27.2 of the SCM Agreement says '... Article 3 shall not apply ...';[91] footnote 59 of the SCM Agreement states that 'Paragraph (e) is not intended to limit ...';[92] Article 13 of the Agreement on Agriculture provides '... notwithstanding the provisions of ...', and Articles 5 and 6 of the SCM Agreement provide 'This Article does not apply ...', while Article 3 of the SCM Agreement states that 'Except as provided in ...';[93] the words 'except' or 'exception' are used in the title of Article XX of the GATT, Article XIV of the GATS, Article 2 of the ATC,[94] Article 30 of the TRIPS Agreement,[95] Article 2.4 of the TBT Agreement,[96] Article 3.1 of the SPS Agreement,[97] and Article 2.2 of the SPS Agreement.[98]

According to the Oxford English Dictionary, the word 'exception' means '1. The action of excepting (a person or thing, a particular case) from the scope of a proposition, rule, etc. [...] 2. Something that is excepted; a particular case which comes within the terms of a rule, but to which the rule is not applicable [...]'.[99] It would be fair to say that all the expressions referred to above either fit this definition of the word 'exception' or convey the same or a very similar idea. Yet, despite the similar meaning of those expressions not all the provisions listed above have been found to be exceptions. Of the provisions above, only Articles

86 With respect to Article XI:2(c), see Appellate Body Report, *US—Wool Shirts and Blouses*, above n 7 (in *obiter dicta*).

87 With respect to Article XXIV:5, see Appellate Body Report, *Turkey—Restrictions on Imports of Textile and Clothing Products*, WT/DS34/AB/R, adopted 19 November 1999.

88 With respect to Article XV:9, see Panel Report, *Dominican Republic—Import and Sale of Cigarettes*, above n 14.

89 With respect to the Enabling Clause, see Appellate Body Report, *EC—Tariff Preferences*, above n 51.

90 With respect to Article II:2(a), see Appellate Body Report, *India—Additional Import Duties*, above n 70.

91 With respect to Article 27.2, see Appellate Body Report, *Brazil—Aircraft*, above n 40.

92 With respect to footnote 59, see Appellate Body Report, *US—FSC (Article 21.5—EC)*, above n 44.

93 With respect to Article 13 of the Agreement on Agriculture, and Articles 3, 5, and 6 of the SCM Agreement, see Panel Report, *US—Upland Cotton*, above n 5.

94 With respect to Articles 2 and 6 of the ATC, see Appellate Body Report, *US—Wool Shirts and Blouses*, above n 7.

95 With respect to Article 30, see Panel Report, *Canada—Pharmaceutical Patents*, above n 14.

96 With respect to Article 2.4, see Appellate Body Report, *EC—Sardines*, above n 34.

97 With respect to Articles 3.1 and 3.3 of the SPS Agreement, see Appellate Body Report, *EC—Hormones*, above n 25.

98 With respect to Articles 2.2 and 5.7 of the SPS Agreement, see *EC—Approval and Marketing of Biotech Products*, above n 35 at paras 7.2969, 7.2976.

99 *The Oxford English Dictionary* (2nd edn, Oxford: Claredon Press, 1989) Tomo V at 498.

XI:2(c)(i), XV:9, XX, and XXIV:5[100] of the GATT, the Enabling Clause, Article XIV of the GATS, footnote 59 of the SCM Agreement, and Article 30 of the TRIPS Agreement are exceptions which must be proved by the defendant.

Based on the wording of Article 2.4 of the ATC, the panel in *US—Underwear* concluded that Article 6 of the ATC is an exception to the general prohibition on the imposition of new restrictions, and that therefore claims under that Article must be proved by the defendant.[101] This interpretation of Articles 2.4 and 6 of the ATC was short-lived. In *US—Wool Shirts and Blouses*, the panel and Appellate Body concluded that Article 6 of the ATC is *not* an exception which must be proved by the defendant; the panel and the Appellate Body did not conduct an analysis of the wording of Article 2.4 in coming to that conclusion with respect to Article 6.

Interestingly, in *Brazil—Aircraft*, the panel and Appellate Body concluded on the basis of the plain meaning of 'shall not apply' in Article 27.2 of the SCM Agreement that developing countries falling under that provision do not fall within the scope of application of Article 3.1(a) of the SCM Agreement. Therefore, according to the panel and Appellate Body, Article 27.2 is not an exception, but rather a provision which excludes the application of another.[102] The panel and Appellate Body did not seem to consider that this fits perfectly within the definition of an exception, ie that an exception is 'a particular case which comes within the terms of a rule, but to which the rule is not applicable'. Similarly, in *US—Upland Cotton*, the panel sought to emphasize the expression 'does not apply' in Articles 5 and 6 of the SCM Agreement while downplaying the word 'except' in Article 3 of the SCM Agreement.[103] When analysing the words 'notwithstanding' and 'exempt' in Article 13 of the Agreement on Agriculture, the panel seems to have realized fleetingly that the difference between an

[100] See Gabrielle Marceau & Cornelis Reiman, 'When and How is a Regional Trade Agreement Compatible with the WTO?' (2001) 28:3 Legal Issues of Economic Integration 297 at 313, for the view that the Appellate Body in *Turkey—Textiles* found that Article XXIV of the GATT is an exception. See also, Petros C Mavroidis, 'Development of WTO Dispute Settlement Procedures Through Case-Law (We Will Fix It)' in F Ortino & E -U Petersmann (eds), *The WTO Dispute Settlement System 1995–2003* (The Hague: Kluwer Law International, 2004) 153 at 172; Alan Yanovich & Werner Zdouc, 'Procedural and Evidentiary Issues' in D Bethlehem et al (eds), *The Oxford Handbook of International Trade Law* (Oxford: Oxford University Press, 2009) 344 at 359. But see Lorand Bartels, 'WTO Dispute Settlement Practice on Article XXIV of the GATT' in F Ortino & E -U Petersmann (eds), *The WTO Dispute Settlement System 1995-2003* (The Hague: Kluwer Law International, 2004) 263 at 272 (noting that 'it is not entirely certain whether a defendant WTO Member bears the onus of proof' with respect to Article XXIV). While the Appellate Body did not expressly say that Article XXIV:5 of the GATT is an *exception* which must be proved by the defendant, it did state that Article XXIV:5 'may be invoked as a possible 'defence' to a finding of inconsistency.' Appellate Body Report, *Turkey—Textiles*, above n 87 at para 45.

[101] Panel Report, *US—Wool Shirts and Blouses,* above n 15 at para 7.16.

[102] Panel Report, *Brazil—Aircraft*, above n 37 at paras 7.50; 7.54; Appellate Body Report, *Brazil—Aircraft*, above n 40 at para 139.

[103] Panel Report, *US—Upland Cotton*, above n 5 at paras 7.275–7.277.

exception and something to which the rule is not applicable is artificial.[104] However, this did not influence the panel's final conclusion that Article 13 is not an exception which must be proved by the defendant. The word 'except' was also downplayed in *EC—Approval and Marketing of Biotech Products*. The panel in that case noted that the language 'except as provided for in paragraph 7 of Article 5' in Article 2.2 of the SPS Agreement indicates that Article 5.7 of the SPS is not an exception but rather a provision that is excluded from the scope of application of Article 2.2.[105]

In *EC—Hormones*, the panel read Article 3.1 of the SPS Agreement as establishing a general obligation to base SPS measures on international standards; this obligation, however, is not absolute since Article 3.1 provides that this rule applies 'except as otherwise provided for in [the] Agreement, and in particular Article 3.3'. The panel viewed the word 'except' in Article 3.1, together with the reference to Article 3.3, as an indication that Article 3.3 is an exception which must be proved by the defendant.[106] The Appellate Body, however, came to a different conclusion. The Appellate Body stated that the general rule that the complainant must establish a *prima facie* case 'is not avoided by simply describing [a] provision as an 'exception' [...]'.[107]

Perhaps because of *EC—Hormones*, the panel in *EC—Sardines* did not rely upon the word 'exception' in Article 2.4 of the TBT Agreement to come to the conclusion that the defendant must bear the burden of proof with respect to the second part of Article 2.4. In that case, the Appellate Body overturned the panel's decision on the grounds that 'as with Articles 3.1 and 3.3 of the *SPS Agreement*, there is no "general rule-exception" relationship between the first and the second parts of Article 2.4.'[108]

In *EC—Tariff Preferences*, the panel and Appellate Body returned to an analysis of the text. They focused on the word 'notwithstanding' and concluded that the

[104] Panel Report, *US—Upland Cotton*, above n 5 at para 7.279. The following were the words of the panel: 'The Panel also notes that Article 13 uses the words "notwithstanding" and "exempt". The ordinary meaning of "notwithstanding" is "in spite of, without regard to or prevention by". The ordinary meaning of exempt is "[n]ot exposed or subject to something unpleasant or inconvenient; not liable to a charge, tax, etc. (Foll. by *from*)" The mere use of these words does not indicate whether the measures provided for in that article fall within or without the scope of the relevant obligations in the listed provisions, any more than merely characterizing a provision as an exception. Read in context, these words do not indicate that domestic support measures provided for in paragraph (b) fall within the scope of the obligations in Articles 5 and 6 of the *SCM Agreement* in light of the clear wording of the last sentence of Article 5 and Article 6.9. Therefore, there is no basis to conclude that the use of those words indicates that export subsidies provided for in paragraph (c) fall within the scope of the obligations in Article 3.1 of the *SCM Agreement* either.'

[105] Panel Report, *EC—Approval and Marketing of Biotech Products*, above n 35 at para 7.2968. For a similar critique of the panel's reliance on the word 'except' in Article 2.2 of the SPS Agreement, see Broude, above n 51 at 219.

[106] Panel Report, *EC—Hormones (Canada)*, above n 22 at para 8.90.

[107] Appellate Body Report, *EC—Hormones*, above n 25 at para 104.

[108] Appellate Body Report, *EC—Sardines*, above n 34 at para 275.

ordinary meaning of this word suggests that the Enabling Clause exempts Members from complying with Article I.[109] Therefore, they concluded that the Enabling Clause is an exception with respect to which the burden of proof is on the defendant.[110] Notably, the panel in *US—Upland Cotton* examined the ordinary meaning of 'notwithstanding' and arrived at the opposite conclusion. The wording of Article 30 of the TRIPS Agreement also seems to have been the basis for the panel's conclusion in *Canada—Pharmaceutical Patents* that 'Article 30 is an exception to the obligations of the TRIPS Agreement' and that, therefore, the burden was on Canada, the defendant, to prove that Sections 55.2(1) and 55.2(2) of Canada's Patent Act complied with the criteria laid down in that Article.[111]

More recently, in *India—Additional Import Duties*, the panel noted that the fact that Article II:2 of the GATT opens with the phrase '[n]othing in this Article shall prevent [. . .]' does not mean that Article II:2 is an exception similar to Article XX of the GATT which reads '[. . .] nothing in this Agreement shall be construed to prevent'.[112] The panel concluded that Article II:2 excludes the application of Article II:1(b) and that, therefore, it was for the United States, the complainant, to demonstrate that the measures at issue did not meet the requirements of Article II:2(a). On appeal, the Appellate Body explained that the wording of Article II:2 of the GATT indicates that Article II:2(a) exempts certain measures 'from the coverage of ArticleII:1(b)'.[113] The Appellate Body, however, did not find that Article II:2 of the GATT is an exception which places the burden of proof on the defendant.[114]

After this brief analysis of the jurisprudence and the wording of some provisions of the agreements, it is reasonable to conclude that the language criterion has not been coherently applied, and that, therefore, it is not a useful tool to predict the outcome of disputes regarding the allocation of the burden of proof.

ii. The US—Wool Shirts and Blouses criteria. The analysis in the next few paragraphs will be divided in two parts according to the two *US—Wool Shirts*

[109] Appellate Body Report, *EC—Tariff Preferences*, above n 51 at para 90. In a dissenting opinion, one of the members of the panel concluded, essentially based on the wording of the Enabling Clause, that there is no general rule-exception relationship between the Enabling Clause and Article I. According to the dissenter: 'The words "Notwithstanding the provisions of Article I of the General Agreement . . ." indicate the relationship between the Enabling Clause and Article I. "Notwithstanding" means nevertheless or in spite of a hindrance of some kind, in this case in spite of the commitments Members had made under Article I. It is a traditional legal term that, even when standing alone, has a long history. The word derives from the Latin term "non obstante", indicating that the king or ruler had granted a licence, charter or some other right despite the law, not as an exception to the law.' Panel Report, *EC—Tariff Preferences*, above n 46 at para 9.13.

[110] Panel Report, *US—Upland Cotton*, above n 5 at para 7.279

[111] Panel Report, *Canada—Pharmaceutical Patents*, above n 14 at para 7.16.

[112] Panel Report, *India—Additional Import Duties*, above n 64 at para 7.148.

[113] Appellate Body Report, *India—Additional Import Duties*, above n 70 at para 153.

[114] Appellate Body Report, *India—Additional Import Duties*, above n 70 at para 195.

and Blouses criteria mentioned above. The first part focuses on the positive rule criterion, while the second part addresses the hierarchical criterion.

The positive rule criterion. It is not entirely clear what the Appellate Body meant when it described Articles XX and XI:2(c)(i) of the GATT as exception provisions because they provide exceptions from obligations under other provisions and are not 'positive rules' establishing legal obligations in themselves.[115] But since this statement was made against the background of Article 6 of the ATC, it may be appropriate to compare the structure of Articles XX and XI:2(c)(i) of the GATT with Article 6 of the ATC to reach a clearer definition of this criterion. A comparison between those Articles suggests that provisions that provide exceptions and are not positive rules establishing obligations in themselves (i) would contain a direct reference to the obligations that they are providing an exception from and (ii) would set down the conditions under which the exception could be invoked. In turn, provisions that contain positive rules establishing obligations in themselves—ie provisions that are not exceptions—would, similarly to Article 6 of the ATC, be self-standing provisions regulating, authorizing, or prohibiting something.

In its first decision regarding the allocation of the burden of proof after *US—Wool Shirts and Blouses*, the Appellate Body did turn to the criterion established in that decision. In *EC—Hormones*, the Appellate Body overturned the panel's characterization of Article 3.3 of the SPS Agreement as an exception. In the Appellate Body's words, Article 3.3 of the SPS Agreement recognizes the 'autonomous right' of a Member to establish a higher level of protection than that implicit in an international standard provided that that Member complies with certain requirements in promulgating SPS measures.[116] The structure of Article 3.3, if read in isolation from Article 3.1, seems to support such a conclusion—there is no reference in Article 3.3 to Article 3.1. In addition, Article 3.3 contains all the elements necessary for it to stand on its own. The same, however, cannot be said of the second part of Article 2.4 of the TBT Agreement, that is, the second part of Article 2.4 is not independent of the first part—the first and second part of Article 2.4 are parts of the same sentence. The Appellate Body, however, did not seem to take this into account when in *EC—Sardines* it overturned the panel's allocation to the defendant of the burden of proof under the second sentence of Article 2.4. In that case, the Appellate Body focused instead on the conceptual similarities between Article 2.4 of the TBT Agreement and Article 3 of the SPS Agreement.

[115] Appellate Body Report, *US—Wool Shirts and Blouses*, above n 7 at 16. See Joost Pauwelyn, *Conflict of Norms in Public International Law: How WTO Law Relates to other Rules of International Law* (Cambridge: Cambridge University Press, 2003) at 184 (explaining that 'WTO rules mostly prohibit the imposition of trade restrictions, they do not impose positive obligations on WTO members to restrict trade'); Broude, above n 51 at 228 (noting that most WTO rules are permissive norms rather than pure obligations).

[116] Appellate Body Report, *EC—Hormones*, above n 25 at para 104.

It was in *Brazil—Aircraft* that the positive rule criterion was for the first time given a different interpretation. Articles 27.2 and 27.4 of the SCM Agreement refer to Article 3.1 of the SCM Agreement and clearly depend on that provision to have any meaning. The panel, however, found that 'although Article 27.4 would not necessarily be the legal basis for a separate claim of violation of the SCM Agreement, Article 27.4 does impose certain obligations'.[117] The panel did not seem to consider, however, that those obligations are not autonomous. Nor did the panel consider that even Article XX of the GATT imposes certain obligations in that, for example, under paragraph (b) measures can only be adopted if they are 'necessary'. In short, it is fair to say that pursuant to the panel's interpretation of the positive rule criterion most, if not every, provision of the WTO agreements would be a positive rule because they all contain some type of requirement which must be observed. The Appellate Body upheld the panel's findings on very similar grounds. According to the Appellate Body, a careful reading of paragraphs 2 and 4 of Article 27 clearly reveals that 'the conditions set forth in paragraph 4 are *positive obligations* for developing country Members, *not* affirmative defences'.[118]

The last sentence of footnote 59 of the *SCM Agreement* contains a clear reference to item (e) of the Illustrative List of Export Subsidies and it is not a provision that could stand on its own. Therefore, it seemed straightforward for the Appellate Body to conclude that footnote 59 contained an exception to item (e) and was not a positive rule establishing obligations in itself. Instead of mirroring its analysis in *US—Wool Shirts and Blouses*, however, the Appellate Body in *US—FSC (Article 21.5—EC)* rephrased the positive rule criterion. According to the rephrased version, an exception does not establish any positive obligations relevant to determining the proper scope of the provisions they are providing an exception from. This suggests that exceptions do contain positive obligations but that those obligations are not relevant to determining the scope of the provisions from which they provide an exception.[119] Such interpretation contradicts *US—Wool Shirts and Blouses* where the Appellate Body said that exceptions are 'not positive rules establishing obligations in themselves.'[120]

The Appellate Body in *US—FSC (Article 21.5—EC)* invoked Article XX of the GATT as an example of a provision that does not establish any positive obligations relevant to determining the scope of other provisions. In the view of the Appellate Body, Article XX merely 'sets out circumstances in which Members are entitled to "adopt or maintain" measures that are inconsistent with the obligations imposed under other provisions of the GATT, such as Article I and III'.[121] However, the Appellate Body did not seem to consider the following point.

[117] Panel Report, *Brazil—Aircraft*, above n 37 at para 7.55.
[118] Appellate Body Report, *Brazil—Aircraft*, above n 40 at para 140 [original emphasis].
[119] Appellate Body Report, *US—FSC (Article 21.5—EC)*, above n 44 at para 127–8.
[120] Appellate Body Report, *US—Wool Shirts and Blouses*, above n 7 at 16.
[121] Appellate Body Report, *US—FSC (Article 21.5—EC)*, above n 44 at para 127.

Article XX defines the scope of the obligations contained in Articles I and III of the GATT when it entitles Members to adopt or maintain measures that would otherwise be inconsistent with those Articles. The fact that panels and the Appellate Body usually examine a measure first under Articles I and III and only if they find an inconsistency with those provisions do they move to Article XX should not prejudge the issue. If for no other reason, the agreements do not prescribe that order of analysis. In addition, an inconsistency with Articles I and III does not constitute a violation of the WTO agreements if a panel finds that the measure at issue complies with the conditions of Article XX.[122] In other words, if the measure meets the requirements of Article XX, panels and the Appellate Body cannot make a recommendation pursuant to Article 19.1 of the DSU.[123] Finally, the rephrasing of the positive rule criterion has arguably given it a totally new meaning, since according to *US—FSC (Article 21.5—EC)* provisions that are not self-standing will qualify as positive rules establishing obligations.

The panel in *US—Upland Cotton* moved even further away from the original positive rule criterion. In that case the panel explicitly recognized that Article 13 of the Agreement on Agriculture does not impose positive obligations.[124] This finding, however, did not influence the panel's final conclusion. The panel instead referred to the rephrased criterion from *US—FSC (Article 21.5—EC)* and found that Article 13 defines the scope of positive obligations contained in Articles 3,5, and 6 of the SCM Agreement and, therefore, it is *not* an exception which must be proved by the defendant. Similarly, the panel found that Articles 3.1, 5, and 6.9 of the SCM Agreement also 'alter the scope of the prohibited and actionable subsidies obligations by reference to the conditions in Article 13'.[125] Consequently, the panel concluded, 'neither those conditions nor Article 13 are an affirmative defence'.[126]

In *EC—Tariff Preferences*, the panel went back to the original *US—Wool Shirts and Blouses* formulation of the positive rule criterion. The Enabling Clause clearly refers to Article I of the GATT and, therefore, is arguably not a self-standing obligation. In the panel's view, the fact that the Enabling Clause contains requirements does not alter the 'basic "non-obligatory" nature of these provisions', because the conditions contained in these provisions 'are only subsidiary obligations, dependent on the decision of the Member to take such measures'.[127] The Appellate Body upheld the panel's finding that the Enabling

[122] This means that in a situation where Article XX applies, there is never a breach of the WTO agreements.

[123] According to Article 19.1: '[w]here a panel or the Appellate Body concludes that a measure is inconsistent with a covered agreement, it shall recommend that the Member concerned bring the measure into conformity with that agreement'.

[124] In the view of the panel, the only positive obligation in Article 13 is the obligation to show due restraint in initiating countervailing duty investigations, but this, the panel noted, is not relevant to this dispute. Panel Report, *US—Upland Cotton*, above n 5 at paras 7.274 and 7.278.

[125] Panel Report, *US—Upland Cotton*, above n 5 at para 7.282.

[126] Ibid.

[127] Panel Report, *EC—Tariff Preferences*, above n 46 at para 7.37.

Clause is an exception which must be proved by the defendant, though it did not make an explicit determination about whether the Enabling Clause is a positive rule containing obligations in itself.

This brief analysis of the jurisprudence suggests that the *US—Wool Shirts and Blouses* positive rule criterion has not been consistently applied. For this reason, it is not a useful tool to predict the outcome of disputes regarding the allocation of the burden of proof.

The hierarchical criterion. The analysis now turns to the second *US—Wool Shirts and Blouses* criterion described above, ie the *hierarchical* criterion. Similarly to *US—Wool Shirts and Blouses*, in *EC—Hormones*, the Appellate Body stated that the right contained in Article 3.3 of the *SPS Agreement* which gives Members the freedom to determine their own appropriate level of sanitary protection is 'an important right'.[128] According to the Appellate Body, this is made clear in the sixth preambular paragraph of the SPS Agreement. In *Brazil—Aircraft*, the Appellate Body made a similar statement with respect to Article 27 of the SCM Agreement to the statement it had made regarding Article 6 of the ATC in *US—Wool Shirts and Blouses*. The Appellate Body noted that 'paragraphs 2 and 4 of Article 27 contain a carefully negotiated balance of rights and obligations for developing country Members'.[129] The Appellate Body also referred in the following paragraph to the purpose of Article 27, that is, to provide special and differential treatment to developing countries in recognition of the fact that subsidies may play an important role in the economic development programmes of those countries.[130]

In *India—Autos*, the panel disregarded India's argument that '[j]ust as Article 6 of the ATC [is] a fundamental part of the rights and obligations of WTO Members under the ATC, Article XVIII:B of the GATT [is] a fundamental part of the rights and obligations of developing countries under the GATT'.[131] But it was in *EC—Tariff Preferences* that the panel and Appellate Body categorically rejected the idea that there is any hierarchy between provisions and that this hierarchy would affect the allocation of the burden of proof.[132] The Appellate Body noted that characterizing the Enabling Clause as an exception would not undermine its importance and diminish 'the right of Members to provide or to receive 'differential and more favourable treatment'.[133]

Accordingly, the analysis above reveals that the importance the drafters placed on a certain provision has not been consistently taken into account by panels and the Appellate Body when determining whether a certain provision is an exception.

[128] Appellate Body Report, *EC—Hormones*, above n 25 at para 172.

[129] Appellate Body Report, *Brazil—Aircraft*, above n 40 at para 139.

[130] Appellate Body Report, *Brazil—Aircraft*, above n 40 at para 140.

[131] Panel Report, *India—Autos*, above n 79 at paras 4.155. and 7.287.

[132] Panel Report, *EC—Tariff Preferences*, above n 46 at para 7.52; Appellate Body Report, *EC—Tariff Preferences*, above n 51 at para 98.

[133] Appellate Body Report, *EC—Tariff Preferences*, above n 51 at paras 95 and 98.

2. Decisions based on alternative grounds

There have also been cases where panels and the Appellate Body did not refer to the distinction between an *exception* provision and an *excluding* provision—though the provisions involved would clearly fall into one of these categories—nor to any of the criteria mentioned above. For example, in *India—Quantitative Restrictions*, the panel placed the burden of proof on the party that *raised* each provision.[134] The panel also specifically noted that India bore the burden of proof with respect to the proviso contained in Article XVIII:11 because India's reference to this proviso was 'in the nature of an affirmative defence'.[135] On appeal, the Appellate Body agreed with the panel that the defendant bore the burden with respect to the proviso. Neither the panel nor the Appellate Body provided further reasons for their findings. The question of the allocation of the burden of proof with respect to Article XVIII:B was raised once again in *India—Autos*, a dispute which arose out of further developments related to the problem presented in *India—Quantitative Restrictions.* Once again, the panel allocated the burden of proof with respect to Article XVIII:B to the party that raised that provision. According to the panel, since the complainants had made no representations concerning Article XVIII:B, the burden of proof was on India, the party invoking that provision.[136]

It is worth noting that the criterion that *the party who raises an issue must bear the burden of proving it* (hereinafter 'pleading criterion') is not followed consistently. For example, in *Brazil—Aircraft*, Canada had not raised any claims under Article 27 of the SCM Agreement; Article 27 of the SCM Agreement was raised by Brazil. The panel and the Appellate Body, nonetheless, imposed on Canada the burden of proving that Brazil did not meet the conditions laid out in Article 27.2 and 27.4 of the SCM Agreement.[137] Similarly, in *India—Additional Import Duties*, India rather than the United States raised Article II:2 of the GATT. The panel and the Appellate Body, however, placed on the

[134] In certain instances this arguably resulted in the burden being allocated to both parties with respect to the same provision since, according to the panel, the United States bore the burden with respect to its claim of violation of Article XVIII:11 and India with respect to Article XVIII:B—Article XVIII:11is a subparagraph of Article XVIII:B. See Panel Report, *India—Quantitative Restrictions,* above n 73 at para 5.119.

[135] Panel Report, *India—Quantitative Restrictions,* above n 73 at para 5.219.

[136] Panel Report, *India—Autos,* above n 79 at para 7.286.

[137] It is important to note that Canada had not included Article 27 in its request for establishment of a panel. Brazil argued before the panel that because Canada had not raised Article 27, Brazil could not be found in violation of Article 3 of the SCM Agreement. Canada, on the other hand, argued that it had no obligation to include Article 27 in its panel request, because Article 27 was an affirmative defence and therefore it was for Brazil to raise this provision. Although the panel found that Article 27 was not an affirmative defence and that it was for Canada to establish that Brazil had not complied with the requirements of Article 27.4, the panel did not impose any sanctions on Canada for not having raised this provision in the panel request. As discussed in Chapter 1, the WTO jurisprudence has established that claims which are not properly raised in the request for establishment of a panel cannot later be considered by the panel.

United States the burden of proving that the measures at issue did not meet the requirements of Article II:2 of the GATT.

The panel in *Dominican Republic—Cigarettes* also did not discuss any of the criteria presented in the previous section. The panel noted that both parties agreed that Article XV of the GATT is an exception and that, therefore, the burden of proof with respect to that Article is on the defendant. The panel agreed with this characterization without providing further explanation.[138] In *Brazil—Aircraft (Article 21.5)*, the Appellate Body also invoked the fact that a party had recognized—even though this had happened in a previous proceeding—that it bore the burden of proof with respect to a certain provision as one of the reasons to allocate the burden of proof to that party.[139] In that case, the Appellate Body again did not discuss any of the criteria presented above. It found that because Brazil was clearly asserting a particular item as a defence, Brazil should bear the burden of proving it.[140] It is important to note that because the allocation of the burden of proof is a question of law, panels and the Appellate Body should not leave the answer to this question to be determined by the parties. However, if *all* the parties in a case expressly agree to a certain allocation of the burden of proof this agreement may be valid for the purposes of that particular dispute.[141]

3. *Final considerations regarding all the criteria*

The discussion above demonstrates that the jurisprudence regarding the allocation of the burden of proof has not followed a clear pattern. Panels and the Appellate Body have set some criteria but have not consistently followed them. This lack of consistency makes it hard to predict the outcome of any future disputes regarding the allocation of the burden of proof.

B. Are the criteria relied upon effective?

In addition to the criticism that none of the criteria that have been discussed up until this point are consistently employed by panels and the Appellate Body, the relevance of those criteria is also questionable. The relevance of those criteria is discussed in the sections below.

1. *Pleading criterion*

The criterion that the party who raises a certain provision must bear the burden of proof with respect to the elements of that provision is easily abused, and,

[138] Panel Report, *Dominican Republic—Import and Sale of Cigarettes*, above n 14 at paras 7.107 and 7.131.
[139] Appellate Body Report, *Brazil—Aircraft (Article 21.5—Canada)*, above n 75 at para 66.
[140] Appellate Body Report, *Brazil—Aircraft (Article 21.5—Canada)*, above n 75 at para 66.
[141] See Pauwelyn, *Conflict of Norms*, above n 115 at 318–21 (arguing that the parties can conclude *inter se* agreements altering DSU procedural rights).

therefore unworkable. The parties to a case could easily draft their claims and submissions in ways that would avoid touching upon issues for which they would not wish to bear the burden of proof. This would force the opposing party to bring up the point and, therefore, bear the burden of proof with respect to it. For example, in a case under the now expired ATC, the complainants could choose to bring a claim only under Article 2.4 of the ATC even though they were aware of the fact that the restrictions imposed on imports originating in its territory would fall under Article 6 of the ATC.[142] In a more drastic example, the complainant, knowing that anti-dumping duties had been imposed on imports originating in their territory, could choose to challenge those duties under Articles I or VI of the GATT, therefore, leaving the defendant to raise and prove any claims under the Anti-Dumping Agreement.

The situation described above arguably occurred in *India—Additional Import Duties*. In that case, notwithstanding the fact that the wording of the measures at issue suggested that they had been adopted under Article II:2(a) of the GATT, the United States did not claim that the measures did not meet the requirements of Article II:2(a).[143] Instead, it claimed that the measures were inconsistent with subparagraphs (a) and (b) of Article II:1 of the GATT, forcing India to raise Article II:2(a) in its submissions. Another factor which indicates that the United States was engaging in opportunistic behaviour is that it did not pursue its claims under Article III of the GATT.[144] In order to prove its claim under Article III:2 of the GATT, the United States would have had to present arguments and evidence which would have been relevant to determining whether the measures at issue were justified under Article II:2(a) of the GATT. The outcome of *India—Additional Import Duties* was that little information was presented on the question of whether the measures at issue met the requirements of Article II:2(a). Unfortunately for the United States, the panel and the Appellate Body found that the burden of proof with respect to Article II:2(a) was on the United States. On account of the fact that there was not enough evidence on the record relating to Article II:2(a), the United States did not prevail on any of its claims.

2. *Prescriptive language*

In *EC—Hormones* and *US—Wool Shirts and Blouses*, the panels and the Appellate Body addressed the question of whether the prescriptive language of certain provisions has any impact on the allocation of the burden of proof.[145] In

[142] This strategy was suggested in Edwin Vermulst, Petros C Mavroidis & Paul Waer, 'The Functioning of the Appellate Body After Four Years: Towards Rule Integrity' (1999) 33:2 Journal of World Trade 1 at 11.

[143] See Appellate Body Report, *India—Additional Import Duties*, above n 70 at para 190 and footnote 367.

[144] Panel Report, *India—Additional Import Duties*, above n 64 at paras 7.402–7.418.

[145] See Panel Report, *EC—Hormones (Canada)*, above n 22 at para 8.55; Appellate Body Report, *EC—Hormones*, above n 25 at para 102; Panel Report, *US—Wool Shirts and Blouses*, above n 15 at paras 5.2 and 7.12.

other words, the question before the panels and the Appellate Body was whether the fact that certain provisions use language such as 'Members shall ensure that ...'[146] suggests that the burden of proof in dispute settlement should be allocated to the party to whom the provision is addressed. While the panel in *EC—Hormones* relied upon the prescriptive language of certain provisions of the SPS Agreement in allocating the burden of proof, the Appellate Body wisely disagreed with the panel.[147]

The prescriptive language of certain provisions is merely intended to impose an obligation on a Member to *do* certain things—as opposed to merely *abstaining* from doing certain things—when adopting certain types of measures, such as phytosanitary measures, which have a recognized impact on trade. This may impose a certain burden on Members adopting those types of measures since they have to ensure that certain procedures are followed in their domestic regulatory process. However, this burden should not be mistaken with the burden of proof in adjudication.

3. Exception provisions versus excluding provisions

The distinction that panels and the Appellate Body have created in the current jurisprudence between provisions that constitute exceptions and provisions that exclude the application of others is an artificial one. Although panels and the Appellate Body have not expressly said so, this distinction seems to have derived from techniques of interpretation to avoid or solve conflicts between legal rules.[148] That is to say, panels and the Appellate Body have resorted to conflict of norms analysis to conclude that while *exception* provisions and the rules they are providing an exception from are in conflict, *excluding* provisions and the rules that they exclude are not in conflict. Panels and the Appellate Body seem to believe that there is conflict between the provisions of the first group, but that this conflict can be solved through the application of the principle of *lex specialis*.[149] Pursuant to this principle, the exception provision would prevail to the extent of the conflict. As for the second group of provisions, panels and the

[146] See Articles 2.2, 2.3, 5.1 and 5.6 of the SPS Agreement.

[147] Appellate Body Report, *EC—Hormones*, above n 25 at para 102.

[148] See Ruth Sullivan, *Statutory Interpretation* (Concord: Irwin Law, 1997) at 220–34; Ruth Sullivan, *Sullivan and Driedger on the Construction of Statutes* (4th edn, Vancouver: Butterworths, 2002) at 262–80.

In *Statutory Interpretation* Sullivan explains that:

When two (or more) legislative provisions apply to the same facts, there are four possibilities:

The overlapping provisions do not conflict, and since both apply, the court gives effect to both.

The overlapping provisions might conflict, but the conflict is avoided through interpretation.

The overlapping provisions do not conflict, but the court concludes that one of the provisions was meant to be exhaustive and therefore applies to the exclusion of the other.

The overlapping provisions conflict and, in order to resolve the conflict, the court applies a conflict resolution rule.

[149] See Steve Charnovitz et al, above n 11 at 257.

Appellate Body maintain that these provisions do not conflict because they have different scopes of application, that is, they do not overlap.[150]

The main criticism of the approach followed by panels and the Appellate Body is that there is no conflict or overlap between the provisions of either group. Therefore, there is no need to resort to this type of analysis. The drafters of the Agreements explicitly dealt with any possible conflict that could arise between the provisions at issue here when they included words and phrases such as 'except', 'notwithstanding', 'nothing in this Agreement shall be construed to prevent', and 'shall not apply'. The language of all the provisions at issue—ie exceptions as well as excluding provisions—explicitly allows for deviations from other rules. Therefore, it is clear that, for example, owing to the action of the drafters there is no conflict or overlap between Articles I and XX of the GATT just as there is no conflict or overlap between Articles 3.1 and 3.3 of the SPS Agreement.[151] Conflict of norms analysis is appropriate when due to legislative oversight courts do not know which provision applies to a certain situation. However, this is not the case when due to legislative action it is clear which provision applies.[152] Finally, and most importantly, the allocation of the burden of proof and determination of which party should raise a certain claim before a panel should be based on considerations specific to the question of proof and the efficient functioning of the legal process rather than an analytical tool developed for completely different purposes.[153]

In addition, the criteria that have been used to differentiate an exception provision from an excluding provision lack substance. The fact that panels and the Appellate Body have rephrased and changed the meaning of the positive rule criterion is an indication of this. The application of this criterion has created artificial differences between provisions. For example, the panel in *EC—Tariff*

[150] It is also possible that panels and the Appellate Body consider that *excluding* provisions are meant to constitute an exhaustive regulation of the matter. However, it is questionable whether the provisions that have been characterized as provisions that exclude the application of others would meet the requirement of exhaustiveness. For more on that requirement, see Sullivan, *Statutory Interpretation*, above n 148 at 223.

[151] In support of the view that there is no conflict between a rule and an explicit exception to that rule, eg between Articles III and XX of the GATT, see Pauwelyn, *Conflict of Norms,* above n 115 at 163, 176, 185, 250, 414.

[152] In most of the cases discussed in this chapter there was no disagreement between the parties over the issue of whether exceptions and *excluding* provisions applied. The main disagreement was over which party had to raise and prove claims regarding exceptions and *excluding* provisions. *Turkey—Textiles* is one of the few cases where the parties seemed to disagree on the issue of whether a provision, ie Article XXIV of the GATT, applied. While the panel found that Article XXIV does not justify 'the introduction of measures otherwise incompatible with the WTO Agreement', the Appellate Body ruled that Article XXIV may be invoked to justify violations of other provisions of the GATT. According to the Appellate Body, the words 'shall not prevent' in the chapeau of Article XXIV:5 should be read to mean 'that the provisions of the GATT 1994 *shall not make impossible* the formation of a customs union'. Panel Report, *Turkey—Restrictions on Imports of Textile and Clothing Products*, WT/DS34/R, adopted 19 November 1999 at paras 9.190, 9.208; Appellate Body Report, *Turkey—Textiles,* above n 87 at para 45.

[153] This question will be explored further below.

Preferences concluded that the Enabling Clause is *not* a positive rule because, similarly to Articles XX, XXI, and XXIV of the GATT, it does not impose an obligation on Members to *do* something, eg provide preferences; the obligations contained in those provisions are subsidiary because they depend on the decision of a Member to adopt certain measures, eg grant tariff preferences.[154] If this understanding is applied, many of the provisions that have been classified as provisions that exclude the application of other provisions would not meet the positive rule criterion. For instance, Article 6 of the ATC does not oblige Members to adopt safeguard measures, nor does Article 3.3 of the SPS Agreement mandate Members to adopt measures that pursue higher levels of protection than international standards. Similarly to the Enabling Clause and Articles XX, XXI, XXIV of the GATT, Article 6 of the ATC and Article 3.3 of the SPS Agreement set out conditions that must be complied with if a Member decides respectively to avail itself of the right to impose a safeguard measure or adopt an SPS measure that guarantees a higher level of protection than an existing international standard.

The distinction created between Article 3 of the SPS Agreement and Article XX of the GATT is particularly instructive. The SPS Agreement is the product of an effort to discipline an area where the domestic regulatory process could potentially undermine the benefits of tariff bargains.[155] It is clear that WTO Members recognized that SPS regulation is often necessary, but this does not mean that Members thought that they could act without constraint when enacting SPS measures. In this context, the SPS Agreement expressed a preference that Members use international standards when possible.[156] This preference is clearly expressed in Article 3.1 of the SPS Agreement which states that 'Members shall base their sanitary or phytosanitary measures on international standards, guidelines or recommendations, where they exist ...'. The fact that Members expressed this preference, however, does not mean that they thought that they could not adopt measures that are not based on international standards. An authorization to adopt such measures was expressly included in Articles 3.1 and 3.3 of the SPS Agreement. This authorization, however, was not a *carte blanche* for Members to do whatever they saw fit. Article 3.3 contains the conditions which must be observed.

It can similarly be said that the drafters of the GATT have also recognized that some kinds of domestic regulation, such as health regulation, are necessary. They also recognized that these regulations may affect international trade by, for

[154] Panel Report, *EC—Tariff Preferences*, above n 46 at paras 7.37–7.38. See Bartels, *The WTO Enabling Clause*, above n 12 at 518 (arguing that a good case could be made 'that the conditions in the Enabling Clause should be seen as "positive obligations" which must be satisfied if a WTO Member wishes to benefit from the exemption applicable to trade preferences for developing countries').

[155] Kevin C Kennedy, 'Resolving International Sanitary and Phytosanitary Disputes in the WTO: Lessons and Future Directions' (2000) 55 Food and Drug Law Journal 81 at 83.

[156] See Horn & Weiler, above n 82 at 252 (arguing that the paradigm shift from local discretion to an internationally determined standard is a germane factor establishing the object and purpose and the context of the TBT and SPS Agreements).

instance, granting imports less favourable treatment than domestic products or by restricting access to the market of the regulating country. They expressed a preference that Members do not do so in, eg Articles III and XI of the GATT. The fact that Members expressed this preference, however, does not mean that they thought that they could not adopt measures under any circumstances that, eg, provide less favourable treatment to imports. An express authorization to do so is contained in Article XX which states that 'nothing in this Agreement shall be construed to prevent the adoption or enforcement ...'. This authorization, however, is subject to certain conditions which are specified in the chapeau and paragraphs of Article XX.

Accordingly, the distinction created between Articles 3.1 and 3.3 of the SPS Agreement, and Article XX of the GATT is not based on the substance or the purpose of those Articles. Moreover, if the references to Article XX(b) contained in the SPS Agreement are taken into account, the fragility of the distinction becomes more evident.[157] The Preamble to the SPS Agreement notes that the SPS Agreement elaborates on the provisions of Article XX(b) of the GATT. In addition, Article 2.4 of the SPS Agreement provides that measures which comply with the SPS Agreement shall be presumed to be in accordance with the obligations of the Members under the provisions of Article XX(b). Article 2.4 suggests that it might not have been the intention of Members to allocate the burden of proof differently in Article XX(b) of the GATT and the SPS Agreement. This is so because if the measure is challenged under the GATT only, under the current rules the burden of proof is on the defendant since Article XX is an exception. However, if the measure is challenged under the SPS Agreement and the GATT, the burden will be on the complainant to show that the measure is not consistent with the SPS Agreement. If the complainant is not able to do so, the measures will be found to be consistent with the SPS Agreement and, therefore, enjoy a presumption of consistency with the GATT. As will be discussed in the next section, this is not to say that the burden of proof with respect to the SPS Agreement should be allocated to the defendant.

4. Hierarchical criterion

The application of the hierarchical criterion has created two classes of provisions. The reasoning goes as follows. If Members intended that a provision be a fundamental part of the scheme of rights and obligations, then they could not have intended that provision to work as an exception. That provision is then characterized as a provision that excludes the application of another, and,

[157] See Jeff Waincymer, *WTO Litigation: Procedural Aspects of Formal Dispute Settlement* (London: Cameron May, 2002) at 554. Waincymer argues that '[t]he different results in Hormones on the one hand and Shirts and Blouses and Reformulated Gasoline on the other are even more stark given that the SPS Agreement uses a number of criteria from Article XX of the GATT 1994 as positive requirements under its own terms'.

therefore, the burden of proof is allocated to the complainant. For obvious reasons, the application of this criterion makes the process of allocation of the burden of proof hostage to value judgments—that is, judgments about what is subjectively considered important or fundamental—and vulnerable to criticism. The Appellate Body seems to have realized this in *EC—Tariff Preferences* when it found that 'characterizing the Enabling Clause as an exception [...] does not undermine the importance of the Enabling Clause within the overall framework of the covered agreements [...] Nor does it "discourage" developed countries from adopting measures in favour of developing countries under the Enabling Clause.'[158]

However, this recognition might have come too late in the process. The prevalent perception is that certain values have been favoured over others, and that in certain situations important values have not been adequately protected. Abbott expresses this concern with respect to Articles 13 and 30 of the TRIPS Agreement, which have been classified as exceptions which must be proved by the defendant.[159] He notes that in *EC—Hormones* the Appellate Body went to some lengths to explain that the European Communities had the right to protect its public and that the burden was on the United States to demonstrate that the European Communities had failed to apply reasonable scientific standards. He then raises the question: 'If exceptions to patent rights allow governments scope to protect the public interest, should the burden be on the Member establishing the exception to demonstrate that it is doing so?'[160] More than demonstrating that the burden of proof was allocated wrongly either in *EC—Hormones* or in *Canada—Pharmaceutical Patents*, this kind of criticism reiterates the problematic nature of the *hierarchical* criterion and the distinction it purports to establish between exceptions and provisions that exclude the application of other provisions. Panels and the Appellate Body are not in a position to determine the importance that Members placed on a certain provision—this is a subjective judgment or at least the manner in which the Appellate Body has referred to it indicates that it is. Nor should they infer from the importance of a provision and in the absence of an indication to the contrary that Members intended to allocate the burden of proof differently than would otherwise be the case.

5. Language criterion

Relying purely on the language of a provision does not constitute a sounder and more predictable method for allocating the burden of proof. As noted above, the

[158] Appellate Body Report, *EC—Tariff Preferences*, above n 51 at para 95.

[159] Frederick M Abbott, 'WTO Dispute Settlement Practice Relating to the Agreement on Trade-Related Intellectual Property Rights' in F Ortino & E -U Petersmann (eds), *The WTO Dispute Settlement System 1995–2003* (The Hague: Kluwer International Law, 2004) 421 at 443.

Joost Pauwelyn has also expressed some concern that 'all the distinctions and complexities added by the AB give the impression that conditional rights [or *excluding* provisions] are more important than exceptions [...]'. See Steve Charnovitz et al, above n 11 at 257.

[160] Abbott, above n 159 at 444.

definition of 'exception' encompasses the idea expressed in the phrase 'shall not apply'. Moreover, it is not clear why the burden of proof should be allocated differently when a provision that establishes an exception is at issue.

It is true that GATT 1947 panels issued a series of decisions embracing the view that the party claiming an exception had the burden of showing that it had satisfied the requirements of that exception.[161] However, WTO panels and the Appellate Body have not blindly followed GATT 1947 panels in many areas including this issue. For example, some GATT 1947 panels considered that the trade remedies provisions constituted exceptions to the general GATT rules. Therefore, the onus was upon parties imposing anti-dumping and countervailing duties to demonstrate before a dispute settlement panel that they had not acted inconsistently with the terms of the provisions granting such exceptions.[162] Relatedly, GATT 1947 panels also held that exceptions had to be interpreted narrowly.[163] WTO panels and the Appellate Body have not supported the view that trade remedies rules are exceptions which must be proved by the party making use of those rules. They have also rejected the view that exceptions must be interpreted narrowly.[164] Accordingly, while there might have

[161] Panel Report, *Panel on Norwegian Procurement of Toll Collection Equipment for the City of Trondheim*, adopted 13 May 1992, BISD 40S/319 at para 4.5; Panel Report, United States—Measures Affecting Alcoholic and Malt Beverages, adopted 19 June 1992, BISD 39S/206 at paras 5.41–5.42; Panel Report, *United States—Restrictions on Imports of Tuna*, September 1991, unadopted, BISD 39S/155 at para 5.22; Panel Report, *United States Section 337 of the Tariff Act of 1930*, adopted 7 November 1989, BISD 36S/345 at para 5.27; Panel Report, *European Economic Community—Restrictions on Imports of Dessert Apples—Complaint by Chile*, adopted 22 June 1989, BISD 36S/93 at para 12.3; Panel Report, *Canada—Import Restrictions on Ice Cream and Yoghurt*, adopted 5 December 1989, BISD 36S/68 at para 59; Panel Report, *European Economic Community—Restrictions on Imports of Apples—Complaint by the United States*, adopted 22 June 1989, BISD 36S/135 at para 5.3; Panel Report, *Japan—Restrictions on Imports of Certain Agricultural Products*, adopted 2 March 1988, BISD 35S/163 at para 5.1.3.7; Panel Report, *Canada—Administration of the Foreign Investment Review Act*, adopted 7 February 1984, BISD 30S/140 at para 5.20. See also Philip M Nichols, 'GATT Doctrine' (1996) 36 Virginia Journal of International Law 379 at 435; Rutsel Silvestre J Martha, 'Presumptions and Burden of Proof' (1997) 14 Journal of International Arbitration 67 at 87.

[162] See, eg Report of the GATT Panel, *United States—Countervailing Duties on Fresh, Chilled and Frozen Pork from Canada*, DS7/R, adopted July 11, 1991, BISD 38S/30, para 4.4; Panel Report, *Swedish Anti-Dumping Duties*, adopted 26 February 1955, BISD 3S/81, paras 15, 22–23. See also Duane W Layton, 'The Litigation of Anti-Dumping Disputes before the World Trade Organization' (2000) 4 Business Law International 294 at 300; James Cameron & Kevin R Gray, 'Principles of International Law in the WTO Dispute Settlement Body' (2001) 50 International and Comparative Law Quarterly 248 at 28; Martha, above n 161 at 87, 90, 95.

[163] See, for example, Report of the GATT Panel, *US—Canadian Pork*, above n 162 at para 4.4.

[164] See Appellate Body Report, *EC—Hormones*, above n 25 at para 104 (where the Appellate Body stated that 'merely characterizing a treaty provision as an "exception" does not by itself justify a "stricter" or "narrower" interpretation of that provision than would be warranted by examination of the ordinary meaning of the actual treaty words, viewed in context and in the light of the treaty's object and purpose, or, in other words, by applying the normal rules of treaty interpretation'). See also Peter Van den Bossche, *The Law and Policy of the World Trade Organization: Text, Cases and Materials* (2nd edn, Cambridge: Cambridge University Press, 2008) at 618 (noting that the Appellate Body has rejected the position that the exceptions contained in Article XX of the GATT should be construed narrowly).

been a GATT practice of allocating to the defendant the burden of proof with respect to exceptions, the Appellate Body broke away from that practice with respect to GATT provisions which were elaborated in entirely new agreements such as the trade remedies agreements. This was so even though those agreements do not expressly allocate the burden of proof to the complainant. Notably, at least in the context of one of those agreements (the SCM Agreement), the United States sought to include a provision to that effect, but was unsuccessful.[165]

In light of the above, and for reasons of consistency, the Appellate Body should have been prepared to reject the whole practice regarding exceptions. In fact, it is worrisome that this rule has not been questioned more vigorously, since there is no indication in the text of the WTO agreements that the burden of proof with respect to provisions that provide exceptions should be allocated to the defendant. Why should we assume that this was the intention of the drafters, particularly in light of provisions such as Article 10.3 of the Agreement on Agriculture which clearly address the question of the burden of proof?

The Appellate Body may have been right when in *EC—Hormones* it found that '[t]he general rule in a dispute settlement proceeding requiring the complaining party to establish a *prima facie* case of inconsistency [...] is *not* avoided by simply describing that same provision as an "exception" [...].'[166] The problem with *EC—Hormones* is that even though the Appellate Body seems to have stated that the fact that a provision is an exception says nothing about the allocation of the burden of proof, the Appellate Body still went to some lengths to explain that Article 3.3 of the SPS Agreement is not an exception, but rather a self-standing provision that excludes the application of Article 3.1 of the SPS Agreement. In other words, the Appellate Body could instead have concluded that even though Article 3.3 is an exception—which seems undeniable from the language of Article 3.1 of the SPS Agreement—in the absence of any indication to the contrary, there is no reason to place the burden of proof on the defendant with respect to that Article.

One of the main problems with allocating the burden of proof to the defendant with respect to exceptions is that this allocation is based on the assumption that there is something special about an exception that would imply that the drafters made such choice of allocation. But what is so special about an exception? Does not an exception merely define the scope of a rule? As Williams explains in criminal law parlance, '[r]ationally regarded, an "exception" merely

[165] See Terence P Stewart (ed), *The GATT Uruguay Round: a Negotiating History (1986–1992)* (Deventer: Kluwer Law and Taxation Publishers, 1993) vol I at 949 (noting that the United States proposed that the new countervailing duties agreement provide that complainants 'have the burden of demonstrating, by clear and convincing evidence, that the investigating authorities have not acted reasonably in implementing their obligations under the GATT Subsidies Code').

[166] Appellate Body Report, *EC—Hormones*, above n 25 at para 104 [original emphasis].

states the limits of an offence. A person whose act falls within the exception does not commit the offence.'[167] Therefore, 'the exception is, rationally regarded, part and parcel of the rule'.[168] In addition, it is often possible to draft provisions in a way that the exception is contained in the rule;[169] thus, the use of words indicating an exception may only have the function of making a provision easier to read and understand.[170] For example, instead of using the word 'except' in Article 3.1 of the SPS Agreement to establish a relationship with Article 3.3, the drafters could have chosen the following wording:

> When a Member chooses a level of sanitary and phytosanitary protection that is similar to the level implicit in an international standard it shall base its measures on that standard. If a higher level of protection is desired, a Member may adopt a measure that is not based on an international standard. In the latter case, the Member shall ensure that it observes the relevant provisions of paragraphs 1 through 8 of Article 5 ...

The fact that an exception is stated in a separate Article should not alter this conclusion. The drafters may have preferred to create a separate provision merely for reasons of convenience, that is, in order to avoid having to incorporate the exception into several or all Articles of an agreement.

In light of the above, the following question seems inevitable. Is it appropriate to assume that the style of drafting chosen for a certain provision represents a considered judgment as to the allocation of the burden of proof? One might argue that the drafters were aware of the rule that the burden of proof with respect to exceptions is allocated to the defendant when they chose to express a certain rule in the form of an exception; thus they implicitly made a choice concerning the allocation of the burden of proof. The truth of this proposition is questionable, particularly because it would be fair to state that there is no general principle of law recognized by civilized nations that an exception must be proved by the defendant.[171]

[167] Granville Williams, 'The Logic of "Exceptions"' (1988) 47:2 Cambridge Law Journal 261 at 262.

[168] Williams, above n 167 at 278.

[169] Williams, above n 167 at 270.

[170] See also Broude, above n 51 at 229 (noting that 'permissions', which include exceptions, can be expressed in 'obligatory semantics, without the use of any distinctively permissive language'. Accordingly, he also concludes that the 'textual structuring of provisions tells us little about [...] their burden-of-proof classification').

[171] It is worth noting that there was a principle in Roman law according to which *reus in exceptione actor est*. The *exceptio* in Roman law referred to any defence put forward by the defendant which went beyond a mere denial of the facts alleged by the plaintiff. The expression *exceptio* is still used in civil law jurisdictions to refer broadly to the defendant's response to the claims put forward by the plaintiff. In this regard, see Antonio Carlos de Araújo Cintra, Ada Pellegrini Grinover & Cândido R. Dinamarco, *Teoria Geral do Processo* (12th edn, São Paulo: Malheiros, 1996) at 272–5; José Vizcarra Dávalos, *Teoría General del Proceso* (9th edn, Mexico City: Editorial Porrúa, 2007) at 141–2. The expression *exceptio* is also used in codes of civil procedure in connection with procedural pleas. For instance, in the French and the Brazilian codes of civil procedure, *les exceptions* and *exceções*, respectively, constitute procedural pleas such as the plea of lack of jurisdiction.

The jurisprudence of the International Court of Justice does not refer to such a principle.[172] As for domestic law, some commentators have noted that in their quest to determine what is essential to a party's case courts in certain jurisdictions have sometimes applied a controversial formula, ie they have sought to distinguish between the constituent elements of a promise or of a statutory command and matters of exception; the plaintiff would have the burden of proving the constituent elements and the defendant the burden of proving exceptions, exemptions, excuses, qualifications, and provisos.[173] The presence of linguistic signposts such as 'except for', 'provided that', and 'subject to' would help in determining whether a certain provision constitutes a matter of exception.[174] It is important to note that most examples of cases where this formula is applied refer to litigation concerning contracts,[175] or cases where the application of this formula resulted from a specific statutory command.[176] Furthermore, in many cases courts employ this formula only to allocate the burden of pleading—in which case the burden of proof remains with the plaintiff.[177] In any event, the formula has been criticized for leading to arbitrary allocations of the burden of proof, as the 'statutory language may be due to a mere casual choice of form by the draftsman'.[178]

Sullivan also notes that 'courts *sometimes* suggest that statutory exceptions are to be strictly construed, or alternatively, that persons seeking to benefit of a statutory exemption or exception must establish clearly that they come within its terms'.[179] She explains that the reason behind this is that the courts are 'concerned that exceptions and exemptions be interpreted in light of their underlying rationale and not used to undermine the broad purpose of the legislation'.[180] In the WTO context, panels and the Appellate Body would in most cases have little legitimacy to make this kind of judgment about the broad

[172] This statement is based on a review of the cases published in the 'International Court of Justice Decisions, Combined' database of <www.lexis.com> (accessed 27 April 2009).

[173] John W Strong (ed), *McCormick on Evidence* (5th edn, St Paul: West Group, 1999) vol 2 at 415; John Sopinka, Sidney N Lederman & Alan W Bryant, *The Law of Evidence in Canada* (Toronto: Butterworths, 1992) at 84.

[174] John Sopinka, Sidney N Lederman & Alan W Bryant, *The Law of Evidence in Canada* (2nd edn, Toronto: Butterworths, 1999) at 84.

[175] See Clifford S Fishman, *Jones on Evidence: Civil and Criminal* (7th edn, Rochester: Lawyers Cooperative Publishing, 1992) at 272; Strong, above n 173 at footnote 15 to page 414.

[176] See, for example Section 101 of the Magistrate's Courts Act 1980 (UK), c 43; Section 18 of the Uniform Narcotic Drug Act 1932 (US).

[177] Strong, above n 173 at 414–15. Strong also notes that when an exception points to an exceptional situation an estimate of the probabilities may suggest that the burden of proof should be allocated to the party relying upon the exception. The use of estimate of probabilities to allocate the burden of proof will be further discussed below.

[178] Strong, above n 173 at 414. See also Julius Stone, 'Burden of Proof and the Judicial Process: A Commentary on *Joseph Constantine Steamship, LTD.* v. *Imperial Smelting Corporation, LTD.*' (1944) 60 The Law Quarterly Review 262 at 281.

[179] Sullivan, *Construction of Statutes*, above n 148 at 396. [emphasis added]

[180] Ibid, at 397.

purpose of the Agreements. Unlike domestic courts, panels and the Appellate Body cannot rely upon a set of fundamental principles such as those found in national constitutions to guide them in that process. Panels and the Appellate Body not only cannot rely upon fundamental principles, but also cannot refer to any legislative expression of policy with respect to certain Agreements or provisions in the Agreements. For example, the Anti-Dumping Agreement and the SCM Agreement do not have a preamble which could provide some guidance as to the policy objectives of those agreements. Scarcity of legislative expressions of policy in the text of the WTO agreements likely reflect the fact that while WTO Members agreed on the text of the Agreements, they often had different views on the policy behind those Agreements. In any event, as noted above, the Appellate Body has expressly rejected the view that exceptions must be strictly or narrowly construed. It may be time to do the same with the rule that exceptions must be proved by the defendant.

III. What are the Alternatives?

Where does the discussion above leave us? Panels and the Appellate Body have not consistently followed the same rules to allocate the burden of proof. The criteria they have set out to distinguish between exceptions and provisions that exclude the application of other provisions, as well as the distinction itself, seem artificial. The criterion that the party who raises a certain provision must bear the burden of proof with respect to the elements of that provision is easily abused. The prescriptive language of certain provisions is merely intended to impose an obligation on a Member to *do* certain things when adopting certain types of measures, that is to say, it does not address the question of the burden of proof in the litigation process. In the light of all this, how is the burden of proof to be allocated? Are there any lessons to be learned from domestic courts and other international courts and tribunals?

A. A look at domestic and international law

1. Actori Incumbit Probatio

It is a general principle of law that the burden of proof lies on the claimant—*actori incumbit probatio* or *actori incumbit onus probandi.* This principle had its origin in the Roman judicial system, and is considered in present times to embody the general rule regarding the allocation of the burden of proof in domestic as well as in international judicial proceedings.[181] The general and abstract character of this

[181] See Bin Cheng, *General Principles of Law as Applied by International Courts and Tribunals* (London: Stevens & Sons, 1953) at 327, 334; Mojtaba Kazazi, *Burden of Proof and Related Issues: a Study on Evidence before International Tribunals* (The Hague: Kluwer Law International, 1996) at

principle has contributed to its widespread acceptance. On account of these characteristics, however, the principle does not provide detailed guidance on how the burden of proof should be allocated, particularly in complex situations.

It is widely understood that the reference to the claimant should not necessarily be equated with a reference to the plaintiff from the procedural standpoint[182]—though the plaintiff is indeed the claimant in most situations.[183] If both the plaintiff and the defendant can be the claimant, it is then necessary to define which claims must be associated with the plaintiff and which claims (or defences *stricto sensu*) must be associated with the defendant.

2. To whose case is the claim essential?

Some common law commentators have noted that in distinguishing between claims that must be proved by the complainant and those that must be proved by the defendant courts often inquire whether a certain claim is essential to the plaintiff's or the defendant's case.[184] However, as Wigmore notes, this only advances the inquiry one step in that 'we must then ask whether there is any general principle which determines to what party's case a fact is essential'.[185] Some civil law jurisdictions have pursued a similar line of inquiry; they have sought to distinguish between facts that give rise to a legal right, those that prevent the formation of that legal right, those that modify a legal right, and those that extinguish a legal right. In this system, plaintiffs who assert a legal right in judicial proceedings must prove the facts on which the right is based. Defendants may oppose by claiming the existence of certain causes preventing

221–2; Chittharanjan F Amerasinghe, *Evidence in International Litigation* (Leiden: Martinus Nijhoff, 2005) at 61–2; Shabtai Rosenne, *The Law and Practice of the International Court, 1920–1996* (3rd edn, The Hague: Martinus Nijhoff, 1997) at 1083; Anna Riddell & Brendan Plant, *Evidence before the International Court of Justice* (London: British Institute of International and Comparative Law, 2009) at 87; Andreas Reiner, 'Burden and General Standards of Proof' (1994) 10 Arbitration International 328, at 333; Harald Koch & Frank Diedrich, Civil Procedure in Germany (The Hague: Kluwer Law International, 1998) at 109. This principle is also embodied in Article 9 of the French Code of Civil Procedure. See Christian Dodd, *The French Code of Civil Procedure in English* (Dobbs Ferry: Oceana Publications, 2005). For arguments against the application of this principle in international law, see JC Witenberg, 'Onus Probandi Devant les Juridictions Arbitrales' (1951) 55 Revue Generale de Droit International Public 321 at 325–7; Mojtaba Kazazi, *Burden of Proof and Related Issues: a Study on Evidence before International Tribunals* (The Hague: Kluwer Law International, 1996) at 224–30.

[182] See Cheng, above n 181 at 332; Kazazi, above n 181 at 221.In this light, Principle 21.1 of the ALI/UNIDROIT Principles of Transnational Civil Procedure provides that 'each party has the burden to prove all the material facts that are the basis of that party's case.' See American Law Institute & UNIDROIT, *Principles of Transnational Civil Procedure* (Cambridge: Cambridge University Press, 2006) at 42.

[183] See for example, Strong, above n 173 at 412; Rosenne (1997), above n 181 at 1083.

[184] Colin Tapper, *Cross and Tapper on Evidence* (9th edn, London: Butterworths, 1999) at 119; Strong, above n 173 at 413; John Henry Wigmore, *Evidence in Trials at Common Law* (Boston: Little Brown and Company, 1981) vol 9 at 288.

[185] Wigmore, above n 184 at 288. See also Fleming James Jr, 'Burdens of Proof' (1961) 47 Virginia Law Review 51 at 59.

the legal effect claimed by the plaintiff, or by claiming that the right has been modified or extinguished. It is upon defendants to prove the facts necessary to establish the causes that prevent, modify, or extinguish the right.[186] Ultimately, this strategy runs into a similar problem to the one noted by Wigmore, that is, we must ask whether there is a general principle which determines what the facts are that give rise to a legal right as opposed to those that prevent, modify or extinguish that right.[187] An answer to the questions 'What is essential to a party's case?' or 'What are the facts that give rise to a legal right as opposed to those that prevent, modify or extinguish that right?' can only be found in the specificities of the substantive law in question.[188]

3. Substantive law

Rules for the allocation of the burden of proof which are based on substantive law may provide guidance or serve as models to some international tribunals adjudicating questions similar to those dealt with by domestic courts, for instance, tribunals resolving property and contractual disputes, of which the Iran–United States Claims Tribunal is an example.[189] However, their relevance is limited to tribunals which are in charge of adjudicating unique issues. This is the case of the WTO, where, for example, the question of who must prove *force majeure* in breach of contract cases is not a question which will come before panels and the Appellate Body since they have no jurisdiction to adjudicate contractual disputes. Not only are the issues not the same, but also the structure and concept of WTO law is not the same. For example, domestic civil/private litigation reflects the existence of reciprocal/mutual relations between the parties— party *A* demands payment whereas party *B* argues that payment has already been made; party *A*

[186] For example, see Article 2697 of the Italian Civil Code; Article 333 of the Brazilian Code of Civil Procedure. The same rule seems to be applied in Japanese civil procedure. See Yasuhei Taniguchi, Pauline C Reich & Hiroto Miyake (eds), *Civil Procedure in Japan* (2nd edn, Yonkers: Juris Publishing, 2002) at para 7.05[14].

[187] See Luiz Eduardo Boaventura Pacífico, *O Ônus da Prova no Direito Processual Civil* (São Paulo: Revista dos Tribunais, 2001) at 129.

[188] Reiner notes that the United States and the Soviet Union considered incorporating rules on the burden of proof in the *UNCITRAL Model Law on International Commercial Arbitration,* but the Commission overseeing the process decided not to do so. One of the reasons behind this decision was that certain aspects of the burden of proof may be more properly classified as issues of substantive, rather than procedural law. Following this line of thought, the *Rome Convention of 1980 on the Law Applicable to Contractual Obligations* provides that the law of the contract governs its construction (Article 10) as well as issues regarding the burden of proof (Article 14). This is, in fact, the general approach adopted in international arbitration. According to Reiner, those arbitral awards which do not refer to the national law governing the merits of the dispute often limit themselves to general statements or rules such as *actori incumbit probatio*. Reiner, above n 181 at 329–35.

[189] For examples of some of the questions regarding the burden of proof which have been decided by the Tribunal, see Allahyar Mouri, *The International Law of Expropriation as Reflected in the Work of the Iran–U.S. Claims Tribunal* (Dordrecht: Martinus Nijhoff, 1994) at 284–8; Kazazi, above n 181 at 111–12 (examples involve contractual claims).

demands damages for destruction of its property whereas party *B* argues that the property was destroyed because *A* placed it in an inappropriate location—and these relations may lead to a variety of types of legal actions. A defendant could even be the plaintiff in another proceeding based on the same fact that she alleges in her defence. Furthermore, private law—the law of contracts and torts, or the law of obligations—is essentially non-prescriptive, that is, it mostly serves as a guide for the conduct of individuals in their interactions with other individuals, and as long as the individuals agree they are not required to behave in a certain manner. Panels and the Appellate Body, on the other hand, have jurisdiction to adjudicate claims under the WTO agreements.[190] The WTO agreements are regulatory treaties setting limits to the actions of its Members in the field of international trade. In other words, WTO Members have agreed to comply with a set of rules and when they do not do so other Members can resort to the dispute settlement mechanism to complain about the inconsistency of those actions with the WTO agreements. The party which initiates dispute settlement proceedings is not required to demonstrate that trade between it and the defendant has been negatively affected.[191] Finally, the principal remedy for a breach of WTO obligations is the removal or amendment of the measure found to be inconsistent with the WTO agreements.[192]

4. *Proof of negatives versus proof of universal statements*

Courts in certain domestic jurisdictions have occasionally allocated the burden of proof on the basis of whether the proposition to be proved is affirmative or negative. The criterion that the burden of proof should not be allocated to the party which would as a consequence have to prove a negative has, however, been subject to much criticism.[193] This criterion is meant to reflect the alleged difficulty of providing proof of a negative. There is, however, no inherent difficulty in proving negative allegations. In fact, parties to legal proceedings often have to

[190] See Article 1.1 of the DSU.

[191] In this regard, see Appellate Body Report, *European Communities—Regime for the Importation, Sale and Distribution of Bananas—Recourse to Article 21.5 of the DSU by the United States*, WT/DS27/AB/RW/USA and Corr.1, adopted 22 December 2008 at paras 463–76.

[192] Pursuant to Article 19.1 of the DSU, '[w]here a panel or the Appellate Body concludes that a measure is inconsistent with a covered agreement, it shall recommend that the Member concerned bring the measure into conformity with that agreement'. Moreover, Article 3.7 of the DSU provides that 'the first objective of the dispute settlement mechanism is usually to secure the withdrawal of the measures concerned if these are found to be inconsistent with the provisions of any of the covered agreements'.

[193] See Strong, above n 173 at 413; Wigmore, above n 184 at 288; Fishman, above n 175 at 260; Tapper (1999), above n 184 at 118–19 (criticizing the criterion because language can be manipulated, and because parties often do have to prove negatives); Pacífico, above n 187 at 63–5 (criticizing the criterion and noting that it is not accepted as a general rule for allocating the burden of proof); James Jr, above n 185 at 58–9 (criticizing the criterion because language can be manipulated).

prove negatives. For example, proving that Peter was at Union Station at 10 am on 3 March 2009 requires the same effort as proving that Peter was not at Union Station at 10 am on 3 March 2009. In order to prove the former a witness may be brought to testify that she sold Peter a coffee at Union Station at 10 am on 3 March 2009. In order to prove the latter, a witness may also be brought to testify that he was having breakfast with Peter at the Renaissance Hotel at 10 am on 3 March 2009. Moreover, language can easily be manipulated so as to state most propositions either negatively or affirmatively. For example, requiring a party to prove that 'John is not sane' is the same as requiring the party to prove that 'John is mentally ill'.

Admittedly, there are propositions whose logical form leads to difficulty in proof but that difficulty is not related to the presence of a negative, but rather the generality or universality of the statement.[194] In other words, the difficulty lies in proving universal statements, which do not focus on a specific individual, event, or set of circumstances. For example, consider the following two statements: (a) *not* every available job is beyond the capability of the complainant; (b) every available job is beyond the capability of the complainant. It is easier to prove the negative one (statement 'a') than the positive one (statement 'b').[195] In order to prove statement 'a', all the party bearing the burden of proof needs to do is to find a single job that is not beyond the capability of the complainant. In contrast, proof of statement 'b' would require the party bearing the burden of proof to show that every available job is beyond the complainant's capability.

However, the problem of proving universal propositions in legal proceedings can be overcome by focusing on the specificities of each case to narrow universal statements, that is, to make them specific. In the example above this can be achieved by requiring the party bearing the burden of proof to show that because of the injuries suffered while on duty the complainant is not capable of performing those jobs which are available for a person with the complainant's qualifications in the area where the complainant lives. The party bearing the burden of proof could then consult a local employment agency to determine what specific jobs are available for a person with the complainant's qualifications. At the same time, its opponent is also likely to identify jobs which he believes the complainant can perform. The party bearing the burden of proof would then have to prove that the complainant was not capable of performing those specific jobs.

Panels and Appellate Body have on occasion had to address the argument that the burden of proof should not be allocated to the party which would have to prove a negative proposition as a consequence of such allocation. This was

[194] See Kevin W Saunders, 'The Mythic Difficulty in Proving a Negative' (1985) 15 Seton Hall Law Review 276 at 277, 279–82; Pacífico, above n 187 at 65.

[195] This example is used in Saunders, above n 194 at 279.

argued, for example, by Peru in *EC—Sardines.*[196] The Appellate Body correctly dismissed that argument in *EC—Sardines*, and it has not otherwise allocated the burden of proof on the basis of whether a negative proposition is involved.[197]

As a general rule, panels and the Appellate Body have also correctly understood that the alleged problem of proving negatives is in fact a problem of proving universal propositions. They have also noted that this problem is not insurmountable. In this regard, the Appellate Body in *EC—Sardines* found that it is not impossible for complainants to demonstrate that an international standard is ineffective or inappropriate to fulfill the objectives of technical regulations adopted by defendants. The Appellate Body noted that among other options complainants can use the process of consultations which precedes the establishment of a panel to obtain information on the objectives of technical regulations or the specific considerations that may be relevant to the assessment of their appropriateness.[198] Complainants can then gather and produce evidence with a view to demonstrating that the international standard is an effective and appropriate means for the fulfilment of the objectives specified by the defendant.

Moreover, the process of narrowing down a universal proposition will often occur during the panel process through the exchange of arguments between the parties. This was what occurred, for instance, in *Canada—Pharmaceutical Patents.* In *Canada—Pharmaceutical Patents,* it was for Canada to prove that the exceptions to the exclusive rights conferred by a patent that it sought to impose did not unreasonably prejudice the legitimate interests of the patent owner. The panel noted that while '[o]ne cannot demonstrate that no legitimate interest of the patent owner has been prejudiced until one knows what claims of legitimate interest can be made', in the case at hand the European Communities had put forward two claims of legitimate interest.[199]

Finally, in certain cases the characteristics of the measure at issue will naturally narrow down the propositions to be proved. This point was recognized by the Appellate Body in *India—Additional Import Duties.* It was clear from the wording of the measure at issue in that case that the measure could potentially be justified under Article II:2(a) of the GATT and, therefore, not constitute a violation of Article II:1(b). The United States argued that it would be burdensome for complainants alleging a violation of Article II:1(b) of the GATT to have to demonstrate first that the measure at issue is not justified under

[196] Panel Report, *EC—Sardines*, above n 30 at para 4.2; Appellate Body Report, *EC—Sardines*, above n 34 at 83.

[197] See also Appellate Body Report, *Japan—Measures Affecting Agricultural Products*, WT/DS76/AB/R, adopted 19 March 1999, DSR 1999:I, 277 at para 137 (where, though not in the context of the *allocation* of the burden of proof, the Appellate Body rejected the view that it is impossible to prove a negative).

[198] Appellate Body Report, *EC—Sardines*, above n 34 at paras 277–80.

[199] Panel Report, *Canada—Pharmaceutical Patents*, above n 14 at paras 7.60, 7.83. For a similar case, see Panel Report, *Canada—Continued Suspension of Obligations in the EC—Hormones Dispute*, WT/DS321/R, adopted 14 November 2008 at paras 7.382–7.383, 7.400–7.402.

subparagraphs (a) to (c) of Article II:2 of the GATT. The Appellate Body disagreed, noting that complainants alleging a violation of Article II:1(b) are not in all cases required to demonstrate that the measure at issue is not justified under Article II:2.[200] However, in the view of the Appellate Body, the characteristics of the measure at issue in the case at hand provided a reasonable basis to believe that the measures satisfied the requirements of Article II:2(a).[201] The Appellate Body concluded, therefore, that it would not be unduly burdensome for the United States to adduce evidence and arguments with respect to Article II:2(a).[202]

In short, the WTO jurisprudence has correctly recognized that the problem of proving universal statements in the context of legal adjudication can be managed.[203]

Finally, it is important to note that the justification for narrowing universal statements in legal proceedings is found in the fact that resources (time and money) are limited. Neither the parties nor the adjudicator can be expected to investigate an unlimited number of possibilities. Accordingly, the focus in legal proceedings is on what would usually occur in light of the circumstances of the case.

5. Criteria related to law and economics

When allocating the burden of proof, courts sometimes also take into consideration the knowledge of the parties with respect to a particular fact including their access to evidence.[204] The fact that a party may have better knowledge and access to evidence is usually only one among other factors justifying the allocation of the burden of proof to that party, and it is not in any way an absolute criterion in that very often parties must prove matters as to which their adversaries have better knowledge and access to proof.[205]

Perhaps the two strongest reasons for not assigning more importance to the criterion of knowledge and access to proof are, first, that it cannot easily be turned into a rule of general application for determining the allocation of the burden of proof. This is because while there could be certain types of cases where it would be possible to determine in advance that one of the parties would in

[200] Appellate Body Report, *India—Additional Import Duties,* above n 70 at paras 192–3.

[201] Appellate Body Report, *India—Additional Import Duties,* above n 70 at para 190.

[202] Appellate Body Report, *India—Additional Import Duties,* above n 70 at paras 192–3.

[203] The difficulty of proving universal statements was also addressed in *US—Gambling.* In that case, the Appellate Body imposed a burden on the opposing party to narrow the universal statement. *US—Gambling* will be further discussed in Section II.C.3 below on the burden of pleading.

[204] See Wigmore, above n 184 at 288; Strong, above n 173 at 413; James Jr, above n 185 at 60. See also Tapper (1999), above n 184 at 129 (arguing that 'there is nothing in the nature of a general rule that the burden of establishing any defence based on facts peculiarly within his knowledge is borne by him').

[205] See Fishman, above n 175 at 267, 271; Strong, above n 173 at 413.

most situations be in possession of the information necessary to discharge the burden of proof, there would be many other types of cases where the information would some times be within the knowledge or possession of one party and at other times of her opponent. Therefore, there would always be situations where a party would be required to prove a fact which is within the knowledge of its opponent or for which its opponent has easier access to relevant evidence. Second, whereas it seems plausible to require a party to put forward evidence which is in its control, there is no reason in most cases to place the burden of proof on that party for that reason alone.[206] This is particularly so because even after the information is placed before the court, the court may still remain in doubt about the matter and may thus have to rule against the party bearing the burden of proof in order to settle the question. These considerations suggest that the problem of access to information in the control of the defendant should to the extent possible be solved through other mechanisms (this issue will be further discussed in Chapter 5). In this regard, it is worth noting that the ICJ in *Corfu Channel* noted that 'a State on whose territory or in whose waters an act contrary to international law has occurred may be called upon to give an explanation'.[207] According to the Court, however, 'this fact, by itself and apart from other circumstances, neither involves *prima facie* responsibility *nor shifts the burden of proof*'.[208]

One factor that has approvingly been used as a tool to allocate the burden of proof involves the drawing of an estimate of the probabilities of the situation.[209] Based on previous knowledge about the factual patterns of a certain type of case, the burden may be allocated to the party who contends that the more unusual event has occurred. Finally, many commentators note that courts often resort to policy considerations when allocating the burden of proof.[210]

[206] See Charles V Laughlin, 'The Location of the Burden of Persuasion' (1956) 18 University of Pittsburgh Law Review 3 at 7.

[207] *The Corfu Channel* (Merits) (United Kingdom v Albania), Judgment of 9 April 1949, International Court of Justice, Reports of Judgments, Advisory Opinions and Orders (1949) at 18.

[208] Ibid at 18 [emphasis added]. On the question of access to evidence and the allocation of the burden of proof, see Panel Report, *India—Additional Import Duties*, above n 64 at para 7.161 (noting that '[t]he mere fact that the responding party, due to greater familiarity with, and readier access to, its domestic laws and policies, might find it easier than the complaining party to supply information to a panel that would aid a determination of whether a particular border charge is equivalent to an internal tax and falls within the scope of Article II:2(a) is not a sufficient reason for shifting the burden of proof onto the responding party').

[209] Strong, above n 173 at 413; James Jr, above n 185 at 61; Stone, above n 178 at 278; Fishman, above n 175 at 272; Wigmore, above n 184 at footnote 3 to page 289.

[210] Laughlin argues that the same kind of policy considerations that determine the rules of substantive law should also determine the allocation of the burden of persuasion. In his view, '[i]t seems incredible that any rule which controls the results of cases, by stating the legal consequences of a failure to have a certain type of knowledge, should be based upon any premise other than consideration of social policy'. Laughlin, above n 206 at 10. Similarly, Stone argues that '[w]here once it has been agreed that there is no applicable rule and no precedent, it is respectfully believed

The criteria discussed here will be elaborated in Section B under a framework developed by law and economics scholars.

6. Absence of a framework

The criteria discussed in the previous paragraphs have not been coherently and systematically applied. When this is combined with rules which are based on substantive law, we are left with the impression that domestic law has failed to build a coherent analytical framework[211] which could provide guidance to panels and the Appellate Body in their task of allocating the burden of proof.

Unfortunately, international law does not provide clear guidance either. International law in general has not developed a systematic approach to the allocation of the burden of proof going beyond the general guidance provided by the principle of *actori incumbit probatio*.[212] The ICJ has only set rules with respect to specific types of cases which have come before the court such as those where both parties lay claim to the same object—of which rival claims to the same territory are an example.[213] In such cases, on account of the fact that each party claims the territory for itself on different grounds, the Court requires each party to establish their own claims to the disputed territory.[214] The Court has also often stated that 'it is the litigant seeking to establish a fact who bears the burden of proving it.'[215]

that the Court should proceed openly to the considerations of policy which in the last resort must base the making of a new rule'. Stone, above n 178 at 283. See also Wigmore, above n 184 at footnote 3 to page 289; Strong, above n 173 at 415.

[211] Many commentators have come to a similar conclusion. See Thomas R Lee, 'Pleading and Proof: the Economics of Legal Burdens' (1997) 1997 Brigham Young University Law Review 1 at 3; Wigmore, above n 184 at 288; Tapper (1999), above n 184 at 118, 120; Sopinka, Lederman & Bryant (1992), above n 173 at 83; Fishman, above n 175 at 239; Stone, above n 178 at 415.

[212] See references in n 181 above. See also, for example, *Salini Costruttori SPA and Italstrade SPA v The Hashemite Kingdom of Jordan*, ICSID Case No ARB/02/13, Award of 31 January 2006 at para 70; *Middle East Cement Shipping and Handling Co SA v Arab Republic of Egypt*, ICSID Case No. ARB/99/6, Award of 12 April 2002 at para 89; *Asian Agricultural Products Ltd v Republic of Sri Lanka*, ICSID Case No. ARB/87/3, Award of 27 June 1990 at para 56.

[213] See Sir Arthur Watts, 'Burden of Proof, and Evidence Before the ICJ' in F Weiss (ed), *Improving WTO Dispute Settlement Procedures: Issues and Lessons from the Practice of Other International Courts and Tribunals* (London: Cameron May, 2000) 289 at 292; Rosenne (1997), above n 181 at 1083; Sir Gerald Fitzmaurice, *The Law and Procedure of the International Court of Justice* (Cambridge: Grotius, 1986) at 576.

[214] See, for example, *The Minquiers and Ecrechos Case* (France v United Kingdom), Judgment of 17 November 1953, International Court of Justice, Reports of Judgments, Advisory Opinions and Orders (1953).

[215] *Case Concerning Military and Paramilitary Activities in and against Nicaragua* (Jurisdiction and Admissibility) (Nicaragua v United States), Judgment of 26 November 1984, International Court of Justice, Reports of Judgments, Advisory Opinions and Orders (1984) at 437, para 101; *Case Concerning the Land and Maritime Boundary between Cameroon and Nigeria* (Preliminary Objections) (Cameroon v Nigeria), Judgment of 11 June 1998, International Court of Justice, Reports of Judgments, Advisory Opinions and Orders (1998) at 319, para 101; *Case Concerning Avena and other Mexican Nationals* (Mexico v United States of America), Judgment of 31 March 2004, International Court of Justice, Reports of Judgments, Advisory Opinions and Orders (2004) at 41, para 55.

This statement, however, is more properly understood as referring to proof of individual facts—ie auxiliary propositions—alleged by the parties in the course of the proceedings[216] rather than the burden of proof *stricto sensu*.

B. Can law and economics analysis help?

Where does this leave us? In this kind of situation, it is always useful to inquire where the problem originated. It seems that panels and the Appellate Body courted confusion when seeking to identify a 'defence' which must be proved by the defendant. This approach is based on the logical proposition that if we know that in general the burden of proof is allocated to the plaintiff, by determining the specific instances when the burden is allocated to the defendant we can solve the problem of the allocation of the burden of proof. In this context, a more fundamental question will be: Why should the burden of proof be allocated to the defendant? Law and economics can help to provide an answer to this question.

Law and economics supports the general understanding that the burden of proof should usually lie upon the plaintiff. The point of departure is the assumption that when allocating the burden of proof courts aim at minimizing a social loss function composed of two kinds of costs: direct or process costs, and error costs.[217] Direct or process costs are those costs incurred in the process of settling a claim—cost of presenting evidence, preparing submissions, resources devoted by the court to deliver and enforce a judgment, among others. Error costs are those costs associated with erroneous legal judgments, for example, the costs associated with the frustration of objectives such as deterrence[218] and the specific objectives pursued by the substantive law.

According to Hay, the costs of allocating the burden of proof to a given party are a function of five parameters: (i) the probability the party is correct; (ii) the party's estimate of that probability; (iii) the party's cost of presenting evidence; (iv) the amount at stake for the party; and (v) the social costs of an erroneous ruling against the party. Hay also demonstrates that when determining the desirability of allocating the burden to a given party, an increase in parameters i, iii, iv, and v 'has the effect of making the opposite allocation more desirable'—parameter ii has no clear bearing on the desirability of the allocation.[219] Taking as a baseline a type of dispute where (i) given the court's knowledge about the type of dispute, the probability that the plaintiff has a meritorious claim for relief is relatively small,[220] and (ii) the parties' costs of presenting evidence, the amount at stake for each

[216] In this regard, see Chapter 2, section I.A.

[217] Lee, above n 211 at 4–5; Bruce L Hay, 'Allocating the Burden of Proof' (1997) 72 Indiana Law Journal 651 at 654.

[218] Error costs include not only the costs of underdeterrence, but also the costs of overdeterrence.

[219] Hay, *Allocating the Burden of Proof*, above n 217 at 675.

[220] Hay argues that considering the universe of all potential disputes, the odds that a given dispute actually involves a meritorious claim for judicial relief are probably quite small.

party, and the social costs of an error in one or the other party's favour are all roughly the same,[221] an analysis of the parameters suggests that the burden of proof should be allocated to the plaintiff.[222] Hay argues that because most cases resemble this baseline case, as a general rule, the burden of proof on contested issues should be on the plaintiff.[223] There could be two negative consequences if under these circumstances the burden of proof is allocated to the defendant instead. First, when the parties are not certain of the merits of a claim 'the plaintiff would be tempted to sue on the slimmest of grounds (when her chances of success were very small), compelling the defendant to present evidence'.[224] In this situation, on the one hand, if the defendant presents evidence, process costs will be incurred. On the other hand, if the defendant does not produce evidence, the result will be error costs. Second, the plaintiff might threaten to sue 'even knowing she had no claim, in the hopes of inducing the defendant to pay her to drop the claim'.[225] Process and error costs in both situations would likely be greater than if the plaintiff bore the burden of proof.[226]

Based on a similar analysis of cost minimization, Lee arrives at the same conclusion that the burden of proof should, as a general rule, be allocated to the plaintiff. Lee's conclusions, however, are based on the idea that when liability is indeterminate the plaintiff is just as likely to be correct as the defendant. In other words, in cases where the court is uncertain about which party should prevail—the kind of cases where the burden of proof determines the outcome of the case—there is a probability of 0.5 that the plaintiff deserves to prevail and an equal probability that the defendant should prevail. According to Lee, there are two justifications for a default rule that assigns the burden of proof to the plaintiff. First, a judgment for plaintiff results in post-judgment direct costs—such as remedy construction costs, enforcement costs, and transaction costs

[221] Hay notes that given modern rules of discovery the parties' costs of presenting evidence are frequently roughly the same. The stakes will also be identical for the parties in most cases—the plaintiff's gain is the defendant's loss, and vice versa. As for the social cost of an erroneous outcome, Hay observes that an erroneous imposition of liability may or may not have the same social cost as an erroneous failure to impose liability. Hay, *Allocating the Burden of Proof*, above n 217 at 674–7.

[222] Hay, *Allocating the Burden of Proof*, above n 217 at 673–7. In another paper, Hay arrives at a similar conclusion based on slightly different theory. Bruce L Hay & Kathryn E Spier, 'Burdens of Proof in Civil Litigation: an Economic Perspective' (1997) 26 Journal of Legal Studies 413.

[223] Hay, *Allocating the Burden of Proof*, above n 217 at 677.

[224] Hay, *Allocating the Burden of Proof*, above n 217 at 677–8. Hay explains that the party bearing the burden of proof will submit evidence to the court only if the result of (i) the party's estimated chance of success multiplied by (ii) the amount at stake for the party is bigger than (iii) the party's cost of presenting evidence. Taking this into account and assuming that the plaintiff's cost of filing a claim are minimal, if the burden of proof is allocated to the defendant the plaintiff will file a suit 'so long as the plaintiff's estimated chance of winning is greater than zero'. However, if the plaintiff bears the burden of proof, 'she will file a claim if and only if the plaintiff's threshold for presenting evidence [—as just described—] is satisfied. For if that threshold is not satisfied, the plaintiff knows she will lose the case (because she will not present evidence), so there is no point in suing'. Ibid, at 661.

[225] Ibid, at 678.

[226] Ibid, at 678.

associated with payment—which would not be incurred if the judgment was for the defendant.[227] Therefore, the default rule assures that these costs will not be incurred when the plaintiff is just as likely to be correct as the defendant.[228] In addition, when liability is indeterminate, post-judgment direct costs cannot be justified on the grounds that they would be offset by a reduction in error costs. Only when liability is not indeterminate and the plaintiff is more likely to deserve recovery will there be an economic argument for incurring the marginal increase in direct costs.[229] Second, but still related to the first point, the default rule can be justified on the grounds that 'it economizes on direct costs by deterring claims based on indeterminate issues of liability'.[230] Lee explains that the default rule seeks to 'encourage only those suits that serve an allocative function (i.e., that decrease error costs)', and this will be the case 'only if the probability that plaintiff is entitled to recovery is greater than 0.5'.[231]

Departures from the general rule that the burden of proof should be allocated to the plaintiff are explained by Lee and Hay on similar cost-saving grounds:[232]

(1) The adjudicator has advance knowledge with respect to the factual pattern of a type of dispute that demonstrates that the plaintiff probably has a meritorious case, that is to say, the defendant is liable in more than 50 per cent of the situations (*theory of a priori judgments*). For example, in a dispute involving payment for services performed for another in an ordinary business or professional context, the burden of proving that the services were offered gratis could be allocated to the defendant.[233] This is so because in general services are not offered gratis in an ordinary business context. In contrast, if the service was performed for members of the immediate family, living together, the burden of proving that the service was performed for a fee could be allocated to the complainant. The reason for such allocation would be that family members do not usually charge other family members for services performed in the context of day-to-day family life.

(2) The plaintiff's costs of presenting the evidence are higher than the defendant's; in other words, the defendant can produce core evidence at a lower cost than the complainant (*relative-cost-of-proof theory*).

[227] In the WTO context, post-judgment costs include costs associated with Articles 21 and 22 of the DSU. For example, the costs incurred in Article 21.3(c) of the DSU arbitrations to determine the 'reasonable period of time', and Article 22.6 of the DSU arbitrations to determine the level of nullification and impairment and the appropriate countermeasures. The costs that the defendant would incur to modify the measure may also be counted as post-judgment costs.

[228] Alex Stein, *Foundations of Evidence Law* (Oxford: Oxford University Press, 2005) at 145.

[229] Lee, above n 211 at 12–14.

[230] Ibid, at 14.

[231] Ibid, at 14.

[232] Hay, *Allocating the Burden of Proof*, above n 217 at 677; Lee, above n 211 at 16, 21, 27–8. Hay mentions a fourth situation where the burden should be allocated to the defendant, ie when 'the plaintiff has more at stake in the case'. This factor, however, can be taken into account in the calculations of the costs associated with a decision against the complainant. Therefore, I opted not to list it above.

[233] This example is based on James Jr, above n 185 at 61.

(3) The costs associated with an erroneous decision in favour of the defendant are higher than those associated with an erroneous decision favoring the plaintiff (*error-cost theory*). If an error in the defendant's favour is more costly than an error in the plaintiff's favour the burden of proof should be allocated to the defendant because if no evidence is produced or the court is not certain about the meaning of the evidence, the higher-social-cost party, ie the defendant, will lose the case.[234]

The discussion above suggests that a cost minimization analysis of the allocation of the burden of proof supports the general rule that in most cases the burden of proof is on the plaintiff. The burden should be allocated to the defendant only in exceptional circumstances, ie those suggested by the theory of *a priori* judgments, the relative-cost-of-proof theory, and the error-cost theory. These theories broadly correspond to the three factors considered in Section III.A.5 above. When courts use an estimate of the probabilities of the situation to allocate the burden of proof to the party whose claim is the most unlikely they apply the theory of *a priori* judgments. The considerations embodied in the relative-cost-of-proof theory are to a large extent the same as those taken into account by courts when they allocate the burden of proof based on a party's knowledge and access to evidence. In this regard, as discussed above, it is not any imbalance in access to evidence which will lead to a reversal of the burden of proof; such imbalance must translate into substantially higher costs for one of the parties. Finally, the error-cost theory provides an objective framework in which to consider policy issues.

Accordingly, it is possible to conclude that law and economics produces a coherent framework for allocating the burden of proof which is closely connected to existing judicial practice. In other words, it organizes into a coherent framework what are otherwise random factors.

C. What are the options for the WTO dispute settlement system?

Based on the analysis described above, there are two alternative courses of action available to panels and the Appellate Body.

[234] Lee provides the following example to illustrate the application of the error-cost theory. According to him, in the United States law of defamation defendants traditionally had the burden of proving the truth of all allegedly defamatory statements because the law valued the individual's interest in reputation more highly than it did the defendant's interest in his money—an erroneous decision in favour of the plaintiff involved a finding of defamation and a transfer of payment for damages, whereas an erroneous decision in favour of the defendant resulted in the wrongful erosion of the good reputation of the plaintiff. In 1986, however, the Supreme Court changed that allocation for cases where the plaintiff is a public figure or where the speech is of public concern. The reason behind this change was that the constitutional policy of ensuring that true speech on matters of public concern is not deterred outweighs the common law policy favouring defamation plaintiffs. The Court believed that erroneous decisions in favour of the plaintiff would deter true speech on matters of public concern. Lee, above n 211 at 22–3.

1. Burden allocated to complainant unless otherwise provided

Panels and the Appellate Body may adopt the view that the kind of considerations required by the theory of a priori judgments, the relative-cost-of-proof theory, and the error-cost theory, belong more properly to the realm of legislative activity. They should, therefore, assume that when WTO Members believed that any of those factors justified an allocation to the defendant, the Members made an express provision to that effect.

This would be the case, for example, of Article 10.3 of the Agreement on Agriculture. The WTO negotiators' decision to provide for a special allocation of the burden of proof in Article 10.3 of the Agreement on Agriculture may be explained on the following grounds. Negotiators had knowledge of the fact that if export subsidies are admittedly provided to a scheduled volume of exports the likelihood that those subsidies are also provided to exports in excess of those scheduled volumes is high—theory of *a priori* judgments. This would be so because it is difficult for the Member providing the subsidy to make sure that no exports over the scheduled volume benefit from the subsidies. Members might also have been concerned with the fact that it is costly for the complainant to prove that subsidies are not provided to exports in excess of scheduled commitments—relative-cost-of-proof theory. Placing the burden of proof on the defendant creates an incentive for the defendant to develop a system to ensure that no subsidies are provided in excess of scheduled commitments and to keep a good record of the transactions

Accordingly, under the first option, panels and the Appellate Body would draw on law and economics to support the view that the burden of proof should be allocated to the complainant absent clear indication to the contrary.

2. Burden allocated according to a priori *judgments, relative-cost-of-proof, and error-cost theories*

Panels and the Appellate Body may adopt the view that the kind of considerations required by the theory of *a priori* judgments, the relative-cost-of-proof theory, and the error-cost theory are not purely in the realm of legislative activity. This is a reasonable premise, since domestic courts often take these kinds of considerations into account when allocating the burden of proof. Under this second option, panels and the Appellate Body would not discard the possibility that the burden of proof should be allocated to the defendant with respect to provisions which do not make an express reference to the allocation of the burden of proof. Accordingly, panels and the Appellate Body could examine provisions that provide for exceptions[235] with a view to determining whether the

[235] An exception here would be defined according to its ordinary meaning, that is, 'the action of excepting (a person or thing, a particular case) from the scope of a proposition, rule, etc. [...] Something that is excepted; a particular case which comes within the terms of a rule, but to which

a priori judgments, the relative-cost-of-proof, and the error-cost theory would justify an allocation to the defendant.[236] If they conclude that an analysis of those three factors indicates that the burden of proof should be allocated to the defendant, they would then have more concrete reasons to find that that was the intention of the drafters.

The advantages of this framework include not only its coherence and logic, but also the fact that it takes into account concerns related to procedure and substance. Furthermore, though the economics behind it may at first suggest that the analysis required to implement the framework is totally foreign to adjudicators, as noted in the previous section, although under a different guise and in an unsystematic manner domestic courts already apply the *a priori* judgment, the relative-cost-of-proof, and the error-cost theories.

It is important to note that in the interests of predictability as well as cost saving,[237] the factors discussed above are not meant to be examined on a case-by-case basis, that is, it should not matter, for instance, that in a particular case before a panel the complainant's cost of presenting evidence is higher than the defendant's if in most similar cases the costs would be roughly the same for both parties. Instead, those factors should generally determine the allocation of the burden of proof with respect to specific provisions.

If panels and the Appellate Body decide to follow the second path, that is, examine provisions that contain words suggesting that they are exceptions with a view to determining whether the burden of proof should be allocated to the defendant, they could develop an analysis similar to that propounded in the next few paragraphs. The following paragraphs briefly discuss how panels and the Appellate Body could use the analytical framework discussed above to allocate the burden of proof with respect to two provisions, Article 3.3 of the SPS Agreement and Article XX of the GATT. These are simply examples of how the analysis could be conducted; the conclusions are not intended to be generalized, that is, they are restricted to Article 3.3 of the SPS Agreement and Article XX of the GATT in their current form.

2.1. Article 3.3 of the SPS Agreement

Article 3.1 of the SPS Agreement states that, except as provided in Article 3.3 of the SPS Agreement, 'Members shall base their sanitary or phytosanitary measures on international standards, guidelines or recommendations'. In turn, Article 3.3 provides that Members may adopt measures which result in a higher level of

the rule is not applicable'. *The Oxford English Dictionary* (2nd edn, Oxford: Clarendon Press, 1989) at 498.

[236] See Horn & Weiler, above n 82 at 262–3, 268 (Horn and Weiler suggest that the Appellate Body take into account the error-cost theory).

[237] If the complainants are given information beforehand which can help them to assess their chances of success, this will reduce the number of cases brought to adjudication and, therefore, save costs associated with likely unsuccessful cases.

protection than would be achieved by measures based on international standards, guidelines or recommendations in two situations: (i) if there is a scientific justification, and (ii) 'as a consequence of the level of sanitary or phytosanitary protection a Member determines to be appropriate in accordance with' the provisions of Article 5 ('Assessment of Risk and Determination of the Appropriate Level of Sanitary or Phytosanitary Protection') of the SPS Agreement. Article 3.3 of the SPS Agreement, therefore, is an exception to the rule contained in Article 3.1; it establishes the conditions Members must fulfil in order to deviate from Article 3.1. If Article 3.3 is an exception, should the burden of proof with respect to that provision be allocated to the defendant? An analysis of Article 3.3 under the law and economics framework suggests that this should not be the case.

First, application of the theory of *a priori* judgments does not indicate that the defendant is liable in more than half of all possible cases. In other words, there is no reason to believe that Members that apply a measure that is not based on international standards do so without a scientific justification or proper consideration of the provisions of Article 5 of the SPS Agreement in more than 50 per cent of the cases.

Second, contrary to what seems to be the case at first glance, the defendant's cost of presenting evidence concerning its own measure are not necessarily significantly lower than the complainant's (relative-cost-of-proof theory). The SPS Agreement contains in Article 5.8 and section 3 of Annex B obligations requiring Members to provide, when requested, information regarding their SPS measures.[238] It is reasonable to expect complainants to conduct an investigation of the situation before beginning a case against a Member applying an SPS measure. In fact, as discussed above, the burden of proof is usually allocated to the complainant exactly to discourage complainants from bringing cases whose merits are questionable. The provisions of Article 5.8 and section 3 of Annex B to the SPS Agreement facilitate that investigation; in other words, they ensure that as a general rule there is no substantial imbalance between the parties with respect to the costs of presenting evidence.[239] It is important to remember that even after evidence that could be more easily presented by the Member imposing the measure is made available, eg the risk assessment, there is still a need to

[238] Article 5.8 requires Members to provide an explanation of the reasons for a sanitary or phytosanitary measure that is not based on an international standard. Section 3 of Annex B requires the creation of enquiry points to provide answers to all reasonable questions from interested Members as well as to provide relevant documents.

[239] Support for this view can be found in *EC—Sardines*, where the Appellate Body noted that the TBT Agreement affords means for the complainant to obtain information about the objectives of technical regulations or the specific considerations that may be relevant to the assessment of their appropriateness—Article 2.4 of the TBT Agreement. For example, information can be obtained under Article 2.5 of the TBT Agreement and through the enquiry points that must be established by the respondent according to Article 10 of the TBT Agreement. Appellate Body Report, *EC—Sardines*, above n 34 at paras 277–80. The role of transparency obligations such as Article 5.8 of the SPS Agreement will be further discussed in Chapter 5.

demonstrate that that risk assessment does or does not comply with the requirements in Article 5 of the SPS Agreement. There is no reason to believe that the costs of presenting the evidence required for such demonstration are necessarily higher for the complainant than for the defendant. For example, as Japan noted in *Japan—Apples*,[240] the exporting country affected by the disease may have more information on that disease than the importing country. It is also worth noting that the Appellate Body in *EC—Hormones* made clear that Members are not required to carry out their own risk assessment. According to the Appellate Body, an 'SPS measure might well find its objective justification in a risk assessment carried out by another Member, or an international organization'.[241] In such cases, it is arguable that the best source of information on the risk assessment is the international organization or the Member which conducted the assessment. Therefore, the relative-cost-of-proof theory would *not* suggest that the burden of proof with respect to Article 3.3 of the SPS Agreement should be allocated to the defendant country.

Third, application of the error-cost theory does not conclusively indicate that the costs of an erroneous decision in favour of the defendant would be higher than the costs of an erroneous decision in favour of the complainant and vice-versa. On the one hand, an erroneous decision in favour of the complainant would result in costs such as those social costs associated with (i) removal of a measure that achieves a Member's correctly determined appropriate level of protection or (ii) removal of a measure that is scientifically sound.[242] Removal of a scientifically sound measure may also result in direct economic costs. For example, the removal of a measure intended to prevent the introduction of a pest capable of destroying the crops of an important commodity could have devastating economic consequences. Erroneous decisions favouring the complainant might also create overdeterrence costs. In other words, it is possible that errors favouring the complainant in litigation may discourage Members from deviating from international standards in situations where it would be efficient to do so; for example, in situations where the international standard needs to be improved. However, overdeterrence might not occur. Instead, the fact that these types of errors might occur may create an incentive for Members to try to change/improve the international standard.

On the other hand, erroneous decisions in favour of the defendant—that is, defendants win when they should lose—would result in little harmonization being achieved which in turn would result in the weakening of international standards. It is worth noting that the preamble to the SPS Agreement and Article 3 refer to harmonization as one of the objectives of the SPS Agreement. The costs of unnecessary diversity may be high; trade will be disrupted because

[240] Panel Report, *Japan—Measures Affecting the Importation of Apples*, WT/DS245/R, adopted 10 December 2003 at para 8.44.

[241] Appellate Body Report, *EC—Hormones*, above n 25 at para 190.

[242] See, similarly, Horn & Weiler, above n 82 at 268.

of the costs of complying with several different standards without any corresponding benefits to human, animal or plant life or health. The fact that governments have devoted resources to establishing standard-setting institutions and negotiating the SPS Agreement is proof that diversity is costly.

In short, the discussion in the previous two paragraphs suggests that there is no clear answer to the question of whether an erroneous decision in favour of the defendant would be more costly than an erroneous decision in favour of the complainant or vice- versa. Notably, if this same analysis were conducted by the WTO Members at the moment they were negotiating the SPS Agreement they could choose to assign more weight to one of those costs. Because those costs are difficult to quantify and there is no indication of whether Members give more weight to one or the other, panels and the Appellate Body should find that those costs cancel each other out. Therefore, the error-cost theory would not suggest that the burden of proof with respect to Article 3.3 of the SPS Agreement should be allocated away from the complainant.

Accordingly, if panels and the Appellate Body were to conduct an analysis along the lines discussed above, they would conclude that there is no reason to deviate in the case of Article 3.3 of the SPS Agreement from the general rule that the burden of proof should be allocated to the complainant. None of the factors—theory of *a priori* judgments, relative-cost-of-proof theory, and error-cost theory—provide a reason to allocate the burden of proof away from the complainant. As discussed before, this conclusion actually corresponds to the conclusion of the Appellate Body in *EC—Hormones*, where, contrary to the panel, the Appellate Body allocated the burden of proof with respect to Article 3.3 of the SPS Agreement to the complainant.

2.2. Article XX of the GATT

The discussion now turns to Article XX of the GATT. Article XX provides that Members may adopt measures which would otherwise be inconsistent with provisions of the GATT if those measures are, for example, (i) necessary to protect public morals, or human, animal or plant life or health, and (ii) provided that those measures are not applied in a manner which would constitute a means of arbitrary or unjustifiable discrimination between countries where the same conditions prevail, or a disguised restriction on international trade. In short, Article XX establishes an exception to obligations contained in other Articles of the GATT; it establishes conditions which Members must fulfill in order to deviate from other GATT rules. If Article XX is an exception, should the burden of proof with respect to that provision be allocated to the defendant? Contrary to the prevailing view in the GATT and WTO jurisprudence, an analysis pursuant to the framework developed above suggests that this should not be the case.[243]

[243] The analysis below is restricted to paragraphs (a), (b), (e), and (g), in combination with the chapeau of Article XX. This does not necessarily mean that an analysis of the other paragraphs would lead to a different conclusion.

The starting point should be the general rule, that is, that the complainant should bear the burden of proof with respect to Article XX. Unless any of the three factors—theory of *a priori* judgments, the relative-cost-of-proof theory, and the error-cost theory—or a combination of them indicates that the burden of proof should be allocated to the defendant, the burden should remain on the complainant.

It is arguable that the theory of *a priori* judgments indicates that the respondent country is liable in more than half of all possible cases. Kometani, for instance, argues that governments tend to favour their domestic producers in designing their laws, that is, domestic regulatory and legislative processes provide greater opportunities to influence regulation and legislation for domestic producers than for foreign producers and domestic constituents which may be negatively affected.[244] Accordingly, it is possible that if we were to examine regulations that are, for example, inconsistent with Articles III ('National Treatment on International Taxation and Regulation') and Article XI ('General Elimination of Quantitative Restrictions') of the GATT, we would conclude that more than half of them are 'protectionist'.[245] However, in the absence of reliable evidence to corroborate this assumption, we may opt to view this factor neutrally.

As for the costs of presenting evidence—relative-cost-of-proof theory—there seems to be no general cost imbalance between the complainant and the defendant. While it is the defendant's measure which is at issue, it is likely that there will be information regarding that measure in the public domain. Perhaps the best evidence of this is the fact that so far in Article XX cases both parties have submitted evidence regarding the requirements of that provision; if the costs of producing evidence were excessively high for one of the parties that party would likely not have presented evidence. In addition, it is arguable that with respect to the conditions in the chapeau complainants are in fact in a better position to provide information regarding how their exports are, for example, being arbitrarily or unjustifiably discriminated against. Regarding the 'necessity' of the measure, the complainant may also in many cases be in a better position to present information regarding less-trade-restrictive measures which could substitute for the measure being challenged. Therefore, it does not seem to be the case that the defendant (or the complainant) could always present evidence at a lower cost than the complainant (or the defendant).

An analysis of the costs of an erroneous decision in favour of either the complainant or the defendant—error-cost theory—does not support the conclusion that the burden of proof should be allocated to the defendant. An

[244] Kazumochi Kometani, 'Trade and Environment: How Should WTO Panels Review Environmental Regulations Under GATT Articles III and XX?' (1996) 16 Northwestern School of Law Journal of International Law & Business 441 at 452.

[245] The word 'protectionist' is used in connection with the requirements contained in Article XX of the GATT.

erroneous decision in favour of the complainant—the defendant loses when it should win—would result in social costs such as the costs associated with the removal of a measure which fulfils an important objective such as the protection of public morals, human, animal or plant life or health.[246] Erroneous decisions in favour of the complainant may also be costly for trade liberalization; such decisions may produce a negative impact on public opinion which may lead governments to adopt a more restrictive approach to trade liberalization. However, erroneous decisions in favour of the defendant may also be costly for trade liberalization; they may lead Members to treat liberalizing offers from other Members with scepticism if they believe that concessions will later be undermined by protectionist measures of the type that would be allowed if liability under Article XX is wrongly determined. Overall, it seems that the costs of erroneous decisions in favour of the complainant would be higher than the costs of erroneous decisions in favour of the defendant. Accordingly, the error-cost theory would recommend that the burden of proof with respect to Article XX remain on the complainant.

Therefore, if panels and the Appellate Body were to conduct an analysis according to the framework set out in this section they would conclude that there is no reason to deviate, in the case of Article XX of the GATT, from the general rule that the burden of proof should be allocated to the complainant. This is so because none of the three factors suggests an allocation to the defendant; even if we considered that the theory of *a priori* judgments might suggest an allocation to the defendant, this would likely have been neutralized by the fact that the error-cost theory indicates that the burden of proof should be allocated to the complainant. If all factors remain neutral, the general rule should remain unaltered, that is, the burden of proof should rest with the complainant.[247]

3. Burden of pleading

One could argue that it is costly to allocate the burden of proof with respect to Article XX to the complainant because the complainant does not necessarily know which of the paragraphs of Article XX the defendant relies upon. The complainant would be in a situation where it would have to prove that the defendant does not comply with the requirements of all of the paragraphs of

[246] The costs associated with the removal of a measure may differ according to the importance that Members attach to the objective pursued by the measure. It is not the objective of this chapter to undertake a careful analysis of all the paragraphs of Article XX of the GATT.

[247] Compare with Pauwelyn, *Conflict of Norms,* above n 115 at footnote 34 to page 250 (arguing that the similarity between Articles 3.1 and 3.3 of the SPS Agreement on the one hand, and Articles III and XX of the GATT on the other hand, 'is a strong argument in favour of revisiting also the "general rule-exception" relationship between GATT Arts. III and XX. [...] Consequently, under GATT Art. XX (as in the case under SPS Art. 3.3) the burden of proof should rest on the complainant').

Article XX. While it is true that it would be costly if the complainant had to prove that the defendant did not comply with the requirements of all paragraphs of Article XX, this situation can be avoided if the defendant is required to specify the paragraph(s) that it relies upon and explain the reasons why it believes it is entitled to justify its measures under that (or those) paragraph(s). In other words, the defendant could have the burden of pleading Article XX.

The requirement for parties to raise or plead certain issues has the function of facilitating efficient communication between parties in litigation or, in other words, it has the function of refining the scope of a case.[248] Similarly to the burden of proof, as a general rule the burden of pleading is allocated to the complainant. Lee explains that an allocation of the burden of pleading to the defendant is economically sound in two contexts. First, when certain issues are unlikely to arise—*probability theory*. In such cases, 'assigning the burden of pleading to the defendant operates as a presumption that saves the cost of raising the issue in most cases'.[249] Second, '[o]n some issues assigning the burden of pleading to plaintiff would require him to make an allegation that would be much broader and more comprehensive than if the burden were assigned to defendant'.[250] In this situation, assigning the burden of pleading to the defendant, the party whose version of the issue in question is more discrete, economizes on direct costs—*relative-cost-of-pleading theory*.

The burden of pleading in WTO dispute settlement is usually on the complainant, which must discharge this burden with its request for establishment of a panel.[251] Although Article 7.1 of the DSU provides that the parties can agree on the terms of reference of the panel within 20 days from the establishment of the panel, the terms of reference are normally determined by the complainant through the request for establishment of a panel.[252] Hence, the first written submission to the panel, following the complainant's first submission, is typically the first occasion where the defendant expresses its views on the scope of the dispute. This is far from ideal, however, because it delays the development of the case when the defendant raises new provisions not addressed by the complainant. It would, therefore, be desirable that defendants also be required to plead provisions such as Article XX of the GATT early in the proceedings. Defendants could be required to file an answer to the request for establishment of a panel before the complainant is required to submit its first written submission. This would allow the complainant to address the provisions raised by the defendant in its first written submission. Such requirement could be included in the Working Procedures of the Panel, whose terms panels have the discretion to establish after consulting the parties to the dispute,[253] or introduced in the DSU

[248] See Lee, above n 211 at 6–7. [249] Ibid, at 9. [250] Ibid, at 8.

[251] According to Article 6.2 of the DSU, the request for establishment of a panel must 'identify the specific measures at issue and provide a brief summary of the legal basis of the complaint sufficient to present the problem clearly'.

[252] See discussion in Section II.C.3.1 of Chapter 1. [253] See Article 12.1 of the DSU.

by the negotiators. Defendants could also be allowed to raise new claims up until their first written submission, in which case they should be required to provide a detailed explanation of the claim covering all the elements of the provision in question.[254] As a matter of fact, most defendants do use their first written submissions to raise provisions which were not otherwise included in the terms of reference of the panel.

In short, the burden of pleading should be understood as a burden of identifying the relevance of a provision within a certain timeframe; a party which does not meet its burden of pleading a provision forfeits its right to invoke that provision at a later stage.

The idea of allocating the burden of pleading to a different party than the party which bears the burden of proof is not alien to the WTO jurisprudence. It was employed by the Appellate Body in *EC—Tariff Preferences*, *US—Gambling*, and *Brazil—Retreaded Tyres*. Although, as will be discussed below, the manner in which the burden of pleading was allocated in those cases is questionable, those decisions can be used to explain how the burden of pleading operates. For this reason they are reviewed below.

3.1. *EC—Tariff Preferences*

In *EC—Tariff Preferences*, the Appellate Body ruled that the Enabling Clause is an exception and therefore the burden of proof with respect to the clause was on the defendant, the European Communities. However, according to the Appellate Body, the complainant, India, was required to indicate in the request for establishment of a panel which of the requirements contained in the paragraphs of the Enabling Clause were not met by the defendant.[255] In the words of the Appellate Body, the responsibility of the complainant 'is merely to *identify* those provisions of the Enabling Clause with which the scheme is allegedly inconsistent, without bearing the burden of *establishing* the facts necessary to support such inconsistency'.[256] While the rationale for allocating the burden of pleading to the complainant and the burden of proof to the defendant in the specific context of the Enabling Clause is questionable, *EC—Tariff Preferences* clearly introduces the concept of the burden of pleading to the WTO jurisprudence.

The following suggests that in this specific case there was no advantage in splitting the burden of pleading and the burden of proof in the manner which the Appellate Body did. The Appellate Body sought to justify its decision to allocate the burden of pleading to the complainant on the grounds of (i) the importance of the Enabling Clause[257] and its special status in the WTO

[254] In this regard, see discussion in Section I.B.1.3 of Chapter 3.

[255] Appellate Body Report, *EC—Tariff Preferences*, above n 51 at paras 113, 115.

[256] Appellate Body Report, *EC—Tariff Preferences*, above n 51 at para 115 [original emphasis].

[257] The Appellate Body noted that because of its vital role in promoting trade as a means of stimulating economic growth and development, the Enabling Clause 'is not a typical "exception",

system;[258] and (ii) the fact that '[e]xposing preference schemes to open-ended challenges would be inconsistent [. . .] with the intention of Members [. . .] to "encourage" the adoption of preferential treatment for developing countries and to provide a practical means of doing so within the legal framework of the covered agreements'.[259] First, it must be noted that placing the burden of pleading on the complaining party is hardly an effective way of achieving the objective of restraining unfounded challenges to a measure taken under the framework of the Enabling Clause. This is so because non-compliance with the rules on the burden of pleading in this situation would have little, if any, negative consequences to the complainant. What would be the consequences of the complainant's failure to raise the Enabling Clause? Would the case be restricted to Article I of the GATT? If this were the case, the complainant would likely benefit from non-compliance with the rule created by the Appellate Body. Second, the reasons provided by the Appellate Body in support of its decision would seem to justify an allocation of the burden of *proof* to the complainant, rather than the burden of *pleading*. If Members place so much importance on encouraging preferential treatment to developing countries, this would suggest that in cases involving the Enabling Clause erroneous decisions in favour of complainants—defendants lose when they should win—are more costly than erroneous decisions in favour of defendants. Therefore, and without a more detailed analysis of all the factors, application of the error-cost theory would suggest that the burden of proof with respect to the Enabling Clause should remain on the complainant.

3.2. *US—Gambling* and *Brazil—Retreaded Tyres*

Following its previous rulings that Article XX of the GATT provides for exceptions which must be proved by the defendant, the Appellate Body in *US—Gambling* found that the burden of proof with respect to Article XIV of the GATS—the GATS equivalent to Article XX of the GATT—is on the defendant. One of the requirements of Article XIV(a) of the GATS is that the measure in question be 'necessary to protect public morals or to maintain public order'. Accordingly, the Appellate Body noted that it is for the defendant to 'show that its measure is "necessary" to achieve objectives relating to public morals or public order'.[260]

or "defence", in the style of Article XX of the GATT 1994, or of other exception provisions identified by the Appellate Body in previous cases'. Appellate Body Report, *EC—Tariff Preferences,* above n 51 at para 106.

[258] According to the Appellate Body, the history of the Enabling Clause demonstrates its special status in the WTO. The Enabling Clause reflects the realization that 'the MFN obligation failed to secure adequate market access for developing countries so as to stimulate their economic development'. Appellate Body Report, *EC—Tariff Preferences,* above n 51 at para 107–109.

[259] Ibid, at para 114.

[260] Appellate Body Report, *US—Gambling*, above n 85 at para 309.

Whether a measure is 'necessary' in the view of the Appellate Body is determined through a process of '"weighing and balancing" and comparison of measures, taking into account the interests or values at stake'.[261] Among the factors to be weighed and balance are (i) the importance of the interests or values pursued by the measure; (ii) 'the contribution of the measure to the realization of the ends pursued by it'; and (iii) 'the restrictive impact of the measure on international commerce'.[262] According to the Appellate Body, after weighing and balancing those factors, '[a] comparison between the challenged measure and possible alternatives should then be undertaken, and the results of such comparison should be considered in the light of the importance of the interests at issue'.[263] If one of the alternative measures is reasonably available and WTO-consistent, the measure at issue will not be considered necessary.[264]

In light of the definition of 'necessary' laid out by the Appellate Body, one would expect that the defendant would be required to prove that the measure it adopted is the only reasonably available measure which would achieve its objectives. The Appellate Body ruled, however, that unless the 'complaining party *raises* a WTO-consistent alternative measure', the defendant is not required to prove that the measure it adopted is the only reasonably available measure which would achieve its objectives.[265] In other words, the Appellate Body imposed on the complainant a burden of pleading WTO-consistent alternative measures. This allocation of the burden of pleading alternative measures was later confirmed by the panel and Appellate Body in *Brazil—Retreaded Tyres* in the context of Article XX of the GATT.[266]

The Appellate Body's justification for allocating the burden of pleading to the complainant in this situation was that requiring the defendant to show that there are '*no* reasonably available alternatives to achieve its objectives' would be 'impracticable and, indeed, often impossible'.[267] In reaching this conclusion, the Appellate Body disregarded its own jurisprudence—discussed in Section III.A.4 above—on the question of proof of negatives and universal statements. According to that jurisprudence, what the defendant should be required to prove in this case is that the measure it adopted is the only reasonably available measure which would achieve its objectives. In order to make such a showing, the defendant could explain why measures which would seem to be alternatives in the circumstances of the case, including measures which the defendant might have considered in the

[261] Appellate Body Report, *US—Gambling*, above n 85 at paras 307, 305.
[262] Appellate Body Report, *US—Gambling*, above n 85 at para 306.
[263] Appellate Body Report, *US—Gambling*, above n 85 at para 307.
[264] Appellate Body Report, *US—Gambling*, above n 85 at para 308.
[265] Appellate Body Report, *US—Gambling*, above n 85 at paras 310–11, 320.
[266] Panel Report, *Brazil—Measures Affecting Imports of Retreaded Tyres*, WT/DS332/R, adopted 17 December 2007 at paras 7.155–7.157; Appellate Body Report, *Brazil—Measures Affecting Imports of Retreaded Tyres*, WT/DS332/AB/R, adopted 17 December 2007 at para 156.
[267] Appellate Body Report, *US—Gambling*, above n 85 at para 309 [original emphasis].

process of adopting the measure at issue, are not reasonably available. If the opposing party or the panel raise other alternative measures, the defendant would have to address those measures as well. In the circumstances of *US—Gambling*, obvious alternative measures would have included the adoption of a regulatory framework similar to that in place in Antigua and other countries which have regulated, rather than banned, internet gambling.[268]

Another problematic aspect of the decision is that the Appellate Body had itself characterized the issue of reasonably available alternative measures as a key element of the definition of 'necessary'. In this context, if no information is presented on the question of reasonably available alternative measures, how can a panel conclude that the measure is necessary? The party bearing the burden of proof with respect to Article XIV(a) should have to demonstrate that all the elements of the definition of 'necessary' are met. Otherwise, there would be obvious reasons to challenge the accuracy of a finding that the measure was necessary.

Moreover, allowing for the imposition of a burden of pleading on the opposing party in circumstances such as these may eventually result in it being used arbitrarily to relieve the claimant from proving certain issues. It is arguable that this might have occurred in *US—Gambling*, where Antigua lost on the issue of 'necessary' because it allegedly failed to identify alternative measures.[269] Although the question of what 'necessary' means had been addressed in many cases under Article XX of the GATT before, this was the first time the Appellate Body found that unless the complainant raises alternative measures the defendant has no obligation to address this issue, and accordingly, Antigua had no reason to believe that it bore a burden of pleading this element of the definition of 'necessary'. Certainly, the issue becomes less controversial once the opposing party knows that it bears the burden of pleading a certain element (or sub-element). In this regard, in *Brazil—Retreaded Tyres* the European Communities openly recognized that based on *US—Gambling* it bore the burden of raising alternative measures in the context of a claim under Article XX of the GATT.[270] This, however, does not change the fact that such use of the burden of pleading may take parties by surprise and be used as a tool to achieve specific results.

[268] It is worth noting that the Appellate Body found that Antigua failed to raise alternative measures. Appellate Body Report, *US—Gambling*, above n 85 at para 320. Such conclusion does not seem accurate however. For example, Antigua put forward several alternatives to address the objective of preventing under age gambling. One such alternative was that 'gambling and betting accounts with Antiguan operators could be opened in person at news agents or other specifically designated shops'. Antigua explained that '[i]n such circumstances the age verification system would be exactly the same as that used by lotteries in the United States'. Panel Report, *United States—Measures Affecting the Cross-Border Supply of Gambling and Betting Services*, WT/DS285/R, adopted 20 April 2005 at para3.291.

[269] Appellate Body Report, *US—Gambling*, above n 85 at paras 320, 326.

[270] Panel Report, *Brazil—Retreaded Tyres*, above n 266 at para 7.153.

3.3. Final note on the burden of pleading

In short, the concept of the burden of pleading could be usefully employed in WTO dispute settlement to refine the scope of a case where certain issues are unlikely to arise or where the claimant would have to raise and prove a broad range of issues. This would be the case, for instance, if the burden of proof with respect to Article XX of the GATT were allocated to the complainant.

However, based on the discussion above, panels and the Appellate Body should avoid allocating to the opposing party the burden of pleading specific elements (or sub-elements) of a claim. This should be particularly the case when such allocation is not indicated *ex ante*. It is worth noting that the opposing party is likely in any event to voluntarily raise issues which will help the claimant narrow the scope of what it has to prove. This is nothing but a corollary of the value of participation.

4. Final considerations

It is important to note that nothing in the agreements, in particular the DSU, would prevent panels and the Appellate Body from conducting an analysis similar to that propounded in this section above. The DSU is completely silent with respect to the question of the allocation of the burden of proof. The absence of rules in the DSU has not so far prevented panels and the Appellate Body from deciding questions regarding the allocation of the burden of proof. In fact, because panels cannot declare *non liquet,* decisions regarding the burden of proof are unavoidable when the evidence is not sufficient to convince panels of the truth or fallacy of a proposition. Accordingly, irrespective of the framework used, when no express provision is made in the agreements, decisions regarding the burden of proof do not add to or diminish the rights and obligations of Members.[271]

The advantage of the approach discussed in this section over the current one is that it provides objective reasons to support a certain allocation of the burden of proof.[272] It can also improve predictability to the extent that the parties themselves can conduct an assessment of whether the *a priori* judgments, the relative-cost-of-proof, and the error-cost theories would suggest an allocation of the burden of proof to the defendant. Predictability, however, would obviously be stronger if panels and the Appellate Body took the path suggested in Section III. C.1, that is, allocate the burden of proof away from the complainant only when the negotiators have expressly provided so.

D. *India—Additional Import Duties*: a paradigm shift?

In *India—Additional Import Duties,* one of the latest decisions on the question of the allocation of the burden of proof, the Appellate Body did not allocate the

[271] Article 3.2 provides that: '[...] Recommendations and rulings of the DSB cannot add to or diminish the rights and obligations provided in the covered agreements'.

[272] See Horn & Weiler, above n 82 at 263ff. Horn and Weiler urge the Appellate Body to develop a more sophisticated analysis with respect to the allocation of the burden of proof.

burden of proof on the basis of whether the provision in question was an exception or a provision that excluded the application of another. Although the parties invoked its previous decisions relating to that distinction, the Appellate Body did not refer to them in concluding that the burden of proof with respect to Article II:2(a) of the GATT was on the United States. Nor did the Appellate Body support the tortuous reasoning through which the panel concluded that Article II:2(a) is a provision that excludes the application of another rather than an exception. Contrary to the panel, which sought to downplay the language of the opening clause of Article II:2 '[n]othing in this Article shall prevent ...',[273] the Appellate Body acknowledged that the wording of Article II:2 clearly exempts measures adopted pursuant to Article II:2(a) from the obligations contained in Article II:1(b).[274]

After addressing the relationship between Articles II:1(b) and II:2(a) of the GATT, the Appellate Body devoted an entirely separate section to the question of the allocation of the burden of proof. The discussion in that section suggests that the burden of proof with respect to Article II:2(a) of the GATT was allocated to the United States because it is for complainants to prove their claims that the measures of another Member are inconsistent with the WTO agreements.[275] Moreover, the Appellate Body disagreed with the United States that it would be too burdensome for a complainant claiming a violation of Article II:1 (b) to have to demonstrate first that the measure at issue does not meet the requirements of Article II:2 of the GATT. According to the Appellate Body, Article II:2 will not be relevant in all instances where a claim of violation of Article II:1(b) is made; however, when the characteristics of the measures at issue or the arguments presented by the responding party indicate 'that the challenged measure may not result in a violation of Article II:1(b) because it satisfies the requirements of Article II:2(a), then the complaining party bears some burden in establishing that the conditions of Article II:2(a) are not met'.[276]

In short, the Appellate Body in *India—Additional Import Duties* seems to have departed from its previous decisions which sought to draw a distinction between provisions that establish an exception to a rule, and provisions that exclude the application of other provisions. Future decisions may clarify whether the Appellate Body consciously chose to break with that line of decisions.[277] In

[273] Panel Report, *India—Additional Import Duties*, above n 64 at para 7.148.

[274] Appellate Body Report, *India—Additional Import Duties*, above n 70 at para 153.

[275] Appellate Body Report, *India—Additional Import Duties*, above n 70 at paras 186–7. The Appellate Body also noted that the United States had stated that 'once a responding party asserts and supports a defence under Article II:2(a), "the ultimate burden would rest with the complaining party to rebut and ultimately disprove that evidence and argument."' Ibid, at para 191.

[276] Appellate Body Report, *India—Additional Import Duties*, above n 70 at para 192.

[277] The Appellate Body might have reacted to recent scholarly criticism of its decisions drawing a distinction between exceptions and provisions that exclude the application of other provisions. For such criticism, see Michelle T Grando, 'Allocating the Burden of Proof in WTO Disputes: a Critical Analysis' (2006) 9:3 Journal of International Economic Law 615 (on which this chapter is based); Broude, above n 51.

light of the reasons presented in the previous sections of this chapter, it is hoped that this hypothesis will be confirmed.

IV. Allocation of the Burden of Proof in Article 21.5 of the DSU Compliance Cases

This section addresses the question of whether the rules regarding the allocation of the burden of proof should be applied differently in compliance proceedings under Article 21.5 of the DSU.

Article 21.5 of the DSU provides that:

> Where there is disagreement as to the existence or consistency with a covered agreement of measures taken to comply with the recommendations and rulings such dispute shall be decided through recourse to these dispute settlement procedures, including wherever possible resort to the original panel. The panel shall circulate its report within 90 days after the date of referral of the matter to it. When the panel considers that it cannot provide its report within this time frame, it shall inform the DSB in writing of the reasons for the delay together with an estimate of the period within which it will submit its report.

The discussion will be divided in two parts. Section A will focus on 'regular' Article 21.5 proceedings, that is, proceedings brought by the original complainant in which it claims that the measures adopted by the original respondent fail to achieve compliance with the WTO agreements. This is the most common type of Article 21.5 proceedings.[278] Section B will address a special type of Article 21.5 proceedings, namely, proceedings resulting from a disagreement between the parties under Article 22.8 of the DSU as to whether the measure found to be inconsistent has been removed so that the authorization for the original complainant to suspend concessions against the original defendant is no longer valid (hereinafter referred to as 'post-suspension of concessions Article 21.5 proceedings'). As of 22 April 2009, no post-suspension of concessions Article 21.5 disputes have been adjudicated.[279] The situation was, however, addressed in *Canada—Continued Suspension* and *US—Continued Suspension*, where the Appellate Body also discussed the question of how the burden of proof must be allocated in this type of disputes.

[278] As of 22 April 2009 there were 26 panel reports issued (and adopted) under Article 21.5 pursuant to a request filed by the original complainant.

[279] There have been Article 21.5 proceedings brought after the original complainant was authorized to suspend concessions. However, those proceedings did not involve a disagreement under Article 22.8 of the DSU. The proceedings were conducted as a regular Article 21.5 proceeding. See Panel Report, *Brazil—Export Financing Programme for Aircraft—Second Recourse by Canada to Article 21.5 of the DSU*, WT/DS46/RW/2, adopted 23 August 2001, DSR 2001:X, 5481; Panel Report, *United States—Tax Treatment for 'Foreign Sales Corporations'—Second Recourse to Article 21.5 of the DSU by the European Communities*, WT/DS108/RW2, adopted 14 March 2006.

A. 'Regular' Article 21.5 proceedings

Panels and the Appellate Body have found that the same rules regarding the allocation of the burden of proof which apply in original proceedings also apply in compliance proceedings under Article 21.5 of the DSU. In other words, the allocation of the burden of proof is not altered because the dispute is brought under Article 21.5 of the DSU.

In *Brazil—Aircraft* (*Article 21.5*), Brazil admitted that its measure, the revised PROEX, was inconsistent with Article 3.1(a) of the SCM Agreement,[280] but argued that its measure was justified by virtue of the first paragraph of item (k) of the Illustrative List of Export Subsidies. The panel placed the burden of proof with respect to this issue on Brazil.[281] On appeal, Brazil argued that the Article 21.5 panel erred in placing on Brazil the burden of proving that it had implemented the recommendations and rulings of the DSB. The Appellate Body began its analysis of this issue by recalling that Brazil had conceded before the original panel that it had the burden of proof with respect to its alleged defence under item (k). In the Appellate Body's view, 'the fact that the measure at issue was "taken to comply" with the "recommendations and rulings" of the DSB does not alter the allocation of the burden of proving Brazil's "defence" under item (k)'.[282]

In *Canada—Dairy* (*Article 21.5*), Canada contended that although it recognized that Article 10.3 of the Agreement on Agriculture normally shifts the burden of proof to the defending party, this should not happen in a dispute under Article 21.5 of the DSU. According to Canada, reports issued by panels and the Appellate Body under Article 21.5 of the DSU uniformly confirm that a Member's measure is presumed to comply with the WTO obligations and, thus, any Member challenging those measures bears the burden of proving any inconsistency. The panel followed the ruling of the Appellate Body in *Brazil—Aircraft* (*Article 21.5*) and held that the 'rules on the allocation of the burden of

[280] Panel Report, *Brazil—Export Financing Programme for Aircraft—Recourse by Canada to Article 21.5 of the DSU*, WT/DS46/RW, adopted 4 August 2000 at para 6.21.

[281] Brazil's defence depended upon the proposition that the first paragraph of item (k) may be interpreted *a contrario,* that is, that if a Member succeeds in proving that its measure is *not* an export subsidy within the meaning of item (k), the measure should then be found to be 'permitted' by the SCM Agreement. The panel rejected the idea that item (k) could be invoked by a defendant as an affirmative defence, but decided nonetheless to assume that item (k) was an affirmative defence and determine whether the PROEX fulfilled the two elements of the first sentence of that provision. Because in the panel's view Brazil did not provide sufficient evidence to support its allegations, the panel ruled that Brazil failed to demonstrate that PROEX payments are not 'used to secure a material advantage in the field of export credit terms' within the meaning of the first paragraph of item (k). *Brazil—Aircraft (Article 21.5—Canada)*, above n 280 at para 6.106. The panel in *Korea—Commercial Vessels* also rejected the idea that the first paragraph of item (k) can be used as a defence. Panel Report, *Korea—Measures Affecting Trade in Commercial Vessels*, WT/DS273/R, adopted 11 April 2005, DSR 2005:VII, 2749 at paras 7.309–7.312.

[282] Appellate Body Report, *Brazil—Aircraft (Article 21.5—Canada)*, above n 75 at para 66.

proof [do not] change simply because a claim is made in the context of Article 21.5 DSU proceedings'.[283]

Finally, in *Chile—Price Band System* (*Article 21.5*—Argentina), Chile argued that 'the Panel did not properly allocate the burden of proof' because it conducted its analysis on the assumption that the revised measure was inconsistent with Article 4.2 of the Agreement on Agriculture.[284] The Appellate Body rejected Chile's claim noting that a careful reading of the panel report revealed that the panel correctly applied the general rules on the burden of proof. Such rules apply in original proceedings and imply that a defendant's measure will be treated as WTO-consistent unless proven otherwise.[285] Accordingly, the Appellate Body found that the burden had correctly been allocated to Argentina, the complainant, to prove that the revised measure was inconsistent with Article 4.2 of the Agreement on Agriculture.

In fact, there seems to be no good reason to adopt a different approach to the allocation of the burden of proof in proceedings under Article 21.5 of the DSU. The mandate of panels in Article 21.5 proceedings is to review the *new* measure—which was adopted by the defendant in order to implement the rulings of the original panel—with a view to determining whether that measure is consistent with the relevant provisions of the WTO agreements invoked by the complainant. Article 21.5 provides for a more expedited procedure to challenge the consistency of a measure which is taken to comply with a previous decision. However, there are no major differences between these two types of proceedings to suggest that the burden of proof should be allocated differently in those cases brought under Article 21.5.

B. Post-suspension of concessions Article 21.5 proceedings

Canada—Continued Suspension is the result of a disagreement between the parties to *EC—Hormones* as to whether (i) the European Communities, the original respondent, had implemented the rulings and recommendations of the DSB in *EC—Hormones*, and thus (ii) the original complainant, Canada, was no longer authorized to suspend concessions against the European Communities.[286] After the panel and Appellate Body reports in *EC—Hormones* were

[283] Panel Report, *Canada—Dairy* (*Article 21.5—New Zealand and US*), above n 3 at para 6.4.

[284] Appellate Body Report, *Chile—Price Band System and Safeguard Measures Relating to Certain Agricultural Products—Recourse to Article 21.5 of the DSU by Argentina*, WT/DS207/AB/RW, adopted 22 May 2007 at para 132.

[285] Appellate Body Report, *Chile—Price Band System (Article 21.5 —Argentina)*, above n 284 at paras 134–6, 140–1.

[286] The European Communities brought a similar case against the United States. The findings of the panel and Appellate Body in the two disputes are mostly the same. Therefore, this chapter will only discuss *Canada—Continued Suspension*. For the United States dispute, see Panel Report, *United States—Continued Suspension of Obligations in the EC—Hormones Dispute*, WT/DS320/R, adopted 14 November 2008; Appellate Body Report, *United States—Continued Suspension of Obligations in the EC—Hormones Dispute*, WT/DS320/AB/R, adopted 14 November 2008.

adopted, the European Communities had a period of time—namely the 'reasonable period of time' provided for under Article 21.3 of the DSU—to implement the rulings contained in the adopted reports. As the European Communities failed to modify its measure within the reasonable period of time, Canada requested and received DSB authorization to suspend concessions against the European Communities pursuant to Articles 22.2 and 22.6 of the DSU. Over four years after Canada received authorization to suspend concessions, the European Communities adopted a new measure which allegedly brought the European Communities into compliance with the WTO agreements.

In *Canada—Continued Suspension*, the European Communities claimed that Canada violated several provisions of the DSU, including Articles 23.1, 23.2(a), and 22.8, by continuing to suspend concessions against the European Communities without having recourse to the DSU to determine whether the measure adopted by the European Communities successfully implemented the rulings and recommendations of the DSB. According to Article 22.8 of the DSU, 'the suspension of concessions or other obligations [...] shall only be applied until such time as the measure found to be inconsistent with a covered agreement has been removed [...]'. While *Canada—Continued Suspension* was not brought under Article 21.5 of the DSU, the Appellate Body ruled in that case that 'panel proceedings under Article 21.5 is the proper procedure for resolving' disagreements over whether the rulings and recommendations of the DSB have been implemented 'and whether, consequently, the resolutive condition in Article 22.8 that requires the termination of the suspension of concessions has been met'.[287] In laying out the procedure to be followed in this type of disputes, the Appellate Body addressed the question of the burden of proof.

The Appellate Body noted that the ultimate issue in a post-suspension of concessions Article 21.5 proceeding is whether the measure found to be inconsistent with a WTO agreement has been removed. In light of this, the main question as to the allocation of the burden of proof is which party should bear the burden of proving substantive compliance.[288] In the view of the Appellate Body, 'the allocation of the burden of proof, in the context of Article 22.8, should not be determined simply on the basis of a mechanistic rule that the party who initiates the proceedings bears the burden of proof'.[289] The Appellate Body then noted that:

> The allocation of the burden of proof in the context of claims arising under Article 22.8 is a function of the following considerations. First, what is the nature of the cause of action that is framed under Article 22.8. Second, the practical question as to which party

[287] Appellate Body Report, *Canada—Continued Suspension of Obligations in the EC—Hormones Dispute*, WT/DS321/AB/R, adopted 14 November 2008 at para 338.

[288] Appellate Body Report, *Canada—Continued Suspension*, above n 287 at para 359.

[289] Appellate Body Report, *Canada—Continued Suspension*, above n 287 at para 360.

may be expected to be in a position to prove a particular issue. Third, consideration must be given to the requirements of procedural fairness.[290]

The Appellate Body did not elaborate on any of these criteria, nor did it clearly explain how the criteria influenced its decision.[291] In the end, however, the Appellate Body seems to have relied mostly on considerations of fairness. In this regard, it referred to the fact that cases involving Article 22.8 are special in that 'the suspension of concessions is a remedy of last resort imposed after an elaborate multilateral dispute settlement process'.[292] That is to say, by the time a post-suspension of concessions Article 21.5 proceeding is instituted the parties will most likely have gone through two panel (and Appellate Body) proceedings,[293] an arbitration under Article 21.3(c) of the DSU to determine the reasonable period of time to implement, and an arbitration under Article 22.6 of the DSU to determine the level of suspension of concessions or other obligations. In light of this, the Appellate Body noted that it is appropriate that the original defendant 'have an onus to show that its implementing measure has cured the defects identified in the DSB's recommendations and rulings'.[294]

According to the Appellate Body, if the original defendant initiates Article 21.5 proceedings with a view to determining that the measure at issue has been removed within the meaning of Article 22.8 of the DSU, it must present a 'clear description of its implementing measure, and an adequate explanation regarding how this measure rectifies the inconsistencies found in the original proceedings' so as to allow the panel to rule in its favour 'in the absence of rebuttal'.[295] In the view of the Appellate Body, however, the original complainant bears the burden of proof with respect to all other issues including 'a claim that the implementing measure is otherwise inconsistent with the covered agreements or that the implementing measure remains wanting for reasons not traversed by the original respondent in discharging its burden of proof'.[296] In other words, the Appellate

[290] Appellate Body Report, *Canada—Continued Suspension*, above n 287 at para 361.

[291] It is worth noting that the second criterion seems to have been rejected by the Appellate Body in previous disputes. For instance, in *EC—Sardines* it noted that '[t]here is nothing in the WTO dispute settlement system to support the notion that the allocation of the burden of proof should be decided on the basis of a comparison between the respective difficulties that may possibly be encountered by the complainant and the respondent in collecting information to prove a case'. Appellate Body Report, *EC—Sardines*, above n 34 at para 281.

[292] Appellate Body Report, *Canada—Continued Suspension*, above n 287 at para 362.

[293] Because original defendants usually adopt measures with a view to achieving compliance within the reasonable period of time to implement, if the original complainants disagree that compliance has been achieved they will usually request the establishment of a panel under Article 21.5 of the DSU before they move to request authorization to suspend concessions or other obligations. This did not occur in *Canada—Continued Suspension* because the European Communities did not modify the original measure within the reasonable period of time. On the relationship between proceedings under Article 21.5 and 22.6 of the DSU, namely, the 'sequencing' problem, see Van den Bossche, above n 164 at 306–7.

[294] Appellate Body Report, *Canada—Continued Suspension*, above n 287 at para 362.

[295] Appellate Body Report, *Canada—Continued Suspension*, above n 287 at para 362.

[296] Appellate Body Report, *Canada—Continued Suspension*, above n 287 at para 364.

Body seems to have allocated to the original complainant the burden of proving that the new measure is inconsistent with provisions which were not part of the rulings in the original proceedings.[297]

Notably, it also seems to have allocated to the original complainant the burden of proof with respect to the same provisions which the original defendant must claim and prove to be in compliance with in order to demonstrate under Article 22.8 of the DSU that the measure found to be inconsistent has been removed. This means, for instance, that if the measure was found in the original proceedings to violate Article 5.1 of the SPS Agreement the original defendant would bear the burden of proving that its new measure complies with Article 5.1 because a risk assessment was conducted so that the measure is now based on a risk assessment. In turn, according to the Appellate Body, the original complainant would also bear the burden of proof with respect to the question of whether the new measure is based on a risk assessment, if the original complainant raises separate allegations against the risk assessment instead of merely denying the allegations put forward by the original defendant. The problem with the Appellate Body's ruling is that because the burden of proof determines the outcome of a dispute when the evidence is equivocal, complainants and defendants cannot bear the burden of proof with respect to the same issues. The only way to reconcile the Appellate Body's findings is to interpret them as relating not to the burden of proof, but rather to the principle that both parties must cooperate in presenting evidence and arguments to the panel. This would mean, however, that the Appellate Body left unaddressed the question of the allocation of the burden of proof in post-suspension of concessions Article 21.5 proceedings.

If the intention of the Appellate Body was to set rules for the allocation of the burden of proof within the meaning discussed in this chapter, it should have pushed its fairness argument to its logical conclusion, namely, it should have allocated exclusively to the original defendant the burden of proof with respect to all provisions with which the original measure was found to be inconsistent. Alternatively, the Appellate Body should have relied on the rule which it expressly rejected, that is, it should have found that the burden of proof should be allocated to the party initiating the post-suspension of concessions Article 21.5 proceedings. This would require the original defendant, when it initiates Article 21.5 proceedings, to bear the burden of proving that its measures are consistent with the provisions which the original measures were found to violate. In turn, it would require the original complainant to bear the burden of proof when it initiates

[297] This would seem to exclude provisions such as Article 5.7 of the SPS Agreement which justify a measure which would otherwise be inconsistent with another provision. In this regard, the Appellate Body noted in *Canada—Continued Suspension* that because the 'European Communities replaced the original definitive ban with a provisional ban and invoked Article 5.7 as an alternative justification to Article 5.1', 'the European Communities had to provide an adequate explanation of how the provisional ban taken under Article 5.7 rectifies the inconsistencies found in *EC—Hormones*'. Appellate Body Report, *Canada—Continued Suspension*, above n 287 at para 716.

proceedings to challenge the consistency of the measures with the same and/or other provisions than the ones analysed in the original proceedings. Contrary to what one would think at first blush, original complainants might have incentives to initiate post-suspension of concessions Article 21.5 proceedings. First, they might have no interest in suspending concessions or other obligations against the original defendant—eg because a tariff increase would hurt domestic consumers. Second, they might have an interest in having a panel and the Appellate Body rule that the measure is inconsistent with the WTO agreements as a way of inducing the original complainant to alter its measure—without such a ruling the original complainant may always contend that its measure is consistent with the agreements and that, therefore, it has no obligation to change it. These might explain, for example, why Canada initiated a second Article 21.5 panel against Brazil's revised measures in *Brazil—Aircraft* (*Article 21.5—Canada II*) even though it had already obtained authorization to suspend concessions against Brazil.[298]

Concluding Remarks

The preceding analysis has shown that the jurisprudence on the allocation of the burden of proof is in a confused state. Panels and the Appellate Body have failed to produce a consistent line of cases which can be used as a predictable model to solve future cases. Furthermore, the jurisprudence has also created what appear to be artificial differences between provisions, which raises questions about the relevance of the criteria employed to distinguish provisions that must be proved by the defendant from those that must be proved by the complainant. Panels and the Appellate Body have become so entangled in the details of those distinctions that they seem to have neglected the basic issues.

The analysis undertaken in this chapter suggests that it may be time to reflect upon the basic question of why the burden of proof should be allocated to a given party. The answer to this question requires recognition of the main purpose of the burden of proof, that is, that the burden of proof is a rule of adjudication which determines the outcome of a case when there is no or little evidence on the record or when the evidence on the record is equivocal. In other words, the burden of proof is a concept which serves to manage uncertainty and the risk of error.

Chapter 1 noted (i) that rational systems of adjudication must manage uncertainty and the risk of error efficiently, and (ii) that seeking the minimization of the social loss function composed of direct and error costs constitutes a valuable tool in designing procedures for that purpose. The framework of analysis developed in Sections III.B and III.C of this chapter is based on the idea

298 Panel Report, *Brazil—Aircraft (Article 21.5—Canada II)*, above n 279.

of minimizing that social loss function. It provides a compelling explanation of why the burden of proof should be allocated in most cases to the complainant and of the reasons that should motivate an allocation to the defendant. Following that framework, panels and the Appellate Body should develop a clearer and more sophisticated analysis. They could adopt two alternative courses of action, assigning two different meanings to the silence of the drafters. Under the first option, silence would be interpreted as an endorsement of the rule that the burden of proof should be allocated to the complainant. Under the second option, the drafters' silence would not be given a specific meaning, that is, panels and the Appellate Body would be free to analyse provisions that do not expressly refer to the question of the burden of proof with a view to determining whether the theory of *a priori* judgments, the relative-cost-of-proof theory, or the error-cost theory would suggest that the burden of proof should be allocated to the defendant.

Given the importance of a concept such as the burden of proof which may determine the outcome of a case, it would be wise for the WTO negotiators to establish clear rules for its allocation. In establishing such rules, they can of course use the analytical framework proposed in Sections III.B and III.C of this chapter. WTO negotiators would, in any event, be in a better position to undertake a more thorough analysis and make value judgments if necessary.

ANNEX

Text of Relevant Provisions from WTO Agreements

GATT Article II

Schedules of Concessions

1. (*b*) The products described in Part I of the Schedule relating to any contracting party, which are the products of territories of other contracting parties, shall, on their importation into the territory to which the Schedule relates, and subject to the terms, conditions or qualifications set forth in that Schedule, be exempt from ordinary customs duties in excess of those set forth and provided therein. Such products shall also be exempt from all other duties or charges of any kind imposed on or in connection with the importation in excess of those imposed on the date of this Agreement or those directly and mandatorily required to be imposed thereafter by legislation in force in the importing territory on that date.
[...]

2. Nothing in this Article shall prevent any contracting party from imposing at any time on the importation of any product:

(*a*) a charge equivalent to an internal tax imposed consistently with the provisions of paragraph 2 of Article III* in respect of the like domestic product or in respect of an article from which the imported product has been manufactured or produced in whole or in part;

(*b*) any anti-dumping or countervailing duty applied consistently with the provisions of Article VI;*

(*c*) fees or other charges commensurate with the cost of services rendered.

*GATT Article XI**

General Elimination of Quantitative Restrictions

2. The provisions of paragraph 1 of this Article shall not extend to the following:

(*c*) Import restrictions on any agricultural or fisheries product, imported in any form,* necessary to the enforcement of governmental measures which operate:

to restrict the quantities of the like domestic product permitted to be marketed or produced, or, if there is no substantial domestic production of the like product, of a domestic product for which the imported product can be directly substituted; or [...]

GATT ARTICLE XV

9. Nothing in this Agreement shall preclude:

(*a*) the use by a contracting party of exchange controls or exchange restrictions in accordance with the Articles of Agreement of the International Monetary Fund or with that contracting party's special exchange agreement with the CONTRACTING PARTIES, or

(*b*) the use by a contracting party of restrictions or controls in imports or exports, the sole effect of which, additional to the effects permitted under Articles XI, XII, XIII and XIV, is to make effective such exchange controls or exchange restrictions.

GATT ARTICLE XVIII:B

9. In order to safeguard its external financial position and to ensure a level of reserves adequate for the implementation of its programme of economic development, a contracting party coming within the scope of paragraph 4 (*a*) of this Article may, subject to the provisions of paragraphs 10 to 12, control the general level of its imports by restricting the quantity or value of merchandise permitted to be imported; *Provided* that the import restrictions instituted, maintained or intensified shall not exceed those necessary:

(*a*) to forestall the threat of, or to stop, a serious decline in its monetary reserves, or

(*b*) in the case of a contracting party with inadequate monetary reserves, to achieve a reasonable rate of increase in its reserves.

[...]

11. In carrying out its domestic policies, the contracting party concerned shall pay due regard to the need for restoring equilibrium in its balance of payments on a sound and lasting basis and to the desirability of assuring an economic employment of productive resources. It shall progressively relax any restrictions applied under this Section as conditions improve, maintaining them only to the extent necessary under the terms of paragraph 9 of this Article and shall eliminate them when conditions no longer justify such maintenance; *Provided* that no contracting party shall be required to withdraw or modify restrictions on the ground that a change in its development policy would render unnecessary the restrictions which it is applying under this Section.*

GATT AD ARTICLE XVIII

Paragraph 11

The second sentence in paragraph 11 shall not be interpreted to mean that a contracting party is required to relax or remove restrictions if such relaxation or removal would thereupon produce conditions justifying the intensification or institution, respectively, of restrictions under paragraph 9 of Article XVIII.

GATT Article XX

General Exceptions

Subject to the requirement that such measures are not applied in a manner which would constitute a means of arbitrary or unjustifiable discrimination between countries where the same conditions prevail, or a disguised restriction on international trade, nothing in this Agreement shall be construed to prevent the adoption or enforcement by any contracting party of measures:

(*a*) necessary to protect public morals; [...]

GATT Article XXIV

Territorial Application – Frontier Traffic – Customs Unions and Free-trade Areas

4. The contracting parties recognize the desirability of increasing freedom of trade by the development, through voluntary agreements, of closer integration between the economies of the countries parties to such agreements. They also recognize that the purpose of a customs union or of a free-trade area should be to facilitate trade between the constituent territories and not to raise barriers to the trade of other contracting parties with such territories.

5. Accordingly, the provisions of this Agreement shall not prevent, as between the territories of contracting parties, the formation of a customs union or of a free-trade area or the adoption of an interim agreement necessary for the formation of a customs union or of a free-trade area; *Provided* that: [...]

Enabling Clause

1. Notwithstanding the provisions of Article I of the General Agreement, contracting parties may accord differential and more favourable treatment to developing countries[1], without according such treatment to other contracting parties.

2. The provisions of paragraph1 apply to the following:[2]

(*a*) Preferential tariff treatment accorded by developed contracting parties to products originating in developing countries in accordance with the Generalized System of Preferences,[3]

ATC Article 2

4. The restrictions notified under paragraph1shall be deemed to constitute the totality of such restrictions applied by the respective Members on the day before the entry into force of the WTO Agreement. No new restrictions in terms of products or Members shall be introduced except under the provisions of this Agreement or relevant GATT 1994 provisions. Restrictions not notified within 60 days of the date of entry into force of the WTO Agreement shall be terminated forthwith. [...]

ATC Article 6

1. Members recognize that during the transition period it may be necessary to apply a specific transitional safeguard mechanism (referred to in this Agreement as 'transitional safeguard'). [...] The transitional safeguard should be applied as sparingly as possible, consistently with the provisions of this Article and the effective implementation of the integration process under this Agreement. [...]

TRIPS Agreement Article 30

Exceptions to Rights Conferred

Members may provide limited exceptions to the exclusive rights conferred by a patent, provided that such exceptions do not unreasonably conflict with a normal exploitation of the patent and do not unreasonably prejudice the legitimate interests of the patent owner, taking account of the legitimate interests of third parties.

SPS Agreement Article 2

[...]
2. Members shall ensure that any sanitary or phytosanitary measure is applied only to the extent necessary to protect human, animal or plant life or health, is based on scientific principles and is not maintained without sufficient scientific evidence, except as provided for in paragraph 7 of Article5
[...]

SPS Agreement Article 5

[...]
7. In cases where relevant scientific evidence is insufficient, a Member may provisionally adopt sanitary or phytosanitary measures on the basis of available pertinent information, including that from the relevant international organizations as well as from sanitary or phytosanitary measures applied by other Members. In such circumstances, Members shall seek to obtain the additional information necessary for a more objective assessment of risk and review the sanitary or phytosanitary measure accordingly within a reasonable period of time.
[...]

SPS Agreement Article 3

1. To harmonize sanitary and phytosanitary measures on as wide a basis as possible, Members shall base their sanitary or phytosanitary measures on international standards, guidelines or recommendations, where they exist, except as otherwise provided for in this Agreement, and in particular in paragraph 3.
[...]

3. Members may introduce or maintain sanitary or phytosanitary measures which result in a higher level of sanitary or phytosanitary protection than would be achieved by measures based on the relevant international standards, guidelines or recommendations, if there is a scientific justification, or as a consequence of the level of sanitary or phytosanitary protection a Member determines to be appropriate in accordance with the relevant provisions of paragraphs 1 through 8 of Article 5.

TBT Agreement Article 2

2.4 Where technical regulations are required and relevant international standards exist or their completion is imminent, Members shall use them, or the relevant parts of them, as a basis for their technical regulations except when such international standards or relevant parts would be an ineffective or inappropriate means for the fulfilment of the legitimate objectives pursued, for instance because of fundamental climatic or geographical factors or fundamental technological problems.

Agreement on Agriculture Article 13

During the implementation period, notwithstanding the provisions of GATT 1994 and the Agreement on Subsidies and Countervailing Measures (referred to in this Article as the 'Subsidies Agreement'):

[...]

(b) domestic support measures that conform fully to the provisions of Article 6 of this Agreement including direct payments that conform to the requirements of paragraph 5 thereof, as reflected in each Member's Schedule, as well as domestic support within *de minimis* levels and in conformity with paragraph 2 of Article 6, shall be:

[...]

(ii) exempt from actions based on paragraph 1 of Article XVI of GATT 1994 or Articles 5 and 6 of the Subsidies Agreement, provided that such measures do not grant support to a specific commodity in excess of that decided during the 1992 marketing year; and

[...]

(c) export subsidies that conform fully to the provisions of Part V of this Agreement, as reflected in each Member's Schedule, shall be:

[...]

(ii) exempt from actions based on Article XVI of GATT 1994 or Articles 3, 5 and 6 of the Subsidies Agreement.

SCM Agreement Article 3

3.1 Except as provided in the Agreement on Agriculture, the following subsidies, within the meaning of Article1, shall be prohibited: [...]

SCM Agreement Article 5

No Member should cause, through the use of any subsidy referred to in paragraphs 1 and 2 of Article 1, adverse effects to the interests of other Members, i.e.:
[. . .]
This Article does not apply to subsidies maintained on agricultural products as provided in Article 13 of the Agreement on Agriculture.

SCM Agreement Article 27

27.2 The prohibition of paragraph1(a) of Article 3 shall not apply to:

(a) developing country Members referred to in Annex VII.
(b) other developing country Members for a period of eight years from the date of entry into force of the WTO Agreement, subject to compliance with the provisions in paragraph 4.

SCM Agreement

Footnote 59 to item (e) of Annex I

Paragraph (e) is not intended to limit a Member from taking measures to avoid the double taxation of foreign source income earned by its enterprises or the enterprises of another Member.

5

The Main Actors in the Process of Fact-Finding and the Development of the Factual Record

Introduction

In general terms, the function of WTO panels and the Appellate Body is to review measures adopted by WTO Members with a view to determining whether those measures are consistent with the WTO agreements. The DSU does not set out in detail how panels are to perform their task of reviewing the measures brought before them. Article 11 of the DSU contains a broad statement describing the role of the panel. According to Article 11, 'a panel should make an objective assessment of the matter before it, including an objective assessment of the facts of the case and the applicability of and conformity with the relevant covered agreements'. Given the broad terms of Article 11, it is not difficult to understand why that Article has been invoked in several different contexts including (i) appeals challenging the panel's appreciation of the evidence as discussed in Section II.C.3.4 of Chapter 1, (ii) cases discussing the question of how much deference panels should accord to different aspects of the domestic decision-making process behind a measure, and (iii) cases discussing the question of whether Article 11 entitles a complaining party to a finding on every specific legal claim brought before a panel, that is, whether the panel is entitled to exercise judicial economy. In sum, the DSU provides no detailed guidance on how panels should perform their review of challenged measures.

A closer examination of the text of the WTO agreements and the cases brought before the dispute settlement system, however, reveals that panels may perform two distinct roles: (i) reviewer *stricto sensu*, and (ii) original-trier-of-facts.[1] Although in a broad sense panels are always 'reviewing' measures, the word 'reviewer' is used in a narrower sense here. Relatedly, the expression

[1] The Appellate Body referred to this distinction in Appellate Body Report, *United States—Countervailing Duty Investigation on Dynamic Random Access Memory Semiconductors (DRAMS) from Korea*, WT/DS296/AB/R, adopted 20 July 2005 at para 188.

'standard of review' may be used to refer broadly to questions regarding the role of the panel in examining domestic measures[2] or more narrowly to the level of scrutiny a panel should apply when acting as a reviewer.[3] The first meaning of the expression encompasses the second.

Panels act as original-trier-of-facts when the agreements impose obligations with which WTO Members must comply but they leave it open for Members to decide whom, how, and what specific criteria are followed to ensure compliance, that is, the agreements do not (or at least not to a substantial degree) regulate the domestic decision-making process. In contrast, panels act as reviewers when the WTO agreements explicitly entrust a domestic authority to make a determination according to procedural and substantive criteria set out in the agreements. In this situation, the panel reviews the determination made by the domestic authority with a view to establishing whether the authority followed the criteria (substantive and procedural) provided for in the agreements. The factual record on which the panel will base its decision will essentially have been developed during the domestic proceedings. Accordingly, the structure of the agreements implies a division of labour between domestic authorities and WTO panels.[4]

Admittedly, there is no absolute separation between the roles of original-trier-of-facts and reviewer. For instance, as a reviewer the panel is still the original-trier-of-facts with respect, for example, to the question of whether the domestic authority was unbiased and objective. In this respect, there may be some scope for relying on evidence which was not part of the record of the domestic authorities.[5] This, however, does not affect the usefulness of this classification because in any given situation one role will clearly predominate over the other.

[2] This seems to be how the expression is used by Ehlerman and Lockhart. See Claus-Dieter Ehlermann & Nicolas Lockhart, 'Standard of Review in WTO Law' (2004) 7:3 Journal of International Economic Law 491 at 493.

[3] This is the meaning given to the expression by Spamann. See Holger Spamann, 'Standard of Review for World Trade Organization Panels in Trade Remedy Cases: a Critical Analysis' (2004) 38:3 Journal of World Trade 509 at 510.

[4] Similarly, see Ehlermann & Lockhart, above n 2 at 502–3.

[5] In the context of a challenge to a countervailing duty determination the Appellate Body in *US—Countervailing Duty Investigation on DRAMS* suggested that panels might have to consider evidence which was not on the record of the domestic authority if an allegation is made that the authority 'failed to investigate sufficiently or to collect certain information'. Appellate Body Report, *US—Countervailing Duty Investigation on DRAMS*, above n 1 at para 187. In the case of challenges to trade remedy investigations, the Appellate Body has indicated that a domestic authority cannot be found *not* to have established the facts properly only because it did not investigate an issue which it was not expressly required to investigate and whose relevance it could not reasonably have discerned from information to which it had access. See Appellate Body Report, *US—Countervailing Duty Investigation on DRAMS*, above n 1 at paras 174–9; Appellate Body Report, *United States—Definitive Safeguard Measures on Imports of Wheat Gluten from the European Communities*, WT/DS166/AB/R, adopted 19 January 2001, DSR 2001:II, 717 at paras 55–6. See also Jesse Kreier, 'Contingent Trade Remedies and WTO Dispute Settlement: Some Particularities' in R Yerxa & B Wilson (eds), *Key Issues in WTO Dispute Settlement: The First Ten Years* (Cambridge: Cambridge University Press, 2005) 46 at 52–3 (regarding the use of non-record evidence in challenges to trade remedy determinations).

The objective of this chapter is to examine how the facts of a case are established, particularly how the record of the proceedings is formed and what the role of the panel and the parties is in that process. This chapter is divided into two main parts. Section I discusses the role of the panel as a reviewer; it explains the limitations which are associated with this role in the context of challenges to domestic trade remedy investigations (Section I.A). It argues that, notwithstanding the views of some commentators, the same restrictions do not apply in cases brought before a panel under the SPS and TBT Agreements, where the panel acts as the original-trier-of-facts (Section I.B).

Section II focuses on the role of the panel as the original-trier-of-facts. It examines how the factual record on which the panel bases its rulings is developed. It explains how the basic structure of the WTO dispute settlement system influences how the factual record is developed (Section II.A). The principal argument throughout this second part is that in order for the facts to be accurately determined and the WTO agreements properly applied it is essential that the disputing parties be forthcoming in providing relevant and necessary information and that the panel be actively engaged in the process of fact-finding.

Section II.B focuses on the role of the disputing parties in the process of fact-finding. It discusses different aspects of the duty of the parties to cooperate in presenting information to the panel such as its scope—including whether it extends to the production of confidential information—when it commences, and how its observance can be ensured. This section also explains that the WTO Members have certain obligations to provide information on their measures even outside the context of the panel process.

Section II.C analyses the role which the panel plays (or ought to play) in the development of the factual record of the proceedings. It begins with a discussion of the reasons supporting an active role for the panel in the process of fact-finding. It then explains how the panel can be active. In other words, it discusses the fact-finding powers of the panel which include the authority to seek and rely upon information from the disputing parties as well as any other relevant source such as WTO Members not involved in the dispute, experts, international organizations, and private parties. The question of the limits of the authority of the panel is then taken up in the last part.

I. The Panel as a Reviewer

A. Trade remedies agreements

Challenges to trade remedy investigations under the Anti-Dumping Agreement, the SCM Agreement, and the Agreement on Safeguards constitute typical examples of cases where panels act as reviewers.[6] These agreements allow WTO Members to impose restrictions, which would otherwise not be permitted under the rules of the GATT, in the form of duties or quotas[7] on imports. In order to impose such restrictions, however, the agreements require a domestic authority to undertake an investigation with a view to determining whether the conditions for the application of restrictions are present. This investigation must be conducted according to pre-established and publicized rules. Restrictions applied without due regard to the procedures demanded by the agreements constitute *per se* violations of the agreements—eg anti-dumping duties imposed solely on the basis of an assessment made by customs authorities at the time of importation would clearly violate the Anti-Dumping Agreement even though dumping and injury may in fact be taking place. Several provisions addressed to the domestic investigating authorities set out in detail the substantive conditions and related factors which must be verified and the procedures which must be followed. The latter include rules regarding: duration of the investigation;[8] use and protection of confidential information;[9] transparency and due process (particularly participation) requirements;[10] and obligation to publish a report setting forth findings and reasoned conclusions.[11] Although the Agreement on Safeguards regulates the activity of investigating authorities in less detail than the Anti-Dumping and the SCM Agreements, it still provides the substantive criteria which must be observed and general guidelines on how the investigation must be conducted.

The task of the panel in challenges to trade remedy investigations is, therefore, not to make the determination that the domestic authority was entrusted to undertake—eg ascertain whether imports are being dumped and causing injury—but rather to review the determination made by the domestic authority with a view to establishing whether the investigating authority observed the procedural and substantive criteria set out in the agreements. Correspondingly, panels do not find that the substantive conditions for the imposition of trade remedies 'do not exist, but rather that the domestic investigating authorities have failed in their national proceedings to establish that they exist'.[12] This division of

[6] It is worth noting that the panel does not act as a reviewer in all cases brought under these agreements. For instance, a panel acts as original-trier-of-facts in 'as such' challenges against the trade remedy statutes of a WTO Member.

[7] Quotas are allowed in the case of safeguards only.

[8] Article 5.10 of the Anti-Dumping Agreement, Article 11.11 of the SCM Agreement, and Article 6 of the Agreement on Safeguards.

[9] Article 6.5 of the Anti-Dumping Agreement, Article 12.4 of the SCM Agreement, Article 3.2 of the Agreement on Safeguards.

[10] Articles 6, 8.3, and 12 of the Anti-Dumping Agreement, Articles 12, 18.3, and 22 of the SCM Agreement, and Article 3.1 of the Agreement on Safeguards.

[11] Article 12.2 of the Anti-Dumping Agreement, Article 22.3 of the SCM Agreement, and Article 3.1 of the Agreement on Safeguards.

[12] Kreier, above n 5 at 57.

labour is implied in the general structure of the agreements and, in the case of the Anti-Dumping Agreement, confirmed in Articles 17.5(ii) and 17.6(i).[13]

Article 17.5(ii) of the Anti-Dumping Agreement states that the panel is established to examine the matter based upon 'the facts made available in conformity with appropriate domestic procedures to the authorities of the importing Member'. Accordingly, this provision makes clear that the panel should focus on reviewing the determination of the domestic authority; it is not for the panel to examine the broader question of whether the conditions to apply a trade remedy are present, since this would require the panel to consider completely new facts. Along these lines, panels have also limited their analysis to the information which was on the record of the investigating authority in challenges to trade remedy investigations conducted under the Agreement on Safeguards and the SCM Agreement.[14] For instance, in a challenge to a safeguard imposed by the United States on certain imports of wheat gluten, the panel noted that it was not its 'role to collect new data, nor to consider evidence which could have been presented to the [domestic authority] by interested parties in the investigation, but was not'.[15] Panels can and have, however, considered information presented to them in a format different from that on the record of the domestic authority,[16] and arguments that were not made by the parties during the

[13] Similarly, see Kreier, above n 5 at 46–51; Ehlermann & Lockhart, above n 2 at 507, 508. But see Spamann, above n 3 at 537–52, 554. Spamann disagrees with this interpretation of the role of panels in challenges to trade remedy investigations. He argues that panels should be able to examine the facts anew with a view to determining whether the substantive conditions for the application of trade remedies exist, that is, in his view the panel should act as an original-trier-of-facts. The points he advances in support of his position may be valid criticisms of the *policy* considerations underpinning the role of the panel as a reviewer; they are less valid as criticisms of the way panels and the Appellate Body have interpreted their actual mandate.

[14] This was the case in Appellate Body Report, *US—Countervailing Duty Investigation on DRAMS*, above n 1 at paras 172–9; Panel Report, *United States—Definitive Safeguard Measures on Imports of Wheat Gluten from the European Communities*, WT/DS166/R, adopted 19 January 2001 at para 8.6; Panel Report, *Korea—Definitive Safeguard Measure on Imports of Certain Dairy Products*, WT/DS98/R and Corr.1, adopted 12 January 2000 at para 7.30; Panel Report, *United States—Measure Affecting Imports of Woven Wool Shirts and Blouses from India*, WT/DS33/R, adopted 23 May 1997 at para 7.21. See also Appellate Body Report, *United States—Transitional Safeguard Measure on Combed Cotton Yarn from Pakistan*, WT/DS192/AB/R, adopted 5 November 2001, DSR 2001:XII, 6027 at paras 78–9 (finding that a panel cannot consider evidence that did not exist at the time of the investigation). See Kreier, above n 5 at 52 (noting that the proposition that panels should focus their work on information that was before the authorities at the time that the determination was made is commonsensical).

[15] Panel Report, *US—Wheat Gluten*, above n 14 at para 8.6.

[16] Panel Report, *European Communities—Anti-Dumping Duties on Imports of Cotton-Type Bed Linen from India*, WT/DS141/R, adopted 12 March 2001 at para 6.43; Panel Report, *United States—Anti-Dumping and Countervailing Measures on Steel Plate from India*, WT/DS206/R and Corr.1, adopted 29 July 2002, DSR 2002:VI, 2073 at 7.13. However, the exception for information presented in a different format does not comprise the case of a study using one of several possible methods to manipulate information on the record. See Panel Report, *United States—Final Dumping Determination on Softwood Lumber from Canada*, WT/DS264/R, adopted 31 August 2004 at paras 7.39–7.41 (where the panel refused to consider a regression analysis which used data on the record of the domestic authority because such regression was beyond 'mere data which [could] be taken at face value').

domestic investigation.[17] Conversely, defences of a domestic authority's determination based on evidence not on the record of the investigation must and have been similarly rejected.[18]

Given the fact that trade remedies can be imposed only after a WTO Member makes a determination pursuant to the provisions of the agreements that the conditions for the imposition of such measures are fulfilled, limiting review at the WTO stage to the record of the domestic authorities also serves to encourage all parties to submit all relevant information at the domestic stage of the process. Otherwise, some parties may be tempted to adopt a wait-and-see attitude during the domestic investigation and, in case of an unfavourable determination, have a WTO panel established to examine the case anew.[19] This would defeat the purpose of domestic investigations and result in waste of resources.

Article 17.6(i) of the Anti-Dumping Agreement in turn explicitly directs the panel to determine 'whether the authorities' establishment of the facts was proper and whether their evaluation of those facts was unbiased and objective'. According to Article 17.6(i), '[i]f the establishment of the facts was proper and the evaluation was unbiased and objective, even though the panel might have reached a different conclusion, the evaluation shall not be overturned'. Article 17.6(i) not only makes clear that the role of the panel is to *review* the domestic authority's determination, but also introduces the question of the level of scrutiny to be applied.[20] In this respect, Article 17.6(i)—and the standard of review

[17] See Appellate Body Report, *United States—Safeguard Measures on Imports of Fresh, Chilled or Frozen Lamb Meat from New Zealand and Australia*, WT/DS177/AB/R, WT/DS178/AB/R, adopted 16 May 2001, DSR 2001:IX, 4051 at paras 113–14. See also Appellate Body Report, *Thailand—Anti-Dumping Duties on Angles, Shapes and Sections of Iron or Non-Alloy Steel and H-Beams from Poland*, WT/DS122/AB/R, adopted 5 April 2001, DSR 2001:VII, 2701 at 94.

[18] See Appellate Body Report, *US—Countervailing Duty Investigation on DRAMS*, above n 1 at para 161. See also Appellate Body Report, *US—Wheat Gluten*, above n 5 at paras 160–3 (where the Appellate Body faulted the panel for relying on clarifications given by the United States in response to the panel's questions rather than the text of the USITC Report in concluding that the 'USITC Report provides an adequate, reasoned and reasonable explanation with respect to "profits and losses" ').

[19] It is not uncommon for companies to refuse to participate in a domestic investigation, particularly because of the costs of doing so. Parties may also be tempted to withhold from the domestic authority information whose value is uncertain, that is, when they are unable to determine whether the information would be favourable to them.

[20] Some commentators have sought to draw a distinction between the standard of review applicable to purely factual findings and that applicable to findings regarding the characterization of the facts in legal terms. This differentiation is not particularly useful, especially because investigating authorities do not establish facts in a vacuum, that is, they do so against the backdrop of the legal rules they have to apply. In light of this, the treatment of the subject by commentators is, to say the least, confusing. For the distinction see, Matthias Oesch, *Standards of Review in WTO Dispute Resolution* (Oxford: Oxford University Press, 2003) at 18, 117–47; Ehlermann & Lockhart, above n 2. Article 17.6(ii) of the Anti-Dumping Agreement addresses the question of the standard of review of purely legal questions, namely, abstract legal interpretations. This question is outside the scope of this study. For more information on this aspect of the standard of review, see: Steven P Croley & John H Jackson, 'WTO Dispute Procedures, Standard of Review, and Deference to National Governments' (1996) 90:2 The American Journal of International Law 193; Oesch, above n 20 at 93–7, 173–229; Ehlermann & Lockhart, above n 2 at 496–500.

elaborated by panels and the Appellate Body for challenges to trade remedy investigations in general—implicitly recognizes the fact that absolute certainties are difficult to come by in legal processes. Accordingly, panels must not overturn the findings of the investigating authority solely on the basis of the fact that, were they the investigating authority, they might have reached a different conclusion.

While Article 17.6(i) expressly requires panels in challenges under the Anti-Dumping Agreement to 'assess if the establishment of the facts by the investigating authorities was *proper* and if the evaluation of those facts by those authorities was *unbiased and objective*',[21] panels and the Appellate Body have found that Article 11 of the DSU requires panels to undertake a similar analysis under the other trade remedy agreements. More specifically, panels must establish whether the factual conclusions 'reached by the investigating authority are reasoned and adequate'.[22] As noted in the introduction to this chapter, Article 11 of the DSU is worded broadly, namely, it does not specifically address the question of the standard of review to be applied by panels in challenges to determinations made by domestic investigating authorities. Because of the broad scope of Article 11 and in the absence of more specific guidelines in the text of the agreements, it seems only natural that panels and the Appellate Body have sought to base their findings regarding the standard of review on Article 11. The Appellate Body's articulation of the standard of review with reference to Article 11 of the DSU in trade remedies cases should not, however, be understood as a universal statement on the standard of review applicable in all WTO cases. This is so because Article 11 is not the only basis for that standard. As noted above, the trade remedies agreements have a particular structure and that structure influences the role of panels in those cases. Importantly, the Appellate Body has recognized that the applicable standard of review is a function of the agreements at issue.[23] It has also noted that certain obligations in those agreements may impose more specific requirements.[24]

[21] Appellate Body Report, *United States—Anti-Dumping Measures on Certain Hot-Rolled Steel Products from Japan*, WT/DS184/AB/R, adopted 23 August 2001, DSR 2001:X, 4697 at para 56 [original emphasis].

[22] Appellate Body Report, *United States—Investigation of the International Trade Commission in Softwood Lumber from Canada—Recourse to Article 21.5 of the DSU by Canada*, WT/DS277/AB/RW, adopted 9 May 2006 at para 93. See also Appellate Body Report, *United States—Definitive Safeguard Measures on Imports of Certain Steel Products*, WT/DS248/AB/R, WT/DS249/AB/R, WT/DS251/AB/R, WT/DS252/AB/R, WT/DS253/AB/R, WT/DS254/AB/R, WT/DS258/AB/R, WT/DS259/AB/R, adopted 10 December 2003, DSR 2003:VII, 3117 at paras 276–9; Appellate Body Report, *US—Lamb*, above n 17 at para 103.

[23] See Appellate Body Report, *US—Countervailing Duty Investigation on DRAMS*, above n 1 at para 184. In support of this view, see Ehlermann & Lockhart, above n 2; Kreier, above n 5 at 51.

[24] See Appellate Body Report, *US—Softwood Lumber VI (Article 21.5—Canada)*, above n 22 at para 92; Appellate Body Report, *US—Lamb*, above n 17 at para 105. With respect to Article 17.6(i) of the Anti-Dumping Agreement, see Appellate Body Report, *Thailand—H-Beams*, above n 17 at para 137.

In light of the fact that investigating authorities must publish their findings and conclusions in a report, panels have taken that report as the starting point for their analysis.[25] In other words, panels scrutinize that report in the light of the evidence on the domestic authority's record with a view to ascertaining whether the factual conclusions of the investigating authority are reasoned and adequate and/or whether the facts were properly established and objectively and unbiasedly evaluated. According to the Appellate Body, when reviewing trade remedies determinations panels 'may not conduct a *de novo* review of the evidence or substitute [their] judgement for that of the competent authorities'.[26] However, they may not be passive either;[27] they have an obligation to examine critically the factual conclusions of the investigating authority.[28] A panel does not discharge its duty by merely considering *in the abstract* whether the 'investigating authority's findings or conclusions appear to be "reasonable" or "plausible" '.[29] Instead, the panel must scrutinize the reasons behind the conclusions of the domestic authority and establish whether the authorities' reasoning is coherent and adequately supported by the evidence on the record of the domestic investigation.[30] In doing so the panel must give due regard to the approach taken by the investigating authority in order to avoid substituting its judgment for that of the domestic authority.[31] This, however, should not interfere with the panel's assessment of whether the reasoning of the authority 'takes sufficient account of conflicting evidence and responds to competing plausible explanations of that evidence'.[32] In sum, while panels are required to accord the domestic authorities a measure of deference in the assessment of the evidence before them, deference is due only (i) if there is evidence on the record which could reasonably support the conclusions of an objective investigating authority, and (ii) if evidence contradicting those conclusions is taken into

25 See, for example, Appellate Body Report, *US—Lamb*, above n 17 at para 105; Appellate Body Report, *US –Steel Safeguards*, above n 22 at paras 276, 298–9.

26 Appellate Body Report, *US –Steel Safeguards*, above n 22 at 299. See also Appellate Body Report, *US—Cotton Yarn*, above n 14 at para 74; Appellate Body Report, *US—Softwood Lumber VI (Article 21.5—Canada)*, above n 22 at paras 93, 99.

27 See Appellate Body Report, *US—Softwood Lumber VI (Article 21.5—Canada)*, above n 22 at para 93; Appellate Body Report, *US—Lamb*, above n 17 at para 106.

28 See Appellate Body Report, *US—Softwood Lumber VI (Article 21.5—Canada)*, above n 22 at para 93; Appellate Body Report, *US—Lamb*, above n 17 at para 106.

29 Appellate Body Report, *US—Softwood Lumber VI (Article 21.5—Canada)*, above n 22 at para 99.

30 See Appellate Body Report, *US—Softwood Lumber VI (Article 21.5—Canada)*, above n 22 at paras 93, 97, 124; Appellate Body Report, *US—Countervailing Duty Investigation on DRAMS*, above n 1 at para 188.

31 See Appellate Body Report, *US—Softwood Lumber VI (Article 21.5—Canada)*, above n 22 at para 99; Appellate Body Report, *US—Countervailing Duty Investigation on DRAMS*, above n 1 at paras 144–152, 157–8.

32 Appellate Body Report, *US—Softwood Lumber VI (Article 21.5—Canada)*, above n 22 at para 97. See also Appellate Body Report, *US—Countervailing Duty Investigation on DRAMS*, above n 1 at para 186; Appellate Body Report, *US—Lamb*, above n 17 at para 106; Appellate Body Report, *US—Cotton Yarn*, above n 14 at para 74.

account and its impact on the conclusions reasonably explained. The criteria discussed in this paragraph, together with the limitation of the review to the facts on the record of the domestic authority, define the broad contours[33] of the standard of review in the broad sense which is applicable to *all trade remedies agreements* –given that Article 11 applies to all agreements and the criteria contained in Article 17.6(i) of the Anti-Dumping Agreement can be interpreted along the same lines.

It is fair to say that the measure of deference owed to the assessments of the domestic investigating authorities is a function of a policy choice to allocate the 'right to error' to those authorities. Such choice is based on (i) recognition of the fact that uncertainty is pervasive and errors are thus inevitable; (ii) belief that the detailed substantive and procedural criteria set out in the trade remedy agreements provide sufficient assurance that the domestic determination will not in general be more prone to errors than WTO adjudication;[34] (iii) respect for the treaty-mandated role of the domestic authority;[35] and (iv) consideration of the fact that trade remedies have a limited life span and that specific procedures for review and revocation at the domestic level of such measures have been provided for in the agreements.[36] Some commentators have also listed the greater resources and expertise of domestic agencies in conducting factual inquiries as a reason for panels to accord some deference to the factual conclusions of the domestic authorities.[37] The alleged greater resources and expertise of the domestic agencies seem, however, to be good reasons for making the information collected by the domestic authorities available to panels, rather than for requiring panels to be deferential to the conclusions drawn from that information.[38]

B. SPS and TBT Agreements

It has been suggested that panels should act as reviewers in challenges to sanitary and phytosanitary (SPS) measures and technical regulations under the SPS

[33] As noted before, specific provisions of the agreements may set out additional criteria.

[34] In other words, the activity of domestic authorities is sufficiently circumscribed so that, for instance, they will not be able to bias the results in favour of domestic producers. Admittedly, there may be problems with the assumption underlying this factor, that is to say, the activity of domestic authorities may not in fact be sufficiently controlled. For example, it is arguable that the domestic authorities' relatively poor knowledge of the local conditions in the exporting Member as compared to the conditions in their own markets may affect the accuracy of their determinations. This particular problem would be minimized if a completely neutral party, such as the panel, with equal knowledge of both markets were ultimately in charge of determining whether the conditions for the application of trade remedies were present. In support of this view, see Spamann, above n 3 at 548–9.

[35] In support of this factor, see Ehlermann & Lockhart, above n 2 at 507.

[36] See Articles 11 and 13 of the Anti-Dumping Agreement, Article 7 of the Agreement on Safeguards, and Articles 21 and 23 of the SCM Agreement.

[37] See Ehlermann & Lockhart, above n 2 at 502; Oesch, above n 20 at 55–6, 106; Croley & Jackson, above n 20 at 208.

[38] Similarly, see Spamann, above n 3 at 551–2.

Agreement and the TBT Agreement respectively. Some of these proposals recommend that panels be even more deferential than in their review of trade remedy determinations; they would require panels to accept a domestic determination as long as the procedure which led to that determination is in accordance with the agreements.[39] This means that panels would not conduct any kind of review of the substantive conditions which must be fulfilled for an SPS measure or technical regulation to be consistent with the WTO agreements—not even an assessment of whether a reasonable domestic regulator could have reached the conclusions which formed the basis of the challenged measure.

The SPS and TBT Agreements, however, do not support such proposals.[40] The structure of these agreements is fundamentally different from the structure of the trade remedy agreements. Neither the SPS Agreement nor the TBT Agreement require a domestic authority to conduct an investigation according to procedures laid out in the agreements as a condition for the adoption of SPS measures or technical regulations. Relatedly, the agreements do not contain detailed guidelines on how the process of formulation of a regulation should be conducted. The agreements only contain basic procedural obligations such as requirements to publish a notice of a proposal to introduce a regulation and to notify other Members at a time when amendments can still be introduced and comments taken into account.[41] It is worth noting that these requirements do not apply to measures which were already in place at the time the SPS and the TBT Agreements came into force. The SPS Agreement does require Members to ensure that SPS measures are based on a risk assessment. However, it does not provide detailed guidance on how this assessment must be conducted; it merely contains a general reference to the 'risk assessment techniques developed by relevant international organizations'. In fact, a Member may base its SPS measure on a risk assessment without conducting an assessment itself, but instead relying upon an assessment undertaken by another country or institution.[42] In

[39] See Andrew T Guzman, 'Food Fears: Health and Safety at the WTO' (2004) 45 Virginia Journal of International Law 1 at 4, 20, 28–9. (Guzman argues that the Appellate Body should defer to the implementing state's evaluation of 'the relevant scientific evidence and the relationship between the measure and the risk assessment'. Curiously, he seems to classify as procedural the following requirements: that a measure not be arbitrarily or unjustifiably discriminatory, that it not be a disguised restriction on trade, and that it not be more trade restrictive than necessary.)

[40] In support of this view, see Ehlermann & Lockhart, above n 2 at 513, 515–16. Green and Epps support a stronger focus on procedure, but they seem to recognize that this is not the approach espoused by the current text of the SPS and TBT Agreements. Moreover, differently from Guzman, their suggestion seems to be to implement a process of review similar to that which takes place in challenges to trade remedy investigations. Andrew Green & Tracey Epps, 'The WTO, Science, and the Environment: Moving Towards Consistency' (2007) 10:2 Journal of International Economic Law 285 at 314–15.

[41] See SPS Agreement, Annex B, paragraph 5, and TBT Agreement, Article 2.9.

[42] See Appellate Body Report, *European Communities—Measures Concerning Meat and Meat Products (Hormones)*, WT/DS26/AB/R, WT/DS48/AB/R, adopted 13 February 1998, DSR 1998:I, 135 at para 190. See also Joanne Scott, *The WTO Agreement on Sanitary and Phytosanitary Measures: a Commentary* (Oxford: Oxford University Press, 2007) at 84.

EC—Hormones, the Appellate Body expressly rejected the view that Article 5.1 contains a minimum procedural requirement which obliges a Member imposing an SPS measure to demonstrate that it has carried out its own risk assessment or that it actually took into account a risk assessment when it enacted or maintained its sanitary measure.[43]

Moreover, the agreements do not require domestic regulators to produce a report embodying the results of the process which led to the enactment of the measure at issue.[44] Accordingly, there will not necessarily be a record of the investigation leading to the adoption of the measure to which the panel can limit its examination—and certainly, the formation of such record is not required by the agreements. In fact, the language of key provisions such as Article 2.2 of the SPS Agreement[45] and Article 2.3 of the TBT Agreement[46] indicate that Members have a *continuing obligation* to ensure, respectively, that there is scientific evidence to support their SPS measures and that the circumstances or objectives which gave rise to the adoption of technical regulations continue to exist[47]—unlike the trade remedy agreements, the SPS and TBT Agreements do not require Members to establish formal procedures to review their measures.

Therefore, when panels review SPS and TBT measures the main focus is not on determining whether the domestic regulator followed the correct substantive and procedural criteria at the time the measure was adopted, but rather whether the substantive criteria are present *at the time the measure is challenged in WTO dispute settlement proceedings*. In light of this, panels should not and do not limit their analysis to the evidence that was considered or was available at the time the domestic regulator enacted the measure at issue.

A review of panel and Appellate Body reports addressing challenges to SPS measures and technical regulations under the SPS and the TBT Agreements reveals that panels have not actually acted as reviewers in these cases but rather as original-trier-of-facts. The Appellate Body has noted that the standard of review—which here must be understood in its broad sense—in SPS cases is that provided for in Article 11 of the DSU, that is, the 'objective assessment of the

[43] Appellate Body Report, *EC—Hormones*, above n 42 at paras 188–190.

[44] Members have only an obligation to publish the measures. See Annex B, paragraph 1 of the SPS Agreement, and Article 2.11 of the TBT Agreement.

[45] According to Article 2.2: 'Members shall ensure that any sanitary or phytosanitary measure is applied only to the extent necessary to protect human, animal or plant life or health, is based on scientific principles and is *not maintained* without sufficient scientific evidence, except as provided for in paragraph 7 of Article 5.' [emphasis added]

[46] According to Article 2.3: 'Technical regulations shall *not be maintained* if the circumstances or objectives giving rise to their adoption no longer exist or if the changed circumstances or objectives can be addressed in a less trade-restrictive manner' [emphasis added].

[47] In this regard, see Ehlermann & Lockhart, above n 2 at 514–16. See also Appellate Body Report, *EC—Hormones*, above n 42 at para 189 (where the Appellate Body interpreted the expression 'based on' in Article 5.1 of the SPS Agreement as referring 'to a certain *objective relationship* between two elements, that is to say, to an *objective situation* that **persists and is observable** between an SPS measure and a risk assessment' [bold emphasis added]).

facts'.[48] It has rejected the application of the standard of review applicable in challenges to trade remedy investigations on several occasions. In *Japan—Apples*, the Appellate Body dismissed Japan's contention that panels should accord a certain degree of discretion to the importing Member in the manner in which it chooses, weighs, and evaluates scientific evidence.[49] Moreover, it noted that 'as regards fact-finding by panels and the appreciation of scientific evidence, total deference to the findings of the national authorities would not ensure an objective assessment as required by Article 11 of the DSU'.[50] In *EC—Hormones* and *Canada—Continued Suspension*, the Appellate Body also rejected the 'deferential "reasonableness" standard' for which the European Communities had argued.[51]

Accordingly, panels act as original-trier-of-facts in challenges to SPS measures and technical regulations. As in most models of adjudication, panels can thus consider all relevant evidence which is placed on the record of the proceedings and they are not under an obligation to defer to the defendant's assessment of that evidence.[52] In this context, references to the standard of review in its narrow meaning—ie whether panels should grant low/high/total deference to a domestic authority's evaluation of the evidence—make no sense.[53] The Appellate Body seems to have said as much when it ruled in *EC—Hormones* that the applicable standard[54] 'is neither *de novo* review as such, nor "total deference", but rather the "objective assessment of the facts"'.[55]

[48] See Appellate Body Report, *EC—Hormones*, above n 42 at para 117; Appellate Body Report, *Japan—Measures Affecting the Importation of Apples*, WT/DS245/AB/R, adopted 10 December 2003, DSR 2003:IX, 4391 at para 165; Appellate Body Report, *Australia—Measures Affecting Importation of Salmon*, WT/DS18/AB/R, adopted 6 November 1998, DSR 1998:VIII, 3327 at 267; Appellate Body Report, *Canada—Continued Suspension of Obligations in the EC—Hormones Dispute*, WT/DS321/AB/R, adopted 14 November 2008 at para 589.

[49] See Appellate Body Report, *Japan—Apples*, above n 48 at paras 161–8. See also Appellate Body Report, *EC—Hormones*, above n 42 at para 119; Appellate Body Report, *Australia—Salmon*, above n 48 at para 267.

[50] Appellate Body Report, *Japan—Apples*, above n 48 at para 165. See also Appellate Body Report, *Canada—Continued Suspension*, above n 48 at para 589.

[51] Appellate Body Report, *Canada—Continued Suspension*, above n 48 at para 587; Appellate Body Report, *EC—Hormones*, above n 42 at paras 113–14.

[52] Note, for example, that in *Australia—Salmon* the Appellate Body responded to 'Australia's contention that the Panel failed to accord "due deference" to matters of fact it put forward' with a statement that panels 'are not required to accord to factual evidence of the parties the same meaning and weight as do the parties'. Appellate Body Report, *Australia—Salmon*, above n 48 at para 267.

[53] The prohibition on *de novo* review reflects the fact that the panel acts as a reviewer rather than original-trier-of-facts. Similarly, see Ehlermann & Lockhart, above n 2 at 513–14.

[54] The Appellate Body's reference to the standard of review must be understood as a reference to the broad sense of the expression.

[55] Appellate Body Report, *EC—Hormones*, above n 42 at para 117. Its statement that 'many panels have in the past refused to undertake *de novo* review, wisely, since under current practice and systems, they are in any case poorly suited to engage in such a review' must be understood as limited to the context of the cases cited in support of the statement, which are all trade remedy cases. Moreover, the Appellate Body made no reference to *de novo* review in its subsequent reports in cases under the SPS Agreement.

Transforming the role of panels in challenges to SPS measures and technical regulations into that of a reviewer which would be required to accord a Member a measure of deference in its assessments in the preparation of regulations would seem to demand changes to the structure of the SPS and the TBT Agreements. Potential changes would include (i) establishing a division of labour between panels and domestic regulators setting out a specific role for the domestic regulators; (ii) laying down detailed substantive and procedural criteria which would provide sufficient assurance that domestic regulators would pursue the objectives of the agreements; (iii) mandate the creation of formal mechanisms at the domestic level for the review of measures. Given the broad coverage of the SPS and the TBT Agreement—the definition of SPS measures and technical regulations is encompassing[56] and the number of domestic entities involved can be high[57]—these amendments may be costly. It is likely that the number and associated cost of the errors which panels make as original-trier-of-facts does not justify the costs of such amendments.[58] Moreover, as discussed in Chapter 4, it must not be forgotten that complainants currently have the burden of proving that the challenged SPS measure or technical regulation is not consistent with the obligations set out in the agreements. Therefore, if the evidence before the panel is not sufficient to allow the panel to conclude at a minimum that the claims at issue are more likely than not to be true, the panel should not be able to find that the SPS measure or technical regulation is inconsistent with the agreements. Furthermore, as discussed in Chapter 3, panels may adopt a higher standard of proof than the preponderance of the evidence (the 'more likely than not') standard, such as the clear and convincing evidence standard, which would reduce the likelihood of erroneous decisions against defendants.

It is worth noting that the fact that panels act as original-trier-of-facts in challenges against SPS measures does not mean that they will find that those measures violate the agreement whenever the majority of the scientific opinion does not support the measure in question. If the panel verifies that the measure is

[56] See Article 1.1 and Annex A, paragraph 1 of the SPS Agreement, and Article 1.3 and Annex 1, paragraph 1 of the TBT Agreement.

[57] The TBT Agreement requires Members to ensure that central government bodies respect the provisions of Article 2 regarding technical regulations. With respect to local government and non-governmental bodies within their territories, Article 3.1 establishes that Members 'shall take such reasonable measures as may be available to them to ensure compliance by such bodies with the provisions of Article 2'. Article 13 of the SPS Agreement provides that 'Members are fully responsible under this Agreement for the observance of all obligations set forth herein.' In addition, Article 13 states that 'Members shall take such reasonable measures as may be available to them to ensure that non-governmental entities within their territories, as well as regional bodies in which relevant entities within their territories are members, comply with the relevant provisions of this Agreement.'

[58] For policy arguments against the idea of transforming the role of panels in challenges to SPS measures and technical regulations into that of a reviewer, see Vern R Walker, 'Keeping the WTO from Becoming the "World Trans-science Organization": Scientific Uncertainty, Science Policy, and Factfinding in the Growth Hormones Dispute' (1998) 31 Cornell International Law Journal 251 at 288–90.

supported by a sound minority opinion, it should find the measure to be maintained with sufficient scientific evidence.[59] This is so because often there is not 'one truth' with respect to scientific matters, and the language of the SPS Agreement does not suggest otherwise. For instance, Article 2.2 of the SPS Agreement states that Members shall ensure that a SPS measure 'is based on scientific principles and is not maintained without sufficient scientific evidence'. Accordingly, as long as the evidence and principles on which the measure is based and maintained can be classified as scientific, the conditions of Article 2.2 are fulfilled. This also means that panels should not weigh all the scientific evidence with a view to establishing which side of the scientific debate is more likely than not to represent the truth.[60] Instead, the panel must weigh the evidence before it with the aim of determining whether there is sufficient scientific evidence—which may well not be on the side of the majority as long as it represents a sound divergent scientific opinion—in support of the measure at issue. A similar analysis must be undertaken under Article 5.1 of the SPS Agreement, which requires SPS measures to be based on a risk assessment. According to the Appellate Body in *Canada—Continued Suspension*:

> a panel reviewing the consistency of an SPS measure with Article 5.1 of the *SPS Agreement* must, first, identify the scientific basis upon which the SPS measure was adopted. This scientific basis need not reflect the majority view within the scientific community but may reflect divergent or minority views. Having identified the scientific basis underlying the SPS measure, the panel must then verify that the scientific basis comes from a respected and qualified source. Although the scientific basis need not represent the majority view within the scientific community, it must nevertheless have the necessary scientific and methodological rigour to be considered reputable science. [...] A panel should also [...] review whether the particular conclusions drawn by the Member assessing the risk find sufficient support in the scientific evidence relied upon. Finally, the panel must determine whether the results of the risk assessment 'sufficiently warrant' the SPS measure at issue. Here, again, the scientific basis cited as warranting the SPS measure need not reflect the majority view of the scientific community provided that it comes from a qualified and respected source.[61]

Moreover, as regards the process of risk assessment, since the SPS Agreement does not regulate in detail this process but instead refers to the 'risk assessment techniques developed by the relevant international organizations',[62] panels must be prepared to accept the different techniques which are recognized by the scientific community.

[59] See Appellate Body Report, *EC—Hormones*, above n 42 at para 194. See also Walker, *Scientific Uncertainty and Factfinding*, above n 58 at 279–81.

[60] Compare with Appellate Body Report, *European Communities—Measures Affecting Asbestos and Asbestos-Containing Products*, WT/DS135/AB/R, adopted 5 April 2001, DSR 2001:VII, 3243 at para 178.

[61] Appellate Body Report, *Canada—Continued Suspension*, above n 48 at para 591.

[62] Article 5.1 of the SPS Agreement.

It is also important to note that the fact that panels act as original-trier-of-facts in challenges against SPS measures—or, in fact, in any other situation where panels act as original-trier-of-facts—does not mean that panels can overrule the policy goals set by WTO Members in the exercise of prerogatives that the agreements have left to them.[63] In the context of the SPS Agreement, a Member's determination of its 'appropriate level of protection' constitutes a good example.[64] The SPS Agreement defines the appropriate level of protection as '[t]he level of protection *deemed appropriate by the Member* establishing a sanitary or phytosanitary measure to protect human, animal or plant life or health within its territory'.[65] Only in the limited circumstances set out in the SPS Agreement can the panel question the appropriateness of the level of protection elected by a Member.[66] But the fact that a panel cannot choose a different policy goal for a Member does not mean that the alleged choice of a certain policy goal cannot be challenged in dispute settlement. In other words, if the defendant alleges that its measure was adopted to reduce child mortality in a given situation to 1 per cent, the complainant may still seek to prove that that is actually not the policy goal motivating the measure.

C. Final considerations

It is beyond the scope of this book to analyse every WTO agreement in order to determine whether they require panels to act as original-trier-of-facts or as reviewers. It is safe, however, to conclude that most WTO agreements impose obligations with which WTO Members must comply, but that those agreements leave it open for Members to decide whom, how, and what specific criteria must be followed to ensure compliance, that is, the agreements do not (or at least do not to a substantial degree) regulate the domestic decision-making process. Accordingly, as a general rule, outside the context of challenges to trade remedy determinations panels act as original-trier-of-facts rather than reviewers.

The next part of this chapter examines how the factual record of the proceedings is developed, including the role of the parties and the panel in that process. While the discussion which follows is not irrelevant to cases where the

[63] Similarly, see Ehlermann & Lockhart, above n 2 at 516–17, 520–21.

[64] For more information on the question of the 'appropriate level of protection', see Scott, above n 42 at 35–40.

[65] Annex A, paragraph 5, of the SPS Agreement [emphasis added].

[66] For instance, according to Article 5.5 of the SPS Agreement, a 'Member shall avoid arbitrary or unjustifiable distinctions in the levels it considers to be appropriate in different situations, if such distinctions result in discrimination or a disguised restriction on international trade.'

It is also worth noting that in *Australia—Salmon* the Appellate Body found that in the limited circumstances 'where a Member does not determine its appropriate level of protection, or does so with insufficient precision, the appropriate level of protection may be established by panels on the basis of the level of protection reflected in the SPS measure actually applied'. Appellate Body Report, *Australia—Salmon*, above n 48 at para 207.

panel acts as a reviewer, the focus is on cases where the panel acts as the original-trier-of-facts. The discussion that ensues is relevant at least in part to cases where the panel acts as a reviewer because, for instance, the record of the domestic proceedings is not automatically transferred to the panel. This contrasts, for example, with the NAFTA Chapter 19 binational panel review of final anti-dumping and countervailing duty determinations, where pursuant to Article 1904.14 the domestic investigating authority must 'transmit to the panel the administrative record of the proceeding'. WTO panels must, therefore, create their own record, even though most of the information which will be on the record of the WTO panel is also part of the record of the domestic authority. The discussion on confidential information in Section II.B.5 is particularly relevant in this regard, because the parties may not be willing to make available to the panel confidential information which is on the record of the domestic authority.

II. The Panel as the Original-Trier-of-Facts

A. Context: institutional and procedural framework

In contrast to cases where the panel acts as a reviewer, when the panel is the original-trier-of-facts the development of the evidence necessary for the panel to determine whether the measure at issue is consistent with the WTO agreements will take place during the WTO dispute settlement process. The manner in which the evidence is gathered and placed on the record of the panel cannot be dissociated from the institutional and procedural framework of the WTO dispute settlement system. Accordingly, the next few paragraphs provide a brief overview of the basic structure of the WTO dispute settlement system in comparison with the archetypal features of the common law and the civil law models of adjudication which have influenced the manner in which the factual record is developed in those systems.

As noted in Section II.C of Chapter 1, the taking and presentation of evidence in WTO proceedings is episodic as opposed to traditional common law proceedings where evidence presentation is temporally concentrated in a single event (the trial). That is to say, in the WTO the factual record of the panel is developed gradually throughout the proceedings. Rather than being introduced through oral testimony during the trial, the evidence (mostly documents) is introduced with the written submissions of the parties, including written answers to questions from the panel and the opposing party. Written submissions explain (or ought to explain) how the evidence appended supports the allegations made. Because the case is presented primarily through written submissions, the function of the oral hearings (ie meetings with the panel) is mainly to provide an opportunity to clarify issues and focus the discussion on the questions which the panel believes are the most important.[67] Accordingly, panel hearings are much shorter than traditional common law trials and they play a secondary role in the development of the factual record. Importantly, short hearings and reliance upon documentary evidence suit well the particular needs of WTO adjudication where the parties and the panel meet away from their home base and the proceedings may be conducted in a language that is foreign to some of them. Predominantly written proceedings allow for substantial time and cost savings, which have made their use a common trend in international adjudication.[68]

The traditional common law concentration of the proceedings in the trial creates the need for a pre-trial procedure—called pre-trial discovery or disclosure—which allows the parties an opportunity to acquire sufficient information (i) to cover a vast array of issues which may (but may well not) be raised during the trial, and (ii) to avoid surprises from their opponents. Although the exact scope of pre-trial discovery and the devices available vary across common law jurisdictions, the term discovery refers to the compulsory disclosure of information relating to the claims and defences of the parties to the dispute. Such disclosure takes place pursuant to rules requiring certain information to be made available automatically[69] or at the request of another party.[70] Pre-trial discovery is typically designed to inform the parties rather than the court; thus the court as a general rule intervenes only where disputes between the parties arise. The United States is known to have the most encompassing pre-trial discovery procedures. According to the Federal Rules of Civil Procedure:

> [p]arties may obtain discovery regarding any matter, not privileged, that is relevant to the claim or defense of any party, including the existence, description, nature, custody, condition, and location of any books, documents, or other tangible things and the identity and location of persons having knowledge of any discoverable matter. [...] Relevant information need not be admissible at the trial if the discovery appears reasonably calculated to lead to the discovery of admissible evidence.[71]

[67] See Eric L White, 'Written and Oral Submissions in WTO Dispute Settlement' in F Weiss (ed), *Improving WTO Dispute Settlement Procedures: Issues and Lessons from the Practice of other International Courts and Tribunals* (London: Cameron May, 2000) 121 at 123–4 (explaining the value of the meetings with the panel).

[68] See Alan Redfern et al, *Law and Practice of International Commercial Arbitration* (4th edn, London: Sweet & Maxwell, 2004) at 320 (noting that '[t]he trend in international arbitration is toward shorter hearings with greater reliance upon documentary evidence. This is a necessary step in the interests of economy of time and costs [...]'); W Lawrence Craig, William W Park & Jan Paulsson, *International Chamber of Commerce Arbitration* (3rd edn, Dobbs Ferry: Oceana Publications, 2000) at 427–8 (noting that the particularities of international disputes favour the civilian approach of short hearings and reliance upon documentary evidence).

[69] For example, US Federal Rules of Civil Procedure, Rule 26(a)(1); English Civil Procedure Rules, Rule 31(6).

[70] For example, US Federal Rules of Civil Procedure, Rule 26(b)(1); English Civil Procedure Rules, Rule 31(12).

[71] Federal Rules of Civil Procedure, Rule 26(b)(1).

Moreover, pursuant to the Federal Rules of Civil Procedure the parties may obtain discovery by depositions,[72] written interrogatories,[73] production of documents or things, entry upon land or other property, physical and mental examinations, and requests for admission.[74] The mechanisms of depositions, written interrogatories, and requests for admission are not generally available in most other common law jurisdictions. In sum, in a system where the trial is *the occasion* where evidence is introduced into the record of the proceedings and connected to the legal arguments of the parties, some form of pre-trial discovery is necessary to allow parties to meaningfully participate—present their case and respond to the case presented by their opponent—in the trial.[75]

WTO proceedings, in contrast, are episodic. This means that although the bulk of the evidence should be introduced into the record of the proceedings with the first set of written submissions to the panel, there are several other occasions where evidence can be placed into the record—namely, the oral hearings, the second set of written submissions, and the answers to questions or specific requests for production of evidence from the panel and the opposing party at or after the oral hearing(s). This is particularly the case of evidence submitted in rebuttal of evidence and/or arguments made by the opposing party. Parties will not be caught in a situation where they will not have an opportunity to respond to evidence submitted by their opponents; if there are no regular submissions scheduled, panels must ensure that upon request the parties are given a chance to respond.

In this procedural setting there is no clear rationale for pre-trial discovery. In fact, because of the absence of a trial properly speaking, pre-trial discovery would have to be understood as 'pre-first submissions' discovery. Certainly, discovery also fulfils the objective of maintaining an evidential balance between the parties,[76] that is, it permits parties to have access to evidence necessary to prove their cases which is in the possession of their opponents and which evidence those opponents may not otherwise produce willingly. However, as will be discussed later in this chapter, such goal can be pursued through means other than pre-trial discovery. Accordingly, even though pre-trial discovery does not fit well with the basic structure of the WTO proceedings, it can be said that certain aspects of the pre-trial discovery process are infused into the different episodes of

[72] Depositions are out-of-court testimonies taken of any person, including a party, upon oral examination or written questions without leave of court. Federal Rules of Civil Procedure, Rule 30(a) and 31(a).

[73] Interrogatories are written questions served without leave of court upon any party to the litigation. Federal Rules of Civil Procedure, Rule 33(a).

[74] Federal Rules of Civil Procedure, Rule 26(a)(5).

[75] See Geoffrey C Hazard Jr, 'Discovery and the Role of the Judge in Civil Law Jurisdictions' (1998) 73:4 Notre Dame Law Review 1017 at 1020; Joachim Zekoll, 'Comparative Civil Procedure' in M Reimann & R Zimmermann (eds), *The Oxford Handbook of Comparative Law* (Oxford: Oxford University Press, 2006) 1327 at 1335.

[76] Neil Andrews, *English Civil Procedure: Fundamentals of the New Civil Justice System* (Oxford: Oxford University Press, 2003) at 597.

the WTO proceedings.[77] As opposed to traditional pre-trial discovery, however, in the WTO scheme, the evidence 'discovered' throughout the proceedings is automatically made part of the record of the panel proceedings.[78]

Another important feature of the WTO dispute settlement system is that disputes are adjudicated by panels composed of individuals chosen for their expertise in the subject-matter of the dispute as opposed to a jury composed of lay persons. Furthermore, panels are in charge of deciding questions of fact and of law. These two features combined with the episodic character of the proceedings enable panels to participate actively in and shape the process of fact-finding. This contrasts with traditional common law proceedings where the jury or the court will learn about the case at the trial, making it more difficult for them to participate actively in the process of fact-finding. In other words, active involvement of the adjudicator in the process of fact-finding presupposes a certain level of knowledge about the dispute which the jury or the courts in the archetypal common law trial do not have; generally speaking they acquire such knowledge too late in the proceedings to have a meaningful impact on the development of the factual record. Moreover, the traditional view that the proceedings have a strictly adversarial character makes it less appropriate for the common law judge to be more active in the process of fact-finding.[79] Such view contrasts with that espoused by the DSU; Article 13 of the DSU expressly grants panels the authority to seek information from the parties and from any individual or body which they deem appropriate. Accordingly, in the WTO dispute settlement system, similarly to civilian jurisdictions, the evidence on

[77] Langbein explains that the process of proof-taking in German civil procedure, a civilian system, 'merges the investigatory function of [the American] pretrial discovery and the evidence-presenting function of [the American] trial'. The same is valid for WTO dispute settlement. John H Langbein, 'The German Advantage in Civil Procedure' (1985) 52:4 University of Chicago Law Review 823 at 829.

[78] In traditional common law proceedings information produced during the pre-trial discovery process may not become part of the court record if the parties do not submit the information to the court. Strict separation between party information (discovery) and court information (trial) occurs particularly in jury trials. According to Sturner, the more recent trend in non-jury trials has been to make the results of the discovery phase known to the court. Rolf Sturner, 'Transnational Civil Procedure: Discovery and Sanctions against Non-Compliance' (2001) 6 Uniform Law Review 871 at 874–5. However, as a general rule, as Hazard Jr notes, 'pretrial discovery [. . .] is a system whose primary function is to inform the advocates, rather than informing either the judge (who ordinarily knows little or nothing of the proofs until trial commences and who will be essentially a neutral umpire come trial) or the jury (which will receive only a small refined residue of the material processed by counsel in discovery)'. Hazard Jr, above n 75 at 1021.

[79] Some common law jurisdictions have revised their positions on this matter. In England, for example, the civil procedure reform which resulted in the 1999 Civil Procedure Rules introduced a more active role for the courts. According to Andrews, while as recently as the early 1980s a civil judge in England was expected to know little or nothing about a case before trial and was required not to interfere significantly with the advocates' presentation of the case, '[u]nder the CPR, the court is now expected to take charge of the conduct of trial. [. . .] the court at trial may "control the evidence by giving directions as to (a) the issues on which it requires evidence" (b) the nature of the evidence which it requires to decide those issues and (c) the way in which evidence is to be placed before the court'. Andrews, above n 76 at 777–8.

which the panel will base its decision is developed through a combination of adversarial presentation and panel intervention.

The hybrid (inquisitorial-adversarial) character of the WTO proceedings and the episodic taking and presentation of evidence also influence the role of the parties in the development of the factual record. The next section examines this question and more generally the role of the parties in the process of fact-finding. The following section then analyses more closely the role of the panel in the process.

B. The role of the disputing parties

1. The general contours of the duty of cooperation

The settlement of disputes between states through adjudication is based on the mutual consent of the states involved. In the context of the WTO, the Members freely agreed to resolve their disputes pursuant to the procedures established in the DSU.[80] Accordingly, as noted in Chapter 1, when a dispute arises, the parties have a duty to cooperate for the smooth development of the process. This obligation has been expressly incorporated into Article 3.10 of the DSU which provides that 'if a dispute arises, all Members will engage in these procedures in good faith in an effort to resolve the dispute'. This general duty of good faith cooperation encompasses the process of fact-finding. In this regard, Article 13.1 of the DSU reinforces the commitment contained in Article 3.10 by providing that Members 'should respond promptly and fully to any request by a panel for such information as the panel considers necessary and appropriate'.[81] In other words, the parties have a duty to cooperate in presenting arguments and evidence with respect to the claims in question so that the panel can accurately determine the facts of the case, which is a necessary precondition for the proper application of the WTO agreements.[82] This is particularly so because the WTO does not have a team of investigators with the power to go into the territory of WTO Members to conduct a thorough investigation—including through the

[80] See Article 23.1 of the DSU, which provides that 'When Members seek the redress of a violation of obligations or other nullification or impairment of benefits under the covered agreements or an impediment to the attainment of any objective of the covered agreements, they shall have recourse to, and abide by, the rules and procedures of this Understanding.'

[81] See Appellate Body Report, *Canada—Measures Affecting the Export of Civilian Aircraft*, WT/DS70/AB/R, adopted 20 August 1999, DSR 1999:III, 1377 at 190 (where the Appellate Body noted that 'the duty of a Member party to a dispute to comply with a request from the panel to provide information under Article 13.1 of the DSU is but one specific manifestation of the broader duties of Members under Article 3.10 of the DSU').

[82] On the general need for the parties to international litigation to cooperate in the production of information, see Chittharanjan F Amerasinghe, *Evidence in International Litigation* (Leiden: Martinus Nijhoff, 2005) at 96–7; VS Mani, *International Adjudication: Procedural Aspects* (The Hague: Martinus Nijhoff, 1980) at 198–9.

issue of warrants—of alleged violations of the WTO agreements.[83] Instead, the WTO dispute settlement system relies to a large extent on the cooperation of the parties to build the record of the proceedings. Generally speaking, the system depends on WTO Members being transparent with respect to the implementation of their WTO obligations.

The duty of cooperation in the presentation of information (arguments and evidence) with a view to assisting the adjudicator to properly apply the law is a common feature of international adjudication and given its widespread acceptance could be said to constitute a general principle of international procedure.[84] While the duty of cooperation is not an exclusive creation of international adjudication, it finds special justification in this context owing to the linguistic, legal, economic, cultural, and political differences between states which make it more difficult for them to understand and present information about activities occurring in the territory of another state. While those differences do not *per se* constitute a reason to require the state whose measures are challenged to prove that its measures do not violate its obligations, they constitute nevertheless a good reason to require that state to provide an elaborate response supported by evidence.

Examples of international instruments making express reference to the duty of cooperation include Article 18.1 of the 1958 International Law Commission Model Rules on Arbitral Procedure [between States] which provides that '[t]he parties shall cooperate with the tribunal in dealing with the evidence and in the other measures contemplated by paragraph 1';[85] Article 75 of the 1907 Convention for the Pacific Settlement of International Disputes establishing that '[t]he parties undertake to supply the Tribunal, as fully as they consider possible,

[83] On a different note, it is worth noting that subject to certain conditions WTO Members have agreed to allow the domestic authorities of another WTO Member to access their territory to collect information from private parties involved in that investigation for the purposes of a domestic anti-dumping or countervailing duty investigation. See Article 6.7 and Annex I to the Anti-Dumping Agreement; Article 12.6 and Annex VI to the SCM Agreement.

[84] See Durward V Sandifer, *Evidence before International Tribunals* (revised edn, Charlottesville: University Press of Virginia, 1975) at 112–18 (referring to several cases and commentary regarding the duty of the parties to disclose to the tribunal relevant information in their possession. He concludes that 'the cases indicate that tribunals tend to require of parties a very full disclosure of evidence in their possession as a condition precedent to an award.'); Mojtaba Kazazi, *Burden of Proof and Related Issues: a Study on Evidence Before International Tribunals* (The Hague: Kluwer Law International, 1996) at 119–21; Mani, above n 82 at 198–9; Anna Riddell & Brendan Plant, *Evidence before the International Court of Justice* (London: British Institute of International and Comparative Law, 2009) at 98–9. The duty of cooperation also finds expression in domestic law and in the adjudication of international disputes between individuals. See, for example, respectively, Article 10 of the French Civil Code, and Thomas H Webster, 'Obtaining Documents from Adverse Parties in International Arbitration' (2001) 17:1 Arbitration International 41 at 57; Thomas E Carbonneau, 'Darkness and Light in the Shadows of International Arbitral Adjudication' in RB Lillich (ed), *Fact-Finding before International Tribunals* (Ardsley-on-Hudson: Transnational Publishers, 1992) 153 at 168.

[85] Adopted by the International Law Commission at its 10th session in 1958, available at <http://untreaty.un.org/ilc/texts/instruments/english/draft%20artides/10_1_1958.pdf> (accessed 20 April 2008).

with all the information required for deciding the case'; and Article 34.3 of the ICSID Rules of Procedure for Arbitration Proceedings (the 'ICSID Arbitration Rules') providing that '[t]he parties shall cooperate with the Tribunal in the production of the evidence and in the other measures provided for in paragraph (2)'. Other instruments refer instead to the right of the tribunal to request the parties to provide information—this other facet will be examined more carefully in Section II.C.1 below.

International tribunals have also long recognized the duty of the parties to cooperate in the presentation of information to the tribunal. In the frequently cited *Parker* case, the United States–Mexico General Claims Commission noted that it is the duty of the parties to 'cooperate in searching out and presenting to this tribunal all facts throwing any light on the merits of the claim presented. The Commission denies the "right" of the respondent merely to wait in silence in cases where it is reasonable that it should speak.'[86] The Commission noted that the honour of the nations binds them to 'full disclosures of the facts' 'so far as such facts are within the knowledge' of the parties or 'can reasonably be ascertained by them'.[87] The Commission referred to Article 75 of the 1907 Convention for the Pacific Settlement of International Disputes in support of its decision. Article 75 of the 1907 Convention was also cited by the Commission in the *Kling* case, where the Commission noted that it is counsel's duty in an international arbitration to produce all possible evidence and argument in support of the government's contentions.[88]

WTO panels and the Appellate Body have also made explicit reference to the duty of the parties to cooperate in providing information to panels.[89] In

[86] *William A Parker (USA) v United Mexican States*, 31 March 1926, 4 Reports of International Arbitration Awards 35 (Millwood, Kraus Reprint, 1974) at 39 or para 6 of the Award.

[87] *William A Parker*, above n 86 at 39 or para 7 of the Award. The brevity of the decision makes it difficult to determine the exact scope of the duty of cooperation imposed by the Commission in this case. The Commission was more specific in the *Kling* case where, for example, it was clear that the Commission had actively requested the parties to provide further information and that Mexico's responses were considered inadequate. *Lillie S Kling (USA) v United Mexican States*, 8 October 1930, 4 Reports of International Arbitral Awards 575 (Millwood, Kraus Reprint, 1974) at 582–4. Mani argues that *Parker* attempts to establish a rigid principle which would impose on the parties a more onerous obligation to present evidence than is the case in diverse municipal legal systems. This, however, seems to be an overly strict reading of *Parker*. The statements of the Commission in *Parker* are of a general nature and can easily be interpreted to allow states under certain circumstances not to disclose information which, for example, would pose a threat to their national security. See Mani, above n 82 at 200.

[88] *Lillie S Kling (USA)*, above n 87 at 582–3.

[89] See, for example, Appellate Body Report, *Canada—Aircraft*, above n 81 at paras 187, 190; Appellate Body Report, *India—Additional and Extra-Additional Duties on Imports from the United States*, WT/DS360/AB/R, adopted 17 November 2008 at para 194; Panel Report, *Turkey—Measures Affecting the Importation of Rice*, WT/DS334/R, adopted 22 October 2007 at paras 5.16, 7.1, 7.7, 7.10; Panel Report, *Japan—Measures Affecting the Importation of Apples*, WT/DS245/R, adopted 10 December 2003 at para 8.48. On the more general duty of the parties to cooperate for the smooth development of the proceedings, see Appellate Body Report, *United States—Tax Treatment for 'Foreign Sales Corporations'*, WT/DS108/AB/R, adopted 20 March 2000, DSR 2000: III, 1619 at para 166.

Argentina—Textiles and Apparel, while refusing to provide evidence of higher quality which was in its possession, Argentina challenged the evidence presented by the claimant, the United States, on the grounds that it was not the best evidence available. The panel dismissed Argentina's challenge noting that '[b]efore an international tribunal, parties do have a duty to collaborate in doing their best to submit to the adjudicatory body all the evidence in their possession'.[90] In a different context, the Appellate Body in *India—Patents* reminded the parties that '[a]ll parties engaged in dispute settlement under the DSU must be fully forthcoming from the very beginning both as to the claims involved in a dispute and as to the facts relating to those claims'.[91] According to the Appellate Body, '[c]laims must be stated clearly. Facts must be disclosed freely. This must be so in consultations as well as in the more formal setting of panel proceedings.'[92]

In a few words, the main premise behind the duty of cooperation is that the parties must engage in the proceedings in good faith with a view to helping the panel to properly apply the WTO agreements—ie help panels to discharge their obligation to 'make an objective assessment of the matter before [them], including an objective assessment of the facts of the case and the applicability of and conformity with the relevant covered agreements'.[93] This inevitably requires the parties to cooperate in producing arguments and evidence to the panel.[94] But how this general principle translates into the practicalities of the process of fact-finding?

Before moving to examine this question, it is worth noting that some commentators have used the expression 'burden of production' or 'burden of producing evidence' in connection with the parties' duty to cooperate in presenting information to the panel. These expressions are consciously not employed in this study for two reasons. First, because these formulations are used in common law

[90] Panel Report, *Argentina—Measures Affecting Imports of Footwear, Textiles, Apparel and Other Items*, WT/DS56/R, adopted 22 April 1998 at para 6.58, see also paras 6.40, 6.53–6.57.

[91] Appellate Body Report, *India—Patent Protection for Pharmaceutical and Agricultural Chemical Products*, WT/DS50/AB/R, adopted 16 January 1998, DSR 1998:I, 9 at para 94.

[92] Appellate Body Report, *India—Patents (US)*, above n 91 at para 94.

[93] Article 11 of the DSU.

[94] Regarding the importance of arguments as opposed to evidence, see Appellate Body Report, *United States—Measures Affecting the Cross-Border Supply of Gambling and Betting Services*, WT/DS285/AB/R, adopted 20 April 2005 at para 140 (where the Appellate Body noted that 'evidence and legal argument' must be 'put forward by the complaining party in relation to each of the elements of the claim. A complaining party may not simply submit evidence and expect the panel to divine from it a claim of WTO-inconsistency'); Appellate Body Report, *Canada—Measures Relating to Exports of Wheat and Treatment of Imported Grain*, WT/DS276/AB/R, adopted 27 September 2004, DSR 2004:VI, 2739 at para 191 (where the Appellate Body stated that 'it is incumbent upon a party to identify in its submissions the relevance of the provisions of legislation—the evidence—on which it relies to support its arguments. It is not sufficient merely to file an entire piece of legislation and expect a panel to discover, on its own, what relevance the various provisions may or may not have for a party's legal position').

jurisdictions as a synonym to the 'burden of going forward'[95] which as seen in Chapters 2 and 3 is not a valid concept in WTO dispute settlement and, second, because there is room for confusing the 'burden of proof' with the 'burden of production'.

2. Practical significance of the duty of cooperation

First of all, it is important to note that while, as seen in previous chapters, only one of the parties bears the burden of proof with respect to any given claim, both parties have an obligation to provide information to the panel with respect to the claims at issue.[96] In this regard, the Appellate Body in *India—Additional Import Duties* noted that 'both parties had a responsibility [...] to adduce relevant evidence at their disposal, both with respect to Article II:1(b) and Article II:2 (a)'.[97] Because in light of the rules on the burden of proof the claimant will receive an adverse ruling if no or insufficient supporting evidence is placed before the panel, the claimant (ie the party bearing the burden of proof) has a direct incentive to provide information to the panel and, therefore, it is generally forthcoming. As will be discussed later, the sanctions resulting from a failure on the part of the respondent to provide information are less clear, which might consequently affect the respondent's incentives to observe its duty to cooperate. However, the mere fact that the sanctions imposed on the respondent are not as clear as that which is imposed on the claimant does not mean that the respondent is not under a duty to cooperate in producing evidence to the panel. As Amerasinghe notes in the context of international litigation '[n]ot only should the adversary not hide the truth, but he is expected to co-operate with the claimant in establishing the truth'.[98] In the same vein, the panel in *Chile—Alcoholic Beverages* noted that the duty of the respondent to cooperate goes beyond merely refraining from obstructing the process of fact-finding.[99]

In fact, the duty of cooperation is more frequently invoked with reference to the *respondent*'s obligation to produce information; but this should not be

[95] See, for example, *Black's Law Dictionary* (8th edn, St Paul: Thomson West, 2004) at 209 (defining the burden of production as '[a] party's duty to introduce enough evidence on an issue to have the issue decided by the fact-finder, rather than decided against the party in a peremptory ruling such as a summary judgment or a directed verdict.—Also termed *burden of going forward with evidence; burden of producing evidence; production burden; degree of proof*).

[96] This view was also adopted by the ALI/UNIDROIT Principles of Transnational Civil Procedure. See American Law Institute & UNIDROIT, *Principles of Transnational Civil Procedure* (Cambridge: Cambridge University Press, 2006) at 42, P-21C.

[97] Appellate Body Report, *India—Additional Import Duties*, above n 89 at paras 193, 231. See also Panel Report, *United States—Section 110(5) of the US Copyright Act*, WT/DS160/R, adopted 27 July 2000, DSR 2000:VIII, 3769 at para 6.15 (noting that '[w]hile a duty rests on all parties to produce evidence and to cooperate in presenting evidence to the Panel, this is an issue that has to be distinguished from the question of who bears the ultimate burden of proof for establishing a claim or a defence').

[98] Amerasinghe, *Evidence in International Litigation*, above n 82 at 97.

[99] Panel Report, *Chile—Taxes on Alcoholic Beverages*, WT/DS87/R, WT/DS110/R, adopted 12 January 2000 at paras 6.26–6.27.

interpreted as suggesting that the claimant is not bound by the duty. Particularly because of the episodic organization of proceedings, not every failure on the part of the claimant to provide information will result in an automatic ruling against the claimant—the arguments and evidence provided by claimants are not always complete, not infrequently because claimants adopt an understanding of the substantive legal standards which does not correspond with the view espoused by the panel, or because they are not aware at the outset of the type of evidence they need to present in order to prove a certain proposition. The fact that claims are not dismissed automatically (or upon the motion of the opposing party) at an early stage of the proceedings because of an incomplete presentation does not mean, however, that the panel is in possession of sufficient information to find that all the elements of the claim advanced by the claimant have been established. In this regard, the panel in *EC—Tube or Pipe Fittings* issued a preliminary ruling at the first meeting with the parties dismissing the European Communities' request for the panel to exclude from the proceedings certain claims which were allegedly vaguely defined by Brazil in its first written submission. The panel noted that 'it is in the nature of the Panel process that the claims made by a party may be progressively clarified and refined throughout the proceeding'.[100] The panel made clear, however, that its decision not to reject Brazil's claim at that stage did not prejudge the question of whether Brazil would ultimately succeed in substantiating its claims.[101] Complainants, therefore, should continue to cooperate throughout the proceedings in producing information to the panel, particularly, but not exclusively, when called on to do so.

In traditional common law proceedings, the parties are under an obligation during the pre-trial discovery stage to exchange materials which may be used as evidence at trial. Each party is then solely responsible for presenting their cases to the court or jury at the trial. It could be said that the parties are under a duty to cooperate in the pre-trial stage but then have no obligation to do so during trial. In contrast, given the episodic character of the WTO proceedings, the duty of the parties to cooperate is not restricted to a specific phase of the proceedings. The duty of cooperation finds expression in procedural obligations throughout the proceedings. Pursuant to these procedural obligations, information must be presented voluntarily at certain stages (automatic production) and specifically upon request.

[100] Panel Report, *European Communities—Anti-Dumping Duties on Malleable Cast Iron Tube or Pipe Fittings from Brazil*, WT/DS219/R, adopted 18 August 2003 at para 7.10 or para 6 of the preliminary ruling. The panel was careful to note that 'if, subsequently in the course of these proceedings, the European Communities considers that Brazil's claims remain insufficiently clear or that these claims have finally become clear at such a late stage that the European Communities considers that it has not had an opportunity properly to respond, it may bring this situation to the attention of the Panel. The Panel will then consider the situation, keeping in mind the due process rights of the European Communities.' Ibid, para 7.10 or para 7 of the preliminary ruling.

[101] Panel Report, *EC—Tube or Pipe Fittings*, above n 100 at para 7.10 or para 9 of the preliminary ruling.

As to automatic production, several provisions of the DSU and established practice indicate that the parties have not only the right but also the obligation to provide information on the claims at issue. Articles 12.5 and 12.6 of the DSU provide that written submissions must be deposited with the Secretariat according to the deadlines set by the panel. Article 12.6 also provides that the 'complaining party shall submit its first submission in advance of the responding party's first submission' and 'subsequent written submissions shall be submitted simultaneously'. Furthermore, paragraph 4 of Appendix 3 (Working Procedures) establishes that '[b]efore the first substantive meeting of the panel with the parties, the parties to the dispute shall transmit to the panel written submissions in which they present the facts of the case and their arguments'. At the first substantive meeting, 'the panel shall ask the party which has brought the complaint to present its case' followed by the opposing party which 'shall be asked to present its point of view'.[102] In addition to having become common practice, some panels have also expressly stipulated in their working procedures that the 'parties shall submit all factual evidence to the Panel no later than during the first substantive meeting, except with respect to evidence necessary for purposes of rebuttals, answers to questions or comments made for purposes of rebutting answers provided by others'.[103] According to paragraph 7 of Appendix 3, '[f]ormal rebuttals shall be made at a second substantive meeting of the panel'; prior to that meeting, the 'parties shall submit [...] written rebuttals to the panel'.

Pursuant to these provisions, the complainant presents its case first; its first written submission should specify its claims and present detailed arguments and supporting evidence.[104] The defendant then submits its written submission containing its own arguments and supporting evidence in response. In the first meeting with the panel the parties (i) put forward their views without necessarily repeating all the information which was introduced in the written submissions, (ii) present evidence which could not be appended to the written submissions, and (iii) ask and answer questions from the panel and the other parties.[105] Although the DSU does not explicitly provide for the right of the parties to ask questions of each other at the meeting with the panel (which are often followed

[102] DSU, Appendix 3 (Working Procedures), paragraph 5.

[103] See, for example, the working procedures in Panel Report, *European Communities—Selected Customs Matters*, WT/DS315/R, adopted 11 December 2006, at Annex E.

[104] In support, see Panel Report, *US—Steel Plate*, above n 16 at para 7.28 (where the panel noted that '[p]aragraphs 4 and 7 of Appendix 3 to the DSU provide that parties shall "present the facts of the case and their arguments" in the first written submission, and that written rebuttals shall be submitted prior to the second meeting. These procedures, in our view, envision that initial arguments regarding a claim should be presented for the first time in the first written submission, and not at the meeting of the panel with the parties or in rebuttal submissions.').

[105] For the authority of the panel to ask questions, see Appendix 3 (Working Procedures), paragraph 8 of the DSU and Article 13 of the DSU.

up in writing) this is an established practice in WTO dispute settlement.[106] The subsequent submissions, which should focus on following up and rebutting arguments and evidence submitted at the initial stage, should be equally detailed and supported by evidence. Accordingly, as in proceedings in civil law jurisdictions, 'both parties have to give a very detailed picture of the (alleged) facts from their point of view and have to react in a substantive manner to the differing standpoint thereon of the opponent'.[107]

The fact that the complainant must present its case in its first written submission[108] requires it to have undertaken substantial preparation and precludes the complainant from setting off the panel process with the objective of 'discovering' a case in the process.[109] If the complainant does not present detailed arguments and evidence in support of its claims, the respondent will not as a consequence be able to respond in an appropriate manner. The insufficiency of supporting information which will likely result from this situation in combination with considerations of due process stemming from the inability of the defendant to respond in an appropriate manner should inevitably lead to the failure of claims which are not thoroughly argued and supported by evidence.[110] This was the case in *US—Upland Cotton* where the panel rejected Brazil's claims that the FSC Repeal and Extraterritorial Income Act of 2000 (the 'ETI Act of 2000') was inconsistent with Articles 8 and 10.1 of the Agreement on Agriculture and Articles 3.1(a) and 3.2 of the SCM Agreement because Brazil had not presented arguments and evidence with respect to those claims.[111] The panel also referred to the 'fundamental concerns of due process and procedural fairness in WTO dispute settlement' in support of its ruling.[112] In *US—Gambling* the Appellate Body provided some general guidance on the minimum level of elaboration required to fulfil the demands of the due process requirement of participation. According to the Appellate Body, the evidence and arguments 'must

[106] See White, above n 67 at 123.

[107] Peter Gottwald, 'Fact-Finding: a German Perspective' in DLC Miller & PR Beaumont (eds), *The Option of Litigating in Europe* (London: United Kingdom National Committee of Comparative Law, 1993) vol 14, 67 at 70 (describing German civil proceedings). See also, Article 138 of the German Code of Civil Procedure; Articles 282, 283, 300, and 302 of the Brazilian Code of Civil Procedure. The ALI/UNIDROIT Principles of Transnational Civil Procedure also adopted this view in Principle 11. See American Law Institute & UNIDROIT, above n 96 at 30.

[108] This is without prejudice to the opportunity to present supplementary information in the responses to questions and the second written submission.

[109] The system of notice pleading embraced by the United States Federal Rules of Civil Procedure allows complainants to start a case on the basis of very general allegations which combined with generous discovery rules permits the complainant to make claims as to whose merits the complainant is uncertain.

[110] This is not to say that the panel cannot exercise its *discretion* to request the complainant to provide clarifications. However, if clarifications are provided, the defendant must then be granted an opportunity to respond. Some aspects of this point are further developed in Section II.C.4.

[111] Panel Report, *United States—Subsidies on Upland Cotton*, WT/DS267/R, and Corr.1, adopted 21 March 2005 at paras 7.959, 7.974, 7.976.

[112] Panel Report, *US—Upland Cotton*, above n 111 at para 7.976.

be sufficient to identify the challenged measure and its basic import, identify the relevant WTO provision and obligation contained therein, and explain the basis for the claimed inconsistency of the measure with that provision'.[113] In that case, the Appellate Body reversed the findings of the panel that eight state laws of the United States were inconsistent with Article XVI of the GATS because those claims were not sufficiently elaborated.[114] According to the Appellate Body, '[i]n none of Antigua's submissions to the Panel was the way in which these measures operate explained in a manner that would have made it apparent to the Panel and to the United States that an inconsistency with Article XVI was being alleged with respect to these measures'.[115] *EC—Bananas III* merits some attention in this respect. In that case, the Appellate Body reversed a decision of the panel which excluded certain claims under the GATS made by Mexico, Guatemala, and Honduras from the scope of the case because in the panel's view those parties' failure to make those claims in their first written submission could not 'be remedied by later submissions or by incorporating the claims and arguments of other complainants'.[116] In reversing the panel, the Appellate Body stated that '[t]here is no requirement in the DSU or in GATT practice for arguments on all claims relating to the matter referred to the DSB to be set out in a complaining party's first written submission to the panel'.[117] This statement must be understood in the context of that specific dispute which, as the Appellate Body noted, involved five co-complainants who had submitted a *joint request for establishment of a panel*.[118] Although the parties filed separate first written submissions, they made all other written and oral submissions jointly. Importantly, the first written submissions of some of the co-complainants did contain arguments and evidence with respect to the GATS claims.

It must be noted that while the complainant should present information on its claims in its first written submission and at the latest the first meeting with

[113] Appellate Body Report, *US—Gambling*, above n 94 at para 141.

[114] The failure of the complainant to elaborate its claim and the consequent failure of the panel to guarantee the due process right of the respondent to participation were at the basis of the Appellate Body's reversal of a ruling of the panel regarding that claim in *Chile—Price Band System.* Appellate Body Report, *Chile—Price Band System and Safeguard Measures Relating to Certain Agricultural Products*, WT/DS207/AB/R, adopted 23 October 2002 at paras 153–77.

[115] Appellate Body Report, *US—Gambling*, above n 94 at para 149. Section 11.C.4 of this chapter argues that the Appellate Body may not have gone far enough in protecting the parties' right to meaningful participation.

[116] Panel Report, *European Communities—Regime for the Importation, Sale and Distribution of Bananas, Complaint by Guatemala and Honduras*, WT/DS27/R/GTM, WT/DS27/R/HND, adopted 25 September 1997 at para 7.57.

[117] Appellate Body Report, *European Communities—Regime for the Importation, Sale and Distribution of Bananas*, WT/DS27/AB/R, adopted 25 September 1997, DSR 1997:II, 591 at para 145.

[118] *European Communities—Regime for the Importation, Sale and Distribution of Bananas*, Request for the Establishment of a Panel by Ecuador, Guatemala, Honduras, Mexico, and the United States, WT/DS27/6, 12 April 1996.

the panel (the second written submission and meeting with the panel are devoted to rebuttals),[119] this is not to say that the complainant must append all evidence (except that which becomes necessary for purposes of rebuttal) to its first written submission if it can otherwise show a good reason not to do so at that time. One such reason would be the fact that the evidence is in the exclusive possession of the defendant. Due process considerations —namely, the right of the defendant to meaningful participation—nonetheless require the complainant to specify the evidence that it would like to submit later when existence of that evidence is known to the complainant.

Under normal circumstances the defendant has an obligation to present an elaborate response as opposed to presenting a general denial.[120] It cannot be expected to do so, however, when it does not know the details of the claims brought against it, because the complainant failed to put forward an elaborate presentation of its claims. Moreover, the defendant does not have an open-ended obligation to search and present information. In other words, the duty of cooperation does not mean that respondents must readily provide information whose relevance is not apparent. The panel (rather than the parties) is, however, the ultimate arbiter of what is 'relevant' or, as per the language of Article 13 of the DSU, 'necessary and appropriate'—this aspect will be further explored in Section II.C below. In addition, as discussed in Chapter 3, the fact that the respondent is under a duty to cooperate should not mean that whenever the claimant has presented some evidence, independently of its strength, the respondent is then placed in a situation where it must demonstrate that the allegations are not true or suffer an adverse ruling against it.[121]

While the respondent has a duty to cooperate, when the case reaches the decision-making stage the respondent must not be sanctioned for failing to rebut a proposition which was not, on the basis of information on the record, shown to be at least more likely than not true.[122] This was made clear in *India—Additional Import Duties* where even though both the panel and the Appellate Body noted that the respondent (India) should have been more forthcoming in producing information, the case was ultimately decided against the claimant (the

[119] DSU, Appendix 3 (Working Procedures), paragraph 7.

[120] With respect to the obligation of the defendant to present an elaborate response in international adjudication, see Kazazi, above n 84 at 121; Amerasinghe, *Evidence in International Litigation*, above n 82 at 98. Civil law jurisdictions also require defendants to provide elaborate responses. See, for example, Gottwald, above n 107 at 70.

[121] Chapter 3 argues that this would in effect place the burden of proof on the respondent when the evidence presented by the claimant in support of a claim is weak.

[122] But see JC Witenberg, 'La Theorie des Preuves Devant les Juridictions Internationales' (1936) 56 Recueil des Cours 5 at 48–50. Witenberg seems to suggest that the principle of cooperation requires the claimant to provide only a 'commencement de preuve' (a beginning of proof or *prima facie* case). He notes that the same is true in common law jurisdictions, from where, according to him, the principle originated. It is not correct to say, however, that claimants in common law jurisdictions only have an obligation to present a *prima facie* case. See Chapters 2 and 3 for details on this point.

United States), which had equally failed to produce information on the questions at issue.[123] The situation is different, however, if the respondent had been requested to provide evidence to which it had exclusive or preferential access—information to which the requested party has preferential access is information which cannot reasonably be obtained from another source. In this situation, as noted in Chapter 3 and further explored in Section II.B.4 below, failure to provide such evidence may result in adverse consequences to the respondent.

In sum, in great part the duty of cooperation means that the parties must voluntarily produce throughout the different steps of the proceedings all information relevant to the claims at issue. In practice, however, the parties will not always automatically disclose all relevant information. This may happen for several reasons. First, while good faith cooperation requires the parties to produce all relevant information including information which is not favourable to their cases, there is always the possibility that some parties will nonetheless decide to act against this requirement in the hope that their non-compliance will not be detected. Second, information may not be provided because the parties may not be aware of its relevance. In this connection, when a party considers that relevant information has not been produced by its opponent, it may request that such information be presented. If the opponent still does not provide the information,[124] the party may petition the panel to exercise its power under Article 13 of the DSU. In this regard, the Appellate Body noted in *India—Patents (US)* that when a party believes that 'all pertinent facts relating to a claim are, for any reason, not before the panel, then that party should ask the panel in that case to engage in additional fact-finding'.[125] This procedure is another aspect of the duty of cooperation, the details of which will be discussed in Section II.C together with the role of the panel.

3. When does the duty of cooperation commence?

As discussed in the preceding paragraphs, the duty of cooperation finds expression in the various procedural obligations of the parties throughout the proceedings. As an aspect of the broader requirement contained in Article 3.10 of the DSU which enjoins all Members, if a dispute arises, to 'engage in [dispute settlement] procedures in good faith in an effort to resolve the dispute', the duty of the parties to cooperate in presenting information is ubiquitous throughout the proceedings. Unless the parties agree on additional preliminary proceedings, the first occasion where the duty of cooperation comes into play is at the time of the first written submissions where the parties must provide detailed information

[123] See, for example, Appellate Body Report, *India—Additional Import Duties*, above n 89 at paras 193–5.

[124] When parties have a valid reason for not producing information, it is advisable that they explain their reasons so that it is clear that they are acting in good faith and are generally willing to cooperate.

[125] Appellate Body Report, *India—Patents (US)*, above n 91 at para 94.

on their positions with respect to the claims at issue.[126] As the moving party, the complainant is required to provide detailed information on its case first. Accordingly, Article 12.6 of the DSU provides that the complainant must submit its first submission in advance of the defendant. The defendant is then given time to consider that submission and file a detailed response. The parties will then meet with the panel to present their cases and discuss their initial written submissions. At this point the panel should have a good understanding of the case and will thus become more involved in the process posing questions,[127] asking explanations[128] and requesting such information from the parties as it deems necessary and appropriate.[129] The parties in turn must cooperate in providing the information requested by the panel. In *Canada—Aircraft*, the Appellate Body made clear that pursuant to Article 13.1 of the DSU, WTO Members are 'under a duty and an obligation to "respond promptly and fully" to requests made by panels for information'.[130] The Appellate Body rightly noted that if Members were not legally bound to cooperate with the panel, the panel's 'right to seek' information 'would be rendered meaningless'.[131] Moreover, individual Members would in effect be given the power to preclude a panel from carrying out the mandate conferred upon it by all Members when they agreed to the rules of the DSU.[132]

Importantly, contrary to what is argued by Kazazi[133] in the context of international adjudication in general and also contrary to what was argued by Canada in connection with WTO dispute settlement in *Canada—Aircraft*,[134] the respondent's duty to cooperate in producing information is not contingent on the establishment of a *prima facie* case by the claimant.[135] The argument that the

[126] Pursuant to Annex V of the SCM Agreement, in cases brought under Article 7.4 of the SCM Agreement, a special procedure for gathering information may take place even before the panel is composed. Paragraph 1 of Annex V provides that '[e]very Member shall cooperate in the development of evidence to be examined by a panel in procedures under paragraphs 4 through 6 of Article 7'. This procedure will be discussed further in Section II.C.3.1.

[127] DSU, Appendix 3 (Working Procedures), paragraph 8.

[128] DSU, Appendix 3 (Working Procedures), paragraph 8.

[129] Article 13.1 of the DSU.

[130] Appellate Body Report, *Canada—Aircraft*, above n 81 at para 187. See also Panel Report, *Turkey—Rice*, above n 89 at paras 5.14–5.16, 7.1 (where the panel rejected the United States' contention that the DSU does not provide for a rule of cooperation).

[131] Appellate Body Report, *Canada—Aircraft*, above n 81 at para 188.

[132] See Appellate Body Report, *Canada—Aircraft*, above n 81 at paras 188–9.

[133] Kazazi, above n 84 at 137–8, 140, 149.

[134] See, for example, paragraph 82 of Appellate Body Report, *Canada—Aircraft*, above n 81. In support of the view advanced by Canada, see Rambod Behboodi, '"Should" Means "Shall": A Critical Analysis of the Obligation to Submit Information under Article 13.1 of the DSU in the *Canada – Aircraft* Case' (2000) Journal of International Economic Law 563 at 573–4, 582. See also Panel Report, *Argentina—Textiles and Apparel*, above n 90 at para 6.40 (noting that the duty of cooperation 'does not arise until the claimant has done its best to secure evidence and has actually produced some *prima facie* evidence in support of its case').

[135] In support of this view, see Jeff Waincymer, *WTO Litigation: Procedural Aspects of Formal Dispute Settlement* (London: Cameron May, 2002) at 562 (according to him, 'the better view is that

claimant must make a *prima facie* case before the respondent incurs an obligation to present information originates from common law proceedings where before presenting its response to the court or jury the respondent can request the court to rule on whether the claimant has discharged its burden of going forward; if the court finds that the claimant failed to present a *prima facie* case, the respondent does not have to submit its response and the question at issue does not advance—this was explained in Chapter 2.[136] Notably, in common law proceedings prior to that stage the parties would normally have gone through pre-trial discovery where they would have had an opportunity to collect information on the claims at issue. In contrast, there is no pre-trial discovery in WTO proceedings. Instead, certain aspects of the discovery process are infused throughout the proceedings. Therefore, if the panel dismisses a claim at the initial stages, it may deny some parties with valid reasons for not attaching evidence to their first submissions a chance to establish their cases. Moreover, under the current situation (in which panels have declined to issue preliminary rulings on the sufficiency of the evidence), the respondent has no means of knowing whether the claimant has made a *prima facie* case—see Chapters 2 and 3. Accordingly, if the respondent could refuse to cooperate in the production of information on the grounds that the claimant had not made a *prima facie* case, the respondent would in effect be granted the authority to act as a judge in its own cause. In this regard, in *Canada—Aircraft* the Appellate Body stated that 'no Member is free to determine for itself whether a *prima facie* case or defence has been established by the other party. That competence is necessarily vested in the panel under the DSU, and not in the Members that are parties to the dispute.'[137] In *Canada—Aircraft*, the Appellate Body rejected Canada's theory that a party's 'duty to respond promptly and fully to a Panel's request for information arises only after the opposing party to the dispute has established a *prima facie* case' that its claim is meritorious.[138] As the information in question had been requested by the panel,[139] the Appellate Body further noted that the

the respondent is not entitled to withhold crucial information and as a result, challenge the complainant for failing to make out a *prima facie* case'). See also Amerasinghe, *Evidence in International Litigation*, above n 82 at 109 (noting that 'the stricter requirement of some common law jurisdictions that the claimant must provide enough evidence to establish a *prima facie* case before the respondent needs to act [...] is probably as such not applicable in international litigation in general').

[136] The origin of the argument is confirmed by Canada's statements in *Canada—Aircraft*. See Panel Report, *Canada—Measures Affecting the Export of Civilian Aircraft*, WT/DS70/R, adopted 20 August 1999 at, for example, para 4.143 (where Canada stated that it was concerned that the panel 'requested the production of evidence in respect of matters where in Canada's view Brazil has clearly not made out a *prima facie* case. Canada notes that the Panel has not ruled on whether Brazil has made out a *prima facie* case on any of the impugned programmes, activities or transactions'). See also Kazazi, above n 84 at 137.

[137] Appellate Body Report, *Canada—Aircraft*, above n 81 at para 192.

[138] Appellate Body Report, *Canada—Aircraft*, above n 81 at paras 185, 192

[139] Brazil had however asked the panel to request Canada to provide information which was in its possession.

'discretionary authority [of the panel] to seek and obtain information is *not* made conditional by [Article 13], or any other provision, of the DSU upon the other party to the dispute having previously established, on a *prima facie* basis, such other party's claim'.[140]

It must be noted, however, that even though the respondent's duty to cooperate is not dependent upon the claimant presenting evidence which would suggest that its claims are true, as far as voluntary production is concerned, the respondent cannot be expected to provide an elaborate response if the respondent is not aware of the case that is being made against it. In addition, if the complainant as the moving party does not pursue a claim which was stated in the request for establishment of a panel, the defendant is entitled to assume that the claim was withdrawn. Finally, the panel is not likely to use its discretionary authority to engage in fact-finding if the complainant does not give any reason for the panel to believe that its claims have merit. In keeping with the spirit of good faith cooperation, the best approach when the complainant does not elaborate on its claims is, as suggested in Chapter 3, for panels on their own motion or on the motion of the respondent to inform the claimants of the existence of major deficiencies in their presentation of arguments and evidence and provide them with an opportunity to remedy those deficiencies.

4. How can cooperation be ensured?

It has been noted throughout this book that the cooperation of the parties is essential for the smooth development of the proceedings and the proper application of the law. Previous chapters and sections have alluded to the fact that failure to cooperate in the production of information during the panel process may place the uncooperative party in an unfavourable position. The threat to impose 'procedural disadvantages' on uncooperative parties is the main, if not the only, means of promoting the observance of the duty of cooperation in a system that cannot otherwise force the parties to be forthcoming. The application of procedural disadvantages lies for the most part within the discretionary authority of panels. They must decide when and how to sanction uncooperative behaviour taking into account the specific facts of each case and the systemic interest in ensuring that the parties produce relevant information in their possession. This section reviews what consequences may flow from a failure to cooperate as well as other factors which may serve as an incentive for the parties to cooperate.

At a general level, as the party bearing the burden of proof, the ultimate sanction for a failure on the part of the claimant to cooperate is the rejection of its claim. As for the respondent, while it does not automatically lose the case when there is no evidence on the record, if it remains quiescent it exposes itself

[140] Appellate Body Report, *Canada—Aircraft*, above n 81 at para 185.

to the risk that the panel will find the evidence presented by the claimant persuasive.[141] Particular instances of non-observance of the duty to produce information may, however, result in more specific procedural disadvantages to the parties.

4.1. Adverse inferences

i. The authority to draw adverse inferences. One of the most common means across legal systems of encouraging parties to cooperate in producing information is the threat that non-production will result in inferences being drawn against the uncooperative party. In other words, if a party does not provide information upon request, the adjudicator is entitled to assume that the information withheld is adverse to the requested party's position. Frequent references to adverse inferences are found in domestic, transnational, and international legal instruments[142] and/or jurisprudence,[143] indicating that the authority to draw such inferences is inherent in the function of adjudicators. Despite the fact that the Statute of the ICJ does not make an express reference to the authority of the court to draw adverse inferences,[144] Judge Jessup, in his separate opinion in the *Barcelona Traction* case, stated that the court should apply the rule that 'if a party fails to produce on demand a relevant document which is in its possession, there may be an inference that the document "if brought, would have exposed facts unfavourable to the party ..."'.[145] The Iran–United States Claims

[141] See, for example, Panel Report, *US—Upland Cotton*, above n 111 at eg paras 7.576–7.583, 7632 (where the defendant, the United States, declined to suggest alternative approaches leading the panel to embrace the analysis presented by the complainant).

[142] Principles 17.3 and 21.3 of the ALI/UNIDROIT Principles of Transnational Civil Procedure provide that courts may draw adverse inferences as a sanction for unjustified non-production. The commentary on principle 17.3 explains that '[i]n all systems the court may draw adverse inferences from a party's failure to advance the proceeding or to respond as required'. American Law Institute & UNIDROIT, above n 96 at 38. For examples of civilian jurisdictions, see Article 359 of the Brazilian Code of Civil Procedure; Article 88 of the Dutch Code of Civil Procedure (previously, Article 19a(4), an English version of which can be found at Jan M Hebly, *The Netherlands Civil Evidence Act 1988* (Deventer: Kluwer Law and Taxation Publishers, 1992) at 72).

The rules and statutes of most international courts and tribunals do not make express reference to the authority to draw adverse inferences. The IBA Rules on the Taking of Evidence in International Commercial Arbitration is one of the few sets of rules that make express reference to adverse inferences. Article 9.4 of the IBA Rules provides that '[i]f a Party fails without satisfactory explanation to produce any document requested in a Request to Produce to which it has not objected in due time or fails to produce any document ordered to be produced by the Arbitral Tribunal, the Arbitral Tribunal may infer that such document would be adverse to the interests of that Party'.

[143] See Sandifer, above n 84 at 150, 153 (noting that '[a]d hoc tribunals have frequently asserted the existence of a rule empowering them to draw adverse inferences from the failure of a party to produce evidence'). See also references in footnote 146 below regarding the jurisprudence of the Iran–United States Claims Tribunal.

[144] Article 49 of the ICJ Statute expressly authorizes the court to take 'formal note' of any refusal to produce any document or to supply any explanations, but it does not refer to the drawing of 'adverse inferences'.

[145] The quoted passage in Judge Jessup's statement is from Wigmore's treatise 'Evidence'. Judge Jessup noted that adverse inferences are applied in common law jurisdictions. Separate Opinion of Judge Jessup, *Case Concerning The Barcelona Traction, Light and Power Company, Limited*, ICJ Reports, 1970 at 215 or para 97.

Tribunal has also interpreted its authority to include the power to draw adverse inferences notwithstanding the fact that its rules of procedure do not explicitly refer to such power.[146] Commentators have also argued that the authority to draw adverse inferences is inherent in the function of international tribunals.[147]

In the same vein, WTO panels and the Appellate Body have confirmed the authority of panels to draw adverse inferences from the refusal of a party to produce information in its possession notwithstanding the silence of the DSU with respect to this question.[148] The only reference to adverse inferences in the WTO agreements is contained in Annex V to the SCM Agreement which provides for a mechanism to gather information in proceedings brought pursuant to Article 7 of the SCM Agreement. According to paragraph 7 of Annex V, '[i]n making its determination, the panel should draw adverse inferences from instances of non-cooperation by any party involved in the information gathering process'. In *Canada—Aircraft*, the Appellate Body ruled that there is no reason to infer that the absence of a similar reference in other provisions of the WTO agreements means that adverse inferences cannot be drawn outside the context of Annex V. According to the Appellate Body, the authority to draw adverse inferences from a Member's refusal to provide information is 'an ordinary aspect of the task of all panels to determine the relevant facts of any dispute involving any covered agreement'.[149]

The view expressed by the Appellate Body in *Canada—Aircraft* is in line with international jurisprudence and the general understanding that the authority of

[146] See Monica Petraglia McCabe, 'Arbitral Discovery and the Iran-United States Claims Tribunal Experience' (1986) 20 International Lawyer 499 at 529; Amerasinghe, *Evidence in International Litigation*, above n 82 at 134.

[147] See Kazazi, above n 84 at 315; Amerasinghe, *Evidence in International Litigation*, above n 82 at 134; Robert Pietrowski, 'Evidence in International Arbitration' (2006) 22:3 Arbitration International 373 at 383–4; McCabe, above n 146 at 529. See also Yves Derains & Eric A Schwartz, *A Guide to the ICC Rules of Arbitration* (2nd edn, The Hague: Kluwer International, 2005) at 283 (noting that an arbitral tribunal operating under the ICC Rules, which do not refer to adverse inferences, is 'free to draw any negative inferences that may flow from a party's refusal to produce the documents requested'); Lucy Reed, Jan Paulsson & Nigel Blackaby, *A Guide to ICSID Arbitration* (The Hague: Kluwer Law International, 2004) at 85 (noting that although the ICSID Arbitration Rules do not expressly say so, 'a party's uncooperative conduct, as in any international commercial arbitration, may lead the tribunal to draw adverse inferences from that lack of cooperation').

[148] Appellate Body Report, *Canada—Aircraft*, above n 81 at paras 202–3; Appellate Body Report, *US—Wheat Gluten*, above n 5 at para 174; Panel Report, *Korea—Measures Affecting Trade in Commercial Vessels*, WT/DS273/R, adopted 11 April 2005 at para 7.162; Panel Report, *Turkey—Rice*, above n 89 at para 7.10. In *Turkey—Rice* the panel, in response to a request from the United States, replaced the expression 'adverse inferences' with 'appropriate inferences'. The panel, however, did not change its reasoning in support of the conclusion that panels may draw appropriate inferences, leading to the conclusion that there is no difference of meaning between the two expressions.

[149] Appellate Body Report, *Canada—Aircraft*, above n 81 at para 202. See also Panel Report, *Korea—Commercial Vessels*, above n 148 at para 7.162.

adjudicators to draw adverse inferences from refusals to provide information is inherent in their function.[150] In fact, as the Appellate Body noted in *Canada—Aircraft*, 'because a party's refusal to collaborate has the potential to undermine the functioning of the dispute settlement system' panels should carefully consider whether the circumstances warrant the drawing of inferences against the uncooperative party.[151] In other words, the 'continued viability of [the dispute settlement] system depends, in substantial measure, on the willingness of panels to take all steps open to them to induce the parties to the dispute to comply with their duty to provide information deemed necessary for dispute settlement'.[152] The Appellate Body correctly understood that the real value of an adverse inference lies in its capacity to induce cooperation rather than in the inference itself. Accordingly, it urged panels to 'expressly remind the parties—during the course of dispute settlement proceedings—that a refusal to provide information requested by the panel may lead to inferences being drawn about the inculpatory character of the information withheld'.[153] In this regard, commentators have noted that the mere possibility that an adverse inference may be drawn 'is an effective tool in compelling the parties to produce evidence'.[154]

ii. Scope of adverse inferences. In the event that the *threat* of an adverse inference does not induce cooperation—ie a party refuses to comply with a request to produce information—the panel then has the discretion to decide whether an inference should be drawn against the uncooperative party. While the authority of adjudicators to draw an adverse inference from a refusal to provide information is widely accepted, the exact scope of the inferences which may be drawn is usually not well defined.[155] The same is true in the case of WTO dispute settlement. While the Appellate Body has made clear that panels have the

[150] In support, see John Ragosta, 'Unmasking the WTO – Access to the DSB System: Can the WTO DSB Live Up to the Moniker 'World Trade Court'?' (2000) 31:3 Law and Policy in International Business 739 at 764 (arguing that 'when a panel requests relevant information within the possession of one government and the government refuses to provide it, the DSU should permit (if not mandate) an adverse inference').

[151] Appellate Body Report, *Canada—Aircraft*, above n 81 at para 204.

[152] Appellate Body Report, *Canada—Aircraft*, above n 81 at para 204.

[153] Appellate Body Report, *Canada—Aircraft*, above n 81 at para 204. Following *Canada—Aircraft* panels have alerted the parties about the possibility of adverse inferences being drawn from refusals to provide information. See, for example, Panel Report, *US—Wheat Gluten*, above n 14 at para 8.7; Panel Report, *US—Upland Cotton*, above n 111 at paras 7.33, 7.609.

[154] Charles N Brower, 'Evidence Before International Tribunals: the Need for Some Standard Rules' (1994) 28 The International Lawyer 47 at 57. See also Jeremy K Sharpe, 'Drawing Adverse Inferences from the Non-production of Evidence' (2006) 22:4 Arbitration International 549 at 550.

[155] See, for example, Sharpe, above n 154 at 550 (noting that while commentators cite the arbitrators' power to draw adverse inferences, they 'offer little practical guidance as to the application of inferences'); KPE Lasok, *The European Court of Justice: Practice and Procedure* (2nd edn, London: Butterworths, 1994) at 387 (noting that while the ECJ may draw inferences from a refusal to provide information, 'there is no obligation on it to do so nor any rules as to what inferences it may draw').

authority to draw adverse inferences, it has not provided a clear definition of the scope of such inferences.

Generally speaking an adverse inference entails the assumption that the information which is not produced is adverse to the requested party's position. The existence of factors which are bound to vary from case to case—such as the specificity of the information withheld, what is known from other sources about that information, what other evidence is on the record related to the evidence withheld or to the fact which it is intended to prove—warrants a broad definition of the scope of adverse inferences. Panels should thus have discretion within the bounds of reasonableness to decide when and exactly what kind of inferences to draw from non-production. This is in line with the freedom which panels enjoy to admit and evaluate evidence. Moreover, it allows panels to take into account the circumstances leading to non-production in each case.[156] For example, the panel can consider the sensitivity of the evidence in question, whether an adequate mechanism to protect confidential information is in place,[157] and the circumstances which led to the non-production of documents controlled by private entities related to the requested disputing party.

Notwithstanding the fact that panels should have discretion to decide when and exactly what kind of inferences to draw from non-production, the drawing of any inferences from non-production must be subject to certain minimum requirements. These requirements are intended to be consistent with the goal of achieving an accurate decision. While the accuracy of a decision may be affected if the panel does not have access to relevant information, unlimited recourse to adverse inferences may equally affect the accuracy of the decision since there is

[156] In this regard, Principle 18.2 of the ALI/UNIDROIT Principles of Transnational Civil Procedure provides that '[t]he court should consider whether [privileges, immunities, and similar protections of a party or nonparty concerning disclosure of evidence or other information] may justify a party's failure to disclose evidence or other information when deciding whether to draw adverse inferences or to impose other indirect sanctions'. American Law Institute & UNIDROIT, above n 96 at 39. See Waincymer, above n 135 at 614 (noting that '[b]efore adverse inferences can be drawn, consideration needs to be given as to the explanation behind the failure to provide information').

[157] In *Canada—Aircraft*, in connection with its ruling on the question of whether the panel had the authority to draw an adverse inference from Canada's refusal to provide information, the Appellate Body noted that the panel had rightly rejected Canada's attempt to justify its refusal on the grounds that the information in question was confidential. In that case, the panel had adopted special procedures to protect confidential business information. While the panel chose not to draw inferences against Canada, the Appellate Body noted that the panel could have done so and that, if it were the panel, it 'might well have concluded that the facts of record did warrant the inference that the information Canada withheld on the ASA transaction included information prejudicial to Canada's denial that the EDC had conferred a "benefit" and granted a prohibited export subsidy'. Appellate Body Report, *Canada—Aircraft*, above n 81 at para 205. See also Panel Report, *Turkey—Rice*, above n 89 at paras 7.103–7.106 (where the panel drew inferences from Turkey's refusal to provide information after it rejected Turkey's attempt to justify its refusal on the grounds that the information in question was confidential).

no guarantee that the inference corresponds to the truth. The next few paragraphs are devoted to a discussion of such requirements.

First, there must be a clear connection between the nature of the information withheld and the inference derived from its non-production.[158] In this regard, as discussed later in this chapter (Section II.C.3.1), to the extent possible a request to produce must provide a detailed description of the information requested so that in case of a refusal to produce the panel can assume that the content of the documents withheld are as described. When a detailed description of the documents to be produced cannot be provided, the probable nature of the documents should be taken into account in deciding whether to assume the truth of the fact which the documents were intended to demonstrate. Naturally, because there must be a connection between the nature of the information withheld and the inference derived therefrom, the information withheld must be—as also discussed in Section II.C.3.1 below—relevant to the issue in question.[159] In this connection, for instance, in *Korea—Commercial Vessels* the panel rejected a request from the European Communities for the panel to draw an adverse inference on the grounds that the document which Korea refused to produce was not relevant to the issue in dispute.[160]

Second, in drawing the inference the panel must give adequate consideration to the evidence which is (or is not) on the record. For instance, there may be strong evidence on the record directly contradicting the inference, in which case an adverse inference may not be warranted.[161] Moreover, where the inference which can be drawn from non-production is one of the links in a chain of auxiliary propositions leading to proof of an element of a claim, the other auxiliary propositions of the chain must be supported by evidence. For example, in *Korea—Commercial Vessels*, the panel refused to draw an inference from the failure of Korea to provide information on the terms of certain transactions because there was no evidence on the record demonstrating that those transactions actually took place.[162] In addition, when a request to produce is broadly

[158] See Sharpe, above n 154 at 558; Craig, Park & Paulsson, above n 68 at 451.

[159] See Kazazi, above n 84 at 320 (noting that the point of departure for the whole process of drawing negative inferences against a party is the determination that the documents in question are relevant and necessary to the resolution of the dispute); Peter Ashford, 'Documentary Discovery and International Commercial Arbitration' (2006) 17 American Review of International Arbitration 89 at 102.

[160] Panel Report, *Korea—Commercial Vessels*, above n 148 at para 7.401.

[161] This was the position adopted by the ICJ in *Corfu Channel* where the Court noted that it could not draw from the United Kingdom's refusal 'to produce the [naval] orders [requested by the Court] any conclusions differing from those to which the actual events gave rise'. *The Corfu Channel* (Merits) (United Kingdom v Albania), Judgment of 9 April 1949, International Court of Justice, Reports of Judgments, Advisory Opinions and Orders (1949) at 32.

[162] The European Communities argued that the panel should infer (because of Korea's failure to provide the relevant information) that certain APRGs were issued at rates higher than those charged by KEXIM. The panel noted that it could not draw any inferences regarding the *terms* on which alleged APRGs were issued because there was no evidence before it indicating that such APRGs were actually issued. Panel Report, *Korea—Commercial Vessels*, above n 148 at para 7.163.

framed, an inference from a refusal to provide the information requested must be supported by some other evidence on the record.[163] In other words, the broader the inference requested, the higher the need for supporting evidence on the record. Compare, for instance, in a subsidy claim the difference between (i) inferring that a 'benefit' has been conferred by a government program to producers of widgets solely from the failure of the defendant to produce a government report allegedly explaining how a government agency has managed a government loan program; and (ii) inferring that a loan was granted at a rate below a specified market rate from a failure to produce a contract indicating the terms of a transaction that is known to have taken place.

The fact that an adverse inference cannot be drawn in a vacuum without due regard to the record of the proceedings was explained by the Appellate Body in *US—Wheat Gluten*. In that case the Appellate Body explained that 'a panel must draw inferences on the basis of *all of the facts of record* relevant to the particular determination to be made'.[164] According to the Appellate Body, the refusal of a party to provide information is an important but not the only fact 'to be taken into account in determining the appropriate inference to be drawn. [...] if a panel were to ignore or disregard other relevant facts, it would fail to make an "objective assessment" under Article 11 of the DSU'.[165]

Third, the information at issue must be shown (i) not to be accessible to or in the possession of (ie not otherwise available to) the party seeking the adverse inference, and (ii) to exist and be in the possession of the requested party.[166] If the requested party is shown to have destroyed the documents which were in its possession, the panel should take into account the conditions under which the documents were destroyed in deciding whether and what inferences to draw.[167] Moreover, in connection with the question of whether the information is not accessible to or in the possession of the party seeking the adverse inference, the panel must determine whether other evidence could be produced which would equally address the issue in question. As a matter of fact, in considering the

[163] See Craig, Park & Paulsson, above n 68 at 456 (noting that the inference which can be drawn from the failure of a party to produce documents 'is insufficient to sustain a claim or defense for which no evidence of record exists.') Some commentators have referred to the requirement that the party seeking the inference must have presented *prima facie* evidence of its claim. For the reasons which have been expounded in other parts of this book, particularly the ambiguity associated with the use of the expressions '*prima facie* evidence' and '*prima facie* case' in WTO dispute settlement, these expressions have been consciously avoided here. It is likely that the ideas expressed here are similar to those of commentators who argue that the party seeking the inference must have presented *prima facie* evidence of its claim. Referring to the *prima facie* requirement, see Sharpe, above n 154 at 564–7; Kazazi, above n 84 at 321; Ashford, above n 159 at 102.

[164] Appellate Body Report, *US—Wheat Gluten*, above n 5 at para 174. See also Panel Report, *Turkey—Rice*, above n 89 at para 7.11.

[165] Appellate Body Report, *US—Wheat Gluten*, above n 5 at para 174.

[166] In support, see Sharpe, above n 154 at 557; Kazazi, above n 84 at 320; Sandifer, above n 84 at 153; Ashford, above n 159 at 102 (requiring the documents to be 'in the control of the requested party').

[167] See Sharpe, above n 154 at 558.

drawing of adverse inferences, panels and the Appellate Body have taken into account the fact that the evidence at issue was in the possession of the requested party. For example, in *Turkey—Rice*, where the panel drew inferences from Turkey's refusal to provide information, the panel explicitly noted that 'the evidence requested by the Panel of Turkey, regarding Certificates of Control approved for the importation of rice, is in Turkey's possession.'[168] In *Canada—Aircraft*, in considering whether the panel could have drawn adverse inferences from Canada's refusal to provide the information requested by the panel, the Appellate Body found it 'safe to assume that the information requested by the Panel was in the possession of Canada because Canada did not indicate otherwise to the Panel'.[169] Moreover, the Appellate Body noted that 'the information requested by the Panel was not publicly available', an indication that it was not accessible to the requesting party.[170]

As discussed below in Section II.C.3.2, an important question with respect to this subject refers to the situation where the evidence requested is in the hands of private parties with an interest in the dispute—for example, in a subsidies dispute, the private party receiving the subsidy at issue in the dispute. Although information which is in the hands of private parties is not strictly speaking in the possession of the requested party, the fact that the relationship between the requested party (the WTO Member) and the private parties holding the information is under consideration in the WTO proceedings suggests that an adverse inference should be drawn from the non-production of evidence in the possession of private parties. This was the position adopted by the panel in *Chile—Alcoholic Beverages* where in the face of a refusal by the *Chilean industry* to produce a report which was in its possession, the panel accepted certain statements made in the Chilean press with respect to the contents of that report. The panel noted that '[w]hile it is the *Chilean government* which is a party to this case, it would be unrealistic and artificial to argue that the panel should not address the issue based on this distinction given the direct underlying economic interest of the Chilean industry'.[171] In contrast, in *Indonesia—Autos* the panel noted that 'because the *Asian Forecast* is not a document to which the complainants can control access, resort to adverse inferences would not appear appropriate'.[172] This was not,

[168] Panel Report, *Turkey—Rice*, above n 89 at para 7.97. See also Panel Report, *US—Upland Cotton*, above n 111 at para 7.631 (where in considering Brazil's request for the panel to draw adverse inferences, the panel noted that the information requested was in the exclusive control of the requested party, the United States); Panel Report, *Korea—Commercial Vessels*, above n 148 at para 7.450 (where the panel found that the EC's request for adverse inferences regarding the KDB report is 'unfounded, since there is nothing on the record to suggest that any such report ever existed').

[169] Appellate Body Report, *Canada—Aircraft*, above n 81 at para 199.

[170] Appellate Body Report, *Canada—Aircraft*, above n 81 at para 199.

[171] Panel Report, *Chile—Alcoholic Beverages*, above n 99 at paras 6.25–6.27 and footnote 390 to para 7.66 (emphasis added).

[172] Panel Report, *Indonesia—Certain Measures Affecting the Automobile Industry*, WT/DS54/R, WT/DS55/R, WT/DS59/R, WT/DS64/R and Corr.1, 2, 3 and 4, adopted 23 July 1998, DSR 1998:VI, 2201 at 14.180.

however, the only (nor the main) reason motivating the panel's refusal to draw adverse inferences. Moreover, the panel only said that it 'would not appear appropriate' to draw an inference. In sum, it seems that the best approach would be for panels to determine in each case whether given the circumstances it was reasonable to expect the requested party to produce information which is in the possession of private parties under its jurisdiction.

Fourth, in order to ensure the observance of the due process requirement of participation, the panel must have informed the requested party of the fact that adverse inferences could be drawn if the information were not produced.[173] Relatedly, the drawing of adverse inferences should be limited to those situations where a request to produce was made in accordance with the criteria discussed below in Section II.C.3.1.

The impact that an adverse inference has on the resolution of an issue in dispute will vary from case to case depending on factors such as the evidence which is already on the record, and the attributes of the information which is not produced. At one end of the spectrum is the situation where the evidence actually on the record is, although not the best evidence, persuasive—that is, it indicates that the proposition at issue is more likely than not true. In this case, a refusal by the party to whom that evidence is unfavourable to comply with a request to produce allows the panel to decide on the basis of the information on the record. In these circumstances, the adjudicator infers that the information which was *not* made available supports the conclusion which can be drawn from the evidence already on the record; if this were not the case, the requested party would have produced the information. In this situation the panel may decide not to make express reference to the inference, but rather support its decision on the evidence on the record.[174] This seems to have been the case in *Argentina—Textiles and Apparel*, where on account of Argentina's refusal to provide evidence of higher quality which was in its possession, the panel relied upon the evidence produced by the complainant, the United States.[175]

At the other end of the spectrum are the cases where the evidence on the record is not sufficient to support the conclusion that the proposition at issue is more likely than not true, and the information withheld is necessary for the resolution of that question—this situation is discussed in more detail in Section III.C of Chapter 3. In this case, an inference from non-production may, combined with the evidence on the record, be sufficiently weighty to support the

[173] In support, see Sharpe, above n 154 at 568–9.

[174] Although some would not refer to this situation as involving the drawing of an adverse inference, as explained above when the panel bases its decision on the evidence on the record it infers that the evidence withheld by the respondent does not contradict such conclusion because otherwise the respondent would have produced it.

[175] Panel Report, *Argentina—Textiles and Apparel*, above n 90 at paras 6.40, 6.51–6.65. See also Panel Report, *US—Upland Cotton*, above n 111 at Section VII.D (eg paras 7.632–7633).

conclusion that the proposition at issue is more likely than not true.[176] In this situation, the adverse inference has a clear impact on the resolution of the issue in question and the panel is bound to refer to the inference to support its decision which would otherwise lack persuasive power. One of the few cases, if not the only case, where a panel has expressly referred to an adverse inference in support of its decision is *Turkey—Rice*. In this case, however, the panel had a fair amount of evidence before it supporting its conclusions, which suggests that the inference might not have been decisive.

There have been few instances where panels have (at least explicitly) drawn adverse inferences from the refusal of a party to provide information. While it is entirely possible that the conditions for the drawing of any such inferences were not present in any of the cases where information was withheld, panels should be aware of the fact that their failure to draw adverse inferences when such conditions are present may have systemic implications. Although there is no guarantee that an adverse inference will lead to an accurate decision in the specific case under examination, an inference may nonetheless be important to foster cooperation and to ensure the proper application of the law in future cases.[177] Importantly, however, when the record contains no evidence in support of a claim or some of its elements, a finding in favour of the claimant exclusively on the basis of adverse inferences is likely not to be appropriate. If the absence of evidence on the record is a reflection of the fact that all evidence related to the claim is in the exclusive possession of an uncooperative respondent—a situation which is the exception rather than the rule and which is likely to be limited to special categories of cases—means other than adverse inferences must be devised by the WTO negotiators to deal with this situation. These may include a different allocation of the burden of proof and, as discussed in Section II.B.5.2, the creation of substantive obligations mandating disclosure of specified information.

4.2. Deadlines

Deadlines are another means of promoting cooperation.[178] Apart from their importance to ensuring the timely resolution of disputes, deadlines promote cooperation because in their absence parties may be tempted to withhold

[176] See in this regard Sharpe, above n 154 at 550 (noting that 'in appropriate circumstances, arbitrators do employ adverse inferences to enable parties to discharge their burdens of proof in the absence of evidence otherwise sufficient to make their cases').

[177] In this regard, it is worth noting that after the Appellate Body clarified in *Canada—Aircraft* that panels have the authority to draw adverse inferences, Canada was more cooperative in a later case brought against its subsidy programs to its regional aircraft industry. See Panel Report, *Canada—Export Credits and Loan Guarantees for Regional Aircraft*, WT/DS222/R and Corr.1, adopted 19 February 2002, DSR 2002:III, 849.

[178] On the importance of enforcing deadlines in international adjudication, see Sandifer, above n 84 at 68–9, 74–5, 459–60.

information which is not clearly in their favour[179] and/or not have sufficient incentives to conduct a reasonable search for information. Non-observance of the duty of cooperation in this context means that the party in question runs the risk that the adjudicator will refuse to consider any evidence submitted after the deadline. Although in the short term the enforcement of deadlines may create a tension with the pursuit of accurate decisions, in the longer term deadlines may encourage cooperation and thus result in more accurate decisions. WTO panels seem to be, in general, aware of these considerations. They have frequently provided in their working procedures that but for 'evidence necessary for purposes of rebuttals, answers to questions or comments made for purposes of rebutting answers provided by others', all other evidence must be submitted to the panel 'no later than during the first substantive meeting'; exceptions to this rule are 'granted upon a showing of good cause'. As a matter of fact, panels have in several occasions declined to consider evidence submitted late in the process when such evidence could have been presented earlier.[180] It has thus been rightly recognized that it is within the discretion of the panel to decide according to the circumstances of each case when to consider evidence that is submitted beyond the prescribed time limit.[181] In other words, the parties do not have a *right* to have untimely submitted evidence considered by the panel.[182] In this connection, the ruling of the panel in *EC—Selected Customs Matters* is somewhat troubling in that it implies that the panels' duty to make an objective assessment of the matter *obliges* panels to accept information submitted in an untimely manner. In that case the panel declined to decide whether the challenged evidence was submitted for the purposes of rebuttals; instead it stated that it would accept the evidence because it did not 'consider that [it] would be abiding by [its] duty in Article 11 of the DSU if [it] were to rule as inadmissible evidence that [could] have a bearing on the Panel's findings'.[183] Although this statement of the panel can be interpreted otherwise, the best way of reading it is that Article 11 gives panels the *discretion* to accept untimely submitted

[179] This includes evidence whose value they cannot determine.

[180] See, for example, Panel Report, *India—Quantitative Restrictions on Imports of Agricultural, Textile and Industrial Products*, WT/DS90/R, adopted 22 September 1999 at para 4.9; Panel Report, *European Communities—Trade Description of Sardines*, WT/DS231/R and Corr.1, adopted 23 October 2002 at para 6.16; Panel Report, *Canada—Measures Relating to Exports of Wheat and Treatment of Imported Grain*, WT/DS276/R, adopted 27 September 2004 at para 6.139–6.140.

[181] Pietrowski lists the following criteria which may be taken into account by an international tribunal in deciding whether to consider untimely submitted evidence: 'whether the evidence was available to the party submitting it at the time when the evidence should have been produced; if so, whether, as a result of developments in the course of the arbitral proceedings the evidence has assumed an importance not apparent earlier; and whether admission of the evidence will unduly delay or disrupt the arbitral proceedings or otherwise prejudice the interests of the other party'. Pietrowski, above n 147 at 400.

[182] See Lasok, above n 155 at 382–3 (referring to the discretion of the ECJ to decide when to admit evidence submitted late); Gottwald, above n 107 at 71 (referring to the discretion of the German courts to decide when to admit evidence submitted late).

[183] Panel Report, *EC—Selected Customs Matters*, above n 103 at para 7.66.

evidence, rather than *requires* them to do so.[184] Importantly, if a panel accepts evidence submitted after the prescribed deadline, due process requires it to provide the opposing party an opportunity to respond.[185]

4.3. Revision upon discovery of new evidence

Another way of promoting cooperation is to allow decisions to be revised if important evidence is discovered after the panel report is issued. As Mani notes in the context of international adjudication, '[r]evisability of the final decision of the tribunal may [. . .] play a not too insignificant psychological role, in persuading a party to act in good faith as regards presentation of evidence'.[186] There is no specific provision addressing this subject in the DSU, namely, the DSU neither allows nor prohibits decisions to be revised in the light of new evidence.[187] With a view to encouraging parties to be forthcoming and in the absence of specific review procedures, Members should be allowed to bring a new complaint in cases where new evidence is unearthed.This view seems to be supported by the Appellate Body. In the face of the respondent's refusal to cooperate and the panel's decision not to draw adverse inferences from this refusal, the Appellate Body noted in *Canada—Aircraft* that Brazil was not 'precluded from pursuing another dispute settlement complaint against Canada, under the provisions of the *SCM Agreement* and the DSU, concerning the consistency of [the same measure] with the provisions of the *SCM Agreement*'.[188] Although in this case the Appellate Body specifically noted that Brazil had '*not proven*' the issue in question,[189] there seems to be no reason to limit review of decisions upon the discovery of important information to situations where a specific finding of 'not proven' has been made.

[184] The Appellate Body referred to the discretion of the panel with respect to this subject in Appellate Body Report, *Argentina—Measures Affecting Imports of Footwear, Textiles, Apparel and Other Items*, WT/DS56/AB/R and Corr.1, adopted 22 April 1998, DSR 1998:III, 1003 at para 81.

[185] The panel in *EC—Selected Customs Matters* did provide the opposing party an opportunity to respond. See Panel Report, *EC—Selected Customs Matters*, above n 103 at para 7.66.

[186] Mani, above n 82 at 201. Also referring to international adjudication in general, Amerasinghe and Kazazi argue that fears of the delay and costs of repeating a proceeding may encourage parties to place all the material evidence in their possession before the tribunal so that the adversary may not be able to use unrevealed evidence as a basis for requesting a revision. Amerasinghe, *Evidence in International Litigation*, above n 82 at 116–17; Kazazi, above n 84 at 151. Admittedly these may not constitute strong incentives in the case of WTO dispute settlement. This is so because delays work for the benefit of defendants and governments may not respond as readily to increased costs as private parties.

[187] The Statute of the ICJ, for example, provides in Article 61 that '[a]n application for revision of a judgment may be made only when it is based upon the discovery of some fact of such a nature as to be a decisive factor, which fact was, when the judgment was given, unknown to the Court and also to the party claiming revision, always provided that such ignorance was not due to negligence'. WTO Members may wish to consider the introduction of a similar provision in the DSU.

[188] Appellate Body Report, *Canada—Aircraft*, above n 81 at para 206.

[189] Appellate Body Report, *Canada—Aircraft*, above n 81 at para 205 [original emphasis].

4.4. Other factors

Other factors which may play a significant role in inducing cooperation are (i) the transparency of the proceedings, and (ii) the naming and shaming of uncooperative parties.[190] On the first factor, public scrutiny may make it more difficult for Members not to cooperate when they can be reasonably expected to do so.

The effect of refusals to cooperate on the willingness of other Members to cooperate in future cases is another factor which may induce Members to be forthcoming in producing information. In other words, the interest of Members in maintaining the viability of the dispute settlement system may lead them to observe their duty to cooperate in the production of information to the panel.

As noted in Chapter 3, the adoption of a mid-range standard of proof such as the preponderance of the evidence may also encourage the production of evidence.[191] This is so because if the standard of proof is set too low the party bearing the burden of proof has no incentive to produce more than the minimal evidence required to satisfy that standard. In contrast, if the standard is set too high, the party that does not bear the burden of proof will have little incentive to produce any evidence.

Finally, if the idea of monetary damages is ever widely accepted as a possible remedy in WTO dispute settlement,[192] consideration could be given to the idea of imposing daily fines on uncooperative parties to induce them to provide information.[193] However, this may not be very effective in that governments are less likely to respond to cost incentives than private parties. Moreover, monetary fines are likely to disproportionally affect developing country Members as

[190] The panel in *US—Upland Cotton* correctly devoted a section of its report to noting the failures of the respondent to cooperate in producing information to the panel. Panel Report, *US—Upland Cotton*, above n 111 at paras 7.609–7.632.

[191] In this regard, see Vern R Walker, 'Preponderance, Probability and Warranted Factfinding' (1996) 62 Brooklyn Law Review 1075 at 1113–15.

[192] Although the DSU does not provide for financial compensation, in *US—Section 110(5) Copyright Act* (*Article 25.3*) the United States agreed to pay financial damages of Euro 1,219,900 per year to the European music industry for as long as the WTO inconsistent legislation was not brought into compliance with the WTO obligations of the United States. The amount of damages was determined by a panel of arbitrators established under Article 25 of the DSU. This is the only case where the parties agreed to financial compensation. Award of the Arbitrators, *United States—Section 110(5) of the US Copyright Act—Recourse to Arbitration under Article 25 of the DSU*, WT/DS160/ARB25/1, 9 November 2001, DSR 2001:II, 667. For a commentary on this case, see Gene M Grossman & Petros Mavroidis, 'United States—Section 110(5) of the US Copyright Act, Recourse to Arbitration under Article 25 of the DSU: Would've or Should've? Impaired Benefits Due to Copyright Infringement' in H Horn & PC Mavroidis (eds), *The WTO Case Law of 2001: The American Law Institute Reporters' Studies* (Cambridge: Cambridge University Press, 2003) 281.

[193] See Carbonneau, above n 84 at 168 (noting that monetary fines could be imposed on uncooperative parties in international arbitration); McCabe, above n 146 at 532 (discussing the idea of using monetary fines in proceedings before the Iran–United States Claims Tribunal and noting that in order to be effective a fine 'should accrue until the obligation to disclose information is fulfilled').

opposed to developed ones. Notably, as a matter of fact, not many legal systems seem to resort to fines to enforce cooperation.[194]

5. The problem of confidential information

5.1. Overview of the problem

WTO dispute settlement frequently requires presentation of confidential information,[195] that is, non-public business or proprietary information and government information which is not accessible to the public. Some of the substantive WTO agreements explicitly recognize the need to protect such information in domestic processes. For instance, Article 12.4 of the SCM Agreement, Article 6.5 of the Anti-Dumping Agreement, and Article 3.2 of the Agreement on Safeguards require domestic investigating authorities not to disclose, without the specific permission of the party submitting it, any information which is by nature confidential or which is provided on a confidential basis by parties to an investigation. Certain provisions connected to transparency obligations (discussed in the next section) state that Members are not required to disclose confidential information which would impede law enforcement or otherwise be contrary to the public interest or would prejudice the legitimate commercial interests of particular enterprises, public or private.[196] Although none of these provisions refer to the panel process—the references are not made in the context of dispute settlement under the DSU—they indicate that Members believe that confidential information is worthy of protection.

As for the process of dispute settlement under the DSU, as noted in Chapter 1, while as a general rule the DSU makes the entire dispute settlement proceedings confidential including the submissions and documents presented by the parties, it does not effectively regulate the submission, use, and protection of confidential information. The most specific provisions of the DSU concerning

[194] According to Sturner, '[t]he majority of Continental rules of civil procedure and those influenced by them impose no direct compulsory sanctions (contempt sanctions) on the parties to litigation, but rely on indirect means of compulsion in the form of procedural disadvantages in the event [...] cooperation in the taking of evidence is refused. [...] French law has adopted two policies that contrast with the other Continental rules of procedure: on the one hand, if a party refuses to cooperate, a court may consider this to the disadvantage of the party; on the other hand, there is the possibility of "astreinte", a form of procedural fine [Article 11 NCCP]. However, in practice, negative evaluation tends to be the rule, with the "astreinte" a very rare exception.' He also notes that English judges seldom resort 'to imprisonment or fines for contempt as the ultima ratio', but that contempt sanctions are 'very common in US proceedings'. Sturner, above n 78 at 877.

[195] See, for example, Behboodi, above n 134 at 566 (referring to the fact that much of the information which Canada had to produce in its defence in *Canada—Aircraft* was of a highly sensitive nature); Olivier Prost, 'Confidentiality Issues under the DSU: Fact-finding Process Versus Confidentiality' in R Yerxa & B Wilson (eds), *Key Issues in WTO Dispute Settlement: the First Ten Years* (Cambridge: Cambridge University Press, 2005) 190 at 198, 202 (referring to the increase in the number of cases potentially requiring the production of confidential information).

[196] See Article X:1 and Article XVII:4(d) of the GATT; Article III *bis* of the GATS; Annex B, paragraph 11(b) of the SPS Agreement.

the subject of confidential information are Articles 13.1 and 18.2. Article 18.2 of the DSU mandates Members to 'treat as confidential information submitted by another Member to the panel or the Appellate Body which that Member has designated as confidential'.[197] Article 13.1 provides that '[c]onfidential information which is provided [to the panel] shall not be revealed without formal authorization from the individual, body, or authorities of the Member providing the information'. In addition, Article 17.7 of the Anti-Dumping Agreement and Article 19.5 of the Customs Valuation Agreement provide that '[c]onfidential information provided to the panel shall not be disclosed without formal authorization from the person, body or authority providing such information'.

Some parties have invoked the confidential character of certain information as a reason not to provide the information to the panel. This position was taken, for instance, by Canada in *Canada—Aircraft*, Turkey in *Turkey—Rice*, and the United States in *Indonesia—Autos*. These attempts to avoid production of information based on the confidential character of the information were rejected by panels and the Appellate Body. In *Canada—Aircraft*, Canada argued that it could not provide certain information on its subsidy programs because it was sensitive confidential business information. It stated that Article 18.2 of the DSU and the special procedures which were eventually adopted by the panel in that case did not afford sufficient protection to the information.[198] The panel 'regret[ted] Canada's refusal to provide the requested information' and noted that it could draw adverse inferences from Canada's refusal—though in the end it decided not to draw such inferences.[199] On appeal, the Appellate Body rejected Canada's argument that concerns for the protection of confidential information justified its refusal to provide information to the panel.[200] In *Turkey—Rice*, Turkey refused to provide information to the panel on the grounds that Turkish law classified the information requested as confidential and imposed penalties for its disclosure.[201] The panel noted that Turkey could not simply rely upon limitations imposed by its own laws. The panel ultimately drew adverse inferences from Turkey's refusal to provide the information.[202] The United States in *Indonesia—Autos* did not provide certain information in support of its claims on the grounds that it was confidential business information. The panel's reaction to the United States' argument was that complainants cannot 'invoke confidentiality as a basis for their failure to submit the positive evidence required' to demonstrate their claims.[203]

Notably, some parties have sought to justify their refusal to produce information to the panel on the basis of provisions, such as Article 3.2 of the

[197] Similarly, see Appendix 3, paragraph 3, of the DSU.
[198] Panel Report, *Canada—Aircraft*, above n 136 at paras 4.124, 4.153–4.155, 4.173–4.176, 6.80.
[199] Panel Report, *Canada—Aircraft*, above n 136 at paras 9.178, 9.181, 9.188–9.190.
[200] Appellate Body Report, *Canada—Aircraft*, above n 81 at paras 195–6, 199.
[201] Panel Report, *Turkey—Rice*, above n 89 at para 7.99.
[202] Panel Report, *Turkey—Rice*, above n 89 at paras 7.106–7.107.
[203] Panel Report, *Indonesia—Autos*, above n 172 at para 14.235.

Agreement on Safeguards, which relate to the protection of confidential information in domestic processes.[204] The argument that the confidentiality obligations contained in provisions such as Article 3.2 preclude the parties from producing information during the WTO dispute settlement process has, however, been correctly rejected in favour of the view (i) that certain information may be necessary for a panel to make an objective assessment of the matter, (ii) relatedly, that Article 13 of the DSU grants the panel the right to seek (and the parties the duty to provide) such information that it considers necessary and appropriate, and (iii) that pursuant to Article 12.1 of the DSU a panel has the authority to adopt special procedures to protect confidential information.[205] This was the case, for instance, in *US—Wheat Gluten*.[206]

In *US—Wheat Gluten* the United States refused to provide certain information on the grounds that Article 3.2 of the Agreement on Safeguards allowed it to withhold the information from the panel. The panel acknowledged the provisions of Article 3.2 but noted that the special procedures it had adopted were 'adequate to protect the confidentiality of information submitted to it'.[207] The United States did not submit the information requested and the panel ultimately decided that the information which was on the record provided 'sufficient basis for [it] to conduct [an] objective assessment of the matter'.[208] On appeal, the Appellate Body emphasized the duty of Members to respond to requests for information made by panels under Article 13.1 of the DSU and the fact that refusals to do so undermine the 'ability of a panel to make an objective assessment of the facts and the matter'.[209] In light of this, the Appellate Body 'deplore[d] the conduct of the United States'.[210]

[204] Article 3.2 provides that: 'Any information which is by nature confidential or which is provided on a confidential basis shall, upon cause being shown, be treated as such by the competent authorities. Such information shall not be disclosed without permission of the party submitting it. Parties providing confidential information may be requested to furnish non-confidential summaries thereof or, if such parties indicate that such information cannot be summarized, the reasons why a summary cannot be provided. However, if the competent authorities find that a request for confidentiality is not warranted and if the party concerned is either unwilling to make the information public or to authorize its disclosure in generalized or summary form, the authorities may disregard such information unless it can be demonstrated to their satisfaction from appropriate sources that the information is correct.'

[205] According to Article 12.1, 'Panels shall follow the Working Procedures in Appendix 3 unless the panel decides otherwise after consulting the parties to the dispute.'

[206] See also Panel Report, *United States—Imposition of Countervailing Duties on Certain Hot-Rolled Lead and Bismuth Carbon Steel Products Originating in the United Kingdom*, WT/DS138/R and Corr.2, adopted 7 June 2000 at paras 6.6–6.7 (where the panellists noted that Article 13 of the DSU grants panels the authority to seek information and that they were 'not persuaded that the proprietary nature of the information preclude[d] [them] from requesting (or the United States from submitting) the information, since it is open to the Panel to implement special procedures to protect proprietary information').

[207] Panel Report, *US—Wheat Gluten*, above n 14 at paras 8.7–8.11.

[208] Panel Report, *US—Wheat Gluten*, above n 14 at para 8.12.

[209] Appellate Body Report, *US—Wheat Gluten*, above n 5 at para 171.

[210] Appellate Body Report, *US—Wheat Gluten*, above n 5 at para 171.

Accordingly, panels and the Appellate Body have found that confidentiality does not provide a justification for parties not to submit information which is otherwise necessary to determine the truth of allegations made in a dispute. This conclusion is correct in that where confidential information is necessary for the proper application of the WTO agreements, allowing parties to withhold information on grounds of confidentiality undermines the dispute settlement system.[211] Moreover, permitting a party to exclude from the proceedings information which it has self-designated as confidential discourages good faith cooperation as parties may abuse or be perceived as abusing their power to designate information as confidential.[212] In other words, confidentiality may become (or be perceived to be) an excuse not to provide information which would disfavour the party in question.

At the same time, there is a strong case for protecting confidential information if its disclosure would (a) provide an undeserved advantage to a person given access to the information or (b) have an adverse effect upon the party supplying the information or upon the person from whom the supplying party acquired the information. Specific concerns which have been raised with respect to the presentation of confidential business information include the fact that (i) the information may fall into the hands of competitors,[213] (ii) a government may be liable under its domestic law for public disclosure of information regarding private parties which was in its possession, and (iii) private parties may not share information with the government for the purposes of WTO dispute settlement if the government cannot provide some assurance that the information will not be made public or fall into the hands of competitors.[214] While

[211] In support of this view, see Kreier, above n 5 at 53–4 (noting that it is difficult to imagine how a panel can review the adequacy of the investigating authorities' determination 'unless it has access to the relevant facts, including confidential information, that were before the investigating authorities').

[212] It may also be the case that a private party who has a direct interest in an eventual WTO dispute auto-designates the information as confidential.

[213] This is a common concern in international arbitration, which has led arbitral institutions to address the issue in their rules. Article 20.7 of the Rules of Arbitration of the International Chamber of Commerce (the 'ICC Arbitration Rules') provides, for instance, that 'The Arbitral Tribunal may take measures for protecting trade secrets and confidential information.' Articles 9.2(e) and 9.3 of the IBA Rules provide, respectively, the tribunal may excuse a party from providing commercial or technical confidential information or instead it may 'make necessary arrangements to permit evidence to be considered subject to suitable confidentiality protection'. See also Emmanuel Gaillard & John Savage (eds), *Fouchard Gaillard and Goldman on International Arbitration* (The Hague: Kluwer Law International, 1999) at 691–2 (explaining the legitimate concern of parties not to reveal certain information such as know-how and pricing information to their competitors and the manner that this subject has been managed in international commercial arbitration); Derains & Schwartz, above n 147 at 284–5 (reviewing the rationale and origin of Article 20.7 of the ICC Arbitration Rules).

[214] With respect to point (iii) see Panel Report, *Canada—Measures Affecting the Importation of Milk and the Exportation of Dairy Products—Recourse to Article 21.5 of the DSU by New Zealand and the United States*, WT/DS103/RW, WT/DS113/RW, adopted 18 December 2001 at para 2.2; Panel Report, *Canada—Wheat Exports and Grain Imports*, above n 180 at paras 4.143–4.144.

these concerns do not necessarily justify excluding confidential information from the panel process, they do warrant the establishment of procedures to protect confidential information. Without such protection, some Members may choose not to produce confidential information, preferring instead to suffer the consequences of their non-compliance, which may be less costly than the damage that would ensue from public disclosure of the information. Sanctioning the recalcitrant party in these circumstances will not necessarily lead the panel to a more accurate decision since the information in question may actually support the position of that party.

5.2. The case for standard procedures to protect confidential information

As noted above, currently, neither the DSU nor other WTO agreements provide for standard procedures to protect confidential information. The general obligations contained in the DSU do not guarantee the protection of information which has been designated as confidential as several reported instances of leakage demonstrate—many others are likely to have occurred but not have become public.[215] In *US—Gambling*, both in the original and the Article 21.5 proceedings, the panel reported that the confidentiality obligations with respect to the interim report of the panel were breached. The panel stressed that the interim report had been expressly designated as 'strictly confidential' and that this had been 'accepted by the parties, as well as reflected in the Panel's Working Procedures and in all relevant correspondence with the parties'.[216] A more extensive leak of the panel's confidential interim report occurred in *EC—Approval and Marketing of Biotech Products* where a substantial part of the interim report was published on the website of a non-governmental organization.[217] In this case, not only was the interim report confidential, but the report actually contained specific information which had been designated by the party

[215] In support, see Hunter Nottage & Jan Bohanes, 'Arbitration as an Alternative to Litigation in the WTO: Observations in the Light of the 2005 Banana Tariff Arbitrations' in Y Taniguchi, A Yanovich & J Bohanes (eds), *The WTO in the Twenty-first Century: Dispute Settlement, Negotiations, and Regionalism in Asia* (Cambridge: Cambridge University Press, 2007) 212 at 232 (noting that 'the text of the DSU as well as practice of the past ten years does not offer parties security that their BCI will be protected').

[216] Panel Report, *United States—Measures Affecting the Cross-Border Supply of Gambling and Betting Services—Recourse to Article 21.5 of the DSU by Antigua and Barbuda*, WT/DS285/RW, adopted 22 May 2007 at paras 5.2–5.6; Panel Report, *United States—Measures Affecting the Cross-Border Supply of Gambling and Betting Services*, WT/DS285/R, adopted 20 April 2005 at paras 5.3–5.5. Similar breaches of confidentiality concerning interim reports were reported in Panel Report, *United States—Restrictions on Imports of Cotton and Man-made Fibre Underwear*, WT/DS24/R, adopted 25 February 1997 at 6.3; Panel Reports, *United States—Definitive Safeguard Measures on Imports of Certain Steel Products*, WT/DS248/R, WT/DS249/R, WT/DS251/R, WT/DS252/R, WT/DS253/R, WT/DS254/R, WT/DS258/R, WT/DS259/R, and Corr.1, adopted 10 December 2003 at para 9.41.

[217] Panel Report, *European Communities—Measures Affecting the Approval and Marketing of Biotech Products*, WT/DS291/R, WT/DS292/R, WT/DS293/R, Corr.1 and Add.1, 2, 3, 4, 5, 6, 7, 8 and 9, adopted 21 November 2006 at paras 6.183–6.185.

submitting it as strictly confidential.[218] Leakage of information which had been specifically designated as confidential also occurred in *EC—Export Subsidies on Sugar (Brazil).* The leak was discovered because an *amicus curiae* brief disclosed information that Brazil had submitted to the panel in confidence.[219]

While the parties to WTO dispute settlement might be more inclined to protect confidential business and/or government information as opposed to interim reports which do not contain such information, leakages of any information which is designated as confidential, including interim reports, discourage those in possession of such confidential information from producing it to the panel. Concerns about the effectiveness of the current obligations to protect confidentiality are reinforced by the facts that (i) the diffusion of panel submissions is wide and unmonitored; (ii) third parties (ie intervening parties) have access to some submissions; and (iii) 'the parties are free to determine the composition of their own delegations (which often include the lawyers for affected private parties or even employees of the [private] parties themselves)'.[220] In this regard, in *Brazil—Aircraft (Article 21.5—Canada II)* the panel found that nothing in Article 18.2 of the DSU, or any other provision of the DSU, indicates that confidential information may not be shared with the advisors of a party, independently of whether they have been designated as Members of its delegation.[221] In the view of the panel, the parties must only ensure that these persons comply with the rules of the DSU regarding confidentiality.[222] The

[218] Although the NGO in question removed part of the strictly confidential information before publishing the report, some parts apparently remained. Moreover, the NGO was not a party to the proceedings, therefore, the fact that it was in possession of the information indicates in and of itself that a breach of confidentiality occurred. The panel noted that it had adopted special procedures to protect the confidentiality of the information designated as strictly confidential; though it did not provide the details of such procedure. Panel Report, *EC—Approval and Marketing of Biotech Products*, above n 217 at paras 6.179, 6.184–6.185, 6.188, 6.190. A similar situation occurred in Panel Report, *European Communities—Measures Affecting the Importation of Certain Poultry Products*, WT/DS69/R, adopted 23 July 1998 at para 191.

[219] Panel Report, *European Communities—Export Subsidies on Sugar, Complaint by Brazil*, WT/DS266/R, adopted 19 May 2005 at para 7.86. Similarly, see Appellate Body Report, *Thailand—H-Beams*, above n 17 at para 64 (where leakage of Thailand's confidential submission to the Appellate Body was discovered because an industry association submitted an *amicus curiae* brief which cited Thailand's submission).

[220] Kreier, above n 5 at 55.

[221] Panel Report, *Brazil—Export Financing Programme for Aircraft—Second Recourse by Canada to Article 21.5 of the DSU*, WT/DS46/RW/2, adopted 23 August 2001, DSR 2001:X, 5481 at paras 3.7–3.8.

[222] Panel Report, *Brazil—Aircraft (Article 21.5—Canada II)*, above n 221 at paras 3.6, 3.10. See also Panel Report, *Korea—Taxes on Alcoholic Beverages*, WT/DS75/R, WT/DS84/R, adopted 17 February 1999 at paras 10.31–10.32 (where the panel noted that 'written submissions of the parties which contain confidential information may [. . .] be provided to non-government advisors who are not members of an official delegation at a panel meeting. The duty of confidentiality extends to all governments that are parties to a dispute and to all such advisors regardless of whether they are designated as members of delegations and appear at a panel meeting'); Appellate Body Report, *Canada—Aircraft*, above n 81 at paras 141, 145 (where the Appellate Body noted that Article 18.2 of the DSU obliges Members to ensure that 'confidentiality is fully respected by any person that a Member selects to act as its representative, counsel or consultant').

absence of control over the number and background of individuals who have access to confidential information may not give the relevant parties confidence that the information will not end up in the hands of persons who may disclose it to the public or derive an advantage for themselves from the information.

Moreover, the currently imperfect regulation of confidential information allows WTO Members to avoid making the necessary adjustments to their domestic laws, and gives them the opportunity to seek to invoke their domestic laws prohibiting disclosure as a reason not to produce information. This occurred in *Canada—Aircraft*,[223] *US—Upland Cotton*,[224] and *Turkey—Rice*.[225] Domestic laws protecting the privacy of individuals and privileging certain categories of information should not automatically excuse Members from producing information which is considered necessary for the proper application of the WTO agreements.[226] This is in accordance with the principle of international law that a state cannot invoke its domestic laws to justify non-compliance with international obligations.[227] If states were allowed to do so, they could effectively undermine the rules to which they had previously agreed. This is not to say however that the international law of procedure should not exclude certain categories of information from production. It means that international procedure, including WTO dispute settlement, must develop its own law of privilege rather than merely enforcing exclusions contained in the domestic laws of WTO Members.[228] As noted in Section II.B.6.1 of this chapter, settlement

[223] Panel Report, *Canada—Aircraft*, above n 136 at para 4.177.

[224] Panel Report, *US—Upland Cotton*, above n 111 at paras 7.23, 7.631.

[225] Panel Report, *Turkey—Rice*, above n 89 at para 7.99.

[226] In the context of investor-state arbitration, see *Biwater Gauff (Tanzania) Ltd v United Republic of Tanzania*, ICSID Case No ARB/05/22, Procedural Order No 2, 24 May 2006 at 8–9 (rejecting Tanzania's objection to a request for production of documents on the grounds that the documents were protected by the doctrine of public interest immunity under Tanzanian law. The tribunal noted that it was mandated to apply international law, and that such doctrine has no equivalent in international law. According to the tribunal, 'if a State were permitted to deploy its own national law in this way, it would, in effect, be avoiding its obligation to produce documents in so far as called upon to do so by this Tribunal. This, in itself, is an international legal obligation arising from the state's consent by way of the BIT to ICSID arbitration'); *Pope & Talbot Inc v The Government of Canada*, Award on the Merits of Phase 2, 10 April 2001 at para 193 (rejecting Canada's objection to a request for the production of documents on the grounds that their disclosure was prohibited by the Canada Evidence Act).

[227] Ian Brownlie, *Principles of Public International Law* (6th edn, Oxford: Oxford University Press, 2003) at 34. See also the Article 27 of the Vienna Convention on the Law of Treaties which states that '[a] party may not invoke the provisions of its internal law as justification for its failure to perform a treaty'.

[228] There seems to be no established law of privileges in international law from which the WTO could borrow. See Pietrowski, above n 147 at 405 (he notes that there are no general rules regarding privileged information in international law). In the context of arbitration under Chapter 11 of the NAFTA, referring to the need to apply the law governing the tribunal rather than the domestic law of the litigating state to resolve claims of privilege, see *United Parcel Service of America v Government of Canada*, Decision of the Tribunal Relating to Canada's Claim of Cabinet Privilege, 8 October 2004 at para 7; *Pope and Talbot v Government of Canada*, Decision by the Tribunal, 6 September 2000 at paras 1.3–1.5.

proposals (and related documents) made during the consultations process are an example of privileged information which is excluded from production in the WTO panel process. In addition, national security information and information confided to certain professionals such as lawyers in their professional capacity, for instance, seem to be strong contenders to be excluded from production.[229]

In sum, provision of clear rules at the WTO level regarding the subject of confidential information would allow Members to adapt their domestic laws accordingly. Those WTO Members that chose not to do so would be effectively precluded from raising their domestic laws as an excuse not to provide information to the panel. In these circumstances, more provisions such as Section 84.2(b) of Canada's Special Import Measures Act may flourish. Section 84.2(b) explicitly authorizes the disclosure of confidential information in WTO dispute settlement. It provides an exception to a rule precluding the disclosure of confidential information submitted by a person in the context of domestic anti-dumping and subsidy countervailing investigations.[230]

Article 12.1 of the DSU grants panels the authority to draw up *ad hoc* procedures to protect confidential information. However, on several occasions panels have declined requests to adopt such procedures,[231] and in others they have adopted rules differing from those requested by the disputing parties.[232] In addition, in many cases the parties were not able to agree on the need to adopt special procedures[233] or on the scope of the procedures.[234] These disagreements are likely to become a point of contention affecting good faith cooperation. For example, in *Canada—Aircraft*, the parties' disagreement with respect to the

[229] In *Canada—Aircraft*, the panel referred to the possibility of privileging national security information upon an explanation from the Member concerned of the basis for the need to protect that information. See Panel Report, *Canada—Aircraft*, above n 136 at footnote 633 to para 9.347. On the latter example above, see Sandifer, above n 84 at 376.

[230] See Section 84(1) and (2) of the Special Import Measures Act, R.S.C. 1985, c. S-15.

[231] See Panel Report, *EC—Export Subsidies on Sugar (Brazil)*, above n 219 at paras 2.12–2.15; Panel Report, *Canada—Dairy (Article 21.5—New Zealand and US)*, above n 214 at para 2.15 (in this case, however, the panel determined that the confidential information was not necessary for the panel to conduct an objective assessment of the matter at paras 2.18–2.20); Panel Report, *Australia—Measures Affecting Importation of Salmon*, WT/DS18/R and Corr.1, adopted 6 November 1998 at para 7.7 (the panel refused to adopt special procedures for the protection of government confidential information; though it adopted two additional rules to the effect that the information must not be disclosed in the report of the panel and that the information must be returned after the conclusion of the dispute settlement proceedings).

[232] See Contribution of Canada to the Improvement of the WTO Dispute Settlement Understanding, WTO Doc. TN/DS/W/41, 24 January 2003 at 2 (where Canada notes that the 'ad hoc procedures adopted by panels, in the absence of specific procedures to protect BCI, have on occasion failed to satisfy disputing parties').

[233] See, for instance, Panel Report, *Canada—Dairy (Article 21.5—New Zealand and US)*, above n 214 at paras 2.2, 2.5 (for divergences between the complainant and the defendant); Panel Report, *EC—Export Subsidies on Sugar (Brazil)*, above n 219 at paras 2.10–2.11 (for divergences between the complainant and the defendant); Appellate Body Report, *Canada—Aircraft*, above n 81 at 134–6 (for the arguments of a third party against the adoption of special procedures).

[234] See, for example, Panel Report, *Canada—Aircraft*, above n 136 at paras 4.152–4.170.

scope of the procedures led Canada to refuse to provide certain information to the panel; and in *EC—Bananas III (US)* (Article 22.6—EC) the European Communities' refusal to agree to the procedures set up by the arbitrators resulted in it being denied access to the confidential information submitted by the United States.[235]

Other limitations and disadvantages of this *ad hoc* approach include, first, the fact that panels cannot impose sanctions for breach of confidentiality that go beyond the panel process. Second, while panels can adopt *ad hoc* procedures for the protection of confidential information they cannot impose such procedures on the Appellate Body. On at least one occasion the Appellate Body declined to adopt confidentiality procedures similar to those which had been adopted by the panel.[236] Third, the negotiation of these agreements consumes valuable resources (time and money)—resource savings are particularly important when the volume of confidential information to be submitted is small. Moreover, the fact that confidentiality procedures are not already in place may inhibit the parties from being forthcoming from the very beginning of the proceedings. These considerations suggest that Members should establish standard procedures for the protection of confidential information.[237] If well designed, such procedures can protect confidential information, improve the accuracy of decisions, save resources, and encourage good faith cooperation, and thus maximizing the realization of the goals of the WTO dispute settlement system. With a view to ensuring some flexibility, provision could be made to allow the parties to modify the standard procedures by agreement.

5.3. Design of the standard procedures to protect confidential information

Canada has put forward a proposal in the DSU review negotiations for the adoption of standard special procedures to protect confidential business information.[238] The proposal reflects to a large extent some of the *ad hoc* procedures which have been adopted in past disputes. Some of the features of Canada's proposal and/or past *ad hoc* procedures[239] include: (i) limitations on access to

[235] *Decision by the Arbitrators, European Communities—Regime for the Importation, Sale and Distribution of Bananas—Recourse to Arbitration by the European Communities under Article 22.6 of the DSU*, WT/DS27/ARB, 9 April 1999, DSR 1999:II, 725 at para 2.6. In the end, the arbitrators noted that it was not necessary for them to rely on the confidential information submitted by the United States in making their ruling. Ibid, at para 2.7.

[236] Appellate Body Report, *Canada—Aircraft*, above n 81 at paras 141–5.

[237] In favour of the adoption of standard confidentiality procedures, see Prost, above n 195 at 197; Claus-Dieter Ehlermann, 'Six Years on the Bench of the 'World Trade Court': Some Personal Experiences as Member of the Appellate Body of the World Trade Organization' (2002) 36:4 Journal of World Trade 605 at 626–7. Downplaying the importance of confidential information and the need for special procedures to ensure its protection, see White, above n 67 at 129–30.

[238] *Contribution of Canada to the Improvement of the WTO Dispute Settlement Understanding*, WTO Doc TN/DS/W/41, 24 January 2003.

[239] See Panel Report, *Canada—Aircraft*, above n 136 at Annex I; Panel Report, *Korea—Commercial Vessels*, above n 148 at attachment 2; Panel Report, *US—Wheat Gluten*, above n 14 at

confidential information to approved persons who have signed a non-disclosure agreement; (ii) prohibition on copying and distribution of documents; (iii) limited physical access to the information including requirements that the information be stored in designated locations or that information be accessed at a neutral location (WTO Secretariat) or at a location which is under the control of the party providing the information; (iv) a requirement that the information be returned or destroyed after proceedings are concluded; (v) a requirement that Members receiving confidential information ensure that their representatives comply with the procedures; (vi) a requirement for the panel not to disclose confidential business information in its report; and (vii) authority of the panel to decline to consider information which it believes is not reasonably entitled to protection.

A feature of certain *ad hoc* procedures which was not incorporated in the Canadian proposal is the classification of confidential information into groups requiring different levels of protection.[240] This feature is useful in that it takes into account the fact that not all confidential information is of the same sensitivity and therefore does not require the same level of protection. Moreover, Canada's proposal focuses exclusively on confidential business information leaving government confidential information unregulated.[241]

Another omission from the Canadian proposal and *ad hoc* procedures is that they do not provide for sanctions for breaches of confidentiality. Sanctions, however, may have an important role in deterring breaches and building confidence in the procedures' effectiveness. Although some Members may have mechanisms in place to sanction breaches of confidentiality by their employees or representatives, this is not necessarily the case with all WTO Members. Members could therefore agree to set up reasonable domestic sanctions for those who violate non-disclosure agreements. Although in a different context, it is worth noting that Annex VI, paragraph 2, of the SCM Agreement contains an obligation for Members to establish sanctions in their domestic law. Paragraph 2 provides that if a domestic investigating authority includes non governmental experts in the on-the-spot investigating team, these individuals must be subject to 'effective sanctions for breach of confidentiality requirements'.

Chapter 19 of the NAFTA could be a model for DSU rules addressing the subject of sanctions for breaches of confidentiality. Article 1904.14 of the NAFTA provides that the rules of procedure for binational panel reviews shall

attachment 4; Panel Report, *Brazil—Export Financing Programme for Aircraft*, WT/DS46/R, adopted 20 August 1999 at Annex I.

[240] *United States—Measures Affecting Trade in Large Civil Aircraft (Second Complaint), WT/DS353; European Communities—Measures Affecting Trade in Large Civil Aircraft*, WT/DS317. In the context of litigation under Chapter 11 of the NAFTA, see *United Parcel Service of America v Government of Canada*, Procedural Directions and Order of the Tribunal, 4 April 2003 at section E.

[241] This is particularly interesting since Canada raised this issue in past disputes. See, for example, Panel Report, *Canada—Aircraft*, above n 136 at para 9.345.

include 'sanctions against persons participating before panels for improper release of' business proprietary, government classified, and other privileged information. In turn, Rule 54 of the rules of procedure refers to the sanctions which are specified in the domestic statutes of the state parties to the NAFTA.[242] A sanction which could be provided for in the DSU (and implemented domestically) is to give the party adversely affected by the breach the right to sue the party that leaked the information in domestic courts for damages.[243] An approach along these lines has been adopted in some cases under Chapter 11 of the NAFTA. Some Chapter 11 Tribunals have established confidentiality agreements referring to the use of domestic courts and remedies to restrain and redress breaches of confidentiality.[244]

It is worth noting that the unqualified prohibition on *ex parte* communications with the panel and the Appellate Body contained in Article 18.1 of the DSU does not allow for *in camera* review of confidential information as provided for in certain legal systems.[245] Accordingly, panels have refused in the past to consider information which a party offered to submit exclusively to the panel.[246] In light of this, Canada's proposal and *ad hoc* procedures have not provided for *in camera* review of information by panels. When highly sensitive information is at issue,[247] an alternative to *in camera* review could be the use of neutral tribunal-appointed experts who would inspect the documents and present their findings to the panels and the parties.[248] Such a solution is provided

[242] According to Rule 54, sanctions are to be imposed 'in accordance with Section 77.034 of the [Canada] *Special Import Measures Act*, as amended, Section 777(*f*) of the [United States] *Tariff Act of 1930*, as amended, or Article 93 of the [Mexico] *Ley de Comercio Exterior*'. The rules of procedure are available at <http://www.nafta-sec-alena.org/en/view.aspx?coniD=823> (accessed 3 August 2009).

[243] See Derains & Schwartz, above n 147 at 285 (referring to the use of confidentiality agreements in international arbitration and how their breach can be the basis of a claim for damages.)

[244] See *United Parcel Service of America v Government of Canada*, Procedural Directions and Order of the Tribunal, 4 April 2003 at Appendix A; *SD Myers v Government of Canada*, Procedural Order No. 11 (concerning confidentiality of materials produced in the arbitration), 11 November 1999 at Appendix A.

[245] See, for example, Lasok, above n 155 at 381 (referring to the practice of the ECJ). Relatedly, see Toshiro M Mochizuki, 'Baby Step or Giant Leap?: Parties' Expanded Access to Documentary Evidence under the New Japanese Code of Civil Procedure' (1999) 40:1 Harvard International Law Journal 285 at 297 (explaining that the New Japanese Code of Civil Procedure allows the 'courts to examine documents *in camera* to see whether they fall within the stated exceptions to the duty to produce'); Kuo-Chang Huang, *Introducing Discovery into Civil Law* (Durham: Carolina Academic Press, 2003) at 194 (referring to the same procedure of in camera review under the New Japanese Code of Civil Procedure).

[246] See Panel Report, *Turkey—Rice*, above n 89 at paras 2.50–67, 7.100, 7.104; Panel Report, *Korea—Anti-Dumping Duties on Imports of Certain Paper from Indonesia*, WT/DS312/R, adopted 28 November 2005 at para 7.17; Appellate Body Report, *US—Wheat Gluten*, above n 5 at para 168; Panel Report, *US—Wheat Gluten*, above n 14 at para 8.10.

[247] Because the tribunal-appointed expert cannot be completely controlled due to information asymmetries, ideally this solution should be restricted to highly sensitive information.

[248] Appointment of a neutral expert may also offer a solution to disputes over whether information is protected by a privilege from production in WTO dispute settlement.

for in Article 3.7 of the IBA Rules on the Taking of Evidence in International Commercial Arbitration (the 'IBA Rules'), and Article 52(e) of the WIPO Arbitration Rules.[249] Article 52(e) of the WIPO Arbitration Rules provides that the tribunal may appoint an expert 'to report to it, on the basis of the confidential information, on specific issues designated by the Tribunal without disclosing the confidential information either to the party from whom the confidential information does not originate or to the Tribunal'. Such a rule would not violate the prohibition on *ex parte* communications with the panel and would restrict access to the information to a very limited number of people (one or two experts), thus more effectively guaranteeing its protection.

Another issue which has yet to be resolved in a satisfactory manner is the question of access to confidential information by third parties. Article 10.3 of the DSU—which provides that '[t]hird parties shall receive the submissions of the parties to the dispute to the first meeting of the panel'—has been interpreted to require third parties to have access to confidential information.[250] Given that any of the 153 Members of the WTO may become a third party to a proceeding, third party access to confidential information produced with the first written submissions of the parties raises serious issues with respect to the effective protection of such information. There seems to be no strong reason for granting third parties access to confidential information since their rights are not directly at stake in the proceedings.[251] Moreover, third parties do not in any event have the same rights of participation as the parties to the dispute. For example, they have no right to receive the second submissions of the parties to the panel or to participate in the second meeting with the panel. Granting third parties the right of access to confidential information has been identified as a problem by several WTO Members in proposals submitted in the negotiations to amend the DSU.[252]

[249] See Giovanni Ughi et al, 'Commentary on the New IBA Rules of Evidence in International Commercial Arbitration' (2000) 2 Business Law International 16 at 23 (referring to the IBA Rules); Derains & Schwartz, above n 147 at 430 (referring to ICC arbitration).

[250] See, for instance,Panel Report, *Canada—Wheat Exports and Grain Imports*, above n 180 at para 6.8.

[251] It is worth noting, for instance, that in proceedings before the European Court of First Instance and the European Court of Justice, interveners may be denied access to 'secret or confidential' information if at least one of the parties to the proceedings opposes access. See Article 116 (6) of the Rules of Procedure of the Court of First Instance of the European Communities of 2 May 1991; Article 93(3) of the Rules of Procedure of the Court of Justice of the European Communities of 19 June 1991.

[252] These proposals provide that third parties 'shall receive a copy of all documents or information submitted to the panel, at the time of submission, except for certain factual confidential information designated as such by the disputing party that submitted it'. See *Proposal by Costa Rica on Third Party Rights*, WTO Doc TN/DS/W/12/Rev.1, 6 March 2003; *Contribution of the European Communities and its Member States to the Improvement and Clarification of the WTO Dispute Settlement Understanding*, WTO Doc TN/DS/W/38, 23 January 2003; *Contribution by the Separate Customs Territory of Taiwan, Penghu, Kinmen and Matsu to the Doha Mandated Review of the Dispute Settlement Understanding (DSU)*, WTO Doc TN/DS/W/36, 22 January 2003; *Proposal by Japan on Amendment of the Understanding on Rules and Procedures Governing the Settlement of Disputes*, WTO Doc TN/DS/W/32, 22 January 2003.

5.4. Final note on the problem of confidential information

Finally, it is important to recognize that the panel must be the ultimate arbiter of the *necessity* of confidential information to the resolution of a dispute. In this regard, panels should balance the goal of protecting confidential information—including the likelihood that the information may leak (account being taken of the confidentiality procedures put in place) and the damage that such disclosure may cause—against the contribution that the information is likely to make to the accuracy of the decision. If the confidential information is not likely to lead to a more accurate decision, the panel may find that the information is not necessary.[253] Moreover, because panels are allowed to exercise judicial economy with respect to certain claims, information which is relevant exclusively to those claims is accordingly not necessary. In the same vein, panels may allow parties to redact the documents to be produced in order to eliminate information which is not necessary for the proper application of the WTO agreement at issue.[254]

6. Cooperation before the establishment of the panel

Even before the panel process is set in motion, and independently of whether it is set in motion, WTO Members have certain obligations to make information regarding their measures available to other Members. One such obligation operates during the process of consultations prior to the establishment of a panel. The WTO agreements have also created many transparency obligations and related surveillance mechanisms which require WTO Members to provide certain information on their measures with a view to allowing the monitoring of the implementation of their obligations.

Importantly, although the main objective of these obligations is not to develop information for the panel process—one of their main objectives is to ensure voluntary compliance with the WTO agreements obviating the need to recur to the panel process—the information collected in consultations and

[253] See, for example, Panel Report, *US—Lead and Bismuth II*, above n 206 at para 6.7 (noting that certain confidential information although relevant was not necessary to resolve the dispute); Panel Report, *United States—Definitive Safeguard Measures on Imports of Circular Welded Carbon Quality Line Pipe from Korea*, WT/DS202/R, adopted 8 March 2002 at para 7.4 (noting that it was not necessary for the United States to produce the whole confidential record of the safeguard investigation).

[254] See, for instance, Panel Report, *United States—Safeguard Measures on Imports of Fresh, Chilled or Frozen Lamb Meat from New Zealand and Australia*, WT/DS177/R, WT/DS178/R, adopted 16 May 2001 at paras 5.63–5.65 (finding that indexed data was 'adequate and sufficient for purposes of [its] review of the USITC's investigation and determination pursuant to [its] terms of reference'); Panel Report, *Argentina—Textiles and Apparel*, above n 90 at paras 6.53, 6.57–6.59 (where the panel accepted customs documents which had been redacted); Panel Report, *US—Upland Cotton*, above n 111 at para 7.25 (where the panel noted that the United States could 'protect the identity of individual producers by, for example, using substitute farm numbers which still permit data-matching'). But see Panel Report, *Canada—Aircraft*, above n 136 at 9.345 (where the panel noted that the material provided by Canada had 'been redacted to such an extent that it [was] simply of no value to the Panel').

through the operation of the transparency obligations and related surveillance mechanisms constitutes an important source of information for the panel process. It is worth noting that while consultations, transparency obligations (and related surveillance mechanisms), and the panel process have their own specific objectives, they share a common general objective, namely, ensuring compliance with the WTO agreements. For this reason, they must not be seen as mutually exclusive but as complementary to each other.

6.1. Consultations

The plea in Article 3.10 of the DSU for Members to 'engage in [dispute settlement] procedures in good faith in an effort to resolve the dispute' applies not only to the panel proceedings but also to the stage which precedes the establishment of the panel, namely, the consultations. Members are thus under a general duty to cooperate in good faith during the consultations with a view to settling the dispute. Such duty indubitably includes exchange of information on the claims and the measure at issue. In this regard, according to Article 4.4 of the DSU the Member requesting consultations must provide in writing 'the reasons for the request, including identification of the measures at issue and an indication of the legal basis for the complaint'. The Member to which the request is directed shall 'reply to the request within 10 days after the date of its receipt and shall enter into consultations in good faith [...] with a view to reaching a mutually satisfactory solution'.[255] Recognizing the impact that consultations may have on the subsequent panel proceedings, the Appellate Body has urged Members to be 'fully forthcoming' in consultations 'as to the claims involved in a dispute and as to the facts relating to those claims'.[256]

As a general rule, Members indeed use the consultations to exchange information on the measure at issue and the potential legal claims—it is true, however, that in certain cases, particularly when Members have already unsuccessfully tried to resolve the dispute in other fora, the process of consultations is approached by some as a mere formality. Typically the Member which requests consultations sends a list of questions to the other Member; such questions, even if not answered in full or in writing, help to frame the exchange of information at the consultation meeting. The prime objective of this exchange is to reach a mutually agreed solution,[257] but even where such solution

[255] Article 4.3 of the DSU.

[256] Appellate Body Report, *India—Patents (US)*, above n 91 at para 94.

[257] The disparity between the number of requests for consultations and the number of requests for establishment of a panel suggests that the exchange of information which takes place during the consultations helps Members resolve many disputes without having to recur to the panel process. Resolution of a dispute without recourse to the panel process encompasses not only mutually agreed solutions but also cases which are not pursued because the Member requesting consultations is satisfied with the explanations given by the Member to which the request for consultations is directed.

A simple comparison between the number of consultation requests and panel requests based on DS numbers (not including requests under Article 21.5 of the DSU) reveals that between January

is not achieved the exchange of information which takes place during the consultations helps to define the scope of the differences between the parties. Along these lines, the Appellate Body noted in *Mexico—Anti-Dumping Measures on Rice* that an important rationale behind the requirement for consultations is 'the exchange of information necessary to refine the contours of the dispute, which are subsequently set out in the panel request'.[258] This is particularly true in those cases where consultations are the first opportunity that the Members have had to discuss the problem raised by the Member requesting consultations.

Except for the general requirement of Article 4.4 of the DSU that the Member requesting consultations provide the reasons for the request, the exchange of information during the process of consultations is unregulated and completely voluntary. In fact, pursuant to Article 4.3 of the DSU, if the Member to which the request is made does not respond or enter into consultations, 'the Member that requested the holding of consultations may proceed directly to request the establishment of a panel'. Moreover, because the process is private—no representative from the DSB is involved—confidential and 'without prejudice to the rights of any Member in any further proceedings',[259] the refusal of a Member to cooperate cannot be the subject of a sanction either at the consultations or at the panel stage.[260] In this regard, the absence of the panel or another neutral figure makes disputes over the necessity and relevance of information insoluble—because at this stage the parties still know relatively little about the details of the case, such disputes are likely to be common. Indeed, panels have refused to examine the adequacy of the consultation process, observing that what takes place in consultations 'is not the concern of a panel'.[261] This is in line with the fact that the 'basic function of consultations is

1995 and 14 September 2007 there were 208 panel requests out of 366 requests for consultation. Examining GATT/WTO dispute settlement data from 1948 to 1999, Busch and Reinhardt conclude that 'in a substantial majority of disputes (roughly 55%), no panel is ever established'. They observe that 'the proportion of disputes for which a panel has been established has not changed appreciably over time'. Marc L Busch & Eric Reinhardt, 'Bargaining in the Shadow of the Law: Early Settlement in GATT/WTO Disputes' (2000) 24 Fordham International Law Journal 158 at 161–2.

[258] Appellate Body Report, *Mexico—Definitive Anti-Dumping Measures on Beef and Rice, Complaint with Respect to Rice*, WT/DS295/AB/R, adopted 20 December 2005, DSR 2005:XXII, 10853 at para 138.

[259] Article 4.6 of the DSU.

[260] This of course does not mean that Members are not under a duty to cooperate in good faith. It just means that the different purposes of the consultations and of the panel process result in differences in the scope of the duty of cooperation. While the panel process is intended to resolve the dispute by the proper application of the law, consultations are intended to settle the dispute by the agreement of the parties—although pursuant to Article 3.5 of the DSU such agreement must be consistent with the WTO agreements and must not nullify or impair benefits accruing to any Member under those agreements or impede the attainment of any objective of those agreements, a mutually agreed solution allows Members to reach compromises.

[261] Panel Report, *Korea—Alcoholic Beverages*, above n 222 at para 10.19; Panel Report, *European Communities—Regime for the Importation, Sale and Distribution of Bananas, Complaint by the United States*, WT/DS27/R/USA, adopted 25 September 1997 at paras 7.19–7.20. See also Appellate Body Report, *United States—Subsidies on Upland Cotton*, WT/DS267/AB/R, adopted 21 March 2005 at para 287.

to force the parties to talk to each other in a meaningful way before they initiate the formal panel process'.[262] Accordingly, even though the consultation process may generate useful information for the panel proceedings, the exchange that takes place during this stage falls essentially in the realm of diplomacy rather than legal adjudication. This distinguishes consultations from common-law (particularly American) pre-trial discovery despite some apparent similarities between the two.[263]

Finally, the fact that '[c]onsultations shall be confidential, and without prejudice to the rights of any Member in any further proceedings'[264] should not be interpreted to mean that all information exchanged during consultations is not admissible into evidence at the panel stage. If information exchanged during consultations would automatically become privileged, some of the most relevant information would be excluded from panel consideration.[265] This could even encourage Members to submit information during consultations with the objective of preventing it from being taken into account by the panel. Such broad privilege would jeopardize accuracy without a clear countervailing benefit. Article 4.6 of the DSU may be interpreted so as to avoid such an extreme result. The rule that consultations are 'without prejudice to the rights of any Member in any further proceedings', may be understood to prevent reliance upon settlement proposals and related documents.[266] This more limited privilege would be justified on the grounds that allowing panels to base their decisions on such information would discourage the parties from making settlement offers. Moreover, admitting such proposals into evidence may not advance the goal of

[262] William J Davey, 'Evaluating WTO Dispute Settlement: What Results Have Been Achieved through Consultations and Implementation of Panel Reports?' in Y Taniguchi, A Yanovich & J Bohanes (eds), *The WTO in the Twenty-first Century: Dispute Settlement, Negotiations, and Regionalism in Asia* (Cambridge: Cambridge University Press, 2007) 98 at 118.

[263] Davey argues that adding 'a discovery function to the consultation process would transform it from a political one into a legal one'. This would likely discourage parties from negotiating a mutually agreed solution and 'would probably work to the disadvantage of developing countries, since it would raise the stakes early in the dispute settlement process before they may have arranged for legal assistance'.Davey, *Evaluating WTO Dispute Settlement*, above n 262 at 118.

[264] Article 4.6 of the DSU.

[265] In support of the view that denying the parties the right to rely upon information obtained during consultations would seriously hamper the dispute settlement process, see Panel Report, *Mexico—Anti-Dumping Investigation of High Fructose Corn Syrup (HFCS) from the United States*, WT/DS132/R and Corr.1, adopted 24 February 2000, DSR 2000:III, 1345 at paras 7.41–7.43; Panel Report, *Korea—Alcoholic Beverages*, above n 222 at para 10.23.

[266] Similarly, see Waincymer, above n 135 at 222–3. This seems to have been the approach adopted by the Permanent Court of International Justice in *Case Concerning the Factory at Chorzow* (Claim for Indemnity) (Merits), Judgment of 13 September 1928, Permanent Court of International Justice, Series A, No 17, (1928) at 51 (where the Court observed that it could 'not take into account declarations, admissions or proposals which the Parties may have made during direct negotiations between themselves, when such negotiations have not led to a complete agreement'.) With respect to international adjudication in general, see also Amerasinghe, *Evidence in International Litigation*, above n 82 at 174; Kazazi, above n 84 at 196; Pietrowski, above n 147 at 403–4.

the proper application of the law since parties may during consultations be willing to compromise on certain issues to reach an agreement. In fact, the panel in *US—Underwear* declined to base its findings on information submitted by Costa Rica relating to settlement offers by the United States. According to the panel, 'the wording of Article 4.6 of the DSU makes it clear that offers made in the context of consultations are, in case a mutually agreed solution is not reached, of no legal consequence to the later stages of dispute settlement, as far as the rights of the parties to the dispute are concerned'.[267]

6.2. Transparency obligations and surveillance mechanisms

i. The scope of the transparency obligations and the role of the committees in the surveillance process. The duty of WTO Members to provide information with respect to their measures is not limited to dispute settlement proceedings under the DSU. Self-standing obligations to provide information ('transparency obligations') have been enshrined in many provisions of various WTO agreements. Hence, the duty of WTO Members to cooperate in providing information is not only a procedural obligation to be observed during dispute settlement proceedings, but also a substantive obligation which must be observed apart from the dispute settlement process. There are essentially four categories of such substantive obligations: (i) publication; (ii) enquiry points; (iii) notification, and (iv) clarification obligations. Examples of the first category include Article X of the GATT which provides that:

> Laws, regulations, judicial decisions and administrative rulings of general application [...] pertaining to the classification or the valuation of products for customs purposes, or to rates of duty, taxes or other charges, or to requirements, restrictions or prohibitions on imports or exports or on the transfer of payments therefor, or affecting their sale, distribution, transportation, insurance, warehousing inspection, exhibition, processing, mixing or other use, shall be published promptly [...]

A similar requirement is contained in other WTO agreements[268] including Article III:1 of the GATS which states that Members 'shall publish promptly [...] all relevant measures of general application which pertain to or affect the operation of this Agreement'. As a general rule, publication requirements refer to measures of general application rather than specific measures directed at one or a few individual operators that are adopted pursuant to a measure of general application.[269] Moreover, the agreements refer to the publication of the measures themselves as opposed to information related to those measures.

[267] Panel Report, *US—Underwear*, above n 216 at para 7.27.

[268] For other examples, see Annex B, paragraphs 1 and 2 of the SPS Agreement; Articles 2.11,5.6.1, and 5.8 of the TBT Agreement.

[269] Article 12.2 of the Anti-Dumping Agreement, and Article 22 of the SCM Agreement are perhaps the closest that the agreements have come to a requirement of publication of specific measures.

Certain agreements such as the GATS, the SPS Agreement, and the TBT Agreement also require WTO Members to establish enquiry points. Enquiry points are in charge of responding to all reasonable enquiries from other Members related to measures falling under the scope of those agreements and, in the case of the TBT and SPS Agreements, providing relevant documents.[270]

Notification obligations are numerous and are contained in many different WTO agreements. These obligations essentially provide that WTO Members shall automatically notify the existence of and changes to certain measures as well as make available certain information on those measures to other WTO Members. Notifications are received by the WTO Secretariat which makes them available to all Members. For instance, Article 25 of the SCM Agreement requires Members to notify their subsidies and provide information on the form of the subsidy, the subsidy per unit or, in cases where this is not possible, the total amount or the annual amount budgeted for that subsidy, the purpose of the subsidy, its duration, and statistical data permitting an assessment of its trade effects.[271]

Finally, some provisions (clarification obligations) grant individual Members the right to directly request other Members to provide information with respect to certain aspects of their measures. Such provisions clearly establish that the requested Member is obliged to provide the information requested. In this regard, Article 2.5 of the TBT Agreement provides that '[a] Member preparing, adopting or applying a technical regulation which may have a significant effect on trade of other Members shall, upon the request of another Member, explain the justification for that technical regulation in terms of the provisions of paragraphs 2 to 4'. Similar provisions are contained in Article 5.8 of the SPS Agreement and Articles 25.8 and 25.9 of the SCM Agreement among others.[272]

One of the main functions of these different categories of obligations to provide information is to monitor the implementation by Members of their commitments under the WTO agreements.[273] This monitoring may be

[270] Annex B, paragraphs 3 and 4 of the SPS Agreement; Article 10 of the TBT Agreement; and Article III:4 of the GATS.

[271] Articles 25.2, 25.3 of the SCM Agreement. Other notification requirements include Articles 25.10–25.12 of the SCM Agreement; Articles 2.9–2.10,5.6.2, and 10.7 of the TBT Agreement; Articles 16.4–16.5, 18.5 of the Anti-Dumping Agreement; Article 12 of the Agreement on Safeguards; Article XVII:4(a) of the GATT; and Articles III:3 and V:7(a) and (b) of the GATS; Articles 18.2 and 18.3 of the Agreement on Agriculture; Article 12.4 and Article 7 of the SPS Agreement together with Annex B, paragraphs 5–8, 10 (for more information on the notification requirements of the SPS Agreement, see Scott, above n 42 at 197–207). According to the Director General of the WTO, Pascal Lamy, only in the area of trade in goods there are currently more than 175 notification requirements. Pascal Lamy, 'Evolving Trade Increases Need for "Active Transparency"', 22 October 2007, Speech given at the Georgetown University Law Center, available at <http://www.wto.org/english/news_e/sppl_e/sppl78_e.htm> (accessed 20 May 2009).

[272] See also Article XVII:4(b) of the GATT.

[273] In this regard, see Lamy, above n 271.

conducted by individual Members on their own or by the whole Membership in the different committees created by the agreements such as the Committee on Sanitary and Phytosanitary Measures,[274] the Committee on Subsidies and Countervailing Measures,[275] and the Committee on Agriculture.[276] The committees review notifications and examine any other issues regarding the implementation of the corresponding agreements brought to their attention by the WTO Membership.[277] Article 25.9 of the SCM Agreement constitutes an example of the latter kind of activity; it provides that if upon request a Member does not make available certain information, the Member requesting the information may bring the matter to the attention of the Committee on Subsidies and Countervailing Measures. Even where a specific provision similar to Article 25.9 does not exist, the right of Members to raise questions and request information at the committees regarding the implementation of WTO obligations by other Members is unquestionable. Such right flows from the transparency obligations contained in the agreements and is supported by established practice. The process of surveillance thus yields information on the measures adopted by Members.

It is also important to note that apart from their monitoring and surveillance functions, some of the committees have also been assigned a more formal role in resolving potential and actual disputes between Members. For instance, Articles XII:4 and XVIII:12 of the GATT together with paragraph 5 of the Understanding on the Balance-of-Payments Provisions of the General Agreement on Tariffs and Trade 1994 ('Balance-of-Payments Understanding') entrust the Committee on Balance-of-Payments Restrictions with the task of carrying out consultations with any Member imposing restrictive import measures for balance-of-payments purposes. Paragraph 5 of the Balance-of-Payments Understanding requires Members imposing balance-of-payments restrictions to enter into 'consultations with the Committee within four months of the adoption of such measures'. Articles XII:4(d) and XVIII:4(d) of the GATT provide that consultations may also be undertaken on the request of a Member that can provide evidence that another Member is applying restrictions that are inconsistent with the balance-of-payments provisions and that its trade is adversely affected thereby. Consultations are conducted on the basis of a basic document submitted by the Member adopting restrictive measures,[278] a factual background paper prepared by the WTO Secretariat,[279] and material supplied by the

[274] Article 12 of the SPS Agreement.

[275] Article 24 of the SCM Agreement.

[276] Article 17 of the Agreement on Agriculture.

[277] See, for instance, Article 26 of the SCM Agreement, Article 12.4 of the SPS Agreement, Article 18 of the Agreement on Agriculture, Article 13 of the Agreement on Safeguards, Article V:7(a) of the GATS, Articles 16 and 18.6 of the Anti-Dumping Agreement, Articles 13 and 15.2–15.3 of the TBT Agreement.

[278] Paragraph 11 of the Balance-of-Payments Understanding.

[279] Paragraph 12 of the Balance-of-Payments Understanding.

IMF.[280] If the Committee concludes that the restrictions are not consistent with Article XII or Section B of Article XVIII of the GATT, it must 'indicate the nature of the inconsistency and *may* advise that the restrictions be suitably modified'.[281] If the inconsistency is of a serious nature and it is found to cause or threaten to cause damage to the trade of any Member, the Committee *shall* make appropriate recommendations for securing conformity.[282] Moreover, when consultations are undertaken pursuant to Articles XII:4(d) and XVIII:4(d) of the GATT, the Committee *shall* recommend the withdrawal or modification of the restrictions if the inconsistent restrictions are found to cause or threaten to cause damage to the trade of the Member which initiated the consultations. According to paragraph 13 of the Balance-of-Payments Understanding, the Committee must produce a report to the General Council indicating its conclusions 'as well as the facts and reasons on which they are based'. Importantly, because the Committee operates under the consensus rule, all Members including the Member imposing the restrictions must agree on the conclusions of the Committee.[283] If consensus cannot be reached, consultations will end without agreed conclusions. In this case, the Committee will present a report to the General Council explaining the main points discussed during the consultations.

Notably, this role of the Committee in resolving potential and actual disputes between Members does not exclude action under the dispute settlement procedures of the DSU.[284] Moreover, nothing precludes relevant information collected during the balance-of-payments consultations from being produced and considered in panel proceedings under the DSU. Nor do the agreements indicate that panels have an obligation to give special deference to the findings of the Committee.[285] Panels can thus freely evaluate information originating from the consultation process. Accordingly, in the event that a complaint is brought under the DSU, the consultation process before the Committee may turn out to be a valuable source of information.

[280] Paragraphs 8 and 9 of the Procedures and Arrangement for Regular Consultations on Balance-of-Payments Import Restrictions, L/3388, 27 April 1970 (BISD 18S/48-53).

Simplified procedures may apply to consultations involving least-developed countries and, under certain circumstances, developing countries. See Paragraph 8 of the Balance-of-Payments Understanding.

[281] Articles XII:4(c)(i) and XVIII:4(c)(i) of the GATT. [emphasis added]

[282] Articles XII:4(c)(ii) and XVIII:4(c)(ii) of the GATT.

[283] See Technical Information on Balance of Payments, available at <http://www.wto.org/english/tratop_e/bop_e/bop_info_e.htm> (accessed 20 May 2009); Oesch, above n 20 at 37.

[284] According to footnote 1 of the Balance-of-Payments Understanding: 'The provisions of Articles XXII and XXIII of GATT 1994 as elaborated and applied by the Dispute Settlement Understanding may be invoked with respect to any matters arising from the application of restrictive import measures taken for balance-of-payments purposes.' See also Appellate Body Report, *India—Quantitative Restrictions on Imports of Agricultural, Textile and Industrial Products*, WT/DS90/AB/R, adopted 22 September 1999, DSR 1999:IV, 1763 at paras 80–109.

[285] In support of this view, see Oesch, above n 20 at 39–40.

In sum, one of the main objectives of the transparency obligations and related surveillance mechanisms is to ensure compliance with the WTO obligations, which is also one of the objectives of the dispute settlement system.[286] Transparency obligations and related surveillance mechanisms may in fact reduce the need for recourse to the dispute settlement system.[287] When this ideal is not achieved, they nonetheless produce valuable information which may then be used in the panel process.[288] In *EC—Sardines*, the Appellate Body stressed that the transparency obligations contained in the TBT Agreement—Article 2.5 provides for a clarification obligation and Article 10 refers to enquiry point obligations—afford potential complainants opportunities to obtain information about technical regulations which may then be used in dispute settlement.[289]

Examples of cases where information derived from the transparency obligations and related surveillance mechanisms was introduced into evidence include *Brazil—Aircraft*, where Canada referred to Brazil's response to questions posed at the Committee on Subsidies and Countervailing Measures to support its allegation that PROEX provided financing for Brazilian exports rather than for sales in the domestic market,[290] and where Brazil noted that its notifications under Article 25 of the SCM Agreement contained information that was relevant to the question of whether it was in compliance with its obligations under Article 27.4 of the SCM Agreement.[291] Information contained in notifications was also presented by the complainants and relied upon by the panel in *EC—Export Subsidies on Sugar*, where the European Communities was found to be exporting sugar in quantities exceeding its commitment level.[292] While in these and many other cases the parties were able to refer in panel proceedings to information which was made available through transparency obligations and the operation of surveillance mechanisms, in other instances non-compliance with the transparency obligations denied the claimants the same opportunity. The

[286] It is worth noting that the GATT predecessor of the DSU addressed not only formal dispute settlement, but also notifications and surveillance. See *Understanding Regarding Notification, Consultation, Dispute Settlement and Surveillance*, L/4907, adopted n 28 November 1979, GATT, BISD 26 Supp. 210 (1980).

[287] Pascal Lamy reports two instances where potential disputes were resolved through committee surveillance, one involving a German piece of legislation limiting residues of sulphur dioxide in cinnamon which prevented Sri Lanka from exporting cinnamon to Germany, and another involving a Swiss draft ordinance concerning measures to reduce particle emissions from diesel engines. Pascal Lamy, above n 271.

[288] As noted below, information produced specifically for the TPRM constitutes an exception to this rule.

[289] Appellate Body Report, *European Communities—Trade Description of Sardines*, WT/DS231/AB/R, adopted 23 October 2002, DSR 2002:VIII, 3359 at paras 277, 279.

[290] Panel Report, *Brazil—Aircraft*, above n 239 at para 4.50.

[291] Appellate Body Report, *Brazil—Export Financing Programme for Aircraft*, WT/DS46/AB/R, adopted 20 August 1999, DSR 1999:III, 1161 at para 66.

[292] Panel Report, *EC—Export Subsidies on Sugar (Brazil)*, above n 219 at paras 4.28, 7.230 and footnote 531. For examples on the different question of how work undertaken in the Committees may influence the *interpretation* of WTO rules by panels, see Scott, above n 42 at 72–3.

lack of notification pursuant to Article 25 of the SCM Agreement of certain subsidy programmes and incomplete notification of others was noted, for instance, by the complainant (Brazil) and the panel in *Canada—Aircraft*.[293] The panel acknowledged in that case the fact that absence of or incomplete notification of subsidy programmes may make it difficult for complainants to obtain the information necessary to support their cases against export subsidies.

ii. Consequences of failure to comply with transparency obligations. Accordingly, the non-observance of the transparency obligations not only affects the WTO Members' understanding of other members' measures and the promotion of voluntary or negotiated compliance, but also has the potential to disrupt the smooth development of the panel process under the DSU. If the WTO is to yield full benefits to Members and their constituencies, it is thus necessary that Members observe their transparency obligations. As is the case with any treaty obligation, transparency obligations are governed by the principle of *pacta sunt servanda* which provides that '[e]very treaty in force is binding upon the parties to it and must be performed by them in good faith'.[294] Members are therefore under an obligation to cooperate in good faith to provide information on their measures either upon request or voluntarily through publication and notification of such measures.

What can be done when Members do not comply with their transparency obligations? A Member can always request the establishment of a panel to determine whether another Member has not complied with its transparency obligations as provided for in the WTO agreements. Such course of action is, however, burdensome and likely to produce unsatisfactory results. The design of the DSU is not well-suited for this type of complaint: first, the time frame of the proceedings is too long and the structure too costly for what are likely to be straightforward claims; second, if a violation is found and the responding Member chooses not to provide the information, the complainant will probably be left without an effective remedy since the criteria for imposition of countermeasures under Article 22 of the DSU are not readily applicable to this kind of violation. Moreover, when information which should have been made available pursuant to transparency obligations is to be used in panel proceedings, it would be unreasonable to require Members to first bring a case for violation of the transparency obligations. The latter situation—ie when the information may eventually be relevant for dispute settlement under the DSU—is particularly relevant to the subject of this book.[295] The best solution to the problem that it

[293] Panel Report, *Canada—Aircraft*, above n 136 at para 4.104, 9.53.

[294] Article 26 of the Vienna Convention on the Law of Treaties. The Appellate Body linked this principle to the transparency obligations in Appellate Body Report, *EC—Sardines*, above n 289 at para 278.

[295] The importance of ensuring compliance with transparency obligations transcends its impact on dispute settlement. Accordingly, more elaborate measures than the ones discussed here may be required to induce Members to comply. On the importance of transparency and the need to create

presents is to establish a link between a failure to provide information pursuant to a transparency obligation and the dispute settlement proceedings for which such information would be relevant.

One option worthy of consideration is to allocate to the defendant the burden of proving—that is to say that the defendant would lose if no or insufficient information is placed on the record—the consistency of its measure with certain obligations upon a showing by the complainant that the defendant failed to comply with a related transparency obligation. This would work in a similar fashion to Article 10.3 of the Agreement on Agriculture.[296] While it would normally be for the complainant to prove that the defendant is providing export subsidies, under Article 10.3, after the complainant has proven that the defendant has exported an agricultural product in quantities that exceed its quantity commitment level recorded in its Schedule, the defendant must prove that no export subsidies have been granted in respect of the excess quantity exported.

Given the facts that the transparency obligations are extensive[297] and that their particular scopes are not always well-defined,[298] a general rule requiring defendants to bear the burden of proof with respect to claims regarding all measures or aspects of measures which are the subject of a transparency obligation with which the defendant failed to comply would have far-reaching consequences. Such a sweeping rule would seem to require the express assent of Members, which is not currently found in the text of the agreements. This view seems to be supported by the Appellate Body. In the context of an appeal regarding the allocation of the burden of proof in proceedings under the SPS

incentives to encourage Members to comply with their transparency obligations, see Lamy, above n 271 (Lamy mentions, for example, a proposal which 'would call for the Secretariat to submit notifications based on best information available for discussion among Members and eventually for a rebuttal by the Member concerned' and a proposal which 'would prohibit Members from taking certain actions in the absence of notifications'). See also Doha Work Programme, *Decision Adopted by the General Council on 1 August 2004, Annex A—Framework for Establishing Modalities in Agriculture*, WTO Doc WT/L/579, 2 August 2004, at paras 19, 48 (referring to the objective of establishing effective transparency provisions and enhancing monitoring); Cairns Group Proposal, *Improving Monitoring and Surveillance, Communication to the Committee on Agriculture Special Session*, 12 June 2007, JOB(07)/88, available at <http://www.cairnsgroup.org/proposals/070614_doc_07_88.pdf> (accessed 20 May 2009).

[296] According to Article 10.3 '[a]ny Member which claims that any quantity exported in excess of a reduction commitment level is not subsidized must establish that no export subsidy, whether listed in Article 9 or not, has been granted in respect of the quantity of exports in question'. For further details on Article 10.3, see Chapter 4 and Appellate Body Report, *Canada—Measures Affecting the Importation of Milk and the Exportation of Dairy Products—Second Recourse to Article 21.5 of the DSU by New Zealand and the United States*, WT/DS103/AB/RW2, WT/DS113/AB/RW2, adopted 17 January 2003, DSR 2003:I, 213 at paras 69–75.

[297] According to Lamy, only in the area of trade in goods there are currently more than 175 notification requirements. Pascal Lamy, above n 271.

[298] See, for example, Article 18.2 of the Agreement on Agriculture which provides that:

'The review process shall be undertaken on the basis of notifications submitted by Members in relation to such matters and at such intervals as shall be determined, as well as on the basis of such documentation as the Secretariat may be requested to prepare in order to facilitate the review process.'

Agreement, the Appellate Body ruled that 'Article 5.8 of the *SPS Agreement* does not purport to address burden of proof problems'.[299] According to the WTO Director General, Pascal Lamy, the idea of requiring Members which fail to notify their measures to bear the burden of proof in dispute settlement has been floated in the current Doha Round of Trade Negotiations.[300] This idea can perhaps be usefully employed in specific areas where Members have been reluctant to notify their measures and where information is otherwise not accessible (or not accessible through reasonable efforts) to other Members. Particularly in the case of notifications, it is important to note that many Members still do not notify their measures because of lack of knowledge about what needs to be notified and scarcity of resources to devote to the notification process.

While a reversal of the allocation of the burden of proof should be a matter to be considered by WTO Members in negotiations, there are other ways in which panels may take into account a failure to provide information pursuant to a transparency obligation. Admittedly, it may be difficult for panels to attach specific consequences to failures to provide information pursuant to transparency obligations which are broad in scope. However, when a transparency obligation is sufficiently specific and an allegation in dispute settlement is directly related to information which should be made available pursuant to that transparency obligation, panels can take a failure to provide that information into account in making their findings. Article 5.8 of the SPS Agreement can be used as an illustration. According to Article 5.8:

> When a Member has reason to believe that a specific sanitary or phytosanitary measure introduced or maintained by another Member is constraining, or has the potential to constrain, its exports and the measure is not based on the relevant international standards, guidelines or recommendations, or such standards, guidelines or recommendations do not exist, an explanation of the reasons for such sanitary or phytosanitary measure may be requested and shall be provided by the Member maintaining the measure.

The example involves claims under Articles 3.1, 3.3, and 5.1 of the SPS Agreement that the respondent has adopted an SPS measure which is not based on an existing international standard and that such measure is not scientifically justified and/or based on a risk assessment. Assuming that the claimant demonstrates to the panel that pursuant to Article 5.8 of the SPS Agreement it requested the respondent to describe the scientific justification of its measure and the respondent did not answer or provided an incomplete response, the panel could draw inferences against the respondent from such behaviour. Because the idea is not to sanction the respondent for not complying with Article 5.8 of the SPS Agreement but rather to encourage the respondent to

[299] Appellate Body Report, *EC—Hormones*, above n 42 at para 102.
[300] Lamy, above n 271.

cooperate, no such inferences should be drawn if the respondent provides the requested information during the panel process. The difference between this situation and the normal circumstances (discussed above in Section II.B.4.1) under which panels are authorized to draw adverse inferences would be that inferences could be drawn even when the respondent did not have exclusive or preferential access to the information requested. This would be so because Article 5.8 imposes a specific obligation on the respondent to make the information available to the claimant upon request. Such solution would be in line with the procedural duty of the parties to cooperate in providing information to the panel and yet it would also take into consideration the substantive obligation to provide information contained in Article 5.8. In addition, providing a role for Article 5.8 in proceedings under the DSU may encourage Members to be forthcoming from the early stages of a dispute and potentially avoid the need for the panel process.

The statement of the Appellate Body in *EC—Hormones* that 'Article 5.8 of the *SPS Agreement* does not purport to address burden of proof problems' should be understood to refer to the allocation of the burden of proof rather than the proposal made here.[301] In fact, in *Japan—Agricultural Products II*, the Appellate Body indicated that a failure by the respondent to 'bring forward scientific studies or reports in support of its [measure]' in response to a request for information under Article 5.8 of the SPS Agreement would constitute 'strong indication that there are no such studies or reports'.[302] The Appellate Body did not make clear whether in its view this failure alone would constitute enough evidence to justify a finding against the respondent. According to the proposal made here, as is the case with other inferences, this failure alone should not be sufficient to justify a ruling against the respondent. That is to say, the inference should be drawn in the light of the other evidence on the record.[303] Otherwise, in most cases the burden of proof would be effectively allocated to the respondent.

iii. The Trade Policy Review Mechanism. The Trade Policy Review Mechanism ('TPRM') also performs an important role in monitoring compliance with the WTO obligations. The stated objective of the TPRM 'is to contribute to improved adherence by all Members to rules, disciplines and commitments' made under the WTO agreements while allowing 'collective appreciation and evaluation of the full range of individual Members' trade policies and practices and their impact on the functioning of the multilateral trading system'.[304] The TPRM essentially allows for peer review of a Member's trade policies and

[301] Appellate Body Report,*EC—Hormones*, above n 42 at para 102.

[302] Appellate Body Report, *Japan—Measures Affecting Agricultural Products*, WT/DS76/AB/R, adopted 19 March 1999, DSR 1999:I, 277 at para 137.

[303] In *Japan—Agricultural Products II*, the Appellate Body noted, for example, that the complainant could also submit an expert opinion attesting that there are no relevant scientific studies or reports. Appellate Body Report, *Japan—Agricultural Products II*, above n 302 at para 137.

[304] Paragraph A(i) of the Trade Policy Review Mechanism.

practices based on reports prepared by the reviewed Member and the WTO Secretariat. In preparing its report, the WTO Secretariat can seek clarification of the reviewed Member's trade policies and practices.[305] Accordingly, the process of reviewing the trade policies and practices of Members under the TPRM has the potential to produce valuable information on those policies and practices. The TPRM makes clear, however, that it is not 'intended to serve as a basis for the enforcement of specific obligations under the Agreements or for dispute settlement procedures'.[306] This precludes Members from introducing into evidence in dispute settlement proceedings information produced specifically for the TPRM which is the case of the reports submitted by the reviewed Member and the Secretariat, and the minutes of the meetings of the Trade Policy Review Body. In this regard, in *Canada—Aircraft*, the panel refused to consider references to the 1998 Trade Policy Review of Canada made by Brazil in support of some of its allegations.[307]

The reason for not permitting Members to introduce such information into evidence is to encourage a dialogue among Members on their policies and practices which allows Members to become acquainted with each other's policies and practices, and to promote voluntary compliance with the WTO agreements. The privilege, however, should not be interpreted so as to shield all information referenced during the trade policy review, that is, Members should still be able to use information referenced in the review which is otherwise available. Moreover, the information exchange which takes place during the review of the trade policies and practices of a Member will inevitably allow other Members to identify potential problems and work for their resolution on a bilateral basis, in the committees, or in formal dispute settlement. This is in accordance with the ultimate objective of the mechanism, namely, to improve adherence by all Members to rules, disciplines and commitments undertaken in the agreements.

iv. A role for private parties? The process of monitoring and ensuring compliance with the WTO obligations, including the dispute settlement stage of this process, could be strengthened through the creation of a mechanism which would allow private parties (or, as a matter of fact, any entity) to have access to information in the possession of government departments related to the implementation of a Member's WTO obligations. Trade-restrictive measures tend to more immediately affect the interests of private parties—which are as a general rule the ones directly engaged in international trade—than governments. Private parties have, accordingly, a strong interest in ensuring that WTO Members comply with their obligations. The incentive which private parties have to monitor compliance should, therefore, be taken advantage of. This is not to argue that private parties should be given direct access to the WTO dispute

[305] Paragraph C(v)(b) of the Trade Policy Review Mechanism.
[306] Paragraph A(i) of the Trade Policy Review Mechanism.
[307] Panel Report, *Canada—Aircraft*, above n 136 at para 9.274.

settlement system. To the contrary, the idea would be to give private parties a role in monitoring implementation allowing them to bring informed complaints to their governments which would maintain their prerogative to decide whether to pursue the issue in WTO committees and/or through an action under the DSU.

Some WTO Members have in fact created certain mechanisms giving their private sector a role in the process of monitoring compliance. This is the case, for instance, of Section 301 of the Trade Act of 1974[308] in the United States, and the Trade Barriers Regulation[309] in the European Union. Those legal instruments allow private parties to petition their governments to conduct an investigation of an alleged violation of the WTO agreements.[310] In other words, Section 301 and the Trade Barriers Regulation provide a channel for private parties to bring complaints related to the implementation of the WTO agreements and to participate in the preparation of an eventual formal complaint before the WTO against the trade-restricting WTO Member.

However, given the entirely domestic nature of those instruments, they do not and could not grant private parties the right to access information in the possession of a foreign government. Accordingly, unless the domestic legislation of the trade-restricting WTO Member provides private parties access to information held by government departments, private parties may not be able to access information which may be necessary to determine whether the WTO Member in question is complying with its WTO obligations. In short, instruments such as Section 301 cannot impose an obligation on foreign government departments to provide information in their possession; without such information, however, private parties may not be able to effectively monitor compliance with WTO obligations.

The proposal advanced here is of a different nature, but nevertheless complementary to legal instruments such as Section 301 and the Trade Barriers Regulation. The idea would be to integrate private parties in the process of monitoring compliance with the WTO agreements by providing them with the means to access information in the possession of a WTO Member government relating to the implementation of its WTO obligations. In order to implement such idea, rules should be negotiated that would create an obligation for WTO Members to (i) guarantee private parties from WTO Members access to enquiry points such as that foreseen in Annex B of the SPS Agreement,[311] and (ii) create

[308] Chapter 12, subchapter III, of title 19 of the United States Code (USC).

[309] Council Regulation No 3286/94, published in OJ L349, 31.12.1994 last amended by Regulation (EC) No 356/95, 20.02.1995 published in OJ L41, 23.02.1995.

[310] For a discussion of the basic features of the Trade Barriers Regulation and Section 301, see Petros C Mavroidis & Werner Zdouc, 'Legal Means to Protect Private Parties' Interests in the WTO. The Case of the EC New Trade Barriers Regulation' (1998) 1:3 Journal of International Economic Law 407.

[311] Currently Annex B of the SPS Agreement refers to enquiries from 'Members'. Article 10 of the TBT Agreement, however, refers to 'enquiries from other Members and *interested parties* in other Members'. [emphasis added]

and implement domestic legislation allowing private parties to have access to information related to the implementation of WTO obligations held by government departments. In both cases, private parties should be guaranteed access to a review procedure before a domestic court in case their request for information is ignored, wrongfully refused, or inadequately answered.

Some WTO Members already have in place broad-ranging freedom of information legislation allowing access to information held by government bodies. An example of such legislation is the United States Freedom of Information Act, and it is worth noting that information collected under that Act has been used in WTO dispute settlement.[312] In fact, the right to access information held by public bodies has been recognized as a fundamental human right, and has been actively promoted in different countries and fora in recent years.[313] According to a report released in 2006 by Transparency International, 65 laws have been adopted globally, 50 of which were adopted after 1990.[314] This number indicates a growing interest in freedom of information legislation, but it also shows that the majority of WTO Members do not have legislation in place. While initiatives to promote broad-ranging freedom of information legislation merit support given the role of such legislation in holding governments accountable to their people, the WTO is likely not the appropriate forum to promote such broad legislation. The WTO obligations could, therefore, be limited to requiring creation of a framework which would allow access to information directly related to the implementation of WTO obligations.

The Convention on Access to Information, Public Participation in Decision-Making and Access to Justice in Environmental Matters (the 'Aarhus Convention'),[315] which is also focused on access to a specific category of information, ie environmental information, could serve as an initial model for future negotiations on access to information obligations within the ambit of the WTO. The Aarhus Convention requires the states parties to ensure that, when requested, public authorities make environmental information available to the public.[316] According to the Convention, the requesting entity is not required to state an interest in its request.[317] Strict deadlines are set for the public authorities to consider a request and accept or reject it *in toto* or partially.[318] Articles 4.3 and 4.4 of the Convention state the grounds under which a request for information may be refused; these include a request which is 'formulated in too general a manner', and a request regarding information the disclosure of which would

[312] See, for example, Panel Report, *US—Upland Cotton*, above n 111 at paras 6.624, 7.21.

[313] Toby Mendel, *Freedom of Information: a Comparative Legal Survey* (New Delhi: UNESCO, 2003) at iii, 1.

[314] *Using the Right to Information as an Anti-Corruption Tool* (Berlin: Transparency International, 2006) at 3.

[315] Adopted at Aarhus, Denmark, on 25 June 1998; entered into force on 30 October 2001. Available at <http://www.unece.org/env/pp/documents/cep43e.pdf> (accessed 20 May 2009).

[316] Article 4.1. [317] Article 4.1(a). [318] Articles 4.2 and 4.7.

adversely affect the 'confidentiality of personal data and/or files'. The Convention also provides that the public authority must state the reasons behind a refusal.[319] Finally, it requires states parties to guarantee the requesting entity access to a review procedure before an independent and impartial body.[320]

C. The role of the panel

1. The basis for an active panel

Section B of this chapter discussed the duty of the parties to cooperate in presenting arguments and evidence with respect to the claims in question with a view to helping the panel to properly establish the facts and apply the law. This section, in contrast, examines the role of the panel in the process of ascertaining the facts for the proper application of the WTO agreements.

As noted in Section A of this chapter, the facts (i) that the panel is composed of experts in the field who are in charge of deciding questions of fact and law and (ii) that the taking and presentation of evidence is divided into several episodes, enable panels to participate actively in and shape the process of fact-finding. It was also noted that not only are panels in a position to play an active role in the process of fact-finding, but that they have in fact been granted the authority to do so. Article 13 of the DSU makes express provision for an active/investigative panel, giving the proceedings a hybrid inquisitorial-adversarial character. According to Article 13 of the DSU:

> 1 Each panel shall have the right to seek information and technical advice from any individual or body which it deems appropriate. [...] A Member should respond promptly and fully to any request by a panel for such information as the panel considers necessary and appropriate. [...]
>
> 2 Panels may seek information from any relevant source and may consult experts to obtain their opinion on certain aspects of the matter. With respect to a factual issue concerning a scientific or other technical matter raised by a party to a dispute, a panel may request an advisory report in writing from an expert review group. Rules for the establishment of such a group and its procedures are set forth in Appendix 4.

Similar authority has been granted to other international courts and tribunals following the model adopted in civilian jurisdictions where judges play an active role in the process of gathering information 'with the aim of having all the relevant evidence available actually presented'.[321] For instance, Articles 49 and

[319] Article 4.7. [320] Article 9.

[321] Michele Taruffo, 'Principles and Rules of Transnational Civil Procedure: an Evidentiary Epistemology' (2006) 25:2 Penn State International Law Review 509 at 512. See also John H Langbein, 'Legal Institutions: Trashing the German Advantage' (1988) 82 Northwestern University Law Review 763 at 769; P Oberhammer & T Domej, 'Germany, Switzerland, Austria (CA.

50 of the Statute of the ICJ provide that the court may 'call upon the agents to produce any document or to supply any explanations' and 'entrust any individual, body, bureau, commission, or other organization that it may select, with the task of carrying out an enquiry or giving an expert opinion'.[322] According to Article 43 of the Convention on the Settlement of Investment Disputes between States and Nationals of other States (the 'ICSID Convention') and Article 34.2 of the ICSID Arbitration Rules, the tribunal may, 'if it deems it necessary at any stage of the proceedings', 'call upon the parties to produce documents' or other evidence and visit places connected with the dispute and conduct inquiries there. Articles 68 and 69 of the 1907 Convention for the Pacific Settlement of International Disputes establish that the tribunal has the right to request the production of papers or documents and demand all necessary explanations. Articles 24.3 and 27.1 of the UNCITRAL Arbitration Rules, which are also part of the Tribunal Rules of Procedure of the Iran–United States Claims Tribunal, provide that the tribunal may 'require the parties to produce documents, exhibits or other evidence' and 'appoint one or more experts to report to it, in writing, on specific issues to be determined by the tribunal'.[323] In fact, the authority of international tribunals to seek information is considered inherent in the adjudicative function of those tribunals.[324] As several commentators have noted, international tribunals have in fact taken the initiative to order the production of evidence and, more broadly, investigate facts which are not clear.[325]

1800–2005)' in CH van Rhee (ed), *European Traditions in Civil Procedure* (Antwerpen: Intersentia, 2005) 103 at 300; Joelle Godard, 'Fact-Finding: a French Perspective' in DLC Miller & PR Beaumont (eds), *The Option of Litigating in Europe* (London: United Kingdom National Committee of Comparative Law, 1993) vol 14, 57 at 61; Gottwald, above n 107 at 61. See also French Code of Civil Procedure, Article 10; German Code of Civil Procedure, Article 139; Brazilian Code of Civil Procedure, Articles 130, 342, 355, 399, 418, 437, 440.

[322] Discussing the authority of the ICJ to seek information, see Andrés Aguilar Mawdsley, 'Evidence before the International Court of Justice' in RSJ Macdonald (ed), *Essays in Honor of Wang Tieya* (Dordrecht: Martinus Nijhoff, 1994) 533 at 535, 548; Riddell & Plant, above n 84 at 56–78.

[323] See also Article 24 of the Statute of the Court of Justice of the European Communities; Article 20 of the ICC Arbitration Rules; Principles 22.2.2 and 22.4 of the ALI/UNIDROIT Principles of Transnational Civil Procedure and Rules 22.2, 25.5, and 28.3 of the ALI/UNIDROIT Rules of Transnational Civil Procedure. Discussing the authority of international tribunals to seek information, see Amerasinghe, *Evidence in International Litigation*, above n 82 at 148–152; Mani, above n 82 at 212.

[324] Amerasinghe, *Evidence in International Litigation*, above n 82 at 152; Kazazi, above n 84 at 166. See also Sandifer, above n 84 at 108 (noting that the view that international tribunals have limited authority 'to require the production of further evidence, so far as it may be available, is not generally accepted.'); Hans Smit, 'Roles of the Arbitral Tribunal in Civil Law and Common Law Systems with Respect to Presentation of Evidence' in AJ van den Berg (ed), *Planning Efficient Arbitration Proceedings: The Law Applicable in International Arbitration* (The Hague: Kluwer Law International, 1996) 161 at 165–6 (referring to arbitral tribunals in general including those adjudicating disputes exclusively between private parties).

[325] See John Crook, 'Fact-Finding in the Fog: Determining the Facts of Upheavals and Wars in Inter-State Disputes' in R Alford & C Rogers (eds), *The Future of Investment Arbitration* (Oxford: Oxford University Press, 2009) forthcoming (referring to investment tribunals); Howard M

Importantly, commentators have called for more active international adjudicators rather than more passive ones.[326] Why is this so? There are several reasons to support active international adjudicators—including WTO panels—that seek to elucidate the facts by requesting production of evidence, discussing the case with the parties, and asking questions: (1) efficiency; (2) accurate outcomes; (3) the absence of exclusionary rules of evidence; (4) the parties' diverse legal background and approaches to presenting evidence; (5) real equality of the parties; (6) good faith cooperation. These reasons are explored in further detail in the next few paragraphs.

An active panel can make adjudication more efficient in that as the neutral figure which will ultimately decide the case the panel knows (or should seek to identify) which issues will be the most important in resolving the dispute.[327] It can therefore narrow the inquiry and indicate to the parties the areas where they should focus. Moreover, the fact that the WTO agreements are relatively new and that many obligations have not yet been clarified may make it more difficult for the parties to know what kind of information to present to the panel in support of their cases. In such circumstances, the parties are likely to benefit from the panel's guidance concerning what it expects.[328] In the absence of such guidance from the panel, some parties may produce scores of irrelevant information, that is, their fear of losing the case may lead the parties to overproduce

Holtzmann, 'Streamlining Arbitral Proceedings: Some Techniques of the Iran-United States Claims Tribunal' (1995) 11:1 Arbitration International 39 at 44 (referring to the Iran-United States Claims Tribunal); Howard M Holtzmann, 'Fact-Finding by the Iran–United States Claims Tribunal' in RB Lillich (ed), *Fact-Finding before International Tribunals* (Ardsley-on-Hudson: Transnational Publishers, 1992) 101 at 109–10 (referring to the Iran–United States Claims Tribunal); Sandifer, above n 84 at 156–160 (referring to international tribunals in general and particularly the Permanent Court of International Justice);Kazazi, above n 84 at 34–5.

[326] See Sandifer, above n 84 at 162–3, 460–1 (arguing that 'Tribunals should be given expanded authority to obtain evidence, if necessary, through their own resources.'); Keith Highet, 'Evidence and Proof of Facts' in LF Damrosch (ed), *The International Court of Justice at a Crossroads* (New York: Transnational Publishers, 1987) 355 at 371 (referring to the ICJ); Holtzmann, *Fact-Finding by the Iran-United States Claims Tribunal*, above n 325 at 132; Crook, above n 325; Ruth Teitelbaum, 'Recent Fact-Finding Developments at the International Court of Justice' (2007) 6 The Law and Practice of International Courts and Tribunals 119 at 152, 157–8; Riddell & Plant, above n 84 at 70–4, 76–7 (referring to the ICJ). Suggesting active adjudicators in the context of international commercial arbitration, see Matti S Kurkela, *Due Process in International Commercial Arbitration* (Dobbs Ferry: Oceana Publications, 2005) at 44–5, 124–6; Holtzmann, *Streamlining Arbitral Proceedings*, above n 325 at 46 (referring to the English arbitration legislation); ICC Commission on Arbitration, *Techniques for Controlling Time and Costs in Arbitration* (Paris: International Chamber of Commerce, 2007) at paras 31–3.

[327] In support of the view that an active adjudicator can make the process of adjudication more efficient, see Redfern et al, above n 68 at 320–1; Derains & Schwartz, above n 147 at 270–1; Mauro Cappelletti, *The Judicial Process in Comparative Perspective* (Oxford: Clarendon Press, 1989) at 252; Gillian Hadfield, 'The Levers of Legal Design: Institutional Determinants of the Quality of Law' (May 2007) USC Legal Studies Research Paper No 07-6 at 20; ICC Commission on Arbitration, above n 326 at paras 31–3.

[328] Noting that the parties to international litigation are likely to benefit from the adjudicator's guidance, see Holtzmann, *Fact-Finding by the Iran–United States Claims Tribunal*, above n 325 at 132; Redfern et al, above n 68 at 320–1.

evidence. Overproduction is costly not only to the parties but also to the panel who will have to sift through and make sense of the information. Accordingly, an active panel can streamline the procedures and reduce the amount of information presented to an optimum.

Relatedly, an active panel can potentially render more accurate decisions. In this respect, it is important to note first that fact-finding is a quest for knowledge and that for such a quest to be effective it must involve the knowledge-seeker, that is, the adjudicator. Such involvement approximates the 'cognitive stance of individuals who make factual inquiries in everyday life. [...] people are in the habit of actively taking part in obtaining knowledge about facts on which their decisions turn'.[329] Moreover, although we have no means of knowing when a decision is correct, as Jolowicz notes, it would 'be extremely odd to describe as "correct" a decision that the judge suspects—or actually knows—to be wrong because he was deprived of information he considered to be relevant'.[330] Similarly, Walker argues that 'having an actual belief seems to be psychologically and logically necessary for having human knowledge'.[331] Therefore, a panel is not justified in finding that a certain proposition is more likely than not true unless the panel actually believes that that is the case.[332] In addition, because any rational fact-finding activity aspires to neutrality, the active participation of the panel ensures that fact-finding in the context of WTO dispute settlement is closer to the demands of dispassionate and rational inquiry—ie the panel is a neutral figure in an otherwise polarized process.[333]

The active involvement of the panel should not mean, however, that the panel is the only actor in the fact-finding enterprise. To the contrary, as in any hybrid inquisitorial-adversarial system, the parties are still required to present information to the panel. The system recognizes that the parties are the most

[329] Mirjan R Damaska, *Evidence Law Adrift* (New Haven: Yale University Press, 1997) at 90.

[330] JA Jolowicz, 'Adversarial and Inquisitorial Models of Civil Procedure' (2003) 52 International and Comparative Law Quarterly 281 at 288.

[331] Walker, *Preponderance, Probability and Warranted Factfinding*, above n 191 at 1091–2.

[332] This contrasts with traditional common law adversarial proceedings where the judge acts as a neutral umpire who simply chooses between the different versions of the facts laid before him by the parties. In this system, the goal of achieving accurate outcomes is secondary. In this regard, see Hazard Jr, above n 75 at 1019; DJ Galligan, *Due Process and Fair Procedures: a Study of Administrative Procedures* (Oxford: Clarendon Press, 1996) at 244–5; EW Thomas, *The Judicial Process: Realism, Pragmatism, Practical Reasoning and Principles* (Cambridge: Cambridge University Press, 2005) at 327; Jolowicz, *Adversarial and Inquisitorial Models*, above n 330 at 286, 288). Moreover, Jolowicz notes that in the traditional common law adversarial proceedings 'it was regarded as a positive advantage that the judge should enter the court-room wholly ignorant of the case he was about to hear'. He notes that at least in England this view is changing. Judges have began to show dissatisfaction 'with the idea that the truth has really very little to do with the solution of litigation if the parties themselves do not wish the truth to be revealed. Not all judges are content to see themselves as mere umpires, still less as photo-electric cells set up to detect the winner of a kind of game.' JA Jolowicz, 'Fact-Finding: a Comparative Perspective' in DLC Miller & PR Beaumont (eds), *The Option of Litigating in Europe* (London: United Kingdom National Committee of Comparative Law, 1993) vol 14, 133 at 142, 146.

[333] See Damaska, above n 329 at 101–2.

important source of information because their involvement in the circumstances which gave rise to the dispute has given them first hand knowledge about some of the facts in dispute. Moreover, their interest in the dispute motivates them to search for information. At the same time, because of their interest in the outcome of the dispute, the parties have little incentive to present information which is not clearly in their favour.[334] Their concern for keeping costs down may also not encourage them to search and present neutral information.[335] In short, the parties are not necessarily interested in giving the panel a complete picture of the situation, but rather a picture that favours their case. Accordingly, their interest in winning the case and reducing their own costs may skew the truth. Furthermore, while in certain circumstances the clash of contrary positions may enable the panel to find the truth, there is no reason to believe that the truth necessarily lies in one of the two different accounts put forward by the parties.[336] In this context, the involvement of the panel in identifying where the information on the record conflicts and where it is incomplete and, relatedly, its active efforts to produce a coherent and complete record may enhance the accuracy of panel reports. In sum, the active participation of the panel in the process of fact-finding may result in more accurate outcomes because the panel is a disinterested party which can lead the inquiry into areas where the parties would otherwise have no incentive to go.

An active panel is also needed to make up for the absence of exclusionary rules of evidence—these rules render certain types of evidence such as hearsay inadmissible in the proceedings. In fact, such exclusionary rules owe their existence to the presence of lay triers-of-fact and the passiveness of the judge in traditional common law proceedings. In such conditions, exclusionary rules are 'a useful instrument by which to pressure the parties and their lawyers to make available the best or the most reliable sources of information to the court'.[337] In contrast, such exclusionary rules are not necessary in a system of expert adjudicators who have the authority in case of need to intervene in the process of fact-finding to complete the factual record. The latter is the institutional regime under which panels operate.

An active approach to fact-finding can also neutralize any differences between the parties which stem from their different legal backgrounds and approaches to

[334] See Damaska, above n 329 at 98–9; Thomas, above n 332 at 327.

[335] Damaska argues that party control over the gathering and presentation of evidence may be particularly problematic where adjudication relies heavily on scientific evidence. He notes that the natural inclination of the parties 'to elicit only favorable information, an inclination that leads to the neglect of undisputed or neutral data', creates problems in disputes involving scientific questions because the fact-finder cannot rely upon its background knowledge to fill-in gaps: 'the material required to complete the necessary inferences is here unavailable'. Damaska, above n 329 at 145.

[336] Doubting whether the clash of contrary argument enables the judge to find the truth, see Jolowicz, *Adversarial and Inquisitorial Models*, above n 330 at 283; Damaska, above n 329 at 100–1.

[337] Damaska, above n 329 at 84–5.

presenting information. This is particularly relevant in the context of the current DSU which provides very little guidance to the parties with respect to the process of fact-finding. Moreover, an active panel can reduce the impact of resource inequalities between the parties[338] as well as inequalities resulting from the fact that in certain cases most of the relevant evidence is in the hands of the responding party.[339] Waincymer, for instance, suggests that the right of WTO panels to seek information could be used 'to put more balance into the resources of the disputants' which may vary greatly depending on their level of development.[340]

Intervention of a neutral figure may also minimize animosity between the parties and encourage the parties to cooperate in the production of information.

Admittedly, an active panel will have more work to do than a passive one. This is where the WTO Secretariat's role in assisting the panels becomes crucial.[341] The establishment of a permanent group of panelists, as suggested by some commentators and WTO Members, may also be a positive development in this regard.[342] The investment in an active panel is ultimately justified in view of the potential gains in the accuracy and legitimacy of the decisions.

Finally, it is important to note that there is no reason to believe that the impartiality of the panel is affected when it takes an active role in the process of fact-finding. Impartiality and passivity are not two sides of the same coin.[343] The belief that an active adjudicator is partial originates from common law

[338] See Damaska, above n 329 at 101 (Damaska notes that a 'competitively organized fact-finding enterprise requires a rough equality of the two sides in dispute in order to be fair'; when the two sides are not roughly equal their accounts cannot 'be expected to cancel out and expose the truth. [. . .] A weak case brought by a resourceful litigant can appear unduly strong').

[339] Judge Owada of the ICJ in the *Iranian Oil Platforms* case urged the Court to adopt a more proactive stance using its powers to ascertain the facts of the case when the parties have asymmetric access to information. *Oil Platforms* (Iran v United States of America), Judgment of 6 November 2003, Separate Opinion of Judge Owada, International Court of Justice, Reports of Judgments, Advisory Opinions and Orders (2003) at 321–3, paras 47, 52. See also Teitelbaum, above n 326 at 132–3.

[340] Waincymer, above n 135 at 567–8.

[341] According to Article 27.1 of the DSU, '[t]he Secretariat shall have the responsibility of assisting panels, especially on the legal, historical and procedural aspects of the matters dealt with, and of providing secretarial and technical support'.

[342] In this regard, see Section II.C.3.2 of Chapter 1. See also Contribution of the European Communities and its Member States to the Improvement and Clarification of the WTO Dispute Settlement Understanding, WTO Doc. TN/DS/W/38, 23 January 2003 at 3–4. See also William J Davey, 'Expediting the Panel Process in WTO Dispute Settlement' in ME Janow, V Donaldson & A Yanovich (eds), *The WTO: Governance, Dispute Settlement, and Developing Countries* (New York: Juris Publishing, 2008) 409 at 430–8 (proposing the creation of a permanent panel body); William J Davey, 'The Case for a WTO Permanent Panel Body' (2003) 6:1 Journal of International Economic Law 177 (proposing the creation of a permanent panel body); Thomas Cottier, 'The WTO Permanent Panel Body: a Bridge Too Far?' (2003) 6:1 Journal of International Economic Law 187 (supporting the creation of a permanent panel body); Andrew W Shoyer, 'Panel Selection in WTO Dispute Settlement Proceedings' (2003) 6:1 Journal of International Economic Law 203 (arguing against the creation of a permanent panel body).

[343] See Cappelletti, above n 327 at 250–1 (noting that judicial activism in fact-finding does not conflict with the ideals of an impartial judge and the parties' right to a fair hearing).

jurisdictions adopting a strictly adversarial conception of adjudication, that is, jurisdictions that believe that the contest between the parties has value *per se*—namely, independently of its worth for accurate outcomes—in the resolution of disputes.[344] In other words, if the parties are seen as contestants in a game where the judge is the umpire, any interference on the part of the judge is seen as an inappropriate intervention in the game. The fact that many systems of adjudication—notably, most civilian jurisdictions—provide for an active role for adjudicators in the process of fact-finding indicates that limiting the role of the adjudicator to that of an umpire is not necessary to avoid bias.[345] In short, there is no *a priori* reason to believe that disinterested adjudicators will use their fact-finding powers to skew the outcome one way or the other.

Admittedly, the exercise of the panel's authority to seek information, including to pose questions to the parties and to request the production of evidence, will have an impact on the outcome of the dispute, that is, on the discharge of the burden of proof. This is, however, implied in any hybrid inquisitorial-adversarial system.[346] It would make no sense to allow the panel to seek information and then prohibit it from relying upon such evidence in deciding the case. Accordingly, as already noted in Chapter 3, panels should make their rulings on the basis of all the information on the record,[347] independently of the origin of such information, provided that the parties were given a meaningful opportunity to express their views on that information.[348] Any other interpretation would conflict with the panel's duty under Article 11 of the DSU to make an 'objective assessment of the matter before it, including an objective assessment of the facts of the case'.

[344] See Mirjan Damaska, 'The Uncertain Fate of Evidentiary Transplants: Anglo-American and Continental Experiments' (1997) 45 American Journal of Comparative Law 839 at 851 (noting that the traditional common law understanding of judicial impartiality 'grew up against the background of a competitive factfinding process—a process, that is, in which it is risky for a third party to intervene in the forensic contest without appearing to offer assistance to one or the other litigant.'). See also Damaska, above n 329 at 82.

[345] See, for instance, L Cadiet, 'The New French Code of Civil Procedure (1975)' in CH van Rhee (ed), *European Traditions in Civil Procedure* (Antwerpen: Intersentia, 2005) 49 at 58 (noting that the French Code of Civil Procedure does not equate impartiality with passivity).

[346] See Kazazi, above n 84 at 156 (noting that '[t]he authority of international tribunals, even if applied with utmost impartiality, affects the burden of proof. For it may lead to clarification of some aspects of a given case to the detriment or benefit of the proponent of the burden of proof').

[347] Article 6.8 of the SCM Agreement, for instance, makes it clear that 'the existence of serious prejudice should be determined on the basis of the information submitted to or *obtained by the panel*'.

[348] This principle is expressly stated in the French Code of Civil Procedure, which is an example of a hybrid inquisitorial-adversarial system. According to Article 7 of the French Code of Civil Procedure: 'The judge may not base his/her decision on facts which are not part of the debate. Provided that a fact has been part of the debate, the judge may take it into consideration even if the parties did not expressly rely upon it to support their claims.'

2. Discretionary authority

The fact that the fact-finding authority of the panel may have an impact on the outcome of the dispute does not mean that the parties are released from their obligation to prove their claims and to adequately support their assertions with evidence. The panel is not meant to replace the parties, but rather to guide and complement their presentations. Particularly, the parties must make their claims and/or allegations seem plausible otherwise the panel may come to the conclusion that those claims and/or allegations are unfounded and thus do not merit attention. This is so because the panel does not have an *obligation* to search for information but rather the *discretion* to do so.

The language of Article 13.1 of the DSU makes clear that the panel has 'the right to seek information' not an obligation to do so. In addition, Article 13.2 provides that the panel '*may* seek information [...] and *may* consult experts'. The duty of panels under Article 11 of the DSU to make an 'objective assessment of the matter before it, including an objective assessment of the facts of the case', should not be interpreted so as to transform the panel's discretion under Article 13 into an obligation. Once the panel demonstrates that it has given proper consideration to measures of inquiry potentially appropriate to the case, its duty under Article 11 of the DSU should be considered discharged.[349]

The Appellate Body has in fact ruled in several occasions that pursuant to Article 13 of the DSU panels have discretion to decide whether or not to seek information.[350] It has also clarified in *EC—Sardines* that:

> A contravention of the duty under Article11 of the DSU to make an objective assessment of the facts of the case cannot result from the due exercise of the discretion permitted by another provision of the DSU, in this instance Article 13.2 of the DSU.[351]

The relationship between Articles 13 and 11 of the DSU was examined again in a recent decision in *US—Continued Zeroing*. Although the Appellate Body did not come to a clear conclusion on the issue, it hinted that it is possible that a panel's exercise of its discretion under Article 13 may lead to a violation of Article 11 of the DSU. This would be so because Article 11 'regulates a panel's exercise of its discretion'—which would include the exercise of the panel's

[349] This approach is also adopted, for instance, by the European Court of Justice and the Court of First Instance. See Jacquelyn MacLennan, 'Evidence, Standard and Burden of Proof and the Use of Experts in Procedure Before the Luxembourg Courts' in F Weiss (ed), *Improving WTO Dispute Settlement Procedures: Issues and Lessons from the Practice of Other International Courts and Tribunals* (London: Cameron May, 2000) 265 at 274.

[350] See Appellate Body Report, *EC—Sardines*, above n 289 at para 302; Appellate Body Report, *United States—Import Prohibition of Certain Shrimp and Shrimp Products*, WT/DS58/AB/R, adopted 6 November 1998, DSR 1998:VII, 2755 at para 104; Appellate Body Report, *European Communities—Anti-Dumping Duties on Imports of Cotton-Type Bed Linen from India—Recourse to Article 21.5 of the DSU by India*, WT/DS141/AB/RW, adopted 24 April 2003, DSR 2003:III, 965 at para 167.

[351] Appellate Body Report, *EC—Sardines*, above n 289 at para 302.

discretion under Article 13.[352] In other words, the Appellate Body seems to have said that while panels have the discretion to decide when, how, and what information to seek, because panels have a duty to make an objective assessment of the matter presented to them that discretion is not boundless.

One instance where the panel should be found to act inconsistently with Article 11 is when it rejects a request for production of information which meets the criteria discussed in Section II.C.3.1 below—among which are the fact that the information requested is relevant and necessary to decide the question at issue—and then finds against the party requesting the information on the grounds that it did not present sufficient evidence in support of its claim. As the Appellate Body has found on several occasions in the context of appeals challenging the panel's assessment of the facts, a panel violates Article 11 of the DSU if it deliberately disregards evidence.[353] The conduct just described would be equivalent to 'disregarding' evidence in that (i) the evidence is clearly relevant and necessary to decide the question at issue, and (ii) the reason why the requesting party does not itself produce the information is because the requested party has exclusive or preferential access to it. Such conduct of the panel could also be interpreted as a violation of the due process right of equal treatment in that one party is allowed to withhold information (to which it has exclusive or preferential access) to the detriment of its opponent.[354] A situation along these lines was presented to the Appellate Body in *US—Continued Zeroing*.[355] In that case, however, even though the Appellate Body reproached the panel for not taking 'the necessary steps to elicit from the parties the information that might [...] "elucidate its understanding of the facts and issues in the dispute before it" ', the Appellate Body declined to find that this led the panel to act inconsistently with Article 11.[356] The Appellate Body preferred to base its decision on

[352] Appellate Body Report, *United States—Continued Existence and Application of Zeroing Methodology*, WT/DS350/AB/R, adopted 19 February 2009 at para 345.

[353] See discussion in Section II.C.3.4 of Chapter 1. See also, for example, Appellate Body Report, *US—Continued Zeroing*, above n 352 at para 331; Appellate Body Report, *United States—Countervailing Duties on Certain Corrosion-Resistant Carbon Steel Flat Products from Germany*, WT/DS213/AB/R and Corr.1, adopted 19 December 2002, DSR 2002:IX, 3779 at para 142.

[354] Along these lines, see *Biwater v Tanzania*, above n 226 at 9 (noting that allowing a party to invoke domestic laws to avoid the production of requested information 'would create an imbalance between the parties.' According to the tribunal, '[i]t is indeed one of the most fundamental principles of international arbitration that the parties should be treated with equality'); *Pope & Talbot v Canada*, Award on Merits, above n 226 at para 193 (deploring Canada's decision not to produce the documents requested, and finding that that decision could be considered a derogation from the principle of equality).

[355] Notably, because neither the DSU nor panels and the Appellate Body have laid out clear criteria for requests to produce information, the European Communities in this case did not make a request which would fulfill the criteria discussed in Section II.C.3.1 below. Instead, in answering a written question posed by the panel, the European Communities indicated that in case the panel considered necessary to examine more direct evidence on the question at issue, it should request such evidence from the United States. See Panel Report, *United States—Continued Existence and Application of Zeroing Methodology*, WT/DS350/R, adopted 19 February 2009 at footnote 20 to para 6.20.

[356] Appellate Body Report, *US—Continued Zeroing*, above n 352 at 347.

other errors committed by the panel. According to the Appellate Body, because of those errors, it could not 'determine whether further inquiry by the Panel pursuant to its authority, including under Article 13, would have yielded greater clarity as to the evidence'.[357]

The fact that the panel has *discretion* to decide when, how, and whether to seek information provides an incentive for the parties to search and present information. In other words, uncertainty as to whether the panel will seek information on its own motion motivates the parties to be active in the proceedings. This is particularly so since the panel may always rely upon the rules on the burden of proof to decide the case if the information before it is insufficient to support a finding that the claim in question is more likely than not true.[358] In this respect, adjudication is not like many other factual inquiries in that it must result in an 'either-or' solution within a reasonable period of time.[359] While delivering a decision on the basis of the allocation of the burden of proof is an unsatisfactory solution, in many cases it is nonetheless a necessary evil of legal adjudication. This was noted, for example, by the panel in *Argentina—Hides and Leather*. In that case, the panel expressly noted that it had difficulties with respect to the development of the facts and that in an attempt to clarify the situation in question it asked the parties an extensive series of questions. Nonetheless, according to the panel, it was left with the feeling that 'there were facts of which we were not aware and which might be of importance and, therefore, we have not been fully satisfied that we have had a truly comprehensive view of some aspects of the situation'.[360] Ultimately, the panel noted, 'the burden of proof in any dispute rests with the complainant to support the claims made'.[361]

Dissatisfaction with the state of the information before the Court—and with the passive attitude of the Court—was expressed by Judge Bustamante of the ICJ in *Barcelona Traction, Light and Power Company, Limited*. In his dissenting opinion, Judge Bustamante noted that evidence was lacking in the proceedings

[357] Appellate Body Report, *US—Continued Zeroing*, above n 352 at 347.

[358] See, for example, Panel Report, *US—Upland Cotton*, above n 111 at paras 7.980–7.986 (where the panel decided not to request the complainant, Brazil, to provide further information on its claim; in light of the insufficiency of the evidence presented by Brazil the panel found that Brazil had not discharged the burden of proving its claim).

[359] It is also worth noting that panels cannot be likened to a domestic investigating authority, eg in a dumping investigation. An anti-dumping investigating authority has the power to apply a trade restrictive measure against imports. In order to do so, it must collect information which shows that dumping is taking place and is injuring (or posing a threat of injury to) the domestic industry. The information collected will also allow the investigating authority to set the level of the anti-dumping duty. In contrast, a panel performs a judicial function—its function is equivalent to that of a domestic court, not that of a domestic investigating authority. Panels are presented with questions which require yes-or-no answers, and they may rely on the concept of the burden of proof when the evidence does not allow them to discern what the correct answer is.

[360] Panel Report, *Argentina—Measures Affecting the Export of Bovine Hides and Import of Finished Leather*, WT/DS155/R and Corr.1, adopted 16 February 2001, DSR 2001:V, 1779 at para 11.14.

[361] Panel Report, *Argentina—Hides and Leather*, above n 360 at para 11.14.

which did not allow him to express a categorical judgment on the issue in question. In his view, it was not:

> unlikely that if the Court, in the exercise of its powers, were *proprio motu* to ask the parties to furnish it with any relevant document or piece of information [. . .] it might be found possible to throw light on one or more of the questions raised above. I naturally accept that in each case the onus of proof is placed on one of the parties, but it is also true that the overriding interests of justice give the Court the faculty of taking such steps as are possible to induce the parties to clarify what is not sufficiently clear.[362]

Reliance on the burden of proof is particularly unsatisfactory when it is clear that the parties actively searched and presented information to the panel but in the end did not cover a specific issue the relevance of which the parties were not aware of. This was the problem, for instance, in *US—Continued Zeroing*, where the panel required authenticated information, but did not inform the parties of this requirement during the proceedings—this resulted in a finding against the party bearing the burden of proof.[363] In this connection, panels should be aware of the fact that opting for remaining passive may, in certain circumstances, not allow them to assist the DSB to make recommendations or rulings able to achieve a 'satisfactory settlement of the matter'.[364]

3. The fact-finding powers of the panel

In *US—Shrimp* the Appellate Body noted that Articles 12 and 13 of the DSU taken together accord a panel 'ample and extensive authority to undertake and to control the process by which it informs itself both of the relevant facts of the dispute and of the legal norms and principles applicable to such facts'.[365] In the Appellate Body's view, that authority 'is indispensably necessary to enable a panel to discharge its duty' under Article 11 of the DSU to 'make an objective assessment of the matter before it, including an objective assessment of the facts of the case and the applicability of and conformity with the relevant covered agreements'.[366] This section discusses what is entailed in the ample and extensive authority of the panel to inform itself of the facts of the dispute. Apart from the question of experts, the focus of this section is on documentary evidence,

[362] *Case Concerning the Barcelona Traction, Light and Power Company, Limited* (New Application: 1962) (Preliminary Objections) (Belgium v Spain), Judgment of 24 July 1964, Separate Opinion of Judge Bustamante, International Court of Justice, Reports of Judgments, Advisory Opinions and Orders (1964) at 80.

[363] That finding was reversed on appeal on the grounds that the panel failed to examine the evidence in its totality. The Appellate Body reproached the panel for not informing the parties of what kind of evidence it would require. It did not, however, find that the panel acted inconsistently with Article 11 of the DSU for failing to do so. Appellate Body Report, *US—Continued Zeroing*, above n 352 at paras 347–8.

[364] According to Article 3.4 of the DSU, '[r]ecommendations or rulings made by the DSB shall be aimed at achieving a satisfactory settlement of the matter [. . .]'.

[365] Appellate Body Report, *US—Shrimp*, above n 350 at para 106.

[366] Appellate Body Report, *US—Shrimp*, above n 350 at para 106.

since witness testimony has been rare (and mostly limited to economic expert witnesses) in WTO dispute settlement.

3.1. Information from disputing parties

i. General overview. Article 13 of the DSU grants panels the right to seek information from any individual, body, or WTO Member, inevitably including the Members which are the parties to the dispute. In addition to Article 13 of the DSU, paragraph 8 of Appendix 3 (Working Procedures) to the DSU provides specifically that 'panel[s] may at any time put questions to the parties and ask them for explanations either in the course of a meeting with the parties or in writing'. Accordingly, panels have the power to seek information from the parties, including the power to request the production of evidence and to interrogate them.

While the degree of their participation may vary from panel to panel, panels do in fact ask questions and demand explanations from the parties particularly after the first and the second meetings of the parties with the panel. The authority of panels to put questions and ask for explanations has been reaffirmed by the Appellate Body in several occasions. For instance, in *Thailand—H-Beams* and *US—Zeroing (EC)*, the Appellate Body rejected claims that by asking certain questions of the parties the panels overstepped the limits of their authority.[367] Referring to its abovementioned statement in *US—Shrimp*, the Appellate Body in *US—Zeroing (EC)* found that the 'ample and extensive' authority of panels to inform themselves of the factual and legal details of the disputes brought before them indicates that panels have a 'broad authority to pose such questions to the parties as [they] deem relevant for purposes of considering the issues that are before [them]'.[368] According to the Appellate Body, '[t]he asking of questions is, after all, part and parcel of the investigative function and duty of panels'.[369] Moreover, in *Thailand—H-Beams* the Appellate Body noted that if the request for establishment of the panel sets out a claim with 'sufficient clarity', such claim is within the terms of reference of the panel and, therefore, 'it [is] within the Panel's mandate to ask questions related to [that] claim'.[370] According to the Appellate Body, the authority of the panel to ask questions is not conditional upon the claimant having made a *prima facie* case.[371]

[367] Appellate Body Report, *Thailand—H-Beams*, above n 17 at paras 135–6; Appellate Body Report, *United States—Laws, Regulations and Methodology for Calculating Dumping Margins ('Zeroing')*, WT/DS294/AB/R, adopted 9 May 2006 at paras 255–62.

[368] Appellate Body Report, *US—Zeroing (EC)*, above n 367 at para 260.

[369] Appellate Body Report, *US—Zeroing (EC)*, above n 367 at para 260.

[370] Appellate Body Report, *Thailand—H-Beams*, above n 17 at para 136.

[371] Appellate Body Report, *Thailand—H-Beams*, above n 17 at para 135. The panel had also expressed its view on this matter in the following terms: 'We as a panel have the mandate and the duty to manage the Panel proceedings and the ability to pose questions to the parties in order to

Naturally, whenever a panel asks questions or requests explanations from a party, it provides an opportunity for that party to clarify its position and present supporting evidence that may ultimately constitute the basis of a panel ruling.[372] Provided that the opposing party is given an opportunity to respond to such information, there is nothing objectionable with this procedure; to the contrary, as already noted, this kind of panel intervention is welcomed for the potential it has to lead to more accurate outcomes. It is worth noting that, as argued in Section I.B.1.3 of Chapter 3, in those cases where the submissions—particularly the first written submission—of the claimant do not pursue or explain in detail a claim that is stated in the request for establishment of a panel, panels should not merely ask questions; instead they should on their own motion or on the motion of the respondent communicate to claimants the existence of such deficiencies and provide an opportunity for the claimants to remedy them.

Panels have also used their authority to seek information to request, on their own motion or on the motion of one of the parties, the parties to produce evidence. For instance, in *Canada—Aircraft* the panel requested Canada to provide detailed information on certain transactions as well as other documents identified in the record of the proceedings;[373] in *US—Upland Cotton* the panel requested the United States to provide information on certain subsidy programs in a specified format;[374] and in *US—Wheat Gluten* the panel requested the United States to provide certain information which had been redacted from the public version of the report of the safeguard investigation at issue.[375]

clarify and distil the legal arguments that are asserted by the parties in support of their claims. [. . .] We believe that [. . .] a panel's extensive authority to put questions to the parties in order to inform itself of the relevant facts of the dispute and the legal considerations applicable to such facts is not conditional in any way upon a party having established, on a *prima facie* basis, a claim or defence. We view this authority as essential in order to carry out our mandate and responsibility under the DSU and the AD Agreement.' Panel Report, *Thailand—Anti-Dumping Duties on Angles, Shapes and Sections of Iron or Non-Alloy Steel and H-Beams from Poland*, WT/DS122/R, adopted 5 April 2001 at para 7.50.

[372] The panel recognized this in *Thailand—H-Beams*. In that case the panel noted that a specific development in the complainant's 'argument might have been prompted by questioning from the Panel'. The panel further noted that it believed 'that questioning from a panel may prompt development of the parties' arguments in order to distil the parties' positions' and that this was fine because 'the fact that the complaining party bears the burden of establishing a violation of a provision of a covered agreement does not "freeze" a panel into inaction'. Panel Report, *Thailand—H-Beams*, above n 371 at para 7.239. See also Appellate Body Report, *Korea—Definitive Safeguard Measure on Imports of Certain Dairy Products*, WT/DS98/AB/R, adopted 12 January 2000, DSR 2000:I, 3 at paras 148–9 (where the Appellate Body states that the panel did not overstep the bounds of its authority in basing its decision on information presented as a result of questioning from the panel).

[373] Panel Report, *Canada—Aircraft*, above n 136 at paras 9.52, 9.176, 9.327.

[374] Panel Report, *US—Upland Cotton*, above n 111 at paras 7.25, 7.32.

[375] Panel Report, *US—Wheat Gluten*, above n 14 at para 8.7. See also Panel Report, *Canada—Aircraft Credits and Guarantees*, above 177 at 7.135–7.136, 7.379–7.382; Panel Report, *Australia—Subsidies Provided to Producers and Exporters of Automotive Leather*, WT/DS126/R, adopted 16 June 1999, DSR 1999:III, 951 at paras 6.9–6.10, 6.13; Panel Report, *Canada—Dairy (Article 21.5—New Zealand and US)*, above n 214 at para 6.82; Panel Report, *US—Line Pipe*, above n 253 at paras 7.4, 7.8; Panel Report, *Turkey—Rice*, above n 89 at paras 7.94, 7.99–7.100.

The authority of the panels to seek information (ie evidence) from the parties has been expressly upheld by the Appellate Body. In *Canada—Aircraft*, the Appellate Body devoted 16 paragraphs of its report to clarifying the right of the panel to seek information from the disputing parties and the related duty of those parties to provide the information sought.[376] The Appellate Body made clear that the authority of the panel to seek information from a disputing party is not conditional 'upon the other party to the dispute having previously established, on a *prima facie* basis, such other party's claim or defence'.[377] In fact, the Appellate Body noted that panels are 'vested with ample and extensive discretionary authority to determine' not only *when* they need information but also *what* information they need to resolve a dispute.[378] In the view of the Appellate Body, there is no textual support in the WTO agreements for a conditional interpretation of the authority of the panel nor could such support be 'derived from a consideration of the nature of the functions and responsibilities entrusted to panels in the WTO dispute settlement system'.[379] According to the Appellate Body, Articles 12 and 13 of the DSU place the control of the information-gathering process in the hands of the panel.[380] Moreover, the fact that the panels have the ultimate control over the process of fact-finding indicates that the disputing parties have an obligation to produce evidence to the panel when requested to do so. If the parties could freely decide whether to answer requests for information from the panel, the panel would in many cases be prevented from ascertaining the facts of a dispute.[381] Consequently, the panel would 'not be in a position to determine the applicability of the pertinent treaty provisions to those facts, and, therefore, it [would] be unable to make any principled findings and recommendations to the DSB'.[382]

Canada—Aircraft clarifies, therefore, that panels have the discretionary authority to determine when and what kind of evidence to request from the parties. Discretion, however, does not mean arbitrariness. This is particularly so given the panel's duty under the DSU to 'make an objective assessment of the matter before it, including an objective assessment of the facts of the case and the applicability of and conformity with the relevant covered agreements'. Moreover, when deciding whether and what kind of information to request, panels should seek to maximize and balance the values of the dispute settlement system,

[376] The findings of the Appellate Body in *Canada—Aircraft* discussed in this paragraph have been referred to in many subsequent panel and Appellate Body reports. See, for instance, Appellate Body Report, *US—Wheat Gluten*, above n 5 at para 171; Panel Report, *Turkey—Rice*, above n 89 at paras 7.1, 7.10.

[377] Appellate Body Report, *Canada—Aircraft*, above n 81 at para 185. Similarly, Panel Report, *Canada—Aircraft*, above n 136 at para 9.89.

[378] Appellate Body Report, *Canada—Aircraft*, above n 81 at para 192.

[379] Appellate Body Report, *Canada—Aircraft*, above n 81 at para 185.

[380] Appellate Body Report, *Canada—Aircraft*, above n 81 at para 188.

[381] Appellate Body Report, *Canada—Aircraft*, above n 81 at para 188.

[382] Appellate Body Report, *Canada—Aircraft*, above n 81 at para 188.

particularly, the values of accuracy, equality, protection of confidential information, and efficient use of resources. The following section discusses guidelines for the panel's exercise of its fact-finding discretion.

ii. Discovery versus panel-controlled disclosure. The discussion in Chapter 4 regarding the allocation of the burden of proof was based on the assumption that both parties would have similar opportunities to access evidence necessary to prove their cases. This assumption does not hold true, however, if the parties are allowed to withhold information which their opponent cannot otherwise access. Likewise, the equality of the parties would also be affected, if one of them is denied access to evidence to which its opponent has exclusive or preferential access. Moreover, allowing parties to withhold relevant information which is necessary to resolve the dispute is likely to negatively affect the accuracy of the decisions. Accordingly, an optimal dispute settlement system must have in place some mechanism to allow the parties (and the panel) to have access to evidence to which their opponent has exclusive or preferential access, and which is not otherwise voluntarily produced.

The question then is: What kind of mechanism? Traditionally, the two major legal systems, the common law and the civil law, have relied upon two basic models: (i) the pre-trial discovery model (common law), and (ii) the court-controlled disclosure model (civil law). These models are to a large extent a reflection of the basic structure of those legal systems. The term 'discovery' is sometimes used in a broad sense to include any mechanism which allows evidence to be accessed by the parties and/or the adjudicator.[383] In the common law, however, the term 'discovery' is traditionally used to describe a pre-trial process in which the parties are under a general obligation to disclose, on demand of another party and without the need of a court order, information related to the dispute. The role of the court in this process is limited to resolving disputes between the parties regarding the scope of discovery requests. The party which resists discovery bears the burden of demonstrating to the court that production of the requested information is not appropriate under the circumstances—such circumstances may include the fact that the documents requested are irrelevant or protected by some privilege such as the attorney-client privilege.[384] Under the US Federal Rules of Civil Procedure the scope of discovery is limited to any matter 'relevant to any party's claim or defense'.[385] 'Relevance' is

[383] Kazazi, for example, refers to adjudicator-controlled disclosure as 'indirect discovery'. Kazazi, above n 84 at 140.

[384] See, for instance, Charles Brower, 'Discovery and Production of Evidence in the U.S.: Theory and Practice' in *Taking of Evidence in the Arbitral Proceedings* (Paris: ICC Publishing, 1990) 7 at 12 (referring to the discovery process under the US Federal Rules of Civil Procedure); Anthony J Scirica, 'Judge's Response to Professors Hazard and Taruffo' (2006) 25:2 Penn State International Law Review 519 at 520 (referring to the discovery process under the US Federal Rules of Civil Procedure).

[385] Rule 26(b)(1). Explaining the scope of discovery under the US Federal Rules of Civil Procedure, see Jack H Friedenthal, Mark Kay Kane & Arthur R Miller, *Civil Procedure* (4th edn, St Paul: Thomson West, 2005) at 399–401.

determined with reference to the pleadings of the parties, which according to Rule 8 must contain only 'a short and plain statement of the claim showing that the pleader is entitled to relief'—this is called notice pleading. The criterion of relevance is also used in other common law jurisdictions. In most jurisdictions, however, relevance is determined with reference to pleadings which must not only give notice of the claims and defences advanced, but also state the facts on which the claimant relies—this is called fact pleading.[386] While the latter system allows for a more strict control of the relevance of the information,[387] the fact that discovery takes place at the initial stage of the litigation, when the court's knowledge of the case is still limited, tends to give the parties wide latitude to access information in the control of their opponents.

In contrast, in the civil law system disclosure is traditionally controlled by the court, which, consistently with their episodic organization, may order the production of evidence at any time during the proceedings. Usually the court will only order the production of documents which are identified in detail and shown by the requesting party to be relevant and necessary to resolve the dispute.[388] The relevance and necessity of the information is determined in the light of the parties' written submissions, which must present a detailed account of the parties' position with respect to the claims and defences at issue and be accompanied by supporting evidence. This will tend to result in limited access to information not otherwise voluntarily produced. A broader right to access documents in the possession of another party exists only where the party in question has a substantive obligation to provide certain information; for example, when the law requires the party to render an account or to issue documents to the other party outside the context of adjudication.[389] The fact that the parties present a detailed account of their positions before the court needs to

[386] See Hazard Jr, above n 75 at 1019.

[387] The system under the US Federal Rules of Civil Procedure is particularly well-known to lead to extensive disclosure of information. In addition to the fact that relevance is determined with reference to notice pleading, broad discovery also results from the fact that pursuant to Rule 26(b)(1) discovery is not limited to information that is admissible at trial but extends to information which leads to the discovery of admissible evidence, that is, train of inquiry information. In this regard, see Geoffrey C Hazard Jr, 'Jury Trial and the Principles of Transnational Civil Procedure' (2006) 25:2 Penn State International Law Review 499 at 500–1; Jan W Bolt & Joseph K Wheatley, 'Private Rules for International Discovery in U.S. District Court: the U.S.–German Example' (2006) 11 UCLA Journal of International Law and Foreign Affairs 1 at 6–7. See also Andrews, above n 76 at 600–1 (explaining that since the enactment of the Civil Procedure Rules, England no longer allows discovery of train of inquiry information under what is now known as 'standard disclosure').

[388] See Damaska, *The Uncertain Fate of Evidentiary Transplants*, above n 344 at 848–9; Sturner, above n 78 at 876; Siegfried H Elsing & John M Townsend, 'Bridging the Common Law–Civil Law Divide in Arbitration' (2002) 18:1 Arbitration International 59 at 60–1; Thierry Bernard, 'The Administration of Evidence in Countries of Civil Law' in PV Eijsvoogel (ed), *Evidence in International Arbitration* (London: Graham and Trotman and Martinus Nijhoff, 1994) 21 at 23–4; Koen Van den Broeck, 'Belgium' in PV Eijsvoogel (ed), *Evidence in International Arbitration Proceedings* (London: Graham & Trotman and Martinus Nijhoff, 1994) 77 at 82; Huang, above n 245 at 44–5.

[389] See Gottwald, above n 107 at 70 (referring to German law); Huang, above n 245 at 176–8 (referring to Japanese law).

decide whether to order the production of documents, combined with the requirement that the requested evidence be specified in detail, allow the courts to more precisely control the relevance and necessity of the information. Accordingly, the amount of information requested and produced is much smaller than under the pre-trial discovery model. Importantly, the civilian court-controlled disclosure model cannot be used to access information of which the requesting party has no specific knowledge. Civilian court-controlled disclosure is not a tool for investigation, but rather a means of making evidence, the existence of which is known, available. Under this system the parties are required to conduct their own investigation before filing a case—one of the objectives of pre-filing investigation is to prevent frivolous cases.

The location of this section within this book reveals the preference of this author for a panel-controlled disclosure mechanism.[390] The main reasons for such preference are (i) the potential efficiency gains which can be derived from the involvement of the panel in the process and (ii) the fact that panel-controlled disclosure is more consistent with the current structure of the WTO dispute settlement system. As for efficiency gains, panel intervention can result in requests for documents that are limited to what is relevant and necessary to resolve the dispute. In contrast, in a party-led mechanism such as pre-trial discovery the parties are likely to demand the production of much more evidence than is necessary for the adjudicator to decide the case. It has been noted with respect to pre-trial discovery that '[w]holesale disclosure of documents is an expensive and time-consuming process for all concerned and rarely reveals the "smoking gun" that is being sought.'[391] Accordingly, panel-controlled disclosure may reduce costs without necessarily compromising the accuracy of the decision. As for the fact that panel-controlled disclosure is more consistent with the structure of the WTO dispute settlement system, it is worth recalling that Article 13 of the DSU already grants panels the right to seek information. Moreover, as discussed in Section II.A of this chapter, the need for a pre-trial (or pre-first submissions) discovery mechanism is questionable in a system such as the WTO dispute settlement system in which the proceedings are episodic.

Finally, the fact that many WTO Members are not familiar with pre-trial discovery suggests that that mechanism, which is essentially party-led, might not function well if implemented in the WTO. In support of this view, it is worth noting that in *EC—Approval and Marketing of Biotech Products* the European Communities urged the panel to issue a formal request for the European

[390] In support of this position, see Davey, *Evaluating WTO Dispute Settlement*, above n 262 at 118–19 (noting that the need for discovery in its broad sense can be effectively met by allowing 'parties to request panels to ask questions of the other party in the panel process').

[391] Redfern et al, above n 68 at 300. See also Andrew Rogers, 'Improving Procedures for Discovery and Documentary Evidence' in AJ van den Berg (ed), *Planning Efficient Arbitration Proceedings: the Law Applicable in International Arbitration* (The Hague: Kluwer Law International, 1996) 131 at 137.

Communities to produce relevant documents. The European Communities argued that certain documents which were important to the resolution of the dispute were to a large extent in the possession of its Member States and that a formal request from the panel would assist it in obtaining those documents.[392]

Indeed, the negotiations of the Hague Convention on the Taking of Evidence Abroad in Civil or Commercial Matters[393] revealed the existence of general hostility against the pre-trial discovery model. Pursuant to Article 23 of the Convention, many states parties to the Convention made declarations to the effect that their courts would 'not execute Letters of Request issued [by the courts of another signatory] for the purpose of obtaining pre-trial discovery of documents as known in Common Law countries'.[394] Opposition is particularly pronounced against the American model of pre-trial discovery embodied in the Federal Rules of Civil Procedure, which leads to broad discovery which is seen as invasive, expensive, and time consuming.[395] Sensitivity to the problems associated with discovery has also led to the more widespread adoption of the court-controlled disclosure model in international and transnational instruments. The court-controlled disclosure model is endorsed, for example, by the ALI/UNIDROIT Principles of Transnational Civil Procedure,[396] the Rules of Arbitration

[392] Panel Report, *EC—Approval and Marketing of Biotech Products*, above n 217 at para 7.40.

[393] Concluded on 18 March 1970 and entered into force on 7 October 1972.

[394] Article 23 of the Convention provides that: '[a] Contracting State may at the time of signature, ratification or accession, declare that it will not execute Letters of Request issued for the purpose of obtaining pre-trial discovery of documents as known in Common Law countries.' A Special Commission in charge of revising the practical operation of the Convention noted that 'Article 23 was intended to permit States to ensure that a request for the production of documents must be *sufficiently substantiated* so as to avoid requests whereby one party merely seeks to find out what documents may generally be in the possession of the other party to the proceeding'. Accordingly, the Special Commission recommended that the signatories to the Convention revise their reservations to pre-trial discovery to allow requests which are sufficiently substantiated, that identify the requested documents in detail, and/or identify the relationship between the evidence or information requested and the pending proceeding. Conclusions and Recommendations of the Special Commission on the Practical Operation of The Hague Apostille, Evidence and Service Conventions (28 October to 4 November 2003) at paras 29–34, available at <http://hcch.e-vision.nl/upload/wop/lse_concl_e.pdf> (accessed 20 May 2009).

[395] Referring to the time and expense that can be consumed in discovery especially in the United States, see Brower, *Discovery and Production of Evidence*, above n 384 at 11; Scirica, above n 384 at 521; McCabe, above n 146 at footnote 1 to page 499; Taruffo, above n 321 at 513–4; Stephen F Black, 'United States Transnational Discovery: the Rise and Fall of the Hague Evidence Convention' (1991) 40 International and Comparative Law Quarterly 901 at 903; Rogers, above n 391 at 137; Zekoll, *Comparative Civil Procedure*, above n 75 at 1334–5; Samuel R Gross, 'The American Advantage: the Value of Inefficient Litigation' (1987) 85:4 Michigan Law Review 734 at 735–6. Huang is one of the few commentators to recognize the costs of discovery but to argue that discovery is nonetheless cost-efficient. Huang, above n 245 at 103–5.

[396] Principle 16.2 provides that 'Upon timely request of a party, the court should order disclosure of relevant, nonprivileged, and reasonably identified evidence in the possession or control of another party or, if necessary and on just terms, of a nonparty.' See also Rule 22 of the Rules of Transnational Civil Procedure. American Law Institute & UNIDROIT, above n 96 at 36 and 130–1 respectively. See also Zekoll, *Comparative Civil Procedure*, above n 75 at 1346–7.

of the International Chamber of Commerce,[397] the IBA Rules,[398] the Rules of Procedure of the Court of First Instance of the European Communities,[399] and the Rules of Procedure of the European Court of Justice.[400]

To be sure, the pre-trial discovery model has been adopted in some international arbitral proceedings such as certain disputes under Chapter 11 of the NAFTA including *United Parcel Service of America Inc v Government of Canada*, *SD Myers v Government of Canada*, *Pope & Talbot Inc v Government of Canada*, and *Glamis Gold Ltd v the United States of America*.[401] In these disputes, the tribunal issued procedural directions providing for party-led discovery to take place before the parties submitted their detailed written submissions.[402] This use of the pre-trial discovery model is, however, largely explained by the fact that the actors (lawyers and arbitrators) involved in those arbitrations are predominantly common law trained and, therefore, more familiar with that model.

[397] Article 20.5 of the Rules of Arbitration of the International Chamber of Commerce provides that '[a]t any time during the proceedings, the Arbitral Tribunal may summon any party to provide additional evidence'. See also Derains &Schwartz, above n 147 at 279–80; Redfern et al, above n 68 at 300.

[398] Article 3.2 of the IBA Rules provides that '[w]ithin the time ordered by the Arbitral Tribunal, any Party may submit to the Arbitral Tribunal a Request to Produce.' Article 3.6 on its turn establishes that '[t]he Arbitral Tribunal shall, in consultation with the Parties and in timely fashion, consider the Request to Produce and the objections. The Arbitral Tribunal may order the Party to whom such Request is addressed to produce to the Arbitral Tribunal and to the other Parties those requested documents in its possession, custody or control as to which the Arbitral Tribunal determines that (*i*) the issues that the requesting Party wishes to prove are relevant and material to the outcome of the case, and (*ii*) none of the reasons for objection set forth in Article 9.2 apply.' See also Ughi et al, above n 249 at 20–1; Hilmar Raeschke-Kessler, 'The Production of Documents in International Arbitration: a Commentary on Article 3 of the New IBA Rules of Evidence' (2002) 18:4 Arbitration International 411 at 415.

[399] Chapter 3, Sections 1 and 2 of the Rules provide for measures of organization of procedure and measures of inquiry which can be adopted by the court. The parties may also use the application foreseen in Article 114 of the Rules to request the court to order the production of documents. See Lasok, above n 155 at 384–5; MacLennan, above n 349 at 273–6.

[400] Chapter 2 of the Rules provide for measures of inquiry and preparatory measures that can be adopted by the court. The parties may also use the application foreseen in Article 114 of the Rules to request the court to order the production of documents. See Lasok, above n 155 at 384–5; MacLennan, above n 349 at 273–6.

[401] The discovery model is also used in international commercial arbitration, particularly when American parties are involved. The general trend in international commercial arbitration is, however, to follow the IBA Rules and to delay requests for production of documents until the arbitrators are familiar with the case.

[402] *United Parcel Service of America Inc v Government of Canada*, Procedural Directions and Order of the Tribunal, 4 April 2003 at section B; *S. D. Myers v Government of Canada*, Procedural Order No 1, 28 May 1999 at paras 5-12; *Pope & Talbot Inc v Government of Canada*, Procedural Order No 4, 29 October 1999; *Glamis Gold Ltd v the United States of America*, Procedural Order No 1, 3 March 2005 at section II. See also *ADF Group Inc v The United States of America*, ICSID Case No ARB(AF)/00/1, Award of 9 January 2003 at para 31 (where the tribunal set out principles to govern the production of documents 'in line with the procedure and practice in the District of Columbia and the caselaw under the U.S. Federal Rules of Civil Procedure (FRCP).').

Importantly, the pre-trial discovery model is to a certain extent reflected on the procedure foreseen in Annex V of the SCM Agreement. Annex V provides for a specific procedure for developing information concerning claims of adverse effects under Articles 5 and 6 of the SCM Agreement. The procedure is essentially party-led[403] and structured to take place without the supervision of the panel. In this regard, in *Korea—Commercial Vessels* the panel ruled that there is no 'scope for intervention by the Panel in procedural issues relating to Annex V'.[404] Instead, a facilitator is appointed by the DSB exclusively to oversee the process and 'to ensure the timely development of the information';[405] however, the facilitator has no power to order the production of information or decide eventual disputes between the parties.

Despite the fact that paragraph 2 of Annex V establishes that the DSB *shall*, upon request, initiate the information-gathering procedures, in at least two instances one of the parties blocked the initiation of the process by refusing to accept the nomination of a facilitator—the Chairman of the DSB understood that a facilitator could not be appointed in the absence of a consensus among the parties. In *US—Upland Cotton*, the United States did not agree to the nomination of a facilitator on the grounds that before information could be gathered on serious prejudice the panel had to decide whether the Peace Clause (Article 13) of the Agreement on Agriculture precluded a claim of serious prejudice under Articles 5 and 6 of the SCM Agreement.[406] In *US –Large Civil Aircraft* the United States did not agree to the initiation of the Annex V procedure with respect to claims included in an additional request for establishment of a panel because in the view of the United States, first, the 'Annex V process could not begin until the parties had mutually agreed on initiation and on modalities'[407] and, second, the European Communities were attempting to resume the original Annex V procedure which had already been concluded.[408]

The information-gathering process under Annex V was instituted in four cases: *EC—Large Civil Aircraft*,[409] *US—Large Civil Aircraft* (the original

[403] This is so even though in the Annex V proceedings which have taken place so far the facilitator appointed by the DSB was put in charge of preparing and submitting a questionnaire to the parties. The questionnaire prepared by the facilitator was based on questions submitted by the parties which also had an opportunity to comment on drafts of the questionnaire. See Panel Report, *Korea-Commercial Vessels*, above n 148 at Attachment 1.

[404] Panel Report, *Korea-Commercial Vessels*, above n 148 at para 7.1.

[405] Paragraph 4 of Annex V.

[406] Minutes of the Meeting of the Dispute Settlement Body held on 31 March 2003, WTO Doc WT/DSB/M/146, 19 May 2003 at para 3.

[407] Minutes of the Meeting of the Dispute Settlement Body held on 17 February 2006, WTO Doc WT/DSB/M/205, 31 March 2006 at para 71.

[408] Minutes of the Meeting of the Dispute Settlement Body held on 14 March 2006, WTO Doc WT/DSB/M/206, 4 April 2006 at paras 14-20, 25; Minutes of the Meeting of the Dispute Settlement Body held on 17 March 2006, WTO Doc WT/DSB/M/207, 26 April 2006 at para 94.

[409] Minutes of the Meeting of the Dispute Settlement Body held on 23 September 2005, WTO Doc WT/DSB/M/197, 10 October 2005 at para 6.

panel),[410] *Indonesia—Autos*,[411] and *Korea—Commercial Vessels*.[412] In these instances, although much information was collected—perhaps even excessively[413]—the process did not unfold smoothly: (i) delays occurred which in turn delayed the panel process;[414] (ii) disputes between the parties regarding non-production were common and could not be resolved given the lack of authority of the facilitator in this regard.[415]

Given the lack of authority of the facilitator and the absence of panel supervision, disputes over the production of information are deferred to the panel process. When this occurs, as in any other proceeding, the panel can use its authority under Article 13 to seek the information in question if it considers necessary and appropriate to do so. Accordingly, the limited experience with Annex V of the SCM Agreement, which sets up a fairly focused information-gathering procedure,[416] provides another indication that the panel-controlled disclosure model is likely better-fitted for WTO dispute settlement in general.

[410] Minutes of the Meeting of the Dispute Settlement Body held on 23 September 2005, WTO Doc WT/DSB/M/197, 10 October 2005 at para 16.

[411] Minutes of the Meeting of the Dispute Settlement Body held on 12 June 1997, WTO Doc WT/DSB/M/34, 8 July 1997.

[412] Panel Report, *Korea-Commercial Vessels*, above n 148 at Attachment 1.

[413] The United States affirmed that it provided more than 40,000 pages of information during the Annex V procedure in *US—Large Civil Aircraft*. Minutes of the Meeting of the Dispute Settlement Body held on 14 March 2006, WTO Doc WT/DSB/M/206, 4 April 2006 at para 17. In *Korea—Commercial Vessels* the panel described the documentation produced as 'extensive' and 'voluminous'. Panel Report, *Korea—Commercial Vessels*, above n 148 at para 7.516 and Attachment 1, para 7. See also Sungjin Kang, 'Comment on Annex V of the WTO SCM Agreement Procedures in the Context of Korea-Shipbuilding Dispute' (2006) 33:2 Legal Issues of Economic Integration 183 at 187 (referring to the high volume of information produced in *Korea—Commercial Vessels*).

[414] Korea noted that in *Korea—Commercial Vessels* the Annex V procedure added six months to the process. Minutes of the Meeting of the Dispute Settlement Body held on 11 April 2001, WTO Doc WT/DSB/M/187, 25 April 2005 at para 12. Delays were also experienced in *US—Large Civil Aircraft* and *EC—Large Civil Aircraft*. First, it took over two months to institute the information-gathering process because of disagreements between the parties; second, after the process began the period for information-gathering had to be extended from 60 to 90 days. See Minutes of the Meeting of the Dispute Settlement Body held on 23 September 2005, WTO Doc WT/DSB/M/197, 10 October 2005 at para 2; Minutes of the Meeting of the Dispute Settlement Body held on 14 March 2006, WTO Doc WT/DSB/M/206, 4 April 2006 at para 17.

[415] Reporting instances of non-cooperation on the part of the United States on the presentation of information requested by the European Communities and vice-versa, see Minutes of the Meeting of the Dispute Settlement Body held on 14 March 2006, WTO Doc WT/DSB/M/206, 4 April 2006 at paras 12, 20; Minutes of the Meeting of the Dispute Settlement Body held on 17 February 2006, WTO Doc WT/DSB/M/205, 31 March 2006 at para 71. See also Panel Report, *Indonesia—Certain Measures Affecting the Automobile Industry*, WT/DS54/R, WT/DS59/R, WT/DS64/R and Corr.1,2,3 and 4, adopted 23 July 1998, DSR 1998:VI, 2201 at paras. 8.30 and 8.106 (where the United States noted that Indonesia refused to provide information which it had requested during the Annex V process).

[416] The procedure under Annex V is to be used to obtain information 'necessary to establish the existence and amount of subsidization, the value of total sales of the subsidized firms, as well as information necessary to analyze the adverse effects caused by the subsidized product' (para 2). Moreover, paragraph 5 of Annex V provides a non-exhaustive list of the type of information which should be collected, namely, 'data concerning the amount of the subsidy in question (and, where appropriate, the value of total sales of the subsidized firms), prices of the subsidized product, prices of the non-subsidized product, prices of other suppliers to the market, changes in the supply of the subsidized product to the market in question and changes in market shares.'

In light of the reasons discussed above, it is submitted that disclosure of evidence not automatically produced by the parties must be controlled and ordered by the panel. This is not to say that the parties should not be encouraged to address requests for documents directly to each other and voluntarily exchange information. However, failure to present information pursuant to a request from another party should not result in adverse inferences being drawn against the requested party. Moreover, the existence of a previous party request should not be a pre-requisite for the panel to order the production of evidence under Article 13 of the DSU.

iii. Requests to produce. Requests for production of information under Article 13 should be made (i) *sua sponte* by the panel or (ii) upon application of a party. The discussion below focuses on the second situation. The same kind of considerations should, however, also guide the panel when requesting production of evidence *sua sponte.*[417] In both situations, if the requested party believes that the criteria discussed below have not been observed, it should be able to raise objections which must then be decided by the panel. Only when a party does not comply with a request for production of documents issued according to such criteria should the panel consider drawing adverse inferences against that party. The parties should of course be informed in advance of the requirements of a request to produce—currently there is no clear guidance on this subject.

In managing requests to produce, panels may consider adopting what has been referred to as a 'Redfern Schedule'.[418] A Redfern Schedule is a spreadsheet with four columns. The first column lists the information requested. The second column contains a short description of the reasons for each request, which should be set out according to the requirements discussed below. The third column provides a summary of any objections raised by the requested party; these would include objections regarding the applicability of any of the criteria discussed below, and those raising a claim of privilege—eg that the documents were created for the purpose of consultations.[419] Finally, the fourth column is reserved for the decision of the panel on each request.

It is submitted that a panel should grant a request for production of information when the requested information is (i) relevant and necessary, (ii) specified in detail in the request, and when the party requesting the information demonstrates (iii) that it is not in possession of the information and cannot otherwise have access to it, and (iv) that the requested information is in the control of the requested party. Points iii and iv can be otherwise expressed as 'information to which the requested party has exclusive or preferential access'.

[417] Here it is important to distinguish between the production of evidence, particularly documents, and information in a broader sense. The panel should not be restricted in its power to *ask questions* which do not imply production of evidence.

[418] The Redfern Schedule is named after Alan Redfern. See Redfern et al, above n 68 at 301–2.

[419] Regarding privileges, see discussion in Sections II.B.5.2 and II.B.6.1 above.

The criteria above are intended to ensure the efficiency and fairness of the disclosure process. They find expression in the practice of some international tribunals and in international instruments such as the IBA Rules. With a view to ensuring the observance of those criteria, parties should be required to address them in their requests to the panel for the production of documents ('request to produce').[420] Along these lines, in *US—Line Pipe* the panel alerted Korea that requests to produce 'should be supported by an explanation as to why the information sought is relevant to Korea's claims and is necessary in order for the Panel to perform an objective assessment of the matter'.[421] A detailed request to produce also facilitates the drawing of adverse inferences in case the request is not honoured since in order to draw inferences the panel must know what the documents sought might prove.[422]

Relevant and necessary. First, the information requested should be shown to be relevant and necessary to the resolution of the question at issue. These criteria work to limit the disclosure of information, thus promoting the efficient use of resources and the protection of certain confidential information, without affecting the overall accuracy of the decision. The criteria of 'relevance' and 'necessity' have guided the Iran–United States Claims Tribunal,[423] the European Court of Justice and the Court of First Instance,[424] and international commercial arbitral tribunals[425] in deciding whether to order the production of information. They have also been embraced by the IBA Rules and the ALI/UNIDROIT Principles of Transnational Civil Procedure.[426] Article 3.3(b) of the IBA Rules provides that a request to produce shall contain 'a description of how the documents requested are relevant and material to the outcome of the case'. Article 3.6 in turn establishes that the arbitral tribunal may order the production of documents as to which it 'determines that (*i*) the issues that the requesting Party wishes to prove are relevant and material to the outcome of the case.'[427] 'Material' in the IBA Rules is synonym for 'necessary'.[428] Commenting on the IBA Rules, Raeschke-Kessler notes that the 'the term materiality means that the arbitral tribunal must deem it

[420] This is the approach adopted by the IBA Rules—Article 3.3.

[421] Panel Report, *US—Line Pipe*, above n 253 at para 7.4.

[422] See MA Polkinghorne, 'The Withholding of Documentary Evidence in International Arbitration: Remedies for Dealing with Uncooperative Parties' (2005) 2:5 Transnational Dispute Management at 14.

[423] See M Aghahosseini, 'Evidence before the Iran–United States Claims Tribunal' (1999) 1:4 International Law FORUM du Droit International 208 at 209–10; McCabe, above n 146 at 515.

[424] See Koen Lenaerts & Dirk Arts, *Procedural Law of the European Union* (London: Sweet & Maxwell, 1999) at 383; Lasok, above n 155 at 369; MacLennan, above n 349 at 278–9.

[425] See Redfern et al, above n 68 at 299; Derains & Schwartz, above n 147 at 282.

[426] Principle 16.2 states that 'the court should order disclosure of relevant [...] evidence'.

[427] Similarly, Article 3.9 provides that 'The Arbitral Tribunal, at any time before the arbitration is concluded, may request a Party to produce to the Arbitral Tribunal and to the other Parties any documents that it believes to be relevant and material to the outcome of the case.'

[428] In the United States, 'materiality' is one of the two components of 'relevance', the other being 'probative value'. In this context, materiality 'looks to the relation between the propositions that the evidence is offered to prove and the issues in the case. If the evidence is offered to help prove a

necessary that the document is needed as an element to allow complete consideration as to whether a factual allegation is true or not'.[429]

Relevance is determined with reference to the proposition at issue. Relevant evidence is evidence that makes the establishment of an elemental proposition (or auxiliary propositions linked to the elemental proposition) more probable or less probable than it would be without the evidence. In turn, necessity is a relative concept which depends on factors such as the availability of alternative sources of information which are more easily accessible, the probative value of the evidence already before the panel, the probative value of the requested evidence, and the analytical approach adopted by the panel to dispose of the case—for instance, because panels are allowed to exercise judicial economy with respect to certain claims, information which is relevant exclusively to those claims is not necessary. Moreover, in determining whether the information requested is 'necessary' the panel must weigh the costs and benefits of ordering production so that the costs associated with production are not disproportionately high when compared to the benefits of examining the documents. In this regard, the panel must determine whether the contribution which the documents are likely to make to the accuracy of the decision justifies the time and monetary expenditures involved in producing and examining the documents requested.[430] Also, if the documents requested contain highly sensitive confidential information and may shed some light on a question at issue but are not likely to be determinative of the outcome of the dispute, the panel may find that the benefit that can be derived from their production is not proportionate to the costs associated with their potential leakage. Along these lines, the panel in *US—Line Pipe* noted that in the light of the interest in protecting confidential information expressed in Article 3.2 of the Agreement on Safeguards panels should show appropriate restraint in ordering the production of confidential information.[431] In that case the panel refused to order the United States to produce the complete confidential record of the safeguard investigation at issue on the grounds that that record was likely to contain information which was not necessary for the panel to perform an objective assessment of the matter before it.[432]

Article 13.1 of the DSU contains a reference to 'necessary and appropriate'. According to Article 13.1, a Member 'should respond promptly and fully to any request by a panel for such information as the panel considers necessary and

proposition that is not a matter in issue, the evidence is immaterial.' Probative value is 'the tendency of evidence to establish the proposition that it is offered to prove'. Kenneth S Broun (ed), *McCormick on Evidence* (6th edn, St. Paul: Thomson/West, 2006) at 306–7. See also George Fisher, *Evidence* (New York: Foundation Press, 2002) at 18–19.

[429] Raeschke-Kessler, above n 398 at 427.

[430] This kind of judgment is frequently exercised by courts following the court-controlled disclosure model. The French Code of Civil Procedure, for instance, instructs the judge to limit measures of inquiry 'to what is sufficient for the resolution of the dispute by endeavouring to select the simplest and least onerous ones' (Article 147).

[431] Panel Report, *US—Line Pipe*, above n 253 at para 7.4.

[432] Panel Report, *US—Line Pipe*, above n 253 at para 7.4.

appropriate'. In the Spanish version the reference is to 'necesaria y pertinente'. 'Pertinente' translates into English as 'relevant, pertinent; appropriate'.[433] Accordingly, there is explicit support in the DSU for limiting production requests to documents which are relevant and necessary for the resolution of the question at issue.

Some panels have, in fact, referred to these criteria—though without much elaboration—when ordering or declining to order production of evidence. In *US—Lead and Bismuth II*, the panel concluded that it was not necessary to order the United States to produce the information requested by the European Communities. In the view of the panel, the dispute could 'be resolved without reference to the precise facts' invoked by the European Communities.[434] In *EC—Selected Customs Matters* the panel noted that since the party asking the panel to request information did not consider the information necessary for the resolution of the question at issue, the panel did 'not see any compelling reason to exercise its discretion under Article 13 of the DSU to request that information'.[435] Finally, in *US—Upland Cotton* after being informed of the problems faced by the complainant to prove a central issue in the case, the panel decided 'that it was both necessary and appropriate to use its powers under Article 13 of the *DSU* to access [certain] data' which 'was in the control of the United States' and not available to the complainant.[436]

Another aspect related to the determination of the relevance and necessity of the evidence relates to the timing of the request to produce. In order for the panel to be able to effectively determine whether the requested information is relevant and necessary—and thus effectively limit disclosure without affecting the accuracy of its decision—it must know the details of the position of the parties with respect to the claims at issue. Given the briefness and generality of the requests for establishment of a panel, as a general rule it will be difficult for panels to make a determination as to the relevance and necessity of evidence before the parties have submitted their first written submissions. Therefore, it is advisable that as a general rule such requests be considered at the earliest after the filing of the first written submissions of the parties.[437] As a matter of fact, in

[433] Collins: *Spanish-English, English-Spanish Dictionary* (4th edn, Glasgow: HarperCollins, 1996) at 553.

[434] Panel Report, *US—Lead and Bismuth II*, above n 206 at para 6.7. Similarly, see Panel Report, *US—Line Pipe*, above n 253 at para 7.11 (where the panel ruled that it was not 'necessary and/or appropriate to issue further requests for information in response to Korea's second written submission').

[435] Panel Report, *EC—Selected Customs Matters*, above n 103 at para 7.83.

[436] Panel Report, *US—Upland Cotton*, above n 111 at para 7.633.

[437] A similar approach is favoured by the European Court of Justice and tribunals adjudicating international commercial disputes. See MacLennan, above n 349 at 275 (noting that the 'court will normally decide whether to order measures of inquiry at the administrative meeting after the close of the written proceedings'); ICC Commission on Arbitration, *Techniques for Controlling Time and Costs in Arbitration* (Paris: International Chamber of Commerce, 2007) at para 54 (suggesting that the most appropriate timeframe for the production of documents is 'likely to be after the parties have set out their cases in full for the first time').

several cases the parties addressed requests to produce to the panel before the first written submissions had been filed.[438] In most of those cases, the panel declined to entertain such requests at that stage. For instance, in *Canada—Aircraft* the panel expressly noted that it did 'not consider it appropriate to seek any information before receiving at least the first written submissions of both parties'.[439]

US—Line Pipe is an exception in this regard in that the panel partially granted a request to produce filed by Korea before its first written submission on the grounds that Korea had established to its satisfaction that some of the information was relevant to the claims advanced by Korea and necessary in order for the panel to perform an objective assessment of the matter.[440] The panel, however, deferred to a later date a decision on the production of some of the information requested at that occasion because it was not 'in a position at [that] time to assess the need for access to [that] information'.[441]

Specificity. Second, the information requested must meet the specificity criterion. A request to produce must refer to a narrow and precisely described piece of information. One of the main objectives of this criterion is to promote the efficient use of resources; narrow requests require fewer resources to be complied with. The requirement that a request for information be specific has been relied upon by the Iran–United States Claims Tribunal,[442] the European Court of Justice and the Court of First Instance,[443] and international commercial arbitral tribunals.[444] It has found expression in the IBA Rules[445] and the ALI/UNIDROIT Principles of Transnational Civil Procedure.[446] Article 3.3(a) of the IBA Rules provides that a request to produce shall contain '(*i*) a description of a requested document sufficient to identify it, or (*ii*) a description in sufficient detail (including subject matter) of a narrow and specific requested category of documents that are reasonably believed to exist.'

[438] Panel Report, *Canada—Aircraft*, above n 136 at para 9.51; Panel Report, *European Communities—Anti-Dumping Measure on Farmed Salmon from Norway*, WT/DS337/R, adopted 15 January 2008 at paras 1.10–1.11; Panel Report, *United States—Subsidies on Upland Cotton*, WT/DS267/R, Corr.1, and Add.1 to Add.3, adopted 21 March 2005 at paras 8.1–8.3.

[439] Panel Report, *Canada—Aircraft*, above n 136 at para 9.50. Similarly, Panel Report, *EC—Salmon (Norway)*, above n 438 at para 1.11; Panel Report, *Canada—Aircraft Credits and Guarantees*, above n 177 at para 7.134.

[440] Panel Report, *US—Line Pipe*, above n 253 at paras 7.2, 7.4.

[441] Panel Report, *US—Line Pipe*, above n 253 at para 7.4.

[442] See McCabe, above n 146 at 515, 517; Jamison M Selby, 'Fact-Finding before the Iran—United States Claims Tribunal: a View from the Trenches' in RB Lillich (ed), *Fact-Finding before International Tribunals* (Ardsley-on-Hudson: Transnational Publishers, 1992) 135 at 140; Holtzmann, *Fact-Finding by the Iran-United States Claims Tribunal*, above n 325 at 120.

[443] See MacLennan, above n 349 at 279.

[444] See Derains & Schwartz, above n 147 at 282.

[445] On the IBA Rules see Raeschke-Kessler, above n 398 at 417–18; Zekoll, *Comparative Civil Procedure*, above n 75 at 1349.

[446] Principle 16.2 states that 'the court should order disclosure of [...] reasonably identified evidence ...'

Some panels have made reference to the requirement of specificity.[447] For instance, in *Canada—Aircraft*, the panel found that it was not appropriate to use its 'authority under Article 13.1 to make generalized requests for information'.[448] In a similar manner, the panel in *Canada—Aircraft Credits and Guarantees* rejected Brazil's application for the panel 'to request from Canada documents and other information concerning the terms of any support from 1 January 1995 onward committed or granted by the Export Development Corporation ("EDC"), Canada Account, Investissement Québec ("IQ"), or any subsidiary organizations thereof, in connection with the sale of regional aircraft by Bombardier.'[449]

Control[450]. Third, the party requesting the information must demonstrate that it does not possess the information requested, that it has made a reasonable effort to obtain the information through other means,[451] and that the requested party is in control of the information. In other words, the requesting party must demonstrate that the requested party has exclusive or preferential access to the information. Information to which the requested party has preferential access is information which cannot reasonably be obtained through other means. For example, information which is in the possession of the requested party and which is deposited in a public archive is *not* information to which the requested party has preferential access. At the same time, if a lengthy and costly lawsuit is required to access the information, the requested party should be considered to have preferential access to the information.

The rationale behind this requirement is that in order for the rules on the burden of proof to work appropriately, particularly in discouraging litigation of claims of doubtful merit,[452] the claimant must be required to search and present evidence in support of its claims. However, when the search reveals the existence of documents which are in the control of the respondent and which the claimant is not able to obtain through reasonable efforts, denying the claimant access to those documents would not advance any legitimate goals; to the contrary, it would impair the achievement of goals such as equality and accuracy. Moreover, the respondent must provide information to which it has exclusive or preferential access because otherwise an imbalance in the cost equation would occur—the costs the claimant would incur to present the information would be substantially higher (arguably even insurmountable, since the information might not be otherwise available at all). Were such an imbalance to occur, as discussed

[447] See, for example, Panel Report, *Canada—Aircraft Credits and Guarantees*, above n 177 at paras 7.134–7.136; Panel Report, *US—Line Pipe*, above n 253 at para 7.4.

[448] Panel Report, *Canada—Aircraft*, above n 136 at para 9.53.

[449] Panel Report, *Canada—Aircraft Credits and Guarantees*, above n 177 at para 7.134, 7.136.

[450] Control may be defined to include physical possession or right to possession.

[451] This should not be interpreted so as to require the requesting party to first address the request directly to the requested party.

[452] See Section III.B of Chapter 4.

in Chapter 4, the burden of proof would probably have to be allocated to the respondent.

The requirement that the requesting party demonstrate that the requested party has exclusive or preferential access to the requested documents has been relied upon by the Iran-United States Claims Tribunal.[453] Article 3.3(c) of IBA Rules requires that a request to produce contain 'a statement that the documents requested are not in the possession, custody or control of the requesting Party, and of the reason why that Party assumes the documents requested to be in the possession, custody or control of the other Party'. This provision does not, at least explicitly, require the requesting party to demonstrate that it has made reasonable efforts to access the information from other sources. An arbitrator operating pursuant to the IBA Rules could, however, on grounds of 'fairness or equality of the Parties' deny a request to produce if it believes that requesting party has not made a reasonable effort to collect the information from another source.[454]

Support for the criterion that the requested party should have exclusive or preferential access to the requested documents can also be found in the WTO jurisprudence. In *US—Upland Cotton* and *Canada—Aircraft* the panel and the Appellate Body referred to the fact that the requested evidence was in the control of the requested party and not available to the requesting party.[455] As indicated in the panel report, in *Canada—Aircraft*, Brazil sought to demonstrate to the panel that it had made reasonable efforts to access the information requested.[456]

An important question with respect to this issue refers to the situation where the evidence requested is in the hands of private parties with an interest in the dispute—for example, in a subsidies dispute, the private party receiving the subsidy at issue in the dispute. Although information which is in the hands of private parties is not strictly speaking in the possession of the requested party, the fact that the relationship between the requested party (the WTO Member) and the private parties holding the information is under consideration in the WTO proceedings suggests that the requested party should be held responsible

[453] See Aghahosseini, above n 423 at 209–10; McCabe, above n 146 at 515, 517; Selby, above n 442 at 140; Holtzmann, *Fact-Finding by the Iran–United States Claims Tribunal*, above n 326 at 120.

[454] Article 9.2 of the Rules provides that '[t]he Arbitral Tribunal shall, at the request of a Party or on its own motion, exclude from evidence or production any document, statement, oral testimony or inspection for any of the following reasons: [...] (g) considerations of fairness or equality of the Parties that the Arbitral Tribunal determines to be compelling.'

[455] Appellate Body Report, *Canada—Aircraft*, above n 81 at para 199; Panel Report, *US—Upland Cotton*, above n 111 at para 7.633.

[456] Panel Report, *Canada—Aircraft*, above n 136 at para 6.157. See also Panel Report, *India—Additional and Extra-Additional Duties on Imports from the United States*, WT/DS360/R, adopted 17 November 2008 at para 7.161. (Although not in the context of a request to produce, the panel noted that the United States was not released from the obligation to present evidence in support of its case just because it might have been easier for India to do so. According to the panel, there was 'no indication that relevant information was not accessible to the United States'.)

for producing that information when requested.[457] This should be particularly the case when the private parties are those that stand to benefit from the non-production of the information requested. For instance, in a subsidies case, while it is the actions of the WTO Member which are challenged in WTO dispute settlement, the private parties receiving the subsidy benefit directly from an outcome which allows the continuation of the subsidy program in question in the proceedings.

An alternative to this solution—which may put the requested party in a difficult situation when the private parties are uncooperative—would be to establish a mechanism which would allow the use of the domestic courts of WTO Members to gather information from private parties. Such mechanism would work in a similar manner to mutual assistance agreements between countries for the taking of evidence in one signatory for use in a proceeding before the courts of another signatory.[458] With a view to respecting the differences between domestic legal cultures, the mechanism could allow WTO Members to choose between (i) giving direct access to their courts to the party (WTO Member) seeking information, (ii) allowing access through the panel, or (iii) allowing access through both means. The United States, for instance, already has legislation in place which could be used for this purpose. Section 1782 of title 28 of the United States Code entitled 'Assistance to foreign and international tribunals and to litigants before such tribunals' provides that:

(a) The district court of the district in which a person resides or is found may *order* him to give his *testimony or statement* or to *produce a document* or other thing *for use in a proceeding in a foreign or international tribunal*, including criminal investigations conducted before formal accusation. The *order may be made pursuant to a letter rogatory* issued, or *request made, by a foreign or international tribunal* or *upon the application of any interested person* and may direct that the testimony or statement be given, or the document or other thing be produced, before a person appointed by the court. By virtue of his appointment, the person appointed has power to administer any necessary oath and take the testimony or statement. The order may prescribe the practice and procedure, which may be in whole or part the practice and procedure of the foreign country or the international tribunal, for taking the testimony or statement or producing the document

457 In support, see Panel Report, *Chile—Alcoholic Beverages*, above n 99 at paras 6.25–6.27 and footnote 390 to para 7.66 (where in the face of a refusal by the *Chilean industry* to produce a report which was in its possession, the panel accepted certain statements made in the Chilean press with respect to the contents of that report. The panel noted that '[w]hile it is the *Chilean government* which is party to this case, it would be unrealistic and artificial to argue that the panel should not address the issue based on this distinction given the direct underlying economic interest of the Chilean industry' [emphasis added]).

458 Examples of such agreements include the Hague Convention on the Taking of Evidence Abroad in Civil or Commercial Matters, concluded on 18 March 1970 and entered into force on 7 October 1972, and in the context of the European Union, Regulation (EC) No 1206/2001 of 28 May 2001 on Cooperation between the Courts of the Member States in the Taking of Evidence in Civil or Commercial Matters.

or other thing. To the extent that the order does not prescribe otherwise, the testimony or statement shall be taken, and the document or other thing produced, in accordance with the Federal Rules of Civil Procedure. A person may not be compelled to give his testimony or statement or to produce a document or other thing in violation of any legally applicable privilege. [Emphasis added]

Section 1782 provides for both options: direct access by any interested person including a party to the international dispute, or access through a request made by an international tribunal.[459] Legislation similar to section 1782, particularly as it concerns a direct application by a disputing party, is not widely available.[460] Therefore, WTO Members would have to agree to introduce such legislation. In practice such agreement would be similar to an agreement for mutual assistance for the taking of evidence in one signatory for use in a proceeding before the courts of another signatory with the exception that the evidence would be taken for use in a WTO dispute settlement proceeding. In order to avoid substantial delays in the WTO dispute settlement proceedings, strict deadlines would have to be agreed to for the execution of the request by domestic courts.

Another alternative for gathering information from private parties would be for the panel to be granted the authority to issue enforceable orders for production of information. In the event the private party in question does not comply with the panel order, the requesting party would then be able to resort to

[459] For more information on section 1782, see John Fellas, 'Using Section 1782 in International Arbitration' (2007) 23:3 Arbitration International 379 (discussing the application of section 1782 for the taking of evidence for use in international arbitration proceedings); John Fellas, 'Obtaining Evidence Abroad for Use in International Litigation: Evidence Located in the United States' (2001) 29:July/August International Business Lawyer 297 (providing general information on section 1782); Roger J Johns & Anne Keaty, 'The New and Improved Section 1782: Supercharging Federal District Court Discovery Assistance to Foreign and International Tribunals' (2006) 29 American Journal of Trial Advocacy 649 (providing general information on section 1782 and explaining the impact of the United States Supreme Court decision *in Intel Corp v Advanced Micro Devices Inc*, 542 US 241 (2004)). See also *In re Oxus Gold plc*, MISC No. 06-82-GEB, 2007 WL 1037387 (DHJ April 2, 2007) (where the US District Court for the District of New Jersey granted discovery under section 1782 in aid of an international arbitration pursuant to the Bilateral Investment Treaty between the Kyrgyz Republic and the United Kingdom); *In re Roz Trading Ltd*, 469 F.Supp.2d 1221 (N.D.Ga. Dec 19, 2006) (where a Georgia district court granted an order for production of documents in aid of a private international commercial arbitration).

[460] In the ambit of international commercial arbitration, UNCITRAL through the UNCITRAL Model Law on International Commercial Arbitration as adopted on 21 June 1985 and modified on 7 July 2006 encourages countries to adopt the following provision in their arbitration acts:
'Article 27. Court assistance in taking evidence
The arbitral tribunal or a party with the approval of the arbitral tribunal may request from a competent court of this State assistance in taking evidence. The court may execute the request within its competence and according to its rules on taking evidence.'
Pursuant to Article 1(2) of the Model Law, this mechanism is only available when the arbitral tribunal has its seat in the territory of the state in question. See Webster, above n 84 at 42 (discussing the problem that as a general rule there are no mechanisms that allow an international commercial arbitral tribunal to enforce a cross-border order for production of documents).

the domestic courts of the WTO Member where the private party is located to enforce the order. In both cases domestic courts would have to be able to impose sanctions for non-compliance with an order to produce. It seems that this is already the case in most jurisdictions.[461]

3.2. Information from non-disputing parties: WTO members, international organizations, private parties, *amicus curiae*, and experts

Panels are not confined to information in the possession of the disputing parties. Pursuant to Article 13 of the DSU panels may seek information and technical advice from any individual, body, or WTO Member, that is to say, they may seek information from any relevant source—they do not, however, have the means to compel or induce cooperation on the part of non-disputing parties. As discussed in previous sections, the authority of the panel to seek information under Article 13 of the DSU is discretionary; panels have the discretion to decide when, how, and whether to seek information. However, as argued throughout this book, the goal of maximizing the values of the dispute settlement system should guide panels in their decisions including, in this case, in the exercise of their discretion under Article 13. When requesting information from non-disputing parties, the delicate balance between accuracy and the efficient use of resources merits special consideration, that is, before requesting information the panel must determine whether the contribution which the evidence is likely to make to the resolution of the dispute justifies the costs of gathering and examining the information. Part of this assessment involves determining whether the information in question is relevant and necessary—a determination which the panel must also make before requesting information from the disputing parties.

It is worth noting again that the fact that according to Article 13 panels have the authority to seek information leads to no other conclusion than that the information sought and received becomes part of the record and as such it may be relied upon by the panels in their decisions. This approach is not only logically supported by Article 13, but is also conducive to accurate outcomes. In other words, as already noted in previous sections, the commanding interest in the proper application of the WTO agreements indicates that the panel should be able to rely upon all relevant information to which it has access. Indubitably, this is not to say that other values of the WTO dispute settlement system such as participation and equality may be sacrificed in the process. A panel can, however, be active in pursuing accurate outcomes and respect the other values of the dispute settlement system at the same time. In this regard, the most important rule which any panel should observe is that the parties must be given a meaningful opportunity to present their views on any piece of evidence which is

[461] See American Law Institute & UNIDROIT, above n 96 at 38–9 (noting that '[a]ll systems authorize direct compulsory measures against third parties').

placed on the record. In this vein, for example, the French Code of Civil Procedure—which lays out a hybrid inquisitorial-adversarial procedure—establishes in Article 7 that:

> The judge may not base his/her decision on facts which are not part of the debate. Provided that a fact has been part of the debate, the judge may take it into consideration even if the parties did not expressly rely upon it to support their claims.[462]

Generally speaking panels have correctly understood that Article 13 of the DSU empowers them to play an active role in the development of the factual record of the proceedings. Invoking their authority under Article 13 of the DSU panels have sought and relied upon information from WTO Members other than the disputing parties, international organizations, private entities, and experts. It is difficult to determine with precision whether before requesting information panels have always carefully considered the balance between accuracy and the efficient use of resources, but the fact that on occasions such as in *Argentina—Textiles and Apparel* the panel refused to seek information from the International Monetary Fund (IMF) because such information would not be relevant to the issue in question suggests that they are aware of that balance.[463] The following paragraphs provide an overview of how panels have used their authority under Article 13 of the DSU to gather and use information from non-disputing parties.

i. WTO Members. Pursuant to Article 13 a panel may seek information from any WTO Member including third parties and Members which are not a party to the dispute. In this regard, Article 13 provides that '*A Member* should respond promptly and fully to any request by a panel for such information as the panel considers necessary and appropriate' [emphasis added]. In *Canada—Aircraft*, the Appellate Body confirmed that 'the discretionary authority of a panel may be exercised to request and obtain information [...] from *any Member* [...]'.[464] Such authority was exercised by the panel in *Turkey—Textiles* where the panel sought information from the European Communities, a WTO Member which was not a party to the dispute, in order to ensure that it had 'the fullest possible understanding' of the case before it.[465] Moreover, evidence submitted by third

[462] Article 7: 'Le juge ne peut fonder sa décision sur des faits qui ne sont pas dans le débat. Parmi les éléments du débat, le juge peut prendre en considération même les faits que les parties n'auraient pas spécialement invoqués au soutien de leurs prétentions.'

[463] Panel Report, *Argentina—Textiles and Apparel*, above n 90 at paras 6.78–6.79 (where the panel rejected the argument that an agreement with the IMF could have excused Argentina from complying with the requirements of Article VIII of the GATT, leading to the conclusion that the information which the IMF could provide would not be relevant to the dispute). The panel's decision not to seek information from the IMF was upheld by the Appellate Body. Appellate Body Report, *Argentina—Textiles and Apparel*, above n 184 at paras 82–6.

[464] Appellate Body Report, *Canada—Aircraft*, above n 81 at para 185 [original emphasis].

[465] Panel Report, *Turkey—Restrictions on Imports of Textile and Clothing Products*, WT/DS34/R, adopted 19 November 1999 at para 4.1.

parties was taken into account by the panel in several instances. For example, in *EC—Sardines* the panel took into account information submitted by Canada, a third party to the dispute, in concluding that European consumers do not associate the term 'sardines' exclusively with the species *Sardina pilchardus.*[466]

ii. International organizations and private entities. As noted already, Article 13 of the DSU grants a panel the authority to 'seek information from any relevant source' including 'any individual or body which it deems appropriate'. This allows panels to seek information from *any* available source, undoubtedly including international organizations and private entities. In this regard, in *India—Quantitative Restrictions*, given controversy over whether Article XV:2 of the GATT requires dispute settlement panels to consult with the IMF,[467] the panel invoked its authority under Article 13 of the DSU to seek certain information from the IMF.[468] The information provided was taken into account by the panel in deciding the claims before it;[469] as a matter of fact, as noted by the Appellate Body, the panel 'gave considerable weight to the views expressed by the IMF'.[470] The panel in *Canada—Continued Suspension* also requested information and met with representatives of several international entities including the Codex Alimentarius Commission (the 'CODEX'), the International Agency for Research on Cancer (the 'IARC'), and the Joint FAO/WHO Expert Committee on Food Additives (the 'JECFA').[471]

Importantly, the panel may not only actively request information, but also receive unrequested information (ie *amicus curiae* submissions) which it

[466] Panel Report, *EC—Sardines*, above n 180 at paras 6.17, 7.132. See also Panel Report, *Korea—Alcoholic Beverages*, above n 222 at para 10.58 (where the panel noted that it considered 'it appropriate to take into consideration information provided by a third party').

[467] Article XV:2 of the GATT provides that the CONTRACTING PARTIES 'shall consult fully with the International Monetary Fund' when considering matters regarding monetary reserves, balance of payments or foreign exchange arrangements. While this obligation is applicable to the WTO as an institution, it is not clear whether it is also applicable to dispute settlement panels. The panel and the Appellate Body preferred not to address this question.

[468] Panel Report, *India—Quantitative Restrictions*, above n 180 at paras 5.12–5.13. But see Panel Report, *Dominican Republic—Measures Affecting the Importation and Internal Sale of Cigarettes*, WT/DS302/R, adopted 19 May 2005 at paras 7.139, 7.142, 7.145 (where the panel requested and considered information under Article XV:2 of the GATT and para 8 of the 1996 Agreement between the International Monetary Fund and the World Trade Organization instead of Article 13 of the DSU). See also Panel Report, *United States—Section 211 Omnibus Appropriations Act of 1998*, WT/DS176/R, adopted 1 February 2002 at para 8.13; Panel Report, *European Communities—Protection of Trademarks and Geographical Indications for Agricultural Products and Foodstuffs, Complaint by the United States*, WT/DS174/R, adopted 20 April 2005 at para 2.16. In both cases the panel requested information from the International Bureau of the WIPO. The information requested, however, regarded the abstract interpretation of certain treaty provisions, rather than the determination of the facts of the case strictly speaking.

[469] Panel Report, *India—Quantitative Restrictions*, above n 180 at paras 5.12–5.13, 5.120.

[470] Appellate Body Report, *India—Quantitative Restrictions*, above n 284 at para 149.

[471] Panel Report, *Canada—Continued Suspension of Obligations in the EC—Hormones Dispute*, WT/DS321/R, adopted 14 November 2008 at paras 1.7, 7.76.

considers relevant. This view was confirmed by the Appellate Body in *US—Shrimp*, where it ruled that '[a] panel has the discretionary authority either to accept and consider or to reject information and advice submitted to it, *Whether requested by a panel or not*'.[472] Although some WTO Members opposed this decision,[473] a contrary interpretation would be incongruous since in any event the panel clearly has the authority to actively request the information which is otherwise voluntarily submitted. In addition, as the Appellate Body noted, Article 12 of the DSU gives panels wide latitude to develop their own Working Procedures.[474] The fact that the panel has the authority to accept and consider unsolicited information does not, however, mean that international organizations and private entities have a *right* to have their submissions accepted and considered by a panel.[475] As the Appellate Body pointed out in *US—Shrimp*, 'under the DSU, only Members who are parties to a dispute, or who have notified their interest in becoming third parties in such a dispute to the DSB, have a *legal right* to make submissions to, and have a *legal right* to have those submissions considered by, a panel'.[476] Accordingly, it falls within the discretion of the panel to decide whether to accept *amicus curiae* briefs, just as it falls within its discretion to decide whether to actively request information from any relevant source.

It is true that the acceptance of unsolicited information may pose problems such as the costs involved in analysing and responding (rebutting allegations and evidence) to submissions which may contain information which is mostly irrelevant to the issues in dispute. Moreover, when such information is one-sided those costs would fall mainly on the disfavoured party, disturbing the equilibrium between the parties. These and other similar problems can, however, be addressed in a manner which would *not* require the panel to reject information which is relevant to the dispute and which may be crucial for an accurate decision.[477] Accordingly, 'relevance' should be the main criterion for accepting *amicus curiae* briefs. Before accepting an *amicus curiae* submission the panel should be required to find that such submission contains information which is

472 Appellate Body Report, *US—Shrimp*, above n 350 at para 108 [original emphasis].

473 See, for example, Minutes of the Meeting of the Dispute Settlement Body held on 6 November 1998, WTO Doc WT/DSB/M/50, 14 December 1998.

474 Appellate Body Report, *US—Shrimp*, above n 350 at paras 105–6.

475 A WTO Member which is not a party or third party to a dispute may also submit an *amicus curiae* brief; such brief will be treated as a brief submitted by a private entity or international organization. See Appellate Body Report, *EC—Sardines*, above n 289 at paras 163–7.

476 Appellate Body Report, *US—Shrimp*, above n 350 at para 101 [original emphasis].

477 In support of the view that *amicus curiae* briefs may contain valuable information for an accurate decision, see Georg C Umbricht, 'An 'Amicus Curiae Brief' on Amicus Curiae Briefs at the WTO' (2001) 4 Journal of International Economic Law 773 at 783; Petros C Mavroidis, 'Amicus Curiae Briefs before the WTO: Much Ado about Nothing' (2001) Jean Monnet Working Paper 2/01, available at <http://www.worldtradelaw.net/articles/mavroidisamicus.pdf> (accessed 22 April 2008) at 11–12.

relevant to the issues in dispute.[478] In order to facilitate the task of the panel, interested entities should be required to apply for a leave to file a submission.[479] Such application must concisely (i) identify the specific issues which the applicant intends to address in its submission, and (ii) indicate how the submission, including the supporting evidence, is relevant to the issues in dispute which the applicant intends to address.[480] Where leave to file a submission is granted, the panel should then determine whether the submission is indeed relevant. At this stage, it would be a good practice for the panel to indicate to the parties which aspects of the *amicus curiae* submission it considers relevant to the issues in dispute.[481] Finally, also in order to facilitate the panel's task of determining the relevance of the information, the application for leave to file a submission (and the submission itself) must be submitted *after* the parties to the dispute have filed their first written submissions, but, so as to prevent delays and provide the parties a meaningful opportunity to respond, *before* the second set of written submissions is due.

iii. Experts. Article 13 of the DSU also grants panels the authority to request *sua sponte* the opinion of experts on scientific and other technical matters raised in the dispute. Article 11.2 of the SPS Agreement and Article 14.2 of the TBT Agreement reinforce that authority in disputes brought under those agreements. Panel-appointed experts are assistants to the panel. They assist the panel in establishing the facts of the case. In cases where technical matters are at issue, experts may play an important role in ensuring an accurate decision. Article 11.2 of the SPS Agreement explicitly acknowledges this fact; it provides that in disputes 'involving scientific or technical issues, a panel *should* seek advice from experts' [emphasis added]. The important role which experts may play in assisting adjudicators to reach accurate decisions is also recognized by other

[478] In favour of such requirement, see Contribution of the European Communities and its Member States to the Improvement of the WTO Dispute Settlement Understanding, WTO Doc TN/DS/W/1, 13 March 2002 at 11. See also Gabrielle Marceau & Matthew Stilwell, 'Practical Suggestions for Amicus Curiae Briefs before WTO Adjudicating Bodies' (2001) 4 Journal of International Economic Law 155 at 180–1 (noting that '[i]nformation may be accepted where it has a "direct bearing" on the case').

[479] In support, see Contribution of the European Communities and its Member States to the Improvement of the WTO Dispute Settlement Understanding, WTO Doc TN/DS/W/1, 13 March 2002 at 11.

[480] I do not purport to discus all the requirements which an application for leave to file an *amicus curiae* submission, and the submission itself, should meet. For other possible requirements, see Contribution of the European Communities and its Member States to the Improvement of the WTO Dispute Settlement Understanding, WTO Doc TN/DS/W/1, 13 March 2002 at 11–12; Communication from the Appellate Body in *European Communities—Measures Affecting Asbestos and Asbestos-Containing Products*, WTO Doc WT/DS135/9, 8 November 2000 (although the requirements contained in this document refer to *amicus curiae* briefs filed at the appellate stage, most of those requirements would be relevant for the panel stage as well).

[481] Similarly, see Marceau & Stilwell, above n 478 at 184.

systems of adjudication which make provision for adjudicator-appointed experts to report on specific questions of fact related to their expertise.[482]

As noted in Section II.C.3.2 of Chapter 1, panels have the discretion not only to decide whether to seek expert advice but also to decide how to seek such advice.[483] The language of Article 13 of the DSU is broad enough to support this interpretation.[484] A panel may opt for establishing an expert review group, in which case Appendix 4 to the DSU and Annex 2 to the TBT Agreement establish basic rules on how such groups should be constituted and how they should operate. Alternatively, a panel may appoint individual experts, which has been the preferred choice of panels.[485] The procedures for individual expert consultations are developed by the panels in each case in consultation with the parties. Typically the panels in consultation with the parties, draft questions covering specific issues raised in the dispute particularly those in which the parties disagree. Such questions are sent to the experts, who are asked to answer

[482] See, for instance, Ughi et al, above n 249 at 30–2 (discussing Article 6 of the IBA Rules); Derains & Schwartz, above n 147 at 276–9 (discussing Article 20.4 of the ICC Rules of Arbitration); McCabe, above n 146 (discussing Rule 27 of the Rules of the Iran–United States Claims Tribunal). Court appointed experts are also common in civilian jurisdictions; in this regard, see Langbein, *The German Advantage*, above n 77 at 839–41; Taruffo, above n 321 at 516–18; Elsing & Townsend, above n 388 at 63–4.

[483] Discussing the advantages and disadvantages of expert review groups versus individual experts, see Joost Pauwelyn, 'The Use of Experts in WTO Dispute Settlement' (2002) 51 International and Comparative Law Quarterly 325 at 327–9; Theofanis Christoforou, 'WTO Panels in the Face of Scientific Uncertainty' in F Weiss (ed), *Improving WTO Dispute Settlement Procedures: Issues and Lessons from the Practice of Other International Courts and Tribunals* (London: Cameron May, 2000) 243 at 255–60.

[484] Article 13.1 states that '[e]ach panel shall have the right to seek information and technical advice from any individual or body which it deems appropriate'. Article 13.2 provides that '[p]anels may seek information from any relevant source and may consult experts to obtain their opinion on certain aspects of the matter. With respect to a factual issue concerning a scientific or other technical matter raised by a party to a dispute, a panel *may* request an advisory report in writing from an expert review group' [emphasis added]. In support, see Appellate Body Report, *EC—Hormones*, above n 42 at paras 146–7.

[485] Panels have appointed individual experts in at least 11 disputes from 1995 to 2008. Panel Report, *United States—Continued Suspension of Obligations in the EC—Hormones Dispute*, WT/DS320/R, adopted 14 November 2008 paras 7.71–7.75; Panel Report, *Canada—Continued Suspension*, above n 471 at paras 7.69–7.73; Panel Report, *EC—Approval and Marketing of Biotech Products*, above n 217 at paras 7.18; Panel Report, *European Communities—Measures Affecting Asbestos and Asbestos-Containing Products*, WT/DS135/R and Add.1, adopted 5 April 2001 at para 8.10; Panel Report, *United States—Import Prohibition of Certain Shrimp and Shrimp Products*, WT/DS58/R and Corr.1, adopted 6 November 1998 at para 7.9; Panel Report, *Australia—Salmon*, above n 231 at para 6.1; Panel Report, *Australia—Measures Affecting Importation of Salmon—Recourse to Article 21.5 of the DSU by Canada*, WT/DS18/RW, adopted 20 March 2000, DSR 2000:IV, 2031 at para 6.1; Panel Report, *Japan—Measures Affecting Agricultural Products*, WT/DS76/R, adopted 19 March 1999 at para 6.2; Panel Report, *European Communities—Measures Concerning Meat and Meat Products (Hormones), Complaint by Canada*, WT/DS48/R/CAN, adopted 13 February 1998 at para 8.7; Panel Report, *Japan—Apples*, above n 89 at para 6.2; Panel Report, *Japan—Measures Affecting Consumer Photographic Film and Paper*, WT/DS44/R, adopted 22 April 1998, DSR 1998:IV, 1179 at para 1.9–1.10.

in writing those questions which fall within their area of expertise.[486] After the panel and the parties have an opportunity to review and comment on the answers of the experts, a meeting is held to discuss those answers allowing the panel and the parties to cross-examine the experts.[487]

The opinion of the experts—either in the form of answers to questions or of a report in case the panel decides to establish an expert review group—is treated as a piece of evidence which the panel has the freedom to evaluate, that is to say, the opinion of the experts is not binding on the panel.[488] Panels, however, usually accord those opinions great weight. In most cases where experts were consulted, particularly those brought under the SPS Agreement, the experts' opinions had a clear impact on the findings of the panels. In cases such as *EC—Hormones*,[489] *Japan—Apples*,[490] and *Australia—Salmon*[491] the panels made numerous references to the views expressed by the experts in support of their findings. In certain instances the expert evidence was crucial for the establishment of a proposition at issue.[492] For example, in *EC—Hormones* the panel relied entirely on the opinion of the experts to support its finding that the treatment of the hormones oestradiol-17β, testosterone, and progesterone 'when used for growth promotion purposes as opposed to the treatment of these hormones which (i) occur endogenously in meat and other foods and (ii) which have been administered for therapeutic or zootechnical purposes, constitute comparable situations in the sense of Article 5.5.'[493] Similarly, in *Australia—Salmon* the opinion of the experts was crucial for the panel's finding that the biological and economic consequences of the introduction of the diseases which Australia sought to prevent would be the same or similar irrespective of whether

[486] See Panel Report, *EC—Approval and Marketing of Biotech Products*, above n 217 at para 7.26; Panel Report, *Japan—Apples*, above n 89 at para 6.2. See also Scott, above n 42 at 134.

[487] Panel Report, *EC—Approval and Marketing of Biotech Products*, above n 217 at para 7.29; Panel Report, *Japan—Apples*, above n 89 at para 6.2. See also Mireille Cossy, 'Panel's Consultations with Scientific Experts: the Right to Seek Information under Article 13 of the DSU' in R Yerxa & B Wilson (eds), *Key Issues in WTO Dispute Settlement: the First Ten Years* (Cambridge: Cambridge University Press, 2005) 204 at 215–16.

[488] Assistance sought under Article 4.5 of the SCM Agreement and in certain cases under Article XV:2 of the GATT (assuming that Article XV.2 applies to dispute settlement panels) is the exception. In such cases, the panel is obliged to accept the conclusions of the Permanent Group of Experts or the IMF respectively.

[489] Panel Report, *EC—Hormones (Canada)*, above n 485.

[490] Panel Report, *Japan—Apples*, above n 89.

[491] Panel Report, *Australia—Salmon*, above n 231.

[492] This is also the view of Cottier. According to Cottier, in *EC—Hormones*, *Australia—Salmon*, and *Japan Agricultural Products II*, 'panels strongly relied upon expert views, and could not have rendered their assessment and recommendation without such independent advice of individual experts'. Thomas Cottier, 'Risk Management Experience in WTO Dispute Settlement' in D Robertson & A Kellow (eds), *Globalization and the Environment: Risk Assessment and the WTO* (Chelthenham: Edward Elgar, 2001) 41 at 51.

[493] Panel Report, *EC—Hormones (Canada)*, above n 485 at paras 8.189–8.190. While the Appellate Body reversed the panel's conclusion that the European Communities acted inconsistently with the requirements set out in Article 5.5 of the SPS Agreement, it did not reverse this specific finding regarding the comparability of the situations.

the disease was introduced by imports of the salmon products in question or by imports of herring used as bait or live ornamental finfish.[494] Moreover, in *Japan—Apples*, the panel relied entirely upon the opinion of the experts in addressing the issue of *apples other than* mature symptomless apples—the panel expressly noted that the United States submitted evidence only with respect to mature symptomless apples.[495] In finding that the last stage of the pathway—namely, the transmission of fire blight from an apple to a host plant—would likely not be completed, the panel again referred exclusively to the evidence provided by the experts.[496] Accordingly, experts have been an important source of information particularly in disputes involving scientific knowledge.

Given their role as assistants to the panel and their influence on the decision-making process, particularly in disputes involving scientific knowledge, it is important that experts be held to similar standards as are panels regarding their independence and impartiality.[497] This much is recognized by the Rules of Conduct which apply equally to panels and panel-appointed experts.[498] When selecting experts, therefore, panels must be careful not to select persons who could be perceived to lack the requisites of independence and impartiality. This issue came up in *Canada—Continued Suspension.* In that case, despite the opposition of the European Communities, the panel appointed two experts who had been involved in the drafting and adoption of the risk assessments which the European Communities did not accept as a basis for its measures and which lay at the centre of the dispute. The panel disagreed with the European Communities that the experts' involvement in the preparation of those risk assessments would affect their objectivity—in fact, the panel saw the experts' involvement as an advantage, since they would be able to assist the panel in understanding the work of JECFA, the institution sponsoring the risk assessments.[499] Whether their objectivity would in fact be affected, however, should not have been the test. The test, as the Appellate Body correctly identified, should have been whether there were any facts that would likely affect or give rise to justifiable

[494] Panel Report, *Australia—Salmon*, above n 231 at para 8.135.

[495] Panel Report, *Japan—Apples*, above n 89 at paras 8.153–8.160. This view is shared by Scott, above n 42 at 130 and footnote 185.

[496] Panel Report, *Japan—Apples*, above n 89 at paras 8.162–8.166.

[497] The Appellate Body has also recognized that '[e]xperts appointed by a panel can significantly influence the decision-making process'. Appellate Body Report, *Canada—Continued Suspension*, above n 48 at para 480. See also André J Faurès, 'Improving Procedures for Expert Testimony' in AJ van den Berg (ed), *Planning Efficient Arbitration Proceedings* (The Hague: Kluwer Law, 1996) 154 at 156 (noting that while an expert witness is an agent of the party which retains it, 'an expert appointed by the tribunal has to be neutral and independent of the parties.'); Erik Schafer, Herman Verbist & Christophe Imhoos, *ICC Arbitration in Practice* (The Hague: Kluwer Law International, 2005) at 106 (noting that tribunal-appointed experts 'are required to be independent and impartial, like arbitrators').

[498] See Rule IV.1 of the Rules of Conduct for the Understanding on Rules and Procedures Governing the Settlement of Disputes, WTO Doc WT/DSB/RC/1, 11 December 1996.

[499] Panel Report, *Canada—Continued Suspension*, above n 471 at paras 6.21, 7.83.

doubts as to the independence or impartiality of the experts.[500] In *Canada—Continued Suspension*, the fact that the two experts were directly involved in issues which were at the centre of the dispute would have met that test. This was recognized by the Appellate Body, which concluded that the panel infringed the due process rights of the European Communities by consulting with the two experts.[501] If the panel was really interested in understanding the work of JECFA, it should have invited the two experts to appear as witnesses, as opposed to appointing them as assistants to the panel.

Finally, it is worth noting that experts have rarely been used in connection with non-scientific technical issues. *Japan—Film* is one of the few if not the only case where experts were used in connection with an issue which did not involve scientific knowledge—in that case the panel appointed translation experts.[502] Given the fact that panels are often called on to examine complex economic questions, it is notable that they have never appointed economic experts. The significant role which experts have played in scientific disputes suggests that more consideration should be given to the idea of appointing economic experts when panels are asked to make complex economic determinations that fall outside their area of expertise.[503]

4. *The limits of the fact-finding powers of the panel*

The previous sections explained that panels have ample authority to seek and rely upon information from any source. Although the fact-finding powers of panels are ample, they are not limitless. This raises the question 'What are the limits of the fact-finding powers of panels?' The activities of panels are limited in several different ways, as discussed throughout this book, such as the obligation in Article 11 of the DSU enjoining panels to 'make an objective assessment of the matter before [them], including an objective assessment of the facts of the case' and, relatedly, a general obligation to act within the bounds of reasonableness. This section focuses on two specific limitations: (i) the terms of reference of a panel; and (ii) due process (ie participation and impartiality). The

[500] Appellate Body Report, *Canada—Continued Suspension*, above n 48 at paras 445, 454, 481.

[501] Appellate Body Report, *Canada—Continued Suspension*, above n 48 at paras 481–2.

[502] See Panel Report, *Japan—Film*, above n 485 at paras 1.9–1.10.

[503] Andre Sapir & Joel P Trachtman, 'Subsidization, Price Suppression, and Expertise: Causation and Precision in *Upland Cotton*' (2008) 7:1 World Trade Review 183 at 205–7 (arguing for the use of economic experts in cases where panels are required to make complex economic determinations). Similarly, see Hylke Vandenbussche, 'Comment: Upland Cotton Case' (2008) 7:1 World Trade Review 211 at 216–17. Suggesting that panels should consider appointing economic experts when the economic issues before them are complex, see Appellate Body Report, *United States—Subsidies on Upland Cotton—Recourse to Article 21.5 of the DSU by Brazil*, WT/DS267/AB/RW, adopted 20 June 2008 at paras 357–8 (where the Appellate Body noted that the 'relative complexity of a model and its parameters is not a reason for a panel to remain agnostic about them'. According to the Appellate Body, 'the Panel could have gone further in its evaluation and comparative analysis of the economic simulations and the particular parameters used').

discussion which follows also clarifies what should *not* constitute limitations upon the authority of panels.

4.1. Terms of reference and due process

Panels have terms of reference which determine the matter which is to be examined and ruled upon by them. Article 7.1 of the DSU provides that the terms of reference of the panel are 'to examine [. . .] the matter referred to the DSB'. The matter referred to the DSB is as a general rule that described in the request for establishment of a panel. According to Article 6.2 of the DSU, which sets forth the requirements of the request for establishment of a panel, the matter at issue consists of two interrelated elements: (i) the 'specific measure at issue', namely, the object of the challenge, and (ii) the 'legal basis of the complaint'.[504] The Appellate Body often refers to the latter element as the 'claim'—while the Appellate Body has not expressly stated so, throughout this book the term 'claim' refers to the statement which links the measure at issue to the obligation which that measure allegedly violates. In short, in the words of the Appellate Body, 'the panel request identifies the measures and the claims that a panel will have the authority to examine and on which it will have the authority to make findings'.[505] In other words, a panel, as do most legal adjudicators, must respect the *non ultra petita* rule which prevents adjudicators from awarding more than what was sought.[506]

Accordingly, as a panel can only rule on a matter that is within its terms of reference, its fact-finding powers cannot be exercised with respect to matters that are outside those terms of reference. The same must apply in those situations where a party renounces one of its claims either directly or indirectly by choosing not to pursue the claim in its submissions; this is so because the parties, particularly the complainant, are the ones that control the terms of reference. This was the case in *Chile—Price Band System*, where the Appellate Body found that the panel 'acted *ultra petita* and inconsistently with' its duty under Article 11 of the DSU to 'make an objective assessment of the *matter before it*' when it ruled on a claim under the second sentence of Article II:1(b) of the GATT.[507] According to the Appellate Body, while 'the terms of reference were broad enough to have included a claim under the second sentence of Article II:1(b)', an examination of the complainant's submissions indicated that the complainant

[504] In this regard, see Appellate Body Report, *Guatemala—Anti-Dumping Investigation Regarding Portland Cement from Mexico*, WT/DS60/AB/R, adopted 25 November 1998, DSR 1998:IX, 3767 at para 76.

[505] Appellate Body Report, *European Communities—Selected Customs Matters*, WT/DS315/AB/R, adopted 11 December 2006 at para 131.

[506] The Black's Law Dictionary provides the following definition of '*ultra petita*': 'Beyond that which was sought. "A judgment or decision is said to be *ultra petita* when it awards more than was sought or sued for in the petition or summons; and the same thing is said of a sentence when it [does] not conform to its grounds and warrants. This affords a good ground for the reversal or reduction of such a decree." John Trayner, Trayner's Latin Maxims 609–10 (4th ed. 1894).' *Black's Law Dictionary* (8th edn, St Paul: Thomson West, 2004) at 1559.

[507] Appellate Body Report, *Chile—Price Band System*, above n 114 at para 173.

did not articulate a claim under that sentence—the complainant had not mentioned the claim during the entire proceedings.[508] The fact that the third parties had submitted arguments on the issue did not alter the Appellate Body's conclusion.[509]

The *non ultra petita* rule is a function not only of the language of Articles 7.1, 6.2, and 11 of the DSU but also of the due process requirement of meaningful participation; a panel must not rule on a claim which the parties did not have a meaningful opportunity to address. This much was recognized by the Appellate Body in *Chile—Price Band System* where it found that the panel deprived the respondent of a fair right of response when it ruled on a claim which was not made by the complainant.[510] In that case, the Appellate Body ruled that the panel acted inconsistently with its duty under Article 11 of the DSU to 'make an objective assessment of the matter before it' when it ruled on a matter that was not before it and, relatedly, when it did not ensure that due process was respected.[511]

The Appellate Body has ruled in several occasions that while a panel cannot rule on a claim which is not before it, the panel is not under an obligation to base its decision with respect to a claim which is before it on the specific arguments put forward by the disputing parties.[512] According to the Appellate Body, a claim is an allegation 'that the respondent party has violated, or nullified or impaired the benefits arising from, an identified provision of a particular agreement', and it must be set out in the request for the establishment of a panel.[513] In contrast, arguments 'are the means whereby a party progressively develops and supports its claims',[514] and they are 'set out and progressively clarified in the first written submissions, the rebuttal submissions and the first and second panel meetings with the parties'.[515] Moreover, as discussed in the previous sections of this chapter, just as the panel does not have to base its decision on the specific arguments advanced by the disputing parties, the panel is not limited to the evidence presented by the disputing parties in support of those arguments. In short, while the parties determine the subject matter of the dispute, they cannot restrict the pool of arguments and evidence which the panel may rely upon in delivering its decision with respect to the matter that is before it. It is worth noting that this is not an exclusive feature of the WTO dispute

[508] Appellate Body Report, *Chile—Price Band System*, above n 114 at paras 165–8, 173.

[509] Appellate Body Report, *Chile—Price Band System*, above n 114 at para 163.

[510] Appellate Body Report, *Chile—Price Band System*, above n 114 at paras 174–7.

[511] Appellate Body Report, *Chile—Price Band System*, above n 114 at paras 173, 176–7.

[512] See, for example, Appellate Body Report, *EC—Hormones*, above n 42 at para 156; Appellate Body Report, *European Communities—Export Subsidies on Sugar*, WT/DS265/AB/R, WT/DS266/AB/R, WT/DS283/AB/R, adopted 19 May 2005 at para 286.

[513] Appellate Body Report, *Korea—Dairy*, above n 372 at para 139.

[514] Appellate Body Report, *Dominican Republic—Measures Affecting the Importation and Internal Sale of Cigarettes*, WT/DS302/AB/R, adopted 19 May 2005 at para 121. See also Appellate Body Report, *Korea—Dairy*, above n 372 at para 139; Appellate Body Report, *EC—Bananas*, above n 117 at para 141.

[515] Appellate Body Report, *Korea—Dairy*, above n 372 at para 139.

settlement system, but a common feature of many systems of legal adjudication, particularly those which grant adjudicators the power to seek information *sua sponte*.[516]

In this context, the only plausible interpretation of the panel's statement in *US—Upland Cotton* that evidence presented by third parties cannot 'alleviate the complainant's burden to establish a *prima facie* case'[517] is that evidence submitted by a third party cannot be used to rule on a claim which was not pursued (ie implicitly renounced) by the claimant during the proceedings.[518] Third parties have no control over the subject matter of the dispute—they cannot make claims. Therefore, if a claim is abandoned during the proceedings, a third party cannot revive it. Along these lines, when the Appellate Body in *Chile—Price Band System* found that the panel erred in ruling on a claim which was stated in the panel request but was never pursued by the complainant, it expressly noted that the fact that third parties had presented arguments on the claim did not alter that conclusion.[519]

4.2. *Japan—Agricultural Products II*

Japan—Agricultural Products II is a particularly problematic case in relation to what has been discussed above, and, therefore, merits special attention.[520] In that case, it was undisputed that the complainant (the United States) had claimed that Japan's varietal testing requirement was inconsistent with Article 5.6 of the SPS Agreement which requires Members to ensure that their sanitary or phytosanitary 'measures are not more trade-restrictive than required to achieve their appropriate level of sanitary or phytosanitary protection, taking into account technical and economic feasibility'. Before the panel, the United States sought to demonstrate that testing by product was a reasonably available less-trade-restrictive measure capable of achieving the level of protection chosen by Japan. The consultations with the experts during the proceedings allowed the panel to identify two other alternative measures which were potentially less-trade-restrictive than the measure which Japan had in place.[521] After examining

[516] See, for instance, Lasok, above n 155 at 365 (noting that the ECJ 'is not obliged to restrict its investigation of the facts to the documents produced in the pleadings; it is not bound to accede to a party's desire to prove a fact by, for example, the testimony of a string of witnesses. The means to prove facts lie within the discretion of the Court to order'); Jolowicz, *Adversarial and Inquisitorial Models*, above n 330 at 291–3 (noting that in France while the parties control the subject matter of the action, they have little control over the evidence).

[517] Panel Report, *US—Upland Cotton*, above n 111 at para 6.54. The panel also noted that information supplied by a third party 'may constitute evidence, in terms of additional context and support, that [panels] may take into account in conducting an objective assessment of the matter before [them]'.

[518] As discussed in Chapter 3, different meanings can be assigned to the supposed requirement that a complainant must establish a *prima facie* case, none of which are in harmony with the basic structure of the WTO dispute settlement system.

[519] Appellate Body Report, *Chile—Price Band System*, above n 114 at para 163.

[520] This case is frequently invoked in challenges to the panel's use of its fact-finding powers.

[521] Panel Report, *Japan—Agricultural Products II*, above n 485 at paras 8.73–8.77.

all three potential alternatives, the panel concluded that one of the alternative measures which it identified—namely, determining whether the sorption level of additional varieties differs from that of the already approved varieties—was a reasonably available less-trade-restrictive measure according to Article 5.6 of the SPS Agreement—the other two measures did not meet all the requirements of Article 5.6.[522] Having determined that an alternative measure meeting all the requirements of Article 5.6 was available, the panel concluded that the varietal testing requirement maintained by Japan was more trade-restrictive than required within the meaning of Article 5.6 and that, therefore, Japan was acting inconsistently with its obligations under that provision. On appeal, the Appellate Body reversed the panel on the grounds that the panel erred 'when it used [the] expert information and advice as the basis for a finding of inconsistency with Article 5.6, since the United States did not establish a *prima facie* case of inconsistency with Article 5.6 based on claims relating to the "determination of sorption levels"'.[523] According to the Appellate Body, a panel cannot use its fact-finding powers 'to rule in favour of a complaining party which has not established a *prima facie* case of inconsistency based on specific legal claims asserted by it', that is, the panel cannot use its powers 'to make the case for a complaining party'.[524] The discussion in the previous paragraphs indicates that this ruling of the Appellate Body is erroneous for at least three reasons: (i) the panel ruled on a matter which *was* before it; (ii) the panel was not obliged to base its decision on the arguments and evidence presented by the parties, but rather it had to consider all the arguments and evidence on the record and deliver a decision which represented an objective assessment of the matter before it; and (iii) there was no indication that the panel was partial. These three reasons are further explored in the sequence.

First, it is clear that the United States had claimed that Japan's measure was inconsistent with Article 5.6 of the SPS Agreement because it was more trade-restrictive than required to achieve Japan's 'appropriate level of sanitary or phytosanitary protection, taking into account technical and economic feasibility'. This claim was stated in the request for establishment of a panel and was actively pursued by the United States during the proceedings. Therefore, the panel ruled on a matter that was before it. It is true that the United States had not *argued* (and presented evidence in support of the argument) that the determination of sorption levels was an alternative measure, but it did make a claim which covered that argument. Accordingly, it is clear that the Appellate Body confused claims and arguments.[525] Further support for the view that the suggestion of a specific alternative measure was an argument rather than a claim can be found in *Canada—Wheat Board*. In *Canada—Wheat Board* in deciding

522 Panel Report, *Japan—Agricultural Products II*, above n 485 at para 8.103.
523 Appellate Body Report, *Japan—Agricultural Products II*, above n 302 at para 130.
524 Appellate Body Report, *Japan—Agricultural Products II*, above n 302 at para 129.
525 In support, see Pauwelyn, *The Use of Experts*, above n 483 at 352.

whether Section 57(c) of the *Canada Grain Act* complied with the 'necessity' requirement of Article XX(d) of the GATT the panel identified on its own a reasonably available alternative measure which was less-trade-restrictive than Section 57(c) and that, therefore, indicated that Section 57(c) was not necessary.[526]

Second, as the Appellate Body has itself found several times, the panel was not obliged to base its decision on the specific arguments and evidence presented by the disputing parties. The Appellate Body's finding that the panel erred 'when it used [the] expert information and advice as the basis for a finding of inconsistency with Article 5.6' is at odds (i) with Article 13 of the DSU, (ii) the Appellate Body's rulings clarifying that Article 13 grants panels ample authority to seek information with respect to the matter before them, and (iii) cases such as *Japan—Apples*, *Australia—Salmon*, and *EC—Hormones*[527] where the information which the panels gathered from the experts was crucial to some of the panels' findings. Moreover, the Appellate Body in *Japan—Agricultural Products II* suggests that only when the arguments and evidence submitted *exclusively by the claimant* have reached the threshold of a '*prima facie* case', the panel is allowed to consider the other evidence on the record. In other words, the Appellate Body suggests that the claimant bears a burden of going forward, a view which was rejected in Chapter 3 as being incongruous with the structure of the WTO dispute settlement system and the Appellate Body's rulings in other cases. Finally, the Appellate Body's ruling that the panel could not rely upon the expert evidence suggests that panels may consciously disregard relevant information which is part of the record when ruling on a matter that is before them, a proposition which is irreconcilable with the panel's obligation to make an objective assessment of the matter before it. In short, the Appellate Body implied that panels can ignore what is proven to be the truth with respect to the matter before them. This was particularly significant in *Japan—Agricultural Products II* because the panel was later shown to be correct when the parties to the dispute reached a mutually agreed solution based on the alternatives which had been identified by the panel in consultation with the experts.[528]

Third, the Appellate Body implied that the panel had 'made the case' for the complainant, but neither the record of the proceedings nor the Appellate Body report indicated that the panel was partial. Given the breadth of the powers granted to the panel under Article 13 of the DSU, the idea that a panel errs when it 'makes the case for a party' must be related to the existence of bias. A different interpretation would be contrary to Article 13 of the DSU because

[526] Panel Report, *Canada—Wheat Exports and Grain Imports*, above n 180 at para 6.229. Similarly, paragraphs 6.308–6.309. See also Appellate Body Report, *EC—Hormones*, above n 42 at paras 155–6.

[527] These cases are discussed in the previous section under the heading 'experts'.

[528] *Japan—Measures Affecting Agricultural Products*, Communication from Japan and the United States, WTO Doc WT/DS76/12, 30 August 2001 at para 2.

information gathered under that provision will inevitably have an impact on the decision in favour of one or the other party. As a matter of fact, that information is expected to influence the decision, otherwise there would be no reason to seek it. Furthermore, there is nothing in the WTO agreements, especially the DSU, which suggests that the claimant must discharge the burden of proof on its own. As noted throughout this book, the WTO dispute settlement system is not a purely adversarial system.[529] Accordingly, it must be accepted that there is nothing objectionable *per se* with an active panel whose neutral fact-finding activities have an impact on the decision of a matter which is before it.[530] Much to the contrary, as discussed in Section II.C.1 of this chapter, there are advantages to active panels.

In exercising their fact-finding powers, however, panels must respect the requirements of due process. This means, as noted in the previous paragraph, that they must be impartial. It also means that panels must ensure that the parties' right of participation is observed. For instance, when seeking information, particularly from non-disputing parties, the panel must inform the parties and give them an opportunity to participate in the process. In general, panels must ensure that the parties have a meaningful opportunity to address the issues which are the subject of their findings. This much is implied in the idea that panels can rely upon any piece of information on the record which the disputing parties had a meaningful opportunity to address. It is arguable that this was the weakness of the panel in *Japan—Agricultural Products II*. Although the parties had an opportunity to comment on the expert evidence, their comments seemed to address the alternative measures suggested by the experts only tangentially.[531] Accordingly, the ruling of the panel under Article 5.6 of the SPS Agreement would have been stronger if the panel had directly requested the parties to provide their views on the alternative measure on which it based its ruling.

4.3. *US—Gambling*

A similar problem occurred in *US—Gambling*, but with more far-reaching consequences. In that case the panel asked the complainant, Antigua, to clarify the measures which the panel had understood Antigua was challenging and on

[529] In support, see Pauwelyn, *The Use of Experts*, above n 483 at 353, (noting that the Appellate Body's focus in *Japan—Agricultural Products II* 'on the record provided by the parties wrongly portrays the panel process as a purely adversarial system').

[530] It should be noted that some Members often argue—mostly, unsuccessfully—that the fact-finding activities of the panel cannot influence the outcome of the dispute. See, for example, Panel Report, *US—Upland Cotton*, above n 111 at paras 7.27, 7.6.14, 7.633 (where the arguments of the United States in that regard are rejected by the panel); Appellate Body Report, *Canada—Aircraft*, above n 81 at para 83 (where Canada argues that the panel advanced Brazil's case).

[531] Panel Report, *Japan—Agricultural Products II*, above n 485 at paras 8.74, 8.91, 8.95, 8.98 including footnotes (where the panel notes that Japan did not contest and the United States did not specifically address the issues on which the panel made findings).

which the panel ultimately ruled.[532] Antigua did not do so.[533] As a consequence, the defendant, the United States, did not directly address those measures either. The panel, however, proceeded to rule on what it had understood to be the challenged measures without the parties having discussed those measures in any detail during the proceedings. The approach adopted by the panel denied the defendant a meaningful opportunity to respond. The same criticism is valid with respect to the defence under Article XIV of the GATS: the panel based its findings under Article XIV on arguments and evidence which the parties had presented with respect to a claim under Article XVII of GATS.[534]

It is arguable that the panel even acted *ultra petita* because it ruled on *measures* which were not part of the matter before it. There was much confusion during the proceedings about what was (were) the measure(s) at issue.[535] The request for establishment of a panel was sufficiently ambiguous with respect to the measure at issue so that it could have been understood in the terms that the panel finally ruled on, that is, that the measures at issue were certain state and federal laws. However, the request for establishment of a panel as well as the first submission of Antigua could also have been understood to support the view that the measure at issue was the 'total prohibition on the cross-border supply of gambling and betting services'[536]—hereinafter the 'total prohibition'. The latter was the position advocated by Antigua particularly in its second written submission; a position which was also supported by the actions of Antigua during the proceedings.[537] Notably, Antigua did not make an elaborate presentation on

[532] For example, the panel addressed the following question to Antigua 'Is Antigua and Barbuda challenging: (i) specific legislative and regulatory provisions that are claimed to amount to a prohibition on the cross-border supply of gambling and betting services as such; and/or (ii) the specific application of such provisions; and/or (iii) the US practice *vis-a-vis* the foreign cross-border supply of gambling and betting services? Please identify all relevant legislative and regulatory provisions.' Panel Report, *US—Gambling*, above n 216 at Annex C, Question 10.

[533] See Panel Report, *US—Gambling*, above n 216 at, for example, para 6.159 and Annex C, Question 10.

[534] Panel Report, *US—Gambling*, above n 216 at paras 6.583–6.58. For instance, the United States argued on appeal that the panel's approach 'unfairly deprived the United States of any opportunity to respond and defend those specific measures' on which the panel ruled. Antigua argued on its turn that it was denied a meaningful opportunity to respond to the defence under Article XIV of the GATS. See Appellate Body Report, *US—Gambling*, above n 94 at paras 11, and 71–2, respectively. See also paras 319–20 which indicate that Antigua's right of participation was indeed negatively affected by the approach taken by the panel.

[535] The panel even noted in its report that 'the issue of which measures we are obliged to consider in this case is not a straightforward one.' Panel Report, *US—Gambling*, above n 216 at para 6.148.

[536] In its request for establishment of a panel, Antigua stated that '[t]he total prohibition of gambling and betting services offered from outside the United States appears to conflict with the United States' obligations under GATS and its Schedule of Specific Commitments annexed to the GATS (and in particular Sector 10.D thereof) for the following reasons . . .'. Request for Establishment of a Panel by Antigua and Barbuda, *United States—Measures Affecting the Cross-Border Supply of Gambling and Betting Services*, WTO Doc. WT/DS285/2, 13 June 2003. See Panel Report, *US—Gambling*, above n 216 at para 6.154 (regarding Antigua's first written submission).

[537] See Panel Report, *US—Gambling*, above n 216 at paras 6.157, 6.166.

the state and federal laws on which the panel ruled; instead it sought to demonstrate that the United States imposed a total prohibition on the cross-border supply of gambling and betting services which was inconsistent with the terms of the GATS.[538] The panel, however, rejected the idea that the 'total prohibition' was a measure which could be challenged in WTO dispute settlement.[539] Assuming that Antigua was in fact challenging the total prohibition, when the panel found that the total prohibition was not a challengeable measure, it should have dismissed the case. Probably realizing that this would be a drastic and formalistic course of action to take in the late stages of the proceedings, the panel decided instead to seize on the fact that the panel request could be interpreted to support its view about the measures at issue.

On appeal, the Appellate Body upheld the panel's finding that 'a complaining party may not challenge a "total prohibition" as a "measure", *per se*, in dispute settlement proceedings under the GATS'.[540] The Appellate Body found that the panel erred in examining the consistency of the state laws with the GATS because Antigua had not made a *prima facie* case with respect to those measures.[541] In contrast, the Appellate Body found that the panel had not erred in examining the consistency of the federal laws, because Antigua did make a *prima facie* case with respect to those measures.[542] The Appellate Body gave short shrift to both parties' allegations that the panel had violated their due process right of participation.[543]

An analysis of a counterfactual, however, demonstrates that the 'real issue' in *US—Gambling* was the violation of the parties' right of participation. In the counterfactual Antigua would have answered the questions posed by the panel[544] with a detailed explanation, including supporting evidence, of why the measures on which the panel ultimately ruled (ie the state and federal laws) were inconsistent with the GATS. In this situation, Antigua would still not have presented

538 In response to a question from the panel, for instance, Antigua explained that it was bringing 'the "total prohibition" itself before the Panel. [...] the United States insists that Antigua must explain to the United States and the Panel exactly how the total prohibition is constructed under United States law. Antigua has consistently taken the position that to force it to do so—in the words of the United States "an impossible task in our view"—is wasteful and would deflect the efforts of the Panel to an exercise in understanding the minute details of the American legal system when such details should not affect the outcome of this proceeding.' Panel Report, *US—Gambling*, above n 216 at Annex C, Question 10.

539 The panel was also of the view that Antigua had not identified the 'total prohibition' as a measure in its panel request. Panel Report, *US—Gambling*, above n 216 at paras 6.169, 6.175, 6.177.

540 Appellate Body Report, *US—Gambling*, above n 94 at para 126.

541 Appellate Body Report, *US—Gambling*, above n 94 at paras 153–4.

542 Appellate Body Report, *US—Gambling*, above n 94 at paras 153–4.

543 For examples of those arguments, see n 534 above. Similarly, see Douglas A Irwin & Joseph Weiler, 'Measures Affecting the Cross-Border Suply of Gambling and Betting Services (DS 285)' in H Horn & PC Mavroidis (eds), *The WTO Case Law of 2004–2005: Legal and Economic Analysis* (Cambridge: Cambridge University Press, 2008) 71 at 106 (noting that the Appellate Body did not take due process all that seriously).

544 For an example of such questions, see Panel Report, *US—Gambling*, above n 216 at Annex C, Question 10.

what the Appellate Body refers to as 'a *prima facie* case' on its own; to the contrary, it would have been induced to do so by the questions of the panel. However, if the parties had fully debated the measures on which the panel ruled as a result of the panel's questions, it is unlikely that the Appellate Body would have reversed the panel for ruling on measures with respect to which Antigua had not made a *prima facie* case.[545] The fact that the parties discussed the federal laws, even though very briefly, could explain the decision of the Appellate Body to uphold the panel's examination of those laws.

In sum, it is submitted that in order to ensure that the parties had a meaningful opportunity to participate, the panel in *US—Gambling* should have notified the parties—ideally at an early stage but certainly before the panel report was issued[546]—of its view that the 'total prohibition' was not a measure within the meaning of the DSU. This would have provided both parties a meaningful opportunity to present arguments and evidence with respect to the measures on which the panel ultimately ruled.

Accordingly, while panels have ample fact-finding powers which can be employed to allow them to arrive at accurate decisions, panels must respect the limits imposed by the due process requirement of participation. As discussed in Chapter 1, this not only gives legitimacy to the proceedings, but ultimately also advances the goal of accuracy.

Concluding Remarks

This chapter examined the role of the panel and the disputing parties in the process of fact-finding. It explained that panels can assume one of two roles: reviewer or original-trier-of-facts. The role of the panel is more circumscribed when it acts as a reviewer. The evidence is essentially developed during the domestic investigation, which is loosely speaking the measure at issue in the panel process. In most situations, however, the panel acts as the original-trier-of-facts.

In its role as the original-trier-of-facts the panel enjoys ample freedom to develop together with the parties the factual record of the proceedings. Although ample, the powers of the panel are not limitless. The panel must respect the due process requirements of impartiality and participation, act within the bounds of its terms of reference, observe its duty under Article 11 of the DSU to make an objective assessment of the matter, and in general seek to maximize the goals of

[545] In support of this conclusion, see Appellate Body Report, *Thailand—H-Beams*, above n 17 at paras 135–6.

[546] There is no indication in the panel report that the panel informed the parties during the proceedings of its views regarding the measures at issue. To the contrary, the panel report suggests that the measures were identified by the panel for the first time in the panel report. See Panel Report, *US—Gambling*, above n 216 at paras 6.204–6.205, 6.209.

the WTO dispute settlement system—namely, accuracy, participation, impartiality, equality of treatment, good faith cooperation, efficient use of resources, and protection of confidential information. It was argued that within these broad constraints, panels not only can, but should, be actively engaged in the process of fact-finding. This is so because the involvement of the panel in the process of fact-finding can result in a more efficient process and in more accurate decisions.

Pursuant to Article 13 of the DSU the panel can request the disputing parties to produce information which is relevant and necessary to the resolution of the claims in question as well as seek information from sources other than the disputing parties. Naturally, the panel must be able not only to gather information but also to rely upon the information gathered. In order to make an objective assessment of the matter before it the panel ought to take into account all the relevant information on the record in making its findings. In this regard, the position of the Appellate Body in *Japan—Agricultural Products II*—where the Appellate Body found that the panel erred for basing its decision on information provided by the experts assisting the panel—must be revised. That decision discourages panels from taking an active stance in the process of fact-finding. It weakens the inquisitorial element of the hybrid inquisitorial-adversarial structure of the WTO dispute settlement system. Such element has an important role to play in the system. For instance, it fulfils some of the functions which are performed by pre-trial discovery in a purely adversarial system.

The disputing parties are the other major actor in the process of fact-finding. Their cooperation is necessary for the accurate determination of the facts and the proper application of the WTO agreements. The parties must present information voluntarily throughout the proceedings as well as when requested by the panel. The parties should not be automatically excused from providing information because of its confidential character. It is important, however, that an appropriate mechanism be developed to ensure the protection of such information. Without such protection information may not be produced and, consequently, the accuracy of the panel's decision may be compromised. Adequate protection being in place, the parties must be required to produce confidential information which is relevant and necessary to decide the claims at issue, or suffer the consequences of their non-compliance with their duty to cooperate. Non-compliance with the duty of cooperation may lead to the imposition of indirect sanctions or procedural disadvantages such as adverse inferences which may ultimately result in a ruling against the uncooperative party.

This chapter has also explained that the duty of the WTO Members to provide information on their measures is not limited to the panel process. The WTO agreements contain substantive transparency obligations which require Members to provide certain information on their measures independently of the adjudication process. The main purpose of these obligations is not to develop information for the panel process, but rather to allow the Membership to monitor compliance with the WTO agreements. The information generated through the operation of those obligations may, however, become valuable evidence in case an eventual disagreement between the parties regarding compliance is not resolved amicably and a panel is established to resolve the dispute. Transparency is, accordingly, necessary to ensure—whether through adjudication or peer review—that the WTO agreements are more than a dead-letter. Therefore, it is of utmost importance that effective mechanisms and incentives are implemented to make sure that WTO Members make information on their measures available. One of the options discussed in this chapter involves the establishment of a clear connection between the substantive transparency obligations and the panel process by either reversing the burden of proof or allowing adverse inferences to be drawn against a party which does not comply with its transparency obligations. Another option would be to require each Member to adopt and implement legislation which would allow any entity, including private parties, to have access to information held by public authorities which is directly related to the implementation of the obligations contained in the WTO agreements.

In sum, this chapter concludes that an active panel and forthcoming parties are essential for the accurate determination of the facts of the case and, consequently, the proper application of the WTO agreements. Accordingly, WTO negotiators, in considering revisions to the agreements, and panels and the Appellate Body, in making their decisions, must seek to strengthen rather than weaken those two elements of the system.

Conclusion

As noted at the outset of this study, the DSU contains few rules to guide panels in the process of fact-finding. The few rules which are set down in the DSU are of a general character and thus do not provide direct answers to specific questions such as the functioning and allocation of the burden of proof, the quantum of proof necessary to prove an issue, and the consequences of a party's failure to provide information to the panel, among others. Panels and the Appellate Body must, therefore, deal with those questions as they arise in the cases. In the light of this, the main objectives of this book have been to determine (i) the extent to which panels and the Appellate Body have set out optimal rules to govern the process of fact-finding through the existing jurisprudence and, to the extent that that has not been the case, (ii) how that goal could be achieved.

The route to optimizing the process of fact-finding

Chapter 1 set out the criteria on the basis of which optimality would be determined. It was argued that an optimal process of fact-finding would (i) maximize the goals of the WTO dispute settlement system—namely, accuracy, participation, impartiality, equality, good faith cooperation, the efficient use of resources (time and money), and the protection of confidential information; (ii) manage uncertainty and the risk of error efficiently; and (iii) be in harmony with the basic structure of the WTO dispute settlement system—the three most salient features of which are (a) the fact that the disputes are decided by expert adjudicators who are in charge of deciding questions of law and of fact; (b) the episodic taking and presentation of evidence; and (c) the hybrid inquisitorial-adversarial character of the proceedings.

Chapter 1 also explained that the accurate determination of the facts of a case is a necessary pre-condition for the proper application of the law. Accurate decisions contribute to the attainment of the objectives pursued by the substantive law, provide appropriate incentives for the observance of the law, inspire confidence in the process of adjudication and contribute to its fairness. Accordingly, it was argued that the pursuit of accuracy is one of the goals, if not the major goal, of adjudication including WTO dispute settlement. Particular attention was therefore devoted throughout this study to the objective of maximizing accuracy especially when this can be achieved without disproportionately affecting the other goals of the WTO dispute settlement system.

Based on the framework set out above, Chapters 2 through 5 analysed the main elements of the process of fact-finding. Those chapters addressed questions ranging from the determination of which party bears the responsibility of ultimately convincing the panel of the truth of a claim, to what quantum of proof is necessary to convince the panel of the truth of a claim, to what the role of the panel and the disputing parties (complainant and defendant) is in the development of the factual record on which the panel bases its decision on a claim. The analysis conducted in those chapters demonstrated that many of the rules governing the process of fact-finding are not optimal. In other words, in developing rules to govern the process of fact-finding, panels and the Appellate Body have not always maximized the goals of the WTO dispute settlement system, have on occasion not given adequate consideration to the basic structure of the system, and have not sought to manage uncertainty and the risk of error in an efficient manner. The discussion below reviews the main findings in this regard as well as the suggestions made for improving different aspects of the process of fact-finding.

Conceptual clarity

Chapter 2 noted that the concept of the burden of proof has been frequently debated in WTO dispute settlement. It was suggested that to a certain extent this is due to the absence of a rigorous definition at the WTO of the concepts related to the process of proof. This 'conceptual vagueness' is particularly problematic given the fact that concepts such as the burden of proof do not have the same meaning in the different systems of adjudication of the world. The premise upon which Chapter 2 was developed is that conceptual indeterminacy is bound to create confusion and consequently result in inefficiencies and mistakes being made. Chapter 2, therefore, clarified the meaning of basic concepts such as the burden of proof, the standard of proof, and presumptions, which were then further analysed in the chapters following.

The prima facie *case requirement*

Chapter 3 argued that panels and the Appellate Body have muddled the operation of the burden of proof by referring to the requirement that the party which bears the burden of proof must present a *prima facie* case. Panels and the Appellate Body have not explained with any clarity what the meaning of a *prima facie* case is. The references to that requirement in panel and Appellate Body reports indicate at times (i) that the requirement to present a *prima facie* case is a threshold requirement which must be met in order for the proceedings to continue or for the panel to begin an examination of all the evidence before it, and at other times (ii) that the *prima facie* case is the standard of proof which authorizes the panel to rule against the respondent. Apart from the confusion (and errors that may have resulted therefrom) which the unexplained references to a *prima facie* case have created, the two possible meanings of the requirement to present a *prima facie* case are problematic from the perspective of the optimization of the process of fact-finding.

If the *prima facie* case is understood as a threshold requirement which the claimant must meet entirely on its own, a purely adversarial element is introduced into the proceedings which are otherwise structured to have a hybrid inquisitorial-adversarial character. In this connection, such requirement would not take adequate account of the fact that there is no pre-trial discovery in WTO dispute settlement and that as an alternative the claimant may request the help of the panel to gather information which is not in its possession. Moreover, if the claimant is required to make a *prima facie* case entirely on its own, the respondent has no incentive to cooperate in producing information. On the contrary, if a claim could be dismissed at an early stage of the proceedings on the grounds that the claimant failed to present a *prima facie* case, the respondent would have an incentive to withhold information. This would have a negative impact on the values of good faith cooperation as well as accuracy. In addition, panels have so far refused to issue intermediate rulings determining whether a *prima facie* case has been made, which suggests that the *prima facie* case has not functioned as a prerequisite for the continuation of the proceedings. But what would be the function of the *prima facie* case as a threshold requirement if the panel waits until the final report to issue a decision on whether a *prima facie* case has been made? At that stage it is more reasonable for the panel to weigh all the evidence before it, rather than first make a determination as to whether the claimant has on its own presented enough evidence to make a *prima facie* case in support of its claim. If the panel were to dismiss a claim without examining all the evidence on the record of the proceedings—but only that submitted by the claimant—the accuracy of its decision could be compromised with no countervailing benefit.

The main objection to the adoption of the *prima facie* case as the standard of proof which authorizes the panel to rule against the respondent is that this standard is too low to promote accurate decisions. A standard of proof which would allow the panel to rule that a measure is inconsistent with the WTO agreements on the basis of evidence which merely suggests that the claim at issue is possibly true would bias the system towards claimants which would be able to win cases on the basis of very little evidence. This would affect not only the accuracy of the WTO decisions but also the equality of the disputing parties.

Accordingly, Chapter 3 recommended that panels and the Appellate Body refrain from referring to a *prima facie* case. This concept does not add anything to our understanding of how the burden of proof functions. The lack of clarity as to its meaning creates confusion, and is bound to lead to errors.

The standard of proof for WTO dispute settlement

Chapter 3 concluded instead that the standard of proof most appropriate for the majority of the WTO disputes (ie those disputes where the interests of the disputing parties are valued similarly) is the preponderance of the evidence, which requires panels to be convinced that the proposition at issue is at least more likely than not true. For the majority of the cases the preponderance of the evidence standard is more likely not only to promote accurate decisions but also to manage uncertainty and the risk of error efficiently. This is so because a mid-range standard such as the preponderance of the evidence (i) adequately recognizes that even deserving claimants would in many cases not be able to prove their claims to a level of absolute certainty due to the difficulty (or in some cases the impossibility) as well as the high costs of presenting evidence which would allow panels to achieve that level of confidence, and, accordingly (ii) seeks to treat equally the similarly valued interests of the claimant and the respondent in the dispute. If instead panels were required to be certain of the truth of a proposition in order to find in favour of the party bearing the burden of proof with respect to that proposition, many erroneous decisions would be made and those decisions would always be against the claimants. The preponderance of the evidence standard is also more likely to maximize accuracy in that (i) by basing its decision on an assessment of whether a certain proposition is more likely than not true the panel pursues its best chance of arriving at a decision that corresponds to the true state of affairs, and (ii) the mid-range standard encourages both parties to provide their account of the facts and submit supporting evidence.

Chapter 3 argued, however, that when errors against the respondent are more costly than errors against the claimant—ie when the interests of the disputing parties are not valued similarly—a higher standard of proof may be justified in order to reduce errors against the respondent, which are more costly. It was noted that a higher standard of proof could be adopted for instance in cases under the SPS Agreement since not only trade, but also human, animal or plant life or health in the territory of the respondent would be at stake.

Determining that the standard of proof is met

Finally, Chapter 3 also argued that in deciding whether the standard or proof has been met, panels must consider and weigh all the evidence before them rather than focus on the evidence presented by one or the other party. This much is required by the value of accuracy. Moreover, this approach takes into account the following features of the WTO dispute settlement system: (i) that the process of fact-finding is unitary (in the sense that there are no intermediate rulings) and dynamic, (ii) that panels are not passive spectators, but instead have the power to seek information and technical advice from any individual or body which they deem appropriate,[1] and (iii) that the parties to a dispute have a duty to cooperate in the development of the factual record of the panel.

[1] Article 13 of the DSU.

Allocation of the burden of proof

Chapter 4 discussed the question of the allocation of the burden of proof. It was explained that the importance of the allocation of the burden of proof lies in the fact that the burden of proof is a rule of adjudication which determines the outcome of a case when there is no or little evidence on the record or when the evidence on the record is equivocal. In other words, the burden of proof, similarly to the standard of proof, is a concept which addresses the related problems of uncertainty and risk of error in adjudication. Chapter 4 demonstrated that panels and the Appellate Body have failed to develop a clear and consistent approach to the allocation of the burden of proof. It was explained that the criteria relied upon to allocate the burden of proof have not been consistently applied to similar situations and, most importantly, that those criteria are not significant.

Chapter 4 concluded that panels and the Appellate Body must recognize the purpose of the concept of the burden of proof—ie to manage uncertainty and the risk of error—and accordingly determine its allocation through the use of analytical tools which are apt to accomplish that purpose efficiently. One such analytical tool is to seek the minimization of the social loss function composed of direct and error costs. An analysis that seeks to minimize that function indicates that in most cases the burden of proof should be allocated to the complainant. An allocation to the defendant would be justified when as a general rule (i) the defendants can produce core evidence at a much lower cost than the complainants; (ii) information is available with respect to the factual pattern of a claim which suggests that in most similar cases the complainants have a meritorious case, that is, the defendants act inconsistently with the obligation in question in more than 50 per cent of the universe of all potential disputes; (iii) when the costs (social and individual) associated with an erroneous decision in favour of the defendants are higher than those associated with an erroneous decision in favour of the complainants. It is arguable that the WTO negotiators are in a better position to take into account these kinds of considerations and that therefore panels and the Appellate Body should allocate the burden of proof to the complainant unless otherwise expressly indicated in the WTO agreements.

Burden of pleading

It has been argued that when the defendant has specific knowledge that would allow him to narrow the scope of a case, the burden of proof with respect to those specific issues should be allocated to the defendant. This study concluded that in these circumstances, the defendant should not be allocated the burden of proof, but instead the burden of pleading. In this connection, the values of efficiency and participation would require defendants to raise new provisions not addressed by the complainants as early as possible. Chapter 3 suggested that defendants be required to file an answer to the request for establishment of a panel before the complainant is required to submit its first written submission. Defendants could also be allowed to raise new provisions up until their first written submission, in which case they should be required to provide a detailed explanation of the claim.

Avoiding decisions based on the burden of proof

Chapter 5 examined the role of the panel and the disputing parties in the development of the factual record on the basis of which the panel must decide whether a claim has been proved. Chapter 5 is based on the premise that if sufficient information is placed on the record of the panel the question of the allocation of the burden of proof becomes only of academic interest. Unquestionably a decision based on evidence which directly addresses the specific questions at issue before the panel is likely to be more accurate and fair than a decision based on a general rule of adjudication, ie the burden of proof. Accordingly, the focus of Chapter 5 was on promoting the development of a factual record as complete as possible while at the same time not neglecting the other goals of the WTO dispute settlement system such as efficiency (in terms of money and time), participation, and the protection of confidential information, among others.

At the outset Chapter 5 explained that panels can assume one of two roles: reviewer or original-trier-of-facts. When acting as a reviewer the panel essentially relies upon the factual record developed by a domestic investigating authority. In this capacity the role of the panel is to determine based on that record whether the conclusions of the investigating authority are reasoned and adequate and/or whether the facts were properly established and objectively and unbiasedly evaluated. The main focus of Chapter 5 was on those cases where the panel acts as the original-trier-of-facts. In this role the panel, together with the parties, develops its own factual record without being constrained by the record of a previous domestic investigation which in fact may not even exist.

Considering the basic structure of the WTO dispute settlement system, this chapter concludes that an optimal process of fact-finding requires that the disputing parties be forthcoming in providing relevant and necessary information and that the panel be actively engaged in the development of the factual record of the proceedings.

Duty of cooperation

Section II.B of Chapter 5, which examines the role of the disputing parties in the development of the factual record of the panel, noted that the general duty of the parties to engage in WTO dispute settlement 'in good faith in an effort to resolve the dispute'[2] encompasses the process of fact-finding. The duty to cooperate in the presentation of information is also explicitly recognized in Article 13.1 of the DSU which provides that WTO Members 'should respond promptly and fully to any request by a panel for such information as the panel considers necessary and appropriate'. Accordingly, the parties are under a duty to present information relevant and necessary to the resolution of an issue before the panel regardless of whether they bear the burden of proof with respect to that issue. Cooperation is particularly important because the linguistic, legal, economic, cultural, and political differences among the WTO Members make it more difficult for a party to understand and present information about activities occurring in the territory of another party. Moreover, the facts that there is no pre-trial discovery in WTO dispute settlement and that the proceedings—including the taking and presentation of evidence—are episodic mean that the parties have an obligation to be forthcoming throughout the panel process.

The role of the panel in promoting cooperation

Chapter 5 noted that panels and the Appellate Body generally recognize the duty of the parties to cooperate in presenting information to the panel. It was argued that given the facts that the cooperation of the parties is essential for the accurate determination of the facts of the case and that there are no direct means of compelling a party to WTO dispute settlement to present information, panels have an important role to play in promoting cooperation. Accordingly, they must use the means at their disposal to encourage the parties to be forthcoming. These include (i) making direct and emphatic requests for information which panels find to be relevant and necessary to the resolution of a question before them, and (ii) showing willingness to impose indirect sanctions—such as exclusion of untimely submitted evidence and adverse inferences—on uncooperative parties. In this regard, it was noted that the panel in *EC—Selected Customs Matters* was wrong in concluding that the panels' duty to make an objective assessment of the matter *obliges* panels to accept information submitted in an untimely manner. It was also noted that the Appellate Body in *Canada—Aircraft* rightly found that panels have the authority to draw adverse inferences and that they should show a willingness to draw such inferences when the circumstances so warrant.

Chapter 5 explained that in deciding whether to impose a sanction panels must balance the long-term systemic interest in encouraging cooperation and accurate decisions with the short-term interest in delivering an accurate decision in the case at issue. The former favours the imposition of sanctions on uncooperative parties. The latter may not necessarily favour a sanction given that, for instance, untimely submitted evidence may be relevant and necessary, and that

[2] Article 3.10 of the DSU.

unrestricted recourse to adverse inferences may result in wrong decisions since the inference may not correspond to the facts.

Alternatives to managing asymmetries of information

Because the means available to panels to induce cooperation such as the threat of adverse inferences are not always effective, a special challenge to accuracy and equality is posed by claims in relation to which respondents usually have exclusive or preferential access to all or almost all information necessary to their resolution. This is so because if the respondent is not forthcoming and not enough information is before the panel to allow it to draw an inference against the respondent,[3] the panel is bound to rule against the claimant. Another problematic situation involves claims whose resolution requires information which is in the hands of uncooperative private entities. Admittedly, these situations seem to be the exception rather than the rule. However, when they arise they put into question the fairness of the system—especially because of the negative impact on the values of accuracy and equality—which is a strong reason to justify the attention of WTO negotiators.

The best way to deal with the problem posed by the first situation is to weaken or eliminate the defendant's 'monopoly' of information. The transparency obligations discussed in Section II.B.6.2 of Chapter 5 have played a role in this regard. They have not, however, functioned perfectly and at least some WTO Members seem to have recognized and sought a solution to this problem in the current Doha Round of negotiations.[4] With a view to helping to solve this problem, Chapter 5 suggested the creation of a new class of transparency obligations which would give private parties (or any interested entity) the right to access information related to the implementation of a Member's WTO obligations in the possession of its governmental departments. Relatedly, more record-keeping obligations along the lines of those contained in the trade remedies agreements could be created—this is not to say that the whole model of review espoused by those agreements should be adopted under other agreements. Other solutions for the problem of claims in relation to which defendants usually have exclusive or preferential access to all or almost all information necessary to their resolution include (i) the reversal of the burden of proof, and (ii) the creation of legal presumptions. The reversal of the burden of proof would be based on the premise that the defendant can produce core evidence at a much lower cost than the complainant. In fact, if the defendant has exclusive or preferential access to all or almost all information necessary to

[3] This is likely to be the case since the respondent has exclusive or preferential access to all or almost all information necessary to the resolution of the claim in question.

[4] See Pascal Lamy, 'Evolving Trade Increases Need for "Active Transparency"', 22 October 2007, Speech given at the Georgetown University Law Center, available at <http://www.wto.org/english/news_e/sppl_e/sppl78_e.htm> (accessed 20 May 2009).

the resolution of the claim at issue, the differences between the parties in the costs of presenting information can be considered insurmountable. Legal presumptions could be created to address those situations in which the complainants have access to evidence which can prove a fact from which another fact could be presumed. In other words, the complainants would be required to prove certain elements of a claim—with respect to which the defendants do not have a monopoly of information—from which elements a conclusion would be drawn with respect to other elements which would be presumed to be proved unless the defendants succeed in proving otherwise—an example of a legal presumption structured along these lines can be found in Articles 6.1 and 6.2 of the SCM Agreement.[5]

As for the situation where the evidence necessary for the resolution of a claim is in the hands of uncooperative private entities, a suggestion was made that a mechanism be created that would allow the use of the domestic courts of WTO Members to gather information from those entities. Such mechanism would operate in a similar manner to mutual assistance agreements between countries for the taking of evidence in one signatory for use in a proceeding before the courts of another signatory. A related alternative would be to grant panels the authority to issue orders for the production of information which could be enforced in the domestic courts of the WTO Members in the event that they were not voluntarily complied with.

Confidential information

Chapter 5 also argued that the duty of cooperation extends to confidential information, that is, the disputing parties cannot invoke the confidential character of information in their possession as an excuse not to produce that information. This view is in accordance with the goal of ensuring the accurate determination of the facts at issue. The lack of effective procedures to protect confidential information, however, currently disserves both the goal of protection of confidential information and the goal of accuracy. Accuracy is affected because in the absence of effective protection the parties may decide not to produce confidential information. Chapter 5 therefore concludes that there is a need to establish standard procedures for the protection of confidential information in order to maximize the values of accuracy and protection of confidential information.

[5] Pursuant to Article 6.1, '[s]erious prejudice in the sense of paragraph (c) of Article 5 shall be deemed to exist in the case of: (a) the total ad valorem subsidization of a product exceeding 5 per cent'. Paragraph 6.2 in turn provides that '[n]otwithstanding the provisions of paragraph 1, serious prejudice shall not be found if the subsidizing Member demonstrates that the subsidy in question has not resulted in any of the effects enumerated in paragraph 3'. Notably, according to Article 31 of the SCM Agreement, the presumption provided for in Article 6.1 is now expired.

Panel-controlled disclosure

As for the need of a mechanism to allow the parties (and the panel) to have access to evidence that is not otherwise automatically produced by the disputing parties, it was argued that such mechanism should be structured around the authority of the panel to seek information. A panel-controlled disclosure mechanism—as opposed to the pre-trial discovery model—is also consistent with the episodic structure of the proceedings and more conducive to the efficient use of resources without necessarily compromising the accuracy of the decisions.

In this connection, guidance must be provided to the parties as to the requirements of a request to produce. Properly formulated requests to produce should: (i) explain why the information requested is relevant and necessary to the resolution of a claim before the panel; (ii) describe the information requested in detail; (iii) explain that the information is not in the possession of, and cannot otherwise be accessed by, the requesting party; and (iv) demonstrate that the requested information is in the control of the requested party. The adoption of these criteria would help panels in deciding whether and what kind of adverse inferences to draw if the information requested is not produced.

Active panel

Finally, Chapter 5 argued that not only has the panel the authority to play an active role in the development of the factual record, but that the active participation of the panel is in fact important to maximize accuracy, efficiency, equality, and good faith cooperation. In other words, it was argued that the structure of the WTO dispute settlement system demands the active participation of the panel. While panels and the Appellate Body have generally recognized the authority of panels to participate actively in the process of fact-finding, there has not necessarily been awareness of the value of the active participation of the panel. The finding of the Appellate Body in *Japan—Agricultural Products II* that the panel erred in basing its decision on information provided by the experts assisting the panel is especially problematic in this regard. Apart from its impact on the accuracy of decisions—since panels are asked to ignore information which is relevant for the resolution of claims before them—the finding of the Appellate Body in *Japan—Agricultural Products II* has served to discourage the active participation of panels. While it is difficult to determine its precise impact, it is a fact that that finding has been frequently invoked by parties wanting to discourage the participation of the panel. Chapter 5 concluded that the active participation of the panel must be encouraged provided that panels respect their terms of reference and guarantee the observance of the values of impartiality and participation.

Final considerations and way forward

In conclusion, it is clear that there are many aspects of the process of fact-finding which have not been optimally designed and which therefore warrant revision. Admittedly, it is difficult to determine the precise impact that those 'design flaws' have had on the resolution of the disputes brought before panels and the Appellate Body. For instance, it is difficult, if not impossible, to establish that panels and the Appellate Body have made more erroneous decisions because of those flaws. We would have to retry the cases in order to come to a conclusion in that regard. The decision of the Appellate Body in *Japan—Agricultural Products II* mentioned above provides nonetheless a clear example of a situation where the decision of the Appellate Body was mistaken. In that case, the panel was shown to be correct when the parties to the dispute reached a mutually agreed solution based on the factual findings of the panel which were reversed on appeal. The fact that it is difficult to determine the exact impact that the many problems discussed throughout this book have had on past decisions does not mean that those problems do not warrant attention.

It is submitted that most of those problems can be addressed by panels and the Appellate Body through changes in the development of the jurisprudence or through the establishment of clear rules in their working procedures. Of course stability and predictability would be enhanced if the WTO Members would themselves fill the gaps which were left in the DSU and which thus have had to be addressed by panels and the Appellate Body. This could be achieved in the context of the ongoing negotiations to amend the DSU. Alternatively, the DSB (perhaps with the help of a group of experts) could take on the task of producing guidelines for the management of the process of fact-finding. Moreover, only the WTO negotiators have the power to fully implement the suggestions made in Chapter 5 to address the problems posed by the lack of standard procedures for the protection of confidential information, and by situations where the defendant usually has exclusive or preferential access to all or almost all information necessary to the resolution of a certain claim and where the evidence necessary for the resolution of a claim is in the hands of uncooperative private entities.

APPENDIX

Understanding on Rules and Procedures Governing the Settlement of Disputes

Members hereby *agree* as follows:

Article 1. Coverage and Application

1. The rules and procedures of this Understanding shall apply to disputes brought pursuant to the consultation and dispute settlement provisions of the agreements listed in Appendix 1 to this Understanding (referred to in this Understanding as the "covered agreements"). The rules and procedures of this Understanding shall also apply to consultations and the settlement of disputes between Members concerning their rights and obligations under the provisions of the Agreement Establishing the World Trade Organization (referred to in this Understanding as the "WTO Agreement") and of this Understanding taken in isolation or in combination with any other covered agreement.

2. The rules and procedures of this Understanding shall apply subject to such special or additional rules and procedures on dispute settlement contained in the covered agreements as are identified in Appendix 2 to this Understanding. To the extent that there is a difference between the rules and procedures of this Understanding and the special or additional rules and procedures set forth in Appendix 2, the special or additional rules and procedures in Appendix 2 shall prevail. In disputes involving rules and procedures under more than one covered agreement, if there is a conflict between special or additional rules and procedures of such agreements under review, and where the parties to the dispute cannot agree on rules and procedures within 20 days of the establishment of the panel, the Chairman of the Dispute Settlement Body provided for in paragraph 1 of Article 2 (referred to in this Understanding as the "DSB"), in consultation with the parties to the dispute, shall determine the rules and procedures to be followed within 10 days after a request by either Member. The Chairman shall be guided by the principle that special or additional rules and procedures should be used where possible, and the rules and procedures set out in this Understanding should be used to the extent necessary to avoid conflict.

Article 2. Administration

1. The Dispute Settlement Body is hereby established to administer these rules and procedures and, except as otherwise provided in a covered agreement, the consultation and dispute settlement provisions of the covered agreements. Accordingly, the DSB shall have the authority to establish panels, adopt panel and Appellate Body reports, maintain surveillance of implementation of rulings and recommendations, and authorize suspension of concessions and other obligations under the covered agreements. With respect to

disputes arising under a covered agreement which is a Plurilateral Trade Agreement, the term "Member" as used herein shall refer only to those Members that are parties to the relevant Plurilateral Trade Agreement. Where the DSB administers the dispute settlement provisions of a Plurilateral Trade Agreement, only those Members that are parties to that Agreement may participate in decisions or actions taken by the DSB with respect to that dispute.

2. The DSB shall inform the relevant WTO Councils and Committees of any developments in disputes related to provisions of the respective covered agreements.

3. The DSB shall meet as often as necessary to carry out its functions within the time-frames provided in this Understanding.

4. Where the rules and procedures of this Understanding provide for the DSB to take a decision, it shall do so by consensus.[1]

Article 3. General Provisions

1. Members affirm their adherence to the principles for the management of disputes heretofore applied under Articles XXII and XXIII of GATT 1947, and the rules and procedures as further elaborated and modified herein.

2. The dispute settlement system of the WTO is a central element in providing security and predictability to the multilateral trading system. The Members recognize that it serves to preserve the rights and obligations of Members under the covered agreements, and to clarify the existing provisions of those agreements in accordance with customary rules of interpretation of public international law. Recommendations and rulings of the DSB cannot add to or diminish the rights and obligations provided in the covered agreements.

3. The prompt settlement of situations in which a Member considers that any benefits accruing to it directly or indirectly under the covered agreements are being impaired by measures taken by another Member is essential to the effective functioning of the WTO and the maintenance of a proper balance between the rights and obligations of Members.

4. Recommendations or rulings made by the DSB shall be aimed at achieving a satisfactory settlement of the matter in accordance with the rights and obligations under this Understanding and under the covered agreements.

5. All solutions to matters formally raised under the consultation and dispute settlement provisions of the covered agreements, including arbitration awards, shall be consistent with those agreements and shall not nullify or impair benefits accruing to any Member under those agreements, nor impede the attainment of any objective of those agreements.

6. Mutually agreed solutions to matters formally raised under the consultation and dispute settlement provisions of the covered agreements shall be notified to the DSB and the relevant Councils and Committees, where any Member may raise any point relating thereto.

7. Before bringing a case, a Member shall exercise its judgement as to whether action under these procedures would be fruitful. The aim of the dispute settlement mechanism is to secure a positive solution to a dispute. A solution mutually acceptable to the parties

[1] The DSB shall be deemed to have decided by consensus on a matter submitted for its consideration, if no Member, present at the meeting of the DSB when the decision is taken, formally objects to the proposed decision.

to a dispute and consistent with the covered agreements is clearly to be preferred. In the absence of a mutually agreed solution, the first objective of the dispute settlement mechanism is usually to secure the withdrawal of the measures concerned if these are found to be inconsistent with the provisions of any of the covered agreements. The provision of compensation should be resorted to only if the immediate withdrawal of the measure is impracticable and as a temporary measure pending the withdrawal of the measure which is inconsistent with a covered agreement. The last resort which this Understanding provides to the Member invoking the dispute settlement procedures is the possibility of suspending the application of concessions or other obligations under the covered agreements on a discriminatory basis vis-à-vis the other Member, subject to authorization by the DSB of such measures.

8. In cases where there is an infringement of the obligations assumed under a covered agreement, the action is considered *prima facie* to constitute a case of nullification or impairment. This means that there is normally a presumption that a breach of the rules has an adverse impact on other Members parties to that covered agreement, and in such cases, it shall be up to the Member against whom the complaint has been brought to rebut the charge.

9. The provisions of this Understanding are without prejudice to the rights of Members to seek authoritative interpretation of provisions of a covered agreement through decision-making under the WTO Agreement or a covered agreement which is a Plurilateral Trade Agreement.

10. It is understood that requests for conciliation and the use of the dispute settlement procedures should not be intended or considered as contentious acts and that, if a dispute arises, all Members will engage in these procedures in good faith in an effort to resolve the dispute. It is also understood that complaints and counter-complaints in regard to distinct matters should not be linked.

11. This Understanding shall be applied only with respect to new requests for consultations under the consultation provisions of the covered agreements made on or after the date of entry into force of the WTO Agreement. With respect to disputes for which the request for consultations was made under GATT 1947 or under any other predecessor agreement to the covered agreements before the date of entry into force of the WTO Agreement, the relevant dispute settlement rules and procedures in effect immediately prior to the date of entry into force of the WTO Agreement shall continue to apply.[2]

12. Notwithstanding paragraph 11, if a complaint based on any of the covered agreements is brought by a developing country Member against a developed country Member, the complaining party shall have the right to invoke, as an alternative to the provisions contained in Articles 4, 5, 6 and 12 of this Understanding, the corresponding provisions of the Decision of 5 April 1966 (BISD 14S/18), except that where the Panel considers that the time-frame provided for in paragraph 7 of that Decision is insufficient to provide its report and with the agreement of the complaining party, that time-frame may be extended. To the extent that there is a difference between the rules and procedures of Articles 4, 5, 6 and 12 and the corresponding rules and procedures of the Decision, the latter shall prevail.

[2] This paragraph shall also be applied to disputes on which panel reports have not been adopted or fully implemented.

Article 4. Consultations

1. Members affirm their resolve to strengthen and improve the effectiveness of the consultation procedures employed by Members.

2. Each Member undertakes to accord sympathetic consideration to and afford adequate opportunity for consultation regarding any representations made by another Member concerning measures affecting the operation of any covered agreement taken within the territory of the former.[3]

3. If a request for consultations is made pursuant to a covered agreement, the Member to which the request is made shall, unless otherwise mutually agreed, reply to the request within 10 days after the date of its receipt and shall enter into consultations in good faith within a period of no more than 30 days after the date of receipt of the request, with a view to reaching a mutually satisfactory solution. If the Member does not respond within 10 days after the date of receipt of the request, or does not enter into consultations within a period of no more than 30 days, or a period otherwise mutually agreed, after the date of receipt of the request, then the Member that requested the holding of consultations may proceed directly to request the establishment of a panel.

4. All such requests for consultations shall be notified to the DSB and the relevant Councils and Committees by the Member which requests consultations. Any request for consultations shall be submitted in writing and shall give the reasons for the request, including identification of the measures at issue and an indication of the legal basis for the complaint.

5. In the course of consultations in accordance with the provisions of a covered agreement, before resorting to further action under this Understanding, Members should attempt to obtain satisfactory adjustment of the matter.

6. Consultations shall be confidential, and without prejudice to the rights of any Member in any further proceedings.

7. If the consultations fail to settle a dispute within 60 days after the date of receipt of the request for consultations, the complaining party may request the establishment of a panel. The complaining party may request a panel during the 60-day period if the consulting parties jointly consider that consultations have failed to settle the dispute.

8. In cases of urgency, including those which concern perishable goods, Members shall enter into consultations within a period of no more than 10 days after the date of receipt of the request. If the consultations have failed to settle the dispute within a period of 20 days after the date of receipt of the request, the complaining party may request the establishment of a panel.

9. In cases of urgency, including those which concern perishable goods, the parties to the dispute, panels and the Appellate Body shall make every effort to accelerate the proceedings to the greatest extent possible.

10. During consultations Members should give special attention to the particular problems and interests of developing country Members.

[3] Where the provisions of any other covered agreement concerning measures taken by regional or local governments or authorities within the territory of a Member contain provisions different from the provisions of this paragraph, the provisions of such other covered agreement shall prevail.

11. Whenever a Member other than the consulting Members considers that it has a substantial trade interest in consultations being held pursuant to paragraph 1 of Article XXII of GATT 1994, paragraph 1 of Article XXII of GATS, or the corresponding provisions in other covered agreements[4], such Member may notify the consulting Members and the DSB, within 10 days after the date of the circulation of the request for consultations under said Article, of its desire to be joined in the consultations. Such Member shall be joined in the consultations, provided that the Member to which the request for consultations was addressed agrees that the claim of substantial interest is well-founded. In that event they shall so inform the DSB. If the request to be joined in the consultations is not accepted, the applicant Member shall be free to request consultations under paragraph 1 of Article XXII or paragraph 1 of Article XXIII of GATT 1994, paragraph 1 of Article XXII or paragraph 1 of Article XXIII of GATS, or the corresponding provisions in other covered agreements.

Article 5. Good Offices, Conciliation and Mediation

1. Good offices, conciliation and mediation are procedures that are undertaken voluntarily if the parties to the dispute so agree.
2. Proceedings involving good offices, conciliation and mediation, and in particular positions taken by the parties to the dispute during these proceedings, shall be confidential, and without prejudice to the rights of either party in any further proceedings under these procedures.
3. Good offices, conciliation or mediation may be requested at any time by any party to a dispute. They may begin at any time and be terminated at any time. Once procedures for good offices, conciliation or mediation are terminated, a complaining party may then proceed with a request for the establishment of a panel.
4. When good offices, conciliation or mediation are entered into within 60 days after the date of receipt of a request for consultations, the complaining party must allow a period of 60 days after the date of receipt of the request for consultations before requesting the establishment of a panel. The complaining party may request the establishment of a panel during the 60-day period if the parties to the dispute jointly consider that the good offices, conciliation or mediation process has failed to settle the dispute.
5. If the parties to a dispute agree, procedures for good offices, conciliation or mediation may continue while the panel process proceeds.
6. The Director-General may, acting in an *ex officio* capacity, offer good offices, conciliation or mediation with the view to assisting Members to settle a dispute.

[4] The corresponding consultation provisions in the covered agreements are listed hereunder: Agreement on Agriculture, Article 19; Agreement on the Application of Sanitary and Phytosanitary Measures, paragraph 1 of Article 11; Agreement on Textiles and Clothing, paragraph 4 of Article 8; Agreement on Technical Barriers to Trade, paragraph 1 of Article 14; Agreement on Trade-Related Investment Measures, Article 8; Agreement on Implementation of Article VI of GATT 1994, paragraph 2 of Article 17; Agreement on Implementation of Article VII of GATT 1994, paragraph 2 of Article 19; Agreement on Preshipment Inspection, Article 7; Agreement on Rules of Origin, Article 7; Agreement on Import Licensing Procedures, Article 6; Agreement on Subsidies and Countervailing Measures, Article 30; Agreement on Safeguards, Article 14; Agreement on Trade-Related Aspects of Intellectual Property Rights, Article 64.1; and any corresponding consultation provisions in Plurilateral Trade Agreements as determined by the competent bodies of each Agreement and as notified to the DSB.

Article 6. Establishment of Panels

1. If the complaining party so requests, a panel shall be established at the latest at the DSB meeting following that at which the request first appears as an item on the DSB's agenda, unless at that meeting the DSB decides by consensus not to establish a panel.[5]

2. The request for the establishment of a panel shall be made in writing. It shall indicate whether consultations were held, identify the specific measures at issue and provide a brief summary of the legal basis of the complaint sufficient to present the problem clearly. In case the applicant requests the establishment of a panel with other than standard terms of reference, the written request shall include the proposed text of special terms of reference.

Article 7. Terms of Reference of Panels

1. Panels shall have the following terms of reference unless the parties to the dispute agree otherwise within 20 days from the establishment of the panel:

"To examine, in the light of the relevant provisions in (name of the covered agreement(s) cited by the parties to the dispute), the matter referred to the DSB by (name of party) in document . . . and to make such findings as will assist the DSB in making the recommendations or in giving the rulings provided for in that/those agreement(s)."

2. Panels shall address the relevant provisions in any covered agreement or agreements cited by the parties to the dispute.

3. In establishing a panel, the DSB may authorize its Chairman to draw up the terms of reference of the panel in consultation with the parties to the dispute, subject to the provisions of paragraph 1. The terms of reference thus drawn up shall be circulated to all Members. If other than standard terms of reference are agreed upon, any Member may raise any point relating thereto in the DSB.

Article 8. Composition of Panels

1. Panels shall be composed of well-qualified governmental and/or non-governmental individuals, including persons who have served on or presented a case to a panel, served as a representative of a Member or of a contracting party to GATT 1947 or as a representative to the Council or Committee of any covered agreement or its predecessor agreement, or in the Secretariat, taught or published on international trade law or policy, or served as a senior trade policy official of a Member.

2. Panel members should be selected with a view to ensuring the independence of the members, a sufficiently diverse background and a wide spectrum of experience.

3. Citizens of Members whose governments[6] are parties to the dispute or third parties as defined in paragraph 2 of Article 10 shall not serve on a panel concerned with that dispute, unless the parties to the dispute agree otherwise.

[5] If the complaining party so requests, a meeting of the DSB shall be convened for this purpose within 15 days of the request, provided that at least 10 days' advance notice of the meeting is given.

[6] In the case where customs unions or common markets are parties to a dispute, this provision applies to citizens of all member countries of the customs unions or common markets.

4. To assist in the selection of panelists, the Secretariat shall maintain an indicative list of governmental and non-governmental individuals possessing the qualifications outlined in paragraph 1, from which panelists may be drawn as appropriate. That list shall include the roster of non-governmental panelists established on 30 November 1984 (BISD 31S/9), and other rosters and indicative lists established under any of the covered agreements, and shall retain the names of persons on those rosters and indicative lists at the time of entry into force of the WTO Agreement. Members may periodically suggest names of governmental and non-governmental individuals for inclusion on the indicative list, providing relevant information on their knowledge of international trade and of the sectors or subject matter of the covered agreements, and those names shall be added to the list upon approval by the DSB. For each of the individuals on the list, the list shall indicate specific areas of experience or expertise of the individuals in the sectors or subject matter of the covered agreements.

5. Panels shall be composed of three panelists unless the parties to the dispute agree, within 10 days from the establishment of the panel, to a panel composed of five panelists. Members shall be informed promptly of the composition of the panel.

6. The Secretariat shall propose nominations for the panel to the parties to the dispute. The parties to the dispute shall not oppose nominations except for compelling reasons.

7. If there is no agreement on the panelists within 20 days after the date of the establishment of a panel, at the request of either party, the Director-General, in consultation with the Chairman of the DSB and the Chairman of the relevant Council or Committee, shall determine the composition of the panel by appointing the panelists whom the Director-General considers most appropriate in accordance with any relevant special or additional rules or procedures of the covered agreement or covered agreements which are at issue in the dispute, after consulting with the parties to the dispute. The Chairman of the DSB shall inform the Members of the composition of the panel thus formed no later than 10 days after the date the Chairman receives such a request.

8. Members shall undertake, as a general rule, to permit their officials to serve as panelists.

9. Panelists shall serve in their individual capacities and not as government representatives, nor as representatives of any organization. Members shall therefore not give them instructions nor seek to influence them as individuals with regard to matters before a panel.

10. When a dispute is between a developing country Member and a developed country Member the panel shall, if the developing country Member so requests, include at least one panelist from a developing country Member.

11. Panelists' expenses, including travel and subsistence allowance, shall be met from the WTO budget in accordance with criteria to be adopted by the General Council, based on recommendations of the Committee on Budget, Finance and Administration.

Article 9. Procedures for Multiple Complainants

1. Where more than one Member requests the establishment of a panel related to the same matter, a single panel may be established to examine these complaints taking into account the rights of all Members concerned. A single panel should be established to examine such complaints whenever feasible.

2. The single panel shall organize its examination and present its findings to the DSB in such a manner that the rights which the parties to the dispute would have enjoyed had

separate panels examined the complaints are in no way impaired. If one of the parties to the dispute so requests, the panel shall submit separate reports on the dispute concerned. The written submissions by each of the complainants shall be made available to the other complainants, and each complainant shall have the right to be present when any one of the other complainants presents its views to the panel.

3. If more than one panel is established to examine the complaints related to the same matter, to the greatest extent possible the same persons shall serve as panelists on each of the separate panels and the timetable for the panel process in such disputes shall be harmonized.

Article 10. Third Parties

1. The interests of the parties to a dispute and those of other Members under a covered agreement at issue in the dispute shall be fully taken into account during the panel process.

2. Any Member having a substantial interest in a matter before a panel and having notified its interest to the DSB (referred to in this Understanding as a "third party") shall have an opportunity to be heard by the panel and to make written submissions to the panel. These submissions shall also be given to the parties to the dispute and shall be reflected in the panel report.

3. Third parties shall receive the submissions of the parties to the dispute to the first meeting of the panel.

4. If a third party considers that a measure already the subject of a panel proceeding nullifies or impairs benefits accruing to it under any covered agreement, that Member may have recourse to normal dispute settlement procedures under this Understanding. Such a dispute shall be referred to the original panel wherever possible.

Article 11. Function of Panels

The function of panels is to assist the DSB in discharging its responsibilities under this Understanding and the covered agreements. Accordingly, a panel should make an objective assessment of the matter before it, including an objective assessment of the facts of the case and the applicability of and conformity with the relevant covered agreements, and make such other findings as will assist the DSB in making the recommendations or in giving the rulings provided for in the covered agreements. Panels should consult regularly with the parties to the dispute and give them adequate opportunity to develop a mutually satisfactory solution.

Article 12. Panel Procedures

1. Panels shall follow the Working Procedures in Appendix 3 unless the panel decides otherwise after consulting the parties to the dispute.

2. Panel procedures should provide sufficient flexibility so as to ensure high-quality panel reports, while not unduly delaying the panel process.

3. After consulting the parties to the dispute, the panelists shall, as soon as practicable and whenever possible within one week after the composition and terms of reference of

the panel have been agreed upon, fix the timetable for the panel process, taking into account the provisions of paragraph 9 of Article 4, if relevant.

4. In determining the timetable for the panel process, the panel shall provide sufficient time for the parties to the dispute to prepare their submissions.

5. Panels should set precise deadlines for written submissions by the parties and the parties should respect those deadlines.

6. Each party to the dispute shall deposit its written submissions with the Secretariat for immediate transmission to the panel and to the other party or parties to the dispute. The complaining party shall submit its first submission in advance of the responding party's first submission unless the panel decides, in fixing the timetable referred to in paragraph 3 and after consultations with the parties to the dispute, that the parties should submit their first submissions simultaneously. When there are sequential arrangements for the deposit of first submissions, the panel shall establish a firm time-period for receipt of the responding party's submission. Any subsequent written submissions shall be submitted simultaneously.

7. Where the parties to the dispute have failed to develop a mutually satisfactory solution, the panel shall submit its findings in the form of a written report to the DSB. In such cases, the report of a panel shall set out the findings of fact, the applicability of relevant provisions and the basic rationale behind any findings and recommendations that it makes. Where a settlement of the matter among the parties to the dispute has been found, the report of the panel shall be confined to a brief description of the case and to reporting that a solution has been reached.

8. In order to make the procedures more efficient, the period in which the panel shall conduct its examination, from the date that the composition and terms of reference of the panel have been agreed upon until the date the final report is issued to the parties to the dispute, shall, as a general rule, not exceed six months. In cases of urgency, including those relating to perishable goods, the panel shall aim to issue its report to the parties to the dispute within three months.

9. When the panel considers that it cannot issue its report within six months, or within three months in cases of urgency, it shall inform the DSB in writing of the reasons for the delay together with an estimate of the period within which it will issue its report. In no case should the period from the establishment of the panel to the circulation of the report to the Members exceed nine months.

10. In the context of consultations involving a measure taken by a developing country Member, the parties may agree to extend the periods established in paragraphs 7 and 8 of Article 4. If, after the relevant period has elapsed, the consulting parties cannot agree that the consultations have concluded, the Chairman of the DSB shall decide, after consultation with the parties, whether to extend the relevant period and, if so, for how long. In addition, in examining a complaint against a developing country Member, the panel shall accord sufficient time for the developing country Member to prepare and present its argumentation. The provisions of paragraph 1 of Article 20 and paragraph 4 of Article 21 are not affected by any action pursuant to this paragraph.

11. Where one or more of the parties is a developing country Member, the panel's report shall explicitly indicate the form in which account has been taken of relevant provisions on differential and more-favourable treatment for developing country Members that form part of the covered agreements which have been raised by the developing country Member in the course of the dispute settlement procedures.

12. The panel may suspend its work at any time at the request of the complaining party for a period not to exceed 12 months. In the event of such a suspension, the time-frames set out in paragraphs 8 and 9 of this Article, paragraph 1 of Article 20, and paragraph 4 of Article 21 shall be extended by the amount of time that the work was suspended. If the work of the panel has been suspended for more than 12 months, the authority for establishment of the panel shall lapse.

Article 13. Right to Seek Information

1. Each panel shall have the right to seek information and technical advice from any individual or body which it deems appropriate. However, before a panel seeks such information or advice from any individual or body within the jurisdiction of a Member it shall inform the authorities of that Member. A Member should respond promptly and fully to any request by a panel for such information as the panel considers necessary and appropriate. Confidential information which is provided shall not be revealed without formal authorization from the individual, body, or authorities of the Member providing the information.

2. Panels may seek information from any relevant source and may consult experts to obtain their opinion on certain aspects of the matter. With respect to a factual issue concerning a scientific or other technical matter raised by a party to a dispute, a panel may request an advisory report in writing from an expert review group. Rules for the establishment of such a group and its procedures are set forth in Appendix 4.

Article 14. Confidentiality

1. Panel deliberations shall be confidential.

2. The reports of panels shall be drafted without the presence of the parties to the dispute in the light of the information provided and the statements made.

3. Opinions expressed in the panel report by individual panelists shall be anonymous.

Article 15. Interim Review Stage

1. Following the consideration of rebuttal submissions and oral arguments, the panel shall issue the descriptive (factual and argument) sections of its draft report to the parties to the dispute. Within a period of time set by the panel, the parties shall submit their comments in writing.

2. Following the expiration of the set period of time for receipt of comments from the parties to the dispute, the panel shall issue an interim report to the parties, including both the descriptive sections and the panel's findings and conclusions. Within a period of time set by the panel, a party may submit a written request for the panel to review precise aspects of the interim report prior to circulation of the final report to the Members. At the request of a party, the panel shall hold a further meeting with the parties on the issues identified in the written comments. If no comments are received from any party within the comment period, the interim report shall be considered the final panel report and circulated promptly to the Members.

3. The findings of the final panel report shall include a discussion of the arguments made at the interim review stage. The interim review stage shall be conducted within the time-period set out in paragraph 8 of Article 12.

Article 16. Adoption of Panel Reports

1. In order to provide sufficient time for the Members to consider panel reports, the reports shall not be considered for adoption by the DSB until 20 days after the date they have been circulated to the Members.

2. Members having objections to a panel report shall give written reasons to explain their objections for circulation at least 10 days prior to the DSB meeting at which the panel report will be considered.

3. The parties to a dispute shall have the right to participate fully in the consideration of the panel report by the DSB, and their views shall be fully recorded.

4. Within 60 days after the date of circulation of a panel report to the Members, the report shall be adopted at a DSB meeting[7] unless a party to the dispute formally notifies the DSB of its decision to appeal or the DSB decides by consensus not to adopt the report. If a party has notified its decision to appeal, the report by the panel shall not be considered for adoption by the DSB until after completion of the appeal. This adoption procedure is without prejudice to the right of Members to express their views on a panel report.

Article 17. Appellate Review

Standing Appellate Body

1. A standing Appellate Body shall be established by the DSB. The Appellate Body shall hear appeals from panel cases. It shall be composed of seven persons, three of whom shall serve on any one case. Persons serving on the Appellate Body shall serve in rotation. Such rotation shall be determined in the working procedures of the Appellate Body.

2. The DSB shall appoint persons to serve on the Appellate Body for a four-year term, and each person may be reappointed once. However, the terms of three of the seven persons appointed immediately after the entry into force of the WTO Agreement shall expire at the end of two years, to be determined by lot. Vacancies shall be filled as they arise. A person appointed to replace a person whose term of office has not expired shall hold office for the remainder of the predecessor's term.

3. The Appellate Body shall comprise persons of recognized authority, with demonstrated expertise in law, international trade and the subject matter of the covered agreements generally. They shall be unaffiliated with any government. The Appellate Body membership shall be broadly representative of membership in the WTO. All persons serving on the Appellate Body shall be available at all times and on short notice, and shall stay abreast of dispute settlement activities and other relevant activities of the WTO. They shall not participate in the consideration of any disputes that would create a direct or indirect conflict of interest.

[7] If a meeting of the DSB is not scheduled within this period at a time that enables the requirements of paragraphs 1 and 4 of Article 16 to be met, a meeting of the DSB shall be held for this purpose.

4. Only parties to the dispute, not third parties, may appeal a panel report. Third parties which have notified the DSB of a substantial interest in the matter pursuant to paragraph 2 of Article 10 may make written submissions to, and be given an opportunity to be heard by, the Appellate Body.

5. As a general rule, the proceedings shall not exceed 60 days from the date a party to the dispute formally notifies its decision to appeal to the date the Appellate Body circulates its report. In fixing its timetable the Appellate Body shall take into account the provisions of paragraph 9 of Article 4, if relevant. When the Appellate Body considers that it cannot provide its report within 60 days, it shall inform the DSB in writing of the reasons for the delay together with an estimate of the period within which it will submit its report. In no case shall the proceedings exceed 90 days.

6. An appeal shall be limited to issues of law covered in the panel report and legal interpretations developed by the panel.

7. The Appellate Body shall be provided with appropriate administrative and legal support as it requires.

8. The expenses of persons serving on the Appellate Body, including travel and subsistence allowance, shall be met from the WTO budget in accordance with criteria to be adopted by the General Council, based on recommendations of the Committee on Budget, Finance and Administration.

Procedures for Appellate Review

9. Working procedures shall be drawn up by the Appellate Body in consultation with the Chairman of the DSB and the Director-General, and communicated to the Members for their information.

10. The proceedings of the Appellate Body shall be confidential. The reports of the Appellate Body shall be drafted without the presence of the parties to the dispute and in the light of the information provided and the statements made.

11. Opinions expressed in the Appellate Body report by individuals serving on the Appellate Body shall be anonymous.

12. The Appellate Body shall address each of the issues raised in accordance with paragraph 6 during the appellate proceeding.

13. The Appellate Body may uphold, modify or reverse the legal findings and conclusions of the panel.

Adoption of Appellate Body Reports

14. An Appellate Body report shall be adopted by the DSB and unconditionally accepted by the parties to the dispute unless the DSB decides by consensus not to adopt the Appellate Body report within 30 days following its circulation to the Members.[8] This adoption procedure is without prejudice to the right of Members to express their views on an Appellate Body report.

Article 18. Communications with the Panel or Appellate Body

1. There shall be no *ex parte* communications with the panel or Appellate Body concerning matters under consideration by the panel or Appellate Body.

[8] If a meeting of the DSB is not scheduled during this period, such a meeting of the DSB shall be held for this purpose.

2. Written submissions to the panel or the Appellate Body shall be treated as confidential, but shall be made available to the parties to the dispute. Nothing in this Understanding shall preclude a party to a dispute from disclosing statements of its own positions to the public. Members shall treat as confidential information submitted by another Member to the panel or the Appellate Body which that Member has designated as confidential. A party to a dispute shall also, upon request of a Member, provide a non-confidential summary of the information contained in its written submissions that could be disclosed to the public.

Article 19. Panel and Appellate Body Recommendations

1. Where a panel or the Appellate Body concludes that a measure is inconsistent with a covered agreement, it shall recommend that the Member concerned[9] bring the measure into conformity with that agreement.[10] In addition to its recommendations, the panel or Appellate Body may suggest ways in which the Member concerned could implement the recommendations.

2. In accordance with paragraph 2 of Article 3, in their findings and recommendations, the panel and Appellate Body cannot add to or diminish the rights and obligations provided in the covered agreements.

Article 20. Time-frame for DSB Decisions

Unless otherwise agreed to by the parties to the dispute, the period from the date of establishment of the panel by the DSB until the date the DSB considers the panel or appellate report for adoption shall as a general rule not exceed nine months where the panel report is not appealed or 12 months where the report is appealed. Where either the panel or the Appellate Body has acted, pursuant to paragraph 9 of Article 12 or paragraph 5 of Article 17, to extend the time for providing its report, the additional time taken shall be added to the above periods.

Article 21. Surveillance of Implementation of Recommendations and Rulings

1. Prompt compliance with recommendations or rulings of the DSB is essential in order to ensure effective resolution of disputes to the benefit of all Members.

2. Particular attention should be paid to matters affecting the interests of developing country Members with respect to measures which have been subject to dispute settlement.

3. At a DSB meeting held within 30 days[11] after the date of adoption of the panel or Appellate Body report, the Member concerned shall inform the DSB of its intentions in

[9] The "Member concerned" is the party to the dispute to which the panel or Appellate Body recommendations are directed.

[10] With respect to recommendations in cases not involving a violation of GATT 1994 or any other covered agreement, see Article 26.

[11] If a meeting of the DSB is not scheduled during this period, such a meeting of the DSB shall be held for this purpose.

respect of implementation of the recommendations and rulings of the DSB. If it is impracticable to comply immediately with the recommendations and rulings, the Member concerned shall have a reasonable period of time in which to do so. The reasonable period of time shall be:

(a) the period of time proposed by the Member concerned, provided that such period is approved by the DSB; or, in the absence of such approval,
(b) a period of time mutually agreed by the parties to the dispute within 45 days after the date of adoption of the recommendations and rulings; or, in the absence of such agreement,
(c) a period of time determined through binding arbitration within 90 days after the date of adoption of the recommendations and rulings.[12] In such arbitration, a guideline for the arbitrator[13] should be that the reasonable period of time to implement panel or Appellate Body recommendations should not exceed 15 months from the date of adoption of a panel or Appellate Body report. However, that time may be shorter or longer, depending upon the particular circumstances.

4. Except where the panel or the Appellate Body has extended, pursuant to paragraph 9 of Article 12 or paragraph 5 of Article 17, the time of providing its report, the period from the date of establishment of the panel by the DSB until the date of determination of the reasonable period of time shall not exceed 15 months unless the parties to the dispute agree otherwise. Where either the panel or the Appellate Body has acted to extend the time of providing its report, the additional time taken shall be added to the 15-month period; provided that unless the parties to the dispute agree that there are exceptional circumstances, the total time shall not exceed 18 months.

5. Where there is disagreement as to the existence or consistency with a covered agreement of measures taken to comply with the recommendations and rulings such dispute shall be decided through recourse to these dispute settlement procedures, including wherever possible resort to the original panel. The panel shall circulate its report within 90 days after the date of referral of the matter to it. When the panel considers that it cannot provide its report within this time frame, it shall inform the DSB in writing of the reasons for the delay together with an estimate of the period within which it will submit its report.

6. The DSB shall keep under surveillance the implementation of adopted recommendations or rulings. The issue of implementation of the recommendations or rulings may be raised at the DSB by any Member at any time following their adoption. Unless the DSB decides otherwise, the issue of implementation of the recommendations or rulings shall be placed on the agenda of the DSB meeting after six months following the date of establishment of the reasonable period of time pursuant to paragraph 3 and shall remain on the DSB's agenda until the issue is resolved. At least 10 days prior to each such DSB meeting, the Member concerned shall provide the DSB with a status report in writing of its progress in the implementation of the recommendations or rulings.

[12] If the parties cannot agree on an arbitrator within ten days after referring the matter to arbitration, the arbitrator shall be appointed by the Director-General within ten days, after consulting the parties.

[13] The expression "arbitrator" shall be interpreted as referring either to an individual or a group.

7. If the matter is one which has been raised by a developing country Member, the DSB shall consider what further action it might take which would be appropriate to the circumstances.

8. If the case is one brought by a developing country Member, in considering what appropriate action might be taken, the DSB shall take into account not only the trade coverage of measures complained of, but also their impact on the economy of developing country Members concerned.

Article 22. Compensation and the Suspension of Concessions

1. Compensation and the suspension of concessions or other obligations are temporary measures available in the event that the recommendations and rulings are not implemented within a reasonable period of time. However, neither compensation nor the suspension of concessions or other obligations is preferred to full implementation of a recommendation to bring a measure into conformity with the covered agreements. Compensation is voluntary and, if granted, shall be consistent with the covered agreements.

2. If the Member concerned fails to bring the measure found to be inconsistent with a covered agreement into compliance therewith or otherwise comply with the recommendations and rulings within the reasonable period of time determined pursuant to paragraph 3 of Article 21, such Member shall, if so requested, and no later than the expiry of the reasonable period of time, enter into negotiations with any party having invoked the dispute settlement procedures, with a view to developing mutually acceptable compensation. If no satisfactory compensation has been agreed within 20 days after the date of expiry of the reasonable period of time, any party having invoked the dispute settlement procedures may request authorization from the DSB to suspend the application to the Member concerned of concessions or other obligations under the covered agreements.

3. In considering what concessions or other obligations to suspend, the complaining party shall apply the following principles and procedures:

(a) the general principle is that the complaining party should first seek to suspend concessions or other obligations with respect to the same sector(s) as that in which the panel or Appellate Body has found a violation or other nullification or impairment;

(b) if that party considers that it is not practicable or effective to suspend concessions or other obligations with respect to the same sector(s), it may seek to suspend concessions or other obligations in other sectors under the same agreement;

(c) if that party considers that it is not practicable or effective to suspend concessions or other obligations with respect to other sectors under the same agreement, and that the circumstances are serious enough, it may seek to suspend concessions or other obligations under another covered agreement;

(d) in applying the above principles, that party shall take into account:

(i) the trade in the sector or under the agreement under which the panel or Appellate Body has found a violation or other nullification or impairment, and the importance of such trade to that party;

(ii) the broader economic elements related to the nullification or impairment and the broader economic consequences of the suspension of concessions or other obligations;

(e) if that party decides to request authorization to suspend concessions or other obligations pursuant to subparagraphs (b) or (c), it shall state the reasons therefor in its request. At the same time as the request is forwarded to the DSB, it also shall be forwarded to the relevant Councils and also, in the case of a request pursuant to subparagraph (b), the relevant sectoral bodies;

(f) for purposes of this paragraph, "sector" means:

(i) with respect to goods, all goods;

(ii) with respect to services, a principal sector as identified in the current "Services Sectoral Classification List" which identifies such sectors;[14]

(iii) with respect to trade-related intellectual property rights, each of the categories of intellectual property rights covered in Section 1, or Section 2, or Section 3, or Section 4, or Section 5, or Section 6, or Section 7 of Part II, or the obligations under Part III, or Part IV of the Agreement on TRIPS;

(g) for purposes of this paragraph, "agreement" means:

(i) with respect to goods, the agreements listed in Annex 1A of the WTO Agreement, taken as a whole as well as the Plurilateral Trade Agreements in so far as the relevant parties to the dispute are parties to these agreements;

(ii) with respect to services, the GATS;

(iii) with respect to intellectual property rights, the Agreement on TRIPS.

4. The level of the suspension of concessions or other obligations authorized by the DSB shall be equivalent to the level of the nullification or impairment.

5. The DSB shall not authorize suspension of concessions or other obligations if a covered agreement prohibits such suspension.

6. When the situation described in paragraph 2 occurs, the DSB, upon request, shall grant authorization to suspend concessions or other obligations within 30 days of the expiry of the reasonable period of time unless the DSB decides by consensus to reject the request. However, if the Member concerned objects to the level of suspension proposed, or claims that the principles and procedures set forth in paragraph 3 have not been followed where a complaining party has requested authorization to suspend concessions or other obligations pursuant to paragraph 3(b) or (c), the matter shall be referred to arbitration. Such arbitration shall be carried out by the original panel, if members are available, or by an arbitrator[15] appointed by the Director-General and shall be completed within 60 days after the date of expiry of the reasonable period of time. Concessions or other obligations shall not be suspended during the course of the arbitration.

7. The arbitrator[16] acting pursuant to paragraph 6 shall not examine the nature of the concessions or other obligations to be suspended but shall determine whether the level of such suspension is equivalent to the level of nullification or impairment. The arbitrator

[14] The list in document MTN.GNS/W/120 identifies eleven sectors.

[15] The expression "arbitrator" shall be interpreted as referring either to an individual or a group.

[16] The expression "arbitrator" shall be interpreted as referring either to an individual or a group or to the members of the original panel when serving in the capacity of arbitrator.

may also determine if the proposed suspension of concessions or other obligations is allowed under the covered agreement. However, if the matter referred to arbitration includes a claim that the principles and procedures set forth in paragraph 3 have not been followed, the arbitrator shall examine that claim. In the event the arbitrator determines that those principles and procedures have not been followed, the complaining party shall apply them consistent with paragraph 3. The parties shall accept the arbitrator's decision as final and the parties concerned shall not seek a second arbitration. The DSB shall be informed promptly of the decision of the arbitrator and shall upon request, grant authorization to suspend concessions or other obligations where the request is consistent with the decision of the arbitrator, unless the DSB decides by consensus to reject the request.

8. The suspension of concessions or other obligations shall be temporary and shall only be applied until such time as the measure found to be inconsistent with a covered agreement has been removed, or the Member that must implement recommendations or rulings provides a solution to the nullification or impairment of benefits, or a mutually satisfactory solution is reached. In accordance with paragraph 6 of Article 21, the DSB shall continue to keep under surveillance the implementation of adopted recommendations or rulings, including those cases where compensation has been provided or concessions or other obligations have been suspended but the recommendations to bring a measure into conformity with the covered agreements have not been implemented.

9. The dispute settlement provisions of the covered agreements may be invoked in respect of measures affecting their observance taken by regional or local governments or authorities within the territory of a Member. When the DSB has ruled that a provision of a covered agreement has not been observed, the responsible Member shall take such reasonable measures as may be available to it to ensure its observance. The provisions of the covered agreements and this Understanding relating to compensation and suspension of concessions or other obligations apply in cases where it has not been possible to secure such observance.[17]

Article 23. Strengthening of the Multilateral System

1. When Members seek the redress of a violation of obligations or other nullification or impairment of benefits under the covered agreements or an impediment to the attainment of any objective of the covered agreements, they shall have recourse to, and abide by, the rules and procedures of this Understanding.

2. In such cases, Members shall:

(a) not make a determination to the effect that a violation has occurred, that benefits have been nullified or impaired or that the attainment of any objective of the covered agreements has been impeded, except through recourse to dispute settlement in accordance with the rules and procedures of this Understanding, and shall make any such determination consistent with the findings contained in the panel or Appellate Body report adopted by the DSB or an arbitration award rendered under this Understanding;

[17] Where the provisions of any covered agreement concerning measures taken by regional or local governments or authorities within the territory of a Member contain provisions different from the provisions of this paragraph, the provisions of such covered agreement shall prevail.

(b) follow the procedures set forth in Article 21 to determine the reasonable period of time for the Member concerned to implement the recommendations and rulings; and

(c) follow the procedures set forth in Article 22 to determine the level of suspension of concessions or other obligations and obtain DSB authorization in accordance with those procedures before suspending concessions or other obligations under the covered agreements in response to the failure of the Member concerned to implement the recommendations and rulings within that reasonable period of time.

Article 24. Special Procedures Involving Least-Developed Country Members

1. At all stages of the determination of the causes of a dispute and of dispute settlement procedures involving a least-developed country Member, particular consideration shall be given to the special situation of least-developed country Members. In this regard, Members shall exercise due restraint in raising matters under these procedures involving a least-developed country Member. If nullification or impairment is found to result from a measure taken by a least-developed country Member, complaining parties shall exercise due restraint in asking for compensation or seeking authorization to suspend the application of concessions or other obligations pursuant to these procedures.

2. In dispute settlement cases involving a least-developed country Member, where a satisfactory solution has not been found in the course of consultations the Director-General or the Chairman of the DSB shall, upon request by a least-developed country Member offer their good offices, conciliation and mediation with a view to assisting the parties to settle the dispute, before a request for a panel is made. The Director-General or the Chairman of the DSB, in providing the above assistance, may consult any source which either deems appropriate.

Article 25. Arbitration

1. Expeditious arbitration within the WTO as an alternative means of dispute settlement can facilitate the solution of certain disputes that concern issues that are clearly defined by both parties.

2. Except as otherwise provided in this Understanding, resort to arbitration shall be subject to mutual agreement of the parties which shall agree on the procedures to be followed. Agreements to resort to arbitration shall be notified to all Members sufficiently in advance of the actual commencement of the arbitration process.

3. Other Members may become party to an arbitration proceeding only upon the agreement of the parties which have agreed to have recourse to arbitration. The parties to the proceeding shall agree to abide by the arbitration award. Arbitration awards shall be notified to the DSB and the Council or Committee of any relevant agreement where any Member may raise any point relating thereto.

4. Articles 21 and 22 of this Understanding shall apply *mutatis mutandis* to arbitration awards.

Article 26.

1. *Non-Violation Complaints of the Type Described in Paragraph 1(b) of Article XXIII of GATT 1994*

Where the provisions of paragraph 1(b) of Article XXIII of GATT 1994 are applicable to a covered agreement, a panel or the Appellate Body may only make rulings and recommendations where a party to the dispute considers that any benefit accruing to it directly or indirectly under the relevant covered agreement is being nullified or impaired or the attainment of any objective of that Agreement is being impeded as a result of the application by a Member of any measure, whether or not it conflicts with the provisions of that Agreement. Where and to the extent that such party considers and a panel or the Appellate Body determines that a case concerns a measure that does not conflict with the provisions of a covered agreement to which the provisions of paragraph 1(b) of Article XXIII of GATT 1994 are applicable, the procedures in this Understanding shall apply, subject to the following:

(a) the complaining party shall present a detailed justification in support of any complaint relating to a measure which does not conflict with the relevant covered agreement;

(b) where a measure has been found to nullify or impair benefits under, or impede the attainment of objectives, of the relevant covered agreement without violation thereof, there is no obligation to withdraw the measure. However, in such cases, the panel or the Appellate Body shall recommend that the Member concerned make a mutually satisfactory adjustment;

(c) notwithstanding the provisions of Article 21, the arbitration provided for in paragraph 3 of Article 21, upon request of either party, may include a determination of the level of benefits which have been nullified or impaired, and may also suggest ways and means of reaching a mutually satisfactory adjustment; such suggestions shall not be binding upon the parties to the dispute;

(d) notwithstanding the provisions of paragraph 1 of Article 22, compensation may be part of a mutually satisfactory adjustment as final settlement of the dispute.

2. *Complaints of the Type Described in Paragraph 1(c) of* Article XXIII*of GATT 1994*

Where the provisions of paragraph 1(c) of Article XXIII of GATT 1994 are applicable to a covered agreement, a panel may only make rulings and recommendations where a party considers that any benefit accruing to it directly or indirectly under the relevant covered agreement is being nullified or impaired or the attainment of any objective of that Agreement is being impeded as a result of the existence of any situation other than those to which the provisions of paragraphs 1(a) and 1(b) of Article XXIII of GATT 1994 are applicable. Where and to the extent that such party considers and a panel determines that the matter is covered by this paragraph, the procedures of this Understanding shall apply only up to and including the point in the proceedings where the panel report has been circulated to the Members. The dispute settlement rules and procedures contained in the Decision of 12 April 1989 (BISD 36S/61-67) shall apply to consideration for adoption, and surveillance and implementation of recommendations and rulings. The following shall also apply:

(a) the complaining party shall present a detailed justification in support of any argument made with respect to issues covered under this paragraph;

(b) in cases involving matters covered by this paragraph, if a panel finds that cases also involve dispute settlement matters other than those covered by this paragraph, the panel shall circulate a report to the DSB addressing any such matters and a separate report on matters falling under this paragraph.

Article 27. Responsibilities of the Secretariat

1. The Secretariat shall have the responsibility of assisting panels, especially on the legal, historical and procedural aspects of the matters dealt with, and of providing secretarial and technical support.

2. While the Secretariat assists Members in respect of dispute settlement at their request, there may also be a need to provide additional legal advice and assistance in respect of dispute settlement to developing country Members. To this end, the Secretariat shall make available a qualified legal expert from the WTO technical cooperation services to any developing country Member which so requests. This expert shall assist the developing country Member in a manner ensuring the continued impartiality of the Secretariat.

3. The Secretariat shall conduct special training courses for interested Members concerning these dispute settlement procedures and practices so as to enable Members' experts to be better informed in this regard.

[. . .]

Appendix 3. Working Procedures

1. In its proceedings the panel shall follow the relevant provisions of this Understanding. In addition, the following working procedures shall apply.

2. The panel shall meet in closed session. The parties to the dispute, and interested parties, shall be present at the meetings only when invited by the panel to appear before it.

3. The deliberations of the panel and the documents submitted to it shall be kept confidential. Nothing in this Understanding shall preclude a party to a dispute from disclosing statements of its own positions to the public. Members shall treat as confidential information submitted by another Member to the panel which that Member has designated as confidential. Where a party to a dispute submits a confidential version of its written submissions to the panel, it shall also, upon request of a Member, provide a non-confidential summary of the information contained in its submissions that could be disclosed to the public.

4. Before the first substantive meeting of the panel with the parties, the parties to the dispute shall transmit to the panel written submissions in which they present the facts of the case and their arguments.

5. At its first substantive meeting with the parties, the panel shall ask the party which has brought the complaint to present its case. Subsequently, and still at the same

meeting, the party against which the complaint has been brought shall be asked to present its point of view.

6. All third parties which have notified their interest in the dispute to the DSB shall be invited in writing to present their views during a session of the first substantive meeting of the panel set aside for that purpose. All such third parties may be present during the entirety of this session.

7. Formal rebuttals shall be made at a second substantive meeting of the panel. The party complained against shall have the right to take the floor first to be followed by the complaining party. The parties shall submit, prior to that meeting, written rebuttals to the panel.

8. The panel may at any time put questions to the parties and ask them for explanations either in the course of a meeting with the parties or in writing.

9. The parties to the dispute and any third party invited to present its views in accordance with Article 10 shall make available to the panel a written version of their oral statements.

10. In the interest of full transparency, the presentations, rebuttals and statements referred to in paragraphs 5 to 9 shall be made in the presence of the parties. Moreover, each party's written submissions, including any comments on the descriptive part of the report and responses to questions put by the panel, shall be made available to the other party or parties.

11. Any additional procedures specific to the panel.

12. Proposed timetable for panel work:

(a) Receipt of first written submissions of the parties:
  (1) complaining Party: 3–6 weeks
  (2) Party complained against:2–3 weeks
(b) Date, time and place of first substantive meeting with the parties; third party session: 1–2 weeks
(c) Receipt of written rebuttals of the parties: 2–3 weeks
(d) Date, time and place of second substantive meeting with the parties: 1–2 weeks
(e) Issuance of descriptive part of the report to the parties: 2–4 weeks
(f) Receipt of comments by the parties on the descriptive part of the report: 2 weeks
(g) Issuance of the interim report, including the findings and conclusions, to the parties: 2–4 weeks
(h) Deadline for party to request review of part(s) of report: 1 week
(i) Period of review by panel, including possible additional meeting with parties: 2 weeks
(j) Issuance of final report to parties to dispute: 2 weeks
(k) Circulation of the final report to the Members: 3 weeks

The above calendar may be changed in the light of unforeseen developments. Additional meetings with the parties shall be scheduled if required.

Appendix 4. Expert Review Groups

The following rules and procedures shall apply to expert review groups established in accordance with the provisions of paragraph 2 of Article 13.

1. Expert review groups are under the panel's authority. Their terms of reference and detailed working procedures shall be decided by the panel, and they shall report to the panel.

2. Participation in expert review groups shall be restricted to persons of professional standing and experience in the field in question.

3. Citizens of parties to the dispute shall not serve on an expert review group without the joint agreement of the parties to the dispute, except in exceptional circumstances when the panel considers that the need for specialized scientific expertise cannot be fulfilled otherwise. Government officials of parties to the dispute shall not serve on an expert review group. Members of expert review groups shall serve in their individual capacities and not as government representatives, nor as representatives of any organization. Governments or organizations shall therefore not give them instructions with regard to matters before an expert review group.

4. Expert review groups may consult and seek information and technical advice from any source they deem appropriate. Before an expert review group seeks such information or advice from a source within the jurisdiction of a Member, it shall inform the government of that Member. Any Member shall respond promptly and fully to any request by an expert review group for such information as the expert review group considers necessary and appropriate.

5. The parties to a dispute shall have access to all relevant information provided to an expert review group, unless it is of a confidential nature. Confidential information provided to the expert review group shall not be released without formal authorization from the government, organization or person providing the information. Where such information is requested from the expert review group but release of such information by the expert review group is not authorized, a non-confidential summary of the information will be provided by the government, organization or person supplying the information.

6. The expert review group shall submit a draft report to the parties to the dispute with a view to obtaining their comments, and taking them into account, as appropriate, in the final report, which shall also be issued to the parties to the dispute when it is submitted to the panel. The final report of the expert review group shall be advisory only.

Bibliography

A. Reports and Proceedings of International Organizations

Using the Right to Information as an Anti-Corruption Tool (Berlin: Transparency International, 2006).

American Law Institute & UNIDROIT, *Principles of Transnational Civil Procedure* (Cambridge: Cambridge University Press, 2006).

Conclusions and Recommendations of the Special Commission on the Practical Operation of The Hague Apostille, Evidence and Service Conventions (28 October to 4 November 2003) available at <http://hcch.e-vision.nl/upload/wop/lse_concl_e.pdf> (accessed 15 January 2007).

ICC Commission on Arbitration, *Techniques for Controlling Time and Costs in Arbitration* (Paris: International Chamber of Commerce, 2007).

International Court of Justice, *The International Court of Justice* (5th edn, The Hague: ICJ, 2004).

Sutherland, Peter, et al, *The Future of the WTO: Addressing Institutional Challenges in the New Millenium* (Geneva: World Trade Organization, 2004).

B. Dictionaries

The Oxford English Dictionary (2nd edn, Oxford: Clarendon Press, 1989).

The New Shorter Oxford English Dictionary (Oxford: Clarendon Press, 1993).

Collins: Spanish-English, English-Spanish Dictionary (4th edn, Glasgow: HarperCollins, 1996).

Black's Law Dictionary (8th edn, St Paul: Thomson West, 2004).

C. Books and Articles

Abbott, Frederick M, 'WTO Dispute Settlement Practice Relating to the Agreement on Trade-Related Intellectual Property Rights' in F Ortino & E -U Petersmann (eds), *The WTO Dispute Settlement System 1995–2003* (The Hague: Kluwer International Law, 2004) 421.

Abi-Saab, Georges, 'The WTO Dispute Settlement and General International Law' in R Yerxa & B Wilson (eds), *Key Issues in WTO Dispute Settlement: the First Ten Years* (Cambridge: Cambridge University Press, 2005) 7.

Aghahosseini, M, 'Evidence before the Iran–United States Claims Tribunal' (1999) 1:4 International Law FORUM du Droit International 208.

Alvarez, José E, *International Organizations as Law-makers* (Oxford: Oxford University Press, 2006).

Amerasinghe, Chittharanjan Felix, *Local Remedies in International Law* (2nd edn, Cambridge: Cambridge University Press, 2004).

—— *Evidence in International Litigation* (Leiden: Martinus Nijhoff, 2005).

Andersen, Scott, 'Administration of Evidence in WTO Dispute Settlement Proceedings' in R Yerxa & B Wilson (eds), *Key Issues in WTO Dispute Settlement: the First Ten Years* (Cambridge: Cambridge University Press, 2005) 177.

Anderson, Terence, David Schum & William Twining, *Analysis of Evidence* (2nd edn, (Cambridge: Cambridge University Press, 2005).

Andrews, Neil, *English Civil Procedure: Fundamentals of the New Civil Justice System* (Oxford: Oxford University Press, 2003).

Applegate, John S, 'The Prometheus Principle: Using the Precautionary Principle to Harmonize the Regulation of Genetically Modified Organisms' (2001) 9 Indiana Journal of Global Legal Studies 207.

Ashford, Peter, 'Documentary Discovery and International Commercial Arbitration' (2006) 17 American Review of International Arbitration 89.

Barcelo, John J, III, 'Burden of Proof, Prima Facie Case, and Presumption in WTO Dispute Settlement' (2009) 42:1 Cornell International Law Journal (forthcoming).

—— 'Product Standards to Protect the Local Environment: the GATT and the Uruguay Round Sanitary and Phytosanitary Agreement' (1994) 27 Cornell International Law Journal 755.

Bartels, Lorand, 'The WTO Enabling Clause and Positive Conditionality in the European Community's GSP Program' (2003) 6:2 Journal of International Economic Law 507.

—— 'WTO Dispute Settlement Practice on Article XXIV of the GATT' in F Ortino & E -U Petersmann (eds), *The WTO Dispute Settlement System 1995-2003* (The Hague: Kluwer Law International, 2004) 263.

Becroft, Ross, 'The Standard of Review Strikes Back: the US–Korea Drams Appeal' (2006) 9:1 Journal of International Economic Law 207.

Behboodi, Rambod, '"Should" Means "Shall" A Critical Analysis of the Obligation to Submit Information under Article 13.1 of the DSU in the *Canada – Aircraft* Case' (2000) Journal of International Economic Law 563.

Bello, Judith Hippler, 'The WTO Dispute Settlement Understanding: Less is More' (1996) 90:3 The American Journal of International Law 416.

Berg, Albert Jan van den (ed), Planning Efficient Arbitration Proceedings: the Law Applicable in International Arbitration (The Hague: Kluwer Law International, 1996).

Bernard, Thierry, 'The Administration of Evidence in Countries of Civil Law' in PV Eijsvoogel (ed), *Evidence in International Arbitration* (London: Graham and Trotman and Martinus Nijhoff, 1994) 21.

Daniel, Bethlehem, 'Submissions on Points of Fact and Law: Written and Oral Pleadings Before the International Court of Justice' in F Weiss (ed), *Improving WTO Dispute Settlement Procedures: Issues and Lessons from the Practice of Other International Courts and Tribunals* (London: Cameron May, 2000) 175.

Bilder, Richard B, 'An Overview of International Dispute Settlement' (1986) 1 Journal of International Dispute Resolution 1.

Bishop, R Doak, James Crawford & W Michael Reisman, *Foreign Investment Disputes: Cases, Materials and Commentary* (The Hague: Kluwer Law International, 2005).

Black, Stephen F, 'United States Transnational Discovery: the Rise and Fall of the Hague Evidence Convention' (1991) 40 International and Comparative Law Quarterly 901.

Block, Michael K, & Jeffrey S Parker, 'Decision Making in the Absence of Successful Fact Finding: Theory and Experimental Evidence on Adversarial Versus Inquisitorial Systems of Adjudication' (2004) 24 International Review of Law and Economics 89.

Bohanes, Jan, & Nicolas Lockhart, 'Standard of Review in WTO Law' in D Bethlehem et al (eds), *The Oxford Handbook of International Trade Law* (Oxford: Oxford University Press, 2009) 378.

Boisseson, Matthieu de, 'Comparative Introduction to the Systems of Producing Evidence in Common Law Countries and Countries of Roman Law Tradition' in *Taking of Evidence in the Arbitral Proceedings* (Paris: ICC Publishing, 1990) 99.

Bolt, Jan W, & Joseph K Wheatley, 'Private Rules for International Discovery in U.S. District Court: the U.S.–German Example' (2006) 11 UCLA Journal of International Law and Foreign Affairs 1.

Brealey, Mark, 'The Burden of Proof Before the European Court' (1985) 10 European Law Review 250.

Broeck, Koen Van den, 'Belgium' in PV Eijsvoogel (ed), *Evidence in International Arbitration Proceedings* (London: Graham & Trotman and Martinus Nijhoff, 1994) 77.

Bronckers, Marco, & Natalie McNelis, 'Fact and Law in Pleadings before the WTO Appellate Body' in F Weiss (ed), *Improving WTO Dispute Settlement Procedures: Issues and Lessons from the Practice of Other International Courts and Tribunals* (London: Cameron May, 2000) 321.

Broude, Tomer, 'Genetically Modified Rules: the Awkward Rule-Exception-Right Distinction in *EC – Biotech*' (2007) 6:2 World Trade Review 215.

Broun, Kenneth S (ed), *McCormick on Evidence* (6th edn, St Paul: Thomson/West, 2006).

Brower, Charles, 'Discovery and Production of Evidence in the U.S.: Theory and Practice' in *Taking of Evidence in the Arbitral Proceedings* (Paris: ICC Publishing, 1990) 7.

—— 'Evidence before International Tribunals: the Need for Some Standard Rules' (1994) 28 The International Lawyer 47.

Brown, Chester, *A Common Law of International Adjudication* (Oxford: Oxford University Press, 2007)

Brownlie, Ian, *Principles of Public International Law* (6th edn, Oxford: Oxford University Press, 2003).

Buergenthal, Thomas, 'Judicial Fact-Finding: Inter-American Human Rights Court' in RB Lillich (ed), *Fact-Finding before International Tribunals* (Ardsley-on-Hudson: Transnational Publishers, 1990) 261.

Busch, Marc L, & Eric Reinhardt, 'Bargaining in the Shadow of the Law: Early Settlement in GATT/WTO Disputes' (2000) 24 Fordham International Law Journal 158.

Buschbeck, Konrad, 'Evidence: Procedures of Judicial Discovery and Burden of Proof' in H Mosler (ed), *Judicial Protection against the Executive* (Dobbs Ferry: Oceana Publications, 1971) 153.

Cadiet, L, 'The New French Code of Civil Procedure (1975)' in CH van Rhee (ed), *European Traditions in Civil Procedure* (Antwerpen: Intersentia, 2005) 49.

Cameron, James, & Kevin R Gray, 'Principles of International Law in the WTO Dispute Settlement Body' (2001) 50 International and Comparative Law Quarterly 248.

Cameron, James, & Stephen J Orava, 'GATT/WTO Panels between Recording and Finding Facts: Issues of Due Process, Evidence, Burden of Proof, and Standard of Review in GATT/WTO Dispute Settlement' in F Weiss (ed), *Improving WTO Dispute Settlement Procedures: Issues and Lessons from the Practice of Other International Courts and Tribunals* (London: Cameron May, 2000) 195.

Cappelletti, Mauro, *The Judicial Process in Comparative Perspective* (Oxford: Clarendon Press, 1989).

Carbonneau, Thomas E, 'Darkness and Light in the Shadows of International Arbitral Adjudication' in RB Lillich (ed), *Fact-Finding before International Tribunals* (Ardsley-on-Hudson: Transnational Publishers, 1992) 153.

Carlucci, Aida Kemelmajer de, 'La Charge de la Preuve dans les Principes et Regles ALI/UNIDROIT relatifs a la procedure civile transnationale' (2001) 2 Revue de Droit Uniforme 915.

Carnelutti, Francisco, *Sistema de Derecho Procesal Civil* (Buenos Aires: Uteha Argentina, 1944).

Charnovitz, Steve, et al, 'The Appellate Body's GSP Decision' (2004) 3:2 World Trade Review 239.

Cheng, Bin, 'Burden of Proof before the ICJ' (1953) 2 International and Comparative Law Quarterly 595.

—— *General Principles of Law as Applied by International Courts and Tribunals* (London: Stevens & Sons, 1953).

Christoforou, Theofanis, 'WTO Panels in the Face of Scientific Uncertainty' in F Weiss (ed), *Improving WTO Dispute Settlement Procedures: Issues and Lessons from the Practice of Other International Courts and Tribunals* (London: Cameron May, 2000) 243.

Cintra, Antonio Carlos de Araújo, Ada Pellegrini Grinover & Cândido R Dinamarco, *Teoria Geral do Processo* (12th edn, São Paulo: Malheiros, 1996).

Clermont, Kevin M, & Emily Sherwin, 'A Comparative View of Standards of Proof' (2002) 50 American Journal of Comparative Law 243.

Cone, Sydney M III, 'The Asbestos Case and Dispute Settlement in the World Trade Organization: the Uneasy Relationship between Panels and the Appellate Body' (2001) 23 Michigan Journal of International Law 103.

Collier, John, & Vaughan Lowe, *The Settlement of Disputes in International Law: Institutions and Procedures* (Oxford: Oxford University Press, 1999).

Collins, David, 'Institutionalized Fact-Finding at the WTO' (2006) 27 University of Pennsylvania Journal of International Economic Law 367.

Cossy, Mireille, 'Panel's Consultations with Scientific Experts: the Right to Seek Information under Article 13 of the DSU' in R Yerxa & B Wilson (eds), *Key Issues in WTO Dispute Settlement: the First Ten Years* (Cambridge: Cambridge University Press, 2005) 204.

Costello, Kevin, 'Administrative Law – The Burden of Proof on Judicial Review' (1993) 15 Dublin University Law Journal 134.

Cottier, Thomas, 'Risk Management Experience in WTO Dispute Settlement' in D Robertson & A Kellow (eds), *Globalization and the Environment: Risk Assessment and the WTO* (Chelthenham: Edward Elgar, 2001) 41.

—— 'The WTO Permanent Panel Body: a Bridge Too Far?' (2003) 6:1 Journal of International Economic Law 187.

Craig, W Lawrence, William W Park & Jan Paulsson, *International Chamber of Commerce Arbitration* (3rd edn, Dobbs Ferry: Oceana Publications, 2000).

Croley, Steven P, & John H Jackson, 'WTO Dispute Procedures, Standard of Review, and Deference to National Governments' (1996) 90:2 The American Journal of International Law 193.

Crook, John, 'Fact-Finding in the Fog: Determining the Facts of Upheavals and Wars in Inter-State Disputes' in R Alford & C Rogers (eds), *The Future of Investment Arbitration* (Oxford: Oxford University Press, 2009).

Cross, Karen Halverson, 'King Cotton, Developing Countries and the "Peace Clause": the WTO's *US Cotton Subsidies* Decision' (2006) 9 Journal of International Economic Law 149.

Crump, David, et al, *Cases and Materials on Civil Procedure* (5th edn, Newark: LexisNexis, 2008).

Czako, Judith, Johann Human & Jorge Miranda, *A Handbook on Anti-Dumping Investigations* (Cambridge: Cambridge University Press, 2003).

Damaska, Mirjan, 'Presentation of Evidence and Factfinding Precision' (1975) 123 University of Pennsylvania Law Review 1083.

—— 'The Uncertain Fate of Evidentiary Transplants: Anglo-American and Continental Experiments' (1997) 45 American Journal of Comparative Law 839.

—— *Evidence Law Adrift* (New Haven: Yale University Press, 1997).

Damme, Isabelle Van, *Treaty Interpretation by the WTO Appellate Body* (Oxford: Oxford University Press, 2009).

Dávalos, José Vizcarra, *Teoría General del Proceso* (9th edn, Mexico City: Editorial Porrúa, 2007).

Davey, William J, 'Expediting the Panel Process in WTO Dispute Settlement' in ME Janow, V Donaldson & A Yanovich (eds), *The WTO: Governance, Dispute Settlement, and Developing Countries* (New York: Juris Publishing, 2008) 409.

—— 'The WTO Dispute Settlement System: the First Ten Years' (2005) 8 Journal of International Economic Law 17.

—— 'The Case for a WTO Permanent Panel Body' (2003) 6:1 Journal of International Economic Law 177.

—— 'Proposals for Improving the Working Procedures of WTO Dispute Settlement Panels' in F Ortino & E -U Petersmann (eds), *The WTO Dispute Settlement System 1995-2003* (The Hague: Kluwer Law International, 2004) 19.

—— 'The WTO: Looking Forwards' (2006) 9:1 Journal of International Economic Law 3.

—— 'Evaluating WTO Dispute Settlement: What Results Have Been Achieved through Consultations and Implementation of Panel Reports?' in Y Taniguchi, A Yanovich & J Bohanes (eds), *The WTO in the Twenty-first Century: Dispute Settlement, Negotiations, and Regionalism in Asia* (Cambridge: Cambridge University Press, 2007) 98.

Dawson, Grant, & Joakim Dungel, 'Compulsion of Information from States and Due Process in Cases before the International Criminal Tribunal for the Former Yugoslavia' (2007) 20:1 Leiden Journal of International Law 115.

Demougin, Dominique, & Claude Fluet, 'Deterrence Versus Judicial Error: a Comparative View of Standards of Proof' (2005) 161 Journal of Institutional and Theoretical Economics 193.

Denning, AT, 'Presumptions and Burdens' (1945) 61 The Law Quarterly Review 379.

Derains, Yves, & Eric A Schwartz, *A Guide to the ICC Rules of Arbitration* (2nd edn, The Hague: Kluwer International, 2005).

Dodd, Christian, *The French Code of Civil Procedure in English* (Dobbs Ferry: Oceana Publications, 2005).

Dworkin, Roger B, 'Easy Cases, Bad Law, and Burdens of Proof' (1972) 25 Vanderbilt Law Review 1151.

Edward, David, 'Fact-Finding: a British Perspective' in DLC Miller & PR Beaumont (eds), *The Option of Litigating in Europe* (London: United Kingdom National Committee of Comparative Law, 1993) vol. 14, 43.

Eggleston, Sir Richard, *Evidence, Proof and Probability* (2nd edn, London: Weidenfeld and Nicolson, 1983).

Ehlermann, Claus-Dieter, 'Six Years on the Bench of the "World Trade Court": Some Personal Experiences as Member of the Appellate Body of the World Trade Organization' (2002) 36:4 Journal of World Trade 605.

—— 'Reflections on the Appellate Body of the WTO' (2003) 6:3 Journal of International Economic Law 695.

—— 'Six Years on the Bench of the "World Trade Court": Some Personal Experiences as Member of the Appellate Body of the World Trade Organization' in F Ortino & E -U Petersmann (eds), *The WTO Dispute Settlement System 1995–2003* (The Hague: Kluwer Law International, 2004) 499.

—— & Nicolas Lockhart, 'Standard of Review in WTO Law' (2004) 7:3 Journal of International Economic Law 491.

Ehring, Lothar, 'Public Access to Dispute Settlement Hearings in the World Trade Organization' (2008) 11:4 Journal of International Economic Law 1021.

Eijsvoogel, Peter V (ed), *Evidence in International Arbitration Proceedings* (London: Graham & Trotman/Martinus Nijhoff, 1994).

Elsing, Siegfried H, & John M Townsend, 'Bridging the Common Law–Civil Law Divide in Arbitration' (2002) 18:1 Arbitration International 59.

Fellas, John, 'Obtaining Evidence Abroad for Use in International Litigation: Evidence Located in the United States' (2001) 29:July/August International Business Lawyer 297.

—— 'Using Section 1782 in International Arbitration' (2007) 23:3 Arbitration International 379.

Field, Richard H, Benjamin Kaplan & Kevin M Clermont, *Civil Procedure* (8th edn, New York: Foundation Press, 2003).

Fisher, George, *Evidence* (New York: Foundation Press, 2002).

Fishman, Clifford S, *Jones on Evidence: Civil and Criminal* (7th edn, Rochester: Lawyers Cooperative Publishing, 1992).

Fitzmaurice, Sir Gerald, *The Law and Procedure of the International Court of Justice* (Cambridge: Grotius, 1986).

Fleming James, Jr, 'Burdens of Proof' (1961) 47 Virginia Law Review 51.

Franck, Thomas M, *Fairness in International Law and Institutions* (Oxford: Oxford University Press, 1995).

Friedenthal, Jack H, Mark Kay Kane & Arthur R Miller, *Civil Procedure* (4th edn, St Paul: Thomson West, 2005).

Fukunaga, Yuka, 'Securing Compliance through the WTO Dispute Settlement System: Implementation of DSB Recommendations' (2006) 9:2 Journal of International Economic Law 383.

Gaffney, John P, 'Due Process in the World Trade Organization: the Need for Procedural Justice in the Dispute Settlement System' (1999) 14 American University International Law Review 1173.

Gaillard, Emmanuel, & John Savage (eds), *Fouchard Gaillard and Goldman on International Arbitration* (The Hague: Kluwer Law International, 1999).

Galligan, DJ, *Due Process and Fair Procedures: a Study of Administrative Procedures* (Oxford: Clarendon Press, 1996).

Gans, Jeremy, & Andrew Palmer, *Australian Principles of Evidence* (London: Cavendish, 2004).

García, Fernando Flores, *Teoria General de la Composición del Litigio* (México DF: Editorial Porrúa, 2003).

Gaskins, Richard H, *Burdens of Proof in Modern Discourse* (New Haven: Yale University Press, 1993).

Gazzini, Tarcisio, 'The Legal Nature of WTO Obligations and the Consequences of their Violation' (2006) 17:4 European Journal of International Law 723.

Genin-Meric, Régine, 'Droit de la Preuve: l'Exemple Français' in JML de Freitas (ed), *The Law of Evidence in the European Union* (The Hague: Kluwer Law International, 2004) 137.

Giverdon, Claude, 'The Problem of Proof in French Civil Law' (1956) 31 Tulane Law Review 29.

Godard, Joelle, 'Fact-Finding: a French Perspective' in DLC Miller & PR Beaumont (eds), *The Option of Litigating in Europe* (London: United Kingdom National Committee of Comparative Law, 1993) vol 14, 57.

Gottlieb, Stephen E, 'The Paradox of Balancing Significant Interests' (1994) 45 Hastings Law Journal 825.

Gottwald, Peter, 'Fact-Finding: a German Perspective' in DLC Miller & PR Beaumont (eds), *The Option of Litigating in Europe* (London: United Kingdom National Committee of Comparative Law, 1993) vol 14, 67.

Grando, Michelle T, 'Allocating the Burden of Proof in WTO Disputes: a Critical Analysis' (2006) 9:3 Journal of International Economic Law 615.

Green, Andrew, & Tracey Epps, 'The WTO, Science, and the Environment: Moving Towards Consistency' (2007) 10:2 Journal of International Economic Law 285.

Griffin, Peter R, 'Recent Trends in the Conduct of International Arbitration: Discovery Procedures and Witness Hearings' (2000) 17:2 Journal of International Arbitration 19.

Gross, Samuel R, 'The American Advantage: the Value of Inefficient Litigation' (1987) 85:4 Michigan Law Review 734.

Grossman, Gene M, & Petros Mavroidis, 'United States—Section 110(5) of the US Copyright Act, Recourse to Arbitration under Article 25 of the DSU: Would've or Should've? Impaired Benefits Due to Copyright Infringement' in H Horn & PC Mavroidis (eds), *The WTO Case Law of 2001: The American Law Institute Reporters' Studies* (Cambridge: Cambridge University Press, 2003) 281.

Gunter, Pierre-Yves, 'Transnational Rules on the Taking of Evidence' in E Gaillard et al (eds), *Towards a Uniform International Arbitration Law?* (Huntington: Juris Publishing, 2005) 129.

Guzman, Andrew T, 'Food Fears: Health and Safety at the WTO' (2004) 45 Virginia Journal of International Law 1.

Hadfield, Gillian, 'The Levers of Legal Design: Institutional Determinants of the Quality of Law' (May 2007) USC Legal Studies Research Paper No 07-6.

Hanotiau, Bernard, 'Satisfying the Burden of Proof: the Point of View of a "Civil Law" Lawyer' (1994) 10 Arbitration International 341.

Hay, Bruce L, 'Allocating the Burden of Proof' (1997) 72 Indiana Law Journal 651.

—— & Kathryn E Spier, 'Burdens of Proof in Civil Litigation: an Economic Perspective' (1997) 26 Journal of Legal Studies 413.

Hazard, Geoffrey C, Jr, 'Discovery and the Role of the Judge in Civil Law Jurisdictions' (1998) 73:4 Notre Dame Law Review 1017.

—— 'Jury Trial and the Principles of Transnational Civil Procedure' (2006) 25:2 Penn State International Law Review 499.

Hebly, Jan M, *The Netherlands Civil Evidence Act 1988* (Deventer: Kluwer Law and Taxation Publishers, 1992).

Herlitz, Georg Nils, 'The Meaning of the Term 'Prima Facie'' (1991) 55 Louisiana Law Review 391.

Herzog, Peter, *Civil Procedure in France* (The Hague: Martinus Nijhoff, 1967).

Higgins, Rosalyn, 'Respecting Sovereign States and Running a Tight Courtroom' (2001) 50 International and Comparative Law Quarterly 121.

Highet, Keith, 'Evidence, the Court, and the Nicaragua Case' (1987) 81 The American Journal of International Law 1.

—— 'Evidence and Proof of Facts' in LF Damrosch (ed), *The International Court of Justice at a Crossroads* (New York: Transnational Publishers, 1987) 355.

Hilf, Meinhard, 'Power, Rules and Principles – which Orientation for WTO/GATT Law?' (2001) 4 Journal of International Economic Law 111.

Hill, Marvin F, Jr, & Anthony V Sinicropi, *Evidence in Arbitration* (2nd edn, Washington: The Bureau of National Affairs, 1987).

Holtzmann, Howard M, 'Fact-Finding by the Iran–United States Claims Tribunal' in Lillich, RB (ed), *Fact-Finding before International Tribunals* (Ardsley-on-Hudson: Transnational Publishers, 1992) 101.

—— 'Streamlining Arbitral Proceedings: Some Techniques of the Iran-United States Claims Tribunal' (1995) 11:1 Arbitration International 39.

Horn, Henrik, & Petros Mavroidis, 'Still Hazy after All These Years: The Interpretation of National Treatment in the GATT/WTO Case Law on Tax Discrimination' (2004) 15 European Journal of International Law 39.

Horn, Henrik, & Joseph HH Weiler, 'European Communities – Trade Description of Sardines: Textualism and its Discontents' in H Horn & PC Mavroidis (eds), *The WTO Case Law of 2002* (Cambridge: Cambridge University Press, 2005) 248.

Howse, Robert, & Petros C Mavroidis, 'Europe's Evolving Regulatory Strategy for GMOs – the Issue of Consistency with WTO Law: of Kine and Brine' (2000) 24 Fordham International Law Journal 317.

Howse, Robert, & Damien J Neven, 'Canada – Export Credits and Loan Guarantees for Regional Aircraft (WT/DS222/R): a Comment' in H Horn & P Mavroidis (eds), *The WTO Case Law of 2002: The American Law Institute Reporters' Studies* (Cambridge: Cambridge University Press, 2005) 88.

Huang, Kuo-Chang, *Introducing Discovery into Civil Law* (Durham: Carolina Academic Press, 2003).

Hudec, Robert E, *The GATT Legal System and World Trade Diplomacy* (2nd edn, Salem: Butterworth, 1990).

Hughes, Valerie, 'Accomplishments of the WTO Dispute Settlement Mechanism' in Y Taniguchi, A Yanovich & J Bohanes (eds), *The WTO in the Twenty-first Century: Dispute Settlement, Negotiations, and Regionalism in Asia* (Cambridge: Cambridge University Press, 2007) 185.

Iida, Keisuke, 'Why Does the World Trade Organization Appear Neoliberal? The Puzzle of the High Incidence of Guilty Verdicts in WTO Adjudication' (2003) 23:1 Journal of Public Policy 1.

Irwin, Douglas A, & Joseph Weiler, 'Measures Affecting the Cross-Border Suply of Gambling and Betting Services (DS 285)' in H Horn & PC Mavroidis (eds), *The WTO Case Law of 2004–2005: Legal and Economic Analysis* (Cambridge: Cambridge University Press, 2008) 71.

Isunza, Gustavo Carvajal, & Fernando Gonzalez Rojas, 'Evidentiary Issues in NAFTA Chapter 11 Arbitration: Searching for the Truth between States and Investors' in T Weiler (ed), *NAFTA Investment Law and Arbitration: Past Issues, Current Practice, Future Prospects* (Ardsley: Transnational Publishers, 2004) 287.

Iwasawa, Yuji, 'WTO Dispute Settlement as Judicial Supervision' (2002) 5:2 Journal of International Economic Law 287.

Jackson, John H, 'The WTO Dispute Settlement Understanding: Misunderstandings on the Nature of Legal Obligation' (1997) 91:1 The American Journal of International Law 60.

—— 'Dispute Settlement and the WTO Emerging Problems' (1998) 1 Journal of International Economic Law 329.

—— *The World Trade Organization: Constitution and Jurisprudence* (London: Royal Institute of International Affairs, 1998).

—— 'Sovereignty-Modern: a New Approach to an Outdated Concept' (2003) 97:4 The American Journal of International Law 782.

—— *Sovereignty, the WTO, and Changing Fundamentals of International Law* (Cambridge: Cambridge University Press, 2006).

Janow, Merit E, & Robert W Staiger, 'Canada – Measures Affecting the Importation of Dairy Products and the Exportation of Milk' (2004) 3:2 World Trade Review 277.

Johns, Roger J, & Anne Keaty, 'The New and Improved Section 1782: Supercharging Federal District Court Discovery Assistance to Foreign and International Tribunals' (2006) 29 American Journal of Trial Advocacy 649.

Jolowicz, JA, 'Fact-Finding: a Comparative Perspective' in DLC Miller & PR Beaumont (eds), *The Option of Litigating in Europe* (London: United Kingdom National Committee of Comparative Law, 1993) vol. 14, 133.

—— 'Adversarial and Inquisitorial Models of Civil Procedure' (2003) 52 International and Comparative Law Quarterly 281.

Jongbloed, AW, 'The Netherlands (1838–2005)' in CH van Rhee (ed), *European Traditions in Civil Procedure* (Antwerpen: Intersentia, 2005) 69.

Joshua, Julian Mathic, 'Proof in Contested EEC Competition Cases: A Comparison with the Rules of Evidence in Common Law' (1987) 12 European Law Review 315.

Josling, Tim, et al, 'Implications of WTO Litigation for the WTO Agricultural Negotiations' (2006) 19 IPC Issue Brief.

Kang, Sungjin, 'Comment on Annex V of the WTO SCM Agreement Procedures in the Context of Korea-Shipbuilding Dispute' (2006) 33:2 Legal Issues of Economic Integration 183.

Kaplan, John, 'Decision Theory and the Factfinding Process' (1968) 20 Stanford Law Review 1065.

Kaplow, Louis, 'The Value of Accuracy in Adjudication: an Economic Analysis' (1994) 23:1 The Journal of Legal Studies 307.

Kaye, David, 'Naked Statistical Evidence' (1980) 89:3 The Yale Law Journal 601.

—— 'The Limits of the Preponderance of the Evidence Standard: Justifiably Naked Statistical Evidence and Multiple Causation' (1982) 7:2 American Bar Foundation Research Journal 487.

Kazazi, Mojtaba, *Burden of Proof and Related Issues: a Study on Evidence before International Tribunals* (The Hague: Kluwer Law International, 1996).

Kennedy, Kevin C, 'Resolving International Sanitary and Phytosanitary Disputes in the WTO: Lessons and Future Directions' (2000) 55 Food and Drug Law Journal 81 at 83

Khalilian, Sayyed Khalil, *The Law of International Arbitration* (North Vancouver: Pacific Arbitration Network, 2003).

Klami, Hannu Tapani, Minna Grans & Johanna Sorvettula, *Law and Truth: A Theory of Evidence* (Helsinki: The Finnish Society of Sciences and Letters, 2000).

Koch, Harald, & Frank Diedrich, *Civil Procedure in Germany* (The Hague: Kluwer Law International, 1998).

Kokott, Juliane, *The Burden of Proof in Comparative and International Human Rights Law: Civil and Common Law Approaches with Special Reference to the American and German Legal Systems* (The Hague: Kluwer Law International, 1998).

Kometani, Kazumochi, 'Trade and Environment: How Should WTO Panels Review Environmental Regulations under GATT Articles III and XX?' (1996) 16 Northwestern School of Law Journal of International Law & Business 441.

Kreier, Jesse, 'Contingent Trade Remedies and WTO Dispute Settlement: Some Particularities' in R Yerxa & B Wilson (eds), *Key Issues in WTO Dispute Settlement: The First Ten Years* (Cambridge: Cambridge University Press, 2005) 46.

Kuijper, Pieter Jan, 'The Appellate Body and the Facts' in M Bronckers & R Quick (eds), *New Directions in International Economic Law: Essays in Honour of John H. Jackson* (The Hague: Kluwer Academic Publishers, 2000) 309.

—— 'The Pre-litigation Stage in the WTO Dispute Settlement Procedure and in the EC Infringement Procedure' in F Weiss (ed), *Improving WTO Dispute Settlement Procedures: Issues and Lessons from the Practice of other International Courts and Tribunals* (London: Cameron May, 2000) 67.

Kurkela, Matti S, *Due Process in International Commercial Arbitration* (Dobbs Ferry: Oceana Publications, 2005).

Lachs, Manfred, 'La Preuve et la Cour Internationale de Justice' in C Perelman & P Foriers (eds), *La Preuve en Droit* (Brussels: Emile Bruylant, 1981) 109.

Lagarde, Xavier, *Reflexion Critique sur le Droit de la Preuve* (Paris: Librairie Generale de Droit et de Jurisprudence, 1994).

Langbein, John H, 'The German Advantage in Civil Procedure' (1985) 52:4 University of Chicago Law Review 823.

—— 'Legal Institutions: Trashing the German Advantage' (1988) 82 Northwestern University Law Review 763.

Lasok, KPE, *The European Court of Justice: Practice and Procedure* (2nd edn, London: Butterworths, 1994).

Laughlin, Charles V, 'The Location of the Burden of Persuasion' (1956) 18 University of Pittsburgh Law Review 3.

Lauterpacht, H, 'The So-Called Anglo-American and Continental Schools of Thought in International Law' (1931) 12 The British Yearbook of International Law (1931) 31.

Layton, Duane W, 'The Litigation of Anti-Dumping Disputes before the World Trade Organization' (2000):4 Business Law International 294.

Lee, Thomas R, 'Pleading and Proof: the Economics of Legal Burdens' (1997) 1997 Brigham Young University Law Review 1.

Lenaerts, Koen, & Dirk Arts, *Procedural Law of the European Union* (London: Sweet & Maxwell, 1999).

Lewis, David, 'Is It Time to Blow the Whistle on the Burden of Proof?' (2002) 31:1 Industrial Law Journal 79.

Lichtenbaum, Peter, 'Procedural Issues in WTO Dispute Resolution' (1998) 19 Michigan Journal of International Law 1195.

Lockhart, Nicolas, 'A WTO Case Study: the Cotton Dispute' in F Ortino & S Ripinsky (eds), *WTO Law and Process: The Proceedings of the 2005 and 2006 Annual WTO Conference* (London: British Institute of International and Comparative Law, 2007) 122.

Losk, Daniel A, 'Section 1782(a) After INTEL: Reconciling Policy Considerations and a Proposed Framework to Extend Judicial Assistance to International Arbitral Tribunals' (2006) 27:2 Cardozo Law Review 1035.

Lowenfeld, Andreas F, *International Economic Law* (Oxford: Oxford University Press, 2002).

—— et al, 'International Aspects of Discovery' (1989) 83 American Journal of International Law 495.

Luxton, Janet L, 'Equality and Sex Discrimination in the European Union – Is Shifting the Burden of Proof the Answer?' (1999) 17 Dickinson Journal of International Law 357.

MacLennan, Jacquelyn, 'Evidence, Standard and Burden of Proof and the Use of Experts in Procedure Before the Luxembourg Courts' in F Weiss (ed), *Improving WTO Dispute Settlement Procedures: Issues and Lessons from the Practice of Other International Courts and Tribunals* (London: Cameron May, 2000) 265.

Magliveras, Konstantinos D, 'Fact-Finding: a Greek Perspective' in DLC Miller & PR Beaumont (eds), *The Option of Litigating in Europe* (London: United Kingdom National Committee of Comparative Law, 1993) vol 14, 87.

Malek, Hodge M, et al (eds), *Phipson on Evidence* (16th edn, London: Sweet & Maxwell, 2005).

Mani, VS, *International Adjudication: Procedural Aspects* (The Hague: Martinus Nijhoff, 1980).

Marceau, Gabrielle, & Cornelis Reiman, 'When and How is a Regional Trade Agreement Compatible with the WTO?' (2001) 28:3 Legal Issues of Economic Integration 297.

Marceau, Gabrielle, & Matthew Stilwell, 'Practical Suggestions for Amicus Curiae Briefs before WTO Adjudicating Bodies' (2001) 4 Journal of International Economic Law 155.

Martha, Rutsel Silvestre J, 'Presumptions and Burden of Proof' (1997) 14 Journal of International Arbitration 67.

Maton, John, and Carolyn Maton, 'Independence Under Fire: Extra-legal Pressures and Coalition Building in WTO Dispute Settlement' (2007) 2 Journal of International Economic Law at 328–9.

Matray, Lambert, 'Les Traits Caracteristiques de L'Administration de la Preuve dans Certaines Procedures de Type Romaniste' in *Taking of Evidence in the Arbitral Proceedings* (Paris: ICC Publishing, 1990) 113.

Mavroidis, Petros C, 'Amicus Curiae Briefs before the WTO: Much Ado about Nothing' (2001) Jean Monnet Working Paper 2/01 <http://www.worldtradelaw.net/articles/mavroidisamicus.pdf> (accessed 22 April 2008).

—— 'Development of WTO Dispute Settlement Procedures Through Case-Law (We Will Fix It)' in F Ortino & E -U Petersmann (eds), *The WTO Dispute Settlement System 1995–2003* (The Hague: Kluwer Law International, 2004) 153.

—— & Werner Zdouc, 'Legal Means to Protect Private Parties' Interests in the WTO. The Case of the EC New Trade Barriers Regulation' (1998) 1:3 Journal of International Economic Law 407.

Mawdsley, Andrés Aguilar, 'Evidence before the International Court of Justice' in RSJ Macdonald (ed), *Essays in Honor of Wang Tieya* (Dordrecht: Martinus Nijhoff, 1994) 533.

McCabe, Monica Petraglia, 'Arbitral Discovery and the Iran–United States Claims Tribunal Experience' (1986) 20 International Lawyer 499.

McGovern, Edmond, *International Trade Regulation* (3rd edn, Exeter: Globefield Press, 1995).

McNaughton, John T, 'Burden of Production of Evidence: A Function of a Burden of Persuasion' (1955) 68 Harvard Law Review 1382.

McRae, Donald, 'The WTO in International Law: Tradition Continued or New Frontier?' (2000) 3:1 Journal of International Economic Law 27.

—— 'What is the Future of WTO Dispute Settlement?' (2004) 7:1 Journal of International Economic Law 3.

Mecarelli, Gabriele, 'Quelques Réflexions en Matière de Discovery' (2001) 6 Uniform Law Review 901.

Megens, Peter, Paul Starr & Peter Chow, 'Compulsion of Evidence in International Commercial Arbitration: an Asia-Pacific Perspective' (2006) 2:1 Asian International Arbitration Journal 32.

Mehren, Robert B von, 'Burden of Proof in International Arbitration' in AJ van den Berg, (ed), *Planning Efficient Arbitration Proceedings: The Law Applicable in International Arbitration* (The Hague: Kluwer Law International, 1996) 123.

Mendel, Toby, *Freedom of Information: a Comparative Legal Survey* (New Delhi: UNESCO, 2003).

Merrills, John, 'The Means of Dispute Settlement' in MD Evans (ed), *International Law* (Oxford: Oxford University Press, 2006) 533.

Merrills, JG, *International Dispute Settlement* (4th edn, Cambridge: Cambridge University Press, 2005).

Mistelis, Loukas A, 'Confidentiality and Third Party Participation UPS v. Canada and Methanex Corp. v. United States' in T Weiler (ed), *International Investment Law and Arbitration: Leading Cases from the ICSID, NAFTA, Bilaterial Treaties and Customary International Law* (London: Cameron May, 2005) 169.

Mitchell, Andrew D, 'A Legal Principle of Special and Differential Treatment for WTO Disputes' (2006) 5:3 World Trade Review 445.

—— 'Due Process in WTO Disputes' in R Yerxa & B Wilson (eds), *Key Issues in WTO Dispute Settlement: the First Ten Years* (Cambridge: Cambridge University Press, 2005) 144.

—— 'The Legal Basis for Using Principles in WTO Disputes' (2007) 10:4 Journal of International Economic Law 795.

Mochizuki, Toshiro M, 'Baby Step or Giant Leap?: Parties' Expanded Access to Documentary Evidence under the New Japanese Code of Civil Procedure' (1999) 40:1 Harvard International Law Journal 285.

Monnier, Pierre, 'Working Procedures before Panels, the Appellate Body and other Adjudicating Bodies of the WTO' in *The Law and Practice of International Courts and Tribunals* (Kluwer Law International, 2002) 481.

Mosoti, Victor, 'Africa in the First Decade of WTO Dispute Settlement' (2006) 9:2 Journal of International Economic Law 427.

Mouri, Allahyar, *The International Law of Expropriation as Reflected in the Work of the Iran–U.S. Claims Tribunal* (Dordrecht: Martinus Nijhoff, 1994)

Murphy, Peter (ed), *Evidence, Proof, and Facts: a Book of Resources* (New York: Oxford University Press, 2003).

Nichols, Philip M, 'GATT Doctrine' (1996) 36 Virginia Journal of International Law 379.

Nottage, Hunter, & Jan Bohanes, 'Arbitration as an Alternative to Litigation in the WTO: Observations in the Light of the 2005 Banana Tariff Arbitrations' in Y Taniguchi, A Yanovich & J Bohanes (eds), *The WTO in the Twenty-first Century: Dispute Settlement, Negotiations, and Regionalism in Asia* (Cambridge: Cambridge University Press, 2007) 212.

Oberhammer, P, & T Domej, 'Germany, Switzerland, Austria (CA. 1800–2005)' in CH van Rhee (ed), *European Traditions in Civil Procedure* (Antwerpen: Intersentia, 2005) 103.

Oberhammer, P, & T Domej, 'Germany, Switzerland, and Austria' in CH van Rhee (ed), *European Traditions in Civil Procedure* (Antwerpen: Intersentia, 2005) 295.

Oesch, Matthias, 'Standards of Review in WTO Dispute Resolution' (2003) 6:3 Journal of International Economic Law 635.

Oesch, Matthias *Standards of Review in WTO Dispute Resolution* (Oxford: Oxford University Press, 2003).

Okowa, Phoebe, 'Issues of Admissibility and the Law on International Responsibility' in MD Evans (ed), *International Law* (Oxford: Oxford University Press, 2006) 479.

Pacífico, Luiz Eduardo Boaventura, *O Ônus da Prova no Direito Processual Civil* (São Paulo: Revista dos Tribunais, 2001).

Palmeter, David, & Petros Mavroidis, *Dispute Settlement in the World Trade Organization: Practice and Procedure* (2nd edn, Cambridge: Cambridge University Press, 2004).

Panizzon, Marion, *Good Faith in the Jurisprudence of the WTO* (Oxford: Hart Publishing, 2006).

Pauwelyn, Joost, 'Evidence, Proof and Persuasion in WTO Dispute Settlement: Who Bears the Burden?' (1998) 1 Journal of International Economic Law 227.

——'The WTO Agreement on Sanitary and Phytosanitary (SPS) Measures as Applied in the First Three SPS Disputes. *EC – Hormones, Australia – Salmon* and *Japan – Varietals*' (1999) 2:4 Journal of International Economic Law 641.

—— 'The Use of Experts in WTO Dispute Settlement' (2002) 51 International and Comparative Law Quarterly 325.

——*Conflict of Norms in Public International Law: How WTO Law Relates to other Rules of International Law* (Cambridge: Cambridge University Press, 2003).

Petersmann, Ernst-Ulrich, 'WTO Dispute Settlement Practice 1995–2005: Lessons from the Past and Future Challenges' in Y Taniguchi, A Yanovich & J Bohanes (eds), *The WTO in the Twenty-first Century: Dispute Settlement, Negotiations, and Regionalism in Asia* (Cambridge: Cambridge University Press, 2007) 38.

Pfitzer, James Headen, & Sheila Sabune, 'Burden-Shifting in WTO Dispute Settlement: The Prima Facie Doctrine' (2008) March:2 Bridges 18.

Pietrowski, Robert, 'Evidence in International Arbitration' (2006) 22:3 Arbitration International 373.

Polkinghorne, MA, 'The Withholding of Documentary Evidence in International Arbitration: Remedies for Dealing with Uncooperative Parties' (2005) 2:5 Transnational Dispute Management.

Posner, Richard A, 'An Economic Approach to the Law of Evidence' (1999) 51 Stanford Law Review 1477.

—— *Economic Analysis of Law* (New York: Aspen Publishers, 2003).

Powell, Stephen J, & Andrew Schmitz, 'The Cotton and Sugar Subsidies Decisions: WTO's Dispute Settlement System Rebalances the Agreement on Agriculture' (2005) 10 Drake Journal of Agricultural Law 287.

Prost, Olivier, 'Confidentiality Issues under the DSU: Fact-finding Process Versus Confidentiality' in R Yerxa & B Wilson (eds), *Key Issues in WTO Dispute Settlement: the First Ten Years* (Cambridge: Cambridge University Press, 2005) 190.

Punt, BC, 'Fact-Finding: a Dutch Perspective' in DLC Miller & PR Beaumont (eds), *The Option of Litigating in Europe* (London: United Kingdom National Committee of Comparative Law, 1993) vol 14, 109.

Quick, Reinhard, & Andreas Bluthner, 'Has the Appellate Body Erred? An Appraisal and Criticism of the Ruling in the WTO Hormones Case' (1999) 2:4 Journal of International Economic Law 603.

Raeschke-Kessler, Hilmar, 'The Production of Documents in International Arbitration: a Commentary on Article 3 of the New IBA Rules of Evidence' (2002) 18:4 Arbitration International 411.

Ragosta, John, 'Unmasking the WTO – Access to the DSB System: Can the WTO DSB Live Up to the Moniker "World Trade Court"?' (2000) 31:3 Law and Policy in International Business 739.

Raustiala, Kal, 'Rethinking the Sovereignty Debate in International Economic Law' (2003) 6:4 Journal of International Economic Law 841.

Redfern, Alan, 'The Practical Distinction between the Burden of Proof and the Taking of Evidence – an English Perspective' (1994) 10 Arbitration International 317.

—— et al, *Law and Practice of International Commercial Arbitration* (4th edn, London: Sweet & Maxwell, 2004).

Reed, Lucy, Jan Paulsson & Nigel Blackaby, *A Guide to ICSID Arbitration* (The Hague: Kluwer Law International, 2004).

Reiner, Andreas, 'Burden and General Standards of Proof' (1994) 10 Arbitration International 328.

Reufels, Martin, & Karl Kelly, 'Transatlantic Discovery: How Useful is the Hague Convention on the Taking of Evidence Abroad in Civil and Commercial Matters?' (2001) 29:July/August International Business Lawyer 291.

Reymond, Claude, 'The Practical Distinction between the Burden of Proof and Taking of Evidence – A Further Perspective' (1994) 10 Arbitration International 323.

Rhee, CH van, 'Introduction' in CH van Rhee (ed), *European Traditions in Civil Procedure* (Antwerpen: Intersentia, 2005) 3.

Riddell, Anna, & Brendan Plant, *Evidence before the International Court of Justice* (London: British Institute of International and Comparative Law, 2009).

Roessler, Frieder, 'The Concept of Nullification and Impairment in the Legal System of the World Trade Organization' in E -U Petersmann (ed), *International Trade Law and the GATT/WTO Dispute Settlement System* (London: Kluwer Law International, 1997) 123.

Rogers, Andrew, 'Improving Procedures for Discovery and Documentary Evidence' in AJ van den Berg (ed), *Planning Efficient Arbitration Proceedings: the Law Applicable in International Arbitration* (The Hague: Kluwer Law International, 1996) 131.

Rosenne, Shabtai, *The Law and Practice of the International Court, 1920–1996* (3rd edn, The Hague: Martinus Nijhoff, 1997).

—— *The Law and Practice of the International Court 1920–2005* (Leiden: Martinus Nijhoff, 2006).

Rubino-Sammartano, Mauro, 'Rules of Evidence in International Arbitration: a Need for Discipline and Harmonization' (1986) 3:2 Journal of International Arbitration 87.

Sanchirico, Chris William, 'The Burden of Proof in Civil Litigation: A Simple Model of Mechanism Design' (1997) 17 International Review of Law and Economics 431.

Sandifer, Durward V, *Evidence before International Tribunals* (revised edn, Charlottesville: University Press of Virginia, 1975).

Sapir, Andre, & Joel P Trachtman, 'Subsidization, Price Suppression, and Expertise: Causation and Precision in *Upland Cotton*' (2008) 7:1 World Trade Review 183.

Saunders, Kevin W, 'The Mythic Difficulty in Proving a Negative' (1985) 15 Seton Hall Law Review 276.

Schafer, Erik, Herman Verbist & Christophe Imhoos, *ICC Arbitration in Practice* (The Hague: Kluwer Law International, 2005).

Scirica, Anthony J, 'Judge's Response to Professors Hazard and Taruffo' (2006) 25:2 Penn State International Law Review 519.

Scott, Joanne, *The WTO Agreement on Sanitary and Phytosanitary Measures: a Commentary* (Oxford: Oxford University Press, 2007).

Segger, Marie-Claire Cordonier, & Markus W Gehring, 'The WTO and Precaution: Sustainable Development Implications of the WTO Asbestos Dispute' (2003) 15:3 Journal of Environmental Law 289.

Selby, Jamison M, 'Fact-Finding before the Iran–United States Claims Tribunal: a View from the Trenches' in RB Lillich (ed), *Fact-Finding before International Tribunals* (Ardsley-on-Hudson: Transnational Publishers, 1992) 135.

Serio, Mario, 'Fact-Finding: an Italian Perspective' in DLC Miller & PR Beaumont (eds), *The Option of Litigating in Europe* (London: United Kingdom National Committee of Comparative Law, 1993) vol. 14, 123.

Shaffer, Gregory, 'The Challenges of WTO Law: Strategies for Developing Country Adaptation' (2006) 5:2 World Trade Review 177.

Sharpe, Jeremy K, 'Drawing Adverse Inferences from the Non-production of Evidence' (2006) 22:4 Arbitration International 549.

Shavell, Steven, 'Optimal Sanctions and the Incentive to Provide Evidence to Legal Tribunals' (1989) 9 International Review of Law and Economics 3.

—— *Foundations of Economic Analysis of Law* (Cambridge: Harvard University Press, 2004).

Shaw, Malcolm N, *International Law* (5th edn, Cambridge: Cambridge University Press, 2003).

Sheppard, Audley, 'The Jurisdictional Threshold of a Prima Facie Case' in P Muchlinski, F Ortino & C Schreuer (eds), *The Oxford Handbook of International Investment Law* (Oxford: Oxford University Press, 2008) 932.

Shoyer, Andrew W, 'Panel Selection in WTO Dispute Settlement Proceedings' (2003) 6:1 Journal of International Economic Law 203.

Smit, Hans, 'Roles of the Arbitral Tribunal in Civil Law and Common Law Systems with Respect to Presentation of Evidence' in AJ van den Berg (ed), *Planning Efficient Arbitration Proceedings: The Law Applicable in International Arbitration* (The Hague: Kluwer Law International, 1996) 161.

Sopinka, John, & Sidney N Lederman, *The Law of Evidence in Civil Cases* (Toronto: Butterworths, 1974).

——, Sidney N Lederman & Alan W Bryant, *The Law of Evidence in Canada* (Toronto: Butterworths, 1992).

——, Sidney N Lederman & Alan W Bryant, *The Law of Evidence in Canada* (2nd edn, Toronto: Butterworths, 1999).

Solum, Lawrence B, 'Procedural Justice' (2004) 78 Southern California Law Review 181.

Soriano, Miguel Virgos & Francisco J Garcimartin Alferez, *Derecho Procesal Civil Internacional* (Madrid: Civitas, 2000).

Spamann, Holger, 'Standard of Review for World Trade Organization Panels in Trade Remedy Cases: a Critical Analysis' (2004) 38:3 Journal of World Trade 509.

Stein, Alex, *Foundations of Evidence Law* (Oxford: Oxford University Press, 2005).

Stewart, Charles E, *German Commercial Code & Code of Civil Procedure* (Dobbs Ferry: Oceana Publications, 2001).

Stewart, Terence P (ed), *The GATT Uruguay Round: a Negotiating History (1986–1992)* (Deventer: Kluwer Law and Taxation Publishers, 1993) vol I.

—— & Amy S Dwyer, *Handbook on WTO Trade Remedy Disputes: The First Six Years (1995–2000)* (Ardsley: Transnational Publishers, 2001).

Stone, Julius, 'Burden of Proof and the Judicial Process: A Commentary on *Joseph* Constantine *Steamship, LTD.* v. *Imperial Smelting Corporation, LTD.*' (1944) 60 The Law Quarterly Review 262.

Strong, John W (ed), *McCormick on Evidence* (5th edn, St Paul: West Group, 1999) vol 2.

Sturner, Rolf, 'Transnational Civil Procedure: Discovery and Sanctions against Non-Compliance' (2001) 6 Uniform Law Review 871.

Subrin, Stephen N, et al, *Civil Procedure: Doctrine, Practice, and Context* (2nd edn, New York: Aspen, 2004).

Sullivan, Ruth, *Statutory Interpretation* (Concord: Irwin Law, 1997).

—— *Sullivan and Driedger on the Construction of Statutes* (4th edn, Vancouver: Butterworths, 2002).

Summers, Robert S, 'Formal Legal Truth and Substantive Truth in Judicial Fact-Finding: Their Justified Divergence in Some Particular Cases' (1999) 18 Law and Philosophy 497.

Sutton, David St J, 'Discovery and Production of Evidence in Arbitral Proceedings: the U.S. and England Distinguished' in *Taking of Evidence in the Arbitral Proceedings* (Paris: ICC Publishing, 1990) 57.

Sykes, Alan O, 'Domestic Regulation, Sovereignty, and Scientific Evidence Requirements: a Pessimistic View' (2002) 3 Chicago Journal of International Law 353.

Tan, Pei-San, *United States – Measures Affecting Imports of Woven Wool Shirts and Blouses* (1998), online: <http://207.57.19.226/journal/Vol9/No1/sr1c.html> (Date accessed: 11 May 2009).

Taniguchi, Yasuhei, 'Understanding the Concept of Prima Facie Proof in WTO Dispute Settlement' in ME Janow, V Donaldson & A Yanovich (eds), *The WTO: Governance, Dispute Settlement, and Developing Countries* (Huntington: Juris Publishing, 2008) 553.

—— Pauline C Reich & Hiroto Miyake (eds), *Civil Procedure in Japan* (2nd edn, Yonkers: Juris Publishing, 2002).

Tapper, Colin, *Cross & Tapper on Evidence* (8th edn, London: Butterworths, 1995).

—— *Cross and Tapper on Evidence* (9th edn, London: Butterworths, 1999).

Taruffo, Michele, 'Principles and Rules of Transnational Civil Procedure: an Evidentiary Epistemology' (2006) 25:2 Penn State International Law Review 509.

Teitelbaum, Ruth, 'Recent Fact-Finding Developments at the International Court of Justice' (2007) 6 The Law and Practice of International Courts and Tribunals 119.

Thayer, James B, 'The Burden of Proof' (1890) 4:2 Harvard Law Review 45.

Thirlway, Hugh, 'Dilemma or Chimera? Admissibility of Illegally Obtained Evidence in International Adjudication' (1984) 78:3 American Journal of International Law 622.

Thirlway, HWA, 'Evidence before International Courts and Tribunals' in R Bernhardt (ed), *Encyclopedia of Public International Law* (Amsterdam: North-Holland, 1995) vol 2, 302.

Thirlway, HWA, 'Procedure of International Courts and Tribunals' in R Bernhardt (ed), *Encyclopedia of Public International Law* (Amsterdam: Elsevier, 1997) vol 3, 1128.

Thomas, Christopher, 'Litigation Process under the GATT Dispute Settlement System: Lessons for the World Trade Organization?' (1996) 30:2 Journal of World Trade 53.

Thomas, EW, *The Judicial Process: Realism, Pragmatism, Practical Reasoning and Principles* (Cambridge: Cambridge University Press, 2005).

Thomas, JC, 'The Need for Due Process in WTO Proceedings' (1997) 31:1 Journal of World Trade 45.

Trachtman, Joel P, 'Trade and ... Problems, Cost-Benefit Analysis and Subsidiarity' (1998) 9 European Journal of International Law 32.

—— 'The Domain of WTO Dispute Resolution' (1999) 40 Harvard International Law Journal 333.

Trebilcock, Michael J, & Robert Howse, *The Regulation of International Trade* (3rd edn, New York: Routledge, 2005).

Twining, William, *Rethinking Evidence: Exploratory Essays* (2nd edn, Cambridge: Cambridge University Press, 2006).

Ughi, Giovanni, et al, 'Commentary on the New IBA Rules of Evidence in International Commercial Arbitration' (2000) 2 Business Law International 16.

Umbricht, Georg C, 'An "Amicus Curiae Brief" on Amicus Curiae Briefs at the WTO' (2001) 4 Journal of International Economic Law 773.

Unterhalter, David, 'The Burden of Proof in WTO Dispute Settlement' in ME Janow, V Donaldson & A Yanovich (eds), *The WTO: Governance, Dispute Settlement, and Developing Countries* (Huntington: Juris Publishing, 2008) 543.

Valencia-Ospina, Eduardo, 'Evidence before the International Court of Justice' (1999) 1:4 International Law FORUM du Droit International 202.

Van den Bossche, Peter, *The Law and Policy of the World Trade Organization: Text, Cases and Materials* (2nd edn, Cambridge: Cambridge University Press, 2008).

Vandenbussche, Hylke, 'Comment: Upland Cotton Case' (2008) 7:1 World Trade Review 211.

Verheyden-Jeanmart, Nicole, *Droit de la Preuve* (Brussels: Maison Larcier, 1991).

Verkerk, R, 'The Netherlands: Powers of the Judge' in CH van Rhee (ed), *European Traditions in Civil Procedure* (Antwerpen: Intersentia, 2005) 281.

—— 'England and Wales: Powers of the Judge' in CH van Rhee (ed), *European Traditions in Civil Procedure* (Antwerpen: Intersentia, 2005) 307.

Vermulst, Edwin, *The WTO Anti-Dumping Agreement: a Commentary* (Oxford: Oxford University Press, 2005).

—— Petros C Mavroidis & Paul Waer, 'The Functioning of the Appellate Body After Four Years: Towards Rule Integrity' (1999) 33:2 Journal of World Trade 1.

Voon, Tania, & Alan Yanovich, 'The Facts Aside: The Limitations of WTO Appeals to Issues of Law' (2006) 40:2 Journal of World Trade 239.

Wade, Sir William, & Christopher Forsyth, *Administrative Law*, 9th ed. (Oxford: Oxford University Press, 2004).

Waincymer, Jeff, *WTO Litigation: Procedural Aspects of Formal Dispute Settlement* (London: Cameron May, 2002).

Walker, Vern R, 'Preponderance, Probability and Warranted Factfinding' (1996) 62 Brooklyn Law Review 1075.

—— 'Keeping the WTO from Becoming the "World Trans-science Organization": Scientific Uncertainty, Science Policy, and Factfinding in the Growth Hormones Dispute' (1998) 31 Cornell International Law Journal 251.

Wallace, Cynthia Day, '"Extraterritorial" Discovery: Ongoing Challenges for Antitrust Litigation in an Environment of Global Investment' (2002) 5:2 Journal of International Economic Law 353.

Watts, Sir Arthur, 'Burden of Proof, and Evidence Before the ICJ' in F Weiss (ed), *Improving WTO Dispute Settlement Procedures: Issues and Lessons from the Practice of Other International Courts and Tribunals* (London: Cameron May, 2000) 289.

Webster, Thomas H, 'Obtaining Evidence from Third Parties in International Arbitration' (2001) 17:2 Arbitration International 143.

—— 'Obtaining Documents from Adverse Parties in International Arbitration' (2001) 17:1 Arbitration International 41.

Weiler, JHH, 'The Rule of Lawyers and the Ethos of Diplomats: Reflections on the Internal and External Legitimacy of WTO Dispute Settlement' (2001) 35:2 Journal of World Trade 191.

Weiss, Friedl, 'Inherent Powers of National and International Courts' in F Ortino & E -U Petersmann (eds), *The WTO Dispute Settlement System 1995-2003* (The Hague: Kluwer Law International, 2004) 177.

Wellens, Karel, *Economic Conflicts and Disputes before the World Court (1922-1995): a Functional Analysis* (The Hague: Kluwer Law International, 1996).

Wetter, J Gillis, 'The Rann of Kutch Arbitration' (1971) 65:2 American Journal of International Law 346.

White, Eric L, 'Written and Oral Submissions in WTO Dispute Settlement' in F Weiss (ed), *Improving WTO Dispute Settlement Procedures: Issues and Lessons from the Practice of other International Courts and Tribunals* (London: Cameron May, 2000) 121.

Wigmore, John Henry, *Evidence in Trials at Common Law* (Boston: Little Brown and Company, 1981).

Wijffels, A, 'France: Powers of the Judge' in CH van Rhee (ed), *European Traditions in Civil Procedure* (Antwerpen: Intersentia, 2005) 269.

Williams, Granville, 'The Logic of "Exceptions" ' (1988) 47:2 Cambridge Law Journal 261.

Witenberg, JC, 'La Theorie des Preuves Devant les Juridictions Internationales' (1936) 56 Recueil des Cours 5.

—— 'Onus Probandi Devant les Juridictions Arbitrales' (1951) 55 Revue Generale de Droit International Public 321.

Yanovich, Alan, & Tania Voon, 'Completing the Analysis in WTO Appeals: the Practice and its Limitations' (2006) 9:4 Journal of International Economic Law 933.

Yanovich, Alan, & Werner Zdouc, 'Procedural and Evidentiary Issues' in D Bethlehem et al (eds), *The Oxford Handbook of International Trade Law* (Oxford: Oxford University Press, 2009) 344.

Yerxa, Rufus, 'The Power of the WTO Dispute Settlement System' in R Yerxa & B Wilson (eds), *Key Issues in WTO Dispute Settlement: The First Ten Years* (Cambridge: Cambridge University Press, 2005) 3.

Zeitler, Helge Elisabeth, '"Good Faith" in the WTO Jurisprudence – Necessary Balancing Element or an Open Door to Judicial Activism?' (2005) 8:3 Journal of International Economic Law 721.

Zekoll, Joachim, 'Comparative Civil Procedure' in M Reimann & R Zimmermann (eds), *The Oxford Handbook of Comparative Law* (Oxford: Oxford University Press, 2006) 1327.

Zoller, Elisabeth (ed), *La Bonne Foi en Droit International Public* (Paris: Editions A Pedone, 1977).

D. WTO Official Documents

Appellate Body Annual Report for 2008, WTO Doc. WT/AB/11, 9 February 2009.

Communication from the Appellate Body in *European Communities – Measures Affecting Asbestos and Asbestos-Containing Products,* WTO Doc. WT/DS135/9, 8 November 2000.

Communication from Chile and the United States, WTO Doc. TN/DS/W/89, 31 May 2007.

Communication from the United States, WTO Doc. TN/DS/W/82, 24 October 2005.

Communication from Chile and the United States, WTO Doc. TN/DS/W/52, 14 March 2003.

Contribution of Canada to the Improvement of the WTO Dispute Settlement Understanding, WTO Doc. TN/DS/W/41, 24 January 2003.

Contribution of the European Communities and its Member States to the Improvement of the WTO Dispute Settlement Understanding, WTO Doc. TN/DS/W/1, 13 March 2002.

Contribution of the European Communities and its Member States to the Improvement and Clarification of the WTO Dispute Settlement Understanding, WTO Doc. TN/DS/W/38,23 January 2003.

Contribution by the Separate Customs Territory of Taiwan, Penghu, Kinmen and Matsu to the Doha Mandated Review of the Dispute Settlement Understanding (DSU), WTO Doc. TN/DS/W/36, 22 January 2003.

Contribution from Thailand to Clarify and Improve the Dispute Settlement Understanding: Panel System, WTO Doc. TN/DS/W/31, 22 January 2003.

Doha Work Programme, Decision Adopted by the General Council on 1 August 2004, Annex A – Framework for Establishing Modalities in Agriculture, WTO Doc. WT/L/579, 2 August 2004.

Minutes of the Meeting of the Dispute Settlement Body held on 12 June 1997, WTO Doc. WT/DSB/M/34, 8 July 1997.

Minutes of the Meeting of the Dispute Settlement Body held on 6 November 1998, WTO Doc. WT/DSB/M/50, 14 December 1998.

Minutes of the Meeting of the Dispute Settlement Body held on 31 March 2003, WTO Doc. WT/DSB/M/146, 19 May 2003.

Minutes of the Meeting of the Dispute Settlement Body held on 23 September 2005, WTO Doc. WT/DSB/M/197, 10 October 2005.

Minutes of the Meeting of the Dispute Settlement Body held on 17 February 2006, WTO Doc. WT/DSB/M/205, 31 March 2006.

Minutes of the Meeting of the Dispute Settlement Body held on 14 March 2006, WTO Doc. WT/DSB/M/206, 4 April 2006.

Minutes of the Special Meeting Held on 20 December 1999, WTO Doc. G/SCM/M/22, 17 December 2000 101.

Proposal by Costa Rica on Third Party Rights, WTO Doc. TN/DS/W/12/Rev.l, 6 March 2003.

Proposal by Japan on Amendment of the Understanding on Rules and Procedures Governing the Settlement of Disputes, WTO Doc. TN/DS/W/32, 22 January 2003.

Singapore Ministerial Declaration, WTO Doc. WT/MIN(96)/DEC, 18 December 1996, available at <http://www.wto.org/english/thewto_e/minist_e/min96_e/wtodec_e.htm> (visited on 1 July 2007).

Understanding Regarding Notification, Consultation, Dispute Settlement and Surveillance, L/4907, adopted on 28 November 1979, GATT, BISD 26 Supp. 210 (1980).

E. Others

Cairns Group Proposal, Improving Monitoring and Surveillance, Communication to the Committee on Agriculture Special Session, 12 June 2007, JOB(07)/88, available at <http://www.cairnsgroup.org/proposals/070614_doc_07_88.pdf> accessed 20 May 2009.

Lamy, Pascal,'Evolving Trade Increases Need for Active Transparency', Speech given at the Georgetown University Law Center (22 October 2007), available at <http://www.wto.org/english/news_e/sppl_e/sppl78_e.htm> accessed 20 May 2009.

Technical Information on Balance of Payments, available at <http://www.wto.org/english/tratop_e/bop_e/bop_info_e.htm> accessed 20 May 2009.

The Project on International Courts and Tribunals: The International Judiciary in Context, Synoptic Chart, November 2004, available at <http://www.pict-pcti.org/publications/synoptic_chart.html>accessed 21 June 2007.

Index

accuracy 10–2, 13, 17–8, 19, 21, 29, 136, 142, 267, 273, 288, 306–9, 316, 318, 320, 326–8, 330, 334–5, 337–8, 351–3, 354, 356–7, 360–3
adjudication
  civil law, *see* **civil law system**
  common law, *see* **common law system**
  definition 22, 27
  DSU 24–28, 33, 66
adversarial
  definition 15–6, 45
  WTO dispute settlement 53, 56, 250, 304, 307, 310, 352, 354, 356
adverse inferences 55, 122, 145, 264–72, 299–300, 325–6, 352–3, 360–1, 363
  Annex V of SCM Agreement 265
  Private party information 270–1
ALI/UNIDROIT Principles of Transnational Civil Procedure 43
amicus curiae 55, 336–8
Annex V of SCM Agreement 323–4
appeal (Appellate Body) 58–66
  Article 11 of DSU 61–5
  facts on appeal 58–65, 136
  remand 65–6
audi alteram partem, *see* **participation**

balancing, *see* **cost-benefit analysis**
burden of pleading 209–215, 358–9
burden of proof 68–9
  actori incumbit probatio 190, 192, 198
  affirmative defense 153, 155, 161–6, 175–6, 178
  allocation (generally) 152–224, 298–300, 313, 318, 331, 358
  Article 2.4 of TBT Agreement 159–160, 170, 172, 174
  Article 3.3 of SPS Agreement 157–8, 160, 172, 174, 177, 182–4, 187–8, 204–7
  Article 5.7 of SPS Agreement 163
  Article 6 of the ATC 155–6, 167, 169, 174, 177, 180, 183
  Article 10.3 of Agreement on Agriculture 152–3, 187, 203, 298
  Article 13 of Agreement on Agriculture 163–4, 170–2, 176
  Article 21.5 DSU 152, 217–20
  Article 22.8 DSU 217, 219–23
  Article 27 of SCM Agreement 160–1, 170–1, 175, 177–8
  Article 30 of the TRIPS Agreement 155, 170–1, 173, 185
  Article II:2(a) of GATT 165–6, 170, 173, 178–80, 195–6, 216
  Article XI:2(c)(i) of GATT 153, 155, 169, 174
  Article XIV of GATS 169, 212
  Article XV of the GATT 155, 170–1, 179
  Article XVIII.B of GATT 166–8, 177–8
  Article XX of GATT 153, 155–9, 161–2, 165, 169–70, 173–6, 182–4, 204, 207–210, 212–5
  Article XXI of GATT 162
  Article XXIV of GATT 162, 170–1, 182–3
  burden of going forward, burden of passing the judge, evidential burden, burden of adducing evidence, burden of evidence, burden of production, burden of producing evidence 74–6, 80, 82–3, 84, 85, 87, 88, 95–6, 107, 111, 115, 253–4, 262, 347
  burden of persuasion 75, 76–7, 80, 82, 83–4, 85, 87, 95–6
  civil law 74, 77–80
  common law 74–7, 83
  conditional right 154
  defences *stricto sensu*, *see* **defences *stricto sensu***
  definition 70–3
  Enabling Clause 162–3, 170–1, 173, 176–7, 183, 211–212
  exceptions 153–6, 161–79, 181–90, 216
  exclusions 154, 160–1, 166, 168, 171–2, 178, 181–7, 190, 216
  footnote 59 to item (e) of Illustrative List SCM Agreement 161–2, 170–1, 175
  international law 80–3
  negative (proof of) 193–5
  prescriptive language 180–1, 190

burden of proof (*cont.*)
shifting (of burden of proof) 83–6, 103–4, 108, 120–3, 124, 126–9, 135
tactical burden 84–5, 128
trade remedies 186–7

civil law system (basic features) 42–3, 44–5, 78–9, 318–9
claim (definition) 6, 49
common law system (basic features) 42–3, 44–5, 246–9, 255, 318
pre-trial discovery, *see* **discovery**
conciliation 22
conflict of norms 181–2
lex specialis 181
cost-benefit analysis 18, 21
balancing 18, 21
costs, direct and error costs 19–20, 21, 199–201, 223, 358
false positives/negatives 20
consultations 24, 46, 160, 289–92, 325
cross-examination 14
confidential information 233, 234
Article 3.2 of Agreement on Safeguards 276–8, 327
Article 6.5 of Anti-Dumping Agreement 276
Article 12.4 of SCM Agreement 276
Article 13 DSU 277
Article 17.7 of Anti-Dumping Agreement 277
Article 18.2 DSU 277, 281
Article 19.5 of Customs Valuation Agreement 277
ex parte communications 286–7
in camera review 286
interim report 280–1
protection of 36–8, 276–88, 283–8, 326, 352, 354, 359, 362, 364
sanctions 285–6
third parties 281, 287

defences *stricto sensu* 116–7
burden of proof 117, 191
developing countries:
WTO dispute settlement 26, 34
diplomatic model of dispute resolution 22–4, 26, 291
discovery
Annex V of SCM Agreement 323–4
common law 45, 141, 247–9, 255, 262, 291, 318–23, 352, 356, 360, 363
court-controlled disclosure 318, 320, 325–34, 363
due process 13, 29–31, 47–8, 66, 116, 117, 234, 257, 259, 271, 274, 312, 342, 344, 348, 350
impartiality, *see* **impartiality**
participation, *see* **participation**
equality of treatment, *see* **equality of treatment**
duty of cooperation 233, 250–76, 359–60
Article 13 DSU 250, 360
see also confidential information
consultations 289–92
deadlines 272–4, 360
see also good faith

efficiency (efficient use of resources) 13, 18, 19, 38–9, 115, 306, 320, 326, 329, 334–5, 354, 358–9, 363
equality of treatment 14, 17, 34–5, 115, 117, 306, 308–9, 312, 318, 330, 334, 354, 356, 361
developing countries 34
evidence 6
admissibility 52, 56
appeal 60–1, 66
conclusive 124–6
deadline for submission 52, 57, 272–4
direct 124
exclusionary rules 306, 308
exclusive or preferential access 260, 300, 312, 318, 325, 331, 361, 364
indirect 124
material 326
necessary 233, 288, 312, 319–20, 325–9, 334, 352, 359–60, 363
non-conclusive 124–5
post-dating the establishing of the panel 56
production request 315–7, 325–34, 360, 363
relevant 233, 259–60, 268, 312, 318–20, 325–9, 334, 337–8, 352, 359–60, 363
unlawful 41
ex parte **communications** 33, 34
exceptions
burden of proof, *see* **burden of proof**
narrow interpretation 186, 190
experts 55–6, 233, 335, 338–42, 347–8
impartiality 341–2

facts
admitted 73–4
auxiliary facts 5, 72–3, 199, 268
elemental facts 5, 72–3
fact/law distinction 58–9, 65
domestic law (as a fact) 71
notorious facts 73–4
on appeal, *see* **appeal**
finality 12–13, 40, 274
fines 275–6
freedom of information legislation 303, 353, 361

good faith
cooperation in dispute settlement 35–6, 118, 250, 253, 260, 263, 279, 283, 289, 306, 309, 354, 356, 363
presumption, *see* **presumptions**
good offices 22

IBA Rules on the Taking of Evidence in International Commercial Arbitration 44
impartiality 14, 16, 17, 32–3, 136, 309, 341–2, 348, 351, 354, 363
independence 16, 32, 341–2
reasoned decisions 14
inferences 93–4, 123–4
adverse inferences, *see* **adverse inferences**
inherent powers 54–5, 305
inquisitorial 45
interim panel report 57–8
intervention, *see* **third parties**

judicial economy 38, 55
jura novit curia 71
jurisdiction (WTO dispute settlement) 49, 55

mediation 22

natural justice, *see* **due process**
non-violation complaints 46, 141, 146
notice, *see* **participation**

obligation to comply with WTO agreements 25, 146

panel (WTO dispute settlement)
Article 11 DSU 311–2, 314, 317, 342–4, 351
Article 12 DSU 314, 336
Article 13 DSU 260, 304, 311, 314–5, 320, 324–5, 328, 334–6, 338–9, 347, 352
composition 50
fact-finding powers 233, 314–42 (*see also* **Article 13 DSU above**)
inherent powers, *see* **inherent powers**
limits to authority 233
original-trier-of-facts 231–5, 241–6, 351, 359
Permanent Panel Body 50–1, 309
request for establishment, *see* **request for establishment of a panel**
reviewer 231–4, 241–3, 245–6, 351, 359
terms of reference, *see* **terms of reference**
participation 14–6, 31–2, 115, 117, 248, 271, 334, 342, 344, 348, 350–2, 354, 358–9, 363
audi alteram partem 14
notice 14, 31–2
cross-examination 14
principe du contradictoire 14, 16
presumptions
Article 6.1 of SCM Agreement 152
Article 2.6 of TBT Agreement 152
Article 3.2 of SPS Agreement 152
burden of proof 94–6, 97
definition 95
good faith 97
inferences, *see* **inferences**
international law 96–7
irrebuttable presumptions 93, 95, 98–100
Morgan presumptions 95–6
presumption of nullification and impairment 98–100
presumption of fact 93–5, 98, 123–4
presumption of law 93–5, 98, 361–2
presumption with basic facts 94
presumption without basic facts 94–5
prima facie case, see *prima facie* case/evidence
rebuttable presumptions 85, 93–6, 98, 123–5, 151
Thayer presumptions 95–6
WTO dispute settlement 96–101
prima facie **case/evidence**
common law 106–7
definition 104–6
duty of cooperation 261–3, 315, 317
jurisdiction 106
presumption 104, 107
standard of proof, *see* **standard of proof**
suggestive evidence 142–4

prima facie **case/evidence** (*cont.*)
threshold question 104–5, 108–114, 116, 355–6
principe du contradictoire, *see* **participation**
principe dispositive 79
privacy 13, 40
privileges 13, 282–3, 291, 318, 325
probabilities of the situation 20–1, 197, 202
procedural fairness, *see* **due process**

Redfern schedule 325
request for establishment of a panel 46–9, 115–7, 178, 210–211, 328, 343–6, 349, 359
revision (of judgments) 274
Rules of Conduct 32–3, 36–7

Section 1782 of 28 U.S.C 332
settlement (amicable) 24–5, 26, 138
situation complaints 46, 141, 146
sovereignty 11, 17, 34–5
standard of proof
beyond a reasonable doubt 76, 77, 87, 89, 90–2, 137
civil law 88–9
clear and convincing evidence 87, 140, 243
common law 87–8
definition 86
international law 89–93
personal conviction of the judge 89, 90, 137–8
preponderance of the evidence (balance of probabilities) 77, 87–8, 89, 92, 108, 126–7, 131–2, 135, 137–8, 139–40, 141–2, 243, 275, 357
prima facie case/evidence 88, 92, 104, 106, 108, 118–35, 137, 142, 145, 259, 355–6
rationale 138–40
WTO dispute settlement 92–3, 138–42, 146–7, 357
standard of review 232
Article 11 DSU 237, 239, 241–2
Article 17.5(ii) of Anti-Dumping Agreement 235
Article 17.6(i) of Anti-Dumping Agreement 235–7, 239
Article 17.6(ii) of Anti-Dumping Agreement 236
SPS Agreement 239–245
TBT Agreement 239–245
trade remedies 233–9

terms of reference 47–9, 342–3, 351
third parties
access to confidential information 281, 287
right to intervene 28, 53, 55
Trade Act of 1974 (Section 301) 302
Trade Barriers Regulation 302
Trade Policy Review Mechanism 300–1
transparency (in trade remedies investigations) 234
transparency (of WTO dispute settlement proceedings) 37, 275
transparency obligations 147, 276, 288–9, 292–304, 352, 361
Article 2.5 of TBT Agreement 159, 205, 293, 296
Article 5.8 of the SPS Agreement 205, 293, 300
Clarification 292–3, 296
Committee on Balance-of-Payments Restrictions 294–5
enquiry points 160, 205, 292–3, 296, 302
freedom of information legislation, *see* **freedom of information legislation**
notification 292–4, 296–7
publication 292, 297

ultra petita 343–4, 349

violation complaints 46